2002
Merry Christmas
with much love
Cher

July 23, 2003
Toni Conway

THE RYDER CUP

The Definitive History of Playing Golf for Pride and Country

Colin M. Jarman

CONTEMPORARY BOOKS

Library of Congress Cataloging-in-Publication Data

Jarman, Colin M.
The Ryder Cup : the definitive history of playing golf for pride and country / Colin M. Jarman.
p. cm.
ISBN 0-8092-2588-3
1. Ryder Cup—History. I. Title.
GV970.J37 1999
796.352'66—dc21 99-26045
CIP

Interior design by Amy Yu Ng

Published by Contemporary Books
A division of NTC/Contemporary Publishing Group, Inc.
4255 West Touhy Avenue, Lincolnwood (Chicago), Illinois 60646-1975 U.S.A.

Printed in the United States of America
International Standard Book Number: 0-8092-2588-3
99 00 01 02 03 04 HP 18 17 16 15 14 13 12 11 10 9 8 7 6 5 4 3 2

Contents

Preface

On September 19, 1981, the *Washington Post* devoted sixteen paragraphs to news of the LaJet Golf Classic, the World Seniors Invitational, and the Green Hill Yacht and Country Club Invitational Rotary Pro-Am. On the same day, the same newspaper gave just four brief paragraphs to the opening day of an international golfing event known as the Ryder Cup.

Such was the overwhelming apathy toward the long-running contest that had seen the omnipotent United States team lose only three times in the first fifty-four years.

A comparatively short leap forward to 1999. . . . The U.S. Ryder Cup team will try to prevent an unprecedented third *successive* defeat at the hands of a European side that came into being only in 1979.

Thankfully, the last twenty years have seen a total transformation in the Ryder Cup, not only on but also off course. The world has fallen in love with what has become one of the great sporting spectacles of the twentieth century. The last seven encounters, epic matches all, have resulted in four European wins, one tie, and only two United States victories. Stark contrast to the previous twenty-five contests, from which the U.S. team emerged with a one-sided win-loss-tie record of 21–3–1.

The original idea of the Ryder Cup competition, in the good old days of the mashie-niblick and stymie, was a gentlemanly transatlantic challenge between the professional golfers of the United States and Great Britain. In today's golf world of fat-cat pros and fat-shafted clubs, the Ryder Cup has assumed a far more competitive edge—one that keeps getting sharper and keener with every renewal of battle.

After fifty years of "competition" in which the United States apparently just had to show up to retain the trophy, the selection rules were relaxed in 1979. The United States would no longer face an opponent as meek and mild as milky Earl Grey tea. The overly oppressed opposing side would now be widened to include not only Britain but also much of Europe, a move that would eventually prove to be as strong as a double espresso.

In 1985, the American Ryder Cup team tasted defeat for the first time in twenty-eight years. And their adversary would only get stronger.

As the contests became more competitive, the media attention grew, which in turned fueled the public's love affair with the event. The mundane match-play format, which for so long had been a load of bull, as far as television was concerned, turned into a cash cow in terms of viewer numbers and advertising revenues.

As the media and public interest increased, so the inherent pressures magnified on the golfers. Beneath television's microscopic gaze, players visibly cracked under the strain of representing their country in sudden-death battles. Four-foot putts that carried no monetary reward now assumed the importance of major-winning proportions; duck hooks quacked their way into a player's previously watertight armor; while mild outbreaks of butterflies pupated into full-blown nervous breakdowns.

Nothing in golf, maybe in all of sports, compares to the pressure exerted on players over the three days of the Ryder Cup. Grown men cry. Strong men become weak-kneed. Atheists mutter silent prayers. Millionaires cannot buy a smooth swing. Each hole shrinks in direct proportion to the increase in the putter's heartbeat. Choking becomes an occupational hazard for which there is little or no relief in the rule book of life. Despite this, every American and European golfer wants to make the Ryder Cup team, and every golf fan wants to watch it.

The recent success and increased awareness of the Ryder Cup match-play format have spawned some major spin-offs, including the Presidents Cup and the Andersen Consulting World Cup. But, however much the moneymen and media people try to copy the unique atmosphere of the Ryder Cup, nothing will ever come close to matching the history and traditions of golf's most endearing international team event.

Hence the reason for this book.

In tracing the complete history of the Ryder Cup, I spent many enjoyable hours of research—on both sides of the Atlantic—reading hundreds of newspaper reports, magazine articles, player biographies, and reference books, even Internet Web pages. The result is this work, covering seventy years of competition, thirty-two contests, and 704 matches (with the United States leading 413½–290½).

In trying to compile the most accurate reports possible on every Ryder Cup match, my task has been made harder by a number of conflicting reports. Golf reporting, in the main, is a very subjective and speculative practice. I have read about putts that have ranged from three feet in one respected source to thirty feet in an equally esteemed authority. Along with estimated length of shots or distances from the green, course yardage, and which club was used, such detail can never truly be 100 percent accurate—that is part of the intrinsic beauty of the game.

More worrying and perplexing were the occasions in which reports conflicted in their facts. A case in point is the differing reports concerning Gene Sarazen in 1931, an obvious instance of legend getting in the way of fact. And I encountered many other examples of differing "facts" throughout the seventy years of reporting and writing on the Ryder Cup. I suppose the lesson to be learned is that even if you are at close hand, it is extremely difficult to report accurately on every single shot in a golf event.

Trying to reconstitute more than seven hundred matches from fragments of original eyewitness reports proved to be a glorious challenge. Where these eyewitnesses shared blurred vision, I have interpreted the events to the best of my judgment. The result is a book from which I hope every reader will derive as much enjoyment and pleasure as I have had in writing it.

Acknowledgments

First, I must express my deepest gratitude to my editor, Rob Taylor, a true gentleman and friend, for showing extraordinary patience and goodwill both on and off the golf course.

Along with John T. Nolan, Nicole Adams, Peter Grennen, Regina Wells, and the invaluable staff at NTC/Contemporary, Rob has somehow managed to mold my wanton abuse of the English language (the literary equivalent of granting me a mulligan) into producing what we had once only dreamed about, a definitive history.

Roger, Kay, Christopher, and Peter for their utmost patience and undying hospitality in putting up with me during my time in the United States.

Walter, Katharina, Dave, and Max for their utmost patience and undying hospitality in putting up with me during my time in the United Kingdom.

The following kind people in some way have helped to make this book possible:

Every Ryder Cup player and captain, whose gallant deeds and gracious misdeeds are faithfully recorded here.

The golf writers and shrewd observers whose carefully chosen words have also contributed in shaping this book.

Sandra Lyda at the PGA of America.

D. Timothy Hayes of Scioto Country Club.

Margaret Maves and Larry Lamberger of Portland Golf Club.

Sidney L. Matthew of East Lake Golf Club.

Bruce Robinson of Laurel Valley Golf Club.

Lynn Ryan-Baker of PGA National Golf and Sports Club.

Dr. James C. Weig of Oak Hill Country Club.

Thomas B. Hand of Ridgewood Country Club.

Paul Lazar of Worcester Country Club.

Stuart Christie at Wentworth.

Jane Swinnerton at the European Tour.

The helpful staff at the following libraries: Harold Washington (Chicago), Nichols Library (Naperville), British Library (Bloomsbury and Collindale, London), and Westminster Reference (London).

The people at the following golf courses, whose "green and pleasant lands" regularly lured me away from my desk during the many months of writing: Springbrook and Fox Bend (Illinois), The Ridge (Kent, England).

Finally, three men who among them gave birth to and resuscitated the Ryder Cup over the years: Samuel Ryder, Bob Hudson, and Jack Nicklaus.

I thank you all.

History of the Ryder Cup

A Rose by Any Other Name . . .

If posterity, like hindsight, had 20-20 vision today's golfing millionaires would gladly endure a few days of unpaid labor for a chance to win the Harnett Cup.

Just as the origins of golf itself are clouded in the mists of time, so it is with the Ryder Cup. What is known for sure is that the Ryder Cup was first played for in 1927, but professional golfers from the United States and Great Britain had met on a couple of occasions prior to that first official contest.

The first officially documented foundation of the Ryder Cup, as we know it today, was laid at an Annual General Meeting of the Professional Golfers' Association of America. On December 15, 1920, the PGA agreed to partly finance the first-ever transatlantic golf tournament. This team event had been the brainchild of a visionary named James Harnett, a circulation manager for *Golf Illustrated*. Harnett's plan was to increase his magazine's readership by establishing a regular golf fixture between the best players of Great Britain and the United States.

In 1921, Harnett selected a team of American pros to take on their British peers, at the historic Gleneagles golf course in Scotland. The reason this first "unofficial match" was played in Britain is that American golfers had to make the arduous ocean crossing anyway to compete in the 2,000 Guineas Match Play championship.

The British made home-field advantage count to the full with a resounding 9–3 win. The seeds had been sown; professional golfers had tasted international team competition for the first time.

Although the first match had been considered a success, it took another five years before the second unofficial match was again played in Britain. This time the match was played at Wentworth, to the west of London, before the American players faced having to qualify for the British Open that year. Once again, the home country triumphed with a near massacre of Little Big Horn proportions: 13½–1½

The star of the British side was undoubtedly Abe Mitchell, who defeated the 1925 British Open champion Jim Barnes by the handy mark of 8 and 7, before teaming up with George Duncan to humiliate Barnes again, 9 and 8—even though the American was partnered by the great Walter Hagen.

A Blooming Good Idea

"I trust that the effect of this match will be to influence a cordial, friendly, and peaceful feeling throughout the whole civilized world. . . .
I look upon the Royal and Ancient game as being a powerful force that influences the best things in humanity."

—Samuel Ryder, BBC Radio broadcast

"Why can't they all get to know each other?"
—*Samuel Ryder*

A most interested spectator at the 1926 match was an anonymous-looking seed merchant from St. Albans, a few miles north of London. Sixty-eight-year-old Samuel Ryder (who did not take up golf until he was past fifty) was pleased with the overwhelming British victory and the performance of Mitchell (his personal golf coach), but what struck him the most was the obvious camaraderie within the two teams. Still, the fact that the two teams did not mix socially before or after the match upset him, and he sought to put that matter to rights.

As hosts, the British celebrated their win in typical fashion with a pot of tea and a hearty round of sandwiches in the magnificent Wentworth clubhouse. Here, Ryder congratulated both sides on their endeavors and asked why they did not play more often.

George Duncan suggested that if there were a trophy to be played for, the competition might become a regular event.

Having given up his father's seed business in the north of England to sell penny packets of seeds in the south, Ryder was not one to stand on ceremony and let grass (or a flower bed) grow under his feet. He made immediate inquiries with the British PGA, which openly encouraged such a tournament, and so Samuel Ryder went to work.

Some newspaper sources report that the Ryder Cup was presented to the winning British captain, Ted Ray, in 1926. But construction of the Cup was not finished until 1927, just in time for the first official event in Massachusetts.

Ryder commissioned a nineteen-inch-high solid gold trophy from the Mappin & Webb Company in Mayfair, London. The strikingly simple trophy was topped off with a figure of a golfer modeled on Ryder's coach and inspiration, Abe Mitchell. The cost of the trophy was split among Ryder, who paid £100, *Golf Illustrated*, which matched Ryder's offer, and the Royal & Ancient Golf Club, which put in £50. And so the Ryder Cup was born.

With Samuel Ryder acting as the driving force behind the contest, the first official match to bear his name took place the following year, 1927, at Worcester Country Club in Massachusetts.

And the rest, as they say, is history.

In 1981, at Walton Heath, Samuel Ryder's daughter attended the matches named for her father, where she met the Duke of Kent. Eighty-year-old Joan Ryder told the Duke that her father (who died in 1937) had been taken aback by the success of his competition. As she later explained, "He had the idea that when the Americans came over for a match, he would give a 'small friendly lunch party' to both teams."

"The Ryder Cup is now one of the most riveting, most exciting, most keenly anticipated, and most closely contested events in all sport. It is golf's Super Bowl, the royal and ancient game's Olympics. It is Big Time in capital letters."
—*Alister Nicol, Golf.com*

"It would be very easy to drool with sentimentality over the Ryder Cup. But, at the end of the day, it is simply two teams trying to knock seven bells out of each other, in the nicest possible way." —Peter Alliss

"The format of the Ryder Cup was no doubt devised by somebody with a shrewd sense of the sadistic." —*Detroit News*

"Waiting for the Ryder Cup to begin is a bit like waiting for an important date to arrive at a restaurant; nervous about how you are going to perform, desperate to impress, and anxious for the first exchanges to begin." —Jock Howard, *Victory* (1995)

1927

Worcester Country Club
Worcester, Massachusetts
United States
June 3–4

United States 9½	**Great Britain and Ireland 2½**
Leo Diegel	Aubrey Boomer
Johnny Farrell	Archie Compston
Johnny Golden	George Duncan
Bill Mehlhorn	Arthur Havers
Gene Sarazen	Herbert Jolly
Joe Turnesa	Fred Robson
Al Watrous	Charles Whitcombe
Al Espinosa (reserve)	George Gadd (reserve)
Playing Captain	**Playing Captain**
Walter Hagen	Ted Ray

The First Cup Is the Deepest

To put the 1927 Ryder Cup into proper perspective, it took the British team three times longer to sail across the Atlantic than it did for them to actually play in the first official tournament.

To put this fledgling event into further context, it was staged in June to coincide with the U.S. Open, to be played the following week. This "double date" made it financially worthwhile for the British players to leave their full-time posts as club professionals and make the arduous six-day sea journey.

Even at this early stage of the Ryder Cup, the honor of playing for one's country was seen as enough inducement to overlook any financial loss, although golfers in these early days did not have the luxury of lucrative sponsorship deals.

The British team arrived in New York without their designated captain and the inspiration behind the Ryder Cup. Abe Mitchell had stayed behind on doctor's orders to have his appendix removed, and was replaced by Herbert Jolly.

Mitchell himself suggested that the 1920 U.S. Open champion, Edward "Ted" Ray, be appointed as the new team captain. At age fifty, Ray was not only the oldest player on the British team but the most experienced as well—having also won the 1912 British Open.

Selected by a committee of three British Open champions (Harry Vardon, James Braid, and J. H. Taylor), the British team also boasted two other winners of its own Open: forty-four-year-old George Duncan (in 1920) and Arthur Havers (in 1923). Apart from these three past Open champions, no other British player in this inaugural team had won a major or would go on to win one.

In an attempt to help fund the cost of the British team's travel, *Golf Illustrated* magazine launched an appeal to all golf clubs in Britain to send donations. Only 216 of 1,750 clubs answered the call, and the magazine had to make up the shortfall.

The American team, led by multiple majors winners Walter Hagen and Gene Sarazen, was much stronger in depth and quality, with the likes of Leo Diegel (who would go on to win the U.S. PGA in 1928 and 1929) and Johnny Farrell (eight-time winner on the U.S. tour in 1927), among others lending fine support. The depth of quality did not stop at the Americans' playing ability, as the visitors were overwhelmed with the hospitality of their hosts and the luxury of their surroundings.

Upon arriving in New York, the members of the British team were royally entertained at the Westchester-Biltmore Country Club before making their way up to Massachusetts. Here the players, still weary from their travels, were immediately faced with another six-hundred-plate official dinner. The tired British team had asked to be excused from the Worcester banquet but, fearing this snub would leave a nasty taste in the mouths of the assembled guests, agreed to stay until 8:30.

"Everywhere we went we were submerged by hospitality and kindness. Suddenly we were in a world of luxury and plenty—so different from home. It was something we had never expected. Even the clubhouses were luxurious, with deep-pile carpets, not like the run-down and shabby clubhouses at home, which is all most of us really knew." —ARTHUR HAVERS

Since this was the inaugural Ryder Cup, many of the playing rules were not yet written in stone. It had been agreed between the two organizing committees that the Ryder Cup should follow the rules of the Walker Cup, which had seen the United States triumph in all four previous meetings. In vain, the U.S. organizers tried to change the playing format from the unfamiliar "Scotch" foursomes to their preferred fourball format—an early example of tinkering with the rules that would oft be repeated in the years to come.

The Americans need not have worried about their lack of familiarity with the more British foursomes (alternate shot), as they ended the first day with a decisive advantage after four matches. And that was the entirety of the first day—there were no separate morning and afternoon matches, as there are today. Instead the original format had four foursomes matches over thirty-six holes—eighteen holes morning and afternoon. Just imagine today's sponsors rushing to pour their dollars into television coverage of such a snore fest! In the 1920s, TV and sponsors were not even a twinkle in anyone's eye, as only a few hundred spectators dotted the course at any one time, and things were done with due reverence to tradition. Jackets and ties—even hats with brims all the way around—were the order of the day for the players.

"To win, they [the British] will have to play their best, better than they have ever done."
—London Evening News

Course Details

Donald Ross, whose handiwork would later play host to four more contests, designed the very first Ryder Cup course.

"The Worcester course, although in excellent condition for the test, has had a bad siege of winterkill." —*New York Times*

Hole	Distance	Par	Hole	Distance	Par
1	380	4	10	161	3
2	558	5	11	388	4
3	372	4	12	420	4
4	232	3	13	196	3
5	478	5	14	344	4
6	179	3	15	534	5
7	398	4	16	407	4
8	177	3	17	462	4
9	410	4	18	326	4
		35			**35 = Par 70 (6,422 yards)**

Course designer: Donald Ross

Day One: 36-Hole Foursomes

"We were surprised to find the winds blow quite lustily in America."
—GEORGE PHILPOTT, British team manager

Walter Hagen and Johnny Golden (USA) v. Ted Ray and Fred Robson (GBI)

Hagen and Golden seized control of the match by winning the twelfth through the fifteenth holes in the morning session to move from three down to one up.

"Ray and Robson went out in 36 and were three up. Ray was putting finely, and sank a beauty to win the seventh after a grand iron shot by Robson. At the ninth Robson played a spectacular slice round some trees to within ten feet of the hole, enabling his side to win the hole. Hagen was rather indifferent going out, but played splendidly coming home. He and Golden won the twelfth, thirteenth, fourteenth, and fifteenth to take the lead. Then Ray left Robson within three yards of the hole at the sixteenth, and the latter sank the putt to square the match. They halved the last two holes. The British pair were round in 75 and the American in 74." —*Times* (London)

Just as the British pair had played their hosts tough during the morning, finishing all square at lunch, they managed to counter the Americans' superior firepower long into the afternoon. Hagen and Golden won three of the first five afternoon holes but proceeded to lose the next three with some shoddy play. Both were to blame at the eighth: Golden's tee shot found a bunker, and Hagen's recovery flew out-of-bounds.

"For a time Ray, despite his fifty years, drove long and well, outdistancing Hagen by many yards, and, for a time, too, he putted gorgeously."
—*William D. Richardson,* New York Times

The British had also let themselves down, particularly on the greens, leaving too many putts short. If Robson had holed any of three short putts that he missed during the match, the result would have been even closer.

Still one up, the U.S. pair had been made to work harder than Hagen would have wished, and his three-foot birdie putt on the sixteenth doubled the lead. With seventeen halved, Hagen and Golden took the opening foursomes 2 and 1, after thirty-five hard-fought holes.

Gene Sarazen and Al Watrous (USA) v. Arthur Havers and Herbert Jolly (GBI)

Sarazen and Watrous faced another close match against the spirited but generally outgunned visitors. Havers and late replacement Jolly won only two holes in the morning, at the sixth and eighteenth, as they struggled to keep their opponents close.

Said Jolly afterward, "I was so amazed by the sheer size of the event in America and the size and scale of everything, including the hospitality, that I didn't play anything like as well as I could. I almost walked around that course with my mouth open and my eyes on everything but the ball. You could put everywhere I'd ever been into one golf course."

Two up after nine holes, Sarazen and Watrous turned up the heat, winning four of the next six holes to lead by six. The British pair reduced some of this surge by parring the final hole to reach lunch five down after a depressing eighty shots. The Americans carded a less-than-ideal 75 as Watrous played with a sore thumb that had almost kept him off the U.S. team.

The British pair took advantage of some slack American play after lunch and won a couple of early holes to seriously worry their opponents. Back to three up, Sarazen and Watrous—who lost only two holes in the whole of the morning session—managed to stem the tide and maintain their lead to the match's conclusion on sixteen.

"The first two holes were halved, but Gene and Al began piling up a slow but sure lead, which left them on easy street by noontime."
—*William D. Richardson,* New York Times

Although the final score of 3 and 2 indicated another hard-fought match, the Americans finished nine over par for its thirty-four holes. In effect, the British had lost the match rather than the Americans actually winning it.

Johnny Farrell and Joe Turnesa (USA) v. George Duncan and Archie Compston (GBI)

With Abe Mitchell missing, the British team looked to George Duncan to be productive on the first day, but the tall Scot and his partner were found severely wanting. Against Johnny Farrell and Joe Turnesa, the British pair started disastrously, losing the par-4 first and third holes with two double bogeys. They stumbled to the turn in 43 strokes, with Duncan singularly failing to find the form expected of him.

To his partner, who had just knocked his shot at the ninth out-of-bounds in the alternate format: "It is *my* ball that you put out of sight, Archie!"
—*George Duncan*

The Americans coasted the back nine to card a 76 against a slightly improved score from their opponents, who came home three shots better than their first nine.

Galvanized by Farrell's long birdie putt on the third hole, Farrell and Turnesa soon doubled their four-hole lunchtime lead by winning four holes in a row. Two pars and another birdie at the par-5 fifth did the damage for the Americans, but they were pegged back to seven up at the seventh, after needing three putts to traverse the green.

Any hope of a British revival was halted when they lost the ninth, although they took the par-3 tenth on Compston's eight-foot birdie putt. Turnesa's finely executed niblick approach to a few feet on the twelfth gained a winning par, to bring the Americans an 8 and 6 win.

This victory stood as the record margin until 1931, when both British players suffered separate maulings. Compston was humiliated 8 and 7 by Sarazen and Farrell, and Duncan was on the receiving end of a 10 and 9 blowout by Hagen and Shute.

Leo Diegel and Bill Mehlhorn (USA) v. Aubrey Boomer and Charles Whitcombe (GBI)

The best action of the first day came in a fluctuating match that saw the young British pair of Aubrey Boomer and Charles Whitcombe fight it out with Leo Diegel and Bill Mehlhorn. The United States won the first two holes of the day but was back level five holes later, and the tenth saw the British ahead for the first time. Despite Diegel's heroics on eleven and twelve, making two monster putts, before chipping over a stymie on thirteen for a half, the British pair arrived at lunch five holes to the good, with an inward card of 36.

The afternoon session did not have quite the excitement of the morning's play, with Diegel and Mehlhorn not able to match their opponents, who won three more early holes to lead by eight after seven holes. The U.S. pair did win the eighth, and the British pair picked up at the ninth, but the Americans were soon dead and buried at the thirteenth, which they also lost.

This 7 and 5 British victory was its only point on the first day.

Having ended the first day down 1-3, Ted Ray and the rest of his team were probably thankful that the Americans didn't like playing foursomes; otherwise they might have been swept.

"We expected to win the foursomes at least. The trouble is that we can't putt." —GEORGE PHILPOTT, British team manager

Day one result: USA 3, GBI 1

Day Two: 36-Hole Singles

"Conditions under which the final matches of the 1927 series were played today were not nearly as good as they were for the 'Scotch foursome matches' yesterday. Auguring perfect weather conditions in the morning when the matches started, the sky clouded around noontime and the afternoon was cold and raw, with a tricky wind that played havoc with many shots." —William D. Richardson, *New York Times*

Bill Mehlhorn (USA) v. Archie Compston (GBI)

In the first match, "Wild" Bill Mehlhorn held off the concerted challenge of Archie Compston. Lunch had seen the match all square after Mehlhorn had gone around in 76. Out in 35 in the afternoon, Compston took a one-hole advantage into the turn, but Mehlhorn leveled at the tenth.

The American took the lead at thirteen and was still one up with one to play, but soon found himself bunkered alongside the final green. Only an excellent recovery and a seven-foot par putt saw Mehlhorn keep his advantage for the narrowest of wins, 1-up.

Compston would further distinguish himself a week later, at the U.S. Open, as the best-placed Briton, with a top ten finish.

Johnny Farrell (USA) v. Aubrey Boomer (GBI)

Despite carding a 72, the best British round of the morning, Boomer could not match the American's touch on the greens, a fate that afflicted the whole British team. As if to emphasize his side's putting prowess, Farrell slammed home a fifty-foot putt on the seventh.

"One of the chief reasons for our failure was the superior putting of the American team. They holed out much better than we did."

—Ted Ray

Boomer had some success, winning the fifteenth and sixteenth to level the match up to lunch, but then luck seemed to fall the American's way. Two up after wins at three and five, Farrell saw his tee shot carom off a side wall and onto the eighth green, while Boomer's well-hit tee shot found the green but unluckily rolled off into a bunker.

On Boomer's replacing the ill Mitchell as Britain's number one player on the team: "You think Boomer is good, but Mitchell is four strokes better per round."
—*Anonymous British player*

Farrell left the eighth with a par three to Boomer's bogey, lifting the American to three up. With two more wins at twelve and fourteen, the American did not drop a hole all afternoon to win 5 and 4.

"I was one of the young ones of the team. I was a kid. They were all older than me, old men. Some of us tried, but some didn't try quite enough."
—AUBREY BOOMER

Johnny Golden (USA) v. Herbert Jolly (GBI)

The next two matches produced even more overwhelming victories for the home side.

Johnny Golden needed only to card a 76 to be six up at lunch over Abe Mitchell's late replacement, Herbert Jolly. With a name straight out of a Wodehousian golfing short, the Englishman played some very indifferent and far from jolly golf, slumping to a hefty 8 and 7 loss.

The British player was philosophical about his defeat, saying, "He holed out from all over the place. I putted beautifully to where the hole wasn't."

Leo Diegel (USA) v. Ted Ray (GBI)

Sportswriter Grantland Rice was quoted as saying: "Ted Ray was usually as dour as an elephant with a sore foot."

Stung into action by a heavy loss on Friday, Lou Diegel handed the British captain Ted Ray a golfing lesson with a 7 and 5 defeat, perfectly mirroring the American's foursomes defeat.

Six up at the break, Diegel's score of 70 was the best of the morning, when 77s were more the order of the day. The American's matchless morning card was a thumping eight shots better than Ray's.

On Leo Diegel's idiosyncratic putting style of using a "center-shafted wooden affair": "I diegel, thou diegels, he diegels, we all diegel."
—*Bernard Darwin,* Times *(London)*

The British captain fared a little better in the afternoon, as Diegel took his time before finally increasing his lead to seven on the thirteenth, to comfortably win the match with five holes to play.

Having won the first four singles, the United States had seven points, good enough to secure its first Ryder Cup win.

Gene Sarazen (USA) v. Charles Whitcombe (GBI)

The first piece of good news for the dispirited British camp came in Charles Whitcombe's titanic struggle with Gene Sarazen, who was fortunate to escape with a halved match. After fifteen holes in the morning, Sarazen was five down, but he turned things around with a spirited finishing burst. Playing some superb golf, Sarazen won the three holes up to lunch to finish just two down.

Said Sarazen, "I was very honored and excited about playing in the Ryder Cup matches. There was no question that Samuel Ryder intended it to be an event of goodwill and sportsmanship. But I can tell you that in those days, playing against the best was a cutthroat proposition. It was very competitive then, and it has remained that way."

With the job half done, Sarazen pulled back level by the seventh the second time around. From here, neither player gave an inch, until Whitcombe eked out a one-hole lead by winning the thirty-fifth hole. Having stared off Sarazen's concerted challenge, the Englishman promptly undid all his fine work by missing a par putt on the last hole and had to settle for a share of the overall spoils.

Whitcombe carded a 74 in the morning to lead by two holes but slumped to an afternoon 80 to halve the overall match. However, this result did give Britain its first (half) point of the singles.

Walter Hagen (USA) v. Arthur Havers (GBI)

Walter Hagen was not at his best for much of this competitive match against Arthur Havers, as the American captain played the morning in 77 and was on course for an 80 in the afternoon. With the U.S. captain one up at lunch, the defining moment of his 2 and 1 victory came, in the afternoon, at the par-5 fifteenth.

Hagen put his first two shots into the rough, his third into a bunker, his fourth ten feet from the hole, and his fifth in the hole! Havers—on in three, down in six—lost the hole.

Two down with three to play, the British player won the sixteenth with a fighting par, but lost his slim chance of sneaking half a point when he allowed Hagen to win the seventeenth in par to seal the match. As Havers explained, "There was never more than a hole in it either way until we got to the seventeenth—and then I was beaten by a stymie. I tried to putt my ball around Hagen's, but it hit it instead and shot off at an angle, six or seven feet away from the hole. I missed that putt, and when Hagen holed his, he went two up—and that was the match. But I'll never forget playing with him. He was a larger-than-life man—a character, a real personality. A great showman."

Al Watrous (USA) v. Fred Robson (GBI)

In another close one, Al Watrous outstayed Fred Robson in a match of indifferent golf. The American went out in 33 in the morning but came back in 45, perfectly mirroring Hitler's rise and fall—though Watrous had no such problem getting out of any bunkers.

Despite the American's horrendous ten over par on the back nine (4-4-5-5-5-6-6-5-5), Robson picked up only four holes and reached lunch one hole up. Watrous leveled the scores by the afternoon turn, then won the eleventh, twelfth, and the par-3 thirteenth, with a bogey four, to set up his 3 and 2 win.

Joe Turnesa (USA) v. George Duncan (GBI)

The last match out was the most exciting of the day. The American was two down after nine holes, one up at lunch, and two up after twenty-seven—to arrive at the last green all square. A long birdie putt by the forty-four-year-old Scot secured the hole and earned Britain's only victory in the singles, 1-up.

HOMEBREDS TAKE SIX OF EIGHT SINGLES AND GAIN TROPHY
—New York Times *headline*

Seconds after Duncan's closing putt had dropped, both sides met on the final green in a show of sporting camaraderie, shook hands in mutual respect, and walked off hand-in-hand.

Reiterating his earlier words on the difference between the two teams, Ted Ray looked to the future: "Our opponents beat us fairly and squarely, and almost entirely through their astonishing work on the putting greens, up to which point the British players were equally good. We were very poor by comparison, although quite equal to the recognized two-putts-per-green standard. I consider that we can never hope to beat the Americans unless we learn to putt. This lesson should be taken to heart by British players."

How true these words—spoken more than seventy years ago—sound now. Just consider how many Ryder Cups have hinged on one putt.

Day two result: USA 6½, GBI 1½
Overall match score: USA 9½, GBI 2½

Recap

After two days of marathon match play, the first Ryder Cup was finally presented to Walter Hagen.

The 9½–2½ final score did not really do justice to the visiting team, who had had barely a week's practice to shake off their sea legs and acclimatize themselves to the foreign soil and luxurious surroundings of the Worcester Country Club.

Without their leading player of the day, the odds were stacked even higher against the British, who were mainly the cream of club professionals sent into battle against the hardened touring pros from America. The match had been made harder by the absence of Britain's top player, but as the British team manager, George Philpott, said after the heavy loss, "Several Abe Mitchells would have been needed to alter this result."

"The Ryder Cup has done so much to foster that great spirit of international rivalry that makes the present-day sport the great thing that it is."
—Golf Illustrated
(June 1927)

Although the first official Ryder Cup is far removed from the media circus that surrounds latter-day events, what had been set in motion was a competition that would stand the test of time. This odd-year fixture would eventually grow into one of the great events on the world's sporting calendar. The Ryder Cup was truly here to stay.

Match Results (Winning side marked in *italics*.)

Friday, June 3—Foursomes

	USA	GBI	Score
1.	*Walter Hagen* *Johnny Golden*	Ted Ray Fred Robson	2 and 1
2.	*Gene Sarazen* *Al Watrous*	Arthur Havers Herbert Jolly	3 and 2
3.	*Johnny Farrell* *Joe Turnesa*	George Duncan Archie Compston	8 and 6
4.	Leo Diegel Bill Mehlhorn	*Aubrey Boomer* *Charles Whitcombe*	7 and 5

Day one result: USA 3, GBI 1

Saturday, June 4—Singles

	USA	GBI	Score
5.	*Bill Mehlhorn*	Archie Compston	1-up
6.	*Johnny Farrell*	Aubrey Boomer	5 and 4
7.	*Johnny Golden*	Herbert Jolly	8 and 7
8.	*Leo Diegel*	Ted Ray	7 and 5
9.	Gene Sarazen	Charles Whitcombe	halved
10.	*Walter Hagen*	Arthur Havers	2 and 1
11.	*Al Watrous*	Fred Robson	3 and 2
12.	Joe Turnesa	*George Duncan*	1-up

Day two result: *USA 6½, GBI 1½*

Overall match score: *USA 9½, GBI 2½*

1929

Moortown Leeds, Yorkshire England April 26–27	**United States 5**	**Great Britain and Ireland 7**
	Leo Diegel	Aubrey Boomer
	Ed Dudley	Archie Compston
	Al Espinosa	Henry Cotton
	Johnny Farrell	Abe Mitchell
	Johnny Golden	Fred Robson
	Gene Sarazen	Charles Whitcombe
	Horton Smith	Ernest Whitcombe
	Joe Turnesa	Percy Alliss [did not play]
	Al Watrous	Stewart Burns [did not play]
	Playing Captain	**Playing Captain**
	Walter Hagen	George Duncan

Less Is Moor

After the 1927 defeat: *"If our young players profit by their experience, we can reasonably hope for a happier fate in the next match for the Ryder Cup. It is a soundly established truism that experience is a good teacher, and the British professionals have every incentive to make the most of it."*

—George Philpott, British team manager

When the American Ryder Cup champions arrived on British soil to defend the trophy they had won so easily at home, few would have bet against their returning with the trophy still in their possession. Once again Walter Hagen was the playing captain, and he brought with him six of the players from his victorious 1927 team.

Just as the British team had been forced to do in 1927, the Americans raised money for their trip—$6,000 by playing exhibition games and $4,700 from equipment sponsors and other benefactors.

The British had a new captain, George Duncan, who welcomed the return of Abe Mitchell (who had missed the 1927 captaincy owing to ill health) and some new faces. Whereas age and experience characterized the first British Ryder Cup team, the second squad of players were much younger—none more so than twenty-two-year-old Henry Cotton.

"It was a big thrill when I got the invitation, and I hastily cabled back my acceptance." —HENRY COTTON

In the history of the Ryder Cup, no fully fit American has ever sat out a whole contest.

Right from the outset, Hagen established a time-honored American playing tradition that has been followed right through to today—namely, that of playing every player selected, on the principle that if you are good enough to be picked, you are good enough to play. The British team had ten players but sat two of them out (Alliss and Burns) in order to play the men in top form.

Hagen had pleaded that foreign-born Americans should be eligible to play for their country, just as they had fought for their country, but his request fell on deaf ears. The American team was composed totally of home-born talent, although the team's heritage was widespread: two Italians, two Germans, one Irish, one Hungarian, one Polish, one Spanish, and two English.

The playing format was exactly the same as that in the first encounter—four foursomes or alternate-shot (thirty-six holes) on day one, followed by eight singles or twosomes (thirty-six holes) on day two.

"Golf is really a selfish game most of the time. Professionals play it for money and do everything they can do to beat their fellow professionals every time they step onto the first tee. But there is something about the Ryder Cup that brings out the team spirit in golfers. Maybe it's the prospect of beating the Americans, who for so long have been the kings of golf. Maybe it's a throwback to their schooldays when team sports, and not individual sports, were the most important aspect of games. I don't know. But I do know that golfers who normally want only to beat their rivals become, that week, the best of pals." —HENRY COTTON

Course Details

The venue for the first Ryder Cup in Britain was the windswept Moortown course, in Yorkshire, in the northwest of England.

It was hoped that the prevailing windy conditions would bring the Americans down to the British way of playing, with the accent more on accurate long irons to the greens than on putting, which had been Britain's undoing in 1929.

Hole	Distance	Par	Hole	Distance	Par
1	499	5	10	586	5
2	415	4	11	445	4
3	450	5	12	170	3
4	183	3	13	425	4
5	380	4	14	146	3
6	221	4	15	390	4
7	412	4	16	425	4
8	150	3	17	345	4
9	350	4	18	410	4
		36			**35 = Par 71 (6,402 yards)**

Course designer: Alister Mackenzie

Day One: 36-Hole Foursomes

The Americans, who were supposed to have been inconvenienced by the cold and blowy spring weather, looked more at home than their opponents, who were well wrapped up against the elements.

Many of the American team did not have the first clue about foursomes play, and Walter Hagen had to give them an impromptu tactical lesson before play started.

Walter Hagen and Johnny Golden (USA) v. Ernest Whitcombe and Henry Cotton (GBI)

Unfortunately for the youthful Cotton, who had spent time in the States trying to pick up an American-golf style, his partner repeatedly let him down. Against the might of Hagen and Golden, this meant mighty big trouble.

Despite the foursomes format, Hagen, the British Open champion, was confident of success before his match: "I shall win anyway. I always do."

After both teams opened with bogey sixes at the first hole in the morning, the 412-yard par-4 seventh witnessed some truly ugly golf. A British double bogey won the hole by default as the Americans could offer only a triple-bogey seven.

Thanks to wins at the final two morning holes, the Americans were two up at lunch, but they failed to dominate their opponents in the afternoon. Despite the lack of support against such illustrious rivals, Cotton fought back from being four down to level, but the courageous comeback was cut short when the U.S. pair took the last two holes to win 2-up.

The standard of play suffered as the bad weather played more of a part in the afternoon. The Americans carded a morning 71 but dropped to a 78 in the afternoon, while the British pair followed its early 73 with a 77.

Gene Sarazen and Ed Dudley (USA) v. Abe Mitchell and Fred Robson (GBI)

Hagen played down suggestions that he should have paired Sarazen with the mercurial Horton Smith instead of the out-of-form and patently overawed Dudley: "It would be unthinkable to bring them all the way from the States without giving each man a chance to strike a blow for his country."

Owing to their age, the pairing of Mitchell and Robson were suspected of being the British weak link on the first day, but they did their country proud. Against Sarazen and a very nervy Dudley, the match—all square at lunch—remained close.

The British held their game together better in the windswept conditions and managed to hold off Sarazen, whose putting stroke staved off a much bigger defeat, for a well-earned 2 and 1 win. This brought the home side their first and only full point of the day.

Leo Diegel and Al Espinosa (USA) v. George Duncan and Aubrey Boomer (GBI)

Following his superb showing in the first tournament, Leo Diegel continued where he had left off, and the U.S. pair hammered the unfortunate Boomer and Duncan into an early submission.

The potent combination of Diegel's deadeye approach work and Espinosa's finishing touch with a hot putter ran the British ragged. Lunch saw the Americans seven up with a fizzing morning score of 66, having played some quite exceptional golf considering the blustery conditions.

Much of the damage was done at the par 3s. Diegel guided three tee shots into four, twelve, and fourteen that resulted in Espinosa birdie putts: a monumental fifty-footer at the fourth, and a couple of two-to-three-yarders on the latter two holes.

During the match, George Duncan's ball struck a little girl on the head, and the Scot was visibly upset. Crowd control had been a problem all day with the galleries spilling onto the fairways, reducing them to narrow avenues—so much so that an estimated 100 balls landed in the crowd during the first day.

"Diegel was using his irons magnificently at the short holes, if the styles he adopted on the tee and green are eccentricities, they are those of genius, and his golf all around was superb."
—*Bernard Darwin,* Times *(London)*

The afternoon brought little joy for the British pair, who did well to go down to a crushing 7 and 5 loss.

Johnny Farrell and Joe Turnesa (USA) v. Archie Compston and Charles Whitcombe (GBI)

In the last match, Duncan sent out his best pairing, Compston and Charles Whitcombe, against Turnesa and U.S. Open champion Farrell.

A close match was made even closer after Archie Compston gave away the sixth hole when he contrived to hit the American ball as well as his own when trying to get out of a bunker.

In what turned out to be a far-from-edifying standard of golf, the lead constantly changing hands during both sessions, the match came down to the thirty-sixth and final hole. With the British one up, the home crowd eagerly awaited the second win of the day. They were to be cruelly disappointed, as neither team deserved to win the hole.

Whitcombe sliced his drive into some heavy gorse, while Farrell's tee shot went to the other extreme, hooking wildly into the deep rough. Following a drop-shot penalty, Compston hit his recovery shot into a bunker from which the British failed to recover. Turnesa hit a wicked hook, sending the ball into more rough, bouncing off an out-of-bounds wall—and leaving his partner an impossible shot over a marquee. Farrell then made the impossible possible, leaving his ball just four feet from the hole.

FARRELL MAKES GREAT SHOT
PITCHES OVER TENT AND HITS FLAG AT 36TH TO SQUARE MATCH
—*New York Times* headline

With the British failing to make any progress from the bunker, Turnesa made the par putt to win the hole and eke out a surprise half.

The British pair came home with a remarkable card—no threes or fives. Seven fours were bookended by a costly pair of sixes at ten and eighteen, for a 40.

At the end of the first day, Hagen—with a 2½-1½ lead—was extremely confident about the next day's proceedings. Having held back a couple of his aces (Smith and Watrous) from the foursomes, the American could taste the victory. Over the years, the Ryder Cup would have a nasty habit of kicking overconfident teams in the pants, and 1929 would go down as the watershed of pants-kicking.

Day one result: USA 2½, GBI 1½

Day Two: 36-Hole Singles

Gamesmanship was not slow in entering the friendly confines of the Ryder Cup, as Hagen refused to submit his list for the singles matches until the foursomes had been completed. Duncan, who had handed in his singles list, hastily withdrew his lineup until Hagen had properly presented his.

Johnny Farrell (USA) v. Charles Whitcombe (GBI)

The Americans were in for a big surprise, and they didn't have to wait long before it hit them. First up for Britain was Charles Whitcombe, who played some of the best golf of the weekend—carding a 70 in the morning to practically blow U.S. Open champion Johnny Farrell away by lunchtime. Four consecutive British wins at the close of the morning session more or less ended the match at the break.

Around in 76, and six down, the American fared a little better in the afternoon but was swamped by some of the best British golf seen in the early Ryder Cup matches. Farrell got off reasonably lightly with an 8 and 6 drubbing.

This win for Britain leveled the match score at 2½ points each, and from there on, they were never behind.

Gene Sarazen (USA) v. Archie Compston (GBI)

Despite being only one down at lunch, Gene Sarazen was surprisingly blown away in the afternoon and lost his second match of the weekend. The morning session against Archie Compston had been close, and no one could have predicted that the British player would come out after lunch and dominate the great American.

"Gene Sarazen tears the ball through the wind as if it did not exist."
—*Bernard Darwin*

Compston blazed out of the blocks after lunch birdie-par-birdie for three wins and a four-hole lead. Sarazen hit back with three wins in a row of his own, as his opponent bogeyed all three holes. In an amazing front nine, Compston then won two of the last three holes with a trio of honest pars, as Sarazen was blighted by the bogey bug.

Three down, Sarazen had no answer to Compston's aggressive play—both physical and mental—as he went on to drop the tenth and eleventh. The American finally went down, 6 and 4, when he failed to par the 146-yard fourteenth.

"The Ryder Cup has gotten to be a big affair now. In our day, we paid all of our expenses and didn't get to travel on the Concorde. We traveled by either ship or train. We were thrilled to death, however, to have the chance to face the best of the British at any time. We purposely had matches before the British Open to get us ready for that championship."
—Gene Sarazen, from "History of the Ryder Cup" (BBC-TV, 1993)

Leo Diegel (USA) v. Abe Mitchell (GBI)

The third singles match was also over and done with fairly early. It seemed that Ryder Cup play had been invented for Leo Diegel, who was still on fire from the foursomes. His unlucky foe this time was Abe Mitchell, whose morning score of 70 would normally have been good enough for a healthy lead. Mitchell sat down to "enjoy" his lunch five shots down!

Always tinkering with his odd elbows-bowed putting style, Diegel even painted his putter a different color just for his singles match. The paint job may have had some effect, as the American holed a thirteen-footer, after recovering from a bunker, to halve the first hole with a birdie four.

Diegel's amazing morning display could have netted him a 63 if he hadn't missed a very short putt on seventeen after chipping up to the hole. He took two shots to get out of a bunker on eighteen and had to settle for a 65.

After the break, Mitchell again reached the turn in a very creditable 35 shots—but found to his dismay that he had lost another two holes to the runaway Diegel. Relief came soon enough for Mitchell, when Diegel finally closed him out 9 and 8 to put an end to the Englishman's suffering.

Diegel was ten under for twenty-eight holes. "I have certainly never played better golf. My driver never failed me, and my iron shots and putting simply couldn't go wrong," said Diegel, who also celebrated his thirtieth birthday the day of his win.

Walter Hagen (USA) v. George Duncan (GBI)

If reigning U.S. Open champion Farrell had been blitzed by Whitcombe in the opening singles, then the reigning British Open champion Hagen was dismantled—piece by piece—by his opposing number, George Duncan. Hagen deliberately placed himself against Duncan, boasting, "There's a point for our team right there."

Said Sarazen afterward, "Walter met me in the men's room to talk about the pairings for the singles. He said, 'We need to get off to a good start, and I'll play against George Duncan.' Little did we know Duncan happened to be in the men's room, and he went out later and whipped Walter, 10 and 8. You should have seen the look on Hagen's face after his match."

Duncan, too, was confident of victory. "This guy has never beaten me in a serious match, and he never will!" he said of the Master.

The eagerly awaited "battle of the captains" was a truly one-sided affair. Only Hagen's own breathtaking brilliance in and around the green saved him from complete annihilation and total embarrassment.

Eight of the first nine holes were halved, and Hagen's bogey at the par-4 fifth gave Duncan a one-hole lead at the turn. The back nine saw Duncan take matters into his own hands as he reeled off five wins to Hagen's only success of the day, at the sixteenth.

Five up at lunch, Duncan more than pressed home his advantage with wins at two and six, as Hagen was made to chew long and hard on his words. At six down, the American captain was served a second helping of humble pie, with Duncan winning the last four holes to permanently ink his name into the record books with a crushing 10 and 8 extermination.

Hagen lost ten of the last nineteen holes played. This was his only loss in four Ryder Cup singles matches, and was the biggest margin of defeat in any Ryder Cup match.

The lopsided win not only taught Hagen a lesson, but, more important for Duncan, also put Britain ahead in the overall match. With the match score at 3½–4½, the stage was set for a close finish. The first four matches ended 8 and 6, 6 and 4, 9 and 8, and 10 and 8, but the remaining four matches proved to be not quite so one-sided.

Joe Turnesa (USA) v. Aubrey Boomer (GBI)

Both Turnesa and Boomer had lost their singles in the first Ryder Cup encounter and were keen not to repeat that performance. Boomer's wins at holes two and five canceled out the Americans' opening-hole win, but with wins at eight and nine, Turnesa turned a one-hole deficit into a lead.

The American stretched his lead with a hole-winning par at the 445-yard eleventh, but the defining stretch of the match came just before lunch. With Boomer two down after fourteen holes, he played the final four holes of the morning 4-4-3-4 to earn a turn-around two-hole lead.

In the afternoon, both players won and lost two holes each on the front nine, but the British player immediately increased his two-hole lead by coming home with winning pars at ten and eleven. Boomer bogeyed thirteen, but Turnesa did the same at the next hole, and a half on fifteen ended the match 4 and 3 in the Englishman's favor.

Two points up, with just three matches to be completed, Britain needed only one precious point to claim the Ryder Cup.

Horton Smith (USA) v. Fred Robson (GBI)

Having sat out the foursomes, Horton Smith—the youngest player on either side at the tender age of twenty-one—took on the wily British veteran Fred Robson, who was twenty-three years his senior.

With only a few days' practice, Smith had to get used to playing with hickory shafts instead of his customary steel ones, which were banned in the United Kingdom.

Horton Smith, the youngest-ever U.S. player (aged twenty-one years and four days), had won eight times on the U.S. tour in 1929.

Proving that golf is a young man's game, the American rookie finally wore down his opponent, who played tough over the first three-quarters of the match. The key shot of the morning came on the eighteenth green, where Smith putted around a stymie to level the match at the break.

With wins at the first and eighth, Robson actually took a two-hole lead in the afternoon, but Smith stepped up his attack with some relentless pressure over the next ten holes. The American won the sixth and seventh but bogeyed the ninth, as Robson clung to his lead at the turn.

On the way home, experience crumbled in the face of youth, with Smith winning five of the last seven holes played. Five pars, a bogey, and a solitary birdie may not look much like a winning performace, but Smith was handed the holes by the wilting Englishman. Robson threw the match away, carding three bogeys and a double at the 425-yard thirteenth to drop three down with four to play.

"I have never played against anyone who makes me so tired."
—*Fred Robson*

Having been handed four wins on a plate, Smith served up a thirty-foot birdie putt on the sixteenth to finally cook Robson's goose. This stunning climax allowed the young American to win 4 and 2, keeping alive the United States's slim hopes of retaining the trophy.

Al Espinosa (USA) v. Ernest Whitcombe (GBI)

This was the only match out of ten that reached the thirty-fifth hole, let alone the last green.

Al Espinosa started brightly with two wins out of three, lost the par-3 fourth, accepted the fifth with a par, but he then bogeyed the last four holes on the front nine.

One down against Ernest Whitcombe, the American retook the lead with wins at twelve and thirteen, but he then bogeyed the par-3 fourteenth to level the match.

With the last four holes of the morning all halved in fours, this was the first match to reach lunch all square. The second match to do so was right behind.

With the match beautifully balanced at the break, both players won and lost three holes to reach the turn still tied. Espinosa started home 5-5-3-5, as Whitcombe posted wins on eleven and thirteen to stake a valuable two-hole lead with the Cup still up for grabs.

As it turned out, the destiny of the Ryder Cup was soon decided elsewhere and the result of this match was merely one of personal pride. From two down with five to play, Espinosa birdied the 390-yard fifteenth and finally got back level when his par on the last hole beat out Whitcombe's bogey five for a halved match.

The result might have been different had the Cup still been an issue.

Al Watrous (USA) v. Henry Cotton (GBI)

Playing against the ever-dependable Al Watrous, the youngest British player, Henry Cotton, found himself in trouble in the morning session. He lost three of the first four holes—halving the third in birdie fours—as the American carded an excellent 33 for the front nine. Cotton kept a cool head on his young shoulders and kept his game in order, as he slowly managed to claw back some of the American's lead.

Only one down with one to play in the morning, Cotton holed a magnificent chip from the rough on eighteen for a crucial birdie to level the match. Despite losing the first hole to par after the break, Cotton hit back to open up a three-hole advantage by the turn with wins at three, five, six, and nine.

The front nine the second time around proved to be the difference between the players, as the consistent Cotton carded 34s in both the morning and afternoon, while Watrous followed his excellent 33 (bettered only by Diegel) with a disappointing and destructive 37.

This final match to finish meant Britain won the singles 5½–2½, and the match 7–5.

With the outcome of the Cup resting heavily on this match, Cotton proved more assured than his older American opponent, who could not match the Englishman's birdie two on twelve. When Cotton bogeyed thirteen to drop back to three up with five to play, the American may have sensed one last outside chance to save the match and the Cup.

The 2½ points the Americans managed in the singles would be their second-worst-ever result on a final day of individual endeavor—eclipsed only by their performance in 1957.

With the local crowd cheering their man's every move, Watrous could not pull back any more ground, and the deed was finally done when he bogeyed the 390-yard fifteenth to hand the match to Cotton, 4 and 3, and the Ryder Cup to Great Britain.

Day two result: USA 2½, GBI 5½
Overall match score: USA 5, GBI 7

Recap

At the ceremony immediately after the last singles match, a proud Samuel Ryder was more than honored to present his trophy to a rather glum-faced British captain. With the Cup in his safekeeping and Walter Hagen's scalp in his overcoat pocket, Duncan soon cracked a smile and proclaimed it "the happiest day of my life."

"The near rout of the men from overseas [in the singles] came as a pleasant surprise to the home folk, for few of the golf fans of the islands thought the golden trophy, symbol of international professional golfing supremacy, could be regained."
—*William D. Richardson*, New York Times

Having come into the singles matches with a one-point advantage and an air of misplaced confidence, personified by their devil-may-care captain, the U.S. team was comfortably beaten in the one-on-one format. Such anomalies as an American defeat or a British win would not occur often in the coming years, as the United States would continue to dominate the Ryder Cup (as they did the 1929 British Open a few weeks later at Muirfield).

Hagen's confidence was restored, after the knock it took at Moortown, when he ran away with the British Open by six strokes. Second was fellow Ryder Cupper Johnny Farrell, as eight Americans made the top ten list. The victorious British team was well represented in its own championship by Abe Mitchell, who finished tied with Percy Alliss, who had sat out the Ryder Cup because of recent bad play.

On his return home, Hagen showed he was not too unhappy about losing the Ryder Cup: "To lose in a game is not a national calamity. Besides, one country cannot always expect to win. If such a thing were to happen, world interest in golf would evaporate. Though naturally disappointed, I cannot help thinking that Britain's triumph is the finest thing that could have happened to the game. It will act as a tonic all around. America will prepare to win the Cup back, while Britain—stimulated by success long deferred—will go from strength to strength."

What the 1929 Ryder Cup, the first to be officially staged in Britain, proved was that the format could be competitive. After this British win, the Americans made sure they would not be so overconfident in the future.

Match Results (Winning side marked in *italics*.)

Friday, April 26 Foursomes

	USA	GBI	Score
1.	*Walter Hagen* *Johnny Golden*	Ernest Whitcombe Henry Cotton	2-up
2.	Gene Sarazen Ed Dudley	*Abe Mitchell* *Fred Robson*	2 and 1
3.	*Leo Diegel* *Al Espinosa*	George Duncan Aubrey Boomer	7 and 5
4.	Johnny Farrell Joe Turnesa	Archie Compston Charles Whitcombe	halved

Day one result: USA 2½, GBI 1½

Saturday, April 27—Singles

	USA	GBI	Score
5.	Johnny Farrell	*Charles Whitcombe*	8 and 6
6.	Gene Sarazen	*Archie Compston*	6 and 4
7.	*Leo Diegel*	Abe Mitchell	9 and 8
8.	Walter Hagen	*George Duncan*	10 and 8
9.	Joe Turnesa	*Aubrey Boomer*	4 and 3
10.	*Horton Smith*	Fred Robson	4 and 2
11.	Al Espinosa	Ernest Whitcombe	halved
12.	Al Watrous	*Henry Cotton*	4 and 3

Day two result: USA 2½, GBI 5½

Overall match score: USA 5, GBI 7

1931

Scioto Country Club
Columbus, Ohio
United States
June 26–27

United States 9	Great Britain and Ireland 3
Billy Burke	Archie Compston
Wiffy Cox	William Davies
Leo Diegel	George Duncan
Al Espinosa	Syd Easterbrook
Johnny Farrell	Arthur Havers
Gene Sarazen	Bert Hodson
Densmore Shute	Abe Mitchell
Craig Wood	Fred Robson
Playing Captain	Charles Whitcombe
Walter Hagen	**Playing Captain**
	Ernest Whitcombe

Columbus Discovers International Golf

Three members of Britain's winning team from 1929 were ineligible to defend the trophy: Boomer and Alliss were no longer British residents (both living in Europe as club professionals), and Henry Cotton had ruled himself out.

The conditions regarding a player's eligibility for the Ryder Cup were clearly laid out in the deed as "professional golfers born and resident into the country which they respectively represent." The British team was selected by a British PGA committee after candidates had played three special trial matches.

Cotton, the young hero from 1929, disagreed with the British PGA ruling that forced players to share all exhibition money made on their U.S. tour, and he was also not happy with the travel plans. So, without three star players, Britain arrived in America to defend the trophy they had so narrowly won at home.

Not only did the British team set sail on HMS *Majestic* without three key players, but also a fourth player, Herbert Jolly, stepped down because of recent poor play. In the United States working for a British newspaper at the Ryder Cup, Cotton, it was hoped, would reconsider his stand, but he was eventually replaced by Bert Hodson, and Arthur Havers substituted for Jolly.

Hodson's inclusion gave the British its second player under the age of thirty, along with Easterbrook.

"I am quite sure we will win. British golf has taken on a new chapter of its history. They had been persuaded by all sorts of Jeremiahs that they were inferior to the Americans, but they are not."
—*Samuel Ryder*

The hosts, on the other hand, picked a team from an abundance of riches. Five players were preselected at the PGA Annual General Meeting, but the rest of the U.S. team was not picked until a few days before the event started. Burke, Cox, Wood, and Shute all booked their places in a special pre–Ryder Cup qualifying event, which showed how serious the Americans had been in trying to recover the trophy.

Course Details

Having hosted the 1926 U.S. Open, the course at Scioto opened its doors to another major tournament. One reason this picturesque course was chosen is that the 1931 U.S. Open was to be held in nearby Toledo, and Scioto would make an ideal companion site to the longer-established championship event.

"This course is certainly a fine one . . . similar to inland courses in Britain." —FRED PIGNON, British team manager

Hole	Distance	Par	Hole	Distance	Par
1	410	4	10	394	4
2	430	4	11	360	4
3	375	4	12	545	5
4	180	3	13	445	4
5	445	4	14	238	3
6	500	5	15	389	4
7	380	4	16	418	4
8	480	5	17	135	3
9	140	3	18	480	5
		36			**36 = Par 72 (6,744 yards)**

Course designer: Donald Ross

Day One: 36-Hole Foursomes

The hundred-degree temperature was tempered by the welcome arrival of wind and rain on the first morning. The visitors had arrived from the cold spring climate at home dressed in long coats and tweeds, totally unsuited to the oppressive heat in Ohio, and they never really managed to adjust to the change.

Ticket prices were $1 for practice day, $3 for a single match day, and $5 for both match days.

Gene Sarazen and Johnny Farrell (USA) v. Archie Compston and William Davies (GBI)

In one of the most unevenly matched starts to an opening day in Ryder Cup history, the first two foursomes barely reached the final nine holes.

Up first, Sarazen and Farrell, who had both suffered separate defeats in the 1929 foursomes, were not about to lose their shirts a second time. Five up at lunch, the Americans had taken Compston and Davies to the cleaners, with a homeward burst of 33 after having been only one ahead after nine.

Sarazen played two magnificent approaches into fourteen and fifteen, as he and Farrell won five holes, dropping the 135-yard seventeenth to Davies's fifteen-foot birdie putt.

After back-and-forth wins on the first and fourth holes in the afternoon, four more American wins in a row from the sixth saw the U.S. team nine up and coasting.

Compston and Davies were finally undone by the impressive score of 8 and 7. This would have been classed as an overwhelming margin of victory had it not been for the carnage in the game behind them.

Walter Hagen and Denny Shute (USA) v. George Duncan and Arthur Havers (GBI)

Forty-eight-year-old George Duncan, who was not originally picked for this trip but was reinstated after a public outcry back in England, must have wished that his adoring fans had kept their collective mouths shut. He and Arthur Havers (two former British Open winners) walked into one of the most one-sided matches the Ryder Cup would ever witness.

When asked why he always hit the ball high, even in the local windy conditions: "I like to hit the ball high because I have never found the rough or bunkers in the sky. At least not yet!"
—*Walter Hagen*

Duncan started better than Hagen, with an opening drive of some 300 yards, eclipsing the great man's dismal departure shot from the tee. This inauspicious start for the Americans was not symbolic of the way they would go on to play, or how Hagen would tee off the next day. Hagen and Shute were untouchable as they actually won the first hole despite the sides' differing fortunes off the tee.

The Americans reached the turn five up. Lunch came with the U.S. pair an amazing ten up and looking as if they would close out proceedings early on the outward nine in the afternoon.

"Practically nothing went right for Duncan today. He did everything but miss hitting the ball entirely, and once or twice he almost did that very thing." —WILLIAM D. RICHARDSON, *New York Times*

It was to the British players' credit that they staved off defeat until the twenty-seventh hole by the margin of 10 and 9, although Hagen and Shute carded only a four-over-par 40 on the front nine to nail down the record win. Fittingly, it was Shute, the best player of the four, who blasted out of a bunker to a few feet of the ninth hole to set up the final win.

The 10 and 9 margin of victory was the biggest win in Ryder Cup history, and will never be beaten unless the format reverts to thirty-six-hole matches. It was equaled in 1947 by Lew Worsham and Ed Oliver.

Leo Diegel and Al Espinosa (USA) v. Abe Mitchell and Fred Robson (GBI)

After Britain's having been humiliated in the first two matches, it was something of a surprise that the venerable pair of Mitchell and Robson made a better go of it. Not only were the British more competitive, but they actually won their match against Diegel and Espinosa. The visitors took an early two-hole lead, but the Americans had leveled by the turn and were two up by lunch.

The only British win of the first day was fashioned on and around the greens, where they one-putted fourteen of thirty-five holes.

After Diegel and Espinosa won the second hole in the afternoon, they immediately dropped three in a row to fall back level. Having been the only British pair to win their foursomes at Moortown, Mitchell and Robson finished the stronger. They won eight and nine to go up, dropped the eleventh, and won the next two on the way to repeating their winning act, 3 and 1.

Billy Burke and Wiffy Cox (USA) v. Syd Easterbrook and Ernest Whitcombe (GBI)

The British captain decided to send out his brother instead of himself in the final foursomes, although many felt he should have shouldered more of the playing responsibility. "All members of the team are triers and gentlemen. If we lose, we will lose like sportsmen," said Charles Whitcombe.

Burke and Cox were up by three early on, only to be pegged back to one as Whitcombe and Easterbrook came back in 34.

The British pair then took over the lead with wins at the second and third holes in the afternoon, but once Cox's approach to the fourth hole set up a tying score, the anxious Americans never looked back.

One up after ten became two when the Americans claimed the eleventh, but they immediately dropped the 546-yard twelfth to the dogged British pair, who resolutely refused to surrender.

Although this final match was not a cakewalk like the first two matches, Burke and Cox held on to ice their British opponents, with two more wins in the next three holes. A half at sixteen was good enough for a 3 and 2 victory for the Americans.

Day one result: USA 3, GBI 1

"What may or may not have saved the British from a complete whitewash was a cooling storm that swept the course during the noon hour, clearing up before the afternoon matches started, but bringing welcome relief from the terrific heat that has had a decidedly adverse effect on the visitors."

—William D. Richardson, *New York Times*

Day Two: 36-Hole Singles

"Hot weather again prevailed, but a brisk breeze was blowing, which made conditions more comfortable than the first day, when the temperature was 100 in the shade." —*Sunday Times* (London)

"We have had one of the coldest and dreariest winters and springs in England. We have hardly seen the sun. We don't mind the wind, a hard match, or any collection of traps, but this hot weather takes something out of us." —Fred Pignon, British team manager

Billy Burke (USA) v. Archie Compston (GBI)

In the qualifying event for the final four places, Billy Burke broke Scioto's course record for seventy-two holes. His 289 eclipsed Bobby Jones's previous mark of 293, set when winning the 1926 U.S. Open.

After winning the fourth and seventh holes, Burke turned for home in even fours, two up on Compston. With both men winning and losing a pair of holes each, inward cards of 35 apiece saw the American retain his advantage at lunch. Compston showed he was not going down without a fight, making a birdie two in fine style on the fourteenth, after Burke had gone three up on the previous hole.

The British player was unable to win any more holes in the afternoon, as Burke took the fourth and fifth on British bogeys. Three U.S. wins in a row from the ninth was enough to hand Compston his second heavy defeat of the contest, 7 and 6, as the British player failed to reach the thirteenth hole in either of his afternoon rounds.

A week later, Burke converted his fine match-play form into even finer stroke play at the nearby Inverness Club by winning the U.S. Open.

Gene Sarazen (USA) v. Fred Robson (GBI)

Sarazen started his match against Robson by winning the first three holes (3-4-4 against 4-6-5). Robson won the fourth with a par three, after Sarazen drove through the green and into a shelter house being used as a refreshment stand. Sarazen's ball came to rest between some wooden boxes, which were moved to allow the American to conjure up a miraculous shot out of a small window and onto the green ten feet from the flag. According to official records, this saga did not have a happy ending: Sarazen missed the par putt while Robson made his to win the hole.

Sarazen's remarkable recovery on the fourth hole has become the subject of legend. A number of different reports exist concerning the shot which the American regarded as greater than his double-eagle shot at the 1935 Masters. The following is Sarazen's account, taken from the *Scioto Country Club History Book.*

"I saw an opening through the window of the shelter house. The ball was resting on one of the grooves they have in concrete, and I knew the way it was resting that it would bounce up when I hit it. The ball went right through the window and onto the green, about ten feet from the cup, and I dropped the putt for a three."

Another erroneous report stated that after Sarazen's ball flew out the window, Robson thought the American had conceded having thrown it back out. The Englishman took some practice putts, then lost the hole when Sarazen appeared to hole out for par.

The Englishman also won the eighth, but Sarazen hit back at the ninth to be two up at the turn. The next two holes were traded in fours against fives, and Sarazen holed a thirty-footer on fourteen just to save his half. A win on seventeen gave the American a comfortable three-hole lead at lunch, which he more than doubled on the outward half in the afternoon. Sarazen wrapped the match up with three pars in a row to the twelfth for America's second 7 and 6 win of the singles.

Johnny Farrell (USA) v. William Davies (GBI)

At lunch, Farrell and Davies were level, after a morning of cut-and-thrust golf by both players. Farrell had gone ahead on the second hole, but Davies leveled on the next and was behind again after five. The American birdied the par-5 eighth but lost the hole to Davies's excellent eagle three. All square at the turn with 37 strokes each, the foes came home in 36 apiece.

The afternoon was a different story, as one player dominated the other for a convincing win, but unlike prior encounters it was the British player who came home the stronger. Davies exacted some swift revenge over Farrell by reversing the form of the previous day's foursomes with an impressive individual 4 and 3 win.

Wiffy Cox (USA) v. Abe Mitchell (GBI)

Having taken a lead over Abe Mitchell on the first with a par four, Wiffy Cox had to hole a twenty-five-footer on the fourth to maintain his lead. The next hole saw Cox extend his lead, but he played himself into trouble on the sixth, and the lead was back to one. Four halves followed, but then the next five holes produced five results—three by a British hand and two by American—to level the match. With the score all square at the eighteenth, Mitchell made a superb birdie to gain the slightest of edges at the break.

Once again the postlunch malaise hit the British team, as Mitchell's form slumped and Cox's stock rose. The Englishman never looked as if he would repeat his four-hole winning burst of the morning against a much more resolute opponent. A win on the seventeenth gave the American, who was already dormie two, a 3 and 1 win.

Despite being Samuel Ryder's inspiration behind the Cup, Abe Mitchell started off his singles career in poor style with two defeats, having lost heavily to Diegel in 1929.

Walter Hagen (USA) v. Charles Whitcombe (GBI)

For the second contest running, the two captains were paired against each other in the singles, although Hagen appeared late on the first tee with a martini in his hand.

Says Jack Nicklaus in *The Greatest Game of All* (1969), "As Hagen stood on the tee with a coat thrown majestically over his shoulders, a waiter appeared from the clubhouse carrying a tray on which was poised a martini in a shining stem glass. Walter took a sip or two of the martini and nonchalantly swung his driver a couple of times with his free hand, his left. He took another sip or two, shifted the martini, and took a couple of swings with his right hand. When his name was announced, he drained the martini with a flourish, and after a few practice swings with both hands on the club, hit a beautiful drive right down the middle of the fairway."

The martini may well have been stirred, but Hagen was quickly shaken. Whitcombe, who had been kept waiting by the American's showmanship, slapped home a sixteen-foot birdie putt on the first to lead. Whether or not Hagen had imbibed a few extra martinis before he emerged from the clubhouse, he had trouble hitting his drives straight. This minor inconvenience made no difference to Hagen; he reached the turn two up, having won or saved five holes from desperate lies in the rough.

On ten it was Whitcombe's time to taste the drink—landing his ball in the brook to go three down. Without so much as a care, Hagen continued to find trouble: the rough on eleven finally beat him, but he beat the sand on fourteen for a win. Four up at lunch, and Hagen only knows how many martinis down.

In the afternoon, Whitcombe hit his second shot on the thirteenth hole from the deep rough and back onto the fairway, where the Englishman discovered he had played the wrong ball. He promptly picked up and conceded the hole. Hagen would have none of it and made Whitcombe go back, find his ball, and play the shot again. Whitcombe's recovery was so good that he actually won the hole.

Nothing in the afternoon approached the morning entertainment, as Whitcombe could not cut back the lead and his opponent was happy to roll along and smell the roses; Hagen flowed to an easy 4 and 3 win.

The American captain's win gave his side the point required to regain the trophy.

Denny Shute (USA) v. Bert Hodson (GBI)

Densmore Shute parred the first two holes and was gifted a couple of easy wins, as Bert Hodson started bogey-bogey.

Shute dropped the third hole in bogey but took the fifth to go back up by two. Hodson cut the lead again on eight with a birdie four and leveled on the eleventh with a three. Having got back all square, the Englishman let it all slip away on the last four holes. Shute birdied sixteen and seventeen, where he made the thirty-foot shot around a semi-stymie. Hodson muffed a shot on the last hole to finish three down to Hagen's dangerous foursomes partner.

As had been commonplace, the American totally destroyed his opponent in the afternoon, winning five of the next twelve holes to land another massive victory, 8 and 6.

Earlier in the week, Shute had played ninety holes of golf in two and a half days just to qualify for the Ryder Cup, so he was well acquainted with the course.

Shute produced the two most one-sided wins by any player in the same Ryder Cup when he followed up his record 10 and 9 foursomes victory with this 8 and 6 shellacking in the singles.

Al Espinosa (USA) v. Ernest Whitcombe (GBI)

In the closest match of the day, Al Espinosa carded a morning round of 73 and took a two-hole lead into the afternoon against Ernest Whitcombe, as the final five holes of the round were all halved.

The afternoon session proved as close as the morning, with neither player able to establish any telling superiority over the other. Try as he might, Whitcombe could not catch the American, who in turn could not finish the British player off until the penultimate hole, 2 and 1.

Craig Wood (USA) v. Arthur Havers (GBI)

Craig Wood must have been rather surprised to turn one up on Arthur Havers, as the American carded a fairly woeful 39 on the front nine. Perversely, Havers, out in 40, must have felt lucky to be only one down. Coming home, Havers started to make some birdies as he won four out of five holes from the eleventh. Still, this sudden change in fortune (3-5-4-3-3 to 5-6-4-4-5) saw the British player reach lunch only two up. But for a much-needed American birdie on the last, after Havers botched his putt for a win, the lead might have been four.

Having come home in six shots fewer than he started with, Havers continued his good form on into the afternoon and was able to turn his advantage into a 4 and 3 win.

Day two result: USA 6, GBI 2
Overall match score: USA 9, GBI 3

"The result of the Ryder Cup may be rather disappointing but can hardly be surprising except to those who regard it as a patriotic duty to expect what they know will not happen." —BERNARD DARWIN, *Times* (London)

Recap

The win-loss ratio of 3:1 for the whole match was probably a fair reflection of the relative playing strengths of the two teams, especially with the match being played in the United States.

For their second visit in a row, the British had been overpowered in nearly every department of the game, as the 9-3 result at Scioto was very close to the Ryder Cup result of 9½-2½ at Worcester.

"So far as one can judge, our men, with one or two exceptions, played more or less as well as could be hoped against a very strong side under extraordinarily difficult conditions. The handicap of playing in the other man's country is not perhaps sufficiently appreciated by those who have not tried it. Cold is the one and only thing that is at all likely to beat the Americans, and when our team won at Moortown, they were greatly helped by the raw and bitter weather. Similarly, heat is our worst enemy."
—BERNARD DARWIN, *Times* (London)

12,000 SEE GOLF MATCHES
[BOBBY] JONES SPENDS ENTIRE DAY WATCHING PERFORMERS AT SCIOTO
—New York Times *headline*

In addition to the obvious physical and mental advantages the Americans had over the British players, it would prove an almost insurmountable hurdle for the British to become competitive on American soil, let alone achieve a victory.

Match Results (Winning side marked in *italics*.)

Friday, June 26—Foursomes

	USA	GBI	Score
1.	*Gene Sarazen* *Johnny Farrell*	Archie Compston William Davies	8 and 7
2.	*Walter Hagen* *Denny Shute*	George Duncan Arthur Havers	10 and 9
3.	Leo Diegel Al Espinosa	*Abe Mitchell* *Fred Robson*	3 and 1
4.	*Billy Burke* *Wiffy Cox*	Syd Easterbrook Ernest Whitcombe	3 and 2

Day one result: USA 3, GBI 1

Saturday, June 27—Singles

	USA	GBI	Score
5.	*Billy Burke*	Archie Compston	7 and 6
6.	*Gene Sarazen*	Fred Robson	7 and 6
7.	Johnny Farrell	*William Davies*	4 and 3
8.	*Wiffy Cox*	Abe Mitchell	3 and 1
9.	*Walter Hagen*	Charles Whitcombe	4 and 3
10.	*Denny Shute*	Bert Hodson	8 and 6
11.	*Al Espinosa*	Ernest Whitcombe	2 and 1
12.	Craig Wood	*Arthur Havers*	4 and 3

Day two result: USA 6, GBI 2

Overall match score: USA 9, GBI 3

1933

Southport and Ainsdale
Lancashire, England
June 26–27

United States 5½	**Great Britain and Ireland 6½**
Billy Burke	Percy Alliss
Leo Diegel	William Davies
Ed Dudley	Syd Easterbrook
Olin Dutra	Arthur Havers
Paul Runyan	Arthur Lacey
Gene Sarazen	Abe Mitchell
Densmore Shute	Alf Padgham
Horton Smith	Alf Perry
Craig Wood	Charles Whitcombe
Playing Captain	Alan Dailey [did not play]
Walter Hagen	**Captain**
	J. H. Taylor

Taylor-Made Victory

In an attempt to professionalize the British team and enable them to compete with their stronger, better-organized opponents, a nonplaying captain was selected to oversee both the selection of the players and their preparation. It had been feared that the British club pro would always struggle to match the hardened touring pro of the U.S. circuit. So the choosing of sixty-two-year-old J. H. Taylor, one of the original Ryder Cup selectors from 1927, as team manager was a step in the right direction.

Whether or not his players actually enjoyed the new regime of early-morning runs along the local Southport Beach, it certainly showed in their play. Taylor's disciplined training appeared to have paid full dividends on the first day. At one stage, Britain was ahead in all foursomes.

Once again, Britain's top player, Henry Cotton, was absent—he was residing in Belgium at the Royal Waterloo club—although Percy Alliss had returned from his club in Germany and was eligible.

Both teams were selected by their respective PGA committees without any trials or qualifying performance.

The Americans had no problems selecting an even stronger team than the one that had won two years earlier. Two new American faces made the transatlantic trip: Dutra and Runyan. Captain for the fourth time, Hagen had no worries over his rookies, and he threw them both into the opening-day foursomes.

Hagen's only real worry was over the way his team looked when they met up in New York prior to boarding the ship. The always immaculately turned out captain sent his players to the finest tailors in the city, and had them dressed to the nines, before cheekily billing the PGA of America.

Course Details

This typical English seaside course is situated only a few miles up the Lancashire coast from the better-known British Open course at Royal Lytham.

Hole	Distance	Par	Hole	Distance	Par
1	210	3	10	455	5
2	522	5	11	378	4
3	411	4	12	357	4
4	418	4	13	359	4
5	449	4	14	326	4
6	380	4	15	157	3
7	481	5	16	490	5
8	180	3	17	452	5
9	492	5	18	363	4
		37			**38 = Par 75 (6,880 yards)**

Course designer: James Braid

Day One: 36-Hole Foursomes

Walter Hagen played his usual waiting game over handing in his foursomes list. Taylor issued an ultimatum when the American failed to furnish his list after being asked for the second time. Taylor threatened to call the whole match off if Hagen missed the third scheduled "list meeting." Hagen relented and made his peace with Taylor, although the two disparate spirits rarely saw eye-to-eye during the week.

Walter Hagen and Gene Sarazen (USA) v. Percy Alliss and Charles Whitcombe (GBI)

Hagen himself led off the match with Sarazen, although some insiders felt this was more of a peace offering than a tactical master plan. It may have been both, but there had long been a friendly feud between the two great stars, and the chemistry sparked with an early lead.

After Hagen's twenty-five-foot birdie putt on the twelfth gave the U.S. pair a two-hole lead, Whitcombe and Alliss reeled off four wins in a row. Alliss started the ball rolling with a fifteen-footer on thirteen, while Hagen bunkered his tee shot at the short par-4 fourteenth, and Sarazen blew a short putt for a half on fifteen as the British went one up.

"I think Walter was, without question, the greatest putter of all time. He could putt any kind of green, under any conditions."
—*Gene Sarazen*

"Sarazen persisted in missing comparatively short putts, which Americans are supposed to hole with the same ease as they light a cigarette."
—George Greenwood, *London Telegraph*

On the par-5 sixteenth, Sarazen overshot the green and Hagen messed up the return chip. Two up with two to play, Whitcombe made the shot of the morning, a 180-yard bunker shot from the second fairway that landed in the shadow of the flag. However, this miracle recovery was only good enough for a half, as the Americans also got their birdie thanks to Hagen's immaculate approach to three feet.

On the final green of the morning, Hagen's putt hit the British ball, knocking them nearer the hole and leaving his partner a putt of the length he had not holed all day. The British took lunch three to the good, having overturned a two-hole U.S. lead.

Sarazen's putting worries haunted him on the first hole after lunch. He missed a five-footer after Hagen had recovered Sarazen's badly overhit four-iron tee shot. Through eight holes after lunch, the British had extended their lead to four, when Hagen failed to control his tee shot.

As if they fed off the challenge of such a bad start, the American stars got their spluttering game into gear. On the ninth Hagen holed a seventeen-footer, and they also won the next two holes with some inspired play from both players to draw within one hole.

Whitcombe, in particular, succumbed to the increasing pressure on the greens, missing two fairly easy putts that cost his side holes. On the eleventh he managed to miss the hole by six inches from only two feet away.

The British went round in 72 and 77, while the Americans slightly improved on the morning 75 with a 74 for the half.

The next four holes were halved, but the sixteenth was lost by another British bogey, despite a poor drive from Hagen. The seventeenth saw the United States hand the lead back, as Sarazen hooked into the unforgiving links rough. On the eighteenth green it was Alliss's turn to falter under the pressure for which Ryder Cups were quickly becoming notorious. Having sliced into a greenside bunker, he then failed to convert Whitcombe's excellent recovery to four feet. This allowed the U.S. team to win the final hole and halve a match they should have lost some five or six holes earlier.

Olin Dutra and Denny Shute (USA) v. Abe Mitchell and Arthur Havers (GBI)

Dutra and Shute took on the somewhat more experienced British pair of Mitchell and Havers. Hagen's gamble soon unraveled, and his young pair came into lunch four down. At no time had they looked capable of threatening their older opponents, who played perfect foursomes—setting each other up for makable putts. The strain began to show most on the large-framed Dutra, who produced a few shaky shots, including finding the rough with his opening tee shot to go one down.

Havers climbed all over the flag with his mashie-niblick approach to the third to quickly go two up. The Americans were back level after ten, but the British strung together four wins in the next six holes. Havers struck a mashie to six feet on eleven, while Dutra's sense of direction off the tee deserted him again on thirteen.

By lunch, the venerable British pairing held a commanding four-hole lead, as they were out in 71, six better than the U.S. pair.

The lead grew to five following the second hole in the afternoon. Although Dutra and Shute won a couple of holes in creditable threes, Mitchell and Havers held too much in reserve to be beaten and trotted out a 3 and 2 win.

Paul Runyan and Craig Wood (USA) v. Syd Easterbrook and William Davies (GBI)

In a close match that was all square at lunch, there was never much daylight between these two evenly matched pairs—who did not exactly set the course on fire with equally nightmarish rounds of 80. The morning would have been worse for Wood and Runyan had the latter not skillfully skipped a stymie on the eighteenth green to level the match.

Davies and Easterbrook finally opened up a two-hole advantage with three to play over the Americans. With certain defeat staring them in the face, the U.S. pair had a chance to strike back at the sixteenth, but Runyan missed a five-foot putt for the win. On seventeen, with their opponents bunkering themselves out of the hole, the U.S. team did pull a hole back.

The final hole saw both pairs encounter more trouble than they needed at such a late stage. Wood's drive all but disappeared into the rough, while Davies put his second into another bunker. Runyan played a remarkable recovery to the front of the green, only to see the British scramble a vital half—and win the match by one hole.

The British team improved on their morning 80 with an afternoon 73, while the U.S. pair carded a 74 the second time around.

Billy Burke and Ed Dudley (USA) v. Alf Padgham and Alf Perry (GBI)

In the final match, the two young Alfs—Padgham and Perry—were four up at lunch and cruising to an easy win over Burke and Dudley. The morning exchanges were highlighted by the rare sight of one golfer hitting another. On the eighth, Padgham's blind shot from the rough hit an unsuspecting Dudley on the leg, and he was rather unfairly (as the British were all but out of the hole) yet correctly penalized the hole for *interfering* with his opponent's ball.

At lunch, Britain had been well up in three foursomes and level in the other.

The tide turned back to the Americans immediately after lunch, when Britain had a two-foot putt to go five up but missed. This mistake swung the momentum toward the grateful Americans, who suddenly found their true form—the cigar-puffing Burke having won the U.S. Open in 1931.

Six holes after lunch, Britain's four-hole lead had evaporated, although the home team managed to stem the flow of lost holes,

Burke and Dudley played their second round of the day in an amazing twelve shots better than the morning session—carding 81 in the morning, followed by a 69. The British had been more consistently circumspect.

reasserted their superiority, and took a one-hole lead with three to play. The Americans laid a courageous chip to within a few feet for a four and the sixteenth hole.

Back level going to the seventeenth, Burke, who had been the mainstay of the American recovery, holed a telling and timely long putt for a U.S. lead, which became a valuable and unexpected win once the thirty-sixth was halved in fours.

Where they might have hoped for a clean sweep over their visitors, the British ended the first day just one point ahead. Since they were always going to be underdogs in the final-day singles, things did not look too promising for Taylor's troops.

Day one result: USA 1½, GBI 2½

Day Two: 36-Hole Singles

An estimated 25,000 thronged the galleries—a record for any golfing event in Great Britain—though some observers believe many turned up to catch a glimpse of the Prince of Wales, who was among their number.

Come lunchtime on the second day, the singles were all square: both sides up in three and level in two.

Gene Sarazen (USA) v. Alf Padgham (GBI)

In a remarkable piece of captaincy, Hagen had seriously considered dropping Sarazen (who had won the previous year's U.S. and British Opens) after his poor play in the foursomes. Sarazen thought otherwise and persuaded his captain to not only let him play but also lead off the American singles. Hagen conceded, thinking Sarazen would lose against Britain's top player, Padgham. Not for the last time, a Ryder Cup captain would be surprised by one of his "weak links."

Sarazen actually played Alliss in the 1937 singles, but he did not partner Hagen that year. He did partner Hagen against Alliss in 1933—no wonder the "little Squire" was confused over whom he played and when.

Sarazen's recollection of this episode is clouded in the mist of time: *"Hagen and myself didn't get along. When we played in the foursomes the day before, he said, 'You're not hitting the ball as well as you used to.' I said, 'Never mind about what I did yesterday; I want to play tomorrow.' He said, 'All right.' So he put me against Percy Alliss."*

—GENE SARAZEN

Padgham started off as expected and established a slim advantage by the first turn, highlighted by his monster putt on the ninth. Having putted like a novice in the foursomes, Sarazen turned in a masterful display on the greens. Carding a three at eleven, a two at fifteen, and another three at seventeen, the American won four holes to go three up. Padgham reduced the lunchtime lead by slamming home another long putt from the back of the eighteenth green.

Whether or not Sarazen ate well at lunch, he feasted royally on the first five holes in the afternoon. Three wins put him five up on Padgham, who had the stuffing knocked out of him—6 and 4—midway through the inward nine.

Olin Dutra (USA) v. Abe Mitchell (GBI)

A morning of high drama and high-jinks typified this up-and-down battle. Dutra holed a monster putt on the first to take the lead, but Mitchell struck back with an equally long putt on the second. By the turn, Dutra had established a three-hole cushion—out in 35—but his rookie nerves and technique failed him.

When Mitchell made a three to win the eleventh, it was the start of something spectacular—as he went on to win the next seven holes in a row as well. Things went from bad to worse for the American when he took two to get out of the bunker on seventeen and lost the last hole of the morning by knocking Mitchell's ball into the hole attempting to avoid a stymie. Having lost eight holes in succession, the American was five down at lunch and in a seemingly hopeless position, having covered the inward nine in 44 strokes.

This was the day that Abe Mitchell played as if he deserved to be on top of a golf trophy.

Dutra's afternoon started as his morning round had—with a long putt to win the first—but his joy was short-lived. Forty-six-year-old Mitchell took control of the game, taking the next five holes to record an astonishing feat of winning thirteen out of fourteen holes. Nine up with twelve to play, Mitchell ended up a very easy winner, 9 and 8.

Walter Hagen (USA) v. Arthur Lacey (GBI)

One of the world's longest hitters, Arthur Lacey had the unenviable task of trying to take a point off Walter Hagen, but the British player quickly established a two-hole lead over the U.S. captain.

Hagen cut this back when the long-hitting Lacey was so far off line on the sixth hole that a lonely spectator found what he took to be a lost ball from a previous day and pocketed Lacey's ball. The unlucky fan was chased down by an angry steward, who made him replace the ball where he had found it.

The British player then missed an eighteen-inch putt on the seventh hole that would have restored his two-hole lead. Another poor English drive on the eighth gifted that hole to Hagen, who played the ninth in far-from-convincing fashion: hooked drive, short chip onto the fairway, long iron to a yard of the pin, and one solid putt for a fighting half in four.

When the Prince of Wales ventured out onto the golf course (followed by more than two thousand people), he chose this match to follow. On seeing the Prince in the crowd, Hagen—against court protocol—made a point of introducing His Royal Highness to his opponent. The Royal spectator saw little of the match, as he was forced to abandon his walk owing to the increasing number of well-wishers crowding around him.

Hagen's approach play was a sight for sore eyes, as he laid another iron shot at the feet of the flag on the eleventh for a winning three, giving the American captain a lead for the first time in the match. Lacey played the twelfth in Hagenesque fashion: a poor drive into knee-length rough, a recovery into a bunker, a second recovery just onto the green, a first putt into the hole for another belligerent half in four. This seemed to unnerve Hagen, who failed to win another hole before the break. Losses came at fourteen, where he sliced his tee shot into a bunker, and sixteen, where he was unable to pinpoint a chip from the back of the green.

At lunch, Hagen was a hole down but looked well in control of the situation. Despite "the Haig's" best efforts, the match remained evenly balanced throughout the afternoon. Hagen finally drew level on the thirteenth after Lacey again waved good-bye to a bad drive. The American's iron play continued to delight the massed crowds that followed him, as he hit the base of the pin on thirteen for another win and the lead. A ball in the sand pegged back Hagen on the fifteenth, then disaster struck Lacey on the sixteenth, where he took four shots to get down from just fifty yards away.

In his inimitable style, Hagen struck a stupendous spoon to the apron of the seventeenth green and needed only one putt for the half that closed out the match 2 and 1.

Craig Wood (USA) v. William Davies (GBI)

With the score all square at lunch between William Davies and Craig Wood, the American played much the better golf in the afternoon to edge ahead and finally dispose of his opponent quite comfortably, 4 and 3.

Paul Runyan (USA) v. Percy Alliss (GBI)

A real Ryder Cup nail-biter right through the morning and afternoon sessions, this match arrived all square at the sixteenth. Both Runyan and Alliss knew how much the point they were playing for meant to their teams, so neither could afford to make the first mistake. Unfortunately for the U.S. team, Runyan was the first to crack. He lost the sixteenth, and on the next hole he could only watch in despair as his bunker shot flew out-of-bounds. This was enough to give Alliss the victory 2 and 1 and add fuel to the British crowd's growing fervor for a home win.

As a symbol of just how close this match was, when both players found the same bunker on the pivotal seventeenth, their balls were touching in the sand. Alliss played his ball out before Runyan blasted his out-of-bounds.

Leo Diegel (USA) v. Arthur Havers (GBI)

Arthur Havers had been all square at lunch against his American rival Leo Diegel, who had sat out the first day. Superior play in the afternoon along with a better acquaintance with the course reaped its reward for the British, as Havers cozily won, 4 and 3, over the ring-rusty Diegel.

Denny Shute (USA) v. Syd Easterbrook (GBI)

Quite simply, this match between Densmore Shute and Syd Easterbrook has gone down as one of the great Ryder Cup singles matches ever.

Shute, thanks to some inconsistent putting by Easterbrook, was three up after as many holes. A magnificent comeback by the British player brought him level, but he was back one down at lunch.

This dogfight continued through the afternoon, with neither player giving an inch. The nearer they got to the clubhouse, the more they realized how important their match was becoming in the grand scheme of things. They were the last pair out on the course, with the overall match score tied at 5½ points each. The destiny of the 1933 Ryder Cup was riding on this one match.

Shute held a one-hole cushion with four holes to be negotiated, but Easterbrook drew level on the par-3 fifteenth with a marvelous birdie putt from more than fifteen feet away. The Englishman made an even longer putt at the next for a four and a saving half. Shute almost took the seventeenth, but his rival refused to let a semi-stymie prevent him from holing out for another gutsy half.

All square on the thirty-sixth tee with the Ryder Cup to play for, both players rather nervously found bunkers with their hooked drives, but Easterbrook found more distance. Shute played out of one pot bunker into another by the left of the green, while Easterbrook opted for safety and found the comfort of the fairway some way back. His approach to the green was matched in length from the pin by the American's fine bunker shot. Still nothing separated the players or the two sides.

In line with his larger-than-life character, the American captain was deep in conversation with the Prince of Wales as Shute and Easterbrook lined up their vital putts on the eighteenth green. Some observers felt that Hagen should have told Shute to lag his putt up for a certain half, good enough to retain the Cup. Hagen later suggested he did not want to insult the Prince by breaking off his "audience" to attend to the game at hand. Said Hagen: "I was wondering if I shouldn't be down there setting Denny wise to how things stood, but I thought it would be discourteous to walk out on the future king of England."

Standing more than twenty feet away from glory, both players pondered their fate. Rather nervously, Easterbrook putted up to within three feet, allowing Shute a putt for the Cup. The American's downhiller was never going to be short, as the ball charged the hole, going six, maybe seven feet past. With the chance of the win gone, Shute knew the whole match rested on his second putt. He took his time, he took aim, and he missed. One putt for the Cup, and the American had three-putted.

The young British player now had the Ryder Cup in the palm of his clammy hand—and from three feet away he struck the ball cleanly. The cheers of the partisan crowd greeted the brave putt that won the 1933 Ryder Cup.

Horton Smith (USA) v. Charles Whitcombe (GBI)

Despite some late heroics to reduce Horton Smith's five-hole lead at lunch, Whitcombe was never really in this matchup. Although the British player, with a valiant comeback, bravely kept his hopes and those of his team alive until the penultimate hole, Smith's superior technique and skill finally wore him down, 2 and 1.

This point for America had leveled the overall match score 5½–5½ and set the scene for the Shute v. Easterbrook match ahead of them.

Day two result: USA 4, GBI 4

After the golf-loving Prince had been "forced" off the course by the swarming hordes of admirers, he took up residence on the clubhouse balcony that overlooked the final green. Down below him was Samuel Ryder, watching his last Ryder Cup match (he did not make the trip in 1935 and died before the contest that bore his name returned to Britain). When Samuel Ryder was buried, he was interred with his favorite mashie club beside him.

Overall match score: USA 5½, GBI 6½

Recap

In a storybook ending, Britain had regained the Ryder Cup and leveled the series at two matches apiece—with no home side having been defeated. The Ryder Cup as a contest looked set for a competitive run of close-fought matches, but this scenario would prove to be far from the reality.

J. H. Taylor was just happy to receive the coveted trophy from the Prince of Wales, who quaintly summed up the feelings of a whole nation: "In giving this cup, I am naturally impartial. But, of course, we over here are very pleased to have won."

In his closing speech, Hagen admitted that he had "a place for the Cup on the table in the *Aquitania* coming over and we told them to reserve a place going back."

Upon receiving the Cup: *"I am the proudest man in the British Commonwealth of people at this moment."* —J. H. Taylor

As was the norm in the early days of the Ryder Cup, both sets of players met up again at the British Open, staged at St. Andrews.

Syd Easterbrook continued his hot streak, finishing fourth, the top-placed home player and the only non-American in the top six. Densmore Shute quickly got over his nerve-racking Cup defeat by dispatching Craig Wood in an equally enthralling play-off.

Match Results (Winning side marked in *italics*.)

Monday, June 26—Foursomes

	USA	GBI	Score
1.	Walter Hagen Gene Sarazen	Percy Alliss Charles Whitcombe	halved
2.	Olin Dutra Denny Shute	*Abe Mitchell* *Arthur Havers*	3 and 2
3.	Paul Runyan Craig Wood	*Syd Easterbrook* *William Davies*	1-up
4.	*Billy Burke* *Ed Dudley*	Alf Padgham Alf Perry	1-up

Day one result: USA 1½, GBI 2½

Tuesday, June 27—Singles

	USA	GBI	Score
5.	*Gene Sarazen*	Alf Padgham	6 and 4
6.	Olin Dutra	*Abe Mitchell*	9 and 8
7.	*Walter Hagen*	Arthur Lacey	2 and 1
8.	*Craig Wood*	William Davies	4 and 3
9.	Paul Runyan	*Percy Alliss*	2 and 1
10.	Leo Diegel	*Arthur Havers*	4 and 3
11.	Denny Shute	*Syd Easterbrook*	1-up
12.	*Horton Smith*	Charles Whitcombe	2 and 1

Day two result: USA 4, GBI 4

Overall match score: USA 5½, GBI 6½

1935

Ridgewood Country Club
Ridgewood, New Jersey
United States
September 28–29

United States 9	**Great Britain and Ireland 3**
Olin Dutra	Percy Alliss
Ky Laffoon	Dick Burton
Sam Parks	Jack Busson
Henry Picard	William Cox
Johnny Revolta	Ted Jarman
Paul Runyan	Alf Padgham
Gene Sarazen	Alf Perry
Horton Smith	Ernest Whitcombe
Craig Wood	Reg Whitcombe
Playing Captain	**Playing Captain**
Walter Hagen	Charles Whitcombe

Summer Stars, Some Are Not

This was the fifth Ryder Cup meeting and the series was all square, with two wins apiece.

Following the British players' protests at playing in the heat of an American summer, this and all future Ryder Cups in the United States were played in the fall. The only other British Ryder Cup match to be played in the summer was at Southport, in 1937.

The original reason for a summer event was to allow the British players to stay on and compete in the U.S. Open that followed (and vice versa in Britain). With this departure from the golfing equivalent of a time-share, the Ryder Cup had finally emerged as a fixture on the golfing calendar in its own right.

"The British players have had four days' practice with the bigger ball—scarcely sufficient to learn its tricks of flight and its rather jumpy behavior in putting."
—*George Greenwood,* London Telegraph

The Americans again agreed to host the event on the East Coast to alleviate any travel problems the British team might have. But despite having their table laid for them in terms of time and place, the British team did not find any real advantage once play started in earnest. Still without their top player, Henry Cotton, deemed a nonresident as a club pro in Belgium, the British team did boast three Whitcombe brothers: Charles, Ernest, and Reg (a newcomer to the team). Other British rookies were Dick Burton, Jack Busson, William Cox, and Ted Jarman (no relation to this book's author).

As captain, Hagen was automatically selected along with Runyan (1934 PGA champion), Dutra, and Parks (the 1934 and '35 U.S. Open winners). The other six selections were based on overall scoring average.

Hagen captained the Americans again, welcoming a few fresh faces of his own: Ky Laffoon, Johnny Revolta, Henry Picard, and Sam Parks. The forty-two-year-old captain decided to omit himself from the singles—a move mirrored by his British counterpart, though both acquitted themselves admirably on the opening day.

Course Details

With a slightly unusual layout, Ridgewood boasts three—East, West, and Center—championship-quality nine-hole courses that are used in three eighteen-hole combinations.

For the Ryder Cup, the following combinations were used morning and afternoon:

Foursomes: West-East A.M., Center-West P.M.
Singles: Center-East A.M., West-East P.M.

The courses, all quite narrow, are lined by mature trees and the regulation depth of rough, with a number of water hazards.

	West		East		Center	
Hole	**Distance**	**Par**	**Distance**	**Par**	**Distance**	**Par**
1	386	4	413	4	373	4
2	393	4	174	3	576	5
3	210	3	578	5	459	4
4	545	5	427	4	535	5
5	425	4	389	4	205	3
6	162	3	213	3	289	4
7	409	4	448	4	407	4
8	575	5	407	4	153	3
9	432	4	392	4	378	4
	3,537	**36**	**3,441**	**35**	**3,375**	**36**

Course designer: A. W. Tillinghast

Originally founded in 1890, Ridgewood is officially recognized as one of the first hundred courses opened in the United States.

The par-4 289-yard sixth hole on the Center course is nicknamed "Five and Dime," because scores between five and ten are regularly made there.

Day One: 36-Hole Foursomes

Walter Hagen and Gene Sarazen (USA) v. Alf Perry and Jack Busson (GBI)

As in 1933, Hagen paired himself with his old nemesis, Gene Sarazen, and this heady combination of legends scarcely played up to their full potential against Perry and Busson, as they were made to fight for the first nine holes.

One up at the turn, with wins at the second (bogey five) and seventh (par), the Americans lost the fourth with a bogey six to a British par. If the front nine had been close, the voyage homeward was most definitely not. The British pair took 40 strokes to negotiate the nine holes and lost four holes without a win of their own. A bogey six on the twelfth was trumped by a double on the par-4 seventeenth as the Americans picked up the pieces for a five-hole lead at the break.

"Walter Hagen goes down in history as the greatest exponent of the dramatic art of turning three shots into two."
—*Henry Longhurst*

Both pairs played horrible golf to open up the afternoon—both out in 40—typified by double-bogey sixes halving the 393-yard second hole. Five up became six when Hagen holed a twenty-footer for birdie on the tenth, and six up became 7 and 6 when Hagen's four-iron tee shot left Sarazen a tap-in from eight feet for a closing birdie two at the 210-yard twelfth.

Although he captained the U.S. side in 1937, this would prove to be Hagen's last Ryder Cup appearance as a player. He ended in some style, with a playing record of 7–1–1, having never lost a foursomes match (4–0–1). His sole singles defeat came in the 10 and 8 humiliation by George Duncan in 1929.

Henry Picard and Johnny Revolta (USA) v. Alf Padgham and Percy Alliss (GBI)

Picard and Revolta almost matched the American leadoff victory with a convincing 6 and 5 win over Padgham and Alliss. The U.S. rookies had a fairly easy introduction to the Ryder Cup, as they opened with par for the first nine holes, but the British carded a 40 to drop four down at the turn. A second set of 40 strokes coming home by the British gifted the rookies a seven-hole lead at lunch, as they had barely broken sweat with a one-over round for the morning.

The British pair was severely hampered by Alliss's stiff neck and head cold, as he was unable to give the British ace Padgham any support.

Amazingly, in the afternoon, Alliss and Padgham carded two sixes and still cut seven shots off their morning round (this time on the Center course), but they could cut only one hole off the Americans' lead. The last four holes were halved as Picard and Revolta accepted the 6 and 5 win with open arms.

Paul Runyan and Horton Smith (USA) v. William Cox and Ted Jarman (GBI)

British rookies Cox and Jarman were unable to match the effort of the U.S. rookies before them and slumped to an even bigger margin of defeat against Runyan and Smith. The Americans found themselves six up after eighteen holes, as Cox and Jarman had troubles on the East course, carding a 39 and dropping five holes in the process.

The afternoon saw little improvement in the visitors' form on the Center course, as they carded their third 39 in a row for nine holes.

The Americans added three more wins to their lead on the front nine; they eventually finished one over par for their round. The 9 and 8 victory was one of the easiest ever achieved in the Ryder Cup, as Cox and Jarman never came to grips with the course or the match-play format.

In twenty-eight holes of play, the British won just two, while the Americans claimed eleven.

Olin Dutra and Ky Laffoon (USA) v. Charles and Ernest Whitcombe (GBI)

Only a sterling effort by the two older Whitcombes prevented an American clean sweep on the first day. The British pair needed all its guile and experience to hold on to defeat Dutra and Laffoon by one hole.

The brothers were unable to convert their distinct superiority off the tee, as they frittered away short putts at the business end of each hole. They lost the first hole with three putts, then returned wins on four and five to take a lead, in defiance of Laffoon's excellent fourteen-foot putt on the fifth. With wins on six and seven, the American pair clawed back into the lead on the twelfth—

thanks to a birdie four—and a British bogey at thirteen saw the U.S. side two up.

Charles's tee shot at the par-3 fifteenth came up six inches short of perfection and was followed by the Americans' smacking two shots into the woods on sixteen to level the match. Lunch was taken with a modicum of parity, both pairs looking back on what might have been.

While addressing his approach shot to the ninth hole, Dutra accidentally made contact with his ball and conceded the hole. The U.S. pair took the next hole with a par, then halved eleven and twelve to leave the sides all square with six to play. Thirteen was claimed by an American par five, but they lost the next two holes, only to post a win at the sixteenth to square the match again.

"But for two old war-horses on the British team, the invaders would have been left completely in the ruck by the American representatives."
—*William D. Richardson,* New York Times

In a day of high scores and poor shots, Ernest Whitcombe produced the shot of the day, as he lifted his recovery out of a deep bunker alongside the seventeenth green (#8 West) to inches of the hole for a crucial half, in bogey fives.

The Americans contrived to lose the last hole and the match by finding the sand when their opponents were putting up to a few inches for the one-hole win.

Day one result: USA 3, GBI 1

"What probably bothered the British players more than anything else here today was the water on the greens. It made the greens so heavy that many times the players used irons rather than putters." —New York Times

Day Two: 36-Hole Singles

The final day started brightly at nine o'clock, as both captains dropped themselves from the singles action.

Gene Sarazen (USA) v. Jack Busson (GBI)

As he had two years earlier, Sarazen led the Americans into battle on the second day—pitted once more against foursomes foe Jack Busson. As on the first day, Sarazen came out on top, but it wasn't all plain sailing for the American.

When Sarazen found the bunker on the par-3 eighth, Busson took a one-hole lead that he defended on the ninth, despite being trapped in a stymie—from which he escaped for a half. After halves at ten and eleven, Busson went on a tear, winning the next three holes with two pars and a birdie climaxed by a forty-foot putt.

After his match against Busson, Sarazen said that it had been the hardest he had played in all five Ryder Cups he had appeared in. High praise indeed from the man who snatched the Masters (from teammate Wood) in electrifying fashion earlier that summer.

Four down, Sarazen got busy on the last three holes of the morning (also par-par-birdie), cutting the lead to one at lunch. Busson lost the sixteenth from the woods. Sarazen took seventeen and beat out Busson's thirty-foot par putt at eighteen with a forty-footer of his own.

Sarazen squared the match on the first hole of the afternoon with a majestic birdie three, but Busson answered in style with a twenty-footer for eagle on the third to move ahead again. The Englishman overhit his approach to the fifth, while Sarazen's birdie squared up the match. Pars were sufficient to claim the next three holes, with Sarazen prevailing at seven and nine for a one-hole lead.

"The former British and American Open champion staggered his youthful rival by holing a fifteen-foot putt for a four [on twelve] and then made a magnificent recovery shot from underneath a tree on the right of the fairway of the next hole. He had an easy three."

—WILLIAM D. RICHARDSON, *New York Times*

His nose in front, Sarazen powered to a typically strong American finish on the back nine, with back-to-back birdies on twelve and thirteen. He lost the fifteenth with a bogey four before closing out the match on the next hole, 3 and 2.

Paul Runyan (USA) v. Dick Burton (GBI)

The British soon found themselves five down in the overall match standings when Paul Runyan handed debutant Dick Burton a lesson in match-play golf with a 5 and 3 victory.

Burton had proved much longer off the tee, but his short game, so vital in this format of golf, did not hold up well against Runyan's well-honed technique. Things looked bleak from the outset when Burton laid a stymie on his opponent and still lost the hole, after Runyan used a mashie-niblick to hole out for his par. The tables were turned on the third, where Burton was stymied. He hit his opponent's ball and missed the hole to go two down.

"The British team could not hole out in a hole the size of the Atlantic."
—*Tom Webster,* London Mail

The Englishman finally won his first hole at the ninth to turn one down. A poor display of putting from Burton allowed his opponent to win some easy holes and increase his lead at lunch to four, the American coming back in 34 strokes.

On the second hole after the resumption, Burton—searching for extra power off the tee—found the trees and went five down after Runyan's birdie three. From here it was a matter of how quickly the end would arrive, but Burton dug in with wins on seven and eight to light up his false hopes, them immediately bogeyed nine to drop back four down.

The end came for Burton in somewhat messy fashion, as he started for home birdie-bogey-bogey to fall five behind. Runyan bogeyed thirteen to offer a slender lifeline to the drowning Englishman, but Burton bogeyed the par-3 fifteenth, sinking to a 5 and 3 defeat.

Johnny Revolta (USA) v. Reg Whitcombe (GBI)

Having seen his two brothers perform heroically on the first day, Reg Whitcombe almost pulled off an equally good result against Johnny Revolta. Three up at the morning turn—with wins at two, three, six, and seven—the Englishman must have fancied his chances of an easy win. However, with wins at twelve and thirteen, Revolta managed to pull back two holes on the inward nine to go into lunch two down.

Whitcombe extended his lead to five after six holes of the afternoon round, but the American fought back—as his opponent's game disintegrated—by winning eight and nine.

"Still enjoying a three-hole lead with only eight more to go, the Briton's game went completely to smash."

—William D. Richardson, *New York Times*

Revolta—who bore the moniker of a gangster's hit man—turned golfing assassin as he shot the lights out of the Englishman's challenge. Three up at the turn, Whitcombe saw his advantage disappear, and more, as he bogeyed all five holes Revolta won on the way home to a 2 and 1 victory.

Olin Dutra (USA) v. Alf Padgham (GBI)

After an opening win on the sixth hole, Olin Dutra found himself two down to Alf Padgham when he lost the next three holes in a row. Two American pars leveled the score with wins at ten and eleven. The British player won the next two holes—capped by a fine birdie at twelve. Dutra took fourteen and gave up the par-3 fifteenth with a bogey.

Sixteen saw Dutra cut the lead back to one as he won another hole with par. While the players had traded wins on the previous seven holes, normality was restored as they halved seventeen and eighteen to give Padgham a one-hole buffer at lunch.

Like Whitcombe before him, Padgham lost his way after lunch and failed to win a hole on the homeward stretch in the afternoon. All square at the turn, Dutra produced an unanswerable burst of wins at ten and eleven, then at fifteen and sixteen, to pull off the fourth U.S. win in the first four singles, 4 and 2.

With Dutra's win, there was no doubt that the Ryder Cup would be returning to the United States. Having lost the first four singles, Britain split the last four, but by then it was too late to save the Ryder Cup.

Craig Wood (USA) v. Percy Alliss (GBI)

In the fifth match out, Craig Wood, who had earlier that year seen his hopes of winning the Masters dashed by Sarazen's "golden eagle," again saw his chances slip away.

Wood took the second hole of the morning after Percy Alliss hit a tree with his recovery from a bunker, and the American added three more wins in a row to open up a four-hole lead by the turn. Alliss won the tenth with a birdie three, before taking thirteen and fourteen with pars to pull back to one down with four to play in the early session. Wood stopped the English surge by winning the last two holes before lunch to stand three up.

In the afternoon, the patient Englishman again whittled away at the lead, pulling two holes back by the ninth with wins on four, five, and nine, while Wood took the eighth. Five of the first six holes on the way home were won or lost, with Alliss taking the lion's share at ten, twelve, and fifteen to level the match.

Holes sixteen and seventeen were halved in pars to set up a nail-biting finale, but Wood underhit his approach, overhit his chip, and mishit his putt to card a bogey five and hand Alliss a one-hole victory.

Horton Smith (USA) v. William Cox (GBI)

Alliss's comeback in the previous match was bettered by teammate William Cox, who found himself five down at lunch against Horton Smith. Having two-putted from six feet on the second, Cox was three down until he won his first hole at the ninth, reaching the turn two down. Coming home in just 33 strokes, the young American increased his lead to five by the break.

Having won the first hole in the afternoon, Smith found more trouble than he could shake a crooked niblick at: woods, bunkers, rough, everything but fairway and green. Smith found hazards and harassment as regularly as his opponent found the hole. The sixth proved most vexatious, as the American visited the sand at least three times.

Having carded a 69, the best round of the morning, Smith went back out in a calamitous 45, playing the last six holes of the front nine in the afternoon without anything better than a five on his card: 6-5-5-5-7-5.

The Englishman held his game together much better as he won six of the first nine after lunch, to briefly go one up. Level again after the tenth, Smith appeared to weather the storm with wins on twelve and thirteen. Unfortunately, the American's storm in a tin cup had not abated, as Cox won the next two holes and halved the final three.

"Cox, built along dreadnaught lines, halved the match after being six down to Horton Smith, after the first hole this afternoon."
—*William D. Richardson,* New York Times

Henry Picard (USA) v. Ernest Whitcombe (GBI)

The Americans' fifth win in the singles came thanks to Henry Picard, who claimed a 3 and 2 victory over Ernest Whitcombe, albeit after the Cup had been won. Five up after the morning session, Picard had taken full advantage of his opponent's inaccurate driving, and it was only the American's lack of a finishing touch on the greens that kept the final score as close as it was.

Whitcombe staged a minirevival after the break, but with the Cup already back in American hands, there was little to play for except pride and honor.

Sam Parks (USA) v. Alf Perry (GBI)

The final singles saw an interesting matchup between the reigning U.S. and British Open champions—Sam Parks and Alf Perry. In a closely fought encounter worthy of their titles, the U.S. player held a slender two-hole lead after nine holes, but the British champion fought back level by the break.

"The movements of Parks are so slow and deliberate that he has been called the 'human tortoise.'"
—*George Greenwood,* London Telegraph

The afternoon proved to be even closer, with the lead changing hands several times, until Perry eked out an invaluable one-hole lead as they approached the final green. Parks produced the longest putt of the two days—from all of forty feet away—to earn an unexpected half and dash Perry's personal bragging rights over the U.S. Open champion.

Day two result: USA *6,* GBI *2*
Overall match score: USA *9,* GBI *3*

Recap

In the first three Ryder Cup matches staged in the United States, the winning scores had been 9½-2½, 9-3, and 9-3, whereas the two British wins at home had been a lot closer, 7-5 and 6½-5½. The Americans had played much tougher in Britain than the British had played in America.

"Better not go at all than to be beaten like this every year."
—The Tatler *magazine*

The weather could not be blamed this time around, as it had rained on the opening day and was pleasantly warm on the second day. The sad realization that dawned on the British party after this defeat was that they were not on the same competitive level as their opponents. The American players had qualified through the rigors of their tough tour, while the British still played with a country club mentality. The Americans practiced long and often on improving their technique, while the British preferred to "sharpen up" with another round of golf.

Despite the one-sided nature of the result and the fact that Britain could manage only two wins from a dozen matches, many British observers felt this had been their country's best team to travel to the United States. That aside, various excuses were cited for the British defeat: too much clover on the fairways, too much water on the greens, too little practice time, using the wrong type of clubs for the course and conditions. On the face of it, the visitors had no room for complaint; they had simply been beaten by a better team, a fact that would haunt British Ryder Cup teams for many years to come.

For the Americans, the result was what had been expected, and considering their dominance, they were probably ruing the four matches they failed to win.

Match Results (Winning side marked in *italics*.)

Saturday, September 28—Foursomes

	USA	GBI	Score
1.	*Walter Hagen* *Gene Sarazen*	Alf Perry Jack Busson	7 and 6
2.	*Henry Picard* *Johnny Revolta*	Alf Padgham Percy Alliss	6 and 5
3.	*Paul Runyan* *Horton Smith*	William Cox Ted Jarman	9 and 8
4.	Olin Dutra Ky Laffoon	*Charles Whitcombe* *Ernest Whitcombe*	1-up

Day one result: USA 3, GBI 1

Sunday, September 29—Singles

	USA	GBI	Score
5.	*Gene Sarazen*	Jack Busson	3 and 2
6.	*Paul Runyan*	Dick Burton	5 and 3
7.	*Johnny Revolta*	Reg Whitcombe	2 and 1
8.	*Olin Dutra*	Alf Padgham	4 and 2
9.	Craig Wood	*Percy Alliss*	1-up
10.	Horton Smith	William Cox	halved
11.	*Henry Picard*	Ernest Whitcombe	3 and 2
12.	Sam Parks	Alf Perry	halved

Day two result: USA 6, GBI 2

Overall match score: USA 9, GBI 3

1937

Southport and Ainsdale Lancashire, England June 29–30	**United States 8**	**Great Britain and Ireland 4**
	Ed Dudley	Percy Alliss
	Ralph Guldahl	Dick Burton
	Tony Manero	Henry Cotton
	Byron Nelson	William Cox
	Henry Picard	Sam King
	Johnny Revolta	Arthur Lacey
	Gene Sarazen	Alf Padgham
	Densmore Shute	Alf Perry
	Sam Snead	Dai Rees
	Captain	**Playing Captain**
	Walter Hagen	Charles Whitcombe

Bringing Home the Cup

The Ryder Cup returned to the Southport seaside course, scene of Britain's dramatic last-hole triumph four years earlier. Sadly, one person who would not be returning was Samuel Ryder, who died in 1936. On a happier note for the home side, they welcomed back Henry Cotton for his first match in eight years.

Thus, the British lineup included the three previous winners of the British Open: Cotton (1934), Perry (1935), and Padgham (1936). Cotton would also go on to lift the claret jug soon after the Ryder Cup, while teammate Dick Burton would be crowned champion in 1939. With only two rookies on their side (Rees and King), this was the strongest British team ever assembled for a Ryder Cup encounter. Since the match was on home turf, never had the anticipation of a British victory run so high.

The Americans, as always, could be expected to counter with some big guns of their own. Sarazen and Shute had won the British Open in 1932 and '33, respectively, while new boy Sam Snead would win the first postwar British Open, in 1946. The United

States also boasted winners of their own Open championship: Manero ('36) and Guldahl ('37 and, later, '38). The team also had 1937 Masters winner and Ryder Cup rookie Byron Nelson, and 1936 PGA champion Johnny Revolta. Of all the U.S. players, only Ed Dudley would fail to register a major win in his career. The British might have their strongest team out, but the U.S. team also looked stronger than ever.

On the fact that six U.S. players were not alone. "The Americans have too many wives with them. It is my experience, or rather I have observed it to be other people's, that women on these trips are an encumbrance equivalent roughly to conceding two shots per round."
—*Henry Longhurst*

"It wasn't long after the Masters that I learned I had been chosen for the Ryder Cup team. Boy howdy, was I excited? I'd never ever been outside the United States before. I didn't think it was possible that the dream I'd had just two years before at Ridgewood could be coming true already."
—BYRON NELSON, *How I Played the Game*

Course Details

The northwest of England once again played host to the Ryder Cup, four years after Britain's close 6½–5½ win in 1933.

Hole	Distance	Par	Hole	Distance	Par
1	210	3	10	455	5
2	522	5	11	378	4
3	411	4	12	357	4
4	418	4	13	359	4
5	449	4	14	326	4
6	380	4	15	157	3
7	481	5	16	490	5
8	180	3	17	452	5
9	492	5	18	363	4
		37			**38 = Par 75 (6,880 yards)**

Course designer: James Braid

Day One: 36-Hole Foursomes

The foursomes faced a strong crosswind off the Irish Sea, which, combined with the lightning-fast and dry fairways, made it extremely difficult to keep the ball out of the heavy links rough.

Byron Nelson and Ed Dudley (USA) v. Henry Cotton and Alf Padgham (GBI)

The number-one British pairing of Cotton and Padgham were two up after three holes but failed to find the next seven greens in regulation and fell back to level after nine holes against Dudley and Nelson. The strong wind caused all four players to misread distances to the pin, Cotton overhitting the fourth green by twenty yards. The Americans took this hole and the next, when Padgham pulled his mashie approach.

Padgham made amends on the ninth, holing from more than fifteen feet to put the British one up at the end of an untidy opening nine holes. The tenth went to the U.S. team after Cotton missed the green by thirty yards, while eleven saw Dudley foozle his short approach to lose the hole with a six to a British par four. Cotton played two fine shots on fourteen, a rousing recovery from the sand and a twenty-foot putt for the hole in four.

The Americans regained ground at sixteen (on Nelson's pinpoint approach) and seventeen (the British three-putting from inside ten feet) to reach the break all square.

The British carried their poor play into the afternoon, taking fifteen shots for the first three holes to slip to three down, as Nelson followed two costly British blunders with a forty-foot birdie putt at the third. Dudley's fifteen-foot putt brought another U.S. win at the fifth, dealing a body blow to the home side as Padgham failed from five feet to halve the hole. Padgham's putting problems multiplied as he blew an eighteen-incher on seven for a win, scarcely looking like a British Open champion.

Dudley found the sand with his tee shot at the tenth and lost the hole, but Padgham's short game fell apart as he scuttled his chip through the green on eleven to go back three down. Nelson then holed a feisty twenty-two-footer on thirteen to go four up. Padgham looked to have pulled a hole back at fourteen when his thirty-footer dropped, but it was followed in by Dudley's heroic hole-saver from twenty feet. The final hole of the round came at sixteen, where the British pair found the rough and a bunker before picking up and conceding the match, 4 and 2, to the more consistent pair of Nelson and Dudley.

"We were unknowns in England, so the headline in the paper the first morning said, 'Hagen Feeds Lambs to the Butcher.' Well, we did get

steamed up over that. I drove against Cotton all day, and on the par 3s, I put my ball inside his every time, and we ended up winning the match. The next day, the headline read, 'The Lambs Bit the Butcher.' It was a great thrill to win, especially against a player like Cotton."

—BYRON NELSON, *How I Played the Game*

Ralph Guldahl and Tony Manero (USA) v. Arthur Lacey and William Cox (GBI)

Hagen sent out his country's two most recent Open champions, Guldahl and Manero, to face Cox and Lacey. The all-around play and scoring was of a better quality than the opening match, and the result was still in doubt until the later holes. With Lacey shanking his approach to the third behind the backs of the astonished crowd, the U.S. pair was soon two up. Manero found the sand on the fifth, where the British prevailed with a par four, and they took the par-3 eighth as Cox's tee shot landed six feet from the cup.

All square at the turn, the United States went two down as Cox first holed a thirty-five-foot putt on ten, with the U.S. pair out of the hole, and Guldahl's accuracy deserted him as it was his turn to find a bunker on eleven. The Americans rallied to win thirteen, but Cox again sent a splendid tee shot into the par-3 green at fifteen, leaving Lacey with a tap-in for a birdie two and a two-hole cushion.

The British pair missed a short putt on seventeen to give the hole to the Americans, while a half at the last hole meant lunch was reached with the visitors trailing by one.

Tony Manero is the name of the character John Travolta played in the movie *Saturday Night Fever*.

The two Americans were not U.S. Open champions for nothing. They won the opening two holes of the afternoon session but found themselves four behind after six holes. Some truly sparkling American play over the next six holes brought them level with six to play. Although Lacey's birdie three at thirteen gave Britain a one-hole lead, the American pair won three of the last four holes played to come back from a four-hole deficit for a 2 and 1 win.

Gene Sarazen and Denny Shute (USA) v. Charles Whitcombe and Dai Rees (GBI)

Against the strongest of the four U.S. pairings, Sarazen and Shute, the British captain paired himself with the twenty-four-year-old rookie Dai Rees. Between them the British reached lunch all square, having posted wins on seventeen and eighteen.

The early play had been very scrappy, with the Americans much troubled by the windy conditions—particularly Shute, who reduced his partner to hacking back onto the course at various junctures. A forgettable front nine was quickly forgotten when Sarazen holed a twenty-five-foot putt for a birdie four and a two-hole lead. Shute continued to pepper the rough, but his waywardness almost went unpunished as the British pair could win only one of the next three holes.

On fourteen, Sarazen found the base of a bush, only to have a fan pick up the ball—reminiscent of Arthur Lacey in 1933. Sixteen fell to the Americans as Whitcombe drove into the sand, while Shute gave the last two holes back to the British with some more inaccurate play.

"This boy Rees is playing the best golf of the lot of us, and he has the best swing." —Gene Sarazen

All square at the halfway stage, this close match never saw more than a single-hole advantage during the afternoon session. Only Rees's nerveless putting on the outward nine enabled the home pair to stay in contention, as the Americans were unable to establish a sizable lead. Rees halved the tenth with another critical putt from ten feet, and the British went ahead as Shute once again hit the sand at eleven. The next hole saw Sarazen hole for a birdie three to level, as his slightly embarrassed partner doffed his hat in apologetic salute.

Sarazen made a miraculous recovery on thirteen, after Shute had missed the fairway for the umpteenth time. Shute almost holed his chip to scrabble another half. Fourteen gave Shute a wonderful chance to erase his previous mishaps, but he only added to them by missing a hole-winning putt from under two feet.

"They [Sarazen and Shute] were certainly impressive, and seemed, with their heavy builds and air of conscious superiority, to be an entirely different race."
—*Dai Rees*

A poor approach by Rees to the fifteenth cost his side a hole, sixteen was best forgotten by both teams, and Rees quickly made amends at seventeen with a hole-winning putt. The youngster was instrumental in holding off the Americans on the final hole. Having missed hole-winning putts from four feet on the previous two holes, Sarazen hit his approach to the putting surface far too hard and ended up on the practice green. Given a free drop, Shute chipped the ball to within a few inches, leaving Rees to hold his nerve as he holed a nasty six-foot putt to halve the hole and the match.

Henry Picard and Johnny Revolta (USA) v. Percy Alliss and Dick Burton (GBI)

Without a win in the first three foursomes, Britain looked to Alliss and Burton to open their full account against Revolta and Picard. Having won the first hole, the Americans retained this advantage all the way through the twelfth.

From here the British assumed ascendancy, as they took the next three holes. Alliss struck a stupefying approach to within five feet, while Burton stuck a thirty-foot birdie putt on the Americans, who were stone dead—Picard having chipped up from a bunker—for par at fourteen. The U.S. team again hit sand on the par-3 fifteenth to go three down, while Picard had a chance to win the eighteenth but blew a four-footer to go in three down.

The Americans opened much the better after lunch, as Picard nailed his tee shot to the par-3 opening hole. Alliss's uncharacteristic error at the second reduced the British lead to one. All square with their opponents after eight, the British went back in front on nine and added to their lead on eleven when Picard's pitch flew way over the green. The British pair then knuckled down to their task and, in halving the last six holes, ground out a workmanlike and much-needed 2 and 1 victory.

Day one result: USA 2½, GBI 1½

Day Two: 36-Hole Singles

If the players and crowd thought the weather on the first day was bad, they were in for a nasty shock on the final day. Walter Hagen must have had a good line into the Meteorological Office: he did not play on either day, having also sat out the final day in 1935.

"More deplorable conditions than those of the morning are hardly conceivable. The wind had moderated and changed to the south, bringing with it persistent and ruthless sheets of rain. The sky was black with never a break, the light was bad; the ground was rapidly getting waterlogged."

—BERNARD DARWIN, *Times* (London)

Ralph Guldahl (USA) v. Alf Padgham (GBI)

For the second Ryder Cup match running (the first being between Parks and Perry in '35, the U.S. and British Open champions met face-to-face, as Ralph Guldahl and Alf Padgham led off their teams on the second day. Before this tournament, there was some doubt over Padgham's selection; he had played woefully since his British Open win the previous year. Whitcombe not only insisted on picking him but also made him his number one and leadoff man.

Padgham rarely found any form in this singles match, and the strength of Guldahl not only tamed the conditions but also beat the Englishman. With the score all square after five, Guldahl sank a whale of a putt in the worsening wet conditions, to go up by one, and he serenely sailed away from Padgham.

From 1933 to '37, Alf Padgham played in six Ryder Cup games and lost them all—a record for futility later matched by Tom Haliburton (1961 and '63).

"Guldahl is a big, strong man, with a not very engaging swing. He has something of a 'duck' in it, but he is very good and very accurate."

—Bernard Darwin, *Times* (London)

More often than not, pars were sufficient for an American win, with the U.S. Open champion six up at the halfway mark as he cruised to an easy 8 and 7 win.

Denny Shute (USA) v. Sam King (GBI)

American Denny Shute produced some remarkable chip-ins and long putts just to remain level at lunch against the rookie Sam King, who had started quickly—3-3-4-3—going two up after four holes. Shute took the sixth and seventh to level, but after King had taken another lead, Shute twice holed out from off the green to finish the first eighteen all square.

After lunch, Shute began to dominate the match as King hit a bad patch, and the American was four up with eleven to play. To King's credit he refused to be beaten and picked up his game, taking the eighth, tenth, and eleventh to pull back within one. The next six holes were halved in fine style, as both players had chances to win and chances to save the holes. King finally squared the match on the seventeenth from twelve feet, then holed a six-footer for a birdie to halve the match with the more experienced American.

Shute had not been beaten in two years of match play.

Byron Nelson (USA) v. Dai Rees (GBI)

Byron Nelson drew another Ryder Cup newcomer in Dai Rees, and it was the American who took the early honors. Three up in the morning session, Nelson was hit by a barrage from the small

Welshman, who won four holes in a row to go one up at lunch. At one stage, the wind and rain was such that Rees had his club slip right out of his grip.

In the afternoon, it was Nelson who failed to keep a firm hold on the feisty Welshman, who was three up after six. Rees bravely held on to shake hands on an impressive 3 and 1 win over the mighty Texan.

Tony Manero (USA) v. Henry Cotton (GBI)

Cotton had little trouble in dispatching the slow-putting Manero, who was two down after eighteen holes and continued to lose ground after lunch.

Although the American won back-to-back holes to reduce the Englishman's lead to just one after nine holes, Cotton hit a purple patch. Playing the next six holes in just twenty-one strokes, Cotton won four holes to post a 5 and 3 win.

Cotton's win meant Britain had won 2½ points to the U.S. team's 1½ in the first four singles, and the overall match score was four points each. From there on, the wheels came off the British wagon.

Gene Sarazen (USA) v. Percy Alliss (GBI)

Percy Alliss faced a barnstorming start by Gene Sarazen, who posted three opening birdies—2-4-3—to jump out to a three-hole lead. Sarazen got another win at the fifth, smiting a mighty brassie into the howling gale to collect a four. In conditions that should have better suited him, the Englishman made a spirited recovery to be only one down at the turn, and was actually ahead by a hole at lunch.

The home lead was due more to Sarazen's finishing 6-5-5, a stark mirror of his opening trifecta. In the afternoon, Alliss had extended his lead to three by the turn, and Hagen felt obliged to remind Sarazen of the importance of the game he was losing. The American responded valiantly by winning three more holes in a row from the tenth, to level the match.

Unperturbed, Alliss took the lead again on thirteen, only to see Sarazen level the match at the following hole. Luck flowed Sarazen's way thanks to a remarkable escape on the par-3 fifteenth. His too-hard tee shot ran through and off the back of the green, landing in a female spectator's lap. She jumped up in such surprise that the ball ran off her lap and back down the bank onto the green. Sarazen took his good luck in stride and made a birdie two to win the decisive hole.

On the last two greens, Alliss was faced with two stymies: he avoided the first for a half from some distance but could not repeat the act from six feet on the final hole. Much to Hagen's relief, Sarazen walked away with a more than fortuitous one-hole victory.

Sam Snead (USA) v. Dick Burton (GBI)

In his Ryder Cup debut, Sam Snead cut a dashing figure in a bright white raincoat that he donned between shots to keep him dry from the torrential English rain. But the weather did little to dampen his resolve as he reached lunch two holes to the good. The highlight of the morning, however, came from Dick Burton, who finessed a hazardous chip shot, from a muddy path, stone dead at the sixth. Burton—a prodigious driver—for once found himself consistently outdistanced off the tee, and forever found himself playing catch-up with Snead.

The afternoon saw the American newcomer steadily press home his advantage to win, 5 and 4. His first Ryder Cup point gave his team enough to retain the trophy, as the U.S. side became the first to win on foreign soil.

Ed Dudley (USA) v. Alf Perry (GBI)

Ed Dudley was more than matched by Alf Perry up to the greens, as both men struggled through the gale. On the wet greens it was a different matter: Dudley's superior putting technique overshadowed his opponent; the American had to feel unlucky not to be more than one up at lunch.

In the afternoon, Perry threatened time and time again to cut into Dudley's lead, but the American repeatedly pulled out hole-saving putts. Time eventually ran out for the gallant Perry on the penultimate hole, where Dudley celebrated a well-earned 2 and 1 win.

Henry Picard (USA) v. Arthur Lacey (GBI)

Britain's Arthur Lacey looked set to arrive at the break with a creditable lead over Henry Picard, having gone through the turn one up. Lacey doubled his lead at the tenth, then not only let this hard-earned advantage slip but allowed Picard to take a one-hole lead into lunch.

Having got back into the match with a narrow lead, the American did just enough to double his tally in the afternoon to win, 2 and 1.

Day two result: USA 5½, GBI 2½
Overall match score: USA 8, GBI 4

Recap

Not only did the U.S. team become the first to win in the other's backyard, but they paved the way for an era of domination that was to last almost fifty years—save for a blip in 1957.

Having lost his acceptance speech notes to a gust of wind, Hagen forgot where he was: *"I am very proud and happy to be the captain of the first American team to win on* home *soil. . . . You'll forgive me, I'm sure, for feeling so at home here."* —WALTER HAGEN

The only comfort that the deflated British could take from this loss was that most of the individual matches were a lot closer than those of previous years, with only one blowout result (Guldahl against a woefully outplayed Padgham). This was the only match that failed to reach the fourteenth hole the second time around.

The reason these matches were so close is that many British players consistently gave up leads to their stronger-finishing opponents. This was further proof that the Americans were tougher—mentally as well as physically. In the cauldron of match-play golf, it is one thing to have your opponent down, and quite another to finish him off. The British, with the exception of Henry Cotton, did not possess this killer touch.

Cable message sent to Walter Hagen: *"To the greatest general in the world congratulations for leading the greatest golfers in the world to a wonderful victory which brings great honor to your country, the PGA and your fellow professionals who are proud of you. Your achievement will go down in golfing history as the greatest of all time; we salute you, admire your courage and honor you as champions and heroes."*

—GEORGE JACOBUS, President of the U.S. PGA

In Samuel Ryder's lifetime, the competition he set up was considered a two-horse race, at least when staged in his homeland. After his death in 1936, his beloved British team would suffer defeat after heavy defeat to an American side that just got stronger and stronger as the years rolled by.

This was to be the last Ryder Cup for ten years, as the Second World War made any official engagements between the nations impossible. It would also be the last Ryder Cup contest played in the summer.

The ten-year hiatus also killed off the Ryder Cup careers of Walter Hagen and Gene Sarazen. Both American Hall of Famers had distinguished themselves in the first five meetings, with Hagen captaining by example each time. In six Ryder Cups together, Hagen (7-1-1) and Sarazen (7-2-3)—the only man to play in all the foursomes and singles matches—put up some fine career figures, losing only three times in twenty-one matches.

On the victorious 1937 U.S. team: "They were the greatest golfing force which has ever come to this country. They presented a splendid spectacle of athletic youth."
—*Golf Monthly*

In the six prewar matches, the U.S. won four and lost two, with a combined points total of 46-26. This overwhelming differential of almost 2:1 showed clearly how dominant the U.S. team had become.

As usual the teams decamped to Scotland for the British Open at Carnoustie, where the British could be said to have gained some revenge on the visitors. Home players took the first four places, with the claret jug again going to their number one player, Henry Cotton.

Match Results (Winning side marked in *italics*.)

Tuesday, June 29—Foursomes

	USA	GBI	Score
1.	*Byron Nelson* *Ed Dudley*	Henry Cotton Alf Padgham	4 and 2
2.	*Ralph Guldahl* *Tony Manero*	Arthur Lacey William Cox	2 and 1
3.	Gene Sarazen Denny Shute	Charles Whitcombe Dai Rees	halved
4.	Henry Picard Johnny Revolta	*Percy Alliss* *Dick Burton*	2 and 1

Day one result: USA 2½, GBI 1½

Wednesday, June 30—Singles

	USA	GBI	Score
5.	*Ralph Guldahl*	Alf Padgham	8 and 7
6.	Denny Shute	Sam King	halved
7.	Byron Nelson	*Dai Rees*	3 and 1
8.	Tony Manero	*Henry Cotton*	5 and 3
9.	*Gene Sarazen*	Percy Alliss	1-up
10.	*Sam Snead*	Dick Burton	5 and 4
11.	*Ed Dudley*	Alf Perry	2 and 1
12.	*Henry Picard*	Arthur Lacey	2 and 1

Day two result: USA 5½, GBI 2½

Overall match score: USA 8, GBI 4

1939

Ponta Vedra Club
Jacksonville, Florida
United States
November

Owing to the outbreak of the Second World War in September 1939, the seventh Ryder Cup, scheduled for Florida in November, was called off.

Cable message sent to the PGA of America offices in Chicago: *". . . When we have settled our differences and peace reigns, we will see that our team comes across to remove the Ryder Cup from your safe-keeping."* —CHARLES ROE, secretary of the British PGA

Both countries had gone as far as to name the majority of their team:

USA: Walter Hagen (nonplaying captain), Vic Ghezzi, Ralph Guldahl, Jimmy Hines, "Jug" McSpaden, Dick Metz, Byron Nelson, Henry Picard, Paul Runyan, Horton Smith, and Sam Snead.

GBI: Henry Cotton (captain), Jimmy Adams, Dick Burton, Sam King, Alf Padgham, Dai Rees, Charles Whitcombe, and Reg Whitcombe.

The Americans also selected a side for 1941, in the hope that the war would soon end, but it was not to be. The U.S. side did play an exhibition match against a team of British-born players in the States, and raised $25,000 for war charities.

Although McSpaden and Ghezzi were selected for both wartime teams, and Hines and Metz were selected in 1939, none of these players ever played in an actual Ryder Cup match.

The team was: Walter Hagen (nonplaying captain), Jimmy Demaret, Vic Ghezzi, Ben Hogan, "Jug" McSpaden, Lloyd Mangrum, Byron Nelson, Gene Sarazen, Horton Smith, Sam Snead, and Craig Wood.

During the war period, the United States selected other "Ryder Cup" teams that played charity matches for the war effort.

It was to be ten long years before the Ryder Cup resumed a normal schedule in 1947.

1947

Portland Golf Club
Portland, Oregon
United States
November 1–2

United States 11	**Great Britain and Ireland 1**
Herman Barron	Jimmy Adams
Jimmy Demaret	Fred Daly
E. J. "Dutch" Harrison	Herbert "Max" Faulkner
Herman Keiser	Sam King
Lloyd Mangrum	Arthur Lees
Byron Nelson	Dai Rees
Ed "Porky" Oliver	Charlie Ward
Sam Snead	Eric Green [did not play]
Lew Worsham	Reg Horne [did not play]
Playing Captain	**Playing Captain**
Ben Hogan	Henry Cotton

West Coast Offense

Still suffering the firsthand effects of the war, Great Britain was hardly in any shape to challenge for the Ryder Cup after a ten-year hiatus. The war still uppermost in people's thoughts, a minor golfing skirmish was not going to raise much attention.

"The modern Ryder Cup has achieved a transcendent importance, but the Marshall Plan, the death of Henry Ford, the disappearance of street cars from Manhattan, and the first reports of flying saucers all got a lot more ink in '47." —Curt Sampson, *Hogan* (1996)

The Americans, themselves, were in a position to host the event only because of the financial benefaction of an Oregon fruit packer—Bob Hudson. This golfing goodwill goes a long way in explaining why the first postwar Ryder Cup was staged in Portland, Oregon, rather than on the East Coast, as had been usual. But it meant that not only did the British players have to undergo an arduous sea journey (albeit on the luxury liner *Queen Mary*), they then had to endure a three-and-a-half-day rail journey.

With the excessive amount of traveling, it is not surprising that the British players were not in the best frame of mind for the game. Even so, terminal optimist Fred Daly had positive thoughts about the eventual outcome: "The trophy's already on the ship. . . ."

The ten-year gap in proceedings meant a major shake-up in the playing personnel, although some familiar American names remained. Gone were Hagen and Sarazen, to be replaced by the equally dominant figures Hogan and Demaret. Only Snead and Nelson survived from the victorious 1937 team.

Hogan easily finished atop the PGA points list with 1,585 points. Demaret, in second, had 1,011, and Herman Keiser was third at 717. Points were awarded for top ten finishes from January 1, 1946, to September 1, 1947, with extra points for the three majors and the Western Open.

Britain could still count on Cotton, Rees, and King from the last match, but brought seven new faces with them.

"Those players who now are met here, the chosen professional golfers of two great kindred peoples, share a common heritage of honest sport and a thousand memories of loyal comradeship. These are the Ryder Cup matches—the traditional classic of golf—played between the picked teams of the British Isles and the United States. Under the code of the ancient game it matters not which side shall win—for there is honor in even losing." —BEN HUR LAMPMAN, 1947 Ryder Cup program dedication

Course Details

No less a judge of a golf course than Bobby Jones described the 500-yard dogleg fifteenth as one of the finest par-5s he had ever played.

The course hosted the 1946 PGA Championship and was home to the annual Portland Open. At only 6,453 yards the course was short, but it played much longer because of a number of natural obstacles, such as Fanno Creek and a plethora of well-placed trees.

Hole	Distance	Par	Hole	Distance	Par
1	397	4	10	512	5
2	425	4	11	376	4
3	333	4	12	210	3
4	135	3	13	368	4
5	515	5	14	396	4
6	360	4	15	500	5
7	355	4	16	357	4
8	205	3	17	125	3
9	362	4	18	522	5
		35			**37 = Par 72 (6,453 yards)**

Course designers: Members of the Portland Golf Club

Day One: 36-Hole Foursomes

It rained so hard for most of the match that it was surprising the local wildlife did not pair up into foursomes and go off in search of a greenskeeper called Noah. The day started well for the small crowd, but by afternoon the weather and playing conditions had changed with the deluge.

"There were only a few hundred spectators present when the match opened under threatening skies and with the turf soggy. The amount of rain which has fallen in the district during the past month has broken a sixty-five-year record for October, and another 1.06 inches fell during the night." —*Times* (London)

Possibly struck by the biblical proportions of the rainfall, Cotton called his men into his hotel room and asked them to offer a prayer to the one-handicapper in the sky. The call for divine intervention fell on deaf ears, as it was the Americans who were to prove "All Mighty."

Lew Worsham and Ed Oliver (USA) v. Henry Cotton and Arthur Lees (GBI)

Instead of offering a prayer, Cotton could have spent the time more usefully on the putting green. By his own admission, he missed eight putts of ten feet or less in just twenty-seven holes, which proved costly against the pairing of Ed Oliver and Lew Worsham.

"A damp Scottish mist and drizzling rain, which increased to a torrent by the time the first pair reached the turn, made play most difficult for both teams. The course was waterlogged in many places, and players were retrieving from almost impossible positions."

—Desmond Tighe, *Sunday Times* (London)

With the British ending eleven over for their efforts, this 10 and 9 victory equaled the largest margin recorded in a Ryder Cup foursomes match, set in 1931 by Hagen and Shute.

By lunch, Cotton and Lees were facing extinction lying six down, and the afternoon session was no easier. The Americans won another four holes on the front nine to devastate the British leadoff pair, 10 and 9. This drubbing only foretold the devastation to come, and was almost enough for Cotton to break his clubs in half and take holy orders.

Lloyd Mangrum and Sam Snead (USA) v. Fred Daly and Charlie Ward (GBI)

Like the one-sided match ahead of them, this one also reached lunch with the Americans—Mangrum (a decorated World War II veteran) and Snead—six up on their beleaguered British opponents, Daly and Ward. Melding magnificently as a twosome, the Americans reached the break in an impressive one-under-par 71.

"The difficulty of the course is shown by the fact that only Snead and Mangrum beat the par of 72 for the first round."

—DESMOND TIGHE, *Sunday Times* (London)

The bulk of their work already done with a dazzling exhibition of match-play golf in horrendous conditions, Snead and Mangrum took it a lot easier in the afternoon, eventually running out easy winners, 6 and 5.

Ben Hogan and Jimmy Demaret (USA) v. Max Faulkner and Jimmy Adams (GBI)

The good news for Britain at lunch was that they stood all square—up in two matches and down in two.

Rookies Faulkner and Adams were not to be overawed by their more illustrious rivals, Hogan and Demaret. They made a birdie on the first hole thanks to Faulkner's two-iron approach and quickly built on this fast start. The British pair reached the turn four up—out in just 33 strokes. With the match slipping away from them, the Americans managed to whittle away half the British lead by lunch.

The tournament officials allowed the players to pick up any ball embedded in the soft fairways . . . but they were not allowed to clean them. Some players found that when they dropped their ball over the shoulder, it plugged in the fairway again.

Winning four of the first seven holes in the afternoon, Hogan and Demaret went out in 33 shots to claim a two-hole lead. Faulkner pulled a shot back at the eleventh thanks to another fine iron approach shot, while Adams pulled the match back level at the fifteenth with a pitch that finished stone dead. Hogan rescued Demaret's bunkered drive on the sixteenth with such a cleanly hit six-iron that Demaret was almost duty-bound to sink the resulting twelve-foot putt. This birdie put the Americans back up, and they finished off matters on the final green to record a win by two holes.

Byron Nelson and Herman Barron (USA) v. Dai Rees and Sam King (GBI)

Here again, the British pairing of Rees and King got off to a better start, but some injudicious shots by Rees caused the lead to dwindle to a single hole by the break. The British pair carded a 74, the best opening round for the side.

Just as King's partner was letting things slip from under the British team, so Byron Nelson's partner, Herman Barron, was having trouble with his game.

The British held their game together better—one up after the tenth hole in the afternoon. With little support from his partner, Nelson took charge of the match. On eleven, he holed a fifteen-foot putt to level the match, while the next two holes saw putts from the Texan to win or halve the hole. His pinpoint accuracy at the par-3 seventeenth ensured a half in twos.

Byron Nelson came out of semiretirement to play in this match.

This was good enough to give the Americans the match, 2 and 1. They recorded the first-ever clean sweep of a day's play, having posted three 3-1 opening-day wins before.

"Maybe tomorrow will be better for us." —Henry Cotton

Day one result: USA 4, GBI 0

Day Two: 36-Hole Singles

His team having swept the first day and needing only 2½ points to win the Cup, an ever-confident Ben Hogan left himself out of the singles to make way for Dutch Harrison.

Dutch Harrison (USA) v. Fred Daly (GBI)

Playing in place of his skipper, Dutch Harrison did not let his captain down against Fred Daly, the reigning British Open and British PGA champion. The Irishman did his chances no favors in the morning by taking 40 shots to reach the turn, for a three-hole deficit.

Three more American wins on the front nine were offset by Daly's sole success at the sixth, as Harrison efficiently extended his lead to five at the second turn to set up a relatively untroubled 5 and 4 win.

Lew Worsham (USA) v. Jimmy Adams (GBI)

Britain's Jimmy Adams had a much-needed finale to his morning round—birdie-birdie—to arrive at lunch just one down to the U.S. Open champion Lew Worsham, who carded 35 strokes to 37.

Nine holes into the afternoon round, Worsham was still one up, but as the American grew stronger, Daly's game fell apart. Worsham broke the game open by taking the tenth and thirteenth holes to finally prevail, 3 and 2.

Lloyd Mangrum (USA) v. Max Faulkner (GBI)

Lloyd Mangrum took a six-shot lead into lunch, courtesy of a faultless round of 72 against Max Faulkner's faulty 77.

With eleven of the thirteen holes in the afternoon halved and only two holes won (Faulkner claiming the second and Mangrum the fifth), the eighth American victory of this Ryder Cup arrived at the thirteenth, 6 and 5.

Ed Oliver (USA) v. Charlie Ward (GBI)

Four down at lunch, Charlie Ward played some of the best golf by a British player on the second day, but even notching a 34 on the outward nine in the afternoon, after winning the first two holes, made no impression on the hard-hitting Ed Oliver. The American took Ward's two early-afternoon blows on the chin and came straight back to win the third and fourth holes to reestablish his four-hole lead.

"He had me four down at the end of the morning round, but I got two back at the start of the afternoon. Then he put two irons up by the pin, and I never could get back after that." —CHARLIE WARD

Going one better than the match ahead of them, this pair then halved the last twelve holes played, as Oliver was content to sit on his lead for another U.S. win, 4 and 3.

Byron Nelson (USA) v. Arthur Lees (GBI)

Despite a morning round of level par, the British player still found himself two holes down to Byron Nelson, around in 70.

Lees then shot a fine 34 on the outward nine in the afternoon, which was matched by Nelson, as both players each won a hole on the outward journey.

With the last eight holes all halved, Nelson possibly ran out a more comfortable winner than the 2 and 1 score suggested.

Sam Snead (USA) v. Henry Cotton (GBI)

With his troops falling before him under the runaway tank of American professional golf, Henry Cotton also got caught in the slaughter. Sam Snead was at the top his game, having won the 1946 British Open and failed by one shot to win the play-off for the 1947 U.S. Open.

Though Cotton started the better, two up after nine holes, Snead—out in 37—won four of the next five holes to take a three-hole lead at the break. Upping his game, Snead came home in a much-improved 35 while Cotton unraveled for a 40.

Unhappy with his game, Cotton had an early altercation with a press photographer and asked for him to be removed from his sight. After composing himself to play his next shot, Cotton promptly hit his ball into a tree. With Cotton hitting at least four trees in his round, it was reported that neither player spoke to each other or even conceded a single putt during the whole match.

Scoring wins at the first two holes, Cotton did all he could to repel Snead's charge as far as the turn in the afternoon, as he also took the ninth after Snead won the sixth. From one up, Snead curtailed Cotton's comeback, unleashing another devastating run, winning four of the next five holes played (5-4-3-4-4 to 6-4-4-5-5) to register a resounding 5 and 4 win.

Jimmy Demaret (USA) v. Dai Rees (GBI)

Jimmy Demaret was one up in the morning against Dai Rees, but the Welshman was ahead at lunch—coming home in just 34 strokes. The Welshman won the tenth and eleventh as the final seven morning holes were halved, both players around in 71.

Rees continued his good work into the afternoon and held on to his one-hole lead after ten holes. Masters champion Demaret reeled off three wins in a row (4-3-3 to 5-4-5) to demoralize Rees and the British supporters, still desperately searching for their side's first point of the contest.

This 3 and 2 win for the U.S. team meant they needed only to win the last match to record a unique sweep over both days.

Herman Keiser (USA) v. Sam King (GBI)

All square with King at lunch, Keiser took a brief lead in the afternoon with a win on the third hole, but King won three out of four holes to the turn (4-4-3-4 to 5-5-3-5) to stake a two-shot lead at the ninth hole.

With the security of this two-hole cushion, King proceeded to take both the eleventh and thirteenth—and a four-shot lead. The British player halved the next two holes to record Britain's only win of the contest, 4 and 3.

Despite having become the first-ever Masters champion the year before, Herman Keiser would not play in another Ryder Cup.

This loss was also the only blemish in two days for the American side.

Day two result: USA 7, GBI 1

The tale of the cards reveals the difference between the two ill-matched teams. The U.S. team carded a combined one under for the 264 holes played, while the visitors united for a calamitous twenty-five over.

Overall match score: USA 11, GBI 1

Recap

U.S. PRO GOLFERS ROUT BRITISH TEAM IN OREGON
—New York Times *headline*

Having come off a scorching summer drought in Britain, the visiting players had great difficulty adapting to the saturated conditions underfoot in Portland.

"On the sodden greens their approaches pitched past the pin, sat down, and then, as a rabbit temporarily stunned, scuttled back, often fifteen feet before lying dead. The British approach shots seemed just as well struck but were usually on the short side and burrowed straight into the turf."
—LEONARD CRAWLEY, *London Telegraph*

Though the weather was a valid excuse, it does not totally explain the near whitewash the Americans slapped on the visitors. Others looked to the effects of rationing still in force in Britain, though Bob Hudson did his best to fatten up his guests.

Such was Bob Hudson's generosity that British players and officials were still receiving Christmas food parcels in 1957. In honor of his spirit and services to the Ryder Cup, Hudson was elected a vice president of the British PGA in 1951—the first person to be so elected from overseas.

The truth of the matter was that the Americans had replaced two superstars with three more: Hagen and Sarazen had been superseded by Hogan, Nelson, and Snead. Also, while the headliners got most of the plaudits, the supporting cast of the American team were stars in their own right. Other than the mercurial Henry Cotton, the British had not had a single superstar on their team at any time—nor would they for many years to come.

Having gone without many domestic luxuries during and after the war, the British golfing world would have to learn to go without for another ten years before the famine finally turned into a feast.

"The better team won. Your players were magnificent. The game was won and lost on the greens, and we just could not match you there. Naturally, we have regrets. I brought the Cup over in 1935 and had hoped to carry it back."
—*Charles Roe, British team manager*

Match Results (Winning side marked in *italics*.)

Saturday, November 1—Foursomes

	USA	GBI	Score
1.	*Lew Worsham* *Ed Oliver*	Henry Cotton Arthur Lees	10 and 9
2.	*Lloyd Mangrum* *Sam Snead*	Fred Daly Charlie Ward	6 and 5
3.	*Ben Hogan* *Jimmy Demaret*	Max Faulkner Jimmy Adams	2-up
4.	*Byron Nelson* *Herman Barron*	Dai Rees Sam King	2 and 1

Day one result: USA 4, GBI 0

Sunday, November 2—Singles

	USA	GBI	Score
5.	*Dutch Harrison*	Fred Daly	5 and 4
6.	*Lew Worsham*	Jimmy Adams	3 and 2
7.	*Lloyd Mangrum*	Max Faulkner	6 and 5
8.	*Ed Oliver*	Charlie Ward	4 and 3
9.	*Byron Nelson*	Arthur Lees	2 and 1
10.	*Sam Snead*	Henry Cotton	5 and 4
11.	*Jimmy Demaret*	Dai Rees	3 and 2
12.	Herman Keiser	*Sam King*	4 and 3

Day two result: USA 7, GBI 1

Overall match score: USA 11, GBI 1

1949

Ganton Golf Course
Yorkshire, England
September 16–17

United States 7	Great Britain and Ireland 5
Skip Alexander	Jimmy Adams
Jimmy Demaret	Ken Bousfield
Bob Hamilton	Dick Burton
Chick Harbert	Fred Daly
Dutch Harrison	Max Faulkner
Clayton Heafner	Sam King
Lloyd Mangrum	Arthur Lees
Johnny Palmer	Dai Rees
Sam Snead	Charlie Ward
Captain	Laurence Ayton [did not play]
Ben Hogan	**Captain**
	Charlie Whitcombe

Hawk the Slayer

Seven months after almost being killed in a horrific car crash in Texas, Ben Hogan was just fit enough to resume his role as captain, albeit in a nonplaying capacity. It was felt at the time that this appointment by the U.S. PGA was a charitable one, since it was assumed Hogan would never play professional golf again. The fact that he later played on the 1951 Ryder Cup team proved the skeptics wrong.

On the meaning of the Ryder Cup: *"We care about who is selected, but we care more about winning."*—BEN HOGAN

Hogan's brush with death did not soften up his resolve to win, as he ruled his team with a rod of iron. On Hogan's scheduling earlier wake-up calls and longer practices than normal: *"Hey, Hawk! We training for golf or the army?"*—JIMMY DEMARET

Another act of kindness came from Bob Hudson, who had supported the 1947 match in Portland. Knowing of the severe food rationing still operating in postwar Britain, he shipped over $1,349

On the furor that surrounded the benefaction of beef: "The subject should be dropped. We came over here to play golf, not talk about meat. If the British public wants it, we'll come over next time with a meat exhibition instead of a golf team."
—*Ben Hogan*

worth of beef, ham, and ribs for both teams and their wives. The British players ate as much of the meat as they could get their hands on, but their wives steadfastly refused—claiming the whole thing smacked of charity.

Hogan managed to upset the British players by complaining about the legality of the grooves on their irons. This was a calculated move by the American captain, in a tit-for-tat protest mirroring a similar complaint made by Henry Cotton in 1947.

As well as being without the playing talents of Hogan, the U.S. team was missing Byron Nelson, who had retired early, and Cary Middlecoff, the U.S. Open champion, who was ineligible as a non–PGA member.

On the Ryder Cup selection procedure: "The PGA is as archaic as the hickory-shafted baffy, the sand tee, and the red golfing jacket."
—*Gene Sarazen (1949)*

The home side was without Henry Cotton, who like Nelson had opted out of full-time golf, but welcomed back seven of the players from the last match. Having been given a severe lesson in golfmanship in 1947, the British players were doubly keen to make amends on home soil.

Course Details

The first postwar Ryder Cup match in Britain was played at Yorkshire, in the northeast of England. Ganton was an inland, heathland course set in the picturesque Vale of Pickering, noted for its very large and unforgiving pot bunkers.

"The Ryder Cup matches were played at Ganton, outside of London, and I can best describe the course as a sort of Pennsylvania Turnpike with tees."
—*Jimmy Demaret,* My Partner, Ben Hogan *(1954). Actually, the course was some way "outside of London," in the far northeast of England.*

Hole	Distance	Par	Hole	Distance	Par
1	373	4	10	168	3
2	418	4	11	417	4
3	416	4	12	363	4
4	334	4	13	499	5
5	157	3	14	282	4
6	449	4	15	437	4
7	431	4	16	448	4
8	392	4	17	252	3
9	494	5	18	400	4
		36			**35 = Par 71 (6,730 yards)**

Course designer: Harry Vardon

Day One: 36-Hole Foursomes

A gusty southwest wind gave way to driving rain in the afternoon.

Johnny Palmer and Dutch Harrison (USA) v. Jimmy Adams and Max Faulkner (GBI)

The tone of the opening singles was firmly set at the par-3 fifth, where Jimmy Adams hit the flag with his tee shot and Max Faulkner holed the putt for a birdie two. Although the Americans were quickly two up after three holes, Dutch Harrison and Johnny Palmer struggled after Adams's arrow at the fifth.

Setting out in level par, the Americans had taken the first hole after Faulkner missed a par putt, and the third fell the U.S. team's way when Adams failed to find the green with his approach. Following Adams's masterstroke on five, the British took the sixth with a birdie four to quickly cancel out their poor start.

Having then gone two down, the U.S. pair had back-to-back wins to level the match, but the British combination went one better, rattling off three wins in a row to take a three-hole lead into the break. The ambushed Americans carded a 73 for the morning, five shots worse than their rivals.

In the afternoon, the British pair increased their lead to four at the fourth. The Americans struck back by taking the fifth, then halved a series of holes in par. Every time the British won a hole, their opponents pulled it back, but they could not level the match.

Four down with four to play, the Americans had to make their final move. Palmer showed his class by strapping his approach around the pin on fifteen to pull to three down. The pressure got to the home pair, who tripped themselves up at sixteen and were dormie two and facing a revitalized couple of Americans. Adams missed the par-3 green at seventeen, finding a bunker to present his rivals with a golden opportunity, but they couldn't do better than a par themselves. Needing to match par for the win, Faulkner pulled out a courageous chip to inside nine feet and stepped back to allow Adams to seal the 2 and 1 win with a defiant putt.

Skip Alexander and Bob Hamilton (USA) v. Fred Daly and Ken Bousfield (GBI)

The second British pair also set a hot early pace, reaching the turn in 33 and winning the short tenth hole to par, giving them a handy three-shot lead. Alexander and Hamilton won three of the next four holes—with a couple of birdies—to level matters. Just before lunch, the Americans undid all their good recovery work by losing seventeen to par and eighteen to a bogey. At lunch, the British were two holes to the good with a morning round of 69 to their name.

In the afternoon, Alexander and Hamilton soon halved the British lead, but Rees and rookie Bousfield reestablished their two-hole superiority and did not allow the Americans back into the match, doubling their lead by the end. Bousfield's magnificent recovery approach to three feet on fourteen more or less sealed the Americans' fate, as they soon went down 4 and 2.

Jimmy Demaret and Clayton Heafner (USA) v. Sam King and Charlie Ward (GBI)

Despite a superb morning of golf by Demaret and Heafner, they reached lunch with only a meager one-hole lead over King and Ward. The Americans played perfect foursomes golf, with Demaret masterful off the tee and to the green, and Heafner putting like a man possessed.

The ever-colorful Jimmy Demaret did not disappoint his legions of fashion-conscious fans with his carefully chosen wardrobe: purple trousers, scarlet sweater, and a bright yellow cap.

The British pair stuck manfully to their task in the morning, but after the break they were completely undone in a magical spell of golf by the Americans. A fantastic finishing burst (3-4-3-3-3-4-3-4), including four birdies in eight holes, ripped the game away from the British, who suddenly found themselves down and out to a score of 4 and 3.

Lloyd Mangrum and Sam Snead (USA) v. Dick Burton and Arthur Lees (GBI)

A fighting finish to their morning by the British pair of Burton and Lees saw the former halve the seventeenth with a glorious chip up to the pin, and the latter make a long hole-saving putt on the eighteenth. All square at lunch, the top American pairing of Snead and Mangrum took an early lead after the break.

The home pair fought back to take a well-earned two-shot lead early in the afternoon, with Burton making two telling putts on the ninth (from eight feet) and tenth (from ten feet), before Lees holed from all of forty-five feet on eleven. The illustrious U.S. couple pulled the match to level after wins at twelve and fourteen, only to give the two-hole lead back at fifteen and sixteen on a couple of pars.

Mangrum halved this lead at the par-3 seventeenth with a magnificent tee shot to set up a birdie, but the British pair survived a nasty scare at the last hole. After Lees put his ball in a bunker and the Americans visited the woods, Mangrum, who had played a wonderful recovery from behind a tree, missed a putt that would have won the hole—and handed the home side a tremendous one-hole victory.

Day one result: USA 1, GBI 3

"We must not shout till we are out of the woods, but it is a self-evident proposition that two points take a very great deal of getting back, even by the doughty fighters that these Americans unquestionably are."
—*Times* (London)

Having been humiliatingly swept in the 1947 foursomes, the British team started much stronger, brushing aside the U.S. team to record its best-ever first-day result.

Day Two: 36-Hole Singles

Needing just 3½ points to win back the Cup, the British started out full of hope on a perfect day for golf, supported by a full gallery cheering their every stroke.

"The weather might have been ordered for the occasion, and a large gallery—on the whole slightly less partisan than yesterday's—was there to watch." —Henry Longhurst, *Sunday Times* (London)

"Weather conditions were perfect, the course was trimmed like a show garden, and sixteen professionals gave an exhibition of golf at its best. Has there ever been a better?" —Leonard Crawley, *London Telegraph*

Dutch Harrison (USA) v. Max Faulkner (GBI)

Poor, poor Max Faulkner. The British leadoff hitter soon came unstuck, and he must have felt as if he'd been run over by a truck at the start of his match with Dutch Harrison.

Making one of the greatest-ever starts to a Ryder Cup singles match, the American opened 3-3-4-3-3-3 in the first six holes. Harrison registered four birdies and emerged with an early four-hole lead.

Carrying on his good morning's work, the popular American played eighteen holes in 67 for a crushing seven-hole lead at lunch.

In the afternoon, Faulkner more or less held his own, but he could not make any impact on Harrison, who soon closed out for the inevitable American victory, 8 and 7—and set the table for the feeding frenzy behind him.

Johnny Palmer (USA) v. Jimmy Adams (GBI)

"Palmer, veteran of twenty bombing missions over Japan, and allegedly 'dead from ten feet' at home, says the Ganton greens are excellent, but he cannot find his touch."
—*Henry Longhurst,* Sunday Times *(London)*

Out in 71, Jimmy Adams was one up at lunch, and the highlight of his win over Johnny Palmer came in a three-hole blitz. After Palmer had carded a succession of threes to take a one-hole lead, Adams played the tenth through the twelfth in just eight strokes (3-3-2).

This devastating midround burst crushed the American, who had no further answer, and Adams eventually earned himself and his team a valuable 2 and 1 win.

Sam Snead (USA) v. Charlie Ward (GBI)

Rounds of 68 in the morning by Snead and Ward saw the American take a one-hole lead into the break. Snead had held a three-hole lead, but Ward played him tough, especially at the par-3 tenth, where he carded a birdie two off the back of a ridiculously long putt.

After lunch, Ward chipped up to ten feet of the first hole and looked as if he would level the match. Snead unleashed a freakishly long putt from the edge of the green to deny the Englishman, who missed his putt and lost the hole. Snead continued his fine run of scoring, starting out 3-4-3-4-3-4-3. Not to be totally overshadowed, Ward posted back-to-back wins at eight and nine, but Snead reasserted his superiority, coming home 2-4-3 to finish seven under par for his thirty-one holes and cap off a convincing 6 and 5 win.

Bob Hamilton (USA) v. Dai Rees (GBI)

The round of the day came from little Dai Rees. The Welshman took Bob Hamilton's creditable 69 apart in the morning, carding a mesmerizing 65, with eight threes, for a four-hole lead after eighteen.

With both players going out in 34 in the afternoon, Rees piled on the agony for the American on the way home. He eventually finished the match 6 and 4, twelve under par—with just one five blotting his card—for thirty-two holes.

At this stage the match score stood at USA 3, GBI 5. The hosts needed only to gain 1½ points from the remaining four singles matches to regain the trophy.

Clayton Heafner (USA) v. Dick Burton (GBI)

With Burton one hole over Heafner at lunch, the American started the better after the break to take a narrow lead. Burton won the eleventh and twelfth in the afternoon session to restore his earlier lead.

One down with six to play, Heafner instantly hit back with an eagle three at thirteen, but worse was to follow for Burton and Britain. On a 3-3-4-4 run, Heafner reeled off three more wins in a row, capped by a match-winning stymie at sixteen, to suddenly snatch an unexpected 3 and 2 win.

The sudden turnaround in fortunes denied Britain one of the valuable points needed for overall victory, and gave the Americans—now only one point behind—hope they might now win the trophy.

Chick Harbert (USA) v. Sam King (GBI)

In the morning, Chick Harbert beat the living daylights out of Sam King, outdriving the Englishman by more than seventy-five yards at times.

On his opponent's long but incredibly accurate driving: *"He was never in the broccoli once."* —SAM KING

Around in 67, the American was not only in the driving seat—with a five-hole lead—but he also wasn't taking on any passengers. The British player had slightly the better of the match after the turn, carding two twos in the first three holes home, to be down by four. This was as far as Harbert let King get to him, as the American held on for a 4 and 3 win, finishing twelve under for fifteen holes.

Jimmy Demaret (USA) v. Arthur Lees (GBI)

Demaret was not the only American to be five up at lunch, but he had done so in his own inimitable and uncompromising style.

Jimmy Demaret certainly brought his own brand of color to this Ryder Cup. For his second appearance on golf's equivalent of the catwalk, Demaret plumped for a more austere color combo: pink trousers, blue sweater, and a vivid green cap.

Arthur Lees had no answer to Demaret's morning round of 68, and he fared little better after lunch, dropping two more holes to the "human kaleidoscope"—who carded another 34 on the way out en route to a crushing 7 and 6 conquest.

Lloyd Mangrum (USA) v. Fred Daly (GBI)

Under normal circumstances Fred Daly's opening round of 66 (34-32) would have meant a healthy lead at the break, but his opponent, Lloyd Mangrum, carded a 65 (32-33). But for a seventeen-foot putt to win the last, the Irishman would have been further behind.

The American's one-hole lead quickly disappeared in the afternoon, when Daly took two of the first three holes with birdies. Mangrum hit back to take the lead, which was canceled out by Daly's two at the tenth hole. Mangrum sealed the win with another amazing series of holes, 3-3-2-4-3, to finish twelve under par for his thirty-three holes and record a 4 and 3 win over the unlucky Daly, who would have beaten any other man on this day.

"This Mangrum is a tremendous fellow. Terrific player, courteous and charming opponent, German bullets bounced off him in France, and at the moment he is unbeatable anywhere by anybody. At any rate that is the impression he gives me." —LEONARD CRAWLEY, *London Telegraph*

Day two result: USA 6, GBI 2
Overall match score: USA 7, GBI 5

Recap

The Americans became the first side to pull back from two points down coming into the singles to win the Ryder Cup. Not only that, but they won the last four singles matches out on the course to do so.

Hogan's team may have been a little overconfident on the first day, but the 3-1 deficit that faced them on Saturday morning before the singles was enough to inspire them to greater deeds. Also, the daunting prospect of having to face an irate Ben Hogan (crutches or not) on the long journey home was more than enough to ensure that the historic comeback was achieved.

Had Daly prevailed over Mangrum in the final match, the scores would have been level at six points each, but it was not to be for the British. They had come a long way since their humiliation in Portland, but the next British win in the Ryder Cup was still a long way off. The next time the Ryder Cup matches came back to England, in 1953, the home side would go one better but still come up one point short of beating its seemingly invincible opponents.

Whether or not the U.S. team had been too confident on the first day, they certainly took no prisoners on the second. Throughout the history of the Ryder Cup, last-day comebacks were rarer than American losses.

"I do not think that a finer collection of golf than the winners' has ever been seen; nor, I am sure, has there ever been a big match better organized than this one was at Ganton."
—Times *(London)*

The day after the match, the U.S. team left the British Isles in a hurry and with their wallets a lot lighter. The British government suddenly announced they had devalued the pound sterling, leaving the unhappy Americans with a lot less spending money. It was fortunate that there was no prize money on offer at the Ryder Cup, as the winners could well have found themselves even more out of pocket.

Match Results (Winning side marked in *italics*.)

Friday, September 16—Foursomes

	USA	GBI	Score
1.	Johnny Palmer Dutch Harrison	*Jimmy Adams* *Max Faulkner*	2 and 1
2.	Skip Alexander Bob Hamilton	*Fred Daly* *Ken Bousfield*	4 and 2
3.	*Jimmy Demaret* *Clayton Heafner*	Sam King Charlie Ward	4 and 3
4.	Lloyd Mangrum Sam Snead	*Dick Burton* *Arthur Lees*	1-up

Day one result: USA *1,* GBI *3*

Saturday, September 17—Singles

	USA	GBI	Score
5.	*Dutch Harrison*	Max Faulkner	8 and 7
6.	Johnny Palmer	*Jimmy Adams*	2 and 1
7.	*Sam Snead*	Charlie Ward	6 and 5
8.	Bob Hamilton	*Dai Rees*	6 and 4
9.	*Clayton Heafner*	Dick Burton	3 and 2
10.	*Chick Harbert*	Sam King	4 and 3
11.	*Jimmy Demaret*	Arthur Lees	7 and 6
12.	*Lloyd Mangrum*	Fred Daly	4 and 3

Day two result: *USA 6, GBI 2*

Overall match score: *USA 7, GBI 5*

1951

Pinehurst Country Club
Number 2 Course
Pinehurst, North Carolina
United States
November 2–4

United States 9½	Great Britain and Ireland 2½
Skip Alexander	Jimmy Adams
Jack Burke, Jr.	Ken Bousfield
Jimmy Demaret	Fred Daly
Clayton Heafner	Max Faulkner
Ben Hogan	Arthur Lees
Lloyd Mangrum	John Panton
Ed Oliver	Dai Rees
Henry Ransom	Charlie Ward
Playing Captain	Harry Weetman
Sam Snead	**Captain**
	Arthur Lacey

For Country and Uncle Sam

The good news for the United States (and bad news for the British) was that Ben Hogan was back as a player. As proof of his full recovery from his car accident, Hogan had won both U.S. Opens since the previous Ryder Cup, and added the 1951 Masters for good measure. Hogan was not reappointed captain of the U.S. team; this honor went to Sam Snead. The American team was as strong as, if not stronger than, the side that almost whitewashed the British at home in 1949.

The British team had only two players new to Ryder Cup play—John Panton and Harry Weetman—relying heavily on the same faces to avenge the humiliation of four years earlier. Very few experts expected them to win more than a couple of points, let alone mount a serious challenge for the trophy.

During a practice round, British Open champion Max Faulkner gave Ben Hogan some advice: "I say, Ben, I think I could help you with that fade. If you'd drop your right hand under the shaft a bit, you'd cure the fade." Hogan stared back at the Englishman and replied, "You don't see the caddie moving any, do you?"

One strange point about this Ryder Cup is that it was the only one not to be played on consecutive days. The organizers had arranged for the teams to attend a North Carolina college football game on the middle day of the tournament. A strange idea, especially after the U.S. team declined the invitation—they probably had their minds on their own game.

Course Details

The Number 2 course at Pinehurst, designed by Donald Ross, is widely regarded as one of the great courses in the world, and it proved a true test of the match-play abilities of both teams. Ross had also designed the course at Worcester Country Club, site of the first Ryder Cup.

Hole	Distance	Par	Hole	Distance	Par
1	427	4	10	593	5
2	448	4	11	433	4
3	340	4	12	419	4
4	528	5	13	378	4
5	440	4	14	444	4
6	211	3	15	206	3
7	394	4	16	492	5
8	488	5	17	186	3
9	156	3	18	424	4
		36			**36 = Par 72 (7,007 yards)**

Course designer: Donald Ross

Day One: 36-Hole Foursomes

"A raw cold day, typical of English golfing weather in November."
—Times *(London)*

Fall this year in North Carolina brought with it some early wintry showers and mist, which required both sides to dress warmly.

Clayton Heafner and Jack Burke (USA) v. Max Faulkner and Dai Rees (GBI)

Britain led off with its top pair—reigning British Open champion Max Faulkner and Dai Rees. The visitors came up against a pair of Americans in the peak of form, as Heafner and Burke played the morning nines in 34 and 35 for a combined 69. It was to the British players' credit that they arrived at lunch only two holes down.

Faulkner and Rees could not sustain their rearguard action through the afternoon, and eventually slid to a rather ungracious 5 and 3 loss. It seemed that when it mattered, the United States could pull a four out of the hat, while the British were always left holding a five. Once again, this failure of the British side to complete the job over thirty-six holes set the tone for the rest of the tournament.

Ed Oliver and Henry Ransom (USA) v. Charlie Ward and Arthur Lees (GBI)

The only setback the Americans received on the first day came against Ward and Lees, who parred the first nine holes in the morning for a well-deserved one-hole lead over Oliver and Ransom. On the six holes up to the break, the British pair put together a typically American burst of scoring (3-3-2-5-3-3), for a three-hole lead.

After lunch, the U.S. team hit back thanks to some uncharacteristic errors by Ward, and with seven holes to play the Americans found themselves just one down. Steeling themselves for another American comeback in the afternoon, the British couple managed to rebuff any U.S. threat—thanks in part to Ransom's fluffing a shot at the twelfth that proved costly to the Americans. A mightily relieved British team took this match 2 and 1 to counter the earlier loss and prevent a repeat of the foursomes sweep of '47.

Lloyd Mangrum and Sam Snead (USA) v. Jimmy Adams and John Panton (GBI)

Snead and Mangrum worked as a well-oiled pairing, with the captain "slamming" the ball hard and long, in typical fashion, while his partner was coolly efficient on the greens. The poor Scottish pairing of Adams and rookie Panton just could not reach the heights scaled by their more illustrious rivals. The U.S. players went out in 34, and the Scots did well for themselves with a pair of sixes on the way home to finish the first eighteen five down, as the U.S. players registered their second 34 in nine holes. From here, there was no recovering, and the U.S. pair closed out the Scots 5 and 4 without too much fuss.

Ben Hogan and Jimmy Demaret (USA) v. Fred Daly and Ken Bousfield (GBI)

Snead had kept his best four players for last, pairing Hogan with the debonair Demaret.

Jimmy Demaret titled his 1954 book *My Partner, Ben Hogan*, the two players having also won their foursomes match in 1947.

Ken Bousfield admitted that just playing with the mighty Hogan was almost enough of a thrill—hardly the mental edge a captain would want from one of his players. Suffice to say, Daly and Bousfield found themselves deep in the mire after just nine holes. Five down, they were staring at the wrong end of a gun barrel called Hogan.

Demaret's inconsistency allowed the British pair to regain some momentum on the inward nine, to reach lunch down by three. In those closing nine holes, they actually outscored the U.S. pair 35-41 but managed to pick up only two holes. Always looking to finish an opponent when he was down, Hogan made sure there would be no such lapses in the afternoon, and the United States soon had its third win of the first day, 5 and 4.

Day one result: USA 3, GBI 1

Day Two: 36-Hole Singles

In stark contrast to the opening-day downpour, a hazy sun shone down from a perfectly blue, cloudless sky.

Jack Burke (USA) v. Jimmy Adams (GBI)

With a three-point deficit to make up, Britain needed a good start; unfortunately, Jimmy Adams did not provide it. Out in 40, he carded far too many fives to sustain any sort of challenge against Jack Burke, who was six up at lunch. The American was never really in trouble in the afternoon; Adams did win back two holes but still went down rather tamely, 4 and 3.

Jimmy Demaret (USA) v. Dai Rees (GBI)

Having been assisted by some fine individual play by Hogan in the foursomes, Demaret pulled his own game together in the singles, and he needed to. Dai Rees, Britain's most consistent Ryder Cupper of this era, hit the American with everything he had and was two up at the turn, one up at lunch.

After the break, Demaret found his true form and, from the eighth hole on, claimed four birdies in five holes. The American's unbelievable bunker play kept him in this match; Rees later claimed Demaret got up and down ten out of eleven times from bunkers in this one match. The killer blow came on sixteen; after Rees had leveled the score with a birdie at fifteen, Demaret was plugged in a greenside bunker. With his rival sitting pretty on the green, Demaret looked at the cup, looked at the plugged ball, and merely brought the two together—holing his recovery, to Rees's chagrin. Demaret saved his half on seventeen with another miracle recovery from the sand to a few inches, and the American also claimed the last to finish two up.

As though to rub salt (or sand?) into Rees's wounds, Demaret presented the Welshman with his "magical" sand wedge, claiming that Rees's own club was "ill-suited" to the demands of modern bunker play.

Clayton Heafner (USA) v. Fred Daly (GBI)

Clayton Heafner covered the opening round in 70 strokes, en route to a three-hole lead over Fred Daly. The American held the same advantage with three holes to play, but the British Open champion proved his mettle by taking sixteen and seventeen. On the last hole, Heafner bunkered his approach while Daly's second found the middle of the green, which was good enough to ensure him a third consecutive win and a brave half from a seemingly impossible position.

Lloyd Mangrum (USA) v. Harry Weetman (GBI)

In his first Ryder Cup contest, Harry Weetman could not convert his powerful shots into holes won against the more experienced Lloyd Mangrum in the morning session. The Englishman had chances in the first five holes but failed to make any headway on the slow-starting American. Once Mangrum got into gear, there was no stopping him, and he reached the break six up.

In the second session, Mangrum did enough—which in truth was not that much—to hold on to his lead and record a 6 and 5 win for the U.S. team's third win in four singles. This point gave the United States enough to retain the Ryder Cup again.

Ed Oliver (USA) v. Arthur Lees (GBI)

With two wins in two days, Arthur Lees became the first British player to record wins in both foursomes and singles.

The one bright spark in British fortunes on this second day of play came from Arthur Lees, who had also done the same on day one. Matched against "Porky" Oliver, Lees took lunch with a handsome two-hole advantage. Oliver tried to mount a charge in the afternoon, but Lees was too strong for him, going out in 34, one shot better than his morning tally. Oliver managed to pull back a couple of holes before the end, but Lees regained the advantage for a 2 and 1 win.

Ben Hogan (USA) v. Charlie Ward (GBI)

Continuing his rich vein of play, Hogan scorched around the first eighteen in 67, which was only good enough for a two-hole lead. The admirable Charlie Ward refused to be blown away by the masterful golf of his famed opponent. One up on fourteen, Ward had missed several short putts to hand the initiative back to Hogan. On sixteen Hogan showed his superiority, covering the 492 yards in two mighty strokes for a birdie and his third win in three holes.

On the par-5 sixteenth: *"Hogan, whose ball left his brassie like a bullet from an anti-tank rifle, was pin-high with his second and got his four with something to spare."* —*Times* (London)

To start off the afternoon, Hogan threw two threes at Ward, but both reached the turn in a spellbinding 33 strokes each. Nothing, it would seem, would upset Hogan, not even being deep in the woods on the tenth. Forced to chip out with his second shot, Hogan hit a colossal three-wood 300 yards to the front of the green, then promptly holed the thirty-yard putt for a half. Hogan stunned Ward with a birdie at the next and knew he had his man beaten. The match finished on the sixteenth, 3 and 2.

Skip Alexander (USA) v. John Panton (GBI)

After playing even golf with Skip Alexander for the first ten holes, British rookie John Panton blew any chances of a memorable win with seven fives on the inward half of his morning round. Five up, Alexander, who like Hogan had also made an amazing recovery from a crash (aero not auto) a year earlier, extended his lead into the afternoon, running out with the biggest victory of the day, 8 and 7.

Sam Snead (USA) v. Max Faulkner (GBI)

The most eagerly awaited match of the day counted for nothing in the end except professional pride. With the trophy long since in American custody, the British Open champion, Max Faulkner, was seeking to dethrone Sam Snead. A morning round of 67 from the American hurt any realistic chances of a British win, with Snead four up at the break.

At one stage during the afternoon, Faulkner managed to halve Snead's lead. The end came—4 and 3—as the American captain put on an exhibition over the last three holes played, carding threes at thirteen, fourteen, and fifteen.

Day two result: USA 6½, GBI 1½
Overall match score: USA 9½, GBI 2½

Recap

The British team lived up to the expectations of the experts, managing to win only 2½ points in one of their worst defeats ever. The Americans barely had to get out of a hack-canter to put this one in the win column.

In addition to the traditional problems faced by the British team, they just did not stack up man-to-man against an American team that boasted an abundance of talent. Looking at the relative strengths and weaknesses of the teams, it is perhaps surprising that the British managed to get as many points as they did.

With a total of 162 holes played, the U.S. team did not card a single six or worse.

If one area of play served to crucially separate the two teams, it was, once again, the British players' putting. The British came close to matching their hosts shot for shot to the green, but they gave away too many strokes and too many holes at the business end of the course. Add to this handicap the unknown vagaries of the American courses, and the Britishers' struggle in the United States is explained.

"A further match, not recorded in the Handbook, was made when the British captain, Arthur Lacey, married a lady from Pinehurst and lived happily ever after."
—*Henry Longhurst*

Match Results (Winning side marked in *italics*.)

Friday, November 2—Foursomes

	USA	GBI	Score
1.	*Clayton Heafner* *Jack Burke*	Max Faulkner Dai Rees	5 and 3
2.	Ed Oliver Henry Ransom	*Charlie Ward* *Arthur Lees*	2 and 1
3.	*Lloyd Mangrum* *Sam Snead*	Jimmy Adams John Panton	5 and 4
4.	*Ben Hogan* *Jimmy Demaret*	Fred Daly Ken Bousfield	5 and 4

Day one result: USA 3, GBI 1

Sunday, November 4—Singles

	USA	GBI	Score
5.	*Jack Burke*	Jimmy Adams	4 and 3
6.	*Jimmy Demaret*	Dai Rees	2-up
7.	Clayton Heafner	Fred Daly	halved
8.	*Lloyd Mangrum*	Harry Weetman	6 and 5
9.	Ed Oliver	*Arthur Lees*	2 and 1
10.	*Ben Hogan*	Charlie Ward	3 and 2
11.	*Skip Alexander*	John Panton	8 and 7
12.	*Sam Snead*	Max Faulkner	4 and 3

Day two result: USA 6½, GBI 1½

Overall match score: USA 9½, GBI 2½

1953

Wentworth
West Course
Surrey, England
October 2–3

United States 6½	**Great Britain and Ireland 5½**
Jack Burke, Jr.	Jimmy Adams
Walter Burkemo	Peter Alliss
Dave Douglas	Harry Bradshaw
Fred Haas, Jr.	Eric Brown
Ted Kroll	Fred Daly
Cary Middlecoff	Max Faulkner
Ed Oliver	Bernard Hunt
Sam Snead	John Panton
Jim Turnesa	Dai Rees
Playing Captain	Harry Weetman
Lloyd Mangrum	**Captain**
	Henry Cotton

Survival of the Weakest

For various reasons the United States fielded its weakest team (compared with its potential) of the Ryder Cup series to date. Hogan and Harrison had been selected but had declined to travel, which meant only four U.S. players from Pinehurst made a reappearance.

The Americans still boasted some pretty big names—Snead, Mangrum, Middlecoff—but there were thoughts at the time that the U.S. team was not taking the British challenge absolutely seriously. The two PGA champions Walter Burkemo (1953) and Jim Turnesa (1952) were added to the team—in place of Hogan and Harrison—along with the automatic qualifiers from the PGA points list.

Ben Hogan found playing thirty-six holes in a day too tiring as a result of his car accident and turned down invites to the Ryder Cup and the PGA Championship. It was not as though his golf game had deteriorated, however; he won the Masters, the U.S. Open, and the British Open in 1953.

After trials held at Wentworth, the British threw two young lions of their own into the cauldron of the Ryder Cup. Peter Alliss (later a respected TV commentator) and Bernard Hunt (a future Ryder Cup captain) were of the next generation, having had no prewar golfing experience. This pair was seen as the way forward for Britain, but hindsight shows that to have been a flawed vision.

Seeking its first win in twenty years, the British side was helped by the team's redoubtable captain, Henry Cotton. He tried to instill some team spirit by having the players stay together and talk about how they could beat the Americans—and how close the hosts came to doing just that.

Course Details

The clubhouse at Wentworth is regarded as the most beautiful in the whole of the United Kingdom.

Having hosted the second unofficial match between the U.S. and Great Britain in 1926, Wentworth was finally given its chance to stage an official Ryder Cup event nearly thirty years later. With four of its last seven tree-lined holes at least 470 yards, the West Course is aptly nicknamed Burma Road.

Hole	Distance	Par	Hole	Distance	Par
1	455	4	10	181	3
2	140	3	11	361	4
3	444	4	12	471	4
4	504	4	13	429	4
5	176	3	14	174	3
6	330	4	15	474	4
7	389	4	16	349	4
8	382	4	17	551	5
9	443	4	18	470	5
		34			**36 = Par 70 (6,723 yards)**

Course designers: Colt, Alison, and Morrison

Day One: 36-Hole Foursomes

Dave Douglas and Ed Oliver (USA) v. Peter Alliss and Harry Weetman (GBI)

Cotton had no hesitation in sending out his raw recruits on the first day. First up, twenty-year-old Peter Alliss joined Irishman Harry Weetman against Ed Oliver and Dave Douglas. Peter Alliss was the son of Percy—making them the first father-son combination to have played in the Ryder Cup. Peter was also Britain's youngest Ryder Cup player at the time.

The young British lions were a little too loose and free off the tees for their own good. This misguided driving ambition cost them two holes to the turn, and set them back immediately after they had won the fourteenth, where the U.S. had three-putted. Thanks to Oliver's hot and cold putter—he made three lengthy putts and missed some much shorter ones—the Americans were only one up at lunch.

Restarting with two wins in three holes, the U.S. was quickly three up, but bogeyed the par-3 fifth and found water on seven. Back to two up after the turn, Douglas cost his side the twelfth with an itinerant drive. Weetman canceled Oliver's twenty-footer at fifteen with an eight-foot putt for a half. Weetman then compounded a poorly played pitch short of the sixteenth with an equally poor five-foot putt to double the Americans' lead.

On the par-5 seventeenth, Weetman again made too many mistakes. He hit his drive only 150 yards, hit a pitch through the green, then missed a hole-winning four-foot putt. Having parked their ball among the cars, the Americans recovered from this out-of-bounds to muster a six, plenty good enough to halve the hole and win the match, 2 and 1.

Lloyd Mangrum and Sam Snead (USA) v. Eric Brown and John Panton (GBI)

Against the might of Mangrum and Snead, the British pair of Brown and Panton stood no real chance. It was just a matter of how long they could survive after lunch, which they reached eight down, even though the Americans carded only a three-under-par 67. The British pair had lost the first four holes in the morning and could have been five down, save for Mangrum's poor drive that cost his side the fifth hole. The Americans won the twelfth to go five up.

The difference between the sides was amply demonstrated in the manner both sides played their second shots to the 471-yard twelfth hole. Giving his brassie all he had, Brown came up eighty yards short of the green, while Snead flicked a four-iron four yards beyond the pin.

Against such firepower the British cracked, losing the next three holes as they blew up on the fifteenth, hitting a bunker and two poor chip shots between them to go eight down at lunch.

The final score of 8 and 7 was a credit to the British players' not losing heart or any more holes after lunch. They played their illustrious opponents head up and manfully held their own until the end came on the eleventh.

Ted Kroll and Jack Burke (USA) v. Jimmy Adams and Bernard Hunt (GBI)

Even more electrifying golf came from Kroll and Burke, who combined seamlessly—out in 32 and back home for a round of 66—one stroke better than Mangrum and Snead before them. Ted Kroll hardly missed a putt all round, while Jack Burke was content to lay the table for his partner with a series of remarkable recoveries and approaches. In this match the British pair—Adams and Hunt—held its own slightly better, going in to lunch only seven down.

The afternoon held the same fate for the home side, as the U.S. pair started up where they had left off, Burke burying another long putt to take the second hole with a birdie two.

The Americans strode on triumphantly to coast to a 7 and 5 win.

Walter Burkemo and Cary Middlecoff (USA) v. Fred Daly and Harry Bradshaw (GBI)

An all-Irish pairing of Daly (from the north) and Bradshaw (the first player from southern Ireland to play in the Ryder Cup) put up a far better fight than their colleagues.

After he had missed a putt from under eighteen inches on the fifth hole of the day: *"My putting's away to hell, Harry. I'll put the ball on the green; you sink it."* —Fred Daly

Burkemo and Middlecoff found themselves three down at lunch, but they opened up the afternoon 4-2 for a couple of wins and a one-hole deficit. With the British safely on the third green in two, Middlecoff conceded the hole after his ball found an unplayable lie in a rhododendron bush.

By the turn, the home side had regained a three-hole advantage, but Burkemo unleashed a string of shots and scores that rocked the British back. On twelve, his approach with a fairway wood set up a win in par, he made a birdie three at the next, and he almost holed a long birdie putt at the short fourteenth. Off the tee on sixteen, Bradshaw lucked out when his dreadful drive hit a spectator, giving Daly a chance to reach the green in two for another half to retain their slender lead.

Burkemo produced another excellent approach to the seventeenth—hitting the flagstick—but Middlecoff could not convert the seven-footer to level the match. Burkemo put his final stamp on the match with another rasping fairway wood to seventeen feet of the last hole. Daly came up short with his second shot, and Bradshaw could only chip to ten feet. Middlecoff again had the chance to halve the match but could only watch as his putt slowly trickled past the lip of the cup. Daly stepped up and took an interminable time to roll his ball ever so slowly toward the hole. The home crowd erupted as the ball just dropped into the hole to secure the one-hole win.

"Only once could British lungs really let themselves go, and that was when Daly, architect of victory in the bottom match, holed a long putt on the last green to give the British team its only win." —Times (London)

Day one result: USA 3, GBI 1

Once again, a last-ditch British win had staved off the threat of another American sweep on the first day. By blooding rookies rather than send out two veterans, Rees and Faulkner, who had more experience between them than the eight who played, the British team was already staring defeat in the face.

Cotton soon felt the backlash from the British media, and he retaliated with a verbal tongue-lashing of his own for his players, threatening to "kick their backsides."

Day Two: 36-Hole Singles

Early-morning fog caused the start of the second-day singles to be delayed by an hour and a half.

Jack Burke (USA) v. Dai Rees (GBI)

Once the fog had sufficiently cleared, Britain's Dai Rees still had difficulty picking out the right line to the flag. After five holes, when the sun finally broke through the mist, he found himself two down to the youngest member of the U.S. team, Jack Burke.

Dai Rees had failed by four shots to catch Ben Hogan in the British Open, finishing tied for second. He would go on to be runner-up twice more (1954 and '61) in a tournament that eluded him his whole career.

In the sunshine, Rees prospered and was level by lunch.

In the afternoon, the Welshman took a lead on the seventh with a lengthy birdie putt but was back on even terms with Burke after the thirteenth, after which the American quickly edged into a lead. Thanks to a fine putt on sixteen, Rees managed to hold the strong American to a one-hole lead with two to play.

Burke settled matters by literally putting the ball from eighty yards to within twelve inches of the flag, and all Rees could offer was three putts in succumbing to another U.S. opening singles win, 2 and 1.

Ted Kroll (USA) v. Fred Daly (GBI)

With their customary winning start behind them, the Americans looked to sew up the whole match as soon as possible.

Daly did not card a single five in his morning of excellence.

They were forced to wait as Fred Daly shot an immaculate 32 on the outward nine in the morning against Ted Kroll, who ate lunch six down. Having played superbly in the foursomes, Kroll was shocked by Daly's morning onslaught and had hardly digested his food by the time Daly finished him off 9 and 7 in the afternoon. Daly's annihilation of Kroll was the largest winning margin in twenty years and the third-largest margin by a British player.

The only two previous British victories that outdid Daly's 9 and 7 were a 10 and 8 (by George Duncan in 1929) and a 9 and 8 (by Abe Mitchell in 1933).

Daly closed the match out with the same cold, calculated efficiency normally associated with the American pros, and became only the second British player to register two wins in one event.

Lloyd Mangrum (USA) v. Eric Brown (GBI)

Cotton: *"Brown! I want two points from you today!"*
Brown: *"You'll bloody well get them!"*

"Brown also started scrappily against Mangrum, immaculately dressed in trousers the color of strawberry mousse."
—Times *(London)*

Fired up by his own captain, the British rookie Brown played his heart out against the U.S. captain Mangrum, and strode into lunch with an unexpected but well-deserved two-hole lead.

The low point of Mangrum's morning had come when he four-putted the multitiered seventh green. He fell victim to the wicked slope, putting up and watching in disbelief as his ball twice rolled back to his feet.

"A feature of the match, which will live long in my memory, was Mangrum's putting from the lower level of the seventh green. His ball ran up, quivered and returned to his feet. He tried again, was short, missed the next and had taken four putts, the first time, I dare say, for twenty years." —Henry Longhurst, *Sunday Times* (London)

Brown fared much better with his putter on fifteen and seventeen, making long birdie putts to go two up at lunch.

Those who thought Brown would collapse under the pressure were proved wrong, as Mangrum could only cut the lead to one at the second turn. From here Brown looked to have taken control of the game, winning the tenth to go back up by two, and halving the next four holes. The American skipper, not to be counted out too soon, struck two fine birdie putts from four to five yards on fifteen and sixteen to stand all square with two to play.

The experts felt Brown would crack, but the newcomer kept his nerve and knocked a superb long iron in to seventeen to grab back the initiative. The Englishman followed this with two more accurate shots up the eighteenth, while Mangrum was only able to make a par five.

Following Mangrum's sluicing of Brown in the foursomes, this turned into a bad-tempered match. On the final green, the Scot protested that the American's bright yellow jumper was a distraction. Brown felt that Mangrum, who had made a five and needed to win the hole to halve the match, was trying to put him off holing out for a match-winning three. Having been disturbed on his eagle putt, Brown bellowed at Mangrum, "I can't have you there, Lloyd. Just come round and stand over here where I can see you."

With Mangrum where he wanted him, Brown lagged his putt to a foot of the hole and expected a concession for the match that was not forthcoming. Mangrum told him, "I guess you can get down in two from there, but let's see you do it anyway."

With the win in his grasp, Brown joked, "You must be expecting me to drop down dead!" Then he beat the American at his own game, mockingly surveying the gimme putt from every conceivable angle before calmly holing out for the two-hole win.

Eric Brown was ten under par for his two full rounds, as he took his captain's orders to heart. "There was a lot of needle—not against Lloyd, of course," Brown said. "But Henry found a way to get the best out of some players. I just couldn't go back and face him with a loss to my name. It became a matter of pride. And I suspect he knew it."

Sam Snead (USA) v. Harry Weetman (GBI)

With two wins out of the first three matches, the home charge quickly gathered momentum. Sam Snead was fully expected to make quick work of Harry Weetman. At lunch, Weetman's chances seemed even more remote—four down to the great man, who had carded a 67. However, having tamely surrendered his 1951 singles match to Mangrum 6 and 5, this was a British player with a definite purpose and steely resolve.

Weetman did well to keep Snead from increasing the lead as they approached the thirteenth, but there was still a lot of work to be done. In one of the greatest swings in Ryder Cup history, Weetman won the next five holes, thanks to some dreadful mistakes by Snead, who found the woods four times with his own woods to finish 6-4-6-6-5-5.

"Put bluntly Snead went to pieces. His drives, which had for so long been as the Americans say 'creamed' down the middle, suddenly began vanishing into the woods and into people's gardens."
—*Henry Longhurst,* Sunday Times *(London)*

Seizing his chance for glory, Weetman managed a heroic four at the last hole to claim a 1-up victory over Snead. With the match score level at 4–4, Britain had its tail up and was looking for more American blood.

This proved to be Sam Snead's only defeat ever in seven singles matches.

Cary Middlecoff (USA) v. Max Faulkner (GBI)

Cary Middlecoff reached lunch three up against a visibly out-of-sorts Max Faulkner, who made too many errors with misguided tee shots and by leaving putts short.

The American, who was four up after the first seven holes played, was pegged back to one up by the tenacious Englishman, until Middlecoff reeled off another two wins to close the up-and-down morning round three up.

Middlecoff had to do very little in the afternoon to hold on to his three-hole lead and duly closed the match out on the seventeenth, 3 and 1.

Jim Turnesa (USA) v. Peter Alliss (GBI)

Henry Cotton had decided to save his young guns, Alliss and Hunt, for the last few singles matches. Under the intense pressure and competition of Ryder Cup play against the best players from America, both rookies wilted and cracked from winning positions.

After shooting a creditable 70 for the morning, Alliss was only one down at lunch against Jim Turnesa. With some positive shot-making, backed by some youthful exuberance, Alliss got himself back in front by a single hole with three to play. News quickly reached him that his point would regain the Ryder Cup.

On sixteen, bad luck was to rob the Englishman of a hole. Turnesa sliced his tee shot into the crowd, where it hit a spectator and rebounded into play rather than ending up unplayable in the trees. The American bunkered his second shot, then proceeded to make a fine recovery for his par. Alliss played a poor chip and missed his par putt to lose the hole—and the lead. On seventeen, under immense pressure, Alliss drove his ball one yard out-of-bounds to lose another hole. Now the Englishman was fighting to save a match that was within his grasp two holes earlier.

On eighteen, Turnesa's luck finally ran out as he sliced another drive deep into the trees on the right. He played a short recovery, which allowed him to knock his third well short of the green. Alliss had hit the perfect drive down the fairway and stroked a six-iron to just off the green. With Turnesa struggling to make bogey, Alliss had the hole at his mercy. He fluffed his simple chip shot, the ball not even reaching the putting surface!

"I had the fear that if my backswing was a little too long, I would hit some of those shoes sticking out from the stands," Alliss said afterward. "I took a long, steady swing at it, and at the last moment I forgot all about the ball and bumbled it a yard short of the green."

The Englishman's second chip shot did reach the green and ran up almost to within a yard of the flag, cheered on by the gathering horde. Turnesa missed a makable putt for his five and took a six. Alliss had a three-and-a-half-foot putt for a five, the hole, and a priceless half. He missed! He took a "ridiculous, incredible, childish, delinquent" six, halved the hole, and lost the match.

"I made an awful bodge of it . . . I feel I've had to live my whole life with the guilt of messing up that chip," he said recently.

Dave Douglas (USA) v. Bernard Hunt (GBI)

With this the last match out on the course when it reached the eighteenth tee, Britain's hopes of a tie now rested firmly on the shoulders of Bernard Hunt. The Americans were hoping that Dave Douglas, the reigning Canadian Open champion, could rescue their fortunes.

With the match all square at lunch, Douglas and Hunt had proceeded quietly enough, without any notion of the turmoil they were about to run into at the end of the day. In the afternoon, Douglas established a three-hole lead, but Hunt turned this around with wins at twelve and thirteen on birdie putts, while Douglas gave up the seventeenth, like Alliss ahead of him, by driving out-of-bounds.

"I will never, never captain an American team again because of the nine thousand deaths I suffered in the last hour."
—*Lloyd Mangrum (he was named as ceremonial captain for 1955)*

So the British rookie Hunt stood on the eighteenth tee one up, where his drive was a good one. His second shot was poor, sliced off to the right. Both players managed to get on in three, but some way from the pin, leaving Hunt two putts for his win. He struck his long putt with confidence, and it rolled up to about the same length Alliss had just missed from. Surely, lightning could not strike twice? Douglas made his five and stepped back for Hunt to hole out for the win. But Hunt missed! He lost his nerve just as Alliss had done. Douglas won the hole and halved the match; the United States had not so much retained the Ryder Cup as Britain had thrown away its best chance since 1933.

Fred Haas (USA) v. Harry Bradshaw (GBI)

Having won his foursomes match the previous day, Irishman Harry Bradshaw was as confident as any British player could be against the Americans. Although Fred Haas had match-play experience from his days on the U.S. Walker Cup team, Bradshaw was not going to be denied his second win in two days.

One down at lunch, Haas, who had not played on the first day, was a little rusty and could not match the Irishman's enigmatic play. He went down 3 and 2 in his only Ryder Cup appearance.

Harry Bradshaw emulated his foursomes partner, Fred Daly, by winning both his games.

Day two result: USA 3½, GBI 4½

On the two missed chances by the British rookies: *"So we lost, and everyone wept for the two youngest members. By these few inches was the Ryder Cup lost. And it would have been such a glorious victory!"*

—Henry Longhurst, *Sunday Times* (London)

Overall match score: USA 6½, GBI 5½

Recap

After two days of closely fought and finely balanced match play, the whole result came down to two brave but raw rookies needing to make par at the final hole. Both carded bogey sixes to allow the Americans to retain the Cup by the same margin that separated the two teams in the 1933 match at Southport. That result twenty years earlier had stood alone as the closest match played, until the woes of Wentworth descended on Alliss and Hunt, who would rebound in great style in later years.

"Our Ryder Cup Men Go Down Fighting."
—Sunday Times *(London) headline*

The tensions and emotions that flowed through both sides revealed to everyone just how much winning and losing the Ryder Cup meant to the players and their supporters. This is what international match-play golf was all about, giving one's all while living and dying on the accomplishments and failures of others. This Ryder Cup, it seemed, had everything—except a British win.

"In no other sport is there a comparable psychological strain on the player. Nowhere is the agony of waiting to play a stroke so protracted or the impress of a crowd so closely felt."
—Times *(London)*

The Ryder Cup would not see such a close result for another sixteen years.

Match Results (Winning side marked in *italics*.)

Friday, October 2—Foursomes

	USA	GBI	Score
1.	*Dave Douglas* *Ed Oliver*	Peter Alliss Harry Weetman	2 and 1
2.	*Lloyd Mangrum* *Sam Snead*	Eric Brown John Panton	8 and 7
3.	*Ted Kroll* *Jack Burke*	Jimmy Adams Bernard Hunt	7 and 5
4.	Walter Burkemo Cary Middlecoff	*Fred Daly* *Harry Bradshaw*	1-up

Day one result: USA 3, GBI 1

Saturday, October 3—Singles

	USA	GBI	Score
5.	*Jack Burke*	Dai Rees	2 and 1
6.	Ted Kroll	*Fred Daly*	9 and 7
7.	Lloyd Mangrum	*Eric Brown*	2-up
8.	Sam Snead	*Harry Weetman*	1-up
9.	*Cary Middlecoff*	Max Faulkner	3 and 1
10.	*Jim Turnesa*	Peter Alliss	1-up
11.	Dave Douglas	Bernard Hunt	halved
12.	Fred Haas	*Harry Bradshaw*	3 and 2

Day two result: USA 3½, GBI 4½

Overall match score: USA 6½, GBI 5½

1955

Thunderbird Ranch
and Country Club
Palm Springs, California
United States
November 5–6

United States 8	**Great Britain and Ireland 4**
Jerry Barber	Harry Bradshaw
Tommy Bolt	Eric Brown
Jack Burke, Jr.	John Fallon
Doug Ford	John Jacobs
Marty Furgol	Arthur Lees
Chandler Harper	Christy O'Connor, Sr.
Ted Kroll	Syd Scott
Cary Middlecoff	Harry Weetman
Sam Snead	Ken Bousfield [did not play]
Playing Captain	**Playing Captain**
Chick Harbert	Dai Rees

Best (and Worst) of British Luck

In America, no British side had ever won more than three points in a twelve-game match, let alone raised any sort of challenge to the home side. In five visits, Britain had gained only 2½, 3, 3, 1, and 2½ points, for a total of 12 points out of a possible 60—a batting average of .200. In the same period, the American record (on the road) was 5, 5½, 8, 7, and 6½, for a total of 32 points out of 60, a .533 batting average in Britain.

In an attempt to professionalize their approach, the British selectors did away with their Victorian committee method and opted for a ranking system based on results in key tournaments leading up to the Ryder Cup. To understand how outdated the British had been, consider that the United States had been using a similar method for thirty years.

The revised British selection method took the top seven players in the Order of Merit after the British Open, then added three more players selected by those players in consultation with their PGA tournament subcommittee.

The Americans had chosen the 1954 PGA champion, Chick Harbert, as their new captain, and he teamed up with just four players from the previous encounter. The new players on the U.S. team were Harper, Barber, Bolt, Furgol, and Ford.

Having led the victorious team in 1953, Lloyd Mangrum was named as the Americans' ceremonial captain.

Britain selected the dynamic Dai Rees as captain in the hope that his brand of Welsh enthusiasm would spread through the side. He, too, was in charge of a few new names: Fallon, Jacobs (the only British player under the age of thirty), Scott, and O'Connor.

Harbert rated this British team as the best to have been sent over and warned his own men about any undue complacency. He need not have bothered.

This contest was also the first time the sides were allowed to choose between playing with the 1.68-inch American ball and the 1.62-inch British ball. Experts and players were divided over which was the better ball to play, as the larger ball was easier to control in and around the greens, while the smaller ball had more distance in it.

The rules also allowed players to choose a different-size ball for each hole. Most players took advantage of this option and used the smaller ball on the par 5s and the larger ball on the shorter holes.

Course Details

"I don't think the British guys had played much desert golf. For that matter, Palm Springs was sort of unexplored territory for us, too. That was in the days before the Bob Hope tournament." —JACK BURKE

Hole	Distance	Par	Hole	Distance	Par
1	394	4	10	388	4
2	439	4	11	377	4
3	538	5	12	348	4
4	393	4	13	374	4
5	435	4	14	233	3
6	216	3	15	546	5
7	541	5	16	206	3
8	149	3	17	403	4
9	413	4	18	450	4
		36			**35 = Par 71 (6,843 yards)**

Course designer: John Dawson

Day One: 36-Hole Foursomes

Playing in the desert had one obvious advantage: sunshine, which was as plentiful as the golf was erratically exciting.

Of the eight drives from the first tee, only two found the fairway—and all four of the British drives went astray.

Chandler Harper and Jerry Barber (USA) v. John Fallon and John Jacobs (GBI)

In glorious morning sunshine, the first match proved to be the most exciting of the tournament. Off the first tee, Fallon found out why it was called Palm Springs, as he immediately sliced his ball into a clump of the tropical trees. Despite making their par four, the British lost the opening hole to Harper and Barber's five-foot birdie putt.

After Fallon nearly pitched in on seven and holed a sixteen-footer on eight, he and Jacobs were back all square at the turn, reached in 35. The score stayed level until the sixteenth, where Barber showed why he had a reputation for the best short game in the States. Harper's tee shot to the par-3 green found bushes, but Barber had enough room to conjure up a chip shot that found the bottom of the cup for a birdie two. A bogey at eighteen by the British gave the U.S. pair a two-hole lead at lunch.

Earlier in the summer, John Fallon had come within two strokes of catching Peter Thomson in the British Open at St. Andrews, but he had to settle for second best.

The second session saw the match swing back toward the British, who held a precarious one-hole lead with nine to play. Barber putted up and down from off the thirteenth green to level, and a trademark Barber chip on sixteen gave Harper the chance to save the hole, but he missed the two-foot putt. The seventeenth was halved after Harper and Jacobs both hit approaches to within a foot of the hole, leaving the U.S. pair one down.

Standing forty feet away off the back of the final green, Barber knocked the ball in from off the putting surface for the third time in the match. Unperturbed, Fallon calmly holed from four feet for the half, which preserved Britain's one-hole advantage. First blood to the British.

Doug Ford and Ted Kroll (USA) v. Eric Brown and Syd Scott (GBI)

Brown and Scott had a horrendous 5-5-7 start to their match to hand the first three holes to the Americans. Brown was unbelievably wayward, hooking his opening drive into the rough and slicing his second shot across the main road alongside the third hole.

Three down at lunch, the British never really recovered from this false start, although they did win the ninth to cut the lead to two. But this revival was short-lived; thanks to three wins from eleven onward, the Americans quickly and clinically closed their rivals out, 5 and 4.

Jack Burke and Tommy Bolt (USA) v. Arthur Lees and Harry Weetman (GBI)

Another perfectly matched encounter saw the British pair of Lees and Weetman complete the morning session in 68, but they could take only one hole off Bolt and Burke. On the back nine in the morning, the British pair did not card a single five, coming home in a remarkable 31 strokes: 3-4-3-3-3-4-3-4-4. The Americans refused to waver in the afternoon, and a 34-stroke outward nine by the British had no effect on their lead.

This lead was eventually reversed, courtesy of Bolt's punishing a couple of British fives at ten and eleven. The pairs exchanged wins on thirteen and fifteen, and the Americans reached the final hole with a one-hole advantage.

On Weetman's tricky putt on the last hole: "That putt was impossible to make."
—*Jack Burke*

Bolt's superb iron to the green stuck within a couple of yards, but Lees's approach was almost as good. Weetman holed the twelve-foot downhill birdie putt to give the British a chance at an overall half, but Burke rattled in his six-foot birdie putt for the one-hole win.

Sam Snead and Cary Middlecoff (USA) v. Harry Bradshaw and Dai Rees (GBI)

Thanks to three British putts on the first green, the powerful U.S. pairing of Snead and Middlecoff swarmed all over an early three-hole advantage.

"Sam Snead carried on a running feud with the photographers and did not seem to be playing at his top form." —*Times* (London)

Putting their opening disaster behind them, Rees and Bradshaw slowly and surely erased the debit by lunch. It was Middlecoff who let the advantage slip by missing a three-foot putt on seventeen, then fluffing a chip shot on the last.

Although Rees and Bradshaw took the lead by winning the first hole after lunch, they could not sustain such a barrage of low scoring. Two hole-relinquishing bogeys followed, and the Americans ran out comfortable 3 and 2 winners in the end.

The British pair was forced to shoot ten threes during the course of the match just to keep pace with the streaky Americans.

Day one result: USA 3, GBI 1

"The plight of all British players today was putting. It is really something when Bradshaw does not make a putt." —Dai Rees

Day Two: 36-Hole Singles

Ken Bousfield had complained of a bad stomachache prior to the match and requested that he not be picked for either day, as he felt Britain's chances were good enough without him.

"Bousfield thinks we still have a chance, and he does not wish to jeopardize that chance. He is a big man for doing it." —Dai Rees

Tommy Bolt (USA) v. Christy O'Connor (GBI)

Tommy Bolt kept up the Americans' remarkable success in the opening singles match by besting rookie Christy O'Connor. Having won the first, Bolt was two up at the turn but lost the twelfth to the Irishman. The American then won two more holes before the break to register a three-hole lead at lunch. O'Connor, however, had the nerve and temerity to quickly pull two holes back on the temperamental American. "Thunder" Bolt—known for his lightning temper—was unnerved by this comeback and started to throw a few clubs in his own inimitable style.

O'Connor, who had played only a handful of matches outside his native Ireland and had probably never seen anything like it before, lost his concentration. This outburst rejuvenated Bolt, who reasserted his authority and clinched the win, 4 and 2.

"If we could have screwed another head on Tommy's shoulders, he would have been the greatest golfer that ever lived."
—*Ben Hogan*

Chick Harbert (USA) v. Syd Scott (GBI)

Having made a bright start to hold a slender lead over Chick Harbert after nine, Syd Scott completely lost his way back home, and he arrived at lunch six down.

After the break, Scott had the better of the outward nine as he reduced the American's lead to four, but he did so in level par as Harbert took things steady.

The American—with plenty in hand as his opponent could cut only one more hole off his substantial lead—coasted through most of his afternoon round for a 3 and 2 win.

Cary Middlecoff (USA) v. John Jacobs (GBI)

Middlecoff and Jacobs produced the best and the closest match of the second day. With birdies at the first three holes, the Englishman held an early two-hole advantage, but Middlecoff—the reigning Masters champion—came back to level at the turn. Both men were out in 32 with ten birdies between them. The American continued his surge and held a two-hole lead at lunch.

In the afternoon, Jacobs was back square after reaching the turn in his second 32 on the front nine. Birdies at twelve and thirteen enabled Jacobs to take a two-hole lead, which he held with three to play.

The sixteenth was halved after Middlecoff conceded Jacobs's three-foot putt, before holing his eight-footer for the half to keep the match alive. Jacobs later said, "I knew I could miss that putt [on sixteen], but here was this man conceding it. Then I realized what he was doing. He wanted to clear his mind of all distracting thoughts—particularly the hope that I might miss mine. He wanted to address his concentration fully to the stone-cold certainty that he *had* to hole his own putt to stay in the match."

With Jacobs close to the hole in three, the American claimed the seventeenth with a twenty-five-foot birdie putt from the back of the green that ran down the slick slope straight into the center of the cup.

On Middlecoff's calculated semi-comeback: "It was possibly the finest piece of competitive play I have ever witnessed. I learned much from Middlecoff's attitude that day."
—*John Jacobs*

With two clutch putts in a row, Middlecoff moved on to the last hole, one down.

On the final green, Jacobs was faced with a very awkward five-footer that broke at least twelve inches right to left, but his rookie nerve held and he holed the putt to win by one hole, having carded a meritorious 65 in the afternoon.

"I never did have that great a record in the singles [1–2–0], but I played well that day. I don't think John ever played that well again in his life."
—CARY MIDDLECOFF

Strangely, this proved to be Jacobs's only Ryder Cup, and he acquitted himself manfully, winning both his matches on the thirty-sixth hole. It would be thirty-six years before another British player would record a perfect 2-0 career record.

Sam Snead (USA) v. Dai Rees (GBI)

Sam Snead started off with his usual firepower, recording four birdies in the first four holes against Dai Rees to reach lunch in 66 strokes—holding a five-hole lead.

Six holes into the afternoon and Rees had won four holes back, recording four threes. Following a badly hooked drive on the seventh, Snead unleashed a scintillating recovery from the base of a palm tree onto the green. He then holed the longish putt for an eagle to keep his narrow lead.

Taking 31 to the turn, Rees lost his way coming home, and his chance finally disappeared when he three-putted the thirteenth with Snead in a bunker—the American getting up and down in two. From there on, Snead was not seriously troubled as he ran out a 3 and 1 winner.

Marty Furgol (USA) v. Arthur Lees (GBI)

In the poorest match of the day, both a woefully out-of-form Marty Furgol and an equally unimpressive Arthur Lees went out in 37. The match was all square at lunch, and neither player had managed to take a lead after nine more holes in the afternoon. Lees played the second round in level par, which was good enough to pick up three holes on the inward nine and to post a 3 and 1 win over Furgol, who never mounted a serious challenge.

This was Arthur Lees's fourth win over the Americans since the resumption of the Ryder Cup series in 1947.

Jerry Barber (USA) v. Eric Brown (GBI)

With Jerry Barber encountering plenty of putting problems on the greens, Eric Brown carded a 69 to take a three-hole cushion into lunch.

Despite going out in the afternoon in 34, Brown found his lead cut to two. Barber could not reproduce the magical short game that he had on the first day, and it was left to Brown to hole a forty-footer on the fourteenth to set up a 3 and 2 win for himself—and Britain.

There were two close matches still out on the course, and two British wins would gain an historic tie.

Jack Burke (USA) v. Harry Bradshaw (GBI)

Having been one up at the turn in the morning, Jack Burke found disaster on thirteen, where he was forced to pick up and concede the hole to Harry Bradshaw. Burke was disappointed to reach lunch all square against the Irishman, as Bradshaw came home in 31, reeling off six threes to peg the American back. Bradshaw's stunning charge was interrupted only on the fifteenth, where Burke holed a chip shot to restore some balance.

After carding an excellent 65, the best round of the morning, Bradshaw could not match this scoring in the afternoon. Out in 33 after lunch, Burke climbed back to a three-hole lead, winning the tenth in par and making birdie at eleven.

Any faint hope of a British comeback was extinguished by a six at the fifteenth. Bradshaw eventually allowed Burke the luxury of a comfortable 3 and 2 victory to win the trophy for the United States.

Doug Ford (USA) v. Harry Weetman (GBI)

Doug Ford had four threes going out in the morning to take a three-hole lead, but Harry Weetman came home in 33 to reduce the American advantage to one.

After lunch, the PGA champion matched Weetman's 33 on the outward nine, and further steady play during the afternoon rewarded Ford with a 3 and 2 win.

Day two result: USA 5, GBI 3
Overall match score: USA 8, GBI 4

Recap

To the credit of the British team, they managed to take all eight of the singles matches as far as the sixteenth hole in the afternoon, and still had a chance until the final two singles matches. Great Britain took some solace from the fact that they recorded their highest points total to date on U.S. soil.

On the American view of gimmes: "One lesson we can learn from them right away, namely that never in any circumstances do they give a short putt. There is the ball, there is the putter, there is the hole—knock it in."
—*Leonard Crawley,* London Telegraph

Once again the Americans proved too strong in a sporting scenario that was becoming worringly familiar. There was talk in some circles that the Ryder Cup should be postponed until the British could field a team capable of giving the Americans a run for their money.

"Although we have lost, we are going back to practice in the streets and on the beaches." —LORD BRABAZON, president of the British PGA

With their best performance in America behind them, Britain could only hope that the team they would face at home in two years' time would not be the strongest to visit their shores, and would be ripe for the taking.

Match Results (Winning side marked in *italics*.)

Saturday, November 5—Foursomes

	USA	GBI	Score
1.	Chandler Harper Jerry Barber	*John Fallon* *John Jacobs*	1-up
2.	*Doug Ford* *Ted Kroll*	Eric Brown Syd Scott	5 and 4
3.	*Jack Burke* *Tommy Bolt*	Arthur Lees Harry Weetman	1-up
4.	*Sam Snead* *Cary Middlecoff*	Harry Bradshaw Dai Rees	3 and 2

Day one result: USA 3, GBI 1

Sunday, November 6—Singles

	USA	GBI	Score
5.	*Tommy Bolt*	Christy O'Connor	4 and 2
6.	*Chick Harbert*	Syd Scott	3 and 2
7.	Cary Middlecoff	*John Jacobs*	1-up
8.	*Sam Snead*	Dai Rees	3 and 1
9.	Marty Furgol	*Arthur Lees*	3 and 1
10.	Jerry Barber	*Eric Brown*	3 and 2
11.	*Jack Burke*	Harry Bradshaw	3 and 2
12.	*Doug Ford*	Harry Weetman	3 and 2

Day two result: USA 5, GBI 3

Overall match score: USA 8, GBI 4

1957

Lindrick Golf Club
Yorkshire, England
October 4–5

United States 4½	Great Britain and Ireland 7½
Tommy Bolt	Peter Alliss
Dow Finsterwald	Ken Bousfield
Doug Ford	Harry Bradshaw
Ed Furgol	Eric Brown
Fred Hawkins	Max Faulkner
Lionel Hebert	Bernard Hunt
Ted Kroll	Peter Mills
Dick Mayer	Christy O'Connor, Sr.
Art Wall, Jr.	Harry Weetman
Playing Captain	**Playing Captain**
Jack Burke, Jr.	Dai Rees

The Americans Lose Their Grip

Having had only two captains in the first eight Ryder Cup contests, the United States then appointed a different captain for the next four contests—Jack Burke, Jr., being the fourth.

Burke's team was light a number of notable names: Sam Snead and Ben Hogan declined the trip, while the U.S. PGA did not select Cary Middlecoff or Julius Boros after they refused to play in the PGA Championship. With half of their headline players missing, the Americans still managed to field a formidable team. Of the nine selected, only Kroll and Hawkins would not win one of the three major U.S. championships.

Such was the depth of the visiting side, but was it strong enough to take on a British team coming off their best result ever in the United States? The last two matches in Britain had seen the U.S. team triumph by only two points and one point, respectively, and this was undoubtedly an understrength visiting side.

So accustomed to keeping the Ryder Cup, the U.S. PGA actually renewed the insurance coverage on the trophy before the team left America to defend it!

"The argument that America's best players were left behind does not ring true. No place can be gained in their team without constant proof of great

ability. It is true that the team did not contain famous names, but reputation is no guarantee of success." —BERNARD DARWIN, *Times* (London)

Using a new system of selection mirroring the U.S. two-year points list, the British team, once again captained by the tigerish Dai Rees, had only one player new to the unique demands of the Ryder Cup: Peter Mills. Having matured and grown into topflight golfers in their own right, Peter Alliss and Bernard Hunt were recalled to a British team that looked to be the strongest ever.

Both PGAs had selection procedures that worked against younger players. The U.S. PGA required players to have been members for five years before they became eligible for the Ryder Cup. Also, all Ryder Cup hopefuls had to have played in the previous two PGA Championships. The British PGA had a rule that no player who turned professional could play for prize money until he had been a member for five years.

Course Details

"The diminutive Welshman [Dai Rees]—like Henry V at Agincourt—was an inspirational leader and a brilliant strategist. First, he hand-chose Lindrick as the field of battle, partly because he knew it like the back of his hand, and partly because he knew the enemy would know virtually nothing about it."
—*Golf World (1998)*

The stage was set at the inland course at Lindrick, just outside of the steel town of Sheffield, for a battle royal. In an attempt to give the home players as much advantage as possible, the course was not watered for some time before the match started. The rough behind the greens was allowed to grow in the hope of snagging the Americans' balls as they flew through the fast greens.

Hole	Distance	Par	Hole	Distance	Par
1	400	4	10	374	4
2	358	4	11	170	3
3	164	3	12	460	4
4	472	5	13	470	5
5	400	4	14	516	5
6	138	3	15	351	4
7	427	4	16	486	5
8	318	4	17	387	4
9	436	4	18	200	3
		35			**37 = Par 72 (6,527 yards)**

Course designer: Tom Dunn

Day One: 36-Hole Foursomes

Jack Burke felt so confident with his team that he left PGA champion Lionel Hebert on the bench for the first day. He was amply rewarded for his belief in the eight men he sent into battle.

On the professionalism of the 1957 U.S. team: *"Dick, Jackie, Tommy, Ted, Doug, Ed, Dow, Art, Fred, and Lionel. No forename dropping there. They were pros, like Benny Goodman sidemen, from start to finish. And for the foursomes they behaved like pros. Our lot were the short-back-and-sides survivors of the famous 1953 battle, a kind of Tobruk if it weren't for the fact they were playing on Wentworth's Burma Road."*

—JOHN SAMUEL, *London Guardian* (1985)

Doug Ford and Dow Finsterwald (USA) v. Peter Alliss and Bernard Hunt (GBI)

The opening American pairing was as strong as they could put out. Doug Ford was the reigning Masters champion, having won the U.S. Open in 1955, while his partner would go on to win the PGA Championship the following year.

Knowing that Alliss and Hunt would be keen to make amends for their individual capitulation in 1953, Rees teamed his young stars to lead off the British challenge.

They walked straight into a buzz-saw start by Ford and Finsterwald, who shot straight threes at the first three holes to take a two-shot lead. Despite being in the rough six times in the first nine holes, the Americans made several excellent recoveries, most notably at the seventh, where Finsterwald's excellent pitch from the left-hand rough won a hole the British pair looked set to take. Ford and Finsterwald, out in 32 to 35, held a three-hole lead over Alliss and Hunt after nine holes.

An American par four at the fifteenth extended the lead to four, but the British came back with three wins in a row to pull to one down with one to play. Blowing a four-foot putt on the eighteenth, Hunt missed a chance to level the match at lunch.

The U.S. pair started the afternoon in even better style, playing the first six holes in just twenty shots—their three at the 318-yard eighth moved them three ahead again. Despite this blitz of low scoring, the Americans could not finish off the brave pair of British youngsters until the penultimate hole, 2 and 1.

Art Wall and Fred Hawkins (USA) v. Ken Bousfield and Dai Rees (GBI)

Matching Ford and Finsterwald's triple-three opening, Wall and Hawkins also dashed off to a fast start, with birdies winning the first two holes against Rees and Bousfield. The British pair again did well to weather this early onslaught, replying with wins at the fourth and tenth, and eventually leveling the match on the final hole of the morning's play with a fourteen-foot putt from Rees.

The Americans almost repeated the same dose in the afternoon as they grabbed another two-shot lead at the third and fourth holes. Once more the British fought back to level by the tenth, and this time they built on their momentum and some American mistakes to close out with a fine home win, 3 and 2, with Bousfield making the winning putt from fifteen feet on the sixteenth.

This win was Dai Rees's first in a foursomes match after six other Ryder Cup appearances. Previously he had managed only a half—at his debut in 1937—and three losses, and had sat out two foursomes matches.

Ted Kroll and Jack Burke (USA) v. Max Faulkner and Harry Weetman (GBI)

In the poorest of the four matches, Ted Kroll and Jack Burke were held close by the British pairing of Harry Weetman and Max Faulkner. The Americans had a one-hole lead after the first nine holes and could not improve on that by lunch.

The afternoon saw a total transformation, with the American pair racking up a four-hole advantage by the turn. Kroll and Burke reached the turn in just 33 strokes as their opponents struggled badly. Weetman suddenly found the fairways too narrow to hit with any regularity, and Faulkner could do no better.

With little resistance from their opponents, Kroll and Burke ran out easy winners, 4 and 3. The two British players virtually ruled themselves out of the singles the following day.

After their poor showing in the foursomes, Rees dropped Faulkner and Weetman from the singles, a controversial move that had some serious and long-term ramifications. A bitterly upset Weetman vowed, "I'll never play in a team captained by Rees again!"

Following this outburst, Weetman was banned from official team events for a year.

Dick Mayer and Tommy Bolt (USA) v. Christy O'Connor and Eric Brown (GBI)

Fresh from his U.S. Open win at Inverness, Dick Mayer was at the peak of his game. He and the mercurial Tommy Bolt formed a redoubtable partnership, shooting 33-34 for the morning eighteen.

Despite this impressive showing, they were only three up, as O'Connor and Brown somehow held on to the American coattails. The British overcame a number of silly little errors to keep Mayer and Bolt as close as they did.

O'Connor and Brown were not so fortunate after lunch, as the Americans quickly turned up the heat. They played the first nine holes in the afternoon one shot better than they had in the morning, for a six-hole lead. The U.S. pair made further birdies at the par-4 twelfth and par-5 thirteenth for good measure, and were amply rewarded with a convincing 7 and 5 win.

Dick Mayer was the reigning U.S. Open champion. He would lose his title in 1958 to his playing partner, Tommy Bolt.

Day one result: USA *3,* GBI *1*

THE OLD, OLD RYDER CUP STORY —*London Telegraph* headline

Day Two: 36-Hole Singles

With a changeable wind that had finally woken up and started to blow, the British felt the conditions might suit their natural game. Also needed was a change in the British playing standards: half of their pairs from the previous day had barely put a foot right on the course.

The greens staff had apparently been misinformed over the starting day and consequently had not cut the greens to their normal playing length for the first day. For the second day, the greens had been trimmed back to regulation length, making them faster and trickier—so much so that six of the Americans needed three putts on the first green before they realized what had happened. After five holes, the home team found themselves up in seven games and all square in the eighth.

Tommy Bolt (USA) v. Eric Brown (GBI)

In an attempt to end the American stranglehold in the first singles match, the British "hard man," Eric Brown, was promoted to the number one spot against Tommy "Thunder" Bolt.

When the two highly combative players were late arriving on the tee, Jimmy Demaret joked that the last time he had seen them, they were standing at fifty paces, throwing clubs at each other.

Brown did not start well, finding the rough and sand with his first two shots as Bolt took the first hole. The Scot was lucky to halve the second, but he quickly found his rhythm and took a three-hole lead on the seventh. Lunch was reached with Bolt four holes to the bad, as Brown recovered from his patchy start to card a resolute 71.

"Bolt found putting difficult and smiling more difficult still."
—*Leonard Crawley,* London Telegraph

The American soon halved this deficit in the afternoon but could not make any further impact on the resilient Scotsman, who actually extended his lead to finish with a morale-boosting 4 and 3 victory. This was only the second opening singles win for Britain in twelve Ryder Cups.

After the ill-tempered match, the players refused to shake hands and Bolt claimed he had not enjoyed himself, to which Brown replied, "I don't suppose you did . . . because even you knew when the games were drawn that you never had an earthly hope of beating me."

In the locker room afterward, Bolt reputedly broke a wedge in half, and he did not put in an appearance at the presentation ceremony.

Jack Burke (USA) v. Peter Mills (GBI)

The sole British rookie, Peter Mills, had been slated to play Ted Kroll, but the American fell ill and could not play. In a sporting gesture, Rees allowed Jack Burke, who had dropped himself from the singles, to fill in—although the British captain could have claimed a point for a forfeited match.

This was an especially generous offer, since Burke was the recognized American ace and many felt that Mills was merely a lamb being led to the slaughter. Mills proved to be a wolf in sheep's clothing, as he was more than up to the task at hand.

Possibly owing to a lack of preparation on his part, Burke shot a woeful 77 in the morning to fall five holes behind. Had Burke not won the 200-yard eighteenth with a bogey four, he would have been languishing six down at lunch.

In the afternoon, there was nothing the American captain could do to overhaul the first-timer, who flatly refused to let the occasion get to him. Mills pulled off one of the biggest surprises in Ryder Cup history with a 5 and 3 win. As well as lifting the British morale even higher, it just as importantly leveled the match score.

Agreeing to play as a late replacement cost Burke his place among the Ryder Cup immortals, as this defeat was his only loss in eight matches played.

Although Peter Mills was selected for the next Ryder Cup, he was too injured to play, and he never made the team again. So he was left with a career record of played one, won one.

Fred Hawkins (USA) v. Peter Alliss (GBI)

The only singles match in which Britain found itself behind after the first nine holes was the one between Peter Alliss and Fred Hawkins. Three down after six, the Englishman produced wins at eight, nine, and ten to level the match.

By lunch, the American was back in front by a solitary hole, and he quickly increased his lead to three after the break. Stung into action, Alliss produced another string of four wins in six holes to take the lead for the first time. One up after ten, Alliss had to hole a fifteen-footer just to halve the eleventh in birdie twos.

As had been the case all day, Hawkins hit back with two birdie fours that produced two wins at fourteen and sixteen, and he held on with a par at seventeen for a 2 and 1 win.

Hawkins's obvious delight at his personal triumph was cut short when he realized the full extent of the carnage going on behind him. "I was concentrating on my match with Alliss and thought we were winning," he said.

Lionel Hebert (USA) v. Ken Bousfield (GBI)

After nine holes Ken Bousfield had a handy four-hole cushion over Lionel Hebert, which he increased to five by lunch, thanks to a gloriously long birdie putt from the back of the eighteenth green.

After the resumption, the British lead stretched to seven, but then Hebert launched a savage counterattack, winning three holes in a row. Bousfield had more than enough in reserve to staunch the flow of lost holes. He played a delightful chip onto the eighth green and sank an eight-footer to go back five up.

"I was driving like an idiot and putting like an angel."
—*Ken Bousfield*

"Those were the days before scoreboards out on the course and walkie-talkies. All of us playing out there would have no idea what was happening in the other matches if it wasn't for Max (Faulkner). He was marvelous. And he seemed to bring good news every time I saw him. He'd nip up to me, 'Rees is winning.' 'Brown's four up.' 'We've got them on the run, Guv'nor.' 'Go on! You can beat this boy.' Then he'd dash off and come back ten minutes later with more good news. We might have won without him, but he was magnificent that day—I'll never forget what he did." —KEN BOUSFIELD

Comparing his historic win with Sam Torrance's in 1985: "The one big difference from Torrance's was that my match finished out in the country, on the fifteenth green. But it wasn't the same sort of emotion. I can understand Sam crying. I didn't in 1957—but I felt like it."
—*Ken Bousfield*

Six down at the turn, Hebert tried to stage another comeback, but despite his winning two holes, it was too little too late. Bousfield halved the fifteenth with an eighteen-inch putt for a 4 and 3 win—and the point that ultimately won the Ryder Cup for Great Britain.

Ed Furgol (USA) v. Dai Rees (GBI)

As he started his morning round, Dai Rees was aware that something special was happening to his team. They were up in every match except one, and the traditional American singles bonanza had been stifled.

As if to celebrate his team's dominating position, Rees opened up like a man with a mission, covering the first nine holes in 33 strokes—the best of the day. A barnstorming birdie at the par-3 eighteenth almost brought the clubhouse down, leaving Rees four up at lunch on Ed Furgol.

Ed Furgol and his brother Marty (1955) were the second set of American brothers to appear in the Ryder Cup. Jim (1953) and Joe (1927 and '29) Turnesa appeared before them.

The American had no answer to the Welshman, who started out the second session with three threes to take a commanding seven-hole lead at the turn. Bolstered by the good news from around the course, Rees easily held on to this considerable advantage to close out the shell-shocked Furgol, 7 and 6.

"It was the most thrilling day of my life. I was so proud of captaining a winning side that it probably made up for all those disappointments I endured in many British Open championships." —DAI REES

Doug Ford (USA) v. Bernard Hunt (GBI)

"Hunt faced the terrifying Ford, who has deservedly acquired the reputation of being unbeatable in match play." —*Times* (London)

Unfazed by Ford's slamming home long putts on seven, eight, and nine, Hunt was one up at the turn, which is how the score stood at the halfway stage.

After lunch, Hunt left his opponent's reputation strewn all over the front nine holes. Out in 32, Hunt won five holes and only lost the sixth hole to a belligerent birdie two by a seriously shaken Ford.

Down by five with a quarter of the match remaining, Ford had no reply to the Englishman's outward onslaught and was forced to raise the white flag on the thirteenth, taking a 6 and 5 hammering on the chin.

Dow Finsterwald (USA) v. Christy O'Connor (GBI)

Despite some poor putting in the morning, Christy O'Connor managed to finish the first eighteen holes against Dow Finsterwald all square. O'Connor had started the match 3-3-3, compared with the American's disastrous 7-4-4, for a three-hole lead, which he let slip over the course of the morning.

"O'Connor, who was generally considered not quite man enough for the great Finsterwald, began like a machine gun loaded with threes, and stood three up on the fourth tee." —Leonard Crawley, *London Telegraph*

Having been pegged back to all square at the break, the Irishman bought a new putter from the Lindrick pro shop and never looked back in the afternoon session. Waving the new putter like a magic wand, O'Connor won six of the first eight holes after lunch, which virtually settled the match.

O'Connor even bit off a huge slice of Irish luck when he holed an audacious recovery shot from underneath a bush alongside the eighth green. Like many of his compatriots before him, Finsterwald was finally gunned down, 7 and 6.

Dick Mayer (USA) v. Harry Bradshaw (GBI)

With the Ryder Cup already won midway through his afternoon round against U.S. Open champion Dick Mayer, Irishman Harry Bradshaw found himself playing for personal pride. He won the first three holes of the match, and brought the crowd to their feet by holing his bunker shot at the short third hole. After this great start, Bradshaw threw away his advantage and allowed Mayer to take a single-hole lead at the break.

Bradshaw got that hole back on the first green in the afternoon with the luxury of a bogey five. From there on in, neither player was ever more than one hole up.

"Suddenly, before anyone could believe it, the deed was done, the Americans had been put to flight as never before. . . . Last of all Bradshaw brought a wonderfully even match with Mayer to its fitting end by getting down in two from well short of the last green. An unforgettable day was done." —PAT WARD-THOMAS

This was the only match of either day that reached the thirty-sixth hole, and the players halved that as they had the previous four holes for an amicable share of the spoils.

Day two result: USA 1½, GBI 6½
Overall match score: USA 4½, GBI 7½

Recap

REES'S IRON MEN BEAT U.S. AT OWN GAME

—*London Telegraph* headline

In coming from two points down, before the singles, to win the match, Rees's British team not only emulated the feat of the 1949 Americans at Ganton but went one better by stretching the winning margin to three points. This five-point turnaround was as unbelievable as it was improbable; the Americans had dominated the one-on-one format since the early days of the Ryder Cup. This was quite easily the worst-ever American singles performance: one win (Hawkins) and a half (Mayer) from eight matches.

"It's wonderful. This is the greatest shot in the arm British golf ever had. My team should receive the freedom of nearby Sheffield and all of Britain." —DAI REES

On the American demise: "Frankly, you could have knocked us down with a feather."
—Times *(London)*

American fears over the lack of superstar names in the lineup were well founded. Once the rout was on, there was no stopping the British running away with the match and reclaiming the trophy that had last stayed on that side of the Atlantic in 1933.

American captain Jack Burke was not short of an excuse or three for his side's sorry performance: "I think we were overtrained. We came here too soon and played ourselves out in a week of practice. The big mistake we made was playing that little British ball. I'm going to suggest that in the future, American teams arrive here no earlier than four or five days before the event. I've known our fellows for a long time, and I've never seen them putt so badly."

The losing skipper also suggested that the pins used were of differing thicknesses and heights, claiming it was difficult to see some from the fairway, while others made it impossible to chip the ball into the hole.

What most pleased Dai Rees and his team was the manner of the American capitulation; all six American defeats on day two came some distance from the final green. This singles rout was not a close thing, where the Americans might have stolen a match here or there; instead, they were put to the sword. For once the packed galleries had something to shout about—and something to tell their grandchildren, because it would be about that long before the Americans would be defeated again.

Tommy Bolt on the vociferous home crowds: *"Individually, they are pretty nice folks. But get them together and they are about as miserable a bunch of people as you could ever have the misfortune to run into in a supposedly civilized world. They cheered when I missed a putt and sat on their hands when I hit a good shot."*
Ed Furgol: *"Pipe down; we were well and truly licked!"*

With only its third win in twelve meetings, Great Britain had waited nearly twenty years to win the trophy back. It would be another twenty-eight before the Americans would be careless enough to lose their grip again, in 1985.

Match Results (Winning side marked in *italics*.)

Friday, October 4—Foursomes

	USA	GBI	Score
1.	*Doug Ford* *Dow Finsterwald*	Peter Alliss Bernard Hunt	2 and 1
2.	Art Wall Fred Hawkins	*Ken Bousfield* *Dai Rees*	3 and 2
3.	*Ted Kroll* *Jack Burke*	Max Faulkner Harry Weetman	4 and 3
4.	*Dick Mayer* *Tommy Bolt*	Christy O'Connor Eric Brown	7 and 5

Day one result: USA *3,* GBI *1*

Saturday, October 5—Singles

	USA	GBI	Score
5.	Tommy Bolt	*Eric Brown*	4 and 3
6.	Jack Burke	*Peter Mills*	5 and 3
7.	*Fred Hawkins*	Peter Alliss	2 and 1
8.	Lionel Hebert	*Ken Bousfield*	4 and 3
9.	Ed Furgol	*Dai Rees*	7 and 6
10.	Doug Ford	*Bernard Hunt*	6 and 5
11.	Dow Finsterwald	*Christy O'Connor*	7 and 6
12.	Dick Mayer	Harry Bradshaw	halved

Day two result: USA *1½,* GBI *6½*

Overall match score: USA *4½,* GBI *7½*

1959

Eldorado Country Club
Palm Desert, California
United States
November 6–7

United States 8½	Great Britain and Ireland 3½
Julius Boros	Peter Alliss
Dow Finsterwald	Ken Bousfield
Doug Ford	Eric Brown
Jay Hebert	Norman Drew
Cary Middlecoff	Bernard Hunt
Bob Rosburg	Christy O'Connor, Sr.
Mike Souchak	Dave Thomas
Art Wall, Jr.	Harry Weetman
Playing Captain	Peter Mills [did not play]
Sam Snead	John Panton [did not play]
	Playing Captain
	Dai Rees

Paradise (and Cup) Lost

The 1959 Ryder Cup came within 9,000 feet of being a fatal disaster.

The light airplane carrying the British team to the Eldorado Country Club encountered severe turbulence over the San Jacinto Mountains and plummeted from 13,000 to 9,000 feet in seconds. Fortunately, the pilot recovered control of the plane and returned to Los Angeles, where the shaken golfers thanked Providence and took a Greyhound bus to their destination.

American Doug Ford had chanced upon the British team at the Los Angeles airport and "thumbed a lift" on their plane. He must have regretted his travel arrangements after the bumpy ride.

The American team waiting to welcome their opponents proved a lot stronger than the one that had relinquished the Ryder Cup two years earlier. Sam Snead returned as captain, along with some new faces: Cary Middlecoff, Julius Boros, Bob Rosburg, Jay Hebert, and Mike Souchak. Fortunately for the visiting side, the roll call of those ineligible under PGA membership rules included: Arnold Palmer (the 1958 Masters champion), Billy Casper (the reigning U.S. Open champion), and Ken Venturi and Gene Littler (both of whom would go on to win U.S. Opens).

Forty-year-old "Moose" Boros had been selected to play in 1957, but he broke his leg and was unable to take part. Jack Burke was also selected, but a badly injured hand ruled him out. He still had a part to play, however: "He was our cheerleader on the course," said Cary Middlecoff.

The British team had no such strength in depth, and just before the tournament, they lost a key player, Peter Mills, to a serious back problem. The hero of 1957 was replaced by John Panton, who did not get to swing a club in anger.

Having had a nightmare just getting to the course, the British team also suffered at the hands of the club members, who refused to give way for their guests during the practice rounds. "Three times, groups of British players were refused permission to go through at the tenth hole after finishing nine. The tedious, friendly games of the gaudily clad members were given priority," wrote Ron Heager of the *London Express*.

"We were paupers in a millionaires' playground. No one offered to give way. I couldn't believe it. But they drove off just as if we didn't exist," Dai Rees said of the event, which drew a glittering crowd, including Bing Crosby, Bob Hope, and Frank Sinatra.

Course Details

Eldorado was a typical desert course, where narrow fairways and small, flat greens and a judicious sprinkling of water hazards were the order of the day.

The par-4, 393-yard doglegged fourth was the signature hole, with—as would be imagined in an arid region—a second shot over water.

Hole	Distance	Par	Hole	Distance	Par
1	507	5	10	377	4
2	175	3	11	437	4
3	439	4	12	217	3
4	393	4	13	518	5
5	379	4	14	423	4
6	368	4	15	403	4
7	189	3	16	194	3
8	394	4	17	519	5
9	466	4	18	470	4
		35			**36 = Par 71 (6,868 yards)**

Course designer: Lawrence Hughes

Day One: 36-Hole Foursomes

The players were greeted with another shiny day in paradise.

"The weather was perfect when play started, with no wind, a warm sun, and the temperature climbing into the eighties." —*Times* (London)

Bob Rosburg and Mike Souchak (USA) v. Bernard Hunt and Eric Brown (GBI)

The match started quietly enough, as Mike Souchak and Bob Rosburg held a narrow one-hole lead over Hunt and Brown after the front nine.

"I had warmed up early in the morning and then waited through the opening ceremony, which took about fifteen minutes. I was so nervous, I heeled my drive, which hardly got off the ground, about 190 yards down the fairway." —Bob Rosburg

Having holed two birdie putts early on, Rosburg sank another on the twelfth to take a two-hole lead. With Hunt knocking his ball in the water on thirteen, the Americans were three up and going away. They reached lunch six to the good.

The British were severely handicapped by Hunt's bronchitis, which almost forced him to concede the match at the halfway stage. With a superb 68, the Americans carded the only sub-par round of the morning. The British coughed and spluttered their way to a 77.

"Mike Souchak has been an All-American footballer (whatever that may mean), but I am sure he gives far more pleasure to spectators playing golf."
—*Leonard Crawley,* London Telegraph

Hunt and Brown had no answer to the Americans in the afternoon, as Rosburg and Souchak took the first two holes to go eight up, and Rosburg laid his chip to the fourth stone dead for another win. Out in 33, the British pair made a slight recovery in the afternoon, but Brown missed two short putts on fourteen and fifteen that ended the match, 5 and 4.

Julius Boros and Dow Finsterwald (USA) v. Ken Bousfield and Dai Rees (GBI)

Dow Finsterwald seemed to be playing a game different from that of the other three in his group. Boros, Rees, and Bousfield played a host of poor shots that lost holes more regularly than holes were earned. Water, bunkers, rough, and trees all came in for target practice as these three squandered chances.

While the others repeatedly missed the green, Finsterwald stood firm. When he was not making long putts, he was making remarkable recoveries to set up hole-winning putts. All square after the first seventeen holes, the British pair contrived to put another ball in the lake, giving the Americans a one-hole lead at the break.

This match was one of many that would be heavily influenced by the seven major water hazards that dotted this desert course.

In the afternoon, neither side could put together a decent run of holes to mount a match-winning charge, and the final hole loomed large again with the Americans still clinging to a one-hole lead. Once again, the water fatally came into play for the British. After two very respectable drives, Finsterwald changed his mind about taking a four-wood to the green and played a much safer four-iron to lay up. Bousfield had no such luxury; he needed to win the 470-yard closing hole for a half, and had to go for the green.

Two small lakes, cut into the front of an equally small green, were an obvious danger to those foolhardy enough to try for the green in two. Bousfield's approach found the kidney-shaped lake to the right of the hole, and any British chance to share the match drowned.

The Americans prevailed by two clear holes, as this fine finishing hole claimed its first victim of the tournament. It would not be the last.

Art Wall and Doug Ford (USA) v. Peter Alliss and Christy O'Connor (GBI)

The home side's strength was demonstrated in the caliber of their third pairing: Art Wall (the Masters champion) and Doug Ford (Masters champion two years earlier).

The major-winning American pair teed off against Peter Alliss (0-for-4 in his Ryder Cup matches to date) and Christy O'Connor, who had played the best golf in the practice rounds.

The American masters showed their prowess when Wall chipped up to three feet on the first green for Ford to slot home the birdie putt to go one up. They gave the hole back when Ford drove into the trees on the fourth, and the British pair continued to win holes to take a two-hole lead at the turn.

"Wall, voted American golfer of the year, was not at his best, particularly with his irons."
—Times *(London)*

The lead doubled after Ford's approach missed the green at eleven and his subsequent tee shot landed behind a wall, leaving his partner no shot at the twelfth green. Alliss gave a hole back on sixteen, bunkering his approach, then missing an eight-footer for the half. Ford's troubles got worse as he hit his second shot to the

519-yard seventeenth only a hundred yards, coming up way short of the green. He was rescued by Wall, who pitched up to five feet for the birdie putt to cut the lead to two, but the British rounded off a good morning by winning the eighteenth.

O'Connor and Alliss turned their three-hole lead into five after twenty-four holes, but the Americans made a concerted effort to fight back and were only two down with three to play. On the par-3 sixteenth, the British combined well for a birdie two and took the match by 3 and 2.

For their win over the top-class Americans, Alliss and O'Connor were four under par for the thirty-two holes played, and they were the only complete British success of the first day.

Sam Snead and Cary Middlecoff (USA) v. Harry Weetman and Dave Thomas (GBI)

The United States closed with their strongest pairing, and by lunch the Americans were a hole to the good over Weetman and Thomas.

The early-morning exchanges had evened out after nine holes. Thomas won the tenth with a ten-foot putt but gave it back with a wayward approach to twelve. Middlecoff coughed one up into the middle of the lake on thirteen, and Thomas sank his twenty-five-footer on fourteen to go up by two. Snead from thirty feet and Middlecoff from six feet both holed putts to win fifteen and seventeen and level the match. Snead took on and cleared the lakes at eighteen for a birdie and a one-hole lead at the break.

The afternoon saw both pairs play some rousing golf as first the U.S. pair went up by two, then the British not only fought back but took a two-hole lead with two to play.

Harry Weetman was back on the British team after being banned following his outburst against Dai Rees's captaincy in 1957.

On seventeen, Thomas had a five-foot putt to close the American aces out, but he missed. The win would have leveled the overall match score at 2-2—a rare occurrence in Ryder Cup play after the first day.

On the eighteenth tee, Thomas produced a terrific drive that affected Middlecoff, who badly hooked his tee shot into the rough. With the British one up and in prime position, Snead tried to produce another of his wonder shots. Aiming at the flag, he powered his ball out of the rough and into the lake on the left of the green. With four shots to halve the hole, Britain found itself in a most enviable position. Only a bonehead decision would prevent the visiting side from squaring the overall match. Inexplicably, Weetman decided not to lay up with a short iron, but instead took on the twin lakes with a five-iron and found the water on the right.

"Why did I not play safe? I never do. It's not my game. I just didn't hit the right shot," Weetman said afterward.

Given a glimmer of hope, the Americans seized their chance, making a five thanks to Middlecoff's chip to ten feet and Snead's ice-cool putt. The stunned British pair could not match this up and down, lost the hole with a double-bogey six, and walked off with a heartbreaking half.

Day one result: USA 2½, GBI 1½

Day Two: 36-Hole Singles

The players were greeted by another perfect California day with temperatures well into the eighties. November 7 was the latest day in the calendar year that a Ryder Cup match has ever been played.

Doug Ford (USA) v. Norman Drew (GBI)

Suffering from a feverish head cold, Bernard Hunt was replaced by Norman Drew at the head of the British lineup. Despite making his debut at such short notice, Drew acquitted himself well against the very much in form Doug Ford.

Irishman Norman Drew became the first player to represent Britain in both the Walker Cup and the Ryder Cup.

Four up after nine holes, Ford looked to be heading for an easy afternoon stroll in the country, but Drew fought back and reduced the American's lunchtime lead to a single hole. Ford had a much busier afternoon than he had expected, as Drew played him tough—only one down right up to the final hole.

Although he had seen two of his teammates find the water on the last hole the day before, Drew had no doubts he could avoid such a fate himself. After Ford safely laid up short of the lakes, Drew took out his trusty spoon and launched his second shot high over the water, finding the center of the green. His ball rolled up to within fifteen feet of the hole, where the brave Irishman (around in 69) was rewarded by winning the hole to halve the match.

Having hitched a ride on the near-fatal plane ride from Los Angeles with the British team, Doug Ford was given an equally bumpy ride in his two matches—he failed to win either.

Mike Souchak (USA) v. Ken Bousfield (GBI)

The early morning belonged to Mike Souchak. He took four holes out of Ken Bousfield by the turn, who had taken 40 strokes to complete the nine holes. The Englishman managed to hold the American to this four-up lead at lunch, despite twice visiting the water during the morning. With an opening round of 69, the well-built Souchak consistently outdrove his opponent, who was always playing catch-up.

Out in eight strokes better than his morning card, Bousfield cut the lead to two after the first nine holes of the afternoon. With the threat of losing his lead, Souchak pressed home his superior distance off the tee and closed Bousfield out by revealing his gentle touch on the greens, stroking in a twenty-five-footer on the sixteenth to win 3 and 2.

Bob Rosburg (USA) v. Harry Weetman (GBI)

All square with Harry Weetman after nine holes, PGA champion Bob Rosburg carded a steady round of 70 for his morning's work and must have been mildly surprised to hold a four-hole lead at the break. Still smarting from his momentous mistake on the first day, Weetman went round in 74, his putting letting him down badly.

"Harry was still shaken up from his experience the day before. I know it bothered him during our match." —Bob Rosburg

After lunch, Rosburg was three under par for the thirteen holes played, in spite of finding two stretches of the water. Not wanting to be completely outdone, the Irishman also found two stretches of water. Five up at the turn, Rosburg continued his steady play and easily beat Weetman 6 and 5, for his second convincing win of the contest.

Sam Snead (USA) v. Dave Thomas (GBI)

Having halved their foursomes match, Snead and Thomas might have thought their solo encounter would also go the distance. The American legend, having been given a lifeline by Weetman's error on the first day, was not going to need any more chances, as he took two holes off the giant Welshman by the turn.

The previous year, Dave Thomas came within a stroke of winning the British Open, but he tied Peter Thomson and lost in a play-off at Royal Lytham.

Snead returned to the clubhouse with a superb 67—six shots up on Thomas, good for a four-hole lead. The big-driving Welshman had his limitations severely exposed by the American, who settled the match in emphatic style. Snead chipped in from twenty-five feet on the twelfth hole before halving the next for another 6 and 5 U.S. win.

This was Sam Snead's last Ryder Cup appearance, having played in a record seven matches. Like the great man himself, Snead's overall playing record was beyond reproach—10-2-1.

Dow Finsterwald (USA) v. Dai Rees (GBI)

Having played in a poor match on the first day, Dow Finsterwald and Dai Rees started this match in much better style. Scores of 4-2-3 on the first three holes gave the American a three-hole lead, which Rees cut to two by the turn. On the homeward stretch, Finsterwald got back in stride and won another three holes to take a five-hole advantage into lunch.

Yet again, Rees refused to lie down and be beaten: he got three holes back on the afternoon's outward stretch. Two up after twenty-seven holes soon became all square for Finsterwald, as Rees leveled on the twelfth. With Finsterwald wondering what he had to do to dispatch this little Welsh terrier, Rees sent his ball into the water and took a six to go one down again.

The next three holes were halved, as neither player would give an inch. Sixteen looked to have decided the issue when Finsterwald prevailed to take a two-hole lead with two to play. Rees answered in unbelievable fashion, firing his second shot to the par-5 seventeenth within a yard of the hole. Although Finsterwald made his birdie, Rees holed out for an eagle to leave the American dormie one.

The final hole saw Finsterwald put his wooden approach through the back of the green, and Rees answered with another magnificent second to twelve feet. Just as the win was slipping away from the United States, Finsterwald produced one of the shots of his life. He coolly chipped back onto the green and watched as his ball slowly rolled up to the flag and almost dropped in. With a certain American par four, Rees had his putt of a dozen feet for the overall half, but he could not produce the magic one last time, and Finsterwald had his revenge, 1-up.

Jay Hebert (USA) v. Peter Alliss (GBI)

Peter Alliss covered the first nine holes in 32 strokes, holing putts from twenty-five, thirty-five, thirty-five, and forty feet, as well as pitching in from 120 yards for an eagle two on the sixth. At the turn, all the Englishman had to show for his splendid work was a one-hole lead, as Jay Hebert all but matched his sub-par scoring. After sinking a seven-footer on the tenth, Alliss had taken just seven putts to cover the previous seven holes but still could not break the American.

Alliss could not keep up the pace of his opening onslaught, as he came home in 38 but still held on to a solitary one-hole lead. With a fast start in the afternoon, Hebert carded nine fours for the outward half, perfectly matched by Alliss except for a costly bogey five at the ninth hole to level the match.

The American had wins on twelve and fourteen, where he made a fourteen-footer before Alliss missed from six feet nearer the hole. The Englishman got a hole back at fifteen, and the pair approached the last with the United States one to the fore.

The water of the thirty-sixth hole again came into play, gratefully accepting Hebert's humble offering as he tried to close out the match. Needing to win the hole to halve the match, Alliss struck a perfect three-iron safely onto the green, then had no trouble making the putt for the win and an overall half.

In his third singles match, and despite recording the best stroke-play score (one over) of the British team, Peter Alliss had yet to record a solo victory, as he had lost both his previous two matches.

Art Wall (USA) v. Christy O'Connor (GBI)

Art Wall started fast against Christy O'Connor and carved out a four-hole lead after nine holes. The American crowned a good morning round of 70 by holing putts from thirty feet at seventeen and twenty-five feet at eighteen for a three. On the same closing holes, the Irishman missed two putts from twelve feet.

Five up at the break became six up at the turn, as the American continued to hold his form. Unable to make any inroads into the American's commanding lead, O'Connor lost another hole after the turn and went down to the biggest defeat of the contest, 7 and 6.

Cary Middlecoff (USA) v. Eric Brown (GBI)

In the last match, which was purely academic as far as the overall match score was concerned, Eric Brown once again proved he was twice the singles player than he was a foursomes partner. The "Brown Bomber" had lost all four of his foursomes, going down to heavy defeats on each occasion: 8 and 7, 5 and 4, 7 and 5, and 5 and 4. But he was a different man in the singles.

Against Cary Middlecoff, he was the only British player to win the first hole, but he three-putted the second. Despite dropping a shot at the eighteenth, Brown still carded a fine 68—the only British player under 70 in the morning. This excellent scoring was sufficient to give Brown a three-hole lead at lunch.

This was Brown's fourth big win in four singles matches. His hit list of great U.S. golfers included Mangrum, Bolt, Barber, and now Middlecoff.

Middlecoff had struggled on the previous day and did not fare any better on his own, as Brown surged to a six-hole lead at the turn in the afternoon. The American finally got some semblance of form back as he managed to cut the Scot's lead by two, but he was eventually downed 4 and 3.

Day two result: USA *6,* GBI *2*

In the eight singles matches, the Americans combined to be twelve under par, while the British players were ten over par. This difference of twenty-two shots was almost three per man, which explains how the United States won the singles 6-2.

Overall match score: USA *8½,* GBI *3½*

Recap

After their best stateside showing in 1955, the British reverted back to their old form on the road (and sea and air). They never looked good enough to mount a serious challenge against a very strong American side that was only going to get better with a long line of superstars waiting in the wings.

Changes were needed, and suggestions were floated around, like (heaven forbid!) opening the British side up to include Europeans. Even British Commonwealth players were thrown into the Ryder Cup melting pot, since they had dominated the British Open for the past few years, with such luminaries as Player, Thomson, Nagle, and Locke (it took the Presidents Cup only thirty-five years to work that one out!).

By the next Ryder Cup in England, one major set of changes would be made, and it had nothing to do with British playing strength.

Match Results (Winning side marked in *italics*.)

Friday, November 6—Foursomes

	USA	GBI	Score
1.	*Bob Rosburg* *Mike Souchak*	Bernard Hunt Eric Brown	5 and 4
2.	*Julius Boros* *Dow Finsterwald*	Ken Bousfield Dai Rees	2-up
3.	Art Wall Doug Ford	*Peter Alliss* *Christy O'Connor*	3 and 2
4.	Sam Snead Cary Middlecoff	Harry Weetman Dave Thomas	halved

Day one result: USA 2½, GBI 1½

Saturday, November 7—Singles

	USA	GBI	Score
5.	Doug Ford	Norman Drew	halved
6.	*Mike Souchak*	Ken Bousfield	3 and 2
7.	*Bob Rosburg*	Harry Weetman	6 and 5
8.	*Sam Snead*	Dave Thomas	6 and 5
9.	*Dow Finsterwald*	Dai Rees	1-up
10.	Jay Hebert	Peter Alliss	halved
11.	*Art Wall*	Christy O'Connor	7 and 6
12.	Cary Middlecoff	*Eric Brown*	4 and 3

Day two result: USA 6, GBI 2

Overall match score: USA 8½, GBI 3½

1961

Royal Lytham and St. Annes *Lancashire, England* *October 13–14*	**United States 14½**	**Great Britain and Ireland 9½**
	Billy Casper	Peter Alliss
	Bill Collins	Ken Bousfield
	Dow Finsterwald	Neil Coles
	Doug Ford	Tom Haliburton
	Jay Hebert	Bernard Hunt
	Gene Littler	Ralph Moffitt
	Arnold Palmer	Christy O'Connor, Sr.
	Mike Souchak	John Panton
	Art Wall, Jr.	Harry Weetman
	Playing Captain	**Playing Captain**
	Jerry Barber	Dai Rees

New Kids on the Block

At the instigation of the British PGA, the Ryder Cup playing format was changed to introduce twice as many matches and points. Eight foursomes and sixteen singles over eighteen holes replaced the four foursomes and eight singles matches over thirty-six holes that had been the format since the first Ryder Cup in 1927. The thinking behind this change was to give the British team a better chance of success.

Over thirty-six holes the best player(s) invariably will win, and they were usually American. By reducing the matches to just one round, it gave the traditionally weaker British team a greater chance of making the Ryder Cup more competitive. Far too many times Britain had been up at lunch, only to fade over the afternoon eighteen.

While some things were changing, others were not. Dai Rees remained British captain for the fourth Ryder Cup, and an American was in trouble over his eligibility. Having easily qualified for the Ryder Cup, Sam Snead decided to take a break from the PGA

Tour and innocently played in a non-PGA pro-am (while the PGA-run Portland Open was on). As a PGA member, Snead was duty-bound not to play in any non-PGA match while an official PGA match was in progress. Realizing his mistake, Snead immediately dropped out of the pro-am after the first round. But the damage had been done, and he was excluded from the Ryder Cup team. (Although Snead would return to the U.S. Ryder Cup team as a nonplaying captain in 1969, he never played again. His record speaks for itself: beaten only once, by Harry Weetman in 1953, in seven singles matches.)

"Snead played in some twopenny-halfpenny affair the other day, and has been suspended for six months. His absence at Lytham will be a grievous blow to many, and at least one family I know have canceled their rooms at Blackpool this weekend." —LEONARD CRAWLEY, *London Telegraph*

Snead's place as a player and his official uniform was literally filled by the experienced Doug Ford, while the diminutive Jerry Barber tried to fill Snead's much larger shoes as captain. The U.S. team did not really miss Snead's presence, since the roster included a trio of outstanding new Ryder Cup talent: Arnold Palmer, Billy Casper, and Gene Littler. How good were these three Ryder Cup rookies? Good enough to be the last three U.S. Open champions!

As usual, the British team had no such draw on strength or major-winning firepower. They also brought in three new faces: Neil Coles, Tom Haliburton, and Ralph Moffitt, who were a par seven short of matching the three new American stars.

The United States had just one player over age forty, Jerry Barber, while Britain had five: Rees, Haliburton, Panton, Bousfield, and Weetman. The United States had no player under thirty, whereas Britain had two: Coles and Moffitt.

The American team lost the Ryder Cup trophy itself a few days before the match started. In what could have been a very embarrassing episode for the American captain, he realized, after arriving at the course in the northwest of England, that he had forgotten to retrieve the trophy deposited in the security vault at the team's London hotel. After a sleepless night for Barber, the Cup was shipped by rail to the course in time to save Barber's blushes. "Gee, we had so much baggage, I clean forgot about that little old Cup."

Course Details

Royal Lytham is classed as a links course, although the course has no direct view of the sea, is bordered on three sides by houses, and has a railway line running down the fourth side. It is thought of as more of a true seaside course than typical Scottish-style links, although it does possess links fairways that are both narrow and undulating, while the tricky greens run off in more directions than a compass can point.

The most striking feature of Royal Lytham is that it has more than two hundred bunkers, an average of eleven per hole.

Hole	Distance	Par	Hole	Distance	Par
1	208	3	10	336	4
2	424	4	11	483	5
3	456	5	12	166	3
4	393	4	13	339	4
5	188	3	14	445	4
6	466	5	15	462	5
7	551	5	16	356	4
8	394	4	17	549	5
9	164	3	18	379	4
		36			**38 = Par 74 (6,759 yards)**

Course designer: George Lowe

Day One: Morning (18-Hole) Foursomes

"The sun hung full of promise only just above the television tower, and shone through mist into the players' eyes. The fairways were drenched with dew." —*Times* (London)

Doug Ford and Gene Littler (USA) v. Christy O'Connor and Peter Alliss (GBI)

In his first Ryder Cup match, Gene Littler must have wondered what all the fuss about pressure was. He and partner Doug Ford could manage only to bogey the par-3 first, but they still won the hole after the British three-putted. Their opponents, Alliss and O'Connor, did not play the next two holes in any fewer strokes, starting out 5-5-5.

Two down, Alliss got the British pair back on track with a superb chip up to the flag on the sixth for a birdie. Here Littler must have got an inkling as to what Ryder Cup play really was all about. From this point on, the British pair did not look back, O'Connor sticking approaches to ten yards and seven feet at the eighth and tenth for Alliss to make winning birdies and take the lead.

With Littler finding a bunker on eleven, Alliss holed a seven-footer to go two up. The Americans conjured up a way to lose the thirteenth to another Alliss seven-footer for a four, while the Englishman laid his chip shot stone dead on fourteen for a half. With the U.S. pair failing to mount any real challenge, the Englishman finished them off with another eight-foot birdie putt at fifteen, to run out quite cozy 4 and 3 winners.

An unhappy Barber subsequently dropped his opening pair from the afternoon foursomes, handing Littler a very rude welcome to the Ryder Cup.

Art Wall and Jay Hebert (USA) v. John Panton and Bernard Hunt (GBI)

Wall and Hebert were in the box seat early on, thanks to another woeful British start, this time by Hunt and Panton, who made four bogeys in the first seven holes. The Americans also bogeyed the fourth but halved the hole, and a birdie at six put them three up. Hunt's approach shot to the seventh found the sand, and the British took another three strokes to hole out at this par 5, carding a bogey to go down by four.

In the practice session on Thursday, the British pair set the course on fire by carding six consecutive threes. They obviously left their form out on the practice course.

From such a poor beginning, the British pairing recovered slightly but still reached the turn four down, out in 40 strokes to an American 36. A fifth British bogey at the tenth saw the U.S. pair five up, but the British made their first and only birdie at eleven to pull back to four down.

Wall and Hebert coasted from here on in and bogeyed the fourteenth to give the British pair an outside chance of an outlandish comeback, at three down with four to play. But the British pair missed their opportunity as they carded another bogey at fifteen to suffer a 4 and 3 loss.

Arnold Palmer and Billy Casper (USA) v. Dai Rees and Ken Bousfield (GBI)

The dream team of Palmer and Casper had a dream debut against the ill-matched Rees and Bousfield. The tone of the encounter was set as early as the second hole, where Palmer knocked in an eleven-footer for a par four, while Rees missed his from five feet. A second British bogey at the par-3 fifth put the U.S. pair two up, but Bousfield's accurate chip to the sixth helped cut the lead to one.

The 551-yard seventh proved to be the pivotal hole. The Americans, looking to have blown their lead, were jubilant when Casper chipped in from fully fifty yards away in the rough for a birdie to double their advantage. The British pair never really recovered—Bousfield's drive at eight just avoided the railway lines, and an American bogey won the par-4 hole.

Palmer and Casper started out with six straight pars, birdied the seventh, but bogeyed the eighth to reach the turn in an even-par 36, while their opponents stumbled out with a 39.

After turning for home three down, Rees and Bousfield gave Palmer and Casper a run for their money. The British pair birdied the tenth and halved the next four holes before another British birdie on fifteen reduced the U.S. lead to just one.

The sixteenth was halved in par fours, and the Americans must have been surprised and a little worried to have been taken as far as the seventeenth hole. With the British tails well and truly up, Casper's unerring six-iron gave Palmer a five-foot putt for the match, 2 and 1. Bearing in mind their illustrious opponents, Rees and Bousfield may well have settled for that score at the start of play.

Bill Collins and Mike Souchak (USA) v. Tom Haliburton and Neil Coles (GBI)

The final match of the morning went the full eighteen, although when the Americans Souchak and Collins set out 2-4-4, the match did not look as if it would last the distance. Souchak's spectacular opening tee shot almost clinched the hole on its own, while Coles's and Haliburton's putting cost them the next two holes—to go three down.

Although they made a winning start, the Americans were not as consistent as they may have liked. With bogeys at five and seven, and a double at the par-3 ninth, Souchak and Collins were only one up at the turn, as the British battled hard to overcome their poor start.

Worse was to follow for the Americans, as their opponents birdied the par-5 eleventh to level the score. As had become almost customary in Ryder Cup play, the Americans immediately thwarted any hopes of British success. Back-to-back birdies at the par-3 twelfth and par-4 thirteenth quickly restored the lead, but the Americans put their tee shot on fourteen out of bounds to drop another hole.

The British refused to surrender and continued to keep themselves in the match, as Haliburton made a match-saving twenty-five-foot putt to halve the seventeenth. But the Americans refused to give up their lead on the last hole, and held on for a hard-fought 1-up win.

Morning foursomes result: USA 3, GBI 1

Day One: Afternoon (18-Hole) Foursomes

Jay Hebert and Art Wall (USA) v. Peter Alliss and Christy O'Connor (GBI)

Fresh from being the sole British success in an otherwise disastrous morning, Alliss and O'Connor again spearheaded the British challenge against another unbeaten pair, Wall and Hebert. The Americans were first to strike after a British bogey at the fourth, but they bogeyed the par-3 fifth, while a British birdie on the sixth gave them a lead.

Alliss duffed a chip (his fatal flaw in Ryder Cup play) on the 164-yard ninth and the match was level at the turn, with both sides out in 36 shots.

The Englishman dropped a six-foot birdie putt on the tenth to regain the lead, but O'Connor's chipping let the side down on thirteen, and the match was back all square. Alliss holed an eight-foot putt on the fifteenth for a much-needed half to keep the match tied.

As befits four players at the top of their games, no pairing was ever more than one hole up at any time. The U.S. pair regained the lead for the first time since the third hole when they took the 356-yard sixteenth with a birdie. Alliss leveled the match with an exemplary approach to twelve feet, for a hole-winning four, at the seventeenth.

On the last tee, Alliss and Hebert did what was necessary and found the fairway with their drives. After O'Connor hit a majestic second to the heart of the green—fifteen feet off the pin—Wall's reply also found the target but slightly farther away from the flag. With the match at stake, Hebert rattled in his twenty-five-foot birdie putt, and Alliss—with a chance at a half—missed his putt to hand the hole and the match to the visitors.

Arnold Palmer and Billy Casper (USA) v. John Panton and Bernard Hunt (GBI)

Having gone down to the Brits' biggest defeat of the morning session, Hunt and Panton were unlucky enough to be drawn against the mighty Palmer and the dependable Casper. If Rees had not been involved in his own late-finishing match in the morning, against these same Americans, he might have thought better of sending out the same British pair again.

Palmer and Casper played even better in the afternoon than they had in their morning win over Rees and Bousfield. A British bogey gifted the second hole to the United States, but Palmer and Casper earned their own corn at the next two holes with a couple of unanswered birdies to go three up after four holes.

The British players held their own for three holes, but another mistake at the 394-yard eighth cost them a bogey and they were four down, as the U.S. pair reached the turn in 34 strokes.

Hunt and Panton managed their first birdie on the par-5 eleventh, but this was matched by the unshakable Americans. Under so much pressure, the suffering Brits bogeyed the thirteenth and eventually endured a worse setback than their first match, going down 5 and 4.

Bill Collins and Mike Souchak (USA) v. Dai Rees and Ken Bousfield (GBI)

Souchak and Collins struggled at the start of their match against the wily old Rees and Bousfield. An American bogey at the par-3 opener was immediately followed by a couple of wayward drives each—onto the nearby railway line—for a triple-bogey seven. The aberrant Americans then bogeyed the par-5 third to plummet to a self-inflicted three-down deficit after three holes, covered in a five-over-par seventeen strokes.

After Collins's excellent approach with a wood to the sixth gained the U.S. pair's first birdie and first win, they continued their woeful display. Three-putting the seventh for another bogey, the Americans easily lost out to Rees, who anchored his approach to three feet for a birdie. The British pair bogeyed the eighth to hand a hole back to the struggling Americans, who were out in a bloated 41 strokes, having posted two sixes and a seven on their outward card.

This was the only one of the eight foursomes matches in which the British were up at the turn. Once again, the Americans had shown the need for a fast start in these shortened eighteen-hole matches.

Steady play on the back nine by Rees and Bousfield never allowed the Americans back into the match, as they fell three behind on eleven to another British birdie. Although Souchak and Collins had a rare win with a par on the 445-yard fourteenth, Rees and Bousfield, playing much better than their morning showing, made hole-winning birdies on fifteen and sixteen. Bousfield nailed down the 4 and 2 win with a twenty-five-footer on the sixteenth.

Jerry Barber and Dow Finsterwald (USA) v. Tom Haliburton and Neil Coles (GBI)

As in their morning match, Coles and Haliburton took their game to the final hole. History also repeated itself with another American win, but not without a spirited British comeback.

A double-bogey six on the second hole and a bogey on the par-3 fifth by the British pair put the U.S. pair two up, with the pairs having halved the par-5 third in birdie. The U.S. captain showed why he was labeled the "world's best short-game player," with three astoundingly accurate short pitches to six, seven, and eight—leaving a total of ten feet to the hole among them. Despite the brilliance of Barber's close shaves, the Americans were only three up at the turn.

Finsterwald revealed his own solid short game by guiding an almost impossible chip shot to within two feet of the eleventh hole for another birdie. Down by four with seven to play, the British pair, mainly on Coles's accurate approach work, carded a trio of hole-winning threes. At the par-3 twelfth, Barber missed his par putt from four feet, while a pair of British eagles at the par-5 fifteenth and seventeenth gave them an outside chance at a half.

Hauled back to one up with one to play, Finsterwald and a very relieved American captain were not to be denied their full point, and they barely held on. Having played a terrible drive, which Finsterwald could only help into a greenside bunker, Barber made amends by chipping out to leave his partner a do-or-die twenty-foot putt on the eighteenth green for the match. With the British pair already sitting on a par four, Finsterwald holed his pressure par putt for a half—to the dismay of the British players and crowd—and a 1-up win.

Cool Putting Helps U.S. to Gain Ryder Cup Lead
—Times *(London) headline*

Afternoon foursomes result: USA *3,* GBI *1*
Day one result: USA *6,* GBI *2*

Day Two: Morning (18-Hole) Singles

The second morning started off very dull, misty, and unpleasantly cold, but the weather improved as the day wore on.

"Another huge crowd assembled this morning, again in perfect weather, and the taller ones among them saw a lot of very fine golf."
—Henry Longhurst, *Sunday Times* (London)

Doug Ford (USA) v. Harry Weetman (GBI)

With his side trailing by four points in the overall standings, Harry Weetman needed and got a fast start as he led his side off in the morning. Doug Ford's bogey four at the opening hole gave Weetman a lead he held until he bogeyed the par-5 seventh. He followed this six with another as he double-bogeyed the eighth to go one down. Having halved the par-5s at three and six in birdies, Weetman made his third birdie at the 164-yard ninth to level the match at the turn.

Both players bogeyed the 336-yard tenth but played the par-5 eleventh much better. Ford carded his third birdie of the round but lost the hole to Weetman's eagle three. One up again, Weetman held his advantage until Ford birdied the 462-yard fifteenth, and sixteen and seventeen were halved in pars.

Harry Weetman had broken his driver at the recent Masters Tournament and had not managed to find a suitable replacement before this match. He did well to take the match to the last hole.

In a quintessentially British twist of fate, Harry Weetman had a putt on the last green to snatch victory from Doug Ford, but he was wide of the mark. With the half still there for the taking, Weetman proceeded to miss his three-foot comeback putt and lost the match 1-down.

Mike Souchak (USA) v. Ralph Moffitt (GBI)

Having sat out the first day, Ralph Moffitt looked as though he had been born to play in the Ryder Cup, as he made a magnificent start with a birdie at the opening hole to go one up. Alas for the British rookie, this was as good as it got, as he failed to keep up with the big-hitting Mike Souchak.

The American reeled off an amazing blitz of wins that saw him five up after eight holes. Souchak carded hole-winning birdies at three, four, and six, as Moffitt carded hole-losing bogeys at two, seven, and eight.

Five up after eight, Souchak coasted to a 5 and 4 win as he and Moffitt halved the final six holes they played. Both players carded back-to-back birdies on eleven and twelve, and Moffitt could not dent the American's large lead.

Unluckily for Moffitt, the American one-putted eight of the fourteen greens he reached and was five under par at the early close. The British rookie was only a couple of strokes over par, but he was denied his second taste of Ryder Cup action when he was overlooked in the afternoon.

This 5 and 4 hammering thus proved to be Moffitt's only appearance ever in the Ryder Cup, as he was never selected again.

Arnold Palmer (USA) v. Peter Alliss (GBI)

Arnold Palmer and Peter Alliss fought an exciting duel all the way to the last.

Palmer was up after two, back level at the next, with Alliss in front at the fourth. Palmer's chip-in on seven leveled the match again, but Alliss recaptured the lead on the eighth. One down at the turn, the American sank his second shot from off the back of the green to halve the tenth in birdie threes.

With four more halves in a row, the match was back all square when Palmer one-bounced his bunker shot into the cup at fifteen—the third time he had holed out from off the putting surface. This clutch chip shot again denied Alliss a short, hole-winning putt.

A delightfully sporting match stayed all square to the final hole, where Palmer's approach ran twenty-five feet past the flag. Trying to emulate his opponent, Alliss played his forty-yard chip shot almost to perfection, as his ball ran up to thirty inches of the hole.

Palmer immediately conceded the Englishman's putt and went to work on his own match-winning effort. Never one to leave a valuable putt short, Palmer charged the hole and ran almost three feet past. Having missed the chance to win the match, Palmer was faced with having to save it. Alliss did not give him the chance: he graciously conceded the missable putt, "That's all right, Arnold, pick it up. We've had a good match; let's leave it that way."

Thanks to Alliss's selfless gesture (he had yet to win a singles match in four matches), this munificent match was halved when both players, around in 70, deserved at least a full point each.

Despite the closeness of this cordial contest, Palmer held a lead for only one hole. Having taken the lead on the second, he lost the next hole to Alliss's birdie four and never led again.

Billy Casper (USA) v. Ken Bousfield (GBI)

Casper and Boulsfield were all square after three holes, having both bogeyed the 424-yard second. After this even start, the Englishman carded successive bogeys to hand Casper a two-hole lead after five holes. The American quickly gave a hole back as he bogeyed the sixth to reach the turn one up on Bousfield, neither player having carded a birdie between them.

With one hole separating them after the 483-yard eleventh had been halved in the first birdies of the round, the match was still there for the taking by either player. Rather than seize his opportunity, Bousfield threw his chance away with both hands. Casper won the last four holes played despite carding three pars and a final birdie four on the par-5 fifteenth. The Englishman never recovered from a dreadful tee shot at the 166-yard twelfth, and made three bogeys in a row to crash to a humiliating 5 and 3 loss.

Casper had already beaten Bousfield in the opening foursomes.

Jay Hebert (USA) v. Dai Rees (GBI)

In true fighting spirit, the British captain leaped out to an early lead over Jay Hebert with a birdie two at the opening hole. The American bogeyed the second to fall two down but was on level terms after back-to-back birdies on five and six.

All square with Hebert at the turn, after the preceding three holes had been halved in regulation, Rees again assumed the ascendancy with two more birdies in a row—at ten and eleven.

With a two-hole lead, Rees kept Hebert at bay as the last five holes were halved and the American could not get back into the match. Rees took the match, 2 and 1, carding a fine three-under for his considerable effort.

Gene Littler (USA) v. Neil Coles (GBI)

Having lost his only foursomes match before being dropped, Gene Littler was keen to show his true form. For the first six holes, British rookie Neil Coles managed to hold then-U.S. Open champion Littler at bay, as both players birdied the par-5 third hole and shared the 188-yard fifth with bogey fours.

All square after six, Littler edged ahead with a birdie at the 551-yard seventh. With the American bogeying the eighth, Coles could not take advantage as he also carded a five.

Littler's one-up lead at the turn soon disappeared as Coles won the 336-yard tenth with a fine birdie. No sooner had Coles leveled the match than the rookie again shocked Littler, whose birdie was blown away by a British eagle at the eleventh.

Coles carded four threes in a row from the 164-yard ninth.

Having taken a lead, Coles protected it manfully for four holes, with both players making birdie at the par-5 fifteenth. Not only was Littler unable to level the match, but Coles had the temerity to double his lead with an eight-foot birdie putt at the 356-yard sixteenth to stand dormie two.

With the match at his mercy, Coles showed Littler some compassion, almost slicing his drive out-of-bounds at the seventeenth. From a deep footprint, the Englishman was able to advance his ball only some thirty yards and was still well short of the green in three. Littler had no such problem and easily made his four, after Coles finally holed out for a six at exactly the wrong time.

With his confidence severely damaged, Coles played the final hole in regulation, but this was not good enough to beat Littler. Having driven off line, the American smashed a magnificent recovery from the rough to five feet of the hole. With the match on the line, Littler showed his class by holing the putt for a second must-make win in the last two holes, earning himself half a point.

In a superb demonstration of stroke play, Littler carded a five-free back nine, coming home in 34—four under par.

Jerry Barber (USA) v. Bernard Hunt (GBI)

Jerry Barber opened with a par at the first hole for a win, as Bernard Hunt started with a bogey. The roles were reversed on the next hole as Barber carded a bogey to Hunt's par.

The third to the sixth holes were halved in strict parity, but Barber made back-to-back sixes on seven and eight to drop two down. The American captain then carded his first birdie of the day to stand one down at the turn.

With the 336-yard tenth halved in par fours, Hunt surprised Barber and most onlookers as he won the next four holes to close out the match. The Englishman ignited his blazing finish with an eagle at eleven, then finished par-par-birdie as Barber stumbled to a bogey-bogey-bogey finish to suffer an embarrassing 5 and 4 loss.

Dow Finsterwald (USA) v. Christy O'Connor (GBI)

In this final singles of the morning, Dow Finsterwald jumped out to an immediate lead as his birdie two accounted for Christy O'Connor's par.

The Irishman opened with six successive pars and fell two behind on the 466-yard sixth when Finsterwald, who had matched the previous four pars, carded his second birdie of the day.

For the fifth time in eight singles matches, the 208-yard par-3 first hole gave up a win.

After both players had played bogey-free golf for the first six holes, the American inexplicably carded a double-bogey seven at the 551-yard seventh, where O'Connor made his first birdie of the day. Finsterwald soon recovered as he made his second birdie at a par-3 to go back up by two after nine.

O'Connor started home with three more threes in a row (birdie-eagle-par) to level the match after twelve. Having finally pegged the American back, O'Connor gave the lead away again on fourteen with a bogey five. Finsterwald finished in scintillating fashion—birdie-birdie-eagle—to win 2 and 1. The unlucky O'Connor matched the American at the final two par 5s and suffered the unusual distinction of being closed out after carding an eagle of his own.

Morning singles result: USA 5, GBI 3

Day Two: Afternoon (18-Hole) Singles

Once the morning mist cleared, sunshine poured all over the course.

Art Wall (USA) v. Harry Weetman (GBI)

Out in 33, Harry "Wild Thing" Weetman must have expected to be holding a healthy lead at the turn, but he found himself down by two against Art Wall, who had taken two fewer shots to that point. The first six holes were all halved, the third and fourth in birdies.

"Art Wall, one of the most demonic of all the American demon putters."
—*Henry Longhurst,* Sunday Times *(London)*

With two more hole-winning birdies on seven and eight, Wall took only one putt on each of the last four outward holes. He snatched the 164-yard ninth away from Weetman by holing a twenty-five-foot putt for a half, carding his fifth birdie on the way out.

Wall's card for his outstanding outward nine of 31 read: 3-4-4-3-3-5-4-3-2. During the two sessions, only two players came close to matching this score, with 33s on the front nine: Wall's opponent in this match, and his teammate Mike Souchak in the morning.

Coming home, Wall kept up his impressive form as Weetman's game slowly unraveled. On the 483-yard eleventh, Weetman missed the green by thirty yards with his long-iron approach. Wall also found the heavy rough with his second but plucked his chip shot out to a matter of inches from the hole for another birdie, to go three up.

Weetman got a hole back on thirteen, where Wall made his first bogey of the round, and two holes later the American carded a second bogey to cut his own lead to one with two to play. Weetman piled on the pressure by making birdie at the par-5 seventeenth, but Wall was up to the challenge, making his seventh birdie of the round to protect his lead. The American topped off a fine round of golf with a safe par four at the final hole, which Weetman was unable to better, and Wall held on for a one-hole win.

This hard-earned point was all the United States needed to retain the Ryder Cup.

Bill Collins (USA) v. Peter Alliss (GBI)

After his epic duel with Arnold Palmer in the morning, Peter Alliss was in the form of his life and accepted Bill Collins's gift of the first hole when the American failed to make his par. Both players posted a par and a birdie at the next two holes, before Collins recorded his second birdie in a row to level the match on the fourth.

Alliss returned Collins's opening favor by bogeying the 188-yard fifth hole to go one down, but quickly posted a birdie of his own at six to level the match. In a tit-for-tat matchup, both players birdied the seventh, but Alliss edged ahead as Collins carded another bogey on the par-4 eighth. The Englishman reached the turn without a five on his card, and held a valuable one-hole lead.

Collins started back with five straight pars, while Alliss matched him except for a hole-winning birdie on the par-5 eleventh to go two up.

On fifteen, the American finally made his first birdie on the way home, but Alliss was already ahead of him with an eagle, to go dormie three up. The end came on the next hole as Alliss and Collins shared the sixteenth in par fours, as Alliss closed out the match, 3 and 2.

This win was Alliss's first singles win in five attempts; he had lost two and halved two beforehand.

Mike Souchak (USA) v. Bernard Hunt (GBI)

Both Mike Souchak and Bernard Hunt made a mess of the second hole, Hunt escaping with a bogey five to the American's double bogey, to take an early lead. Both players then stepped up and birdied the par-5 third, and Souchak made another birdie at the short fifth hole to draw level. The pair shared another par five in birdies on the 551-yard seventh, before it was Hunt's turn to birdie a par-3 to go back up by one after nine.

Both players started home in great style, with birdies at ten and eleven, but Hunt stumbled with a bogey on the short twelfth. Stung by his own ineptitude, Hunt slotted home another birdie putt on thirteen to go back up by one.

Just when it seemed Hunt would finally wear down the American, the game swung dramatically in the other direction. Souchak tore the heart out of Hunt's game as he carded four birdies (3-4-3-4) on the bounce to convert a one-down score line into a 2 and 1 win.

Not only had Souchak turned his own match around in sensational style, but he had also earned a point vital toward retaining the Ryder Cup. (Art Wall's point, earned a few minutes later, would seal the overall win.)

Arnold Palmer (USA) v. Tom Haliburton (GBI)

Arnold Palmer was given a much rougher ride in his first two singles matches than he could have imagined. After his sporting half against Alliss in the morning, Palmer faced another tricky encounter with fellow rookie Tom Haliburton. The Englishman started well, carding two deuces on the first and fifth holes, to build a surprise two-hole lead.

Within two holes, Palmer was back level as the first eight holes produced only one halved hole—the 393-yard fourth. Palmer had leveled for the first time on the second hole with a birdie three, but he bogeyed the third to go back down by one. Haliburton's second two of the round doubled his lead after five, but Palmer birdied the sixth to pull back to one down.

Haliburton caused his own downfall as he bogeyed the seventh and eighth holes—missing a couple of five-foot par putts—to hand Palmer a lead he would not give up.

The American consistently outdrove his opponent by forty yards, and this extra distance gave Palmer the upper hand on the journey home. The lead stretched to two when Palmer birdied the par-5 eleventh, then Haliburton bogeyed the 445-yard fourteenth to drop three down with four to play. With the fifteenth halved in par fives, Haliburton kept his game alive with a fighting birdie at the 356-yard sixteenth and followed this with another birdie at the par-5 seventeenth, but so did Palmer.

This final halved hole gave Palmer a 2 and 1 win and his first singles win in the Ryder Cup.

With the Ryder Cup won, the four Americans left out on the course may well have relaxed their game. The home side then reeled off three wins and a half to complete the match and bring some respectability to the final score.

Doug Ford (USA) v. Dai Rees (GBI)

Forty-eight-year-old Dai Rees's career record of 7–10–1 barely revealed the contribution he had made to the British team over the previous twenty-five years. In singles play, Rees batted .500, as he won five and lost five of his ten matches.

After a magnificent Ryder Cup career spanning almost twenty-five years and ten matches, Dai Rees played his last game, against Doug Ford. Having already posted two wins in his first three matches, the British captain went out in a blaze of glory with a 4 and 3 victory. Rees took the lead on the third with a birdie four and held this narrow advantage for six holes.

Ford's bogey at the tenth doubled Rees's lead, which the Welshman immediately extended to three with his third birdie of the round at the par-5 eleventh. Ford had no answer to his rival's relentlessly steady play, and the next three holes were halved in par. Rees finally bade farewell to Ford and the Ryder Cup with his fourth win of the round on the fifteenth. In true combative style, Rees did not lose a single hole and made only one bogey—on the halved second hole.

Jerry Barber (USA) v. Ken Bousfield (GBI)

In one of the closest-fought matches in the entire history of the Ryder Cup, Jerry Barber bogeyed the 424-yard second hole to drop one down. The next seven holes were then halved in par except for birdies at the par-5 third.

Barber broke the stalemate by holing out for a birdie two on the 164-yard ninth. The next seven holes were again halved—all in par, except the two par-5s at eleven and fifteen that fell to birdies.

"Barber must be almost the greatest short-game player in the world today and nearly drove Bousfield mad by continually getting down in two when he might be expected to take three."

—Henry Longhurst, *Sunday Times* (London)

All square with three to play, Bousfield dropped the key birdie putt on sixteen to win his second hole of the round and take his second lead. Both players birdied seventeen for another half, and Barber could not break the trend of halves at eighteen, which was also shared in par, and lost by one hole.

Dow Finsterwald (USA) v. Neil Coles (GBI)

Finsterwald found himself down by two against Coles with five to play. With his first bogey of the round coming at the par-4 fourteenth, the British rookie looked to have cracked under the strain of never being behind in this match. Coles pulled himself together on the par-5 fifteenth, as both players made crucial birdies, and retained his one-hole advantage.

The 356-yard sixteenth was also halved as the American tried to break the British player down, and Finsterwald got him on the par-5 seventeenth. Coles managed a very creditable birdie four under the circumstances, but Finsterwald went one better with an eagle to send the match to the final hole. Coles closed out the match with his fourth four in a row, and this time it was enough to win a hole: Finsterwald was the one who blew up under the strain, carding a bogey five to lose by one hole.

Gene Littler (USA) v. Christy O'Connor (GBI)

After the first two holes had been halved in a joint par-bogey opening, the next seven went one way or the other. Littler had hole-winning birdies on three and nine, but these were canceled out by hole-losing bogeys on five and eight. O'Connor birdied the fourth and seventh but bogeyed the 466-yard sixth.

Despite being the current U.S. Open champion, Gene Littler was shown little respect by his British opponents. He failed to win a single match, ending his first Ryder Cup with two halves in the singles and an opening-day loss.

The Irishman had been two up after eight but was only one to the good at the turn. After the mad rush of wins and losses on the front nine, the back nine was much more sedate, with Littler running in a birdie putt on the 166-yard twelfth to level the match.

Both players then conspired to cover the last six holes in straight fours, with birdies at fifteen and seventeen to finish up with a half each.

Afternoon singles result: USA 3½, GBI 4½
Day two result: USA 8½, GBI 7½
Overall match score: USA 14½, GBI 9½

Recap

The new format of morning and afternoon matches quickly sounded the death knell for the player-captain role. Both Barber and Rees found the strain of balancing a captain's duties with those of a player too much to handle. In the future there would be only one more player-captain—an indefatigable Arnold Palmer in 1963.

"If the afternoon pairings are only to be decided after the morning round, it seems that a nonplaying captain should be appointed. The strain of playing in the match, then spending one's lunchtime gathering information about the morning form and making up one's team, seems to me too much to ask of any one player."

—HENRY LONGHURST, *Sunday Times* (London)

Matches of eighteen holes may have favored the British, but of the seven matches that reached the eighteenth with the outcome still at stake, two were halved and the other five were won by the United States. This amply demonstrated that even over the shorter distance, the Americans were still the match-play kings.

Match Results (Winning side marked in *italics*.)

Friday, October 13—Morning Foursomes

	USA	GBI	Score
1.	Doug Ford Gene Littler	*Christy O'Connor* *Peter Alliss*	4 and 3
2.	*Art Wall* *Jay Hebert*	John Panton Bernard Hunt	4 and 3
3.	*Arnold Palmer* *Billy Casper*	Dai Rees Ken Bousfield	2 and 1
4.	*Bill Collins* *Mike Souchak*	Tom Haliburton Neil Coles	1-up

Friday, October 13—Afternoon Foursomes

	USA	GBI	Score
5.	*Jay Hebert* *Art Wall*	Peter Alliss Christy O'Connor	1-up
6.	*Arnold Palmer* *Billy Casper*	John Panton Bernard Hunt	5 and 4
7.	Bill Collins Mike Souchak	*Dai Rees* *Ken Bousfield*	4 and 2
8.	*Jerry Barber* *Dow Finsterwald*	Tom Haliburton Neil Coles	1-up

Day one result: USA *6,* GBI *2*

Saturday, October 14—Morning Singles

	USA	GBI	Score
9.	*Doug Ford*	Harry Weetman	1-up
10.	*Mike Souchak*	Ralph Moffitt	5 and 4
11.	Arnold Palmer	Peter Alliss	halved
12.	*Billy Casper*	Ken Bousfield	5 and 3
13.	Jay Hebert	*Dai Rees*	2 and 1
14.	Gene Littler	Neil Coles	halved
15.	Jerry Barber	*Bernard Hunt*	5 and 4
16.	*Dow Finsterwald*	Christy O'Connor	2 and 1

Saturday, October 14—Afternoon Singles

	USA	GBI	Score
17.	*Art Wall*	Harry Weetman	1-up
18.	Bill Collins	*Peter Alliss*	3 and 2
19.	*Mike Souchak*	Bernard Hunt	2 and 1
20.	*Arnold Palmer*	Tom Haliburton	2 and 1
21.	Doug Ford	*Dai Rees*	4 and 3
22.	Jerry Barber	*Ken Bousfield*	1-up
23.	Dow Finsterwald	*Neil Coles*	1-up
24.	Gene Littler	Christy O'Connor	halved

Day two result: USA 8½, GBI 7½

Overall match score: USA 14½, GBI 9½

1963

East Lake Country Club
Atlanta, Georgia
United States
October 11–13

United States 23
Julius Boros
Billy Casper
Dow Finsterwald
Bob Goalby
Tony Lema
Gene Littler
Billy Maxwell
Johnny Pott
Dave Ragan, Jr.
Playing Captain
Arnold Palmer

Great Britain and Ireland 9
Peter Alliss
Neil Coles
Tom Haliburton
Brian Huggett
Bernard Hunt
Geoff Hunt
Christy O'Connor, Sr.
Dave Thomas
Harry Weetman
George Will
Captain
John Fallon

Arnie Leads His Army

With the success of the playing format introduced in 1961 at Royal Lytham, a further change was made at the players' request and to increase the gallery revenue. A third day was added, with morning and afternoon sessions of fourball (better-ball) sandwiched between the existing format. Rather than make the overall score any closer, these extra games merely exaggerated the Americans' superiority.

At the peak of his career, Arnold Palmer led his country as the last playing captain ever to appear in the Ryder Cup; his opposite number in the British camp, John Fallon, held a purely nonplaying role. Palmer was riding high on the crest of a golfing wave, having won the Masters and defended his British Open title at Troon since the two sides last met.

Palmer arrived at East Lake with a seriously nagging shoulder injury that he feared might be bursitis (a potentially career-ending injury), but luckily it was diagnosed as a temporary tendon problem. Despite this easing of his worries, the shoulder still proved extremely painful throughout the week, but Palmer did not let it affect his game or his demeanor.

The American captain was supported by another powerful American lineup, which Palmer proudly boasted could beat the rest of the world combined. New faces in the U.S. team photo were Tony Lema, Bob Goalby, Billy Maxwell, Johnny Pott, and Dave Ragan. U.S. Open champion Julius Boros returned to fill out the team with Casper, Finsterwald, and Littler. No wonder the captain was so confident in his players' abilities on the world stage.

Great Britain faced the same problems it always had when it visited the States: how to mount and maintain a serious challenge. Six of the team from Lytham made the transatlantic journey, undertaken for the first time by plane rather than by sea. Neil Coles took the surface route aboard a cruise liner because he did not like to fly.

The three new British players were Geoff Hunt (who joined his brother Bernard), George Will, and Brian Huggett (a Welshman who would adequately fill the shoes of the now retired Dai Rees).

The Hunts were the second set of brothers to turn out for Britain, after three Whitcombes played together in the '20s and '30s.

On the news that the Americans were rated as overwhelming favorites by the British bookmakers: "That's preposterous! Except for Palmer, we're as good as their side."
—*John Fallon*

Although the British bookmakers had the United States as favorites, the British media were expecting an upset, "The British will beat the United States. Every American golfer, proud in the belief that the United States dominates one of the world's greatest participant sports, will be shaken right down to his golf spikes by this result," predicted one British golf magazine.

Course Details

"The course plays at 6,898 yards with a par of 70, which only a few were able to match on the first day. No fewer than seventy-three extra bunkers have been put in specifically for the match, and for the past year fertilizer has been put on the rough. With the flags often very close to bunkers or at the very back of the green, East Lake presents a most exacting test."

—HENRY LONGHURST, *Sunday Times* (London)

Hole	Distance	Par	Hole	Distance	Par
1	418	4	10	411	4
2	194	3	11	235	3
3	410	4	12	408	4
4	470	4	13	377	4
5	470	4	14	442	4
6	180	3	15	483	5
7	380	4	16	470	4
8	395	4	17	410	4
9	515	5	18	230	3
		35			**35 = Par 70 (6,898 yards)**

Course designer: Tom Bendelow, with revisions by Donald Ross and George Cobb

Day One: Morning (18-hole) Foursomes

Arnold Palmer and Johnny Pott (USA) v. Brian Huggett and George Will (GBI)

On learning that he was paired with his skipper, Palmer: *"Hell, don't do me any favors. Put me with somebody who'll be just as nervous as I am."* —Johnny Pott

The British captain did not waste any time in blooding his new boys, sending two twenty-six-year-olds, Huggett and Will, out first. Palmer had similar ideas: he partnered himself with a very nervous U.S. rookie—Johnny Pott—in the hope he could bring him through the ordeal.

On his entrance onto the first tee: *"Bands were playing 'The Star-Spangled Banner' and 'God Save the Queen'; it was like the start of a football game."* —Johnny Pott

An unruffled George Will smote a magnificent opening drive. A high-strung Pott, however, put his drive far into the rough, but Palmer managed to rescue with a superb recovery that finished forty feet from the flag. Pott's frightfully fainthearted putt pulled up five or six feet shy of the hole, and Palmer's failure to hole his par putt lost the first hole.

On his rookie partner's poor first putt: *"Don't ever leave me short again!"* —ARNOLD PALMER

Will's poor tee shot at the 470-yard fifth cost his side the hole, and another poor drive from Will at the par-5 ninth was saved by a supreme three-wood from Huggett that carried the water to the green.

"They have gone to great trouble sending us over here to play the Americans. Palmer is an American—the best. Should we win, we will have beaten the best. Should we lose, we will have lost to the best."
—*George Will*

Out in 37, the British pair of rookies was one up on the Americans in a game littered with more mistakes than memorable moments. Palmer battled bravely on his own as Pott contributed little to his side's cause, summing up his round by admitting, "I played like a fourteen-handicapper."

On eleven, Will had to hole from eight feet just for a half, as Palmer strove to pull the game back on his own. Palmer finally leveled the match on the 377-yard thirteenth, as Pott holed the putt set up by Palmer's magical approach.

The American recovery was short-lived. Will holed a ten-footer on fourteen to regain the lead, then chipped up from forty yards away to two feet of the hole on fifteen, for a birdie four and a two-hole lead. Firing in a wayward approach, Pott failed to find the sixteenth green, and Palmer's chip shot hit the branch of a tree and fell into a bunker. The Americans were unable to stave off defeat from this position and went down 3 and 2, finishing an embarrassing eight over par for their sixteen holes.

Billy Casper and Dave Ragan (USA) v. Peter Alliss and Christy O'Connor (GBI)

If the play in the first match was poor, the standard in the second was even worse. Alliss and O'Connor, playing together for the fourth time in succession, came unstuck with a nasty round of 80. This was almost matched by some mediocre play from Casper and Ragan, who managed to win the match on the last hole—1-up.

"Casper is the original 'pop' putter, giving the ball a sharp pop instead of a smooth stroke, and is one of the best putters in the world."
—*Henry Longhurst,* Sunday Times *(London)*

All four players found it tough to hit the fairways. Alliss missed three fairways off the tee and even drove out-of-bounds on the par-4 third. The Americans went out in 36, six shots better than their struggling opponents, but this advantage brought only a two-hole lead at the turn.

On the way home, it was the Americans' turn to suffer. They allowed the British pair to level the match with wins on fourteen and sixteen.

But having clawed their way back into the match with two holes to play, the British players wasted their chance. O'Connor's poor approach at seventeen prevented his side from taking advantage of an American mistake, and the hole was halved.

The Americans pulled themselves together on the final hole, a mammoth 230-yard par 3 over a long stretch of water. With the British failing to make par again when it mattered, the Americans holed out in regulation for the narrow win.

Gene Littler and Dow Finsterwald (USA) v. Dave Thomas and Harry Weetman (GBI)

Following Thomas's excellent second to eight feet of the first hole, Weetman holed the birdie putt to put Britain one up. Finsterwald and Littler were soon back on level terms and converted this momentum into a two-hole lead after Finsterwald's superb approach to the 395-yard eighth left Littler with a birdie putt.

The Americans were out in 34 but held only a single-hole lead after they dropped the ninth. With the next three holes halved, Thomas's missed putt from two feet on thirteen gave the United States a two-hole lead. Again three holes in a row were halved until Finsterwald made a hash of his approach to seventeen as the U.S. pair was unable to close out the British.

The eighteenth proved to be an exciting finishing hole, as this was the second match in a row to go the distance. The broad-shouldered Thomas almost knocked the flagstick out of the hole as his tee shot clanged into the pin. With Littler bunkering his tee shot and the British ball a few feet from a birdie, Finsterwald needed and played a beautiful recovery to inches from the flag. This shifted the pressure onto Weetman to hole out from three feet for a birdie two, which he promptly did for a gutsy half.

Julius Boros and Tony Lema (USA) v. Neil Coles and Bernard Hunt (GBI)

Boros and Lema faced an almighty battle with the older Hunt and Coles, who made a fine putt on the second to take a lead. The experienced American players slowly fought their way back into the match to take a two-hole lead of their own. Once again, Coles stepped up to hole a curving putt on the 380-yard seventh to cut the lead to one at the turn. Both pairs went out in 35 strokes and appeared to be the best-matched players of the morning.

This four-way dogfight continued over the back nine, with the British pair unable to peg back the Americans after seventeen hard-fought holes. One up, Boros and Lema needed only to halve one more hole to claim victory, but they had to take on the British pair and the unforgiving eighteenth hole.

"Julius is all hands and wrists, like a man dusting the furniture."
—*Tony Lema*

Boros's tee shot missed the green to the right and landed among the gallery, while Hunt made no mistake and safely found the elevated putting surface. Lema chipped on to within eight feet, while Coles missed his long birdie putt for the win. Having hit a poor tee shot, Boros made a hash of the eight-foot par putt which allowed Hunt to hole from four feet.

This final turnaround gave the British a hard-earned half that saw the sides with two points apiece after the morning session. This was the first time that the first session had finished at two points apiece, and the first time the Americans had not had a lead after the first four matches on their own turf.

Morning foursomes result: USA 2, GBI 2

Day One: Afternoon (18-Hole) Foursomes

After their best result in the opening foursomes on American soil, the British team set out full of confidence on the afternoon session.

Billy Maxwell and Bob Goalby (USA) v. Dave Thomas and Harry Weetman (GBI)

In a very scrappy affair, fresh partners Maxwell and Goalby went out in 38—three over par—for a one-hole lead over the pairing of Thomas and Weetman. Thomas found the tight course totally at odds with his "rip-it-and-see" power game, while the Americans held their game together with some wonderful sand recoveries.

"The big difference between us is experience with the greens. I seem to leave everything short on the greens. When I make up my mind not to be short, I'm yards past." —DAVE THOMAS

On the inward nine, the Americans started out winning the 411-yard tenth with a par to go two up. Two more pars were sufficient to extend the American lead, and they closed out the match on the par-5 fifteenth, 4 and 3.

Arnold Palmer and Billy Casper (USA) v. Brian Huggett and George Will (GBI)

With Arnold Palmer keen to avenge his morning defeat, he relieved himself of rookie chaperone duties and hooked up with Billy Casper. This formidable partnership won the first two holes, as Huggett was wide of the first green with his approach, and Palmer chipped up to six feet on the second.

The Americans continued their charge as Palmer holed a twenty-five-foot putt on the 180-yard sixth. Casper followed this with a sand save to two feet, and Palmer tapped in. With Casper in incomparable form around the green, the U.S. pair was four up at the turn, out in 33.

George Will had to hole a ten-footer on the tenth for a half, but this merely prolonged the inevitable, as Palmer and Casper closed out the match on the fourteenth, 5 and 4.

"I just tagged along and watched Billy play magnificent golf."
—*Arnold Palmer*

Gene Littler and Dow Finsterwald (USA) v. Neil Coles and Geoff Hunt (GBI)

Coles and Hunt three-putted the fourth green to give Littler and Finsterwald the lead, but the Americans returned the favor by three-putting on the fifth. Coles brought some credibility to the match with a tee shot to ten feet on the sixth hole, and Hunt made the birdie putt to put Britain one up for the first time.

The match was back all square after nine holes, but the British pair took another lead when Finsterwald failed to hit the eleventh green with his tee shot. Hunt's miss from four feet for par on the 442-yard fourteenth leveled the match, and Coles doubled the British anguish when he blew a two-footer on the next hole after Finsterwald had sunk a twelve-footer for birdie. With his putter locked on shoot-to-kill, Finsterwald murdered a ten-footer for a four on the seventeenth to finish off the British challenge, 2 and 1, as the Americans closed out at level pars for their round.

The Americans finished with ten fours in a row.

Julius Boros and Tony Lema (USA) v. Tom Haliburton and Bernard Hunt (GBI)

Not taking too many risks with his afternoon selection, Palmer sent out his third set of veterans in a row, as Boros and Lema took on Bernard Hunt and a flu-ridden Tony Haliburton. Things did not go the Americans' way on the outward nine, and the British pair clung to a one-hole lead at the turn.

The Americans leveled the match after fourteen holes, lost the 470-yard sixteenth, and were back all square after Haliburton drove into the rough on seventeen en route to a hole-relinquishing bogey.

The pairs were deadlocked after seventeen holes of nip-and-tuck match play, and the eighteenth loomed large again. Hunt badly pulled his tee shot, leaving a nightmare chip back down the wickedly sloping putting surface, while Lema came up short from the tee. Haliburton did his best, sliding his recovery twenty feet past the hole. With the Americans sitting on a par putt after Boros chipped up to two feet, Hunt was unable to get his uphill return putt to drop as it ran agonizingly over the cup. This final and fatal British bogey gave the match to the Americans by another one-hole margin.

Afternoon foursomes result: USA 4, GBI 0

This was only the second clean sweep of a session, the first being the American sweep in the 1947 thirty-six-hole foursomes.

Day one result: USA 6, GBI 2

Day Two: Morning (18-Hole) Fourball

"This was just about the hottest day we have had so far, and thirty-six holes of fourball became quite a feat of human endurance."

—HENRY LONGHURST, *Sunday Times* (London)

Julius Boros and Gene Littler (USA) v. Peter Alliss and Bernard Hunt (GBI)

Palmer kept shuffling his pairings as he matched up Boros and Littler to take on Bernard Hunt and Peter Alliss. Like many of the other matches, this one was very close—all square after nine holes.

The Americans went ahead on the 411-yard tenth and dodged a bullet on the eleventh, where Hunt missed a short putt to level. Another fine approach by Hunt gave him a chance to atone for his putting mistake on the previous hole, but he blew another short putt for the win.

With his partner failing to convert his accurate approaches, Alliss decided to take charge, firing a second shot into the 377-yard thirteenth and rolling home the ten-foot putt for a birdie three to level the score. After the Americans had taken the lead again, it was Alliss who got the visitors back all square with a par four on the 470-yard sixteenth.

Having kept his pairing in the match, Alliss knocked his approach fifteen feet past the pin on seventeen, which Hunt improved on with his second to nine feet. With Boros on the green but a long way away, Littler found sand and was not a threat. Boros putted right up to the hole for a concession, leaving the British pair with a putt apiece to go dormie. Alliss almost pulled it off, but his ball stayed out, and Hunt's shorter putt didn't threaten the hole.

Littler again failed to make his ball count on the par-3 finishing hole, while Boros holed a tricky six-footer over the slope for par. Hunt missed his fourth short putt on the back nine, leaving the match in Alliss's large and capable hands. From a yard out, the Englishman stroked home the par putt for half a point.

In a match that took only 3¾ hours to finish—in sweltering heat—both pairs were round in 67, and made only seven fives between them in the seventy-two holes played.

Dow Finsterwald and Arnold Palmer (USA) v. Brian Huggett and Dave Thomas (GBI)

Palmer and Finsterwald took on the best of the British in Thomas and Huggett. Unfortunately, the best of the British was not nearly good enough for the American captain and his ever-reliable partner.

This was the third straight time that Palmer played Huggett—with the score even at a win each after the first two meetings. Palmer had previously paired up with Pott (loss) and Casper (win).

The Americans cruised to the turn in 31 better-ball strokes and a four-hole lead, as the Welshmen had no answers to their opponents or the course. With birdies at the 235-yard eleventh and 377-yard thirteenth, and three pars at the intervening holes, the U.S. pair easily fought off the challenge of Huggett and Thomas, 5 and 4.

Finsterwald admirably repaid Palmer's faith in him, registering three birdies to his captain's two in their win. The Americans were so dominating, they did not lose a single hole out of the fourteen played.

Billy Casper and Billy Maxwell (USA) v. Harry Weetman and George Will (GBI)

The two Billys outplayed the two Ws over the opening nine holes as the less well known of the two Americans put on a putting display.

Maxwell holed out from more than twenty feet on the second green for the lead, then sank another winning putt from sixteen feet on the 470-yard fourth. He increased the U.S. lead with an eight-footer for a birdie three on the fifth hole.

In reply, Will landed a thirteen-foot putt on the par-4 seventh, but it did not stop the Americans, out in 32, from carrying a three-hole lead into the back nine. Casper got in on the putting show-case, draining a twenty-footer on the par-4 tenth, as the Americans coasted to a solid 3 and 2 win.

Bob Goalby and Dave Ragan (USA) v. Neil Coles and Christy O'Connor (GBI)

The best golf of the morning came in this final match. Although they started poorly, Goalby and Ragan were out in 34 and had a real tussle with Coles and O'Connor, who went out in just 33 strokes for a one-hole lead.

After a string of halved holes, the Americans leveled the match with a birdie at the par-4 thirteenth, and followed this with another birdie at the par-5 fifteenth to go ahead. With the momentum swinging away from them, the British pair struck back to win the 470-yard sixteenth. All square, the seventeenth was halved to set up another showdown on the eighteenth.

Ragan's tee shot ended twelve feet from the target, and Goalby almost chipped in for a birdie two from sand. After a rasping iron off the tee, O'Connor ran in a near-impossible thirty-foot birdie putt that Ragan could not match from closer in. The American's putt dramatically lipped out to give the British a one-hole win, their only win of the morning.

Morning fourball result: USA 2½, GBI 1½

Day Two: Afternoon (18-Hole) Fourball

Tony Lema and Johnny Pott (USA) v. Peter Alliss and Bernard Hunt (GBI)

After nine holes, the American combination of Lema and Pott held a one-hole lead over Alliss and Bernard Hunt until the 377-yard thirteenth hole. Here, Hunt pitched to five feet and holed for the win to level the match. On the next hole, Hunt had an opportunity to make another short hole-winning putt, but his woes from the morning returned to haunt him and he blew the chance.

The British then lost the fifteenth to go one down again. Hunt missed another two-foot putt on sixteen, but luckily for him, Alliss nearly chipped in for an eagle, then made his birdie putt to win the hole and level the match. Like Hunt, Johnny Pott was also having his troubles and was still playing poorly, but he hit a fine pitch to seven feet for a birdie on seventeen and a crucial lead.

With Hunt nervously hovering around a five-foot birdie putt on the last green, Lema made the Englishman's putt redundant as he holed from all of thirty feet for a half and the overall win, 1-up.

Billy Casper and Billy Maxwell (USA) v. Tom Haliburton and Geoff Hunt (GBI)

Palmer retained the two Billys, who repaid their captain's faith by accounting for the two Hs with another solid performance.

The British went out in an encouraging 33 strokes—but to no avail, as the Americans carded a 31 for a two-hole cushion at the turn. Hunt and Haliburton dug in and fought hard to get the two holes back with three to play.

Having struggled back into the match, the British pair threw it away with four hands. They lost the sixteenth and seventeenth holes to American pars—both British players took a turn at missing a makable putt for a half—to go down 2 and 1.

Arnold Palmer and Dow Finsterwald (USA) v. Neil Coles and Christy O'Connor (GBI)

Against Coles and O'Connor, the only British winners from the morning, Palmer retained Finsterwald as his partner, and the duo continued their breakneck pace in the afternoon.

As was becoming an irritating habit, Finsterwald badly pulled his opening tee shot, smacked his three-wood recovery into a bunker, then chipped in from fifteen yards away to win the opening hole. And so the contest went—very much the Americans' way. Palmer's approach to six feet bought a second birdie at the 194-yard second, but the Americans squandered short putts on the next couple of holes and failed to extend their lead.

O'Connor came up short with his chip, while Coles three-putted to lose the fifth hole. The sixth hole was remarkable in that O'Connor landed his tee shot eleven feet off the flag but was farthest away. Palmer was eight feet shy, Finsterwald four feet, and Coles's tee shot hit the flag and rebounded to two feet away. O'Connor and Palmer missed their putts, but their partners holed out for a half in twos.

On the 380-yard seventh, Palmer dropped a forty-foot bomb, then followed this with an approach to three feet for a five-hole lead. On the 515-yard ninth, Palmer got up and down from a bunker for a birdie four, and the American pair was on fire, out in 29. Coles and O'Connor carded a 34, one shot worse than their morning round, when they held a one-hole lead.

The red-hot Americans made fourteen birdies in a twenty-three-hole burst during the day.

Having torched the course on the way out, Palmer and Finsterwald were content to rest on their laurels. The British pair clawed a couple of holes back before finally succumbing to a 3 and 2 defeat.

Not only were Palmer and Finsterwald imperious against Coles and O'Connor, but their record-setting 29 on the front nine would have beaten by one hole the best-ball from all eight British players, who combined for a 31.

Bob Goalby and Dave Ragan (USA) v. Brian Huggett and Dave Thomas (GBI)

Americans Goalby and Ragan took on the Welsh pair of Huggett and Thomas and were two up at the turn. Out in 34 strokes, the British pair pulled back to square the match with one hole to play.

Forty-five minutes behind the match in front, this one finished as the sun was setting on the final green. Thomas unleashed the best tee shot of the four, carving a five-iron to six feet of the hole. Having putted up from almost forty feet away, Ragan holed a par putt from seven feet, but Thomas missed his birdie putt for the win, and the sides settled for a half.

Afternoon fourball result: USA 3½, GBI ½
Day two result: USA 6, GBI 2
Overall match score: USA 12, GBI 4

With sixteen singles remaining, the Americans could afford to lose twelve of them and still retain the Cup.

Day Three: Morning (18-Hole) Singles

The final day got under way with the weather more blustery than that of the first two days.

Some years before Peter Fonda and Dennis Hopper rode a couple of Harleys across the United States: AMERICA ALL SET FOR ANOTHER EASY RYDER CUP VICTORY

—*Sunday Times* (London) headline

Tony Lema (USA) v. Geoff Hunt (GBI)

Hardly playing the best golf of his career, Tony Lema was given an easy ride by Geoff Hunt in the opening singles match. Lema won four of the first six holes to more or less wrap the match up a third of the way through. The American reached the turn in a two-over-par 37, still holding a four-hole lead, as Hunt struggled out with a 41.

Hunt's poor play allowed Lema to win both the 411-yard tenth and the 235-yard eleventh to go six up with seven to play. He did manage to pull one hole back on his opponent, who ran out an easy winner, 5 and 3.

Johnny Pott (USA) v. Brian Huggett (GBI)

Brian Huggett went one worse than Lema in the match ahead of him, reaching the turn in 38, but was down to Johnny Pott, also out in 38, who showed early signs of settling his nerves in his Ryder Cup debut.

The American won the first hole with a tidy birdie to set him on his way, but he could not build on this promising start, although he was ahead by one at the turn.

Huggett leveled with a win on the tenth, a par four to Pott's bogey five, and from here on in, the American lost his way. The

Welshman had wins on fourteen and sixteen before sealing a 3 and 1 victory on the 410-yard seventeenth.

Huggett played the final eight holes in one under par to turn a one-hole deficit into a 3 and 1 win. The Welshman complained of stomach pains during his match and sat out the afternoon.

Billy Casper (USA) v. Neil Coles (GBI)

After a tightly contested outward nine that ended all square, Billy Casper was two up with two to play against Neil Coles, who had kept himself in the match with an extraordinary putting display. Dormie two down, the Englishman saw his good fortune continue over the final two holes.

On the 410-yard seventeenth, Casper strafed a bunker with his second shot and could not match Coles's more accurate approach—the lead was down to one. Casper misdirected another approach and had to chip onto the final green, leaving a two-footer for par. Coles, who had been wielding the magic putter all morning, made another putt disappear from twenty feet to win both closing holes for a well-earned half.

Despite suffering from a recurring hand injury that had kept him sidelined for half of the season, Billy Casper emerged as the top player in this contest. He won all four of his pairs matches and halved his only singles encounter.

Arnold Palmer (USA) v. Peter Alliss (GBI)

In a repeat of their encounter two years earlier, Palmer and Alliss put on another wonderful display of golf, which again went right down to the wire. Palmer took the first but lost the seventh when he found sand. Early on, Alliss had played the better golf to the green, but his putter was cold—he missed a couple of crucial six-footers. However, the Englishman was one up at the turn, after a momentous approach over the water on the 515-yard ninth hole set him up for a seven-foot birdie.

After holing a clutch putt to halve eleven, Alliss increased his lead on the 408-yard twelfth with an eight-foot birdie putt, but he blew a two-footer on the next. Having missed the opportunity to build a big lead on the great man, Alliss had to fight hard to hold on to his two-hole advantage, at least until the sixteenth. Here, right on cue, Palmer hit back to win the par-4 hole with a ten-foot putt.

On seventeen, Palmer held sway with his approach, finishing just two feet from the flag. With a lukewarm putter, Alliss finally got hot—he sank a tricky thirteen-footer to halve the hole in birdie threes and retain his slender lead. On the final green, Alliss's putter performed some more magic, persuading the ball to roll up close to the flag from nearly sixty feet.

"I still wasn't convinced I was safe. Not against Arnold. The atmosphere was electric. The crowd was shouting, 'Go get him, Arnie!', and I didn't blame them. On the green I laid my approach putt stone dead. But I still wasn't happy. Arnold is the kind of man who can do anything. I fully expected him to hole his own putt. Then, blow me, he leaves his putt a yard short of the hole. I just couldn't believe it." —Peter Alliss

Failing to hole his putt from the back of the green, Palmer sportingly conceded the Englishman's putt to halve the final hole, and Alliss had won the match 1-up.

"I spanked his bottom. . . ." —*Peter Alliss, on* ESPN TV *(1998)*

Gene Littler (USA) v. Christy O'Connor (GBI)

It was a case of what might have been for Christy O'Connor, who missed a couple of ridiculously short putts on the first three holes that would have given him a lead against Gene Littler. The American weathered the Irishman's opening salvos, and both players reached the turn all square.

Once again, it was the American player who came home in front. Littler eased his way to a three-hole lead, only to see O'Connor pull a couple of late holes back to make the 1-up defeat on the last hole a little more palatable.

Julius Boros (USA) v. Harry Weetman (GBI)

Harry Weetman produced one of the rounds of his life against the reigning U.S. Open champion, Julius Boros. Out in 35, the Englishman was two up, but Boros showed his class by squaring the match on the 470-yard sixteenth with a well-crafted birdie putt.

Rebutting the American's comeback, Weetman showed his own gritty fighting qualities by playing the last few holes in style. A twelve-foot putt put him one up, and he held on until the last to take the match by a solitary hole.

This was Weetman's first singles success since he shocked Sam Snead in 1953.

Bob Goalby (USA) v. Dave Thomas (GBI)

Burly Dave Thomas had struggled more than anyone on the tight course all week long, and he found no solace in his singles match against Bob Goalby. Although the match was level after nine holes, it was only a matter of time before the American made his superiority on the greens count.

Goalby played a patient waiting game and pressed ahead on the inward nine to record a comfortable 3 and 2 win, pulling away from the Welshman.

Dow Finsterwald (USA) v. Bernard Hunt (GBI)

At the turn, Dow Finsterwald and Bernard Hunt were nip and tuck in a contest that was broken apart only by the American's taking two sixes coming home. His double bogey at the 377-yard thirteenth was the less costly, since Hunt made a birdie three to sew up the hole. A bogey at the par-5 fifteenth proved more expensive, because Hunt struggled to make his own par to win the hole.

The American recovered to make a brilliant birdie three at seventeen to save the match, but Hunt, round in 68, made his own clutch par-three on the last hole to win the match by two holes.

This gutsy final win by Hunt prevented the Americans from winning the Ryder Cup outright before lunch. As it was, the home side needed only one point from a possible eight in the afternoon to win the Cup.

Morning singles result: USA 3½, GBI 4½

The British had hung tough and not only prevented the Americans from claiming before lunch, but actually came out on top after eight singles (for the first time in the United States). Their previous best singles performance had been a 5–3 loss in 1955.

Day Three: Afternoon (18-Hole) Singles

"Our team was one of the best. They cooperated fully. For example, when Pott was not playing well, he asked to be left out of the lineup. This afternoon, Billy Casper said he'd like to sit it out." —ARNOLD PALMER

Arnold Palmer (USA) v. George Will (GBI)

With his side needing only one point to secure the Cup, Palmer was out first against George Will, who had not played in the morning. The Englishman's rustiness showed when he missed a short putt to bogey the first hole, but he went on to par the next seven holes before bogeying the ninth. Palmer, in the meanwhile, went about his usual business and reached the turn in 37—unsatisfying for him, but still good enough for a three-hole lead.

Will played so well in the closing stages—preventing his opponent from extending his lead with a typical Arnie charge—that Palmer openly wondered why Will had not played in the morning singles. The Englishman had fought so hard that Palmer, five under par coming home, did not increase his lead.

Will was unable to prevent the inevitable, however, and the American playing captain recorded his fourth outright win of the contest, 3 and 2.

Dave Ragan (USA) v. Neil Coles (GBI)

Neil Coles was unable to reproduce his morning form and ran out of steam against Dave Ragan, who had sat out the morning session. The American was three up at the turn after Coles had frittered away some early chances.

Just as Ragan looked as though he would pull away to a decisive margin of victory, Coles dug in and went down by only 2 and 1.

Tony Lema (USA) v. Peter Alliss (GBI)

Peter Alliss was another British player to feel the stress and strain of three days of unrelenting play and pressure. He held all the aces in the early skirmishes with Tony Lema but once again faded toward the end.

Two down after nine, Lema fought back to be one down with two to play. On the last hole, Alliss must have had visions of his 1953 debut, as he put his tee shot through the par-3 green and left his ball in the rough with his second shot. Lema also missed the green with his tee shot but chipped up to twenty-five feet, where he ended the match on a high note by draining his par putt to win the hole and earn a half.

"Lema holed a putt across the length of the last green to half, but we were beaten by twenty-six points anyway." —PETER ALLISS, ESPN TV (1998)

This was the only match of the afternoon the Americans did not win.

Gene Littler (USA) v. Tom Haliburton (GBI)

Ryder Cup posterity will always show Tom Haliburton in a negative light, but he did his chances of redemption no good at all when he started his match against Gene Littler with five fives. All in all, Haliburton—the oldest player at forty-eight—opened with four bogeys and a double at the second, while Littler rubbed salt in the wounds with a tormenting two at the par-3 sixth.

Against a player of Littler's class and demeanor, this cold start could mean only one thing; seven down after nine, the Englishman had no way back into the game. Every time he managed a par, Littler threw a birdie at him. Haliburton managed to pull one hole back on the brief journey home—to suffer the dual ignominy of a 6 and 5 loss and the knowledge that his "white-flagged" point meant the United States retained the Ryder Cup.

Tom Haliburton played in six matches over two Ryder Cups (1961 and '63), and lost them all—a record in futility that he shares with Alf Padgham in the 1930s. To be fair to Haliburton, in his six games he did face some of the greatest golfers that ever swung a club anywhere.

Julius Boros (USA) v. Harry Weetman (GBI)

In the only rematch from the morning session, Julius Boros was given the opportunity for some instant revenge against Harry Weetman. Starting much the stronger, Boros turned the tables on Weetman and held a constant edge in this reprise. Weetman's long game, which had served him well in previous matches, let him down on a couple of occasions, and the American was quick to take advantage.

This reversal in the afternoon spurred Weetman on. He kept the result in doubt until the end, but the Englishman was unable to keep up the pressure on Boros, who avenged his earlier loss by a 2 and 1 score.

At the end of three days of competition, many of the players complained of being overly tired, but not the oldest American. At forty-three, Julius Boros was quite pragmatic about the strain: "I have an advantage. I'm always tired."

Billy Maxwell (USA) v. Christy O'Connor (GBI)

No British player felt the rigors and demands of two matches a day more than Christy O'Connor. In his fluctuating match against Billy Maxwell, the Irishman was all over the American on the outward nine. Three up after five—he turned two up and looked to be in complete command.

Fatigue took its toll on the inward nine, as the fresh-legged Maxwell not only caught but overtook his tiring opponent. The American overturned a three-hole deficit and came home with a fine 2 and 1 win over the weary O'Connor.

Dow Finsterwald (USA) v. Dave Thomas (GBI)

Dow Finsterwald had his hands full against a rejuvenated Dave Thomas and could muster only a one-hole lead after nine holes. Finsterwald had already beaten Thomas twice in the earlier pairs matches.

Like so many of his colleagues ahead of him, Thomas was unable to match the American's spirit on the closing holes, and Finsterwald ran out a cozy 4 and 3 winner.

Thomas carded a bone-crushing 77 to Finsterwald's tidy 71 and was probably content not to have gone down to a bigger defeat.

Rookie Dave Thomas, one of the workhorses of the British side, finished like a broken-down Welsh pit pony, suffering four defeats in his six matches, and consoled himself with his two halves.

Bob Goalby (USA) v. Bernard Hunt (GBI)

With the Ryder Cup long gone, Bernard Hunt did his best against Bob Goalby, but the Englishman's best was not good enough.

One down after four, Goalby turned things around to lead by one after nine holes. The American had a few scares on the way home but held off Hunt for a 2 and 1 win.

Having swept the British in the afternoon foursomes, the Americans almost swept their opponents in the final eight singles. Only Peter Alliss and his half against Tony Lema saved his side from complete humiliation.

Afternoon singles result: USA 7½, GBI ½
Day three result: USA 11, GBI 5
Overall match score: USA 23, GBI 9

Recap

Although Great Britain had been more than competitive in the three morning sessions—they actually shared the spoils, 8-8—the afternoon sessions were their undoing. Just as in previous thirty-six hole formats, the British continued to struggle in the post-lunch phase of the Ryder Cup.

"We know, and have known all along, since the game of golf got under way in America in the '20s, that good players were in great numbers there, and with the sun throughout the year, practice facilities, and huge rewards, we were up against an insoluble problem. The present top home players, by no means poor performers, are leagues outside the tough American ones." —HENRY COTTON

"Though there were one or two points lost which might have come our way, there were others which did come our way and might not have done. Any team which gets 25 percent in America is doing quite well." —*Henry Longhurst*

On this occasion, they were not just outscored but annihilated in the afternoon sessions, fifteen points to one—an amazing and inexplicable turnaround from their splendidly consistent and competitive morning form. In fact, the British did not win a single match out of the sixteen they played in the afternoon, just a pair of halves.

One crumb of comfort for the deflated British team was the fact that they had proved more competitive when the chips were down on the final hole. Of the thirteen matches to reach the eighteenth green, the Americans won four, the British three, with six halves.

The superiority of the American players may not have been the only reason for such a wide differential from morning to afternoon. It may have been some defect in the British players' preparation—both physical and mental. Arnold Palmer felt the British work ethic was not as engendered as the American, saying, "I think our boys work harder. Whenever our players were not on the course, they were practicing, while the British stayed around the clubhouse."

Opening the Ryder Cup up to three days proved a runaway financial success for the U.S. organizers, as crowds of more than ten thousand saw the matches. This was a substantial increase over previous years.

Many of the Americans believed the real difference between the teams was in the ball used. The slightly smaller British ball flew farther through the air, but it created problems by burying itself deeper in sand or deep rough around the greens. This made recovery shots much more difficult and resulted in more dropped shots from around the green than their opponents had. It is for this reason that the British lost the Ryder Cup by such a lopsided margin, many of the Americans believed.

Match Results (Winning side marked in *italics.*)

Friday, October 11—Morning Foursomes

	USA	GBI	Score
1.	Arnold Palmer Johnny Pott	*Brian Huggett* *George Will*	3 and 2
2.	*Billy Casper* *Dave Ragan*	Peter Alliss Christy O'Connor	1-up
3.	Gene Littler Dow Finsterwald	Dave Thomas Harry Weetman	halved
4.	Julius Boros Tony Lema	Neil Coles Bernard Hunt	halved

Friday, October 11—Afternoon Foursomes

	USA	GBI	Score
5.	*Billy Maxwell* *Bob Goalby*	Dave Thomas Harry Weetman	4 and 3
6.	*Arnold Palmer* *Billy Casper*	Brian Huggett George Will	5 and 4
7.	*Gene Littler* *Dow Finsterwald*	Neil Coles Geoff Hunt	2 and 1
8.	*Julius Boros* *Tony Lema*	Tom Haliburton Bernard Hunt	1-up

Day one result: USA 6, GBI 2

Saturday, October 12—Morning Fourball

	USA	GBI	Score
9.	Julius Boros Gene Littler	Peter Alliss Bernard Hunt	halved
10.	*Dow Finsterwald* *Arnold Palmer*	Brian Huggett Dave Thomas	5 and 4
11	*Billy Casper* *Billy Maxwell*	Harry Weetman George Will	3 and 2
12.	Bob Goalby Dave Ragan	*Neil Coles* *Christy O'Connor*	1-up

Saturday, October 12—Afternoon Fourball

	USA	GBI	Score
13.	*Tony Lema* *Johnny Pott*	Peter Alliss Bernard Hunt	1-up
14.	*Billy Casper* *Billy Maxwell*	Tom Haliburton Geoff Hunt	2 and 1
15.	*Arnold Palmer* *Dow Finsterwald*	Neil Coles Christy O'Connor	3 and 2
16.	Bob Goalby Dave Ragan	Brian Huggett Dave Thomas	halved

Day two result: USA 6, GBI 2

Overall match score: USA 12, GBI 4

Sunday, October 13—Morning Singles

	USA	GDI	Scorc
17.	*Tony Lema*	Geoff Hunt	5 and 3
18.	Johnny Pott	*Brian Huggett*	3 and 1
19.	Billy Casper	Neil Coles	halved
20.	Arnold Palmer	*Peter Alliss*	1-up
21.	*Gene Littler*	Christy O'Connor	1-up
22.	Julius Boros	*Harry Weetman*	1-up
23.	*Bob Goalby*	Dave Thomas	3 and 2
24.	Dow Finsterwald	*Bernard Hunt*	2-up

Sunday, October 13—Afternoon Singles

	USA	GBI	Score
25.	*Arnold Palmer*	George Will	3 and 2
26.	*Dave Ragan*	Neil Coles	2 and 1
27.	Tony Lema	Peter Alliss	halved
28.	*Gene Littler*	Tom Haliburton	6 and 5
29.	*Julius Boros*	Harry Weetman	2 and 1
30.	*Billy Maxwell*	Christy O'Connor	2 and 1
31.	*Dow Finsterwald*	Dave Thomas	4 and 3
32.	*Bob Goalby*	Bernard Hunt	2 and 1

Day three result: USA *11,* GBI *5*

Overall match score: USA *23,* GBI *9*

1965

Royal Birkdale Golf Club
Lancashire, England
October 7–9

United States 19½	**Great Britain and Ireland 12½**
Julius Boros	Peter Alliss
Billy Casper	Peter Butler
Tommy Jacobs	Neil Coles
Don January	Jimmy Hitchcock
Tony Lema	Bernard Hunt
Gene Littler	Jimmy Martin
Dave Marr	Christy O'Connor, Sr.
Arnold Palmer	Lionel Platts
Ken Venturi	Dave Thomas
Johnny Pott [did not play]	George Will
Captain	**Captain**
Byron Nelson	Harry Weetman

Byron Lords It Over the British

With only one loss since the Second World War, the Americans could have been accused at times of being complacent, even disdainful, over their rivals' chances. Which side would have refused to include a player who had won the U.S. Open, the PGA Championship, and two Masters in the previous three years? The U.S. side did, and the player's name is Jack Nicklaus.

The Golden Bear had not served his full PGA apprenticeship and was not eligible. Another sign of the Americans' purported superiority came when Johnny Pott badly injured his ribs and was declared unfit to play. Instead of sending for a replacement (it would have been Mike Souchak), the American captain, Byron Nelson, gave his nine remaining players a vote of confidence by going with them alone.

The PGA of America gave a vote of confidence to Byron Nelson—twenty years after he had retired from the Tour. The British PGA gave their captain a vote of absolution, as Harry Weetman was finally forgiven for his outburst against Dai Rees in 1957.

For the record, Rees was on hand at Birkdale, working as a TV commentator.

The British captain was not short of confidence in his ten players, but he knew they could not stack up man for man against the might of the United States. All he could hope for was a bright start by his men in the first session, because once the Americans were ahead, they were a mighty hard nut to crack.

"The Americans are in for a tough three days. Most of them are going to have to play six rounds of golf." —HARRY WEETMAN

Course Details

"The fellows love the course. We don't have this type of terrain at home, and the conditions are excellent."
—*Byron Nelson*

One of the reasons Birkdale was chosen to host this contest is that the British organizers hoped the stiff winds and rain from off the Irish Sea would trouble the visitors. But the best-laid plans of mice and men . . . The weather was calm and warm and very American. The rain that had fallen in previous weeks had softened the fairways, and the lack of wind put a premium on driving—a distinct advantage for the Americans.

"No domestic tabby of a course, but a full-grown tiger."
—Golf Digest

The finishing holes at the Birkdale course were a big hitter's dream, with four par 5s (all more than 500 yards) in the last six holes.

Various reports on this match indicate that the first and eighteenth par 5s may have been shortened to par 4s in one or more of the sessions.

Hole	Distance	Par	Hole	Distance	Par
1	493	5	10	393	4
2	427	4	11	412	4
3	416	4	12	190	3
4	212	3	13	517	5
5	358	4	14	202	3
6	533	5	15	536	5
7	158	3	16	401	4
8	459	4	17	510	5
9	410	4	18	513	5
		36			**38 = Par 74 (7,140 yards)**

Course designer: George Lowe, with modifications by Fred Hawtree and J. H. Taylor

Day One: Morning Foursomes

As feared by the British team and as forecast by the British weatherman, the skies were clear and the wind was barely a breeze. The unseasonably mild weather drew a crowd of more than twenty thousand who were treated to a day of superb stroke play and magnificent match play.

Julius Boros and Tony Lema (USA) v. Lionel Platts and Peter Butler (GBI)

The first British pair out, rookies Butler and Platts, hardly endeared themselves to their captain with a 5-5-5 start to drop three holes down to Lema and Boros (4-4-4). Over thirty-six holes, the British may have had a chance to fight back from such a poor start, but with just fifteen holes to play, their fate was more or less already settled.

Platts did give the British some hope by making a birdie two on the 212-yard fourth, but the Americans proved unwavering in their resolve. On seventeen, Platts again breathed some life back into the British hopes with a twelve-foot putt that reduced the lead to one with one to play.

In seven foursomes matches between 1959 and 1967, Julius Boros never lost a single one. He had a record of 5–0–2.

On the 513-yard eighteenth, Butler's twelve-foot putt could have halved the match, but Boros was up to the task and holed his eight-foot birdie putt for a much narrower win than expected.

Arnold Palmer and Dave Marr (USA) v. Dave Thomas and George Will (GBI)

Against Palmer and rookie Dave Marr, the second British pair of Thomas and Will started out much better: 4-3-3. Thomas fired a four-iron right at the flag on the first and then holed a fourteen-footer on the second; his teammate holed a twenty-footer on the third.

"At the start I was nervous, and by the third hole I was downright embarrassed." —Dave Marr

This start stunned the Americans, who were unable to get back on anything like level terms and were behind all the way around.

Marr later recounted, "What made me realize that this was something different was when I saw Arnold's hand shaking as he pegged up his ball on the first tee. That scared me to death, and my golf thereafter certainly didn't help Arnold—some of the places I put him in weren't even on the golf course."

For the second contest in a row, Arnold Palmer partnered a rookie in his opening foursomes and was badly beaten.

Reaching the turn in 33 strokes, the British pair continued its avalanche of attacking golf, as Thomas unleashed another mighty wood to reach the front of the 517-yard thirteenth green in two. It was fitting that Thomas, whose prodigious driving and long-iron play set up the win, should hole the birdie putt. The Americans were swamped, 6 and 5, as they failed to win a single hole.

Billy Casper and Gene Littler (USA) v. Bernard Hunt and Neil Coles (GBI)

Despite taking three shots to reach the first green and carding a six, Littler and Casper emerged with a half, as Hunt's five-foot putt ran around the cup and stayed out. The British pair took the par-4 second and halved the next for a one-hole lead.

Littler and Casper quickly found their form by winning four of the next five holes. On the 212-yard fourth hole, Casper's twenty-five-footer was good for a birdie two, while Coles made two costly errors on the par-5 sixth and par-3 seventh. Littler added to the British woes, leaving his approach to the eighth inside of three yards for Casper to drain the birdie putt.

Three American putts on the twelfth cut into their own lead, but Casper's snaking putt on the 536-yard fifteenth dropped for a birdie four to restore a two-hole lead. Two more halves were enough to settle the match, as the Americans overcame a spirited British pair, 2 and 1.

Ken Venturi and Don January (USA) v. Peter Alliss and Christy O'Connor (GBI)

At age forty-nine, Don January was the oldest player in U.S. Ryder Cup history to date. Raymond Floyd was a bit older when he played in 1991.

After taking three to reach the first green, Venturi and January were never in their match against the seemingly inseparable Alliss and O'Connor, who birdied three of the first four holes. Alliss actually squandered a short putt on the second green that would have given him another birdie.

Spurred on by his bad miss, the Englishman did make birdie putts from twelve and nine feet on the next two holes. But he blew another hole-winning short putt on the 358-yard fifth and had to settle for a half.

With the British reaching the turn in 33, the Americans found themselves two down after nine and proceeded to lose three of the next six holes, three-putting the par-4 eleventh. When Venturi drove into a ditch at the par-5 thirteenth and had to drop out, the Americans were dead and buried at four down.

The end came on fourteen, where O'Connor powered home a long par putt that could not be matched by the Americans, who suffered a 5 and 4 mauling.

Morning foursomes result: USA 2, GBI 2

For the second straight contest, the opening foursomes resulted in a 2-2 tie. This had not occurred in the first fourteen meetings.

Day One: Afternoon Foursomes

Arnold Palmer and Dave Marr (USA) v. Dave Thomas and George Will (GBI)

Stung by their humiliating defeat in the morning, Palmer and Marr devoted their lunch break to practice. Given the chance to avenge their loss against Thomas and Will, the Americans, proving that practice does indeed make perfect, started out on fire. They carded six threes from the second to the seventh, reaching the turn in an almost unprecedented 30 strokes.

Having been trounced in the morning match, Palmer thoroughly enjoyed himself in the afternoon on the course where he had won the 1961 British Open, although the conditions were far easier this time around. "I never thought I'd see it so quiet," he said.

Reigning PGA champion Marr, who had been the self-confessed weak link in the morning, holed a thirty-footer for a birdie three on the 427-yard second, which inspired Palmer to make a twenty-five-foot putt on the third. The fourth was halved in par, then Palmer came close to holing his chip shot on the par-4 fifth. Another perfect Palmer putt from twenty-five feet claimed the 533-yard sixth, then the Americans' sixth consecutive three halved the short seventh.

On his appalling morning showing: "I knew I had to improve or get the next train out of town."
—*Dave Marr*

Had Palmer's putt on the ninth dropped instead of lipping out, the Americans would have had an outward 29. Thomas and Will reached the turn in a commendable 34 strokes to lie four down.

Palmer and Marr made two more threes after the turn, including a clinching eagle on the 517-yard thirteenth. Having played thirteen holes in seven under par, the back-in-the-harness Americans quickly disposed of the British pair in a tit-for-tat 6 and 5 win. In just thirteen holes played, the Americans combined for eight threes.

Will and Thomas, only two shots off their morning pace, were heavily beaten. Having not dropped a hole in the morning win, they did not manage to win a single hole in the afternoon.

Billy Casper and Gene Littler (USA) v. Peter Alliss and Christy O'Connor (GBI)

Despite playing the first nine in just 31 shots, Alliss and O'Connor held only a slender one-hole lead over Casper and Littler. The highlight of a fascinating front nine was Casper's pitching in from more than eighty yards out on the fifth for an eagle two.

The match was level after the par-5 thirteenth, where O'Connor's birdie putt lipped out from ten feet and the Americans took the hole with a four. Alliss's chip up to the flag on the 202-yard fourteenth for a half was followed by O'Connor's twenty-foot putt that regained the lead on the longest hole on the course—the 536-yard fifteenth.

Although he had just finished playing one match ahead, Arnold Palmer had a part to play in this one. On the sixteenth, the British pair found that their ball had come to rest in the long rough against a plaque—the one that celebrated Palmer's magnificent shot during the 1961 British Open. Alliss was granted a free drop, which significantly improved his lie. His long iron to the green was good enough for a half to retain the precarious British lead.

The Englishman then played the defining shot of the back nine—another calculated chip shot that ran right up to the seventeenth hole. This was enough to win the hole and bring a 2 and 1 win for the match—the British pair's second victory of the day.

Julius Boros and Tony Lema (USA) v. Jimmy Martin and Jimmy Hitchcock (GBI)

With wins on holes three, four, and five, the strong pairing of Boros and Lema once again made quick work of their opponents.

This time the Americans were not going to let their winning start dwindle away. With four birdies on the front nine, Boros and Lema proved far too strong for the British rookies, who had replaced the equally ineffectual rookie partnership of Platts and Butler.

The experienced Americans finished three under par for their fourteen holes, to close out the overpowered British pair 5 and 4.

Ken Venturi and Don January (USA) v. Bernard Hunt and Neil Coles (GBI)

Bernard Hunt opened up in truly magnificent style, scorching his second shot to three feet on the 493-yard first hole. Neil Coles tapped in one of the simplest eagle putts in Ryder Cup history, and the British were one up.

Having been rocked by this English eagle, the Americans played chicken on the next two holes. January sent a wicked hook into impenetrable rough on the second, and Venturi's nightmare topped drive of only twenty yards on the third gave Coles and Hunt more than enough impetus to dominate this match.

"On paper January and Jacobs were supposed to be my weakest pair, but they rose to the occasion."
—*Byron Nelson*

Hunt added to the lead with a thirty-foot putt on the 393-yard tenth, and Coles made a miracle happen on the par-4 eleventh, having to sit on a gorse bush to play his shot. The resultant recovery ended up two feet from the hole for a wonderful half that must have demoralized the Americans even further.

Two up on the sixteenth, Hunt holed a monster putt of sixty feet for a birdie three that settled the match, 3 and 2.

Afternoon foursomes result: USA 2, GBI 2
Day one result: USA 4, GBI 4

In a day of low scoring and high excitement, players from both teams combined for forty-eight birdies and three eagles.

"I've never seen anything like it. It was an unbelievable day of golf."
—Byron Nelson

Day Two: Morning Fourball

On the second day, the weather was as benign and beautiful as on the first, and the course was equally placid, as both teams took the card apart.

Don January and Tommy Jacobs (USA) v. Dave Thomas and George Will (GBI)

Out in 33 shots, Thomas and Will held a commanding four-hole lead over January and Jacobs. Thanks to a birdie-three putt at the tenth, the British were rolling home four up with seven to play. The Americans would have been five down had January not holed from ten feet on the eleventh to secure a half.

The British charge faltered as both players failed to make par at the short twelfth and fourteenth holes. January followed up with a crucial fifteen-foot birdie putt to win on fifteen, while Jacobs added two winning putts of his own—on the par-4 sixteenth and par-5 seventeenth.

From almost being five down with six to play, the Americans surprisingly stood on the last tee one up. A bogey six was sufficient for the U.S. pair to halve the last hole, as Thomas and Will obviously peaked too soon and ran out of steam against the never-say-die Americans.

Billy Casper and Gene Littler (USA) v. Lionel Platts and Peter Butler (GBI)

In contrast to the bad start on the first morning, Platts and Butler started with three birdies (4-3-3) for a three-hole lead over Casper and Littler. The rejuvenated British players increased their lead when Butler made a birdie two at the seventh. Casper managed to claw one hole back on the eighth with a birdie, but the British pair reached the turn in 33 strokes with a handy three-hole lead.

Platts got a birdie at the tenth, and the British held their four-hole cushion with four to play. With little hope of salvation, the Americans needed the British to falter on a grand scale. Outdoing the collapse by Thomas and Will in the first match out, Butler started the rout by three-putting the fifteenth when two putts would have claimed the match, allowing the Americans to claim this decisive hole with a birdie four.

Littler made the British pair pay with two enormous birdie putts at the next two holes to reduce the lead to one. On the eighteenth, Littler again proved to be the Americans' savior, chipping up to the flag for another birdie to halve the match, the second American comeback charge in as many matches.

The Americans should have been staring at an 0-2 start to the day, but thanks to some fighting fourball play, they were actually up 1½-½ on the deflated British.

Arnold Palmer and Dave Marr (USA) v. Peter Alliss and Christy O'Connor (GBI)

With the Irishman suffering the effects of a nasty head cold, the top British pair of O'Connor and Alliss was no match for a fit American pairing of Palmer and Marr.

Having halved the first four holes, the dynamic U.S. double act took the fifth, sixth, and eighth holes (in birdie-birdie-par) to reach the turn three up. Out in 33 strokes, the Americans had further wins at ten and thirteen with two more birdies.

The British were so overwhelmed by their domineering opponents that they did not manage to win a single hole. A half on the short fourteenth was enough to wrap up a convincing 5 and 4 win for the Americans, who did not card a five (eight fours and six threes) in their wonderfully consistent round.

Julius Boros and Tony Lema (USA) v. Bernard Hunt and Neil Coles (GBI)

This encounter saw both pairs—Hunt and Coles and Boros and Lema—open with explosive eagle threes at the first. Neither pair carded a five on the outward nine, which they both finished in an immaculate 32 strokes. Seven of the first nine holes were halved, the U.S. pair taking the par-4 second with a three, which the British matched on the par-4 fifth.

All square at the turn, the British inched into their first lead of the match on ten, thanks to Hunt's birdie three. With eight holes to play, the match looked to be either pair's to win. The next seven holes were all halved, as neither side could establish authority over the other.

With the British one up on the par-5 eighteenth, the Americans tried desperately to square, and Lema nearly did so with a fine pitch that finished stone dead. But Hunt, to every Britisher's relief, holed his short putt for a birdie four and victory, 1-up.

This was a morning of what could have been for the British and a great escape for the Americans. If the British had held on to their large leads in the first two matches, the morning result would have read USA 1, GBI 3—and the overall match score 5-7. But the British let the Americans not only get back into the match but also take a one-point lead into the afternoon.

Morning fourball result: USA 2½, GBI 1½

Day Two: Afternoon Fourball

Arnold Palmer and Dave Marr (USA) v. Peter Alliss and Christy O'Connor (GBI)

Having easily beaten Alliss and O'Connor in the morning, Palmer and Marr were confident of repeating in the afternoon, but this rematch proved to be a lot closer.

The Americans did strike first, taking a lead on the third hole that they held until the sixth. The next seven holes were all won or lost, with the British combination coming out on top. British wins at six (American bogey), seven (O'Connor's twenty-foot birdie putt), nine (British birdie), eleven (O'Connor's birdie from thirteen feet), and twelve (Alliss making a treacherous curling putt from the edge of the green for birdie) brought a two-hole lead.

The Americans answered these five home wins with two of their own—on eight (British bogey) and ten (U.S. birdie)—and reduced the lead to one with a birdie four on the fifteenth.

With the match poised for a dramatic finish, the 401-yard sixteenth was halved, while Palmer missed a golden opportunity on seventeen to level the match. After O'Connor had failed to hole his ten-foot birdie putt, Arnie blew a six-footer to leave the British one up with one to play.

With his opponents short of the final green in two, Alliss unleashed one of the best and most telling approach shots of the three days. His fairway wood scampered up onto the green and ran on to eight feet of the hole. Needing to hole his own approach, Marr almost succeeded, but his pitch ran some way from the flag and the Americans kindly conceded Alliss's two putts for the match, 2-up.

Don January and Tommy Jacobs (USA) v. Dave Thomas and George Will (GBI)

Thomas and Will took the first hole when January and Jacobs both failed to make par, and the British pair held this lead as the next six holes were all halved. An untidy six at the eighth was all the British could manage between them, and their lead had disappeared by the time the teams reached the turn in 35 shots each.

With everything to play for coming home, the Americans blew the match apart with consecutive birdie threes at ten and eleven. It took the British four holes to cut into this two-hole lead: Thomas's extra strength and length enabled him to birdie the extra-long par-5 fifteenth and cut the U.S. lead to one hole.

With the next two holes halved in par, only a fighting seventeen-foot birdie putt from January on the last for a half saved the American triumph by one hole.

History had repeated itself. The consistent American pairing, with their second consecutive round of 69, had handed the British their second one-hole loss of the day.

Billy Casper and Gene Littler (USA) v. Lionel Platts and Peter Butler (GBI)

History is apt to repeat itself more than once, especially when the Ryder Cup is at stake. Casper and Littler had halved their morning match with Platts and Butler, and the same four players had the same result in the afternoon.

Once again, the British pair threw away a four-hole lead, this time—less dramatically—with ten to play. The British had carded four consecutive threes from the fourth hole onward, but they reached the turn only two up, in 33 strokes.

The Americans eventually pulled level—thanks to a brace of Casper birdies at the par-3 twelfth and the par-5 fifteenth.

All square at the last, the inspirational Casper found the sand by the green. After a gritty recovery, he needed all his steely resolve to slot home a testing ten-foot putt for par to halve the match.

Ken Venturi and Tony Lema (USA) v. Bernard Hunt and Neil Coles (GBI)

Having taken the 427-yard second hole in par, Venturi and Lema found themselves two down after nine to Coles and Hunt. The British pair made telling birdie twos at the fourth and seventh holes, sandwiched around another birdie at the 358-yard fifth.

With his side out in 35, Lema made back-to-back birdie threes at ten and eleven to level the match. Not content with his handiwork, Lema made a twelve-foot birdie putt at the 202-yard fourteenth to give the United States a lead for the first time since the third hole. They almost gave up the lead on the 536-yard fifteenth but scrambled a birdie to match the British effort.

Having made six birdies thus far, Coles and Hunt were unable to better par on the remaining three holes. They even allowed the Americans to defend their minimal lead, with a scrambling half in fives on the last, for a one-hole win.

Afternoon fourball result: USA 2½, GBI 1½

Seven of the eight matches on day two finished on the final green. The only exception was Palmer and Marr's 5 and 4 drubbing of Alliss and O'Connor. The British had three eagles and thirty-four birdies on the day, while the Americans carded thirty-eight birdies and two eagles.

Day two result: USA 5, GBI 3
Overall match score: USA 9, GBI 7

Day Three: Morning Singles

The British hopes for overcoming the two-point deficit were hit hard when O'Connor's feverish cold ruled him out of the morning singles.

Arnold Palmer (USA) v. Jimmy Hitchcock (GBI)

Up against the British weak link in Hitchcock, Palmer was able to start off with a rusty six at the first hole and still walk off with a half. Another bogey on the third by Hitchcock handed Palmer an early lead, which was doubled when Arnie birdied the fifth.

Finding his feet, Hitchcock surprised the great man by making birdies at six and seven to level the match. Realizing he had a serious fight on his hands, Palmer took the eighth, ninth, and eleventh for a three-hole lead. Still the British player refused to go down without a fight, and he came back to win the next two holes, reducing Palmer's lead to just one.

Fourteen was halved, then Palmer finally wrestled the match away from his pugnacious opponent with birdies at fifteen and sixteen—to seal a slightly more difficult 3 and 2 win than Palmer might have expected.

Julius Boros (USA) v. Lionel Platts (GBI)

In a close match with only an American win on the 416-yard third to separate them, Boros held a one-hole lead over Platts as he reached the turn in a commendable 34 strokes.

The Englishman lived up to his reputation as a money player by leveling the match with an accomplished birdie on the tenth. Boros took the twelfth before blistering home with consecutive birdies on fourteen, fifteen, and sixteen for a 4 and 2 win.

Tony Lema (USA) v. Peter Butler (GBI)

Up against the winless Peter Butler, Tony Lema enjoyed being back on the windswept Birkdale course, having just failed to retain his British Open title there earlier in the summer. With wins at the first, fourth, and eighth against Butler's sole outward-nine success—the fifth—Lema reached the turn in 33 strokes and carrying a comfortable two-hole lead.

Butler immediately halved this lead with his second birdie at ten, then followed it up at sixteen with a well-judged downhill putt for birdie to level the match. Seventeen was halved in par fives, but Butler's nerve let him down with a poor tee shot at eighteen. Finding a bunker on the right of the fairway, the Englishman could not reach the green in two and allowed Lema to win the hole with a five, taking the match 1-up.

Dave Marr (USA) v. Neil Coles (GBI)

Having started by claiming the first and fourth holes, Neil Coles was hit by a stinging salvo from Dave Marr. In the next five holes, the American failed to win only the par-3 seventh and reached the turn in 34 shots for a turnaround two-hole lead.

The first five holes home were all halved, but the American marred his card with a bogey six at fifteen that was more than bettered by Coles's four. Having cut the lead to one with three to play, Coles could finish only 5-5-5 to Marr's equally erratic 4-6-4. This up-and-down scoring allowed the American to win two holes and lose one—and eke out a two-hole win on the final green.

The U.S. side had won the first four singles of the day and held an ever-increasing six-point lead.

Gene Littler (USA) v. Bernard Hunt (GBI)

Like two of his four teammates before him, Bernard Hunt lost the first hole. With this sort of encouragement, it was hardly surprising that the Americans were having the better of the morning singles. Hunt and Littler halved the next five holes, before Hunt pulled the match back by making a birdie two at the seventh. Both players reached the turn in 34 strokes with the match delicately balanced.

Littler made the first mistake on the way home by bogeying the par-3 twelfth to give up the lead for the first time in the match. Both players made birdie twos at fourteen, with Hunt having to hole a thirty-footer for his half. Littler made another critical mistake off the tee on fifteen, and the British lead was two.

Hunt was unable to fully capitalize on Littler's mistakes, and the American recovered his composure to stake a win on the 401-yard sixteenth. Seventeen was halved in regulation fives, leaving Great Britain one up with one to play.

Needing to win the final hole, Littler was unable to match Hunt's faultless play as the Englishman knocked his second shot to within six feet of the hole, then held his nerve to hole the vital putt for the first British win of the morning, by two holes.

Littler may have had too many things on his mind, as he had gone four matches without a win after his success on the first day.

Billy Casper (USA) v. Peter Alliss (GBI)

Despite taking just thirteen putts to cover the first nine holes in 33 shots, Billy Casper found himself one down to Peter Alliss, who had already beaten him in the opening foursomes. The unusually consistent Alliss matched Casper on the greens and shaved one stroke off the American's midway total. The Englishman was only the second home player to win the first hole, and also had outward success on four and nine, while Casper prevailed on three and six.

The American made birdie at the par-4 eleventh to level the score, but he took two more shots than Alliss's birdie four on thirteen to fall behind again. Seizing his chance, Alliss was content to play out the last five holes with halves, as Casper could not make the necessary breakthrough.

Casper thought he had a chance on the last green when he holed a ten-foot putt to put the pressure on Alliss. His hopes were dashed, however, when the broad-shouldered Englishman responded with a spirited five-foot putt to cling to his precarious one-hole lead and secure the win.

Tommy Jacobs (USA) v. Dave Thomas (GBI)

Things also seemed to be going Britain's way in this encounter, as Thomas was well in control of Jacobs, reaching the turn in 34. Thomas was two up thanks to wins at seven and nine, which came after he had taken a lead on the second and then dropped the fifth.

No sooner had the mighty Welshman reached the turn than his game disintegrated. He failed to complete the tenth, made a six at thirteen, and lost his ball in the deep rough on fifteen. From two up to two down with two to play, the bespectacled British player had played himself out of the match. Jacobs needed only two pars to finish off the match, 2 and 1.

Thomas's play was so bad in the morning that he asked to sit out the afternoon session.

Don January (USA) v. George Will (GBI)

Once again a British player lost the first hole, but George Will would eventually finish the stronger in a match that he never led. Don January started out with six consecutive fours to take a one-hole lead, which grew to two when he birdied the par-4 ninth hole.

The final nine holes threw up eight wins or losses, with only the par-5 seventeenth producing a half. From the ninth to the fourteenth, both players traded consecutive wins. Will's play was most inconsistent as he sandwiched an excellent pair of cock-a-twos on twelve and fourteen by picking up his ball on thirteen.

January, on the other hand, having made his string of fours to start the match, made only one four on the way home. When Will broke the alternating win sequence by also taking the fifteenth, the match was back level. January immediately kept another four off his card by making a birdie three at sixteen to restore his lead, then halved seventeen to guarantee at least half a point.

And that is all the American got or deserved, as he faltered on the last hole with a six to Will's hole-winning four and had to settle for a half.

Morning singles result: USA 5½, GBI 2½

Losers of the first four singles matches, Great Britain had salvaged some pride by winning two and halving one of the final four matches. Despite this mini-comeback, the Americans started the afternoon singles needing just two points from eight matches to win the Ryder Cup.

Day Three: Afternoon Singles

"The sun continued to shine, the band struck up, thousands of people picnicked on the sandhills, and the Prime Minister (Harold Wilson) duly arrived for an afternoon off."

—HENRY LONGHURST, *Sunday Times* (London)

Arnold Palmer (USA) v. Peter Butler (GBI)

Palmer was again allowed a soft start when he halved the first hole with a bogey, but Butler's generosity ended there as he birdied both the par-3 fourth and par-4 fifth to take a shocking two-hole lead. Palmer quickly hit back with consecutive wins at six and eight to level the match, but Butler once again shocked Palmer by winning the ninth in par.

One down at the turn, in 37 shots, Palmer knew he had a fight on his hands. He made his first move on twelve, where a par three was sufficient to take the hole, and he followed this with birdies for wins on thirteen and fourteen.

In the third match out, Lema swiftly secured the first of the two points necessary to win the Cup. So, it became a matter of personal honor between Palmer and Boros, in the first two matches out, as to who would secure the winning point.

Attempting to deny Palmer his moment of glory, Butler cut his opponent's lead to one by taking the 401-yard sixteenth. When the seventeenth was halved in par fives, this assured the United States half of a point, enough to retain the Ryder Cup.

With that decided, Palmer produced a most spectacular three-wood to the final green that not only reached the putting surface but breathtakingly arced by a bunker. His ball ran up to within three feet of a flag that had been placed in a supposedly unreachable position. Needless to say, Arnie holed his eagle putt for the win—a point that came a few seconds too late for Palmer's own Ryder Cup glory, as Boros had pipped him on the seventeenth green.

Julius Boros (USA) v. Jimmy Hitchcock (GBI)

Striving to get that valuable Cup-winning point before his teammate ahead of him, Boros went out in 35, two shots better than

Palmer but all square with the tenacious Hitchcock. Boros had taken a lead with a birdie at the par-4 third hole, then Hitchcock leveled affairs on six and even had the temerity to take a lead on eight.

Boros leveled with a par on the ninth, and the pair proceeded to halve the next three holes. The American struck on thirteen to snatch an important one-hole advantage, which he held to the par-5 seventeenth.

Boros holed out for par on seventeen to take the hole and the match, following Hitchcock's disappointing bogey six. Moments later, after hearing the crowd noise from Palmer's match ahead on eighteen, Boros knew that his own hard-earned point had won the Cup for America by a matter of seconds.

Tony Lema (USA) v. Christy O'Connor (GBI)

With his country needing him, Christy O'Connor shrugged off the effects of his cold and took on the hale and hearty Tony Lema. Even a fully healthy Irishman probably would not have been a match for Lema, who was in one of his effervescent "champagne" moods.

Lema got off to a good start, grabbing the second, third, and fourth holes. He did lose the fifth, but he won the seventh to hold a three-hole lead at the halfway stage, which he reached in a vintage 33 strokes. The American then produced an even better run of scores—3-3-2-5-2—to close out the sadly suffering O'Connor, 6 and 4.

In bringing his team to within one point of winning the trophy, Lema was six under par for the fourteen holes played.

This was to be Tony Lema's last Ryder Cup, because he tragically died in a plane crash the following year. A fitting epitaph to his spirit and success, this final singles win made him the top American points scorer for the event, with five wins out of six matches.

Ken Venturi (USA) v. Peter Alliss (GBI)

In the first dozen holes, both Venturi and Alliss managed to win one apiece. The American had taken the lead with a birdie three on the 427-yard second and held this advantage for five halved holes—until Alliss took the eighth with a par four to Venturi's five.

The next four holes were halved as the American began to lose his way. Venturi picked up on the par-5 thirteenth and conceded to Alliss's par. The short fourteenth was halved in threes, but Alliss doubled his lead by claiming fifteen with a birdie four. Sixteen was halved in par fours, but Alliss won the next hole with another staggering birdie putt. This was more than enough to finish off the stuttering Venturi, who went down 3 and 1.

This win completed a highly successful campaign by Peter Alliss. His unbelievable record of five wins from six games was one of the greatest performances by a non-American player in a single Ryder Cup.

Billy Casper (USA) v. Neil Coles (GBI)

Although Neil Coles started in customary fashion for a British player by losing the first hole, he soon got back on track with a birdie at the second hole. Billy Casper returned the favor of Coles's opening gift at the par-3 fourth; the genial Englishman seized his chance and would not relinquish the lead. His birdie two on seven was swiftly negated when he took three times as many strokes on the par-4 eighth.

Coles birdied the tenth, shared the next four holes, and was gifted the par-5 fifteenth when Casper could do no better than a six. A half in fours on the 401-yard sixteenth brought Coles the reward he had worked so hard for—a 3 and 2 win over the highly touted American.

Gene Littler (USA) v. George Will (GBI)

Gene Littler managed to overcome an embarrassing oversight and the penalty of two lost holes to eventually defeat George Will. Halfway up the third fairway, Littler suddenly realized that he had Don January's seven-iron in his bag. Since he already had the full complement of his own fourteen clubs, this constituted a breach of the playing rules, and he reported it to the officials. The match-play penalty for carrying too many clubs was two holes. When Will realized the situation, he asked match referee Robert Sangster to nullify the two-hole penalty. But rules are rules, and match referees are match referees. The penalty stood.

At the turn, Will held a fortuitous one-hole lead over Littler—having gone out in 35 strokes. The Englishman increased his lead on eleven when his four beat Littler's bogey five, but gave the hole back when he bogeyed the par-3 twelfth.

With thirteen and fourteen halved in pars, Will let the game slip away from him. He made bogey sixes at fifteen and seventeen, which sandwiched Littler's excellent birdie three at the sixteenth. Will's second bogey six was enough to give the match to Littler, 2 and 1.

Dave Marr (USA) v. Bernard Hunt (GBI)

Having lost the third hole with a bogey five, Dave Marr won three of the next four to take a two-hole lead over Bernard Hunt after seven holes. The American bogeyed the par-4 eighth to reach the turn in 36 strokes with a one-hole lead.

Hunt won the tenth with a birdie three to level the match, and the next three holes were halved. Marr took the lead again by making his par on the short fourteenth, but Hunt birdied the 401-yard sixteenth to level matters with two to play.

The Englishman was unable to make his par on the long seventeenth. Marr had a few worries of his own on the equally long last hole, and could make only a nervous five. With the prospect of half a point dangling in front of him, Hunt could only match Marr on the closing green, and the American won by one hole.

Tommy Jacobs (USA) v. Lionel Platts (GBI)

Having given up the traditional British offering of the opening hole, Platts was soon back level when Jacobs made bogey on the third. Another bogey by Platts on the par-3 fourth gave the American back his lead, which was squandered with another bogey on a par 3 at seven.

Off yet another American bogey on eight, Britain took a lead it was not going to give up. This lead was extended to two on the next hole as Jacobs made the sixth hole-losing bogey of the front nine. Platts reached the turn two up in a dismally poor 38 strokes, two shots better than the error-prone American.

Platts's first birdie of the match came on the tenth, and it stretched his lead to three. Unfortunately, the spate of bogeys did not dry up: Platts gave two holes back with a four on the par-3 fourteenth and a six on the par-5 thirteenth.

The second British birdie of the round came when Platts tamed the 536-yard fifteenth, but he blotted his card with yet another bogey on sixteen. One down with two to play, Jacobs had an outside chance of padding the final team score, and he finally made his second birdie of the round. This rare American success was matched by Platts's third birdie, which kept his lead intact.

Between them, Platts and Jacobs made nine bogeys in eighteen holes. To cap it all, this was Platts's first win in five matches.

With Jacobs needing a win on the last hole to halve the match, it was perhaps fitting that both players carded a final-hole bogey to put the exclamation point on a lamentable display of golf at the end of three days of otherwise excellent entertainment.

Afternoon singles result: USA 5, GBI 3
Day three result: USA 10½, GBI 5½

For the two rounds of singles, Byron Nelson put his best three players (Palmer, Boros, and Lema) out at the top of the order, and they repaid their captain by winning all six of their matches.

Overall match score: USA 19½, GBI 12½

Recap

On calls for Great Britain to include Commonwealth players in their ranks: "All they need is two more really good players."
—*Peter Thomson, Australian winner of the 1965 British Open*

Having been level after the first day (4-4), the United States comfortably won the next two days 15½-8½—to end up dominating yet another Ryder Cup. Having matched their more illustrious opponents stroke for stroke for much of the week, the British team could look back at a few points that slipped away from them, especially in the fourball matches.

On the American and British players: "We were all club professionals. We knew our way around. We'd play practice rounds together and have dinner together. When the Ryder Cup matches ended, we all went back to selling sweaters in our golf shops."
—*Peter Alliss*

Again the matches were consistently closer than earlier encounters, with half of the thirty-two matches reaching the final green—where the U.S. side won eight, the British won five, and three were halved.

The U.S. captain refused to see the seven-point margin as a fair measure of the difference between the two teams. One underlying difference between the teams, he said, was the U.S. players' accuracy with the pitching wedge. So often they got close to the hole from sixty to seventy yards away, whereas Great Britain liberally peppered the green.

Match Results (Winning side marked in *italics*.)

Thursday, October 7—Morning Foursomes

	USA	GBI	Score
1.	*Julius Boros* *Tony Lema*	Lionel Platts Peter Butler	1-up
2.	Arnold Palmer Dave Marr	*Dave Thomas* *George Will*	6 and 5
3.	*Billy Casper* *Gene Littler*	Bernard Hunt Neil Coles	2 and 1
4.	Ken Venturi Don January	*Peter Alliss* *Christy O'Connor*	5 and 4

Thursday, October 7—Afternoon Foursomes

	USA	GBI	Score
5.	*Arnold Palmer* *Dave Marr*	Dave Thomas George Will	6 and 5
6.	Billy Casper Gene Littler	*Peter Alliss* *Christy O'Connor*	2 and 1
7.	*Julius Boros* *Tony Lema*	Jimmy Martin Jimmy Hitchcock	5 and 4
8.	Ken Venturi Don January	*Bernard Hunt* *Neil Coles*	3 and 2

Day one result: USA *4,* GBI *4*

Friday, October 8—Morning Fourball

	USA	GBI	Score
9.	*Don January* *Tommy Jacobs*	Dave Thomas George Will	1-up
10.	Billy Casper Gene Littler	Lionel Platts Peter Butler	halved
11.	*Arnold Palmer* *Dave Marr*	Peter Alliss Christy O'Connor	5 and 4
12.	Julius Boros Tony Lema	*Bernard Hunt* *Neil Coles*	1-up

Friday, October 8—Afternoon Fourball

	USA	GBI	Score
13.	Arnold Palmer Dave Marr	*Peter Alliss* *Christy O'Connor*	2-up
14.	*Don January* *Tommy Jacobs*	Dave Thomas George Will	1-up
15.	Billy Casper Gene Littler	Lionel Platts Peter Butler	halved
16.	*Ken Venturi* *Tony Lema*	Bernard Hunt Neil Coles	1-up

Day two result: USA *5,* GBI *3*

Overall match score: USA *9,* GBI *7*

Saturday, October 9—Morning Singles

	USA	GBI	Score
17.	*Arnold Palmer*	Jimmy Hitchcock	3 and 2
18.	*Julius Boros*	Lionel Platts	4 and 2
19.	*Tony Lema*	Peter Butler	1-up
20.	*Dave Marr*	Neil Coles	2-up
21.	Gene Littler	*Bernard Hunt*	2-up
22.	Billy Casper	*Peter Alliss*	1-up
23.	*Tommy Jacobs*	Dave Thomas	2 and 1
24.	Don January	George Will	halved

Saturday, October 9—Afternoon Singles

	USA	GBI	Score
25.	*Arnold Palmer*	Peter Butler	2-up
26.	*Julius Boros*	Jimmy Hitchcock	2 and 1
27.	*Tony Lema*	Christy O'Connor	6 and 4
28.	Ken Venturi	*Peter Alliss*	3 and 1
29.	Billy Casper	*Neil Coles*	3 and 2
30.	*Gene Littler*	George Will	2 and 1
31.	*Dave Marr*	Bernard Hunt	1-up
32.	Tommy Jacobs	*Lionel Platts*	1-up

Day three result: USA 10½, GBI 5½

Overall match score: USA 19½, GBI 12½

1967

Champions Golf Club
Houston, Texas
United States
October 20–22

United States 23½	Great Britain and Ireland 8½
Julius Boros	Peter Alliss
Gay Brewer	Hugh Boyle
Billy Casper	Neil Coles
Gardner Dickinson	Malcolm Gregson
Al Geiberger	Brian Huggett
Gene Littler	Bernard Hunt
Bobby Nichols	Tony Jacklin
Arnold Palmer	Christy O'Connor, Sr.
Johnny Pott	Dave Thomas
Doug Sanders	George Will
Captain	**Captain**
Ben Hogan	Dai Rees

United States Gets Kicks on Rout '67

The match was originally scheduled for June, but it was then decided that month would be too hot for the players, so the date was switched to September and later to October.

The American team, once again under the captaincy of Ben Hogan, was still without Jack Nicklaus—far and away the world's best golfer. Nicklaus had added a U.S. Open, a British Open, and a Masters title to his tally in the two years since the last match, but he had not had time to accumulate enough Ryder Cup points to make the team.

Hogan's new heroes were Gardner Dickinson, Bobby Nichols, Doug Sanders, Gay Brewer (Masters champions), and Al Geiberger. Not the greatest influx of talent an American Ryder Cup team has been privileged to welcome, but they could have walked in blindfolded and shackled to face the British team.

"I had just nine months and not the full two years in which to collect Ryder Cup points."
—*Jack Nicklaus,* The Greatest Game of All *(1969)*

On his making a 72 and 79 in the first two rounds of the '67 Masters: "151 was a stroke too many to make the cut. When I missed it, I missed the Ryder Cup team."
—*Jack Nicklaus*

On Ben Hogan's succinct introduction of his team at the opening ceremony: "*'Ladies and gentlemen, the United States Ryder Cup team—the finest golfers in the world.' Storm of applause, and the British ten down before a ball had been hit."* —PETER ALLISS

In an attempt to rekindle former glories, the British appointed Dai Rees as nonplaying captain, the Welshman having been the captain of the last British team to win the Ryder Cup, in 1957. Rees took over a team with only three rookies: Anthony Jacklin (who would make his mark as a winning captain later on in his Ryder Cup career), Hugh Boyle, and Malcolm Gregson. Underlying the British lack of depth, neither Boyle nor Gregson picked up a point between them, but then, the rest of the British team didn't score that many points either. This contest would prove to be one of the most one-sided in Ryder Cup history.

"Americans playing on their home ground are no more likely to lose to the British than Boston is likely to apologize for the tea party."
—*Mark McCormack*

In contrast to the diplomatic and democratic demeanor of his opposing number, Hogan was a demonic disciplinarian and a dictator when it came to ruling his team. He decreed no late nights (a 10:30 curfew) and no social events, as he wanted his men to concentrate solely on the match at hand.

Hogan also insisted that all U.S. players use the smaller British ball, explaining that if his players did not know enough about golf to use the small ball, they should not be on his team in the first place.

One of the Ryder Cup's legendary incidents revolved around the use of the small ball. Palmer locked horns with his skipper before the first practice round:

Palmer: "Say, Ben, is that right we are going to play the small ball?"

Hogan: "That's what I said!"

Palmer: "Well, supposing I haven't got any small balls?"

Hogan: "Who said you were playing? And by the way, are you sure you've brought your clubs, or would you like to borrow those as well?"

Course Details

"The course itself is on very much the standard pattern of the period—tree-lined fairways with very little thick rough, plenty of water—you can in fact get caught in it at seven holes—and huge greens.'"
—*Henry Longhurst,* Sunday Times *(London)*

Set some thirty miles outside of Houston, a metropolis where less is definitely not more, not only was the Champions course a monster at well over 7,000 yards, but the greens were also oversized, with huge breaks sweeping across them.

The course was built by two former Masters champions and 1951 Ryder Cup teammates: Jack Burke and Jimmy Demaret—

who had a combined 13–1 record, spoiled only by Burke's shock defeat as last-minute replacement in 1957.

Hole	Distance	Par	Hole	Distance	Par
1	454	4	10	448	4
2	452	4	11	466	4
3	397	4	12	230	3
4	228	3	13	544	5
5	513	5	14	430	4
6	418	4	15	428	4
7	428	4	16	180	3
8	180	3	17	420	4
9	510	5	18	440	4
		36			**35 = Par 71 (7,166 yards)**

Course designer: Ralph Plummer

Day One: Morning Foursomes

"A beautiful day, cloudless and windless, greeted the small crowd. . . . The early fairways had been swept of heavy dew, which had turned the rich grass pale. A hot day with temperatures in the eighties . . . and the long par 5s were soon brought within range of two strokes."

—Peter Ryde, *Times* (London)

Julius Boros and Billy Casper (USA) v. George Will and Brian Huggett (GBI)

The day started very brightly for the British, with Huggett and Will taking the first two holes off Casper and Boros.

Casper's opening putt traveled almost ninety feet right over the hole and seven feet beyond, from where Boros was unable to hole the return putt. Meanwhile, Huggett had rolled his lengthy putt up nearer the hole, and Will obliged with a par putt for the lead.

"When the starter on the first tee says, 'And now playing for the United States . . . ,' it's an experience you can never forget."
—*Billy Casper*

When the Americans two-putted the next green as well, the visitors were two up, having barely drawn a breath. But the homespun generosity was short-lived, as Casper holed from nine feet for a birdie on the par-3 fourth.

Will's wayward drive found the rough and gifted the sixth hole to the Americans, as Huggett missed a six-foot putt to level the match. Huggett made amends with a birdie on the 180-yard eighth.

Both pairs were out in 35, but the British held a vital lead until the par-5 thirteenth. Here both British players found the sand and lost the hole. Worse was to follow on fourteen, as Will drove into a tree before Huggett hit a three-wood into the water to put the United States one up.

After Huggett's long drive on fifteen, Will pitched up to a yard for a birdie to tie the match. The next two holes were halved to set up a showdown on the 440-yard, par-4 eighteenth. Neither pair deserved to win the hole or the match, as they played out a half in scrappy fours.

Arnold Palmer and Gardner Dickinson (USA) v. Christy O'Connor and Peter Alliss (GBI)

Palmer and Dickinson faced a seriously hard battle on the outward nine against Alliss and O'Connor, and the pairs turned all square. The first inkling of a crack in the British resistance came on the lengthy par-4 tenth, where an American par won the hole.

Having finally got themselves in front, the Americans wasted no time in pushing home their advantage. Following Palmer's superb six-iron to the eleventh green, Dickinson holed an eight-footer to go two up, but the British quickly pulled the hole back.

On the fifteenth, Dickinson holed a ten-foot birdie putt to go back up by two. The final two holes played were both halved as the Americans trotted out a 2 and 1 win.

Doug Sanders and Gay Brewer (USA) v. Tony Jacklin and Dave Thomas (GBI)

A poor first nine from Sanders and Brewer allowed Jacklin's rookie nerves to settle, and, in the company of the long-hitting Thomas, the British pair went out in 35 for a two-hole lead.

Brewer chipped to nine feet for an opening go-ahead birdie, but a poor drive by Sanders on the third saw Britain on level terms. On the fifth, a Brewer miscue cost his side the hole and the lead. Both Americans combined to three-putt the par-4 sixth, giving the British a two-hole lead.

Matters improved slightly for the Americans, as Thomas was forced to hole a seven-footer for a half on the 428-yard seventh. Having shown his finesse on the putting surface, Thomas opened his broad shoulders to reach the par-3 ninth in two for a birdie.

The Americans finally got something going on the par-4 eleventh with a birdie to halve the British lead. But then Brewer shot his side in the foot by missing a three-footer to go back two down.

"It is a long way to Tipperary but an even longer way to Texas, and I am not surprised that fifteen hours in a narrow seat in an aeroplane brought on David Thomas's old back trouble."
—*Henry Longhurst,* Sunday Times *(London)*

Thomas's accurate approach to the par-5 thirteenth green gave Jacklin the chance for another birdie four to put their side up by three. With the Americans unable to mount any further challenge, the British increased their lead for a 4 and 3 win.

Round in 71, Jacklin and Thomas had combined for the only British win of the morning, a feat they would repeat in the afternoon.

Bobby Nichols and Johnny Pott (USA) v. Bernard Hunt and Neil Coles (GBI)

The last match out was a noncontest, as Nichols and Pott destroyed an out-of-sorts Hunt and Coles.

Three up after nine, the Americans doubled their advantage in the next four holes to record a thumping 6 and 5 win. The two pairs would meet again the following day.

Morning foursomes result: USA 2½, GBI 1½

Day One: Afternoon Foursomes

With the fine weather and an encouraging start by the home side, the crowd grew to over five thousand.

"Britain's task was not made easier by a decision to cut the fast-growing greens and to change the pin positions between the first and second series. One or two players expressed difficulty in judging the nap on such newly grown greens." —Peter Ryde, *Times* (London)

Julius Boros and Billy Casper (USA) v. Brian Huggett and George Will (GBI)

This rematch of the opening-morning halved match was an equally close-fought encounter. After Huggett and Will had cleaned up at the first two holes, Casper and Boros pulled back level by winning the next two holes. The 513-yard fifth hole was halved, but then the British blew up at the par-4 sixth to hand the hole and the lead to the Americans. After the second halved hole of the round at the 428-yard seventh, the British fought back to level on the par-3 eighth with a birdie two.

The ninth was halved, then Huggett missed a par putt from less than three feet on the par-4 tenth; the Americans parred the hole, giving them back the lead. Having almost reached the 544-yard thirteenth in two, Huggett found his putting touch with a seventeen-foot birdie for the win. The match was level again.

Will struck a damaging hook off the fourteenth tee, which translated itself into an American win and a lead they did not relinquish over the closing four holes.

Arnold Palmer and Gardner Dickinson (USA) v. Malcolm Gregson and Hugh Boyle (GBI)

The British captain decided to send out an all-rookie pairing of Boyle and Gregson, but they ran smack into the Palmer and Dickinson express.

The latter holed three huge putts from ten, twenty, and thirty feet on the front nine, and made a supreme sand save on the 510-yard ninth. Out in 32, the Americans blitzed the shell-shocked rookies, who thanked their stars they were only five down.

Having done the damage on the opening stretch, Palmer and Dickinson eased off the pedal and stayed on cruise control for much of the journey home, recording a comfortable 5 and 4 win.

Gene Littler and Al Geiberger (USA) v. Tony Jacklin and Dave Thomas (GBI)

For nine holes, this match promised to be too close to call, but the normally consistent Littler and first-timer Geiberger lost their way after reaching the turn all square. In contrast, Jacklin and Thomas played faultless bogey-free golf coming home.

By transgressing the first law of match play, "Thou shalt not lose a hole to par," the Americans lost three holes to regulation and were handed a 3 and 2 defeat for their sins.

Bobby Nichols and Johnny Pott (USA) v. Peter Alliss and Christy O'Connor (GBI)

With the American pairing of Nichols and Pott one up after nine against the experienced British pair of Alliss and O'Connor, the match turned and turned again in the first three holes coming home.

Following two superb shots to the par-4 tenth, Alliss sank a birdie putt to level the match. The Americans rolled off back-to-back wins at eleven and twelve to establish a two-hole lead. Alliss and O'Connor were unable to break down their opponents over the closing five holes, as Nichols and Pott continued their morning form into the afternoon by handily accounting for the best of the British, 2 and 1.

Afternoon foursomes result: USA 3, GBI 1
Day one result: USA 5½, GBI 2½

Day Two: Morning Fourball

In a surprising move, Hogan dropped Palmer from the morning session. When a brave reporter asked him why, the U.S. captain simply answered, "Because I chose not to play him!"

Having already fallen afoul of his captain's wrath over the small ball, Palmer acquiesced with Hogan's wishes: "You're the captain. You make the pairings. Whatever you decide suits me fine."

But behind his captain's back, Arnold confided to a teammate, "Ben thinks I'm too tired. I played thirty-six holes Friday, and I am a little tired."*

Billy Casper and Gay Brewer (USA) v. Peter Alliss and Christy O'Connor (GBI)

Trailing by three points, Dai Rees put his faith in his top pairing to get his side back on the winning trail. Having formed a partnership that was the envy of many a marriage in Reno, Alliss and O'Connor halved the first two holes with Brewer and Casper.

Brewer made the first positive American move when he birdied the 397-yard third hole for the lead. A pair of par threes

*Actually, Palmer played only thirty-one holes on the first day.

offset the fourth before Casper got in on the birdie act with a four at the 513-yard fifth to go two up.

The intense heat finally took its toll on Peter Alliss's caddie, who fell ill with heat exhaustion and was replaced. Early reports in the clubhouse suggested the caddie was CUI (caddying under the Influence).

The next three holes were all halved in regulation, then the British couple carded its ninth straight par. Marital bliss is one thing, but winning fourballs demands birdies at the very least.

The Americans made the British pay for their perfect but unprofitable parity when Brewer birdied the par-5 ninth to go three up. O'Connor almost broke the British par sequence, but he left his birdie putt on the lip of the ninth cup.

With the British unable to break par, Brewer bagged his third individual birdie with a seven-foot putt on the par-3 twelfth. Having spotted the Americans a four-hole lead, Alliss decided it was time to open up the British birdie account. He did so in some style on the par-5 thirteenth, getting up and down from a bunker with a ten-foot birdie putt.

The U.S. lead now down to three, Alliss missed two more chances to cut the lead further. The Englishman blew birdie putts on fifteen and sixteen to slam the door in his own team's face, as Casper and Brewer triumphed 3 and 2.

Following this sad display of fourball play by his aces, with only one birdie between them in sixteen holes, Rees split up his number one partnership in the afternoon.

Bobby Nichols and Johnny Pott (USA) v. Bernard Hunt and Neil Coles (GBI)

Although Hunt and Coles showed vastly improved form over that of the previous day, they still did not have enough firepower or finesse to prevent Nichols and Pott from beating them for a second time in two days.

The Americans took an early lead when a par won them the first hole. The next seven holes were evenly contested, but Coles and Pott both reached the par-5 ninth in two. Pott sank an enormous eagle putt from thirty feet that Coles could not match, settling for a birdie as the U.S. pair went two up.

On the par-4 tenth, Coles made another birdie that actually counted, cutting the U.S. lead to one. Nichols finally got in on the act, making back-to-back birdies on twelve (with an eighteen-foot birdie two) and the par-5 thirteenth to go three up. The British answered Nichols's double-birdie blast by posting wins on the next two holes to set the match up for a fascinating finale with the U.S. team just one up with three to play.

Unfortunately, the British had no more ammunition left and allowed the Americans to halve the final three holes to hold on for a 1-up win.

Gene Littler and Al Geiberger (USA) v. Dave Thomas and Tony Jacklin (GBI)

In a repeat of a foursomes match from the day before, Littler and Geiberger were given a chance to gain revenge on Jacklin and Thomas. The first hole was set alight by Geiberger's twenty-five-foot birdie putt that Jacklin had a chance to cancel. The English rookie missed his birdie putt from a mere six feet to go one down.

Jacklin soon made amends by holing his birdie putt at the 397-yard third to level, but Littler regained the lead with his own birdie putt on the fifth. Showing the sort of fighting qualities that would mark him as a future captain, Jacklin hit straight back and made a six-footer for birdie on the 418-yard sixth.

A tremendous battle got even better when Thomas put his name on the birdie list. His tee shot almost torpedoed the flag on the par-3 eighth to send the British one up. Not to be forgotten, Geiberger finished the outward nine as he had started—with a birdie, this time to level the match.

Despite being the youngest member of the British team, Tony Jacklin was producing by far the best golf from the visiting camp.

With the tenth and eleventh holes halved, Jacklin gave his side back the lead, needing only a par on the treacherous 230-yard twelfth to do so. Two holes later, the Americans were back level when Geiberger unleashed another lengthy birdie putt to win the par-4 fourteenth. Littler's birdie on fifteen put the U.S. side up for the first time in nine holes.

Jacklin was out-of-bounds and out of the hole on the par-4 seventeenth, and the contest swung on Thomas's putt, which would square the match again. The Welshman's putt missed, however, allowing Littler and Geiberger to take the match on the final green, 1-up.

Gardner Dickinson and Doug Sanders (USA) v. George Will and Brian Huggett (GBI)

With Palmer missing from the lineup, Dickinson was paired with Doug Sanders, and the pair barely missed a beat against Huggett and Will. After the British took the lead when George Will birdied the short fourth, the Americans quickly leveled the match and were one up at the turn.

The game was blown apart on fourteen and fifteen, where back-to-back wins gave the Americans a three-hole lead with three to play. A safe par at the 180-yard sixteenth gave the new pairing a 3 and 2 win over the British pair, who tasted defeat yet again.

Ben Hogan had the last laugh on those doubters who had criticized him for dropping Arnold Palmer from the morning session. This final Palmer-less win completed a clean sweep of the morning matches for the Americans, only the third four-match sweep in Ryder Cup history, following similar U.S. domination in '47 and '63.

Morning fourball result: USA 4, GBI 0

Day Two: Afternoon Fourball

Billy Casper and Gay Brewer (USA) v. Bernard Hunt and Neil Coles (GBI)

Having swept the British in the morning, the Americans set out as though they were going to repeat the feat in the afternoon. First up were Casper and Brewer, who reached the turn two to the good against Hunt and Coles.

The dispirited British pair had already been beaten twice by Nichols and Pott, and found no sympathy from this fresh but no friendlier set of American opponents. Casper and Brewer steadily built on their halfway lead and closed out their forlorn foes, 5 and 3.

Gardner Dickinson and Doug Sanders (USA) v. Peter Alliss and Malcolm Gregson (GBI)

Having been proved right in his pairing of Dickinson and Sanders, Hogan did not hesitate to send them out again. Conversely, Rees made the decision to split up Alliss and O'Connor—the first time the pair were split up after seven consecutive matches together—and paired the Englishman with his fellow countryman Malcolm Gregson.

Alliss's new partnership fared little better than the old one: they reached the turn three down to the rampaging Americans.

The British managed to hold their own on the way home but could not prevent themselves from going down 3 and 2.

With this win, the United States had won seven matches in a row from the last match on the first day.

Gene Littler and Al Geiberger (USA) v. Dave Thomas and Tony Jacklin (GBI)

The only crumb of comfort for the British on one of their darkest days in the Ryder Cup—and they had had some days that were pitch black—came from their most consistent pair of the match. Having seen their country go down in all the previous matches on the second day, Jacklin and Thomas battled bravely for a half.

Their opponents were Littler and Geiberger, the same pair they had beaten the previous afternoon and lost to in the morning fourballs. So it was fitting that, after two close contests, honors would be shared.

The British team, who were looking for anything to cheer, must have roared themselves hoarse as Thomas holed his opening approach from a hundred yards or more to go one up. From this mighty opening, things soon got bleak for the British, however, as the Americans fought back to take a one-hole lead into the turn.

Jacklin and Thomas managed to level the match soon after turning for home. They took the lead on the 180-yard sixteenth when Thomas knocked his tee shot to three feet for a birdie putt. Once again, the British celebrations were cruelly cut short: Thomas found the water on seventeen, and Jacklin's approach took a sandy detour. Unable to recover, the British lost the hole to level the match.

In deteriorating light, Thomas hit another superb approach to six feet of the final flag, but the bespectacled Welshman could not read the run of the large green in the dusk and could not make the all-important putt to win the match.

"I could not read the grain in that light and did not hit the ball hard enough." —Dave Thomas

The match was halved, but as far as the British were concerned, it had halted the flood of American wins.

Thomas and Jacklin Brighten Day for British Isles

—*Times* (London) *headline*

Remarkably, the pair of Jacklin and Thomas had earned two and a half of Britain's paltry total of three points in the match's first two days.

Arnold Palmer and Julius Boros (USA) v. George Will and Hugh Boyle (GBI)

The Americans' strength was proved by the fact that the U.S. team swept the British in the morning while their star Palmer was having a well-earned rest. Arnie might have been excused for being a bit rusty in the afternoon, as he and Boros watched Boyle and Will reach the turn in a startling 30 shots to go four holes up.

Will capped a scintillating opening nine holes by holing an eagle putt, but his good work was undone when Boyle—the only player to find the green with his second shot—three-putted the tenth to lose it.

Three down when they should have been five adrift, the Americans knuckled down and won three of the next four holes with birdies, to sensationally level a match it had appeared they would lose.

After the American birdie blitz came three halved holes, setting up a thrilling finish on the last hole.

Palmer and Boros merely had to play safe to take the spoils in this anticlimax. In failing light, Will completely misjudged his second shot, while Boyle, who had up to this point played well, savagely cut his approach onto the practice ground. The Americans gladly accepted the gift and ran out winners on the eighteenth by one hole—a remarkable five-hole swing in nine holes.

After this momentous day of domination, the Americans enjoyed the biggest single-day margin in Ryder Cup history, and had built the largest-ever lead going into the final-day singles.

Afternoon fourball result: USA 3½, GBI ½
Day two result: USA 7½, GBI ½
Overall match score: USA 13, GBI 3

RYDER CUP MEN UP CREEK IN TEXAS . . .

"This is a moment perhaps to ask whether it is really fair to expect the Americans to go on with this match, not that conditions have changed so fantastically since the days when Samuel Ryder presented his Cup. There is little public interest in it in America and no company regards it as worth televising . . . a week for the Ryder Cup, with thirty-six holes a day for three days, may seem an exhausting and profitless proposition. . . . The chances of a British team ever beating the USA again are, however much one may bang the patriotic drum, virtually nil."

—HENRY LONGHURST, *Sunday Times* (London)

Day Three: Morning Singles

A thick blanket of fog over the course delayed the start of play. To make up for lost time, the morning matches started on the first and tenth tees.

Billy Casper (USA) v. Peter Alliss (GBI)

In the leadoff singles match, a birdie three at the seventh gave Billy Casper the lead against Peter Alliss, which the American maintained to the turn.

Alliss quickly squared the match on the way back, but no sooner had he fought back level than the Englishman let slip a loose drive on thirteen and three-putted on sixteen to drop back by two.

Casper had no problem making a half on seventeen to win, 2 and 1.

Gay Brewer (USA) v. Hugh Boyle (GBI)

With a fast break, Gay Brewer won the first two holes, from which point on Hugh Boyle faced an uphill task that was beyond him. The British player pulled back one hole by the turn, but Brewer won three of the next five holes to close out with a 4 and 3 win.

Julius Boros (USA) v. Brian Huggett (GBI)

Having benefited from sitting out the previous afternoon, Huggett started like a man possessed—out in 33, and three up after nine on Boros. The American managed to claw two holes back, but the Welshman tigerishly held on to his diminishing lead until the final green. There he halved the match to pick up Britain's first point of the day, 1-up.

Arnold Palmer (USA) v. Tony Jacklin (GBI)

Arnold Palmer gave his massed ranks of fans something to cheer about on the first green. He dropped a bomb from almost sixty feet to go one up on his shell-shocked opponent. Playing as though Palmer's explosive start had unnerved him, Jacklin saw his putting touch desert him. He three-putted the second to go two down, then lost two more early holes by three-putting and was five down at the turn.

The Englishman pulled himself and his putting game together, reeling off three wins in a row, including putts of twelve and fifteen feet. Palmer responded to the fight back and knocked his pitch five feet from the hole on the 418-yard fifteenth (in reality the sixth). The American made his birdie putt to go back up by three, then closed out Jacklin, 3 and 2, on the next hole.

Gene Littler (USA) v. Dave Thomas (GBI)

Dave Thomas opened up with a one-hole lead over Gene Littler at the turn, and extended this lead to two up with two holes to play. Having failed to par the seventeenth in two previous visits, Thomas took three putts for a bogey five on his bogey hole.

His lead now one, the Welshman tried to make amends on the final hole. With too much power for his own good, the brutish British player went through the final green and carded another five. Littler, however, kept his head, and was rewarded with half a point.

Al Geiberger (USA) v. Malcolm Gregson (GBI)

Three up at the turn, Al Geiberger had a fairly easy match against Malcolm Gregson, slowly turning the screw and closing out the Englishman 4 and 2 with another win on the sixteenth.

Bobby Nichols (USA) v. Bernard Hunt (GBI)

Having beaten Bernard Hunt two times in the first two days, Bobby Nichols was unable to make it three. All square after nine holes, the match could have gone either way in the closing stages, but it was the British player who relinquished the upper hand at the finish.

One up on the last, Hunt blew his chance as he bogeyed to throw a lifeline to the American, who was grateful for the half because it kept his unbeaten record intact.

Despite dropping his first half-point of the competition, Bobby Nichols had delivered the half-point the U.S. side needed to retain the Cup.

Doug Sanders (USA) v. Neil Coles (GBI)

In one of the few bright spots of an otherwise disastrous three days for the visitors, Neil Coles beat Doug Sanders 2 and 1.

Having looked out of sorts on the first two days, losing all three of his matches, Coles was a revelation on the final day, winning both of his singles. This sudden change in form might be explained by his travel method: averse to flying, he had come over by boat rather than plane, and seemed to take an extra couple of days to shake off his sea legs.

Morning singles result: USA *5,* GBI *3*

Day Three: Afternoon Singles

Although the Americans had won the Cup midway through the morning session, the players agreed to play out the afternoon for the benefit of the gallery. Consequently, very little was reported at the time on the final eight matches.

Arnold Palmer (USA) v. Brian Huggett (GBI)

Determined to prove to Hogan that he was not to be taken lightly again, Palmer went after his opponent the same way he went after the flag. Four up on Huggett at the turn, Palmer was out in 34 and soon disposed of the Welshman, 5 and 3.

With this win, Palmer was 5-0 for the contest. The only match he did not win was the one he sat out on the second morning.

Gay Brewer (USA) v. Peter Alliss (GBI)

Peter Alliss was back out firing on all cylinders for the British, this time against Gay Brewer. The match all square with three holes to play, Alliss grabbed the advantage with a fine tee shot to the par-3 sixteenth, then holed his birdie putt to go one up.

Alliss, who had never trailed his opponent in this engaging encounter, shut the door on Brewer in scintillating fashion, holing a thirty-foot putt on seventeen for a 2 and 1 win.

Gardner Dickinson (USA) v. Tony Jacklin (GBI)

The only difference between Dickinson and Jacklin was that the American continued his hot putting from the first two days, while Jacklin three-putted on the sixteenth to hand victory to the American, 3 and 2.

Having partnered Arnold Palmer twice on the first day, Dickinson—in this his Ryder Cup debut—equaled Arnie's perfect haul for the week by going 5-0.

It had been a most disappointing introduction for future Ryder Cup legend Jacklin. After winning both his foursomes matches, he had only a half to show for his last four matches. Jacklin would qualify for the U.S. PGA Tour in 1968, and soon become the dominant British player of his era.

Bobby Nichols (USA) v. Christy O'Connor (GBI)

Another American rookie, Bobby Nichols, rounded off a fine week as he remained undefeated in five matches. His fourth win came at the expense of Christy O'Connor.

One up after nine, Nichols increased his lead to post a 3 and 2 victory, while recording the best round of the day, a four-under-par 67.

Johnny Pott (USA) v. George Will (GBI)

The match between Johnny Pott and George Will stayed close until the thirteenth hole, where the American took control and ran out the winner, 3 and 1.

Pott, who had suffered badly with severe nerve problems during his debut in 1965, was almost unrecognizable the second time around, as he went 4-0.

Al Geiberger (USA) v. Malcolm Gregson (GBI)

In their second meeting of the day, Al Geiberger was held a lot closer by Malcolm Gregson in the afternoon.

All square after nine, Geiberger finished the stronger and defeated his opponent for the second time. This time around, Gregson managed to halve the morning deficit, going down 2 and 1.

Doug Sanders (USA) v. Neil Coles (GBI)

In another repeat performance from the morning, both Doug Sanders and Neil Coles went out in 33. With both men playing well, Sanders started home 3-4-3, but then picked up only one hole on his obstinate opponent.

Having taken Sanders's best shots, Coles took control with a couple of birdie threes to take his second 2 and 1 win over Sanders of the day.

Julius Boros (USA) v. Bernard Hunt (GBI)

Both players in this match had something to prove. Julius Boros had lost his morning match to Brian Huggett, while Bernard Hunt had blown a chance of a win over Bobby Nichols.

Neither player gave anything away as they finished the outward nine all square. Hunt finally took a lead onto the eighteenth hole, where, for the second time in the day, he made a bogey five and settled for a half.

Afternoon singles result: USA 5½, GBI 2½
Day three result: USA 10½, GBI 5½
Overall match score: USA 23½, GBI 8½

Recap

This was the fifth American win since the last British success in 1957, in which time the United States had won an average of two-thirds of the points available—the same average the Americans had posted in the first eleven matches before the 1957 loss. So whatever format was played—two days of thirty-six holes or three days of double eighteens—the U.S. team had always been superior by a margin of 2:1.

Statistically this was the sixth biggest win in Ryder Cup history, as the U.S. team won 73 percent of the points available. It also marked the last time the United States would win more than two-thirds of the points.

Just how superior the Americans had been in Ryder Cup play is open to debate. Of the ten matches that reached the eighteenth hole at the Champions Club, the United States lost only one (Boros against Huggett in the opening singles). These final-hole "deciders" accounted for almost a third of the overall result, yet another clear indication of how much more proficient the U.S. team was at the business end of a match—whether it be eighteen or thirty-six holes.

Ben Hogan ended his association with the Ryder Cup with a perfect record. He won all three matches as a player (in 1947 and '51), and all three Ryder Cup matches in which he served as captain (1947, '49, and '67).

The American captain felt that since his team had halved five matches, and won four by one hole and four by the margin of 2 and 1, "one putt could have made a great difference."

By that logic, the British had come close to winning thirteen matches, and they had failed to take only five matches to the sixteenth green. But, as they say, close counts only in horseshoes and hand grenades.

"I was so, so disappointed at lunchtime [on the final day]. I wanted so much to be 4-for-4 in man-to-man combat. We have all our writers here, and I know they will send back stories saying we were routed. But I guess they have a right to. The points are up there on the scoreboard."

—DAI REES

Another indication of the relative strengths of the two teams is that only one British player won more games than he lost. Dave Thomas went 2-1-2 in a heroic but vain individual attempt to take on the mighty Americans. Such an overwhelming lack of depth and strength prompted Dai Rees to suggest that the teams be reduced to eight a side so as to make the British more competitive, since their weakest two players were always far weaker than their American counterparts.

Relative unknowns Nichols and Pott played three pairs together and three singles between them, dropping only half a point out of a possible six.

One change that did come out of this humiliation for the British was that their PGA agreed to switch to the larger American ball in all of its tournaments from 1968 on. Still, whatever the British decided to do to strengthen their team, they knew another American battleship was waiting offshore to blast them out of the water in 1969. Jack Nicklaus was ready for his Ryder Cup roll call.

"An analysis of statements on our Ryder Cup failure reveals that we have been losing because:

a. Our players cannot putt.

b. They can putt but can't hit accurate approach shots.

c. They can hit accurate approach shots but can't drive.

d. They were robbed by Dame Fortune, who kept stretching out a hand and hurling the ball on the green no matter how the Americans hit it.

e. The small ball.

f. The large ball." —MICHAEL GREEN, *Sunday Times* (London)

Match Results (Winning side marked in *italics*.)

Friday, October 20—Morning Foursomes

	USA	GBI	Score
1.	Julius Boros Billy Casper	George Will Brian Huggett	halved
2.	*Arnold Palmer* *Gardner Dickinson*	Christy O'Connor Peter Alliss	2 and 1
3.	Doug Sanders Gay Brewer	*Tony Jacklin* *Dave Thomas*	4 and 3
4.	*Bobby Nichols* *Johnny Pott*	Bernard Hunt Neil Coles	6 and 5

Friday, October 20—Afternoon Foursomes

	USA	GBI	Score
5.	*Julius Boros* *Billy Casper*	Brian Huggett George Will	1-up
6.	*Arnold Palmer* *Gardner Dickinson*	Malcolm Gregson Hugh Boyle	5 and 4
7.	Gene Littler Al Geiberger	*Tony Jacklin* *Dave Thomas*	3 and 2
8.	*Bobby Nichols* *Johnny Pott*	Peter Alliss Christy O'Connor	2 and 1

Day one result: USA 5½, GBI 2½

Saturday, October 21—Morning Fourball

	USA	GBI	Score
9.	*Billy Casper* *Gay Brewer*	Peter Alliss Christy O'Connor	3 and 2
10.	*Bobby Nichols* *Johnny Pott*	Bernard Hunt Neil Coles	1-up
11.	*Gene Littler* *Al Geiberger*	Dave Thomas Tony Jacklin	1-up
12.	*Gardner Dickinson* *Doug Sanders*	George Will Brian Huggett	3 and 2

Saturday, October 21—Afternoon Fourball

	USA	GBI	Score
13.	*Billy Casper* *Gay Brewer*	Bernard Hunt Neil Coles	5 and 3
14.	*Gardner Dickinson* *Doug Sanders*	Peter Alliss Malcolm Gregson	3 and 2
15.	Gene Littler Al Geiberger	Dave Thomas Tony Jacklin	halved
16.	*Arnold Palmer* *Julius Boros*	George Will Hugh Boyle	1-up

Day two result: *USA 7½, GBI ½*

Sunday, October 22—Morning Singles

	USA	GBI	Score
17.	*Billy Casper*	Peter Alliss	2 and 1
18.	*Gay Brewer*	Hugh Boyle	4 and 3
19.	Julius Boros	*Brian Huggett*	1-up
20.	*Arnold Palmer*	Tony Jacklin	3 and 2
21.	Gene Littler	Dave Thomas	halved
22.	*Al Geiberger*	Malcolm Gregson	4 and 2
23.	Bobby Nichols	Bernard Hunt	halved
24.	Doug Sanders	*Neil Coles*	2 and 1

Sunday, October 22—Afternoon Singles

	USA	GBI	Score
25.	*Arnold Palmer*	Brian Huggett	5 and 3
26.	Gay Brewer	*Peter Alliss*	2 and 1
27.	*Gardner Dickinson*	Tony Jacklin	3 and 2
28.	*Bobby Nichols*	Christy O'Connor	3 and 2
29.	*Johnny Pott*	George Will	3 and 1
30.	*Al Geiberger*	Malcolm Gregson	2 and 1
31.	Doug Sanders	*Neil Coles*	2 and 1
32.	Julius Boros	Bernard Hunt	halved

Day three result: USA 10½, GBI 5½

Overall match score: USA 23½, GBI 8½

1969

Royal Birkdale Golf Club
Lancashire, England
September 18–20

United States 16	Great Britain and Ireland 16
Tommy Aaron	Peter Alliss
Miller Barber	Brian Barnes
Frank Beard	Maurice Bembridge
Billy Casper	Peter Butler
Dale Douglass	Alex Caygill
Raymond Floyd	Neil Coles
Dave Hill	Bernard Gallacher
Gene Littler	Brian Huggett
Jack Nicklaus	Bernard Hunt
Dan Sikes	Tony Jacklin
Ken Still	Christy O'Connor, Sr.
Lee Trevino	Peter Townsend
Captain	**Captain**
Sam Snead	Eric Brown

Golden Bear Necessities

If ever a Ryder Cup contest reached both extremes of sportsmanship, this was surely the year. From the very outset, the British captain, the irascible, bald-headed Eric Brown, forbade his players from helping their rivals look for any lost balls in the rough. Brown later said he was concerned his players would tread on the "lost" ball and forfeit the hole. Sadly, this type of unsporting conduct was seen through too many matches, though thankfully, in the end, sportsmanship shone through like a chivalrous shaft of sunshine.

The man responsible for restoring the sporting status quo was none other than Jack Nicklaus, finally appearing in his first Ryder Cup—seven years after winning the 1962 U.S. Open (his first PGA Tour win).

"Jack will give this wonderful contest a completely new and inspiring dimension."
—*Arnold Palmer*

With the increasing stress and strain on the players, both sides agreed to increase the team size to twelve. Of the twenty-four players this year, fifteen were fresh to the unique demands of Ryder Cup play; maybe it was this that brought about the unforgettable result.

"Sam Snead did a good job of preparing us . . . He even let us vote on who we wanted to play with—secret ballot, of course."
—*Frank Beard,* Making the Turn *(1992)*

Reinstalled as U.S. captain, Sam Snead had ten rookies to deal with, only Casper and Littler having played in the Ryder Cup before. Although technically Ryder Cup rookies, the American new blood was hardly unseasoned: Nicklaus, Trevino, Floyd, Hill, Beard, and Aaron were already of the highest quality.

Eric Brown had five new faces, all under twenty-four: Bernard Gallacher, Alex Caygill, Maurice Bembridge, Peter Townsend, and Brian Barnes; none was in the same class as Snead's rookies.

The only major change in the playing conditions was the "compulsory use of the big ball." From time immemorial, the pro tours in Great Britain and the United States had used different-size balls, but after constant lobbying from the British players, their PGA relented and joined the U.S. players in using the 1.68-inch ball.

Since the 1955 Ryder Cup, players on both sides had been allowed to choose which ball they used. With the new rule, everyone was playing not only on the same surface but also with the same-size ball. This meant the British critics had one fewer excuse to scream about after every Ryder Cup battering. If nothing else, this change would bring a halt to all the endless discussion over the merits of the larger or smaller ball. The ball was still round and white, with too many dimples to count with the naked eye.

Course Details

The Ryder Cup returned to the Lancashire links course, which had hosted the matches in 1965, when the U.S. side won 19½–12½.

Hole	Distance	Par	Hole	Distance	Par
1	493	5	10	393	4
2	427	4	11	412	4
3	416	4	12	190	3
4	212	3	13	517	5
5	358	4	14	202	3
6	533	5	15	536	5
7	158	3	16	401	4
8	459	4	17	510	5
9	410	4	18	513	5
		36			**38 = Par 74 (7,140 yards)**

Course designer: George Lowe

Day One: Morning Foursomes

Having waited six years to make his Ryder Cup debut, Jack Nicklaus was forced to wait a few hours more, as Snead decided not to include him in his morning foursomes. Nicklaus eventually made his long-awaited start in the final pairing of the day.

Miller Barber and Raymond Floyd (USA) v. Brian Huggett and Neil Coles (GBI)

Barber and Floyd took a lead on the par-3 fourth, thanks to a British bogey, and Barber holed his chip shot on the eighth to protect the lead from the first British birdie of the round. Huggett and Coles were soon level, as the Americans made a minor hash of the ninth.

The next three holes were halved in regulation, with the Americans scrambling to a three on the 190-yard twelfth after Barber's tee shot had missed the green. The second British birdie of the round won the thirteenth, after Barber found the sand, to trigger a run of three straight British wins.

Fourteen was gift-wrapped by the U.S. pair with another bogey, after Barber again missed a par-3 green from the tee. Barber's woes multiplied when he found the dense shrub-cum-rough on the 536-yard fifteenth, and the Americans conceded the hole to go three down in triple-quick time.

Rookie Ray Floyd played his way onto the U.S. Ryder Cup team by winning the PGA Championship.

A half at the par-4 sixteenth was all the British pair needed to close out the match 3 and 2. First blood to the home team, who knew the importance of a lead after the first day.

Lee Trevino and Ken Still (USA) v. Bernard Gallacher and Maurice Bembridge (GBI)

Trevino and Still birdied four of the first five holes but, in spite of this trailblazing start, were only one up. This was due to some combative play by Bembridge and Gallacher, who made birdies at the first and fifth, coupled with an American bogey at the par-3 fourth.

By the eighth, the British pair was back on level terms, courtesy of a second American bogey, and looking like the more dangerous side.

Twenty-year-old Gallacher became the youngest player in the Ryder Cup.

Whether or not the increasing pressure got to rookie Ken Still, his actions were not in keeping with the level of sportsmanship that had typified Ryder Cup play in the past.

When Bembridge asked the American to move out of his line of sight on the thirteenth tee, Still overreacted and made a great show of asking everyone else on the tee to also move back. This obviously upset Still more than it did Bembridge, as the American badly hooked his tee shot into the rough. Trevino's attempted recovery plugged in the top of a bunker, from where Still half-blasted the ball out, which appeared to hit the bunkered player. Trevino asked his partner if the ball had hit him on the shoulder. Still ignored the question, so Trevino immediately told him to pick up the ball to concede the hole. Trevino's honesty on thirteen meant that the United States dropped to two down, but they got a hole back at fifteen with a birdie.

After fifteen holes, Trevino was clearly frustrated by his opponents: *"These British boys are surely burning things up. We have scored six birdies in all, and here we are one down."* —LEE TREVINO

Gallacher needed a hole-saving chip to three feet at the sixteenth to retain the slim advantage, while an American par at the seventeenth was more than matched by the British. Bembridge's pitch to ten feet was converted by Gallacher for a birdie four and the overall win.

Trevino's sportsmanship and honesty had been a major factor in this 2 and 1 defeat, with the conceded thirteenth hole a turning point in the contest.

Dave Hill and Tommy Aaron (USA) v. Tony Jacklin and Peter Townsend (GBI)

In contrast to the American fast starts in the first two matches, Hill and Aaron were fast-started upon, by Jacklin and Townsend. A birdie putt by Townsend at the 427-yard second hole was swiftly followed by Townsend's nine-iron to four feet for a Jacklin birdie and a two-up lead.

Hill and Aaron fought hard to pull back to one down after the turn, but they took a six after being in the scrubby stuff, while the British pair carded a birdie four for good measure and a two-hole cushion again.

The Americans again played tough but could not eat into the lead, and they stood on the seventeenth tee two down. The hole and the match, however, were sealed by Townsend's second, an immaculate three-wood to the long par-5 green. His shot finished six feet from the hole, forcing Hill to try to hole his long putt from the very front of the green. His ball charged nine feet past the hole, and when Aaron missed the comebacker, Jacklin had two putts for the match. But he sank a psychological nail into the American team's heart by drilling home his eagle putt for a convincing 3 and 1 win.

"Jacklin's presence could be the spark that will light another bonfire such as the one that consumed the United States at Lindrick in 1957."
—*Leonard Crawley,* London Telegraph

The triumphant British pair had completed seventeen holes in a superb (dare one say "Americanlike"?) seven under par.

Billy Casper and Frank Beard (USA) v. Christy O'Connor and Peter Alliss (GBI)

Alliss and O'Connor, who were literally inseparable from each other in Ryder Cup matches, had a drawn-out, shoot-'em-up dogfight with Casper and Beard.

The first hole went to a British birdie but was negated by their bogey on three. A second successive British bogey at the par-3 fourth gave the United States a lead for just two holes—they conceded the sixth to a second British birdie.

"My first year on the Ryder Cup team, 1969, I couldn't believe the intensity of my teammates, the screaming and hollering."
—*Frank Beard,* Making the Turn *(1992)*

This seesaw match soared again as Alliss and O'Connor took the par-3 seventh with a third birdie, but once again their lead was short-lived as the U.S. pair birdied the par-4 ninth. The next three holes were halved in par, as the Americans took their turn holding a brief lead. Their birdie at the par-5 thirteenth was immediately undone by another hometown birdie. The match was all square with four holes to play, as no side proved capable of breaking out beyond a one-hole lead.

Having won the first three matches in the morning, Britain had a golden opportunity to whitewash their visitors, but the pride and experience of Casper and Beard pulled through. On eighteen, Casper blasted out of a bunker to five feet, and Beard stroked home the par putt for the only U.S. half-point of the opening session.

Snead had been forced to play seven rookies in the opening session (to Britain's three), and the results were not good. The only American veteran on display was Casper, and he steered his rookie partner to a face-saving half.

In their best opening morning ever, a resurgent British team had almost swept the mighty Americans off the board. It was only the third time that the U.S. team had spotted the British a lead after the first session of play, and the first time since 1949.

Morning foursomes result: USA ½, GBI 3½

Day One: Afternoon Foursomes

Sam Snead read his team the riot act at lunch, and did the only thing that he could do under the circumstances: he threw his one remaining veteran (Littler) into the fray. Rees, on the other hand, spent lunch slapping his players on the back in delight, then went with his three winning pairs from the morning.

Dave Hill and Tommy Aaron (USA) v. Neil Coles and Brian Huggett (GBI)

Hill and Aaron quickly found themselves two down against Coles and Huggett, having bogeyed the first two holes and lost the third to a British birdie three. The Americans slowly battled back to take the fifth with a par four, before reeling off three wins in a row from the par-3 seventh (birdie-par-birdie) to take a two-hole lead into the turn.

Coles's thirty-footer for a birdie three cut the lead to one after ten, then some evenly matched golf saw the next four holes halved in par threes and fives.

Then came the fiasco of the fifteenth. This par-5, 536-yard hole typified the poor play from both pairs, particularly the Americans, who found sand three times as the British reluctantly took the hole with a bogey six.

On Hill's match-winning putt on the eighteenth: "A shaky putt but a solid point to the Americans."
—*Peter Ryde,* Times *(London)*

All square after sixteen and seventeen were halved in par, it took Hill's three-foot birdie putt, the ball rolling right round the cup before it dropped, to grab the one-hole victory on the final green.

Lee Trevino and Gene Littler (USA) v. Bernard Gallacher and Maurice Bembridge (GBI)

Having halved the first four holes and been stung into action when Bembridge and Gallacher took a lead on the fifth, Trevino and Littler hit back by reeling off three straight wins, with a couple of birdies leading the way. The ninth was halved in par, and the Americans reached the turn three under, in 33 strokes, to hold a two hole lead.

The Americans played the front nine without a five or a bogey on their card—4-4-4-3-4-4-2-4-4—as the visitors finally seemed to have come to grips with the course and the match-play format.

With the 393-yard tenth also halved in par, the next four holes were claimed in turn by each side's mistakes rather than sub-par play. The British took eleven with a par and thirteen after their opponents conceded; the U.S. pair won twelve and fourteen, both par 3s, to par. Some normality returned to the scorecard as the next two holes were halved in regulation to set up a tense finish, the Americans still two holes to the good.

Seventeen fell to the first full birdie of the back nine, as Gallacher and Bembridge fought for their lives and cut the lead to one with one to play. Sadly for the home side's hopes, Gallacher hit an errant drive into the rough on the eighteenth, and their spirited challenge fizzled out. Up ahead, Littler's delicate chip shot rolled right up to the hole for birdie, gaining the U.S. side's second victory of the afternoon on the final green, 2-up.

Billy Casper and Frank Beard (USA) v. Tony Jacklin and Peter Townsend (GBI)

Casper and Beard were twice ahead after claiming the first two par 3s in nothing more spectacular than par. Jacklin and Townsend twice pegged the Americans back, with a birdie at the par-5 sixth, while the Americans conceded on the ninth to turn all square.

The English pair started out with eight consecutive fours, and this sequence was broken only by a birdie three at the 410-yard ninth.

The Americans regained the lead after Jacklin drove into trouble on the eleventh, and Casper blew a birdie putt on twelve that would have doubled the U.S. lead. The American's misery was compounded when his dreadful drive on thirteen resulted in a bogey six to level the scores again. Casper continued to have trouble off the fifteenth tee, as he almost hooked into foul territory. Luckily for the American, Jacklin's approach found a bunker and they were able to scramble a half in par 5s.

Peter Townsend described Casper's increasingly wayward drives as "the worst shots he could have hit for years."

Another wicked hook by Casper off the seventeenth tee finally proved to be costly. A fine recovery and a great chip were not enough to prevent losing to a Jacklin birdie putt for a four. The Americans found themselves down for the first time in the match.

For once it was the British pair who came up the eighteenth with victory in sight. Beard's excellent approach stopped fifteen feet short of the flag, but the British held on thanks to Townsend's delectable chip over a bunker. This was good enough for a valuable half in four—and a one-hole win.

Having been the only American pair not to lose in the morning, Casper and Beard were the only U.S. duo to do so in the afternoon.

Jack Nicklaus and Dan Sikes (USA) v. Peter Butler and Bernard Hunt (GBI)

Dan Sikes had the honor of partnering Jack Nicklaus in the latter's first Ryder Cup match, both having been left out of the morning session.

The fresh pair proved they were far from rusty, taking a one-hole lead on the 427-yard second against Hunt and Butler's double bogey. This promising start was soon blighted by their own bogey at the par-4 third which was bettered by a British birdie.

A par three on the fourth bought the American pairing a lead they held for eleven straight holes, as the two teams matched each other stroke for stroke.

In the previous seven years, while he waited to become eligible for the Ryder Cup, Jack Nicklaus had not wasted his time or energy. He won the U.S. Open twice (1962 and '67), the Masters three times (1963, '64, and '66), the PGA Championship in 1963, and the British Open in 1966.

It took an American bogey, on sixteen, to break this string of consecutive halves. Nicklaus proved to be the unlikely culprit, as his first putt came up well short and required two more taps to reach the target. This putting irregularity leveled the match with two to play.

Both pairs felt the pressure at seventeen, which was halved in bogey sixes. Once again, Nicklaus showed himself to be as affected by Ryder Cup pressure as any mortal golfer. His second shot found some bushes, and save for Hunt's blowing a par putt, the U.S. pair would have found itself one down.

All square after seventeen meant that all four afternoon matches had made good use of the final hole. Again Nicklaus succumbed to the mounting pressures of international match play, as he hit his drive into the rough. Stepping out from the shadow of his more illustrious partner, Sikes showed he was a world-class player in his own right. He extracted a terrific recovery from the rough that finished just short of the green, where Nicklaus made up for his poor tee shot by leaving his wedge shot a few feet from the flag. The British failed to convert their nine-foot putt, lost the hole to a birdie four, and lost the match by one hole—again.

Having almost been swept in the morning foursomes, the Americans took heed of their captain's words at lunch and came close to turning the tables.

In a nail-biting climax to the afternoon, all four matches went to the last green, with the U.S. side out-toughing the Brits, 3-1.

Afternoon foursomes result: USA 3, GBI 1
Day one result: USA 3½, GBI 4½

Day Two: Morning Fourball

Dave Hill and Dale Douglass (USA) v. Christy O'Connor and Peter Townsend (GBI)

Dave Hill and Dale Douglass, in his first match, immediately found themselves down after the first hole, as O'Connor nailed his approach to the first green and Townsend sank the birdie putt. The British hit double trouble on the 416-yard third hole, where both players hit bad drives into deep rough. Neither could recover to challenge an American par, but the Irishman got the lead back on the 212-yard fourth with a twenty-five-foot birdie putt.

O'Connor severely strained his shoulder digging out of the rough on the third hole, and although he completed this round, he was forced to sit out the afternoon round.

The Americans made a birdie at the sixth to level the match again, which is how it remained after nine holes, with both pairs out in 35. The British retook the lead off the back of O'Connor's ten-foot birdie putt, but the Americans refused to let the British get away, as Hill's birdie on twelve pegged them back.

Townsend made short work of the 517-yard thirteenth, reaching in two majestic shots and beating out an American birdie with his own eagle from more than a dozen feet away. The Americans pulled back on the next hole with another birdie, but they had no answer to O'Connor. Following a deft chip over a bunker, the Irishman holed a birdie putt from eight feet on the par-5 fifteenth to go back up by one.

Even a fine birdie-birdie finish by Hill and Douglass could not make any impact on the narrow British lead, as the birdies were matched, allowing Townsend and O'Connor to hold on to their hard-fought 1-up victory.

Townsend and O'Connor wrapped up the match four under for the last six holes (3-4-4-4-4-4), with an eagle and three birdies at the four closing par 5s, and a bogey at the final par 3.

Raymond Floyd and Miller Barber (USA) v. Brian Huggett and Alex Caygill (GBI)

Floyd and Barber took the first hole with a birdie four, but Huggett and Caygill were one up after making birdies at the par-4 third and par-5 sixth.

A second U.S. birdie on the 410-yard ninth leveled the score line, which remained in stasis as the next seven holes were all halved. The Americans should have won the sixteenth after both British players missed the green with their approaches, but the hosts recovered to make par for the seventh half in a row.

This was Alex Caygill's only appearance in a Ryder Cup match. He stands as one of only six British players never to lose a match in the history of the contest.

On seventeen, American tee shots disappeared into the rough. Barber never found his, while Floyd managed to recover sufficiently to land his third within six feet of the flag. With Barber out of the hole, both opponents with birdie putts, and a tie ball game, Floyd was under pressure to make his birdie putt. He missed from inside six feet to give the opponents their first lead since the second hole.

Raymond Floyd is not the type of player to let a missed putt upset him. He made up for his error in truly magnificent style by holing a twenty-foot eagle putt on the last to halve the match.

In a solid game of fourball, both pairs carded a six-under-par 68 on their best ball.

Lee Trevino and Gene Littler (USA) v. Brian Barnes and Peter Alliss (GBI)

Cometh the hour, cometh the golfer. And that golfer was Lee Trevino.

Off his own ball, Trevino single-handedly took the game to Barnes and Alliss, as Gene Littler struggled to make any impact on the match.

After seven holes, Trevino was three up on the British pair. He birdied a par 3, a par 4, and a par 5 for wins, having also birdied the par-5 first hole, for an opening half.

On the strength of Trevino's display, the U.S. pair was out in 32 against a British 34.

"With Nicklaus and Casper struggling to make an impact, the Americans were looking for a new hero at the head of their team. Trevino came as near as anyone to filling that role."

—PETER RYDE, *Times* (London)

To counter Trevino's one-man crusade, Barnes retaliated with four birdies in seven holes. The ninth, tenth, thirteenth, and fifteenth all fell to Barnes's birdie blitz. In the midst of this Barnes-storming display, Trevino managed to squeeze in a birdie of his own to claim the par-4 eleventh.

With the match all square after fifteen exhilarating holes of "two-man fourball," the tempo slowed . . . for one hole. The sixteenth was halved rather disappointingly in par fours. Ever the showman, Trevino was not yet finished. He birdied the par-5 seventeenth with a magical putt from more than twenty feet to grab a late lead for his side.

Not only did Trevino give his side the lead, but he also sensationally salvaged a half on the last hole with his seventh birdie of the match, securing the one-hole win.

"Trevino practically carried Littler round the course to defeat Barnes and Alliss." —LEONARD CRAWLEY, *London Telegraph*

The Americans were round in 67—the lion's share of the scoring came off Trevino's ball—while the British combined for a 68, unable to beat Trevino between themselves.

Jack Nicklaus and Dan Sikes (USA) v. Tony Jacklin and Neil Coles (GBI)

Paired again, Jack Nicklaus and Dan Sikes covered the first nine holes in an impressive four-under-par 32 strokes, which was matched by Tony Jacklin and Neil Coles. Only three holes were halved going out.

Playing a hunch, Eric Brown had decided to sever the only 100 percent pair from the first day and saddle them up with new partners, in the hope that they would win two matches apart instead of just one together. The British captain's gamble would pay off handsomely, as both Townsend and Jacklin paired up separately for two more wins on the second morning.

The Americans birdied the opening hole, but the British leveled with their own birdie on the 427-yard second. After the third hole was halved, Dan Sikes showed he was not going to settle for being Nicklaus's sidekick, and he pinned his tee shot eighteen inches from the flag. Nicklaus made a two-foot birdie putt on five to go two up, then almost albatrossed the 533-yard sixth after his one-iron approach crept within five feet of the hole: he missed his eagle putt, and his second putt was only good enough to halve the hole in birdie fours.

This was an expensive miss by Nicklaus, as Coles birdied the seventh with an eight-foot putt, while Jacklin mirrored his partner's birdie putt on the eighth to level the score. The 410-yard ninth was the third hole to be halved in this action-packed outward journey.

The ninth match in a row had gone to the last green.

Jacklin sank another eight-foot birdie, at the par-4 tenth, to go one up, and the British retained the lead as the next four holes were halved. Once again, Dan Sikes stepped out of Nicklaus' shadow to birdie the 536-yard fifteenth for a share of the action. Jacklin made a critical putt for a half on sixteen, holing from fifteen feet, to avoid dropping one down.

All square with two to play, the U.S. pair rated as favorites with Nicklaus's longer power game, but the Golden Bear found the golden sand with his second to seventeen, preventing him from putting any pressure on Coles's crucial birdie putt.

Having failed to stop the British from taking a lead with one to play, Nicklaus committed a similar snafu on eighteen, finding a bunker for the second hole in a row. Sikes was unable to bail his partner out this time, and the British were happy with a half on the final green for a one-hole win.

To beat Nicklaus and Sikes, the British pair carded the best round of the morning. Jacklin and Coles shot a nine-under-par 65, one better than their rivals.

In his first two matches, Jack Nicklaus had shown that Ryder Cup pressure even gets to the greats. Partnering Dan Sikes both times, Nicklaus was twice taken to the final hole and emerged with one win and one loss. Not the greatest of starts by one of the greatest of players.

Morning fourball result: USA 1½, GBI 2½

Day Two: Afternoon Fourball

Billy Casper and Frank Beard (USA) v. Peter Butler and Peter Townsend (GBI)

In a lackluster match in which both Casper (badly sprained wrist) and Townsend (3-for-3 in his matches so far) showed the stresses and strains of earlier battles, Beard's touch on the greens proved to be the difference between the sides.

A birdie four at the first hole saw the United States off to a winning start, though Townsend landed two long birdie putts on the fourth and fifth holes to take the lead. The American response was swift and devastating—an eagle on the par-5 sixth—but Townsend and Butler went back on top with a birdie two on the seventh.

The front nine was put to rest with an American birdie to level the match.

The U.S. players went out in 32 strokes, one better than their opponents, but gave that extra stroke away when they bogeyed the tenth to go one down. Despite his bad wrist, Casper managed to drain a thirty-foot birdie putt on the 190-yard twelfth hole to level again. A second consecutive birdie by Casper gave the United States a lead they would not surrender.

At this time, Billy Casper was playing as well as anyone else in the world except Jack Nicklaus. Casper had been the only player besides Nicklaus to win the U.S. money title since 1964, finishing first in 1966 and in 1968.

On sixteen, Butler must have thought his thirty-footer for a birdie three would win the hole, but the Americans conjured up their own birdie to halve the hole and stay one up. Seventeen was halved in par fives, as Casper and Beard—both rested in the morning—outstayed the increasingly tired and increasingly inaccurate Townsend and mostly ineffective Butler, who could not compete with the Americans' power and extra distance.

With a final birdie four on the last hole to give them a two-hole victory, the Americans could consider themselves lucky, as the British challenge had simply petered out.

This two-hole win by the Americans meant the previous ten matches had all reached the last green—with the United States winning five, Britain three.

Dave Hill and Ken Still (USA) v. Brian Huggett and Bernard Gallacher (GBI)

The seventeen holes of this encounter have gone down in Ryder Cup history as the most bad-tempered and controversial of all matches ever played.

Having suffered Trevino's wrath during the opening session, Ken Still had been left out of the intervening two sessions, and the sportsmanship so prevalent on course seemed to pass him by.

The acrimony among the players started on the very first green. As he was about to putt, Huggett first asked Hill to stop moving about, then requested that Still not stand so close behind him.

On the next hole, deliberately interrupting Gallacher's putt, Still shouted to his caddie that he shouldn't be tending the flag and told him to leave it for one of the British caddies. These niggling little incidents lit a smoldering fuse that blew up on the seventh.

With his side two up, Hill missed a putt and holed out from two feet, much to Gallacher's obvious annoyance: the Scotsman told Hill, in no uncertain terms, that he had putted out of turn. Before the match referee could make a ruling, Still picked up Gallacher's marker to his three-foot putt, and said, "You can have the hole and the goddamn Cup!" Still and Huggett got into a shouting match as they marched off up the eighth fairway, and by now the crowd had got in on the act, jeering the suddenly unpopular Americans.

"If looks could kill, Ken Still would have been on quite a few murder charges."
—*Brian Huggett*

More drama than on a daytime soap was to follow on the eighth green. Gallacher conceded Still's short putt to prevent him from holing out and giving Hill a clear line of sight, for a potential hole-winning putt. Drawing upon some colorful language, Still explained to Gallacher that he should not have touched his ball and had conceded the hole. Still was wrong on both counts, but Hill made his putt to win the hole. This gave the Americans a two-hole lead, which they quickly increased on the ninth, after a British bogey.

"As I recall, Dave Hill practically got into a fistfight with one of the Brits, and then one of their guys, Bernard Gallacher, had to be pulled off one of ours. Feelings ran so high that players were getting into arguments with their own teammates. Davey and I had a few words over something, I don't remember what. It was that intense."

—FRANK BEARD, *Making the Turn* (1992)

The British pulled two holes back on eleven and thirteen with a birdie and an eagle to keep this ill-tempered match alive and very much kicking. Hill thankfully settled proceedings, as all true golfers should, firing two perfect shots up the par-5 seventeenth. This set up a ten-foot eagle putt that gave the United States the win, 2 and 1.

Despite the win, Hill refused to shake hands with the match referee.

On the plane journey back to the States, which players from both sides made to travel to a tournament, Ken Still (who had already apologized for his on-course behavior) sought out Brian Huggett and offered to play a practice round with him when they arrived at the course. Whether they kissed and made up was never reported.

Tommy Aaron and Raymond Floyd (USA) v. Maurice Bembridge and Bernard Hunt (GBI)

In a remarkable match, Aaron and Floyd halved twelve holes in a row with Bembridge and Hunt. After halving the first two holes (birdie-par), the Americans birdied the third for a one-hole lead, which they held until the sixteenth, including an amazing run of halved holes from the fourth to the twelfth, nine holes of which were played in strict par, as none of the players could manage a birdie.

With the par 5s at thirteen and fifteen halved in birdies, the British pair finally broke the sequence of halves with an unmatched birdie at sixteen. It was the side's only win of the round—more important, it leveled the match.

True to form, the final two holes were both halved in par fives, though not without some anxiety. History repeated itself as Floyd missed a five-footer for a birdie on the seventeenth—for the second time in the day—while Bembridge missed an even shorter putt on eighteen as the game played out in the descending gloom for an honorable half.

Each pair had won only one hole out of the eighteen played: the United States took the third and the British—who never led—won the sixteenth.

Lee Trevino and Miller Barber (USA) v. Tony Jacklin and Neil Coles (GBI)

Jacklin and Coles must have feared the worst when they drew Lee Trevino in the final match out. After his all-universe performance in the morning, the British pair prepared for a battering (both physical and verbal, in view of the American's reputation).

Trevino's partner, Miller Barber, came into the match in no better form than Gene Littler had shown, and he was still looking for his first win in three games.

Trevino was unable to repeat his morning's opening salvo of birdies, and the British players jumped out to the better start, with two birdies of their own at the first and third holes, to go two up.

The Americans pulled one hole back at the 358-yard fifth, halved the par-5 sixth with a second birdie, and leveled the match on Trevino's twenty-five-foot birdie two at the eighth.

Both pairs went out in 33 strokes to stand all square at the turn.

When Lee Trevino returned to Birkdale in 1971, he would walk off with his first British Open title.

The first bogey of the round cost the Americans the tenth hole and the lead, but Barber equalized the score with a birdie on the 202-yard fourteenth. With darkness falling, the last four holes were halved in par, though the gathering gloom did little to staunch the quality of the golf on display.

Having birdied the first four par 5s on the course, the British pair did not card a five until the very last hole, when another birdie four would have won the hole and the match.

The par 5s at fifteen and seventeen gave up a couple of matching birdies, then both Americans faced eight-foot birdie putts that would snatch a last-gasp win on the final hole. Neither Barber nor Trevino was up to the task, and the Americans settled for a halved match.

In his book *They Call Me Super Mex*, Trevino claims that he was distracted from holing his crucial final putt when his Scottish caddie, Willie, broke an ankle while talking to some fans. Instead of winning the hole, Trevino halved. He later joked, "Hell, the British should have given Willie a team blazer."

A number of players complained about the physical and mental stress of playing two rounds in a day: "With great strain placed on stamina by the intrusion of this extra day, the desirability of having it at all must surely be reconsidered."
—*Peter Ryde,* Times *(London)*

Afternoon fourball result: USA 3, GBI 1

After the British team had raced out to win the opening three matches of the contest, they had only three more wins in the remaining ten pairs matches, as the United States struck back with six wins and four halves to level the standings.

This also completed a remarkable run of matches that finished on the last hole—twelve of the previous thirteen matches had all gone the distance, the only exception being the bad-tempered Hill and Still match, which reached the seventeenth.

Day two result: USA 4½, GBI 3½
Overall match score: USA 8, GBI 8

Day Three: Morning Singles

Raymond Floyd (USA) v. Peter Butler (GBI)

Mirroring the tied match score at the start of the day, Raymond Floyd halved the first five holes with Peter Butler. Butler then made back-to-back birdies on six and seven, and held Floyd at bay to the end.

The American won just two holes all match—the eleventh and fourteenth, albeit both with pars. One down on the last green, Floyd finally managed to make his first and only birdie, but this was matched by Butler, who held on doggedly for a 1-up win.

Butler went out in 35 to Floyd's 37, and these opening nine holes proved to be the difference between the players at the end.

Ken Still (USA) v. Maurice Bembridge (GBI)

Maurice Bembridge drew the short straw against the man with the short fuse, Ken Still. These two had met in Still's first match, in which the British player had come out on top.

Despite playing on his best behavior, Still was down after the opening two holes, losing them both to British birdies. The score remained two up to Bembridge as the next eight holes were all halved in regulation. Still fell four down over the next two holes, bogeying them both.

Four down with six to play seemed a hopeless cause, but Still raised his game and reeled off four wins in the next five holes to level matters after seventeen. Birdie, par, and a Bembridge concession gave Still the three holes from thirteen on. The 401-yard sixteenth was halved in par fours, and the American leveled with a birdie on the par-5 seventeenth.

Just when it seemed Still had got the measure of his opponent, Bembridge produced a telling birdie at the last to cruelly claim the full point.

Frank Beard (USA) v. Christy O'Connor (GBI)

Even though he was still complaining of a sore shoulder, Christy O'Connor did not have to exert himself too much to fend off the disappointing challenge put up by Frank Beard. Out in 40, five more than O'Connor, the American was three down, thanks in the main to bogeys at the first, fifth, and eighth holes.

Frank Beard was in the midst of one of his most profitable years. He was on course to finish atop the U.S. money list for the first and only time, with $175,000 in earnings.

The two early holes Beard did win were both thanks to bogeys by his opponent on a less-than-inspiring front nine of golf

Three up, O'Connor started home in slightly the better form, making hole-winning birdies at eleven and thirteen to run out an easy 5 and 4 victory.

Tommy Aaron (USA) v. Neil Coles (GBI)

Having been off his form in his previous three matches (1-1-1), Tommy Aaron was seen practicing in the darkness in an attempt to get his game sorted out. The long hours seemed to have paid off when Aaron overturned Neil Coles's two-hole lead after ten by winning the next three holes in a row.

The Englishman produced some spectacular golf of his own to wrestle the match from the American. On the par-4 sixteenth, Coles holed a seventeen-footer for a birdie and the hole. On seventeen, he nailed a fairway-wood to a few feet of the flag for an eagle, to grab back the lead. Both players birdied eighteen, giving Coles a one-hole win.

Coles's win meant Britain had won the first four singles matches in the morning, three of them on the final hole.

Dave Hill (USA) v. Peter Townsend (GBI)

Dave Hill put the antagonism of the previous afternoon's fourball fracas behind him, reaching the turn in 32 against Peter Townsend. After the first three holes had been halved in fours, Hill hit a purple patch, winning four of the next five holes.

A weary Townsend was unable to recapture his sparkling form of the previous two days, posting just one win in the fourteen holes played. His birdie at eleven reduced Hill's lead to three, but the American won the next two holes with an ugly bogey four at the twelfth and a much prettier birdie at thirteen.

With a half in par at the 202-yard fourteenth, Hill quickly wrapped up his match, 5 and 4, for America's first point of the day.

Hill did not have a five or worse on his card in fourteen holes—nine fours and five threes for a four-under-par total.

Jack Nicklaus (USA) v. Tony Jacklin (GBI)

Jack Nicklaus had been given an easy time by captain Sam Snead, who had decided to save his rookie ace for the final two singles matches. Snead's plan backfired in the morning, as Nicklaus struggled against the British Open champion, Tony Jacklin.

Level after five holes, Jacklin took the lead with a par five—after Nicklaus found more trouble than he could cope with—on the 533-yard sixth.

Jacklin was out in 34, two better than Nicklaus, who struggled to stay with the Englishman. Jacklin was lifted at every corner of the course by the raucous home crowd.

After twelve holes, Jacklin had trebled his lead with wins at nine, off his own birdie three, and at twelve, where Nicklaus again bogeyed to go three down. Sensing it was time to get busy and start playing some real golf, Nicklaus eagled the 517-yard thirteenth for his first win of the round. Jacklin replied with match-winning birdies at fourteen and fifteen, while Nicklaus closed out with his third bogey of the round.

This gave the Englishman a valuable 4 and 3 win and the prized scalp of the world's greatest golfer, who had been bedeviled by a number of missed short putts.

Billy Casper (USA) v. Brian Barnes (GBI)

The first hole was birdied in superb style as both players looked to grab the early advantage. Barnes kept his momentum going on the third and fourth holes, while Casper bogeyed both holes to drop two down.

As one of the veterans of the team, Casper knew that a lot was riding on his shoulders and claimed two wins by the turn, both on Barnes errors. With only his second birdie on the front nine, Barnes also won the 533-yard sixth hole for a one-hole lead at the turn.

The Scot increased his lead with a birdie two at the twelfth and was still two up with four to play, looking set to record another singles victory for his team on this seemingly triumphant morning.

Casper had other ideas. He proceeded to do nothing less than birdie the last four holes (4-3-4-4) in a remarkable finish that knocked the stuffing out, the ample-framed Barnes.

The astonished Scot also birdied the last hole, but it was too late. Casper made a half with his fourth birdie in a row for a shocking come-from-behind one-hole win.

Lee Trevino (USA) v. Peter Alliss (GBI)

This was the last Ryder Cup match for Peter Alliss, stalwart of the British team since 1953. With an early spring in his step, Alliss birdied the first two holes, but Trevino soon leveled and went ahead on the tenth with a birdie.

Despite being two under for his round, Alliss putted poorly in his 2 and 1 loss. He claimed afterward that he had consistently struck his approach shots nearer to the flag than the American had.

With no confidence in his putting game, Alliss requested to sit out the afternoon session for the good of the team—and gallantly bowed out of the Ryder Cup.

This was only the fifth time in eighteen Ryder Cup matches that Britain won the opening singles.

After nine Ryder Cups, Peter Alliss finished with a playing record of 10-15-5, having endured some of the leanest years the British had suffered. He actually had a winning record on his own, 5-4-3, but a poor doubles record of 5-11-2 blighted his figures.

Morning singles result: USA 3, GBI 5

Day Three: Afternoon Singles

Miller Barber (USA) v. Maurice Bembridge (GBI)

Although the American did not make any birdies in his first nine holes—just eight pars and a bogey at the seventh for a half—Miller Barber turned into the golfing equivalent of Sweeney Todd on the back nine, cutting Maurice Bembridge down to size.

With a double bogey on the ninth, Bembridge had lost the plot quicker than a stage prompter in a blackout. He reached the turn four down, in a six-over-par 42, to hand the match to Barber, who was out in 37.

The American quickly picked up a couple more birdies to finish the match off early on the twelvth.

Barber's 7 and 6 destruction of Bembridge was easily the biggest win of the week.

Lee Trevino (USA) v. Bernard Gallacher (GBI)

In spite of taking the lead twice, at the first and fifth holes, Lee Trevino reached the turn one down. Bernard Gallacher, out in 33, had birdies at eight and nine, to go along with a birdie at the third.

Out in 35, Trevino also lost the twelfth, after the Scot left his sweet-as-a-nut two-iron tee shot close enough for another winning birdie putt.

Trevino also lost the fourteenth and fifteenth with two bogeys, as twenty-year-old Gallacher closed out, 4 and 3, with a six-foot par putt to win.

GALLACHER'S LION HEART TYPIFIES BRITISH SPIRIT
—London Telegraph *headline*

This afternoon singles defeat ended Trevino's run of four straight wins in the previous three days. Having played in all six matches, Trevino had lost only his first foursomes match—when he sportingly conceded a hole while partnering Ken Still on Friday morning—against Gallacher.

Dave Hill (USA) v. Brian Barnes (GBI)

Out in a four-under-par 32, Dave Hill built a commanding lead over Brian Barnes, who may have still been suffering from his late-morning capitulation against Billy Casper.

Hill needed only two hole-winning birdies to establish a comfortable three-hole lead by the turn as Barnes bogeyed the sixth and ninth holes.

Coming back home, Hill managed to card four fives in the seven holes played but still increased his advantage. The Englishman bogeyed the last three holes he played to stagger to a second, even more demoralizing, loss of the day, this time by 4 and 2.

Dale Douglass (USA) v. Peter Butler (GBI)

Peter Butler was three up on Dale Douglass after just four holes, but the American fought back to level on the tenth. With birdies on five and six, the American was one down at the turn and drew level when his bogey at ten was a shot better than Butler's second six of the round.

Butler pulled his game together, winning the par 5s at thirteen and fifteen with birdies, and taking fourteen in par, to go three up. The Englishman finished off the match, 3 and 2, with an offsetting bogey at the par-4 sixteenth.

Before the contest, many thought that thirty-seven-year-old Butler (a golf pro since 1948) was too old for the rigors of a three-day match-play format. Although he was winless (0-5-2) his previous seven times out, he proved his critics wrong with two priceless victories in the last-day singles.

Gene Littler (USA) v. Christy O'Connor (GBI)

Gene Littler started fast, making birdies on the first three holes to quickly jump out three up against Christy O'Connor. Out in 35, the American was still three up at the turn.

With a British lead of two points coming into the final singles session, Sam Snead gambled by saving his only two veterans—Littler and Casper—to the end, knowing he had Jack Nicklaus to come.

Although O'Connor managed to win three holes coming home, Littler posted a couple of wins at eleven and twelve to hold on for a 2 and 1 win over the Irishman.

The overall match could not have been any closer. With just two matches still out on course, Great Britain needed one and a half points to win the Cup, while the United States needed just one point to retain the Cup.

Billy Casper (USA) v. Brian Huggett (GBI)

In a match both players knew would be crucial to the final outcome, the lead changed hands three times on the outward nine, with Casper up by one after the tenth, following back-to-back bogeys from the Welshman.

The next six holes were halved, and then the American failed to get out of a bunker on sixteen. After he picked up, Huggett was back level with two to play.

Casper fared much better on seventeen, leaving his chip, from off the back of the green, hard by the flag. Huggett was faced with the sort of six-footer that makes pro golfers take up needlepoint. The Welshman held his nerve and holed the putt to send the match up the final fairway all square.

On Huggett's six-footer on seventeen: *"That has to be the greatest putt of the whole deal."* —DAN SIKES

Both players safely reached the final green in two. Casper failed to hole his eagle putt, opening the door for Huggett to win the hole, but Huggett ran his ball a few feet past. As the Welshman faced another tricky five-footer for a precious half, a tremendous roar swept in from the seventeenth. Huggett thought that the tumultuous crowd noise could mean only one thing—Jacklin had won his match.

The wee Welshman thought that he was standing over a putt to win the Ryder Cup. He took a deep breath, eyed up the hole, and stroked the ball home. Having halved the hole, Huggett shook hands with Casper, then burst into tears, thinking he had achieved a lifelong ambition—to win the Ryder Cup for his country.

Unfortunately, the match behind had not exactly worked out as Huggett had hoped or dreamed. He later recalled, "I heard this enormous roar from the seventeenth green. It was a winning roar. So, being very good at math, you see, working it out, I thought, now if you pop this one in, we're going to win the Ryder Cup. So I thought, 'That's it.' I broke down and shed a few tears, only to learn at the side of the green that the enormous roar was Tony holing to get level with Jack Nicklaus."

Both of Snead's veterans came through for him in the clutch. Littler gained a win, while Casper battled for a valuable half.

Dan Sikes (USA) v. Neil Coles (GBI)

Dan Sikes was two up after nine against Neil Coles, owing in part to sixes at the par-4 second and the par-5 sixth. Struggling to go the distance after playing in all six matches, Coles reached the turn in 40 shots, two worse than his opponent, who was not finding the going any easier.

The standard of play did not improve on the way home. Sikes won three of the next four holes and lost the other, as a wild profusion of bogeys resulted in holes being lost rather than won.

Coles was hoping for a repeat of his earlier foursomes win over his opponent.

With history being set in the matches fore and aft, it was a welcome relief when these two finally stepped off the course with Sikes having claimed a 4 and 3 victory.

Jack Nicklaus (USA) v. Tony Jacklin (GBI)

This was a much-anticipated rematch of the morning singles that had seen Tony Jacklin triumph over Jack Nicklaus. This time Nicklaus drew first blood on the fourth with a birdie two, but the Englishman leveled at the sixth and took the lead on eight—thanks to two birdies of his own.

Nicklaus played the "least worst" golf on the ninth, winning with a bogey five to Jacklin's double bogey, to level once again. After further changes of lead, the two golfers teed off all square at sixteen, which Nicklaus took after the Englishman found a bunker with his headstrong drive.

FINAL ACT IN RYDER CUP IS WELL CAST
—Times *(London) headline*

With the overall match score at 15½ points apiece, and the Ryder Cup slowly slipping from his grasp, Jacklin needed something special on the seventeenth. Both players hit fine tee shots, Jacklin's five-iron approach stopping at the front of the green, fifty-five feet short of the distant flag. Nicklaus laid his seven-iron much nearer to the hole to take a crucial psychological advantage. Faced with losing the hole and the Cup, Jacklin rammed his oh-so-long putt straight at the hole. As his ball disappeared into the cup for a miraculous eagle, the crowd, which had stayed solemnly silent as if in mass prayer, erupted.

This was the tumultuous noise Huggett heard way up on the final green. When Nicklaus missed his longish putt, Jacklin had leveled the match—not won it, as Huggett had wrongly surmised.

The stage was set for the final showdown between the countries' two big guns. All that was at stake—after thirty-one (and seventeen-eighteenths) keenly contested matches—was the Ryder Cup.

Nicklaus (as the pair walked off the final tee): "How do you feel, Tony?"

Jacklin: "Bloody awful!"

Nicklaus: "I thought you might, but if it's any consolation, so do I."

The pair stood on the eighteenth tee and traded praiseworthy drives down the fairway, Jacklin's slightly ahead.

Nicklaus guided his approach to the center of the green, twenty-four feet from the flag. Under the extreme pressure of twenty thousand watching eyes and ten thousand beating hearts, Jacklin overhit his eight-iron approach. The crowd's initial joy, as the ball bounced just beyond the flag, turned to dismay. The ball rolled onto and almost off the back of the green—thirty feet away.

First to putt, Jacklin again sent his ball straight on line for the hole, but it was always going to come up short, slowing and stopping eighteen inches shy of the cup. Even Golden Bears have dreams, and Jack Nicklaus must have dreamed of this moment. He had a putt that could win the Cup for America. He struck the ball confidently, too confidently, misjudging the weight as his ball ran four feet too far.

With Jacklin well inside him, Nicklaus found the tables had turned, and he almost certainly needed to hole his putt to save the Ryder Cup. His second putt was straight and true, which meant the United States could not lose the trophy. Such were the alternating fortunes thrust on these two men on the final green.

Everyone's attention switched to Jacklin, who looked as fidgety and apprehensive as the awestruck gallery. Before Jacklin could even contemplate holing his putt, Nicklaus bent down, picked up Jacklin's marker, and carved himself an enormous niche in sports history.

Nicklaus handed Jacklin his marker and said, "I don't think you would have missed that putt . . . but in these circumstances I would never give you the opportunity."

With that one gesture Nicklaus not only settled the outcome of the Ryder Cup but also erased much of the bitterness that remained from the petty sniping that had gone on before. Great men rise to great occasions, and they come no greater than Jack Nicklaus from Columbus, Ohio.

Both players went out in 33 and returned in 36 to card five-under-par rounds—very creditable, considering the pressure heaped on them.

"I didn't think he was going to concede it. I rather think his gesture was more of a personal gesture to me. . . . A two-foot putt, it was missable, unquestionably. . . . And that meant all the good work I had done by winning the British Open would have been undone if I had a heart seizure or a brain seizure over that two-foot putt." —Tony Jacklin

Unfortunately for Jacklin and his par-5-size ego, Nicklaus had other ideas about the concession: *"I don't care if it was Tony Jacklin. It doesn't matter who the Ryder Cup player might have been. To put that on his shoulders is wrong. It's not in the spirit of the game to turn away a whole week's golf, a whole golfing continent against another golfing continent, on a twenty-inch putt."* —Jack Nicklaus

On the conceded putt: "I'm sure that's exactly what Samuel Ryder had in mind when he donated the Cup."
—*Dave Marr*

This day in Ryder Cup history can also lay claim to adding another small part to the Nicklaus legend. For the first time in his pro career, Nicklaus had to play two full rounds in a day. Finding himself overly tired and listless after his two matches against Jacklin, Nicklaus decided to shed some weight. He dropped from 210 to 180 pounds in five weeks.

Afternoon singles result: USA 5, GBI 3
Day three result: USA 8, GBI 8
Overall match score: USA 16, GBI 16

Recap

And so the Ryder Cup was shared for the first time in thirty-eight years, with the United States officially retaining the trophy, since they were its holders coming into the match.

To prove how close this Ryder Cup was, eighteen of the thirty-two matches went to the last green. The United States won six, the British won six, and six matches were halved—it could not have been more equal.

In a sporting gesture as magnanimous as Nicklaus's on the eighteenth green, the president of the PGA of America, Leo Fraser, announced at the postmatch banquet that both countries would hold the trophy for a year each. He handed the Ryder Cup to his British counterpart, Lord Derby, and it was the first time in a dozen years that the British had got their hands back on the gold trophy (albeit just one hand). The Cup would be passed back to the U.S. PGA after twelve months. Even Eric Brown managed to crack a smile or two.

This had been the first time since 1957 that America had not won the match outright, but it was a result that Jack Nicklaus was happy with. He had waited a long time to get his first shot at the Cup, and he made sure that his rookie year would not be forgotten for a long time.

Not everyone on the U.S. team was as sportingly minded as Jack Nicklaus. Said Frank Beard in *Making the Turn* (1992), "Oh, we were irate. I was, for sure. It may have been a great gesture for Jack, but the other eleven of us had worked very hard and wanted to win. He just arrogantly assumed that the team and the country, individually and together, would want him to make this sporting gesture. . . . Looking back, I recognize the conceded putt as the act of a man of considerable class and sophistication. But I guarantee you, if I'd had the same decision to make, Jacklin would have had to show us he could make a four-footer with the weight of a whole nation on his shoulders."

Sam Snead was of a similar mind: "When it happened, all the boys thought it was ridiculous to give him that putt. We went over there to win, not to be good ole boys. I never would have given a putt like that—except maybe to my brother."

Match Results (Winning side marked in *italics*.)

Thursday, September 18—Morning Foursomes

	USA	GBI	Score
1.	Miller Barber Raymond Floyd	*Brian Huggett* *Neil Coles*	3 and 2
2.	Lee Trevino Ken Still	*Bernard Gallacher* *Maurice Bembridge*	2 and 1
3.	Dave Hill Tommy Aaron	*Tony Jacklin* *Peter Townsend*	3 and 1
4.	Billy Casper Frank Beard	Christy O'Connor Peter Alliss	halved

Thursday, September 18—Afternoon Foursomes

	USA	GBI	Score
5.	*Dave Hill* *Tommy Aaron*	Neil Coles Brian Huggett	1-up
6.	*Lee Trevino* *Gene Littler*	Bernard Gallacher Maurice Bembridge	2-up
7.	Billy Casper Frank Beard	*Tony Jacklin* *Peter Townsend*	1-up
8.	*Jack Nicklaus* *Dan Sikes*	Peter Butler Bernard Hunt	1-up

Day one result: USA 3½, GBI 4½

Friday, September 19—Morning Fourball

	USA	GBI	Score
9.	Dave Hill Dale Douglass	*Christy O'Connor* *Peter Townsend*	1-up
10.	Raymond Floyd Miller Barber	Brian Huggett Alex Caygill	halved
11.	*Lee Trevino* *Gene Littler*	Brian Barnes Peter Alliss	1 up
12.	Jack Nicklaus Dan Sikes	*Tony Jacklin* *Neil Coles*	1-up

Friday, September 19—Afternoon Fourball

	USA	GBI	Score
13.	*Billy Casper* *Frank Beard*	Peter Butler Peter Townsend	2-up
14.	*Dave Hill* *Ken Still*	Brian Huggett Bernard Gallacher	2 and 1
15.	Tommy Aaron Raymond Floyd	Maurice Bembridge Bernard Hunt	halved
16.	Lee Trevino Miller Barber	Tony Jacklin Neil Coles	halved

Day two result: USA 4½, GBI 3½

Overall match score: USA 8, GBI 8

Saturday, September 20—Morning Singles

	USA	GBI	Score
17.	Raymond Floyd	*Peter Butler*	1-up
18.	Ken Still	*Maurice Bembridge*	1-up
19.	Frank Beard	*Christy O'Connor*	5 and 4
20.	Tommy Aaron	*Neil Coles*	1-up
21.	*Dave Hill*	Peter Townsend	5 and 4
22.	Jack Nicklaus	*Tony Jacklin*	4 and 3
23.	*Billy Casper*	Brian Barnes	1-up
24.	*Lee Trevino*	Peter Alliss	2 and 1

Saturday, September 20—Afternoon Singles

	USA	GBI	Score
25.	*Miller Barber*	Maurice Bembridge	7 and 6
26.	Lee Trevino	*Bernard Gallacher*	4 and 3
27.	*Dave Hill*	Brian Barnes	4 and 2
28.	Dale Douglass	*Peter Butler*	3 and 2
29.	*Gene Littler*	Christy O'Connor	2 and 1
30.	Billy Casper	Brian Huggett	halved
31.	*Dan Sikes*	Neil Coles	4 and 3
32.	Jack Nicklaus	Tony Jacklin	halved

Day three result: USA 8, GBI 8

Overall match score: USA 16, GBI 16

1971

Old Warson St. Louis, Missouri United States September 16–18	**United States 18½**	**Great Britain and Ireland 13½**
	Miller Barber	Harry Bannerman
	Frank Beard	Brian Barnes
	Billy Casper	Maurice Bembridge
	Charles Coody	Peter Butler
	Gardner Dickinson	Neil Coles
	Gene Littler	Bernard Gallacher
	Jack Nicklaus	John Garner
	Arnold Palmer	Brian Huggett
	Mason Rudolph	Tony Jacklin
	J. C. Snead	Christy O'Connor, Sr.
	Dave Stockton	Peter Oosterhuis
	Lee Trevino	Peter Townsend
	Captain	**Captain**
	Jay Hebert	Eric Brown

Winning Spirit of St. Louis

The British team arrived in the United States as all visiting Ryder Cup teams had been welcomed—as overwhelming underdogs. Despite the British heroics in winning a share of the trophy in 1969, few felt that the Americans would be such a soft touch at home.

After receiving a less-than-courteous welcome from their hosts, Eric Brown said, "We went to an official dinner and the food was cold. We came out and had to stand around like tramps because there was no transport to our hotel. These things have made the boys angry. I'm pleased to see that they are just a little bit niggled and they can't wait to get at the Yanks."

American captain Jay Hebert held four aces in Nicklaus, Palmer, Casper, and Trevino. The rest of the playing cards he could shuffle around were not too shabby either.

Lee Trevino was a Triple Crown winner, having won the U.S., British, and Canadian Open championships in 1971.

New blood came in the form of master putter Dave Stockton, Masters champion Charles Coody, Mason Rudolph, and J. C.

Snead. (J. C. Snead was the nephew of Sam, making them the first uncle and nephew pair to have played in the Ryder Cup.)

Eric Brown was retained as British captain as a reward for guiding his team to the half in 1969, but he had few of the riches that Hebert had. Tony Jacklin had won the U.S. Open the previous year, but the rest of the team seemed to be mere also-rans as far as the Americans were concerned. Brown's green recruits came in the shape of Bannerman, Garner, and, the one light on the horizon, the future Ryder Cup Hall of Famer Peter Oosterhuis.

With eight players under age thirty, the youngest-ever British team averaged twenty-nine years of age, while the hosts—with five players over forty—were nearly thirty-five years old per man.

Course Details

Old Warson is set in a suburb of St. Louis. Water comes into play on at least seven holes, but this Robert Trent Jones course is balanced by four right-hand and four left-hand dogleg par 4s.

Hole	Distance	Par	Hole	Distance	Par
1	421	4	10	441	4
2	381	4	11	448	4
3	206	3	12	590	5
4	393	4	13	188	3
5	468	4	14	360	4
6	530	5	15	458	4
7	208	3	16	620	5
8	465	4	17	220	3
9	419	4	18	456	4
		35			**36 = Par 71 (7,272 yards)**

Course designer: Robert Trent Jones

Day One: Morning Foursomes

The one-hundred-degree heat encountered in the practice days was replaced by much cooler weather—in the mid-seventies—after a rainstorm delayed the start by seventy-five minutes. This unscheduled early-morning downpour meant the postponement of the opening ceremony until the next day.

Billy Casper and Miller Barber (USA) v. Christy O'Connor and Neil Coles (GBI)

Opening the match for the United States, Casper and Barber fell behind after O'Connor left his tee shot to the third twelve feet from the flag, after which Coles buried the birdie putt.

The Americans recovered and had the match all square by the turn, but they got hit by a one-two sucker punch on ten and eleven to drop two down.

"So much rainwater had accumulated on the ninth green, that the officials ordered a new cup to be cut before play got under way."
—*Lincoln A. Werden,* New York Times

Following a fine birdie three at the eleventh, the British pair combined for an ugly seven on the much longer twelfth.

Coles struck back at the par-3 thirteenth, holing a lengthy putt for a birdie, although Casper missed a much simpler two-footer for the half. Back two up, Coles and O'Connor halved the last four holes played for a creditable and rare 2 and 1 opening win for the British.

Arnold Palmer and Gardner Dickinson (USA) v. Peter Townsend and Peter Oosterhuis (GBI)

With his first putt in the Ryder Cup, Oosterhuis announced himself as a star in the making, holing from more than sixty feet on the first green to win the hole with a birdie three.

Palmer and Dickinson soon fought back, and on the strength of Palmer's fifteen-foot birdie putt at the ninth, they reached the turn in 34, one up on Townsend and Oosterhuis. Dickinson stroked an approach to five feet of the par-5 twelfth, and Palmer rolled home the birdie putt to increase the U.S. lead.

The Americans lost the fourteenth when Dickinson almost sliced his tee shot into a parking lot and Palmer duffed his pitch, unable to force his backswing through a hedge.

Troubles of this nature were few and far between for the Americans, who came to the last hole one up. Palmer, who had saved the best for last, played a magnificent controlled approach, screwing back his six-iron some twenty feet to within a matter of inches. This great shot, under pressure, set up Dickinson for birdie and a two-hole win.

Frank Beard and Charles Coody (USA) v. Peter Butler and Maurice Bembridge (GBI)

One down after six, the American pairing of Coody and Beard fell further behind as Bembridge and Butler won the next two holes. Bembridge dropped a twelve-footer on the 208-yard seventh for a hole-winning birdie, while the U.S. pair's failure to make par cost the side the eighth.

"Our golfers, who had practiced in 100-degree heat, obviously relished the cooler weather following overnight rain which delayed the start by more than an hour."
—*Michael McDonnell,* London Mail

Just as the game seemed to have slipped away from the Americans, it was given back to them with a horrendous run of British blunders after the turn. Carding five bogeys in a row (5-5-6-4-5), the British blew apart their good work and managed to level the match, as the Americans bogeyed a couple of holes themselves.

In spite of this sudden slump in their form, the Britishers pulled their game together over the closing holes.

A fighting four at the last, thanks to a brilliant recovery and a clutch par putt by Butler, was enough to see the visitors through to a one-hole win on the final green, after Coody's drive had found the trees and Beard's recovery hit a branch en route to bogey.

Jack Nicklaus and Dave Stockton (USA) v. Tony Jacklin and Brian Huggett (GBI)

The long-hitting Nicklaus partnered the sure-putting Stockton in a pairing that the U.S. captain thought would pay dividends, but the theory did not work out in practice. The two ill-suited partners failed to sparkle.

The American pair went out in 39, four over par, to be three down to Jacklin and Huggett.

It was Jacklin and Huggett who had the better of the early exchanges; they did not have to break par on their way to a three-hole lead after nine. The Americans dropped the tenth with another bogey, then almost fought their way back into the match on the back nine.

Having let his partner down with his long game, Stockton showed why he was more at home with a putter in his hands. He holed birdie putts at thirteen and fourteen to halve the British lead. With the Americans' tails up, Nicklaus poured a twelve-footer into the cup at fifteen, but Jacklin spoiled the American celebrations by matching the birdie to keep the lead at two.

The Americans were unable to four-peat, as they could manage only a par on the sixteenth, but the British combined superbly all the way up the 620 yards to the hole, where a final twenty-five-foot birdie putt from Jacklin won them the match, 3 and 2.

This was the fourth time Tony Jacklin had faced Jack Nicklaus in five Ryder Cup matchups. The Englishman had managed to win three and halve one.

Morning foursomes result: USA 1, GBI 3

The 3-to-1 score after the first session was the best start ever made by a British team in the Ryder Cup in the United States. Somehow the British had worked out how to play the first session, having recorded their best start ever in 1969 with a 3½-½ opening burst.

On the surprise British lead at lunch on the first day: "I'm glad it's working out this way. Palmer said it would be a cinch. He shouldn't shoot his mouth off."
—*Anonymous U.S. player*

Day One: Afternoon Foursomes

Billy Casper and Miller Barber (USA) v. Harry Bannerman and Bernard Gallacher (GBI)

Eric Brown made only one change to his triumphant morning pairings. Despite their fine victory in the morning, Brown rested the oldies Coles and O'Connor, and in their place inserted the youth movement of Bannerman and Gallacher—with equally good effect.

In their first match, the all-Scottish twosome was paired against Casper and Barber, who had been beaten in the morning by the sidelined British oldies.

Brown was on a roll with his selections. His youngsters doubled the Americans' misery by inflicting defeat by the same score they had suffered in the morning, 2 and 1.

Arnold Palmer and Gardner Dickinson (USA) v. Peter Oosterhuis and Peter Townsend (GBI)

Having prevailed by 2-up in the morning over the same opponents, Palmer and Dickinson found themselves down to Oosterhuis and Townsend for most of this close match.

One up after fourteen, the British pair fatefully missed the fifteenth green to allow the Americans to draw level.

At the inordinately long 620-yard sixteenth, Dickinson wedged his third shot close enough for Palmer to birdie. Having won two holes in a row, the Americans closed up shop and halved the final two holes to record their second win of the day over the two Peters, who were not disgraced in carding a 69.

Lee Trevino and Mason Rudolph (USA) v. Tony Jacklin and Brian Huggett (GBI)

All square after sixteen, Jacklin and Huggett appeared to have thrown the match away when they failed to find the seventeenth green in regulation. Trevino and Rudolph won the hole and took a one-hole lead to the eighteenth.

Pumped up, Trevino smashed his approach way over the final green and onto the clubhouse lawn. Jacklin muffed his approach, and Huggett left his pitch shy of the putting surface. With the American ball deemed still in play, Rudolph delicately chipped off the hallowed club turf to the regulation green. Still not on the green, Jacklin chipped in from thirty-five feet for par—to the obvious delight of his excitable and overemotional partner.

JACKO SUPER-SHOT CLINCHES BEST-EVER START IN U.S.
—London Mail *headline*

Trevino had a long, long putt to halve the hole and win the match, but he failed to deliver and the British pair escaped with a last-ditch half, having parred the last hole without the use of a putter.

Jack Nicklaus and J. C. Snead (USA) v. Maurice Bembridge and Peter Butler (GBI)

At the first tee of his first foursomes match: "Jack, I have never done this before. You tell me if I do anything wrong."
—*J. C. Snead*

Nicklaus had not been happy with his ill-fitting partner from the morning, and his captain was quick to pair him with a more made-to-measure companion. Hebert chose the equally long-hitting rookie J. C. Snead in the afternoon, and the pair hit it off immediately—out in 34.

The Americans lost just one hole on the front nine, and that only came about when Butler chipped in on the ninth for a hole-winning birdie.

Not only did the U.S. partners match each other with their long drives and irons, but they also combined well in and around the greens, carding only one bogey in the fifteen holes played.

Against this welter of consistent scoring, and outdistanced by their too-powerful opponents, Bembridge and Butler—who were one over par for their round—had no answer, crashing to a 5 and 3 defeat.

Afternoon foursomes result: USA 2½, GBI 1½
Day one result: USA 3½, GBI 4½

"This is the first time a British team in America has gone into the second day with a lead." —Eric Brown

Day Two: Morning Fourball

Britain had not won the fourball format since its inception in 1963: *"Our crisis will come on the second day in the fourball matches when the Americans, with 'two-barrels' to fire at every hole, will be deadly."*
—Michael McDonnell, *London Mail*

Unfortunately for the high-flying British team, their captain did not know the meaning of "If it ain't broke, don't fix it!" Eric Brown tinkered with his winning pairings, dropping his top player as he tried to fix what was not broke.

Lee Trevino and Mason Rudolph (USA) v. Brian Barnes and Christy O'Connor (GBI)

All square at the turn, this match stayed close until the eleventh, when Trevino and Rudolph asserted their authority to pull out a 2 and 1 win over O'Connor and Barnes.

"Barnes and O'Connor were level par when they shook hands with Rudolph and Trevino. Britain were playing well—but the Americans were playing better." —Rex Bellamy, *Times* (London)

Frank Beard and J. C. Snead (USA) v. Neil Coles and John Garner (GBI)

Eric Brown was forced to make a last-minute change to his starting lineup when Peter Butler fell ill and was confined to his hotel bed. In his place came rookie John Garner to partner Neil Coles against the pairing of Frank Beard and J. C. Snead.

All square at the turn, this match followed a pattern similar to that of the first, with the Americans finishing the stronger for a 2 and 1 win.

Arnold Palmer and Gardner Dickinson (USA) v. Peter Oosterhuis and Bernard Gallacher (GBI)

Two down after three holes, Palmer and Dickinson went one up on Gallacher and Oosterhuis with three wins in a row of their own, climaxed by Palmer's birdie four at the sixth.

CADDIE'S CHAT COSTS US A VITAL HOLE
—London Mail *headline*

Palmer stuck a glorious tee shot six feet from the flag on the 208-yard seventh, and Gallacher's American caddie innocently asked Palmer what club he had used. Palmer told him a five iron. The players finished the hole in par threes, but the British pair lost the hole. The match referee explained to the dumbstruck British pair that when Gallacher's caddie had asked Palmer what club he had used, he had transgressed the rules by asking for advice from an opposing player. The penalty was the loss of the hole, putting the British down by two. Although Palmer asked for the penalty to be overruled, his plea went unanswered.

Gallacher's fifty-five-year-old caddie, Jack McLeod, was deeply upset after the match. "I've been a Palmer fan for years," he said. "I just admired his great shot and asked him out of interest what club he took. It was natural. I just didn't think." McLeod was not as upset as Eric Brown, who complained, "It's lousy. Why should we be responsible for the caddies the Americans give us?"

Having won four holes in a row on the front nine, the Americans almost repeated the feat on the back nine; they notched three more wins in a row from the twelfth, with two birdies followed by a par.

With the momentum running in their favor, Palmer and Dickinson finally ran out easy 5 and 4 winners.

In the end, losing the seventh on a technicality did not really prove too decisive or costly to the British, who were thoroughly beaten on the back nine.

In this, their fifth and last match together, including the '67 competition, Palmer and Dickinson set a Ryder Cup record as the most productive U.S. pair, with five victories and no defeats.

Jack Nicklaus and Gene Littler (USA) v. Peter Townsend and Harry Bannerman (GBI)

As with the first two matches, the Americans—this time Nicklaus and Littler—prevailed 2 and 1.

"Bannerman and Townsend were three under par when they lost—which fairly indicates the quality of golf Littler and Nicklaus were playing."
— Rex Bellamy, *Sunday Times* (London)

Morning fourball result: USA 4, GBI 0

After a record lead on the first day, the British crumbled on the second morning, suffering a humiliating 4-0 sweep. With three birdies among them at the first hole, for a brighter-than-usual start to the morning, the British pairs then fell away, losing all four matches. That three of these defeats came as late as the seventeenth hole was little comfort for the visitors.

Day Two: Afternoon Fourball

Lee Trevino and Billy Casper (USA) v. Peter Oosterhuis and Bernard Gallacher (GBI)

Casper and Trevino were made to work hard by Oosterhuis and Gallacher just to remain all square after nine. So it came as no surprise when the British pair opened up a two-hole lead with wins on ten and eleven.

The Americans were not going to go down without a fight, and they leveled the match before Oosterhuis struck the shot of the round to regain the lead. On the monster sixteenth, the English rookie played his pitch across the water to seven feet to win the hole.

Gallacher made a gallant four on the last hole to hold off the final American thrust, and the British pair held on for a morale-boosting win by one hole.

The British had gone round in a four-under-par 67, with the Americans two shots back.

Gene Littler and J. C. Snead (USA) v. Tony Jacklin and Brian Huggett (GBI)

With both Littler and Snead playing (with different partners) in the morning massacre, a rested Jacklin and Huggett must have liked their chances of success in the afternoon.

All square after eleven holes, both sides had claimed a brace of birdies to that point. At the 590-yard twelfth, Littler's twelve-footer was good enough for a British six. One up soon became two when, at the short thirteenth, Littler's fine tee shot sailed over the water to set up a birdie two.

From here the British pair had no answer and went down rather too tamely to a 2 and 1 defeat.

Jack Nicklaus and Arnold Palmer (USA) v. Peter Townsend and Harry Bannerman (GBI)

The dream pairing of Palmer and Nicklaus did not disappoint the large crowd that followed them around. They completed the first nine holes in an amazing 30 strokes but found themselves down to the unsung pair of Townsend and Bannerman, who had more than matched the two maestros all the way in the best match of the week. Against mere mortals, six British birdies in the first seven holes should have been worth at least a four-hole lead—but Townsend and Bannerman were not playing mere mortals in Nicklaus and Palmer.

The first hole was a signal to how the rest of this enthralling match would be played. Townsend lofted his approach to two feet of the flag for an opening birdie, but Palmer answered with a much longer birdie putt for the half. Bannerman sank a ten-footer for an unanswered birdie on the second and repeated the dose on the third to go two up.

After the fourth had been halved, Townsend had less luck than his partner in choosing where to birdie holes, as he made three in succession and did not win a single hole. Nicklaus matched one birdie, while Palmer accounted for the other two.

This was Townsend's fourth match of the contest, almost all of which had gone to the last hole, and he had lost all four! He would also lose his second singles match on the last hole.

The undisputed highlight of the front nine came when Nicklaus won the eighth with a see-it-or-don't-believe-it eighty-foot putt that never looked as if it would miss the hole. With the ninth hole halved in birdie twos, the British were out in an amazing 29 strokes, one better than the American legends.

Back to only one down after nine, the golfing gods moved heaven and earth on their way to erasing the lead. Credited with a 66 off his own ball, Nicklaus proved the match winner as he chipped out of the rough to within a few inches on the fourteenth to level the match, then drained a sixteen-footer on the last for his sixth birdie and the win.

After the youthful British pair had gone round in 65 only to be beaten by the U.S. pair, who shot a 64, Arnold Palmer said, "They played some great golf. They gave us a hell of a battle."

Charles Coody and Frank Beard (USA) v. Christy O'Connor and Neil Coles (GBI)

Coody and Beard made a breathtaking start to their match against Coles and O'Connor, racing to four up after just five holes.

But . . . by the ninth the British pair had come back level, after carding four consecutive birdies for four wins. O'Connor birdied the sixth, and a white-hot Coles fired in birdies at the next three holes.

The American pair took twelve and thirteen, before Coles made two more birdies, at sixteen and seventeen, in what was turning into a personal duel between him and the Americans.

O'Connor almost got in on the act at the last hole, where his birdie putt stopped right on the edge of the cup and refused to drop. With darkness making the players almost invisible from the clubhouse, Beard rolled home a four-footer to halve the hole and the match.

After all his teammates had retired for the night: "Perhaps it is early to bed for them tonight, hah! But will they sleep? It is not what time you get to bed that counts, it's the quality of the sleep you enjoy when you are there."
—*Christy O'Connor, as he downed another cold beer*

Afternoon fourball result: USA 2½, GBI 1½
Day two result: USA 6½, GBI 1½
Overall match score: USA 10, GBI 6

Day Three: Morning Singles

Lee Trevino (USA) v. Tony Jacklin (GBI)

With the United States holding a four-shot advantage in the match, a dispirited Tony Jacklin knew that the weight of the British reply rested on his slim shoulders. He was not up for the task of savior. Trevino, who knew the benefit of a fast start, proceeded to win four of the first five holes against an opponent who did not seem to have the stomach for the contest.

More by luck than design, Jacklin battled his way back into the match, catching a couple of lucky breaks along the way. The branches of a tree stopped his ball from flying out-of-bounds after one wayward shot, and an overhit approach to another green snagged in the flag and dropped down by the cup.

Having battled back to one down, Jacklin saw his luck run out and went down by one hole on the final green.

Dave Stockton (USA) v. Bernard Gallacher (GBI)

This was the American's first match since the disappointing loss alongside Jack Nicklaus in the opening foursomes. The Scot, however, had enjoyed two fine wins in the pairs over Billy Casper, having suffered his only setback against the unbeatable Palmer and Dickinson combo.

Playing on his own suited Stockton, who was able to find his rhythm, but he needed to be at his best just to get a hard-fought half with Gallacher, who once again rose to the occasion in the Ryder Cup.

Mason Rudolph (USA) v. Brian Barnes (GBI)

Coming into this all-rookie encounter, Rudolph had already recorded a halved match and a 2 and 1 win. That defeat had been Barnes's only outing so far, but he showed more than enough fighting spirit in the singles to suggest he might have been better utilized.

As in the previous two matches, this was another close one, where Barnes did enough to come out on top with a valuable one-hole victory.

Gene Littler (USA) v. Peter Oosterhuis (GBI)

Rookie Oosterhuis lost his first three matches before registering his first ever success in the afternoon fourball. The Englishman quickly followed up with his second win in a row, easily overcoming the lackluster challenge of a previously unbeaten American.

Littler, who did not play at all on day one and won both his pairs matches on day two, sat out the afternoon singles after this 4 and 3 defeat.

Jack Nicklaus (USA) v. Peter Townsend (GBI)

The *Times* (London) sent its top tennis correspondent, Rex Bellamy, to cover the event, which explains the following line: "Townsend had a restlessly athletic gait reminiscent of Roy Emerson changing ends."

Jack Nicklaus quickly put his opening foursomes loss behind him as he proceeded to rattle off three wins in a row in his remaining pairs matches. Townsend, who had narrowly lost all four of his matches, including both fourballs against Nicklaus, fared little better on his own against the great man.

For the third match in a row, Nicklaus proved too strong for the Scot, recording his biggest victory over him by 3 and 2 for his fourth straight win and Townsend's fifth straight loss.

Gardner Dickinson (USA) v. Christy O'Connor (GBI)

Dickinson, coming to the tee 8-0 lifetime in the Ryder Cup and 3-0 in this contest, proved way too strong for the Irishman, who was 1-1-1 after winning the opening foursomes match of the contest.

Dickinson encountered little trouble in his 5 and 4 win, as he extended his (then) record winning sequence to nine; the next best ever 100 percent playing record was Jimmy Demaret's 6-0 from the 1940s to 1950s.

Arnold Palmer (USA) v. Harry Bannerman (GBI)

Beaten by Palmer (and Nicklaus) on the final hole of the previous afternoon's fourball, Bannerman almost caused a solo upset over the 4-0 American. The Scot had the better of the early exchange, taking a two-hole lead after he won the twelfth.

Hanging on to his unbeaten record, Palmer fought back and again took the match to the eighteenth. The cigar-smoking British player's hopes of a win went up in smoke on the last green when he failed to get down in par and lost the hole—and his chance for glory—to halve the match.

Frank Beard (USA) v. Neil Coles (GBI)

The final singles match out in the morning also pitted two players who had faced off against each other in the previous day's fourballs. Eighteen more holes in the morning singles resulted in an even contest.

Morning singles result: USA 4½, GBI 3½

In what turned out to be a fairly even morning's play, five matches went to the last green, with three halved matches and a win apiece. If the American supremacy (6½-1½) on the second day was ignored, the overall score would have been level at eight points each, going into the final singles. Instead, the Americans needed only two points to claim the Cup, and the British were again staring down the wrong end of a gun barrel.

Day Three: Afternoon Singles

Five points down with just eight singles to go, the British team hoped to stage one of the most amazing golfing comebacks since Ben Hogan won back-to-back U.S. Opens in the '50s. At one spot in the afternoon session, the British were up in six of the eight matches, but one by one the leads dropped away.

Lee Trevino (USA) v. Brian Huggett (GBI)

Trevino continued his barnstorming act in the singles by hammering the luckless Brian Huggett.

On his wonder shot at the fourth: "After I hit that shot, I looked at Huggett and he looked at me, and I said, 'I'm as surprised as you are.'"
—*Lee Trevino*

On the fourth hole, Trevino produced a piece of magic even he did not believe. After his tee shot finished up underneath a tree, Trevino could play only a left-hand reverse wedge shot that flew over a hundred and twenty yards onto the green. Two normal putts earned an amazing half for the master showman.

Cashing in on this remarkable recovery, Trevino reached the turn in 33 with a comfortable four-hole cushion, which he plumped up with three wins on the next three holes to register a 7 and 6 thumping.

J. C. Snead (USA) v. Tony Jacklin (GBI)

Jacklin had to sink a monster putt on seventeen against Snead to take the match to the last hole, where the Englishman failed to make par and handed the game back to Snead, 1-up.

This point gave the United States enough to win the Ryder Cup. "That's great, because I didn't know what the others were doing out there," said Snead

With four wins out of four, Snead was the only player to remain unbeaten in the three days of play.

Miller Barber (USA) v. Brian Barnes (GBI)

Barnes won his second singles match of the day, beating Miller Barber, 2 and 1, after the American ruined his chances by carding a 40 to the turn. Three down at the halfway stage was too much of a deficit for Barber to cut into, although he got one hole back.

Dave Stockton (USA) v. Peter Townsend (GBI)

After Stockton's bright start, Townsend was three down with seven to play. By the last hole, the Scot had leveled the match, but Stockton's birdie three won the last hole and gave him a one-hole victory.

Charles Coody (USA) v. Bernard Gallacher (GBI)

After making par for a win on the third hole, Gallacher was never behind against the Masters champion, as the young Scot reached the turn in 34 strokes to Coody's 36. The American was unable to mount a fight back and eventually went down by 2 and 1.

Jack Nicklaus (USA) v. Neil Coles (GBI)

Nicklaus quickly found himself on the wrong end of a three-hole lead. Neil Coles won three of the first four holes, the American losing his ball in a pond at the first hole.

After such a promising start by the British player, the bottom dropped out of his world. Nicklaus won eight of the next ten holes played, with the assistance of only two birdies. Coles's game disintegrated as Nicklaus romped home to the easiest 5 and 3 win of his career.

Arnold Palmer (USA) v. Peter Oosterhuis (GBI)

Having bested Littler in the morning, Oosterhuis again registered a double success in the singles by handing the previously unbeaten Palmer a 3 and 2 loss in the afternoon.

The American lost his form, particularly on the greens, as Oosterhuis, out in 33, was four up at the turn and held on to inflict Palmer's first loss in six matches in this event, after a 4-0-1 start.

This was only Palmer's fifth loss in a total of twenty-seven Ryder Cup matches.

Gardner Dickinson (USA) v. Harry Bannerman (GBI)

With a most enviable record of played nine, won nine, Gardner Dickinson was brought down to earth by the cigar-smoking Harry Bannerman . . . and his own caddie.

On the par-3 seventh, the American's bag man inadvertently picked up his player's ball, which had rolled up to the hole. Bannerman had not wanted to concede the short putt right away, as he was going to use it as a guide to his own putt. Thanks to his caddie, Dickinson lost the hole.

From there to the 2 and 1 finish on the seventeenth, the match was played in silence.

This defeat was the only blot on Dickinson's Ryder Cup record. He narrowly missed becoming the first player to go 10-0.

Afternoon singles result: USA 4, GBI 4
Day three result: USA 8½, GBI 7½
Overall match score: USA 18½, GBI 13½

Recap

If this match had been played ten years earlier, it would have been halved, as fourball was not played in 1961, and the United States came close to sweeping the day-two format this time around, 6½-1½. These five points were the difference between the sides at the end of three days. The British actually won the first day, and lost the singles by only one point—so they were competitive for two-thirds of the match.

Since fourball matches had been introduced in 1963, the United States had dominated the format by a whopping 25–7, although the last two matches had seen the Americans blow the British away, 14–2 on the second day.

Even with their poor fourball performance, the British had achieved their best-ever result in the United States. Still, some criticized Eric Brown's handling of his players, notably his selecting John Garner as a wild card—Garner was not suited to the long course—and then playing him in only one match. So, despite leading his country to their best away trip in Ryder Cup history and masterminding the tied match in 1969, Brown was not asked to captain the team again.

The victorious Americans had no such problems. They had regained full ownership of the Cup, and, with their four aces in the hole, everything looked rosy for the Stars and Stripes for many years to come. The only downside to the American Ryder Cup dream was the almost complete lack of media attention, which translated into a disconcerting level of public apathy. The next few encounters, also one-sided, would do little to improve the profile of the biennial matches in the United States.

Although the attention from the media and the public in the United States was waning, this would be the last match staged west of the Eastern time zone. This change would allow the event to always be shown live in Britain, where the matches were still eagerly awaited.

Match Results (Winning side marked in *italics*.)

Thursday, September 16—Morning Foursomes

	USA	GBI	Score
1.	Billy Casper Miller Barber	*Christy O'Connor* *Neil Coles*	2 and 1
2.	*Arnold Palmer* *Gardner Dickinson*	Peter Townsend Peter Oosterhuis	2-up
3.	Frank Beard Charles Coody	*Peter Butler* *Maurice Bembridge*	1-up
4.	Jack Nicklaus Dave Stockton	*Tony Jacklin* *Brian Huggett*	3 and 2

Thursday, September 16—Afternoon Foursomes

	USA	GBI	Score
5.	Billy Casper Miller Barber	*Harry Bannerman* *Bernard Gallacher*	2 and 1
6.	*Arnold Palmer* *Gardner Dickinson*	Peter Oosterhuis Peter Townsend	1-up
7.	Lee Trevino Mason Rudolph	Tony Jacklin Brian Huggett	halved
8.	*Jack Nicklaus* *J. C. Snead*	Maurice Bembridge Peter Butler	5 and 3

Day one result: USA 3½, GBI 4½

Friday, September 17—Morning Fourball

	USA	GBI	Score
9.	*Lee Trevino* *Mason Rudolph*	Brian Barnes Christy O'Connor	2 and 1
10.	*Frank Beard* *J. C. Snead*	Neil Coles John Garner	2 and 1
11.	*Arnold Palmer* *Gardner Dickinson*	Peter Oosterhuis Bernard Gallacher	5 and 4
12.	*Jack Nicklaus* *Gene Littler*	Peter Townsend Harry Bannerman	2 and 1

Friday, September 17—Afternoon Fourball

	USA	GBI	Score
13.	Lee Trevino Billy Casper	*Peter Oosterhuis* *Bernard Gallacher*	1-up
14.	*Gene Littler* *J. C. Snead*	Tony Jacklin Brian Huggett	2 and 1
15.	*Jack Nicklaus* *Arnold Palmer*	Peter Townsend Harry Bannerman	1-up
16.	Charles Coody Frank Beard	Christy O'Connor Neil Coles	halved

Day two result: USA 6½, GBI 1½

Overall match score: USA 10, GBI 6

Saturday, September 18—Morning Singles

	USA	GBI	Score
17.	*Lee Trevino*	Tony Jacklin	1-up
18.	Dave Stockton	Bernard Gallacher	halved
19.	Mason Rudolph	*Brian Barnes*	1-up
20.	Gene Littler	*Peter Oosterhuis*	4 and 3
21.	*Jack Nicklaus*	Peter Townsend	3 and 2
22.	*Gardner Dickinson*	Christy O'Connor	5 and 4
23.	Arnold Palmer	Harry Bannerman	halved
24.	Frank Beard	Neil Coles	halved

Saturday, September 18—Afternoon Singles

	USA	GBI	Score
25.	*Lee Trevino*	Brian Huggett	7 and 6
26.	*J. C. Snead*	Tony Jacklin	1-up
27.	Miller Barber	*Brian Barnes*	2 and 1
28.	*Dave Stockton*	Peter Townsend	1-up
29.	Charles Coody	*Bernard Gallacher*	2 and 1
30.	*Jack Nicklaus*	Neil Coles	5 and 3
31.	Arnold Palmer	*Peter Oosterhuis*	3 and 2
32.	Gardner Dickinson	*Harry Bannerman*	2 and 1

Day three result: USA *8½*, GBI *7½*

Overall match score: USA *18½*, GBI *13½*

1973

Muirfield
(Honorable Company of Edinburgh Golfers)
Gullane, Scotland
September 20–22

United States 19	Great Britain and Ireland 13
Tommy Aaron	Brian Barnes
Homero Blancas	Maurice Bembridge
Gay Brewer	Peter Butler
Billy Casper	Clive Clark
Lou Graham	Neil Coles
Dave Hill	Bernard Gallacher
Jack Nicklaus	Brian Huggett
Arnold Palmer	Tony Jacklin
Juan "Chi Chi" Rodriguez	Christy O'Connor, Sr.
J. C. Snead	Peter Oosterhuis
Lee Trevino	Eddie Polland
Tom Weiskopf	John Garner [did not play]
Captain	**Captain**
Jack Burke, Jr.	Bernard Hunt

The Times They Are A-Changin'

A year for two major changes.

The Ryder Cup was played for the first time outside of England and the United States—in Scotland. Muirfield, for so long one of the main courses on the British Open circuit, now had its chance to shine as a major match-play venue.

The second change was in the playing conditions: afternoon fourball would now follow morning foursomes on days one and two. The thinking behind this was that fourball takes much longer to play than the twoball foursomes, and having eight fourballs in one day was putting too much strain on players, who were under enough pressure as it was.

The American captain was Jack Burke, Jr., fondly remembered in Britain as the captain who last lost the Ryder Cup, in 1957. Burke remarked that if he was to lose a second Ryder Cup in Britain, he might not be allowed back into the United States.

"The responsibility of this job is terrible. We're supposed to win, and if you don't, don't come home. I think it's an awful job myself."
—*Jack Burke, Jr.*

Burke welcomed four rookies: British Open champion Tom Weiskopf, Homero Blancas, Chi Chi Rodriguez, and Lou Graham.

With the fully functioning central nervous system of PGA champion Nicklaus, Palmer, Trevino, and Casper, along with current Masters champ Aaron, the U.S. team was still a most formidable foe.

Snead, Casper, and Palmer had just scraped enough points together in the last few qualifying tournaments to guarantee their place, while U.S. Open champion Johnny Miller still had not served all of the five years on the PGA Tour needed to be eligible for Ryder Cup consideration.

At thirty years of age, Tom Weiskopf was the youngest player on a team of players whose average age was just over thirty-six.

"I'll be very surprised if the Americans win this year. Everyone on my side is very keen and very confident."
—*Bernard Hunt*

Britain named former player Bernard Hunt as their captain, and he was brimming with confidence when he took over the reins. The fact that his players had been using the bigger American ball for five years meant that their game was now more like that of their opponents. However, Hunt had three rookies of his own and was worried about how well they would stack up against the seasoned U.S. pros.

A complex British selection procedure ended with Hunt's having taken the top twelve point scorers from the qualifying tournaments, although he was allowed to replace at least three players if they were out of form or injured. Surprisingly, Hunt did not take advantage of this clause, even though John Garner sat out the whole three days, having lost his only previous match in 1971. Eddie Polland got only two games, Clive Clark one, and neither played in the vital singles matches. This showed the complete lack of depth in the British side: Hunt had no one good enough to replace these three players.

Because of a mix-up over travel arrangements, the U.S. team arrived late and had only two full days of practice on the course. Jack Nicklaus flew in on his own from Miami after staying behind to watch a Dolphins football game.

Course Details

A regular host of the British Open, Muirfield ranks as one of the great Scottish links courses, with none of the annoying trickery of false bunkers, hidden hazards, and blind shots. It is regarded as the fairest of the major courses.

"I wish I had come over here when I was playing competitively. I think I could have done well. But it's not a course you can learn in two days. I think we should have given ourselves more time."

—Jack Burke, Jr.

This course inspired Jack Nicklaus to name his course Muirfield Village, a venue that would later host the 1987 Ryder Cup.

Hole	Distance	Par	Hole	Distance	Par
1	442	4	10	473	4
2	349	4	11	386	4
3	379	4	12	381	4
4	181	3	13	153	3
5	558	5	14	447	4
6	471	4	15	396	4
7	185	3	16	188	3
8	444	4	17	542	5
9	495	5	18	447	4
		36			**35 = Par 71 (6,917 yards)**

Course designer: Old Tom Morris

Day One: Morning Foursomes

A mild breeze blowing off the choppy waters of the Firth of Forth estuary cooled the pale September sunshine, causing the temperature to drop ten degrees before the first match got under way.

Lee Trevino and Billy Casper (USA) v. Brian Barnes and Bernard Gallacher (GBI)

" 'On the tee, Lee Trevino of the United States,' says the starter. Like a heavyweight champion before the fight, Trevino crosses himself. In the crowd someone laughs. 'What's funny about that?' asks Trevino testily. And so in deadly earnest the great match gets under way."

—John Woodcock, *Times* (London)

For the first-ever Ryder Cup match in Scotland, the English captain led off with his all-Scottish pairing.

First up, Trevino drove into the rough, as he and Casper combined to three-putt the opening hole. This false start allowed Barnes to play out of sand, leaving Gallacher with a par putt to win the hole.

The U.S. pair fared even worse, each taking a turn to get out of a bunker on the second and conceding before the British had putted.

With this bad start behind them, the Americans played steadily, winning the fifth—after Barnes had found the deep rough off the tee—and the 471-yard par-4 sixth. The match stayed level through nine, where Gallacher was forced into making a thirteen-foot putt to halve the hole.

The Scots won the par-4 tenth, and the lead seesawed over the next few holes. After an American birdie on the par-3 thirteenth leveled the match, a Scottish win on fourteen gave them back the lead, before another U.S. birdie two on sixteen tied the match again.

"The Scots struck with the terror of skirling bagpipes and saw off Trevino and Casper."
Dudley Doust, Sunday Times *(London)*

With the match still within their grasp, the Americans were short of the 542-yard seventeenth green in two, and Gallacher powered his fairway wood approach shot over the green. Barnes chipped back to five feet for his fellow Scot to hole out for another birdie. Trevino missed his shortish putt and the Americans fell behind with one to play.

The Scots looked to have lost their chance on the last, when Gallacher pushed his tee shot into a bunker. With Barnes's great recovery still coming up short of the putting surface, Gallacher atoned for his poor drive with an excellent chip shot to twelve feet. Trevino found the green with his approach for a certain four and Barnes did the rest, holing the uphill putt to win the match by one hole.

Tom Weiskopf and J. C. Snead (USA) v. Christy O'Connor and Neil Coles (GBI)

After carding a stupefying 61 in the practice round on Tuesday, forty-eight-year-old Christy O'Connor joked, "It was the right score on the wrong day."

In his tenth Ryder Cup, Irishman Christy O'Connor put on a magical display with his short game, and he proved to be the difference, partnering Neil Coles against Weiskopf and Snead.

Weiskopf's putt for a par on the 471-yard sixth hole gave the Americans a lead, which they held on to despite O'Connor's clever chip up to the eighth hole for a half. The next saw Weiskopf drive into some almost impenetrable rough, allowing O'Connor to hole from more than thirty feet to take the ninth with a birdie four.

All square after nine holes, and with a hot hand, the inspirational Irishman made a great sand save on the par-4 tenth for the win and the lead. Coles responded to his partner's actions with a twelve-foot birdie putt on eleven to go two up. This was the British pair's third win in as many holes, and it looked to have done in the Americans.

Having taken control of the match, the British three-putted the par-4 fourteenth, only to be reprieved when the Americans did the same on the fifteenth. At the par-3 sixteenth, O'Connor rounded off a fine inward spell with a rasping six-iron to eight feet. Coles's birdie putt snuffed out the Americans, 3 and 2.

Lou Graham and Chi Chi Rodriguez (USA) v. Tony Jacklin and Peter Oosterhuis (GBI)

A British birdie four accounted for the first hole, and Jacklin and Oosterhuis proceeded to halve the next eleven holes with U.S. rookies Rodriguez and Graham.

The Americans won the next two holes thanks to costly mistakes by Oosterhuis (bunkered on thirteen) and Jacklin (muffed chip on fourteen). The home side was back level after sixteen, where Graham left his long "Texas Wedge" attempt well short of the hole and the U.S. pair needed two more putts to get down.

All square with two to play, the Americans got themselves out of jail on the 542-yard seventeenth. They were outplayed in struggling up to the green and in danger of losing this vital hole, their ball still thirty-five feet from the flag. Then, with a flourish of Zorroesque panache, Rodriguez holed from downtown on the dance floor to stay square.

On the last hole, Oosterhuis and Graham played fine seconds to ensure a closing half, as Chi Chi could not reproduce the same magic from seventeen, and Jacklin also blew his birdie putt for the match.

Jack Nicklaus and Arnold Palmer (USA) v. Maurice Bembridge and Eddie Polland (GBI)

The Americans had saved their best for last, and Palmer and Nicklaus did not disappoint their legions of fans. Six up after eleven holes, the U.S. superstars gave the poorly matched Bembridge and Polland little room to maneuver.

The round started badly for the rookie Polland, who missed a short putt to bogey the first hole. From this bad start, things only got worse for the British. Two scorching woods from the Americans made an eagle a formality on the 558-yard fifth.

Polland and Bembridge played the sixth so poorly, they were forced to concede a seven-foot putt for the hole. Palmer needed no such charity on the par 3 seventh, drilling his tee shot to eight feet for Nicklaus to sink the birdie putt. The Americans sailed to the turn in 33, owners of a five-hole cushion that everyone expected them to pad out on a short journey home.

Nicklaus put a wrench in the works when he made the Americans' first and only error of the round, landing his tee shot in a bunker on the tenth. With this temporary blip out of the way, the U.S. legends resumed normal service to curtail the one-sided match, 6 and 5.

"They told me they were throwing me in the deep end—but that was a bottomless pit. I'm glad in a way I wasn't playing well, because I would have hated to have shot my best golf and still lost. Palmer was the backbone of his side."
—*Eddie Polland*

Morning foursomes result: USA 1½, GBI 2½

Day One: Afternoon Fourball

Tommy Aaron and Gay Brewer (USA) v. Brian Barnes and Bernard Gallacher (GBI)

Against a rampaging Barnes and Gallacher, the unfortunate U.S. pairing of Aaron and Brewer did not stand a chance. The British launched their offensive from the outset, and were three up after four as they hit the Americans with everything they had. On the 444-yard eighth hole, Barnes hit his bunker shot more than 150 yards to set up a twenty-five-foot birdie putt. The burly Scot followed this with another fine approach and birdie putt at the ninth, and the British turned for home four up.

"We've been four down before and lived." —Gay Brewer

Barnes proved to be a one-man wrecking crew as he demolished the tenth green with a sixty-foot putt for his third consecutive birdie to go five up. In a forlorn gesture, Brewer made birdies at eleven and twelve to cut the lead to three, but Gallacher halted this comeback attempt with a ten-foot birdie at the par-3 thirteenth. A comfortable hole-winning par 4 at the 447-yard fourteenth gave the British victory, 5 and 4.

This loss, the biggest U.S. defeat in the fourballs to date, went the way Brian Barnes had planned. "We just took things in our stride, and decided we were going to get on top early and stay there."

The Scottish pairing did not card a five between them in the fourteen holes.

Jack Nicklaus and Arnold Palmer (USA) v. Maurice Bembridge and Brian Huggett (GBI)

Having been torn apart by Nicklaus and Palmer in the morning, Maurice Bembridge expected to sit out the afternoon. He learned of his inclusion in the afternoon fourballs while he was enjoying a beer in the clubhouse bar. Although his partner had changed, his opponents had not.

The alcoholic refreshment Bembridge had taken may have helped loosen him up, because he made a telling fifteen-foot putt on the first hole for a half. After that confident start, he played some miraculous golf: he squared the match with an inch-perfect six-iron approach to the sixth, at seven he made a par three for the lead, and he eagled the 495-yard ninth after planting a two-iron within fourteen feet of the flag.

Two down at the turn, the Americans may not have recognized Bembridge—in the morning, they had turned five up. Whatever the U.S. powerhouse pair threw at him, Bembridge seemed to have all the answers.

On fourteen, when his side looked as if they might be caught, Bembridge chipped in from seventy yards to go two up. Nicklaus and Palmer could find no way around or through their tormentor; Bembridge and the redoubtable Huggett ran out surprising winners, 3 and 1.

Tom Weiskopf and Billy Casper (USA) v. Tony Jacklin and Peter Oosterhuis (GBI)

Against another powerful American pair, Casper and Weiskopf, the British aces lived up to their billing, as they opened with seven consecutive birdies. Oosterhuis opened with three birdies of his own, Jacklin stepped in with another at the fourth, Oosterhuis nailed his fourth birdie in five holes, and Jacklin nipped in again on the sixth and added a two at the par-3 seventh. If Jacklin's birdie putt from off the green at the 444-yard eighth had not lipped out, the Americans would have been dead and buried.

After Jacklin just failed to make it eight out of eight birdies: *"That's too bad. I thought you were going to have eighteen in a row. I just hope you boys are enjoying yourselves."*—BILLY CASPER

"The British golf has been just unbelievable. We knew they could play, but we didn't know they could play this well."
—*Jack Burke, Jr.*

As it was, the U.S. pair hung in with the blistering start made by their opponents, and they were only three down after eight, thanks to Weiskopf's making his birdie after Jacklin lipped out. The same two players made birdies at the 495-yard ninth to give the British an outstanding outward card of 28 to the Americans' 31.

Another British birdie at ten was matched by the Americans, but Casper made two good putts for unanswered birdies at twelve and thirteen to pull the lead back to one. Mistakes by both Americans on fifteen allowed the British pair to claim the hole to par. Casper's hooking problems twice plagued him on the fifteenth, while Weiskopf took three to get down from the perimeter of the green.

On seventeen, when Weiskopf missed the eight-footer that he needed to keep the match rolling, the British pair had triumphed in sensational fashion, 3 and 1.

After his second defeat of the day, Weiskopf had tears in his eyes, and when asked who had beaten them, he replied simply, "Pete!"

Lee Trevino and Homero Blancas (USA) v. Neil Coles and Christy O'Connor (GBI)

At times, Blancas appeared so nervous that he had trouble keeping a firm grip on his clubs.

Trevino and Blancas were all square with Coles and O'Connor after a roller-coaster opening nine holes. Coles started the ball rolling with an accurate approach to a couple of feet of the second pin, for the lead. O'Connor missed a four-footer on the par-3 fourth to give up the lead, but holed from more than twenty feet on the next par 3 to edge ahead again after seven holes. Blancas balanced out the first nine holes with a cheeky chip-in on the 495-yard hole.

Having been relatively quiet on the front nine, Trevino birdied the first two holes coming home to put the United States up by two. O'Connor made a birdie on twelve to close the gap, but neither British player managed a par on the par-4 fourteenth and they dropped back two down.

Once again the Americans finished the stronger to record a vital 2 and 1 win in the face of some concerted British golf, preventing a sweep of the afternoon matches.

A U.S. defeat in this last match would have left the British five points ahead after the first day.

This was just the second time the Americans had been beaten in a fourball session—the first being in '69—since the introduction of the format in 1963.

"I'm happy but not surprised. The critics are surprised. But I kept saying all along that I had a good team in heart. I expected them to play well, and they did. They know there's still a long way to go. But they know it's possible to win." —Bernard Hunt

Afternoon fourball result: USA 1, GBI 3
Day one result: USA 2½, GBI 5½

Day Two: Morning Foursomes

Jack Nicklaus and Tom Weiskopf (USA) v. Brian Barnes and Peter Butler (GBI)

With his regular accomplice Bernard Gallacher laid low by a nasty stomach bug, Brian Barnes took on the American power of Nicklaus and Weiskopf with a new partner. Butler was still sound asleep in bed when he was called upon, as he had not been scheduled to play.

Two up after three, the Americans powered to a three-hole lead after five holes, and the match stayed that way until the par-3 188-yard sixteenth. Nicklaus hit a magnificent tee shot straight at and over the flag, the ball coming to rest a few feet away, for a certain match-winning birdie. Looking down and out, Butler, armed with a three-iron, played the only shot that could keep his side alive—a hole-in-one!

"You're playing not only for the team but millions of Brits throughout the world. If you make a mistake, you feel you've let them down."
—*Brian Barnes*

Suddenly, the makeshift British pair was only two down with two to play. They seized their chance at seventeen, where Butler again proved to be the savior, holing a massive putt to win the hole.

Fortunately for the United States, Nicklaus and Weiskopf still had plenty in reserve and held on at the last to win by one, thanks to an exquisite chip by Nicklaus from the back of the green.

Arnold Palmer and Dave Hill (USA) v. Peter Oosterhuis and Tony Jacklin (GBI)

Most players would give their eyeteeth to play in the Ryder Cup, especially on a true links course, but not the temperamental Dave Hill. He was less than enthusiastic about playing in Britain, and consequently this was his only appearance, although he was restricted by a knee injury.

"I appreciate the traditions of the game, but I don't have any warm spot in my heart for Britain. As far as I'm concerned we've refined the game tremendously over here and I don't get any thrills out of going back and roughing it. Give me running water every time."

—DAVE HILL, *Teed Off* (1977)

Arnold Palmer unluckily drew the homesick and limping Hill, and the Americans were rarely in the match against Jacklin and Oosterhuis. Three up after twelve, the British pair almost let Palmer take over the match. Arnie laid a long iron close to the hole on fifteen for a win to generate a spark of light for his pair.

In spite of his reluctance to play, Hill almost holed his approach on seventeen after Oosterhuis fluffed a chip. One down with one to play, the Americans suddenly realized half a point was there for the taking. Having sparked the comeback, Palmer doused the flames by failing to get out of a bunker on the eighteenth, and the U.S. pair went down by one hole.

Chi Chi Rodriguez and Lou Graham (USA) v. Maurice Bembridge and Brian Huggett (GBI)

Although Bembridge and Huggett won this match quite easily, 5 and 4, it was in fact the amateurish Rodriguez and Graham who lost it. Out in 39, the Americans were fortunate not to be more than two down.

The back nine saw no improvement in the Americans' play, and the British pair coasted to a virtually uncontested win.

Carding seven fives and a six, the woeful Americans were an unsightly eight over for fourteen holes. The end was as poor as any poor ending could be: bogey, double, double. Graham in particular still suffered from his lingering malaise on the greens.

Lee Trevino and Billy Casper (USA) v. Neil Coles and Christy O'Connor (GBI)

With the first six holes halved, Trevino and Casper took a lead on Coles and O'Connor at the par-3 seventh. Casper's miss from five feet on the ninth was quickly followed by O'Connor's five-foot birdie putt.

Back level, Casper made amends by holing a ten-footer for a birdie three on the tenth. Both Casper and O'Connor contrived to miss shortish putts at the thirteenth that would have won their side the hole.

"When I missed a five-foot putt for a birdie at the thirteenth, I was sick. Then Christy failed with a nasty four-footer. I knew then we had got it."
—Billy Casper

This proved the last real chance for the older British pair, whose age began to tell on their weary bones. They appeared to physically weaken over the final few holes, allowing the Americans to run out 2 and 1 winners to split the morning foursomes.

Morning foursomes result: USA 2, GBI 2

Day Two: Afternoon Fourball

Facing a three-point deficit going into the afternoon fourball, Jack Burke called a team meeting at lunchtime to pull his side together. Not wanting to become the first captain to lose twice overseas, Burke led off with some tough talking, before diplomatically putting the matter in the players' hands.

"We talked about the situation and we decided we needed to win all four of the afternoon matches." —Gay Brewer

Off his game coming into the event, and with no improvement through two matches thus far, Lou Graham volunteered to step down from the next session. Arnold Palmer (who had asked for the afternoon off) replaced Graham, as the Americans decided to go with their strength. "We needed to get the momentum on our side," said Lou Graham, who also sat out both singles.

Arnold Palmer and J. C. Snead (USA) v. Brian Barnes and Peter Butler (GBI)

On shepherding his second links rookie of the day round the difficult seaside course: "I had meant to rest on the second afternoon, but we needed all we had. Some of our new players just haven't had any idea of how to play this course."
—*Arnold Palmer*

Peter Butler was unable to repeat his one-shot heroics of the morning, and he proved to be the weak link in his partnership with Brian Barnes. Against them were Palmer (replacing Lou Graham) and Snead, who won the first hole but were unable to cut loose, owing mainly to Barnes's excellence on the greens.

The brawny Scot knocked in a twenty-five-foot birdie putt on the second to level the match. The U.S. pair took the sixth to go back up, but Barnes sank a putt from off the putting surface at the eighth. All square after nine, the American pair again finished stronger than the British.

With the match still level on the seventeenth green, Snead was the only player to birdie the par-5 hole, for a one-hole lead.

"I saved myself for that last hole."
—*Arnold Palmer*

Palmer, who had been unusually quiet for most of the round, sank the all-important birdie putt from sixteen feet on the last green to ease out a two-hole win.

In a remarkable Ryder Cup career, Arnold Palmer played twenty-one pairs matches and never halved a single one (16-5-0).

Gay Brewer and Billy Casper (USA) v. Tony Jacklin and Peter Oosterhuis (GBI)

Jacklin and Oosterhuis—the top British pair—struggled to find their previous form against Casper and Brewer. Three up after seven holes, the Americans were at the top of their game, coming within two holes of a 62 for their better-ball round.

"Tony Jacklin is playing like he's dead beat. The ball is going everywhere."
—*Billy Casper*

A trio of American wins from the twelfth on proved crucial. After the British had contrived to lose the twelfth with a bogey, Brewer made a twenty-five-foot birdie putt at the short thirteenth, then chipped in from thirty yards away in a bunker at fourteen.

Against such consistently low scoring the tired-looking British pair had no answers, but they hung on until the sixteenth, where they finally went down to a 3 and 2 defeat.

Jack Nicklaus and Tom Weiskopf (USA) v. Eddie Polland and Clive Clark (GBI)

With Coles and O'Connor finishing dog tired in the morning, they were replaced—against Hunt's plans—by Clark and Polland, who were immediately in trouble against the fired-up pair of Nicklaus and Weiskopf.

Both members of the British pair were very new to the Ryder Cup. Polland was making only his second start, having lost on the opening morning, while Clark was playing in his only match ever.

In the first seven holes, the Americans carded five threes—the highlight coming on Weiskopf's twenty-two-footer for birdie at the sixth. Two up became three on the twelfth, and when the next four holes were halved, the game was well beyond the backup British pair. With a five-under round to their credit, Nicklaus and Weiskopf closed out the match, 3 and 2. The Americans had won the first three matches out.

Lee Trevino and Homero Blancas (USA) v. Maurice Bembridge and Brian Huggett (GBI)

By far the closest match of the afternoon, this was a real nail-biter between a couple of 100 percent pairings. Trevino and Blancas had scored in the first fourball, and Huggett and Bembridge had won both their matches together.

Trevino played the best golf of the four—he needed to, just to keep his side in the match. The British pair held a brief one-hole lead after thirteen holes, but lost the fourteenth before halving the next two holes. On the par-5 seventeenth, Trevino had a long putt for an eagle and the go-ahead hole, but he just missed making it count.

The eighteenth was reached all square, where Trevino's approach was long to the back of the green. With Huggett safe up by the hole, the American was faced with a testing downhill putt.

"When I hit the putt, I just stared at the ground. I didn't dare look how the ball was going." —Lee Trevino

Trevino's tricky putt finished near enough the hole for his four. After two fine opening shots, Huggett had the best chance on the green to take the hole, and the match, but his birdie putt just failed to drop and the match was halved.

This halved match prevented an American clean sweep after their rousing lunchtime council of war.

In a repeat performance from the preceding Ryder Cup in Britain, the teams were dead-locked at eight points each going into the final day of singles.

Afternoon fourball result: USA *3½,* GBI *½*
Day two result: USA *5½,* GBI *2½*
Overall match score: USA *8,* GBI *8*

On his team's giving up a three-point lead from the first day as well as the much-needed momentum of the earlier success: *"I'm a little disappointed, naturally. I anticipated a little slide back today, but not this bad. But I'm very confident."* —Bernard Hunt

Day Three: Morning Singles

With confidence restored to his team, who now had the belief they had conquered the course, Burke led off with Casper and Weiskopf and held back Trevino and Nicklaus as his anchors. At one stage in the morning, every American player was up or level in his match. Not only had the tide turned, but the USS *America* was sailing for home.

Billy Casper (USA) v. Brian Barnes (GBI)

In spite of being fourteen years younger and a good few pounds lighter than his opponent, Brian Barnes was quickly worn down by Billy Casper.

Barnes had played in all four matches before the singles, but so had Casper, which makes Barnes's postmatch comments even more mystifying: "He was fitter than I was. It's becoming just a commando course out there."

Although Barnes had hole-winning birdies at eight and nine, that he had nine fives in seventeen holes was the decisive factor. But whatever the reason, the United States had again struck first in the important singles matches, with Casper posting a 2 and 1 win to lead his country off.

Tom Weiskopf (USA) v. Bernard Gallacher (GBI)

Summoned from his sickbed, Gallacher took on the fit and in-form Tom Weiskopf, and of course the American prevailed. The gutsy Gallacher gave Weiskopf a run for his money, however. One up after the first, Weiskopf let his lead slip with a bogey five on the tenth.

With even his fully "fit" teammates complaining of fatigue, it was no surprise that Gallacher was too weak to keep up the pressure, and he fell behind by two after sixteen. A poor tee shot from Weiskopf on seventeen opened the door for Gallacher, but he topped his own approach shot and lost the match, 3 and 1.

Homero Blancas (USA) v. Peter Butler (GBI)

Homero Blancas had much the easiest match of the morning. The American opened steadily—par-par-birdie—and won each hole, as Butler never got going. Up by four after nine, Blancas remained on cruise control. The final score of 5 and 4 flattered the inept Englishman.

"Peter Butler, for some reason that defies understanding, was sent into battle. Huggett was left out. With this weakened team, disaster swept across the course with the virulence of the bugs in Gallacher's tummy. At one stage the home team was trailing in all matches."

—Dudley Doust, *Sunday Times* (London)

Having started the day all level, the Americans were three points up after the first three singles.

Tommy Aaron (USA) v. Tony Jacklin (GBI)

Arnold Palmer had asked for the previous afternoon off, but instead he played a leading role in the fourball romp. He was finally granted his respite in the morning singles, as Burke replaced him with Tommy Aaron.

Britain looked to the team's one world-class player, Tony Jacklin, to stop the rot at the top of the singles. The Englishman was fortunate to come up against a Masters champion suffering from a bad back. Furthermore, Aaron was playing in only his second match and never came to terms with the undulating course. Even so, it took a string of Jacklin wins from the eighth, triggered by a birdie on the par-4 hole, to secure the match.

Against the sacrificial lamb of the U.S. side, Jacklin still needed sixteen holes to put Aaron out of his misery, 3 and 2.

Britain had begun the singles with a great chance of winning the Cup outright, but Jacklin's victory over Aaron was the hosts' only win of the morning.

Gay Brewer (USA) v. Neil Coles (GBI)

Having already missed two crucial putts, Neil Coles was one up with one to play over Gay Brewer. The Englishman had another short putt—from inside three feet—on the last green that would give his team a vital win, but he missed his second putt and the match was halved.

J. C. Snead (USA) v. Christy O'Connor (GBI)

J. C. Snead outlasted the tired old man Christy O'Connor, but he could have sewn up the match much earlier, having taken a three-hole lead after nine holes. The Irishman fought back to level the match, but Snead won the seventeenth and held on at the last for a one-hole victory.

Jack Nicklaus (USA) v. Maurice Bembridge (GBI)

Neither Nicklaus nor Bembridge played well enough to deserve the outright win. So it was fitting that in a match where par was enough to win many a hole, they finished all square.

Two up with two to play, Nicklaus, contrary to his normal style, decided to play safe on the closing holes. In so doing he allowed Bembridge to close the gap for an unexpected half against America's best player.

Lee Trevino (USA) v. Peter Oosterhuis (GBI)

In the best matchup of the morning, Lee Trevino took on Peter Oosterhuis. The match was close throughout, with the tall Englishman having the best chances to win. Alas, he three-putted the fourteenth and topped his approach to seventeen into a bunker, letting Trevino off with a half.

Morning singles result: USA 5½, GBI 2½

A Man-to-Man Massacre

—*Sunday Times* (London) headline

Day Three: Afternoon Singles

Homero Blancas (USA) v. Brian Huggett (GBI)

Having surprisingly sat out the morning session, Brian Huggett was sent out first for Britain, in an attempt to cut into the U.S. three-point match lead. In this matchup of the only unbeaten players in the contest, Homero Blancas struck first.

At the outset it seemed that the American was going to overpower the Welshman: he was two up after just six holes, having halved the first four holes. With a solid start behind him, Blancas lost his grip on the match, losing the eighth and ninth holes after some poor shots.

Both players let themselves down on the tenth, which was halved in bogeys, as Huggett hit back—and hit back hard. With his fervent pride bubbling over, the Welshman carded six consecutive threes from eleven to sixteen—four of these treys for birdie. This dynamic run set up a much-needed, morale-boosting British win, 4 and 2.

Captain Bernard Hunt's decision not to play Huggett in the morning singles was even less understandable after Huggett's clear-cut win in the afternoon. The Welshman was the only player on either side to remain unbeaten, 3-0-1.

J. C. Snead (USA) v. Brian Barnes (GBI)

For the first and only time in this contest, Brian Barnes did not lead his side off.

After complaining of feeling tired in his morning loss, Barnes started off like a fresh quarter horse, with wins on the first two holes. Snead got credit for an assist at the first with a bogey to Barnes's par, but the Englishman got all the credit with his birdie on two. This was as good as it got for the home side, as Snead reeled off three wins in a row from the fourth to go one up.

After his match, Barnes again complained about being overworked and overtired, claiming that not enough of the workload was shared by the rest of the team. "I'm so tired, I just couldn't concentrate," he said.

Two up after claiming the eighth, Snead never looked back, although Barnes did claw a hole back on the thirteenth with a forlorn looking birdie. The coup de grâce for both Barnes and the British team came on the sixteenth when Snead holed a putt worthy of winning the Ryder Cup from almost forty feet away. This monster putt guaranteed the United States the half-point they needed to retain the Cup.

This was the second contest in a row in which Snead had been responsible for "winning" the Cup, having earned the decisive point in 1971 with his victory over Tony Jacklin.

Snead wrapped up the 3 and 1 win on the next hole with a par five, as Barnes's game completely fell apart.

Gay Brewer (USA) v. Bernard Gallacher (GBI)

With the British needing a fast start and early points, it had seemed a strange lineup that the British captain sent out: Huggett, not good enough for the morning, to lead off; Barnes, who was obviously too tired and in the wrong frame of mind, at two; and the obviously ailing Bernard Gallacher at three.

After winning four of the first five holes with par figures, Gay Brewer showed no mercy as he went on to give Gallacher an old-fashioned 6 and 5 pasting to prove that the Scot was in no condition to play match-play golf.

"I certainly wasn't feeling a hundred percent. The illness took more out of me than I thought." —BERNARD GALLACHER

This need to play a sick man, again, underlined the woeful lack of depth on the British team. In the Scot's defense, Brewer carded the best round of the afternoon—two under par—when most players were feeling the strain.

Billy Casper (USA) v. Tony Jacklin (GBI)

Forty-something Billy Casper, playing in his sixth match out of six, seemed to hold up better than many of the younger players. Against a dispirited Tony Jacklin, who would surely have been better utilized leading off his team, Casper was more than good enough to hold on to win, 2 and 1.

Lee Trevino (USA) v. Neil Coles (GBI)

"Trevino had Coles beaten on the first tee, and he ran clean away from a man who was mentally exhausted."
—*Michael Williams,* London Telegraph

After his emphatic 6 and 5 win over an equally tired-looking Neil Coles, Lee Trevino echoed Brian Barnes's sentiments, claiming he felt "whacked-out!"

Tom Weiskopf (USA) v. Christy O'Connor (GBI)

In his last Ryder Cup match, at the age of forty-eight, the grand old man of the British team, Christy O'Connor, bowed out with a typically gutsy half against Tom Weiskopf.

The final highlight of the Irishman's Ryder Cup career came on the last green, where he got up and down from a bunker to halve the hole and the match.

For his record ten Ryder Cup appearances (later beaten by Nick Faldo in 1997), O'Connor's overall playing totals were 11-21-4. His singles stats were unbelievably poor: 2-10-2.

The best indication of how tired and jaded the players felt came on the eleventh tee when Christy O'Connor yawned twice while waiting for Weiskopf to hit his drive.

Jack Nicklaus (USA) v. Maurice Bembridge (GBI)

Having let a golden opportunity for a win slip through his fingers against the same opponent in the morning, the Golden Bear did not make the same mistake twice. Once again, Maurice Bembridge did not flinch from taking on Jack Nicklaus, and managed to take the rematch all the way to the last hole again.

"Well, who would expect to hold Jack Nicklaus out there over thirty-six holes? Yet, there is that little guy staying with him toe-to-toe all the way."

—Jack Burke, Jr.

Nicklaus, determined to end the contest with a win, was more attacking over the closing holes—finishing birdie, birdie, par—to come out on top, 2-up.

Despite facing Jack Nicklaus four times, Maurice Bembridge ended the week with a very creditable three points from his six matches. Nicklaus himself ended the week as the overall points leader, with four and a half (4-1-1). Casper and Trevino ended with four points each, while Weiskopf chipped in with three and a half.

After the "unknown" Bembridge had taken him all the way for the second time in the singles: "Hey! You sonofabitch! You can play this game!"

—*Jack Nicklaus*

Arnold Palmer (USA) v. Peter Oosterhuis (GBI)

Having beaten Arnold Palmer in an earlier foursomes, Peter Oosterhuis claimed the great man's scalp in the singles, with an emphatic 4 and 2 win. With three wins and two halves from his six matches, Oosterhuis was the top points scorer for the British team.

Although the Americans had retained the Cup in some style, this final match signaled, in hindsight, a great American loss. With this defeat, his third in five matches, Arnold Palmer bowed out of the Ryder Cup as a player. He would return in 1975 as a nonplaying captain. His remarkable record of 22-8-2 from six matches will continue to be among the very best of all time.

"I've heard that a lot of the boys are tired out, but I'm feeling strong. I could go out and play another eighteen holes right now."

—*Peter Oosterhuis*

Afternoon singles result: USA 5½, GBI 2½
Day three result: USA 11, GBI 5

On the final-day rout that saw the United States win nine matches to Britain's three: *"I've played in a lot of Ryder Cup matches, but this is the first one I've watched. And I think the thing that impressed me the most was the strength of the U.S. players. They were as strong at the finish as they were at the start. I suppose that is because they play so much more than we do. But we're catching up here in that department with more old players traveling the world. Getting right down to it, though, I guess they are still a bit better than we are."*—BERNARD HUNT

Overall match score: USA 19, GBI 13

Recap

"It was the beating on the first day that welded the team together. We just weren't going to lose."
—*Jack Burke, Jr.*

"The British players were real good, but when you face this much power, it finally gets you."
—*Jack Burke, Jr.*

The match had started badly, very badly, for the all-powerful American team, with opening-day defeats of their Fantastic Four: Nicklaus, Palmer, Trevino, and Weiskopf. Licking their wounds with a halfway deficit of three points proved to be the catalyst for an impressive American comeback, and they won the second half of the match 14½-5½—losing just three matches out of the final twenty played.

The British, on the other hand, were mightily disappointed over not only throwing away this considerable halfway lead, but also failing to improve upon their recent results. Having halved in 1969, and then recorded their best-ever result in the United States (18½-13½), the British actually took a step back at Muirfield, with their worst result in three meetings. Just as it seemed the Ryder Cup was getting to be more competitive, the Americans proved they were still too strong—even after spotting their opponents a three-point start.

The relative strength of the teams can be gauged by the fact that Britain selected but never played John Garner, considered by his captain as not having enough length to compete over the testing links course (prompting one to ask why he was selected in the first place). Conversely, the U.S. captain had the luxury of bringing the Masters champion, Tommy Aaron, off the bench, and then using him as a last-minute replacement for his weary ace, Arnold Palmer.

The next meeting, at Laurel Valley in 1975, would not prove any easier for the British visitors, as three more American star rookies were chafing at the bit to be unleashed. Hale Irwin, Johnny

Miller, and Bob Murphy were the next superstars off the U.S. production line, with Larry Wadkins and Tom Watson waiting their turn in the wings. In view of this prospect, and the way the British performed in the second half of this match, questions were again raised about opening up the selection process to other countries.

Replying to a sportswriter's question as to the likelihood of a third term in charge: "I have already informed the PGA, 'Don't call me; I'll call you!'"
—*Jack Burke, Jr.*

"For me, and I think a lot of other golfers who've been fortunate to participate in them, international team contests are the most enjoyable events in golf. If the game has one drawback, it is its individuality, its self-concernedness—its selfishness, to be blunt about the matter. Playing for a team, and particularly for your country in someone else's country, really brings a group of players together." —Jack Nicklaus

Match Results (Winning side marked in *italics*.)

Thursday, September 20—Morning Foursomes

	USA	GBI	Score
1.	Lee Trevino Billy Casper	*Brian Barnes* *Bernard Gallacher*	1-up
2.	Tom Weiskopf J. C. Snead	*Christy O'Connor* *Neil Coles*	3 and 2
3.	Lou Graham Chi Chi Rodriguez	Tony Jacklin Peter Oosterhuis	halved
4.	*Jack Nicklaus* *Arnold Palmer*	Maurice Bembridge Eddie Polland	6 and 5

Thursday, September 20—Afternoon Fourball

	USA	GBI	Score
5.	Tommy Aaron Gay Brewer	*Brian Barnes* *Bernard Gallacher*	5 and 4
6.	Jack Nicklaus Arnold Palmer	*Maurice Bembridge* *Brian Huggett*	3 and 1
7.	Tom Weiskopf Billy Casper	*Tony Jacklin* *Peter Oosterhuis*	3 and 1
8.	*Lee Trevino* *Homero Blancas*	Neil Coles Christy O'Connor	2 and 1

Day one result: USA 2½, GBI 5½

Friday, September 21—Morning Foursomes

	USA	GBI	Score
9.	*Jack Nicklaus* *Tom Weiskopf*	Brian Barnes Peter Butler	1-up
10.	Arnold Palmer Dave Hill	*Peter Oosterhuis* *Tony Jacklin*	1-up
11.	Chi Chi Rodriguez Lou Graham	*Maurice Bembridge* *Brian Huggett*	5 and 4
12.	*Lee Trevino* *Billy Casper*	Neil Coles Christy O'Connor	2 and 1

Friday, September 21—Afternoon Fourball

	USA	GBI	Score
13.	*Arnold Palmer* *J. C. Snead*	Brian Barnes Peter Butler	2-up
14.	*Gay Brewer* *Billy Casper*	Tony Jacklin Peter Oosterhuis	3 and 2
15.	*Jack Nicklaus* *Tom Weiskopf*	Eddie Polland Clive Clark	3 and 2
16.	Lee Trevino Homero Blancas	Maurice Bembridge Brian Huggett	halved

Day two result: USA *5½,* GBI *2½*

Overall match score: USA *8,* GBI *8*

Saturday, September 22—Morning Singles

	USA	GBI	Score
17.	*Billy Casper*	Brian Barnes	2 and 1
18.	*Tom Weiskopf*	Bernard Gallacher	3 and 1
19.	*Homero Blancas*	Peter Butler	5 and 4
20.	Tommy Aaron	*Tony Jacklin*	3 and 2
21.	Gay Brewer	Neil Coles	halved
22.	*J. C. Snead*	Christy O'Connor	1-up
23.	Jack Nicklaus	Maurice Bembridge	halved
24.	Lee Trevino	Peter Oosterhuis	halved

Saturday, September 22—Afternoon Singles

	USA	GBI	Score
25.	Homero Blancas	*Brian Huggett*	4 and 2
26.	*J. C. Snead*	Brian Barnes	3 and 1
27.	*Gay Brewer*	Bernard Gallacher	6 and 5
28.	*Billy Casper*	Tony Jacklin	2 and 1
29.	*Lee Trevino*	Neil Coles	6 and 5
30.	Tom Weiskopf	Christy O'Connor	halved
31.	*Jack Nicklaus*	Maurice Bembridge	2-up
32.	Arnold Palmer	*Peter Oosterhuis*	4 and 2

Day three result: USA *11,* GBI *5*

Overall match score: USA *19,* GBI *13*

1975

Laurel Valley
Ligonier, Pennsylvania
United States
September 19–21

United States 21	**Great Britain and Ireland 11**
Billy Casper	Brian Barnes
Raymond Floyd	Maurice Bembridge
Al Geiberger	Eamonn Darcy
Lou Graham	Bernard Gallacher
Hale Irwin	Tommy Horton
Gene Littler	Brian Huggett
Johnny Miller	Guy Hunt
Bob Murphy	Tony Jacklin
Jack Nicklaus	Christy O'Connor, Jr.
J. C. Snead	John O'Leary
Lee Trevino	Peter Oosterhuis
Tom Weiskopf	Norman Wood
Captain	**Captain**
Arnold Palmer	Bernard Hunt

The New Power and Old Glory

If this wasn't the best team ever put out by the United States, it still had unimpeachable references: seven U.S. Open winners, three British Open winners, two Masters champions, and four PGA champions. Only two U.S. players—Snead and Murphy—had not won a major. The stellar cast list did not include the current British Open champion, Tom Watson, who had not qualified as a full PGA member, or a young Lanny Wadkins, whose time in the Ryder Cup was yet to come.

Another nonplayer was Arnold Palmer—who was handling the captain's role at the club where he used to be the touring professional.

"I have achieved many honors in golf, but this one tops them all, especially since we are playing the matches at Laurel Valley, [which] has been a second home to me." —Arnold Palmer

Although he had not gained enough points to qualify as a player for the U.S. team, after wins in the British PGA and Spanish

"It must be psychologically upsetting to the British to know that their best player is captain of the U.S. team."
—*Sports Illustrated*

Open, Arnold Palmer would have easily qualified for the British team. "Wouldn't that be great if I could play for the other side. I could probably win a few points," he said.

The writing was on the wall a few weeks before the Ryder Cup match got under way. Eight members of the British team competed in the World Open at Pinehurst, making little or no impression on the final leader board. This event went to Jack Nicklaus, who admitted he was playing the best golf of his life, having also taken that year's Masters, PGA Championship, Doral, and Heritage titles.

The Americans had only three new players: Hale Irwin, Bob Murphy, and the mercurial Johnny Miller (whose final Masters rounds of 65 and 66 had just failed to catch Nicklaus).

Of the twelve U.S. players, only Billy Casper had failed to win a tournament in 1975, although he managed a creditable sixth place in the Masters. Eight of the British dozen were in their twenties (average age twenty-nine), while only Johnny Miller of the Americans was under thirty (average age thirty-five).

Britain, on the other hand, had six rookies: Horton, Darcy (the youngest at twenty-three), Hunt, Wood, O'Leary, and, continuing the almost time-honored O'Connor dynasty, Christy Jr., who had followed after his uncle "retired" in 1973.

"The British are a team that has not proved it could master even the American Walker Cup team."
—Golf World

The British oddsmakers refused to take any bets on an outright American win, assuming it was a foregone conclusion. The shrewd moneymen, not blinded by patriotic duty, offered odds only on the final score of the British defeat: 21–11 being the early favorite.

"Statistics, it is true, can be made to prove anything except when it comes to the Ryder Cup. No matter how the facts are juggled, not even Perry Mason could make a plausible case for the British chances."

—MICHAEL MCDONNELL, *London Mail*

Course Details

Located fifty miles outside of Pittsburgh, Laurel Valley was built in 1959 on the 260-acre site of a former pheasant farm, and hosted the PGA Championship in only its sixth year. Seven large lakes are the main feature of the course, with thousands of trees having been added over time.

The saving grace of the heavy rain before and during the contest was that it caused the cancellation of a pro-am match between the two captains and entertainers Bob Hope and Perry Como. The softening of the greens also played very much into the hands of the hosts, who were used to the demands of accurate target golf.

"If you're not six feet tall and weigh two hundred pounds, you'll pay a heavy penalty if you get in the rough stuff."
—*Tommy Horton*

Hole	Distance	Par	Hole	Distance	Par
1	440	4	10	412	4
2	400	4	11	563	5
3	540	5	12	446	4
4	431	4	13	397	4
5	205	3	14	190	3
6	505	5	15	373	4
7	382	4	16	448	4
8	218	3	17	218	3
9	430	4	18	447	4
		36			**35 = Par 71 (7,045 yards)**

Course designers: Dick Wilson and Bob Simmons

Day One: Morning Foursomes

Heavy rain washed out much of the practice rounds, and for a time it looked as though the downpour would threaten the actual match.

Jack Nicklaus and Tom Weiskopf (USA) v. Brian Barnes and Bernard Gallacher (GBI)

The British pitched their best pairing, Barnes and Gallacher, into the first match, only to see them face the American aces, Nicklaus and Weiskopf.

The Americans' form in the opening holes was far from inspiring: they missed fairways, finding sand, wood, and rough on a number of occasions. The British pair was unable to take advantage of this slipshod start and actually fell behind after four holes, while Barnes had difficulty finding the fairways on the fifth and six holes. Nicklaus played a pathetic pitch at seven, failing to clear the water in front of him, then Weiskopf rescued the hole with a glorious chip up to the pin.

The Americans were both former Ohio State Buckeyes.

Nicklaus regained his touch on the ninth, knocking his approach to six feet for a birdie, and followed this by holing a long birdie putt to extend the Americans' lead to five after twelve holes.

Even when the British looked as if they would win a hole, the Americans produced something spectacular to rob them. On the fourteenth, Weiskopf holed out from more than thirty feet for a two to snatch a half. Not only did this long putt prevent the British from winning the hole, but it also gave the Americans an impressive 5 and 4 win, setting the tone for the morning.

Living up to their billing as the top U.S. partnership, Weiskopf and Nicklaus carded a five-under-par score for their fourteen holes.

Gene Littler and Hale Irwin (USA) v. Norman Wood and Maurice Bembridge (GBI)

Gene Littler was making his seventh appearance in the Ryder Cup, having been forced to miss the 1973 encounter while he recuperated after treatment for cancer. At the start of this match, he was the third-highest American points scorer, with twelve, and was also third in U.S. wins, after Palmer and Casper.

On the power of the opening two American pairings: *"Weiskopf and Nicklaus, Littler and Irwin . . . my God! The course is as American as it can be, where distance is the big factor. Our men are not accustomed to this length."* —TONY JACKLIN

This match turned on one shot at the 218-yard par-3 eighth hole. With the British ball safely on the green, Irwin tried to extricate Littler's drive from the long grass underneath a tree to the side of the green. Figuring there was not much he could do about a bad situation, Irwin took a carefree swing at the ball and managed to flop it out. The ball took a couple of friendly bounces on the green and rolled into the hole for a brazenly audacious birdie two. Instead of being all square, the British found themselves two down to the slightly fortuitous Americans.

Irwin and Littler secured the match with a run of three telling birdies on the twelfth through fourteenth holes en route to a 4 and 3 win.

Al Geiberger and Johnny Miller (USA) v. Tony Jacklin and Peter Oosterhuis (GBI)

Unusually, Jacklin and Oosterhuis played as if they were on different pages of the coaching manual. Geiberger and Miller took advantage of this lack of British cohesion and staked a two-hole lead after nine holes.

Geiberger and Oosterhuis were best of friends and sometime practice partners on the PGA Tour. "I try to copy Al's swing, and every time I do I play like a dream," the Englishman explained.

This round obviously was not one of those "dream" days.

It was only a matter of time before the British pair clicked, and a birdie on the 563-yard eleventh cut the U.S. lead to one.

This rebirth of the old partnership did not last long. Jacklin's pinpoint pitch to ten feet on the thirteenth hole gave Oosterhuis a putt to level the match, but he blew his chance. At the par-3 fourteenth, Jacklin piled agony upon agony by putting his tee shot into the water. On the next hole, coming back around the water, Oosterhuis deposited his drive in the drink and Britain was three down.

By the end, the Americans were one over par for their 2 and 1 win, while the misfit Brits were four over.

Lee Trevino and J. C. Snead (USA) v. Tommy Horton and John O'Leary (GBI)

Against the pairing of Trevino and Snead, Irishman John O'Leary started his Ryder Cup campaign with an embarrassing shank. Ten holes later he achieved something no other British player had been able to do on the first morning: give his side a lead. He did so by sinking a birdie-four putt from just off the eleventh green, which marked the first and only time any British pair would be in front.

After O'Leary's humble stumble on the first, the British pair had come back level with Trevino and Snead after nine holes. O'Leary's long putt on eleven put them down, but the Americans quickly countered to win the 446-yard twelfth and level the score again.

Trevino overshot the 397-yard thirteenth green and left Snead with a nasty bunker shot back. With the opponents licking their lips at another potential win, Snead holed his recovery for a birdie three to keep the game even. From here the Americans gave no more chances.

Snead continued to torment the British, sinking a putt across the width of the par-3 fourteenth green to regain the lead. Perhaps trying too hard, O'Leary sent his approach to fifteen through and beyond, dropping another hole.

In reply to Horton's magnificent fairway-wood to the heart of the sixteenth green, Snead pressed too hard and topped his own approach, much to his partner's amusement. Trevino ran over and carried Snead the few yards down the fairway to his ball, threatening to "carry him all the way home."

Having dropped the sixteenth in comic fashion, the Americans got serious on the next hole to close out the British pair, 2 and 1.

After the perfect beginning: "I wonder if we can beat these guys 32 points to nothing." —*Hale Irwin*

The United States started fast in all four singles, and their dominance was complete as they swept the morning session, 4–0. This winning start was in contrast to the losing starts they had made in the previous three matches. It was only the second time in Ryder Cup history that the opening session had resulted in a whitewash. America had first swept their opponents in 1947, en route to the biggest-ever victory.

Morning foursomes result: USA 4, GBI 0

Day One: Afternoon Fourball

The afternoon of the first day seemed a mighty early time to be making plans for a rearguard action, but Bernard Hunt had no other option, having been swept in the morning. He knew the Americans were not going to slacken, so he sent out his best pair to try to generate some momentum.

"The weather was humid and overcast . . . but after lunch the sun struggled through, giving an oppressive but not excessive warmth to the day."
—PETER RYDE, *Times* (London)

Billy Casper and Ray Floyd (USA) v. Tony Jacklin and Peter Oosterhuis (GBI)

Billy Casper had turned up late for the opening ceremony and was sidelined by Palmer for the morning session. With a 4–0 lead, the American captain was in a forgiving mood and sent Casper out first in the afternoon.

After their poor display in the morning, Jacklin and Oosterhuis came up trumps with a fighting 2 and 1 win over Casper and Floyd.

Although Oosterhuis birdied the first from ten feet for a lead, the highlight of the outward nine came at the 205-yard fifth, where Casper's twenty-five-foot birdie putt was matched by an equally fine British birdie.

Three successive birdies from the eleventh on put the British pair in the driving seat. Jacklin holed from six feet on eleven before Oosterhuis chipped in on twelve, but Oosterhuis's second birdie in a row was offset by Casper, gaining a modicum of revenge for the fifth hole.

This triple-birdie burst put Britain two up, and they held this lead until the seventeenth, where Oosterhuis made a birdie two for a half to win the match, 2 and 1.

On the only British win of the afternoon: "That's a bit of a relief. I thought we we're going to get wiped out altogether."
—*Tony Jacklin*

Tom Weiskopf and Lou Graham (USA) v. Eamonn Darcy and Christy O'Connor (GBI)

Continuing his red-hot form from the morning, Tom Weiskopf went out in 30 strokes on his own ball. This proved to be a baptism of fire for the Irish rookies Darcy and O'Connor, as Weiskopf and U.S. Open champion Graham proved to be a mighty formidable pair to meet first up.

Showing no rookie nerves in the slightest, Darcy opened with two birdies after two mesmerizing approach shots hypnotized the flag from a yard away. Unfortunately for the Irishman, neither strike won a hole: Weiskopf matched the first birdie, Graham the second.

"Who else in history has scored birdies on his two opening Ryder Cup holes?"
—*Dudley Doust,* Sunday Times *(London)*

After Weiskopf birdied the fifth on his own, Darcy was again denied on the seventh—his twenty-five-foot birdie putt was matched by Graham from fifteen feet closer in. The Irishman was probably wondering what he had to do to win a hole, when Graham showed him. The American slammed his tee shot to within a stride of the eighth hole to make a birdie two, then Weiskopf followed this with a twenty-five-footer for another birdie at nine for a three-hole lead.

Though the British rookies started in good style, three under for nine holes, the Americans combined for a six-under tally. Graham holed another monster from almost thirty feet on thirteen to push the lead to four, but Darcy's six-footer birdied fifteen to force another hole out of the Americans.

"I think there is more pressure than when you are playing for money. The main pressure is you don't want to let your partner down."
—*Lou Graham*

"These matches are exciting. There is a lot of pressure, and a lot of compassion too, more than you see on the tour." —Tom Weiskopf

Having played manfully in the white-hot cauldron of Ryder Cup competition, the Irish pair emerged with their heads held high but a 3 and 2 defeat hanging around their necks.

Jack Nicklaus and Bob Murphy (USA) v. Brian Barnes and Bernard Gallacher (GBI)

Nicklaus and Murphy faced some resolute golf from Barnes and Gallacher, who took an early lead when Barnes holed a forty-yard bunker shot for an eagle three at the third hole. The British players continued their good work and reached the turn four under par, but they held only a one-hole lead, the Americans having matched them all the way.

On the 563-yard eleventh, Nicklaus drove into some wretched rough but found a good lie. With 250 yards to go, he hit a perfect three-wood that split some distant fir trees. His ball found the green, and the great one took two putts for a birdie to go level. This strike was the key to the match: the next seven holes failed to separate the teams, and both pairs carded a five-under 66.

This, the seventh match out, was the first (and only) match of the opening day to reach the foreboding eighteenth hole, a sharp dogleg right across an expansive lake to an elevated green.

Lee Trevino and Hale Irwin (USA) v. Tommy Horton and John O'Leary (GBI)

O'Leary and Horton built upon their encouraging start of the morning, playing the outward nine in just 33 strokes. Unfortunately for the British rookies, Trevino and his own rookie, Irwin, went one stroke better and held a one-hole lead.

The next seven holes were halved, the eleventh and fourteenth in birdie fours and twos, respectively, and the Americans still held their precarious lead as they approached the par-3 seventeenth.

The British pair had a chance to halve the hole and keep the match alive, but they missed the vital putt to suffer their second 2 and 1 loss of the day.

Afternoon fourball result: USA 2½, GBI 1½
Day one result: USA 6½, GBI 1½

Day Two: Morning Fourball

The playing format was slightly changed for the second day, as the fourball preceded the foursomes.

"Fourball play is more freewheeling than foursome competition—the players find it more fun and they let it fly at the pin."

—John S. Rodasta, *New York Times*

Billy Casper and Johnny Miller (USA) v. Tony Jacklin and Peter Oosterhuis (GBI)

This match came down to two bunker shots on the last green. With the score all square, Oosterhuis and Miller (who three-putted for a five) were mere spectators as their partners both had a chance to win the match—from sand. Tony Jacklin blasted his wedge shot to within inches of the hole for a certain half. Not to be outdone, Billy Casper got his ball out of the bunker but finished seven feet from the pin. Casper made a pressure putt to finish all square.

"The embattled Jacklin matched the Mormons, putt for putt, on the moist and slippery greens."
—*Dudley Doust,* Sunday Times *(London)*

In what had been a close match throughout, both pairs finished with a better-ball score of 67.

Jack Nicklaus and J. C. Snead (USA) v. Tommy Horton and Norman Wood (GBI)

Wood and Horton gave Nicklaus and Snead a hard time for the first ten holes. At eleven, Snead holed his bunker shot to win the hole; this body blow spelled an end to the British resistance, and the Americans ended up easy winners, 4 and 2.

Gene Littler and Lou Graham (USA) v. Brian Barnes and Bernard Gallacher (GBI)

Littler and Graham handed Barnes and Gallacher their second heavy defeat of the contest, gaining a 5 and 3 win en route to a 66 for their round.

The length of the holes and the length of the Americans' driving soon became apparent to Gallacher. "It's really exhausting hammering away just to keep up with these guys," he said.

Al Geiberger and Raymond Floyd (USA) v. Eamonn Darcy and Guy Hunt (GBI)

Geiberger and Floyd were held close by Darcy and Hunt for much of the encounter, with Geiberger and Hunt doing the lion's share of the scoring. Despite Hunt's early heroics in matching Geiberger's approach to three feet on the first hole, then winning the third with a well-judged chip, the British were one down after seventeen holes.

Darcy played the final hole the best, hitting a magnificent four-wood over 220 yards to within fifteen feet, before holing the winning birdie putt to deservedly halve the match. Both pairs had tamed the course with resolute 66s.

Morning fourball result: USA 3, GBI 1

Day Two: Afternoon Foursomes

The continual rain made playing conditions very heavy, and the scoring suffered accordingly.

Lee Trevino and Bob Murphy (USA) v. Tony Jacklin and Brian Huggett (GBI)

Brian Huggett came off the bench for the British side, having sat out the first three sessions—and soon made an impact.

Trevino and Murphy took an early two-hole lead on Jacklin and Huggett but were staggered by the British combo on the 430-yard ninth. Huggett unleashed a four-wood second around a fir tree and up to the elevated green. Jacklin finished off the job, making a fifteen-foot downhill putt look as simple as fifteen-foot downhillers can ever look.

This birdie under their belts, the British reeled off three more, with Huggett, again to the fore, holing a bunker shot from sixty yards out on the twelfth. The British players proceeded to convert their two-hole lead into a 3 and 2 win on the sixteenth.

Tom Weiskopf and Johnny Miller (USA) v. Christy O'Connor and John O'Leary (GBI)

Weiskopf and Miller had the rare luxury of finishing over par, as they recorded an emphatically easy 5 and 3 win over O'Connor and O'Leary, who carded too many fives for their own good.

Hale Irwin and Billy Casper (USA) v. Peter Oosterhuis and Maurice Bembridge (GBI)

At forty-four years of age, Billy Casper was playing in a record ninth consecutive Ryder Cup for the United States. Casper's 12½ points made him the second-most-productive U.S. player after Arnold Palmer.

Irwin and Casper, who hardly set the course alight, were over par for their round. But they recorded an incisive 3 and 2 win over Oosterhuis and Bembridge, who were five over par for the first twelve holes.

"We ought to have been beaten 6 and 4. But they played worse."
—*Hale Irwin*

Al Geiberger and Raymond Floyd (USA) v. Eamonn Darcy and Guy Hunt (GBI)

Geiberger and Floyd crowned another wholly miserable day for the British with a solid 3 and 2 win over Darcy and Hunt, who did themselves no favors as they went out in 40.

Overall the British players seemed to struggle more than their opponents in the wet conditions, but then again, they had struggled all week whatever the conditions.

Afternoon foursomes result: USA 3, GBI 1
Day two result: USA 6, GBI 2
Overall match score: USA 12½, GBI 3½

Day Three: Morning Singles

"Because of the recent rains the course played longer today than its surveyed 7,045 yards. Ligonier also is hilly. What with the mud and the hills, the players found walking eighteen or thirty-six holes hard work."

—John S. Radosta, *New York Times*

Bob Murphy (USA) v. Tony Jacklin (GBI)

Leading off for Britain, Tony Jacklin knew he was playing for nothing more than his country's and his own pride.

Jacklin took a lead over Bob Murphy on the fourteenth, then let his advantage and the match slip away with careless drives. Three bad tee shots in a row cost the Englishman each hole, handing Murphy a gift-wrapped 2 and 1 victory.

"I am so tired, I can't even turn on the TV. I fall asleep in three minutes. In the Piccadilly Match Play Championship, which is just as grueling, you get beat and you go home. But here, you get beat and you have to come back for more." —TONY JACKLIN

Johnny Miller (USA) v. Peter Oosterhuis (GBI)

The British number two, Peter Oosterhuis, took up the slack following Jacklin's loss by making an impressive comeback.

Needing to set an example at the top of his order, Bernard Hunt sent out his best three players—Jacklin, Oosterhuis, and Gallacher—with mixed results: loss, win, and half.

Having taken the eleventh, Johnny Miller was two up and held the definite edge on the twelfth green. But Oosterhuis holed a fifty-foot putt, Miller missed his six-footer, and Miller's lead had been cut to one hole. This was not the first hole Oosterhuis had won by holing a putt longer than his rookie opponent's.

With the momentum now on his side, Oosterhuis made five more threes in a row to end with a two-hole victory over a stunned Miller, who won the seventeenth with a birdie two to temporarily prolong his agony, which came when he failed to find the last green in two.

Lee Trevino (USA) v. Bernard Gallacher (GBI)

Trevino and Gallacher must have been sick of the sight of each other as they crossed swords for the sixth time in four contests. The American definitely had something to prove: he had scored only one win (in 1969 in the afternoon foursomes) over the Scot in their previous five meetings.

Gallacher carded a 76 on his way to halving the match with Trevino, who again came up winless against his younger opponent.

Gene Littler (USA) v. Brian Huggett (GBI)

Littler went out in a three-over 38 to be four up against the misfiring Huggett, who couldn't buy a hole. Matters got even worse for the Welshman after the turn.

Despite having spent many hours on the practice ground trying to improve his game, Littler came home with three fives in a row. Still, he lost only one hole in that poor stretch, having been let off by the Welshman, who played even worse. Littler steadied himself and finished the match with a win on the sixteenth for a less-than-pleasing 4 and 2 victory.

With three wins out of three, Littler failed to add to his U.S. record of playing in eight halved matches.

Jack Nicklaus (USA) v. Brian Barnes (GBI)

A combination of his own fine play and the carelessness of his opponent gave Brian Barnes the prized scalp of Jack Nicklaus.

A couple of smooth, twenty-foot-long birdie putts gave the pipe-smoking Englishman the first two holes. Barnes then bogeyed the fifth, which Nicklaus birdied. Nicklaus three-putted the seventh, and Barnes pitched to eight feet on the ninth for a three-hole lead by the turn.

Brian Barnes wore Bermuda shorts and puffed incessantly on a meerschaum pipe that left his mouth only during shots.

Barnes was out in a most creditable 34 strokes, Nicklaus having trouble concentrating after the Cup had been retained.

The American fell four down when he hit a bad drive on the tenth, got one back at fourteen, but lost the match with another bogey on sixteen. Barnes played admirably to hold on to his early advantage for a famous 4 and 2 victory.

Hale Irwin (USA) v. Tommy Horton (GBI)

Hale Irwin started fast and was three up in as many holes on Tommy Horton. Two American birdies were capped by a British bogey to set Irwin on his way, but the Englishman was not to go down without a fight and eventually leveled on the fourteenth.

With the momentum drifting his way, Horton won the seventeenth when his chip rolled close enough for a concession. Dormie at the last, Horton threw away all his good work getting back into and ahead of the match by overplaying his drive, which allowed Irwin the final win for a half.

Hale Irwin had shown he could handle the competitive pressures of the singles format, having won the 1974 World Matchplay title at Wentworth.

Tom Weiskopf (USA) v. Guy Hunt (GBI)

Out in 33, Tom Weiskopf was only two up against the resilient Guy Hunt. Another blistering round of sub-par golf saw Weiskopf finish six under, and he wrapped up his match 5 and 3.

"We've got so much depth, it's like the Green Bay Packers against a high school team."
—*Tom Weiskopf*

Fittingly, it was Weiskopf, who had played the best golf of the contest (winning all four of his matches), who earned the point that retained the Cup for the United States.

The match score immediately after Weiskopf's win was a totally dominating 16½-5½.

Billy Casper (USA) v. Eamonn Darcy (GBI)

The only saving grace for the Irish rookie was that his fourth match without a win came against Billy Casper, playing in his thirty-seventh and last Ryder Cup match.

Casper had been the backbone of the U.S. Ryder Cup effort since 1961, and Darcy became his sixth solo victim in ten matches. The two-time U.S. Open champion coasted to a convincing 3 and 2 win, bowing out in the style to which he had become accustomed.

Casper bowed out of the Ryder Cup with a 20-10-7 record for a total of 23½ points—which was unmatched until 1997.

Morning singles result: USA 5, GBI 3

On the United States winning the morning singles, 5-3, to take a 17½-6½ lead: GREAT BRITISH DESCENT INTO VALLEY OF SHADOW

—*Times* (London) headline

Day Three: Afternoon Singles

Although the Ryder Cup had been settled before the afternoon singles started, the eight matches were still played out. In this friendly finale to the contest, Great Britain took the remaining honors by the score 4½-3½.

With the Ryder Cup already decided, very little was reported in the media on these last "meaningless" matches, with the exception of the final revenge match.

Raymond Floyd (USA) v. Tony Jacklin (GBI)

Jacklin was unable to shoulder the responsibility of being the team's number one player, and his final record of 2-3-1 was indicative of the pressure of expectation he was under. In his Ryder Cup debut, Ray Floyd was keen to make another mark in the win column, and he did so with a 1-up victory.

J. C. Snead (USA) v. Peter Oosterhuis (GBI)

Oosterhuis's second triumph of the day, a 3 and 2 win, gave him 3½ points out of 6, another superb exhibition of match-play golf. It was a pity there were not eleven more like him back home. Snead, who won his first two pairs matches, sat out the second afternoon with a bothersome cyst on his right knee but turned out for the final singles at the last minute, allowing Casper and Weiskopf to sit the final afternoon out.

Lou Graham (USA) v. Tommy Horton (GBI)

Horton spoiled Graham's perfect record coming into the afternoon with a 2 and 1 victory.

Al Geiberger (USA) v. Bernard Gallacher (GBI)

With this half, Geiberger finished unbeaten, with two wins and two halves from his four matches, while Gallacher lost two and halved three of his five outings.

Hale Irwin (USA) v. John O'Leary (GBI)

With this 2 and 1 win, Hale Irwin finished his first Ryder Cup with four wins and a half in five matches, while his rookie opponent O'Leary went 0 for 4.

Bob Murphy (USA) v. Maurice Bembridge (GBI)

Having played a backup role in the pairs (0-1-1), Bob Murphy won both his singles 2 and 1.

Lee Trevino (USA) v. Norman Wood (GBI)

Even though Lee Trevino had been complaining for years about playing both morning and afternoon sessions, this 2 and 1 loss was a major upset, since Wood had been well beaten in his first two pairs matches.

Jack Nicklaus (USA) v. Brian Barnes (GBI)

Palmer sneaked a peak at the British singles lineup and inserted Nicklaus against the player who had humiliated him in the morning.

"I remember Jack saying to me on the first tee, 'You've beaten me once, but there ain't no way you're going to beat me again.' And then he started birdie, birdie, and I didn't think I would. But I did."
—*Brian Barnes*

Looking for revenge, Nicklaus gave Barnes a dose of his own medicine by starting out with two birdies. Barnes fought back to level by the turn, but a three-footer for birdie on the tenth gave Nicklaus back the lead.

The British player was not to be denied a second victory over the world's number one, and he fought back again and more. Two birdies on eleven and twelve put him one hole to the fore. Nicklaus may have had trouble in concentrating on a "meaningless" match, but he had actively sought the rematch in a bid to get even.

Barnes's par three at the short fourteenth increased his lead, and he managed to keep Nicklaus at bay with three halved holes to close out the match. The Scot (who was All-World for one day) was one under par after seventeen, when he claimed his second win over the mighty Nicklaus, 2 and 1.

"What was Nicklaus trying to do, anyway, get Barnes a knighthood? Or a tickertape parade down Piccadilly?"
—*Dudley Doust,* Sunday Times *(London)*

"I still, all these years on, have difficulty in getting away from it. Whenever I attend a company day or a dinner, I am introduced as the man who twice beat Nicklaus head-to-head. I never consider it as that fantastic. Certainly I enjoyed it at the time, but in my own mind I soon forgot it."
—BRIAN BARNES

Strangely, the last five matches all ended 2 and 1. There had been only five 2 and 1 wins in the previous twenty-seven matches.

With this rousing finish to the match, Britain had won 4½ of its total 11 points after the Cup had been lost.

Afternoon singles result: USA 3½, GBI 4½
Day three result: USA 8½, GBI 7½
Overall match score: USA 21, GBI 11

Recap

Having been the successful skipper in 1969, Arnold Palmer became only the second U.S. captain to have a perfect record after leading his team more than once. Ben Hogan is the other.

In an attempt to give the gallery more value for their money, Palmer performed an impromptu air show in his plane after the match was over.

The fact that 3½ of the 6½ points the visiting side gained up to lunch on the final day had been earned by the two players plying their trade on the U.S. professional circuit spoke volumes about the state of British golf. Apart from Brian Barnes's freakish double over Nicklaus on the final day, the only two players who could consistently stack up *mano a mano* against the Americans were Oosterhuis and Jacklin, whose games had developed on the toughest golf tour in the world. Britain had shown it could produce world-beaters, but not if they were restricted to the powder-puff British tour.

DEATH OF THE RYDER CUP
—London Mail *headline*

Some notable voices began to raise old issues:

Jack Nicklaus: "I know national pride is involved, but at some point reality must prevail if the event isn't to decline into little more than an exhibition bout—and especially if it is to remain a vital part of the U.S. golfing calendar. When you consider that the golfing population of the United States is roughly equivalent to that of the rest of the world, maybe a World–versus–United States format would make the most sense."

Henry Poe, U.S. PGA president: "Under the present format, we are going to win more and more matches. But it's not for us to approach the British—just because we think they are not good enough."

Even so, some voices were happy with the way things were:

Arnold Palmer: "There are occasions even in professional sport when who wins by how much isn't everything, and the Ryder Cup is most certainly one of them. I do not think it should be dropped just because the Americans usually win. There has never been a punch pulled yet in the Ryder Cup."

Match Results (Winning sides marked in *italics*.)

Friday, September 19—Morning Foursomes

	USA	GBI	Score
1.	*Jack Nicklaus* *Tom Weiskopf*	Brian Barnes Bernard Gallacher	5 and 4
2.	*Gene Littler* *Hale Irwin*	Norman Wood Maurice Bembridge	4 and 3
3.	*Al Geiberger* *Johnny Miller*	Tony Jacklin Peter Oosterhuis	2 and 1
4.	*Lee Trevino* *J. C. Snead*	Tommy Horton John O'Leary	2 and 1

Friday, September 19—Afternoon Fourball

	USA	GBI	Score
5.	Billy Casper Raymond Floyd	*Tony Jacklin* *Peter Oosterhuis*	2 and 1
6.	*Tom Weiskopf* *Lou Graham*	Eamonn Darcy Christy O'Connor	3 and 2
7.	Jack Nicklaus Bob Murphy	Brian Barnes Bernard Gallacher	halved
8.	*Lee Trevino* *Hale Irwin*	Tommy Horton John O'Leary	2 and 1

Day one result: USA 6½, GBI 1½

Saturday, September 20—Morning Fourball

	USA	GBI	Score
9.	Billy Casper Johnny Miller	Tony Jacklin Peter Oosterhuis	halved
10.	*Jack Nicklaus* *J. C. Snead*	Tommy Horton Norman Wood	4 and 2
11.	*Gene Littler* *Lou Graham*	Brian Barnes Bernard Gallacher	5 and 3
12.	Al Geiberger Raymond Floyd	Eamonn Darcy Guy Hunt	halved

Saturday, September 20—Afternoon Foursomes

	USA	GBI	Score
13.	Lee Trevino Bob Murphy	*Tony Jacklin* *Brian Huggett*	3 and 2
14.	*Tom Weiskopf* *Johnny Miller*	Christy O'Connor John O'Leary	5 and 3
15.	*Hale Irwin* *Billy Casper*	Peter Oosterhuis Maurice Bembridge	3 and 2
16.	*Al Geiberger* *Raymond Floyd*	Eamonn Darcy Guy Hunt	3 and 2

Day two result: USA 6, GBI 2

Overall match score: USA 12½, GBI 3½

Sunday, September 21—Morning Singles

	USA	GBI	Score
17.	*Bob Murphy*	Tony Jacklin	2 and 1
18.	Johnny Miller	*Peter Oosterhuis*	2-up
19.	Lee Trevino	Bernard Gallacher	halved
20.	*Gene Littler*	Brian Huggett	4 and 2
21.	Jack Nicklaus	*Brian Barnes*	4 and 2
22.	Hale Irwin	Tommy Horton	halved
23.	*Tom Weiskopf*	Guy Hunt	5 and 3
24.	*Billy Casper*	Eamonn Darcy	3 and 2

Sunday, September 21—Afternoon Singles

	USA	GBI	Score
25.	*Raymond Floyd*	Tony Jacklin	1-up
26.	J. C. Snead	*Peter Oosterhuis*	3 and 2
27.	Lou Graham	*Tommy Horton*	2 and 1
28.	Al Geiberger	Bernard Gallacher	halved
29.	*Hale Irwin*	John O'Leary	2 and 1
30.	*Bob Murphy*	Maurice Bembridge	2 and 1
31.	Lee Trevino	*Norman Wood*	2 and 1
32.	Jack Nicklaus	*Brian Barnes*	2 and 1

Day three result: USA 8½, GBI 7½

Overall match score: USA 21, GBI 11

1977

Royal Lytham and St. Annes
Lancashire
England
September 15–17

United States 12½	**Great Britain and Ireland 7½**
Raymond Floyd	Brian Barnes
Lou Graham	Ken Brown
Hubert Green	Howard Clark
Dave Hill	Neil Coles
Hale Irwin	Eamonn Darcy
Don January	Peter Dawson
Jerry McGee	Nick Faldo
Jack Nicklaus	Bernard Gallacher
Ed Sneed	Tommy Horton
Dave Stockton	Tony Jacklin
Lanny Wadkins	Mark James
Tom Watson	Peter Oosterhuis
Captain	**Captain**
Dow Finsterwald	Brian Huggett

Fortune Rookies

Another change to the playing format saw the morning and afternoon sessions disappear. Many of the players from the last Ryder Cup match, at Laurel Valley, had complained bitterly about the physical stresses and strains of thirty-six holes of pressure-packed match play. So the powers that be decided to reduce the number of matches, with half an eye on the fact that with fewer matches, the play might be a little more competitive.

The revised format had five foursomes on day one, five fourballs on day two, and ten singles on the third day. This meant that there were only 20 points to be won, the magic number was 10½, and there was less chance of another Great American Blowout. It also meant that the quality of the matches should be high, each side putting out its best players with little fear of fatigue.

Both sides welcomed a large transfusion of new blood under first time-captains Dow Finsterwald and Brian Huggett—both with respectable Ryder Cup playing careers behind them.

Finsterwald had played in four Ryder Cups (9-3-1), while Huggett had experienced six as a player (9-10-6), making his debut the year Finsterwald played his last match. In 1963, the pair faced off in the morning fourball, with the American (partnered by Palmer) rubbing the Welshman's nose in it, 5 and 4.

"In America the Ryder Cup rates somewhere between the Tennessee Frog Jumping Contest and the Alabama Melon Pip Spitting Championship, although the players themselves have always taken it seriously until Tom Welskopf declined to play in favor of a week's holiday shooting sheep."
—*Peter Dobereiner,* London Observer *(1978)*

Finsterwald's rookie charges were Tom Watson, Lanny Wadkins, Jerry McGee, Hubert Green, and Ed Sneed. The American star from 1975, Tom Weiskopf, declined the chance to play, preferring to stay home and go hunting instead.

"It was a classic gray English day, and the ceremony was behind the clubhouse at Royal Lytham and St. Annes. Just as the flags were being raised, a gust of wind blew through and the flags unfurled perfectly, just stood straight up and out. Dow Finsterwald was our captain, and he talked about what it meant to be part of a Ryder Cup, about all the great players who had taken part and how honored he was to follow in the footsteps of all the captains who had come before him. I just stood there with these shivers going down my back, thinking, 'I want to do that someday.' "

—TOM WATSON, who would be named U.S. Ryder Cup captain in 1993

Huggett's new nuggets were Nick Faldo, Mark James (named captain in 1999), Ken Brown, and Peter Dawson.

Having taken up the game only six years earlier, after watching a tournament on TV, Nick Faldo became the youngest-ever Ryder Cup player at twenty years, one month, and twenty-eight days of age.

The Ryder Cup was forever demonstrating that the two countries were still separated by a common language, especially when it came to interpreting rules of golf. The British had been experimenting with a rule that allowed them to tap down spike marks on the green, a practice that is illegal in the United States. Huggett felt that the practice had to be allowed, since his players were used to it, and any infringements would cost them the hole. Finsterwald was not happy with relaxing the rules, but he relented.

Course Details

The Ryder Cup returned to the links course in the northeast of England, sixteen years after the United States had won 14½-9½.

Hole	Distance	Par	Hole	Distance	Par
1	206	3	10	334	4
2	436	4	11	542	5
3	458	4	12	201	3
4	393	4	13	339	4
5	212	3	14	445	4
6	486	5	15	468	4
7	551	5	16	356	4
8	394	4	17	453	4
9	162	3	18	386	4
		35			**36 = Par 71 (6,822 yards)**

Course designer: George Lowe

Day One: 18-Hole Foursomes

The opening-day foursomes were played in light and bright autumnal conditions, with a slight breeze gently persuading the leaves to part company with the trees.

"If the present weather continues, there could be some remarkable scoring. It is superfluous to say which of the two teams is the more accustomed at that." —PAT WARD-THOMAS, *London Guardian*

Lanny Wadkins and Hale Irwin (USA) v. Bernard Gallacher and Brian Barnes (GBI)

Given the undoubted honor of leading off the competition, Wadkins and Irwin teed it up against Gallacher and Barnes, neither pairing showing why they had been handpicked to lead off the contest. The quality of play was not that normally associated with the Ryder Cup, especially in view of the fact that the new five-handed format was supposed to improve the level of performance.

Each pair did manage to win two holes on the front nine—all four to opposing bogeys. The British produced the only birdie going out, on the par-5 sixth, where the Americans took a bogey six to make doubly sure of losing the hole.

The mediocre match of mistakes and misses was all square at the turn, when the teams found their real form. Irwin finally persuaded his red-raw rookie partner Wadkins to leave his woods in the bag when common sense dictated irons, and the Americans immediately went ahead on the par-5 eleventh with their first birdie.

Lanny Wadkins was in prime form, having won two prestigious events in the previous month: the PGA Championship and the World Series of Golf.

British threes at the next two holes swung the lead away from the Americans, and it seemed the momentum had swung with it. One up with five to play, and finally into the birdie habit, the British pair threw the match away. Barnes sliced his approach to fourteen, Gallacher missed a six-footer for par on fifteen, then Barnes blew an even shorter one on sixteen. Three British bogeys and three American wins put the visitors two up with two to play.

Having parred fourteen through sixteen to take the two-hole lead, Wadkins and Irwin cozily closed the match out with a finish that was not in keeping with the rest of the match. Irwin hit a thumping three-iron to three yards of the flag for Wadkins to nail the birdie putt for an opening 3 and 1 win.

Dave Stockton and Jerry McGee (USA) v. Neil Coles and Peter Dawson (GBI)

Peter Dawson was the first left-hander to play in the Ryder Cup.

Despite the magic in Dave Stockton's putter, he and Jerry McGee struggled to the turn against Dawson and Coles.

On the fifth hole, Stockton sank a twenty-five-footer to level the match, but the British regained their lead on the sixth. Stockton had to hole an eight-footer on the seventh to avoid going further behind, but he leveled the match again with a twenty-footer on the eighth. Like clockwork, Stockton's good work was undone as Dawson and Coles edged into the lead again on the next hole. If not for Stockton's hot putter, the British would have turned for home more than one up, having gone out in a blistering 31 strokes.

Over the next six holes, Britain wasted a handful of chances to put the match away, then proceeded to throw the match away over the final three holes.

"The greens were receptive and easy paced. Ask Stockton; he should know. He has lived by his putter for years, but seldom with the brilliance he showed today." —PETER RYDE, *Times* (London)

Two down with three to play, Stockton and his putter were back in business. On sixteen, he holed from twenty-five feet for the win, and went one better on the following green. McGee drove wildly into a fairway bunker on seventeen, leaving Stockton no other option but to hack out. McGee's approach found a remote part of the putting surface, some fifty feet from the hole. The British pair also had its problems, as Coles's overzealous long iron ran through the green and Dawson's comeback chip was well wide of the mark.

Consumed with the confidence that few men ever experience while standing on a green with a putter in their hands, Stockton delivered a fifty-foot bomb, sending shock waves through his opponents. With all the pressure of a fast-disappearing lead, Coles blew his much shorter putt, and the teams were level.

On the eighteenth, it was the British pair's turn to drive into a bunker, Coles the culprit this time. Unlike the Americans, they could not recover to challenge for the hole and went down ignobly—with a double-bogey six—having dominated the match until the final few holes.

"We outplayed Stockton and McGee, but it wasn't enough. They putted like hell."
—*Neil Coles*

Raymond Floyd and Lou Graham (USA) v. Nick Faldo and Peter Oosterhuis (GBI)

After this match, it was announced that newcomer Nick Faldo had been suffering from glandular fever and his participation had been in doubt. What was not in doubt was how much talent this youngster possessed, and under the guidance of Peter Oosterhuis the pair gradually climbed back into the match against Floyd and Graham.

Faldo's illness and rookie nerves may have affected his play, as his first start in the Ryder Cup was less than auspicious. He missed a horrid short putt on the first hole, and he and Oosterhuis went on to drop the first three holes against the Americans, who were out in 32 and comfortably two up.

The tenth brought another U.S. birdie to go three up, and with eight holes to play, the Americans' game began to unravel at the seams. Thanks to some second-rate play, they dropped two holes at eleven and twelve, and their lead was down to one. At fourteen, Faldo hit a fine fairway wood to the green to set up another win to square the match, then Oosterhuis hit an equally good two-iron into fifteen to take the lead.

In a greenside bunker on seventeen, Floyd claimed that the British ball safely on the green was farther away from the hole. A minor disagreement occurred as to who should play first, then Oosterhuis decided to take the psychological advantage and made Faldo putt right up to the hole. Floyd blasted his bunker shot past the hole, and Graham missed the return putt, handing victory to the British, 2 and 1.

The Americans had blown their three-hole lead by finishing 6-5-4-5-5-4-5—six over par for the last seven holes played. The British pair did nothing more spectacular than finish with seven straight pars to win five holes.

Ed Sneed and Don January (USA) v. Eamonn Darcy and Tony Jacklin (GBI)

In this topsy-turvy match, only two holes were halved on the front nine, as January and Sneed were up twice early on against Jacklin and Darcy but faltered to the turn one down.

Jacklin doubled this lead with a chip shot to a yard on the tenth, setting up a birdie putt for Darcy. The Americans gladly claimed the twelfth through the inadequacies of their opponents, who were forced to concede the hole after a series of minor disasters. The British were soon back up by two, courtesy of an American bogey at fourteen.

After Jacklin's excellent sand save, Sneed somehow holed a difficult-looking nine-footer on fifteen to prevent his side going dormie three down. With a win in its sights, the British pair failed to make pars on the next two holes. On sixteen, Jacklin's awful wedged approach found the bunker, giving the United States an advantage they pounced on to cut the lead to one.

Jacklin hit a terrible drive off seventeen, leaving Darcy with little hope of finding the green, to gift another hole to the United States and square the match. The eighteenth was halved—only after Sneed had missed a ten-foot putt for the win—and so the honors were shared.

Yet another match they had been winning got away from the overly hospitable hosts.

Jack Nicklaus and Tom Watson (USA) v. Tommy Horton and Mark James (GBI)

For the last match out, the United States unleashed another dream Ryder Cup pairing. Earlier in the year, Watson, the reigning Masters champion, had thrilled the crowds at Turnberry when he finished with two 65s to snatch the British Open from Nicklaus. On this day, they were on the same side and the British were the common enemy.

As the home crowd feared, Horton and rookie James were no match for the Americans, who had two birdies at the first three holes, adding a third at the seventh. The British pair did manage a solitary win on the front nine, a birdie four at the sixth, but the Americans reached the turn four up in just 32 strokes, carding five threes on the way.

Nicklaus and Watson, who would team up four times in Ryder Cup play and never lose a match, started out 3-3-3-4-3 for a three-hole lead.

"For the British pair it was like finding themselves in a cage with a couple of lions and only their golf clubs to defend themselves with."
—JOHN WOODCOCK, *Times* (London)

The Americans momentarily eased off the power, halving the first three holes coming home, but Nicklaus could not resist trying to drive the 339-yard thirteenth, and failed to do so by only a few yards. This act of bravado set up another hole-winning birdie three, which was almost repeated on the fourteenth, but Watson's putt finished an inch short of the hole. This gimme par four secured the match 5 and 4, and so as not to disappoint the large crowd that had followed the Americans, they agreed to play out the final four holes in an exhibition for the gallery.

Tongue-in-cheek reflection at the 1995 Ryder Cup press conference: *"I played my first Ryder Cup match against Nicklaus and Watson and we held them to 5 and 4. We weren't intimidated, but we had sort of an inkling that they might be slightly better than us, and so it proved."* —MARK JAMES

The general idea of this new five-game format was to give the home side a competitive edge. It did just that, up to a point, as the British were up in four matches with the finishing post in sight, but fell away (again), winning only one match outright and halving a second. Maybe the answer was to play the matches over twelve holes?

Day one result: USA 3½, GBI 1½

Day Two: 18-Hole Fourball

"A cool easterly breeze . . . had changed from the previous day, burnishing the scene with bright light and altering the course completely."
—PAT WARD-THOMAS, *London Guardian*

Tom Watson and Hubert Green (USA) v. Brian Barnes and Tommy Horton (GBI)

Against Barnes and Horton, who never won a hole, Tom Watson returned his second 5 and 4 win in two days, this time in partnership with another "rookie," Hubert Green.

Opening with a forty-foot putt, Watson was the inspiration of the American pair, making birdie twos on all three par 3s on the way out—climaxed by his chip-in on the ninth for a five-hole lead at the turn.

If Watson dominated the par 3s, Green held sway on the other six holes going out. His putting kept Barnes and Horton at bay, particularly on the seventh, where he holed a monster par putt to deprive the British of their only real opportunity of a win in fourteen holes.

The U.S. pair was out in 29, while the British couple encountered some communication difficulties and struggled to keep the game remotely close.

"On the third hole, Brian drove in the rough. When he reached his ball, he yelled across the fairway to ask where my ball was. I replied it was in the fairway, but before I had the chance to add 'in a terrible lie,' the Big Man had his ball in his pocket." —TOMMY HORTON

With the five holes on the back nine all halved in regulation, except for offsetting birdies at the par-4 thirteenth, the match rolled on to its inexorable conclusion with a spanking 5 and 4 victory.

Ed Sneed and Lanny Wadkins (USA) v. Neil Coles and Peter Dawson (GBI)

"Sneed, a strong, handsome man, has a lazy looking swing which conceals a rare acceleration of the club."
—*Pat Ward-Thomas,* London Guardian

Like Tom Watson before them, the American pairing of Wadkins and Sneed combined to card three twos at the short holes on the front nine.

An American bogey at the 458-yard third brought their match against Coles and Dawson back level after their opening deuce, thanks to Sneed's chipping in from a bunker. The second American birdie at the 212-yard fifth put them one up again. A third U.S. birdie at the 551-yard seventh was negated by Dawson's fighting three-foot putt, but he and Coles both bogeyed the eighth to go two down.

As the British pair struggled to keep in contact, Dawson was again the home savior, matching Wadkins's birdie two at the 162-yard ninth.

On his own ball, Lanny Wadkins covered the five holes from nine through thirteen in fifteen strokes: 2-3-4-3-3.

Two up at the turn, in 31 strokes, the Americans went further ahead on the next two holes. At ten, both their opponents again failed to make birdie putts from less than six feet. Then, at eleven, Coles found the trees with his wild and woolly second, and Dawson missed another short par putt.

Four up with seven to play, the Americans consolidated their commanding lead by halving the next three holes, with the shortish par-4 thirteenth covered in birdie threes. On fifteen, the eighth birdie of their round gave Wadkins and Sneed a well-deserved 5 and 3 win that was unfairly overshadowed by Watson and Green before them.

On the one-sided nature of the British pair's play, which the *Times* (London) headlined as "Partnership Fires on One Cylinder": *"Peter Dawson is one of the finest wedge players I have ever seen."*

—Lanny Wadkins ("Danny Wadwins" in the *Times*)

Jack Nicklaus and Raymond Floyd (USA) v. Nick Faldo and Peter Oosterhuis (GBI)

Against the imposing pair of Nicklaus and Floyd, the young Nick Faldo not only held his own but proved to be more than their equal on occasion. With his partner Peter Oosterhuis suffering off the tee, Faldo was left to battle the mighty Americans single-handedly over the opening few holes. He won the second on his own after a languid long-iron approach, scraped a heroic half at the third, and scrabbled a heart-stopping half with Nicklaus on the sixth, having dumped himself in the sand hills with his wayward approach.

Faldo was unable to prevent the Americans from winning the fourth with a birdie, but he maintained a level course until the eighth hole, where his partner finally woke up like a slumbering giant.

"For the first seven holes, Nick was on his own as I played poorly. But he is a solid player and utterly dependable." —Peter Oosterhuis

Oosterhuis took a one-iron and a four-iron to cover all but ten of the 394 yards to the eighth pin, then promptly holed the birdie putt for the lead. Back in touch with his game, Oosterhuis struck again, almost holing his five-iron to the par-3 ninth.

The British were two up and out in 32, two shots better than their slightly stunned opponents, who rallied to birdie the tenth to engender faint hopes that disappeared over the next three holes.

FALDO AND OOSTERHUIS ALONE WALK TALL
—London Guardian *headline*

With his partner back in stride, Faldo completely took over the match, crowning a fine bunker recovery with an eighteen-foot birdie putt on the eleventh to go back up by two. On twelve, his six-footer was for a half, which he quickly followed with a hole-winning birdie from three feet on thirteen.

On the long par-4 fourteenth, with Oosterhuis sitting on a six-foot birdie putt, Floyd hammered home a thirty-footer for the half. The next hole was halved in par, while Nicklaus claimed the 356-yard sixteenth with a six-foot birdie putt to pull back to two down with two to play.

"I was concerned only to make par at one of the last two holes. If they made two birdies, they would deserve to halve." —PETER OOSTERHUIS

Raymond Floyd was the only American to lose both his pairs matches.

With a generous following wind, Oosterhuis was able to reach the 453-yard seventeenth with a drive and a nine-iron for a half, sealing the win 2 and 1 in a joint six-under round.

Dave Hill and Dave Stockton (USA) v. Tony Jacklin and Eamonn Darcy (GBI)

The two Daves, Hill and Stockton, combined well to record the United States' third crushing win of the day by another five-hole margin. Jacklin and Darcy never really played themselves into the picture; Jacklin was woefully off his game, still suffering from the effects of a fever.

On Jacklin's off day: *"Although no one kept scores, I don't think Jacklin would have broken 83 today."* —DOW FINSTERWALD

The Americans again won the first hole when neither of their rivals could rustle up a par between them. The first American birdie at the second par-3 hole was enough for a two-hole cushion, only for the United States to be quickly pulled back by Darcy's lethal putter. On the par-5 sixth and seventh, Darcy dropped a couple of bombs from forty and thirty feet for birdies to level the match.

"Darcy did his best to hold his side together in a match which, so wayward were Jacklin and Hill, developed into a contest between himself and Stockton." —Pat Ward-Thomas, *London Guardian*

Both pairs reached the turn in 34 strokes, with Jacklin contributing very little off his own ball, as Darcy (also not feeling a hundred percent) tried his best to take on both Americans. All square at the turn soon turned into a rout as Stockton and Hill won five of the next six holes with fine figures of 3-4-3-3-4-3, which Darcy could not match on his own.

"Jacklin was playing so poorly that we thought we were playing only Eamonn Darcy." —Dave Stockton

Having previously extolled the high standard of the greens, which was like da Vinci praising a canvas, Stockton filled the cup with a fifteen-footer on the fifteenth to complete a second-half demolition job and a 5 and 3 victory.

Hale Irwin and Lou Graham (USA) v. Mark James and Ken Brown (GBI)

The closest match of the day also saw the worst play as Irwin and Graham took on Brown and James. An opening birdie two by the Americans was promptly followed by a win on the third with a par.

Three of the five American pairs on day two opened with a birdie at the par-3 206-yard first hole. No British pair managed the feat, and Jacklin and Darcy were the only pair to bogey the opening hole.

The British followed their bogey with a birdie on the fourth to cut the lead to one. The pairs halved the next two holes with a par and a birdie apiece, but the British bogey on seven was xeroxed by an American blight on eight.

With neither pair finding any consistency in its game, the Americans took a one-hole lead into the turn almost by default.

Another U.S. bogey at eleven leveled the match, but the British pair returned the favor by bogeying the 339-yard thirteenth. With the Americans one up with five to play, the final holes were all halved in par fours, but not without the British pair's trying manfully to make a fight of it.

James made telling putts at sixteen and seventeen to keep the deficit to one, while Brown saw his canny little chip from off the back of the last green just fail to make the final revolution into the hole for a hole-winning birdie. This last-gasp half in par gave the Americans their fourth win of the day, 1-up.

Day two result: USA 4, GBI 1

In the ten pairs matches, the Americans lost only twice—both times to Faldo and Oosterhuis. Apart from their number one pairing, the British still could not find a formula for success, and the other eight matches produced just half a point (from Darcy and Jacklin on the first day).

Overall match score: USA 7½, GBI 2½

Day Three: Singles

Finsterwald left out Sneed and Stockton as his side went in search of the three points needed to retain the Cup.

With only two players to leave out of the singles, British captain Brian Huggett made the controversial decision to omit Tony Jacklin (as well as Ken Brown). Rumors persisted that Huggett had been unhappy with the way Jacklin had supported the team out on the course.

"Tony is not a hundred percent," said Huggett about his decision. "He is not playing well. He was ill earlier in the week. For the good of the team, I have to leave him out because we have a hard enough job on our hands anyway."

"I'm a big boy now, and I do what the captain says," Jacklin responded.

After the match, Jacklin revised his diplomatic view of Huggett's captaincy: "I doubted the wisdom of the way he did things. He didn't consult; he just scribbled away in his room."

Lanny Wadkins (USA) v. Howard Clark (GBI)

Having led his side off on the first morning, Lanny Wadkins was fired up to go out first again, looking to record his third win in three days. Poor Howard Clark had not played on the first two days, but in a surprise move he was sent out first by captain Huggett, whose side needed a solid start if they were to have any chance of upsetting the Americans.

The pumped-up PGA champion made short work of the twenty-three-year-old Englishman, who never got a grip on the match, finishing two over for the fifteen holes. Wadkins got his third win in three starts—an emphatic 4 and 3 victory that led the United States off in style.

Hale Irwin (USA) v. Brian Barnes (GBI)

A very close match between Hale Irwin and Brian Barnes stood all square after twelve holes, when the Englishman stamped his authority on the match with back-to-back wins. Barnes held his two-hole cushion until the 356-yard sixteenth, where Irwin played a sensational second shot to six feet for a decisive birdie three.

Barnes barely clung to his one-hole lead on the par-4 seventeenth, as Irwin came close to leveling the match. On the eighteenth the Englishman, anxious to avoid the bunkers on the left, let his drive drift into some bushes on the right. He was very fortunate to be able to get a shot at his ball, and did well to move the ball to a position pin high, left of the green, up against the crowd barriers. From there Barnes dropped into one of the allocated dropping zones, chipped a dozen feet past the hole, and to his delight holed the comeback putt for the required half, securing the 1-up victory.

Carding a 68, Barnes recorded his fifth singles win out of nine, but only his first on home soil, as he added Irwin to his growing list of singles victims, having already beaten Nicklaus (twice), Barber, and Rudolph.

Lou Graham (USA) v. Neil Coles (GBI)

Having won one and lost one of his earlier matches, Lou Graham made short work of Neil Coles. Mismatched all week, Coles ended up losing all three of his matches.

A former U.S. Open champion, Graham quietly closed the match out 5 and 3 on the 468-yard fifteenth, leaving the United States one point short of retaining the Cup.

This was Neil Coles's last appearance after eight Ryder Cups. He had never been on the winning side, posting a miserable career record of 12-21-7. He played in the most singles matches, 4-8-1, in his fifteen solo ventures. Coles also tied Christy O'Connor for most career losses.

"None of my experienced players did anything for me all weekend."
—*Brian Huggett*

Don January (USA) v. Peter Dawson (GBI)

Despite a bad back, Peter Dawson delayed the inevitable American celebration by handing a 5 and 4 beating to veteran Don January, at forty-seven the oldest player in the contest.

Reaching the turn in 34, Dawson was well placed at four up, then quickly added to his lead at ten and eleven. January hung tough for a couple of holes as he posted wins on twelve and thirteen.

Dawson's five-footer on the 445-yard fourteenth sewed the match up. It was one of the few bright spots of the week for a dispirited British side.

Jack Nicklaus (USA) v. Bernard Gallacher (GBI)

Before the singles started, and with the Ryder Cup as good as won by the Americans, it was suggested in some quarters that Jack Nicklaus should be given a chance to avenge his two defeats by Brian Barnes at Laurel Valley. The American captain quickly quashed any such idea and inadvertently set a nasty bear trap for the Golden One.

Two things appeared to work against Bernard Gallacher. First, he had to use a new putter, after his old one had been stolen from the practice area. Second, he was playing Jack Nicklaus. As it happened, the new putter worked wonders, while the old Nicklaus did not.

The Scot was four up after four holes, as Nicklaus uncharacteristically dropped shots at each.

On his disastrous start: *"I just can't find the golf course."*

—JACK NICKLAUS

"It's a relief to play Jack in a singles match, because you can go out there and have a go at the golf course. But you'd better shoot a good score or he's going to trample you."
—Bernard Gallacher

With such a bountiful beginning to his match, Gallacher heroically held his own as Nicklaus did all he could to stay in the match. The American finally pulled himself together with wins on seven and eight. He continued to wear the Scot down and leveled affairs after back-to-back birdies on fifteen and sixteen. When it seemed Nicklaus would blitz his way to a famous comeback victory, Gallacher proved he was not a young man to buckle under pressure, even with a new putter in his hands.

Just as most observers expected him to fold, the Scot stunned his opponent by drilling an eighty-foot "Hail Mary" of a putt across the length of the seventeenth green for an outrageous birdie three to recapture the lead.

To prove that this monster putt had not been a fluke with a new putter, Gallacher calmly holed a four-footer on the last for the half and a memorable win over Nicklaus.

After handing Nicklaus his third straight singles defeat, Gallacher said, "Sorry about that, Jack, but everybody wants to beat you, and I'm no exception."

Nicklaus replied, "It's you Scots who keep beating me. I can't handle you guys."

This defeat left Nicklaus with just one win in his previous five singles matches.

Dave Hill (USA) v. Tommy Horton (GBI)

Before this match, Dave Hill had asked to sit out the singles because he was playing so poorly. Finsterwald could not persuade him otherwise, and it was only at the urging of his wife that Hill relented and took his cuts.

Reluctant or not, when Hill effortlessly disposed of Tommy Horton in fourteen holes by the score of 5 and 4, he carved himself a small niche in Ryder Cup history. His point was enough to guarantee that the Cup stayed with the United States.

Hubert Green (USA) v. Eamonn Darcy (GBI)

U.S. Open champion Hubert Green fought off a spirited challenge by Irishman Eamonn Darcy, who had a chance to level the match on the last hole.

With Green one up with one to play, Darcy allowed the American to halve the hole with a bogey five and secure the one-hole victory.

Raymond Floyd (USA) v. Mark James (GBI)

Ray Floyd must have counted himself unlucky in his first two matches. He had twice come up against the only British pair (Faldo and Oosterhuis) to win a match—and they did it twice against him.

As luck would have it, Floyd almost found himself drawn against one of his vanquishers for the singles, as his name came perilously close to theirs on the captains' lists. Luckily, he drew Mark James, who had also lost both of his matches.

In this battle of the 0-2s, it was James who dropped to an 0-3 record, as Floyd proved the stronger with a 2 and 1 win.

Tom Watson (USA) v. Nick Faldo (GBI)

After his second win in two days in his debut match: *"I've never been beaten on this course. I also won the English Championship here, so I'm keen to keep my record."* —NICK FALDO

On his lucky course, Faldo started in fine fashion, taking an early lead against the world number one, Tom Watson. Keen to press home his advantage off the tee, he comfortably outdrove Watson on the 486-yard sixth and then proceeded to float a five iron onto the green for a twenty-five-foot eagle and a two-hole lead.

Not wanting to give the young pretender too much of a start, Watson fought back to level by the turn. Again Faldo eked out a small lead coming home, to stand two up after twelve. For the second time, Watson dug in and drew level with one hole to play after Faldo faltered on the 453-yard seventeenth.

Fate had decreed it was not to be for the American, who found a bunker with his final drive and may well have holed a fifty-foot putt from off the green had it not bounced off the pin. Watson actually elected to putt with his caddie minding the flag; had the pin not been in the hole, the ball would almost certainly have dropped.

Watson's final-hole bogey meant Faldo's par was the difference between the two golfers after eighteen hard-fought holes.

"Nick Faldo, making perhaps the finest debut for Britain and Ireland in the fifty-year history of the Ryder Cup."
—*Dudley Doust,* Sunday Times *(London)*

On winning all three of his matches against Nicklaus, Floyd, and Watson: *"I never thought that I would be thrown in at the deep end against all these great players, but I'm really rather enjoying it. It's quite like a lot of fun, and I'm not as nervous as I thought I might be."*

—NICK FALDO

Jerry McGee (USA) v. Peter Oosterhuis (GBI)

With another strange piece of captaincy, Brian Huggett kept his two best players until last. Rather than send Faldo and Oosterhuis out early in the hope of igniting a comeback, the British captain kept the pair back until the Cup had been irretrievably lost.

Ryder Cup rookie Jerry McGee, far from overawed at being the American anchorman or taking on a 3-for-3 singleton in Oosterhuis, won the opening two holes. Having got off to another slow start, the giant Englishman slowly fought his way back into the match and drew level after twelve holes.

With momentum shifting his way, Oosterhuis took a one-hole lead up the eighteenth fairway, from where he launched another searching approach to the final green. Just as Tom Watson's had done before him, his shot hit the pin and stayed out. Having narrowly missed out on an eagle, Oosterhuis had to make do with a birdie three to claim the final hole for a two-hole win.

Only three players returned 100 percent records over all three days: Wadkins, Faldo, and Oosterhuis (who also retained his perfect singles record in four matches).

Comparing his world-class form in Ryder Cup play with his second-class form on the U.S. PGA Tour: *"I don't understand it. Here I am beating the top Americans, yet for the rest of the year I'm struggling to stay in the top sixty."* —Peter Oosterhuis

Day three result: USA 5, GBI 5

On his team's up-and-down showing in the singles: *"It's not every day you beat Nicklaus and Watson. And we had some very close ones, didn't we?"* —Brian Huggett

"A couple of matches and the result would have gone the other way."
—*Dow Finsterwald*

Overall match score: USA 12½, GBI 7½

After the closing ceremony, Brian Barnes had a few heartfelt words of his own for both teams: "And now for the most important business of the week. We all get drunk together."

Trying to put Britain's 3-18-1 Ryder Cup record into perspective, Jack Nicklaus said, "Stop regarding this contest as a knock-down, drag-out affair. It was always meant to promote international goodwill through golf. It was meant to be a happy affair; of course there will be some close matches, but we will always be the stronger side. That's the way it is."

Recap

Other than the glory of proudly representing their country, the American team took little professional pleasure out of their eighteenth win in twenty-two matches. Their overmatched opponents had managed 7½ points, of which 4 had come from two players, the other ten members of the British team combining for 3½.

"The American golfers are quite happy to treat this match as a goodwill gesture, a get-together, a bit of fun. But here in Britain, it's treated differently. The people here seem to want a serious, knock-'em-down match.

"The future of the Ryder Cup is again, and inevitably, raised. Should the team to face the Americans include other nationals? To do so would spoil the traditions of the Cup and cause administration and selection headaches."
—*Dudley Doust,* Sunday Times *(London)*

If that's what's wanted, there has to be stronger opposition. Something has to be done to make it more of a match for the Americans."

—JACK NICKLAUS

"It's the same every time we lose a Ryder Cup. There is not much difference in the striking of the ball, but when it comes to making that twelve-foot putt, the Americans are superior. They are hardened in their tournaments to the need for making those important putts."

—BRIAN HUGGETT

"The PGAS of Britain and America must simply stop jockeying around with the format and come up with something better."
—*Dow Finsterwald*

The time had come to open up the British team, which had failed to challenge the Americans since the early days of the competition, which was born of a different generation of gentleman golfer, far removed from the professional world of the 1970s. The much-needed outside assistance would come not, as many had forecast, from the British Commonwealth but from the burgeoning European Tour.

On the lack of depth in the last-ever all-British side: "We had Oosterhuis and Faldo . . . our best two players, and the rest of us weren't exactly hitting a cow's ass with a banjo."
—*Mark James*

The next Ryder Cup, at The Greenbrier in 1979, would see other changes as well, most notably in the playing format. The five-handed pairs format was a complete disaster from the players' standpoint, because it resulted in too little golf. Tom Watson complained that he had played only 158 shots in his three days (excluding the impromptu exhibition with Nicklaus on day one) and "would have liked to play more golf." Nicklaus also felt that more should be made of the three days, if only for the benefit of the spectators.

The 1977 engagement at Royal Lytham and St. Annes will always be regarded as the watershed of the modern-day Ryder Cup competition, when common sense talked loud and the game of golf won through.

Match Results (Winning side marked in *italics*.)

Thursday, September 15—Foursomes

	USA	GBI	Score
1.	*Lanny Wadkins* *Hale Irwin*	Bernard Gallacher Brian Barnes	3 and 1
2.	*Dave Stockton* *Jerry McGee*	Neil Coles Peter Dawson	1-up
3.	Raymond Floyd Lou Graham	*Nick Faldo* *Peter Oosterhuis*	2 and 1
4.	Ed Sneed Don January	Eamonn Darcy Tony Jacklin	halved
5.	*Jack Nicklaus* *Tom Watson*	Tommy Horton Mark James	5 and 4

Day one result: USA 3 ½, GBI 1 ½

Friday, September 16—Fourball

	USA	GBI	Score
6.	*Tom Watson* *Hubert Green*	Brian Barnes Tommy Horton	5 and 4
7.	*Ed Sneed* *Lanny Wadkins*	Neil Coles Peter Dawson	5 and 3
8.	Jack Nicklaus Raymond Floyd	*Nick Faldo* *Peter Oosterhuis*	2 and 1
9.	*Dave Hill* *Dave Stockton*	Tony Jacklin Eamonn Darcy	5 and 3
10.	*Hale Irwin* *Lou Graham*	Mark James Ken Brown	1-up

Day two result: USA 4, GBI 1

Overall match score: USA 7 ½, GBI 2 ½

Saturday, September 17—Singles

	USA	GBI	Score
11.	*Lanny Wadkins*	Howard Clark	4 and 3
12.	Hale Irwin	*Brian Barnes*	1-up
13.	*Lou Graham*	Neil Coles	5 and 3
14.	Don January	*Peter Dawson*	5 and 4
15.	Jack Nicklaus	*Bernard Gallacher*	1-up
16.	*Dave Hill*	Tommy Horton	5 and 4
17.	*Hubert Green*	Eamonn Darcy	1-up
18.	*Raymond Floyd*	Mark James	2 and 1
19.	Tom Watson	*Nick Faldo*	1-up
20.	Jerry McGee	*Peter Oosterhuis*	2-up

Day three result: USA 5, GBI 5

Overall match score: USA 12½, GBI 7½

1979

The Greenbrier
White Sulphur Springs, West Virginia
United States
September 14–16

United States 17	**Europe 11**
Andy Bean	Seve Ballesteros (Spain)
Lee Elder	Brian Barnes (England)
Hubert Green	Ken Brown (Scotland)
Mark Hayes	Nick Faldo (England)
Hale Irwin	Bernard Gallacher (Scotland)
Tom Kite	Antonio Garrido (Spain)
John Mahaffey	Tony Jacklin (England)
Gil Morgan	Mark James (England)
Larry Nelson	Michael King (England)
Lee Trevino	Sandy Lyle (Scotland)
Lanny Wadkins	Peter Oosterhuis (England)
Fuzzy Zoeller	Des Smyth (Ireland)
Captain	**Captain**
Billy Casper	John Jacobs (England)

Europe Expects Every Man to Do His Duty

No longer would Great Britain and Ireland bear the sole responsibility of dueling the United States for the Ryder Cup. In an attempt, championed by Jack Nicklaus (who, ironically, failed to qualify for the U.S. team), to make the event more competitive, it was agreed by both sides to open up the British selection process to European players.

"By the time of the 1977 contest at Royal Lytham . . . it had become clear to me that the imbalance inherent in pitting a nation that then possessed about fifteen million golfers against two countries, Britain and Ireland, with barely a million between them was turning the match into a non-event, at least as far as the American public was concerned, and also to some extent for its top players." —Jack Nicklaus, *My Story*

As it turned out, only two Spaniards made the grade, and they managed to win only one point between them—despite both playing in every session. But the precedent had been set.

"Whether this team will play with the same fire under the European banner as the Ryder Cup teams did, I take leave to doubt, just as I doubt whether the public interest (and with it the public income) will be as intense. . . . We shall see in due course. I only wish they would provide a new trophy and a new name for this new competition."

—PETER DOBEREINER, "Ryder Cup Requiem" in *London Observer* (1978)

Yet another change was made to the playing format. The unanimously disliked "five-a-day" experiment from 1977 was immediately dispensed with and replaced by a system that still operates today: three days of competition encompassing four foursomes and four fourballs on each of the first two days, followed by twelve singles matches on the third day. This meant that every player chosen to represent his country would have the opportunity to do just that, if only in the singles. This playing system also gave rise to the magic number 14½—the points needed to win the Ryder Cup outright.

"A marvelous mishmash of match play, spread over three days."
—*Barry Lorge,* Washington Post

The two captains for this historic encounter were Billy Casper and John Jacobs, and both ran into trouble during the contest—Jacobs having by far the worse of it over the behavior of two of his younger charges. Mark James arrived at London's Heathrow Airport without his official uniform, and upon arrival at The Greenbrier, he and Ken Brown managed to miss an important team meeting in favor of a shopping trip, then tried to disrupt the official team photograph.

Upon returning to England, both players were fined. Brown (who also had made disparaging remarks over having to wear a uniform) was suspended from international team golf for a year and also missed the 1981 Ryder Cup. The golfing outlaw and rebel Mark "Jesse" James, on the other hand, was quickly forgiven, played in five more Ryder Cups, and eventually was named captain for 1999 (with Brown as his number two). Brian Barnes was rumored to have threatened to punch James unless he changed his attitude, though James denies this.

On the rebellious James and Brown: "I'd have told them both to pack their bags."
—*Tony Jacklin*

"Some unfortunate things happened, but it wasn't simply a case of me misbehaving. There were many other factors involved and people wrote things about me that were completely untrue."

—MARK JAMES, *Golf World* (1998)

The home side had eight new faces, but as with all American rookies, they were a talented group: Bean, Elder, Hayes, Kite, Mahaffey, Morgan, Nelson, and Zoeller.

Jacobs's rookies were twenty-one-year-old Lyle (winner, the previous week, of the European Open by seven strokes), King, Smyth, and the two Spaniards—Garrido and twenty-two-year-old Ballesteros (the British Open champion).

Casper's troubles were of a more domestic nature. A phone call from Kansas City in the wee hours of Thursday morning summoned record money-winner Tom Watson back home to assist his wife Linda in the birth of their first child (it was a girl) and reduced the American cast of experienced players to four. In trying to fill Watson's vacant golf shoes, Casper called up Mark Hayes.

On the eventful day before competition started: *"September 13: Tom Watson flew home to be with his wife and newborn first child. Lee Trevino was concerned about his son, hospitalized in Texas. Hubert Green worried about his home and family, threatened by Hurricane Frederick. Jack Nicklaus, scheduled to appear as course architect, couldn't make the opening ceremony because his father-in-law died. Officials openly feared bad weather. Andy Bean borrowed his captain's three-iron to kill a copperhead on the tenth hole. Otherwise, there wasn't much out of the ordinary happening."* —Barry Lorge, *Washington Post*

Having previously turned down a Ryder Cup invitation, Tom Weiskopf was also selected to play for the United States, but he, too, withdrew to be at home for the birth of his first child.

Billy Casper also got into domestic hot water at the prematch gala banquet when he introduced Lee Trevino's wife as Rose, who was actually *Lee Elder*'s wife! And this would not be the end of the American skipper's problems with Lee Trevino's name.

In a portent of things not to come, there was a semiserious Writer Cup competition on Wednesday, when a team of British sportswriters beat the American media. Since there was no one on hand to report on the matches, the details are somewhat sketchy.

Course Details

The historic Greenbrier course, home of the Greater Greensboro Open, is set in the picturesque Allegheny foothills of West Virginia.

Recently redesigned by Jack Nicklaus, the tight course had been lengthened to just over 6,700 yards to conform to PGA Championship requirements. Nicklaus left a number of his trademark ridges across the greens, which were made even more treacherous by the heavy rains. The newly laid greens were extremely fast and susceptible to damage from spike marks.

The speed of the putting surface and the extremely tough rough did not meet with the visitors' approval, as Seve Ballesteros complained (not for the last time) that the course was set up to favor the home team.

Hole	Distance	Par	Hole	Distance	Par
1	428	4	10	347	4
2	409	4	11	175	3
3	483	5	12	516	5
4	167	3	13	415	4
5	546	5	14	306	4
6	455	4	15	440	4
7	210	3	16	412	4
8	501	5	17	158	3
9	203	3	18	550	5
		36			**36 = Par 72 (6,721 yards)**

Course designer: Seth Raynor, with revisions by Jack Nicklaus

Day One: Morning Fourball

During the morning, play was delayed almost three-quarters of an hour, as the side effects of Hurricane Frederick skirted the course, flooding a number of greens.

"The competition began today in what could uncharitably but accurately be described as 'British weather.' It was gloomy, as was the visitors' performance." —BARRY LORGE, *Washington Post*

Lanny Wadkins and Larry Nelson (USA) v. Antonio Garrido and Seve Ballesteros (EUR)

For the first match, Jacobs had no hesitation in sending out his only two continental players, who had won the 1977 World Cup together. The American pair did not wait long to roll out the welcome mat to the first continental Europeans to play in the Ryder Cup.

Opening in great style with a couple of "transcontinental" putts, Garrido birdied the first two holes, as if to show what the Great Britain team had been missing. Unfortunately for the new golfing nation known as Europe, the old golfing nation known as the United States also carded two threes to start with, to keep the match level.

On the previous practice day, the Larry and Lanny combination carded a 59 in fourball play to suggest to Billy Casper that they should go out first. Having played so well together in the practice rounds, Nelson and Wadkins combined flawlessly for a betterball score of 28 over the first nine holes in the actual match. They posted six threes on their way out, with a two on the 167-yard fourth hole, and six birdies overall, along with a crowning eagle at the 501-yard eighth. The Americans' perfect sub-par 9 was "marred" only by par threes at seven and nine.

The twenty-nine-year-old Virginian Wadkins was the senior partner, owing to the fact that he had some match-play experience whereas Nelson had little to none. From the get-go, Wadkins instilled in his partner a burning desire to win every hole for his country.

Larry Nelson claimed he had played under match-play rules only once before in his career, when he lost his club championship at Kennesaw, Georgia, seven years earlier.

Rookie Larry Nelson was on a hot streak, having made three top five finishes in his last three Tour qualifying events, including a win at the Western Open. Making the U.S. team had not been high on Nelson's agenda for the year. "I wasn't very excited about the Ryder Cup when I got here, but the more I talked to the players and learned of the history of the matches, the more excited I got," he said. "And then Lanny really got me pumped up."

The outward blitz of scoring gave the Americans a lead on the tenth that they did not relinquish. Thanks to some more spirited golf from Nelson on the way home, the United States took the first match, 2 and 1.

Lee Trevino and Fuzzy Zoeller (USA) v. Ken Brown and Mark James (EUR)

This noncontest had been settled before the first drive had been struck, because James came into the match with a torn rib cartilage that seriously hampered his swing.

"They drove the ball poorly," said Trevino later. "I think that was the only department in which we were stronger. You could see the pain in James's face when he was hitting the ball. He was either blocking it or hitting far left. Very few times were the two of them in on the same hole, and it's very difficult to play best-ball two against one."

With James contributing little to his team's cause, Brown barely played any better—nor, it seemed, did he want to. After their prematch behavior, one wondered what these men thought they were up to in (mis)representing their continent.

"One notably disappointing British player, Ken Brown, played as if he didn't care if it rained on his parade."
—*Barry Lorge,* Washington Post

The American pair was hardly stretched in sixteen holes of fairly ordinary golf that both sides will probably want to forget. Even the upbeat Trevino had difficulty smiling after this 3 and 2 stinker.

"Trevino and Zoeller, a duo that does not lack for mirth or the gift of the gab, produced little extraordinary shotmaking but also complemented nicely and chatted their way past Brown and injured James."
—Barry Lorge, *Washington Post*

Andy Bean and Lee Elder (USA) v. Peter Oosterhuis and Nick Faldo (EUR)

The British players started much better than they finished, with Oosterhuis draining a forty-foot putt on the 409-yard second for the lead. They followed this with three more birdies in a row but could not stretch their lead, as each strike was matched by the Americans.

Forty-five-year-old Lee Elder was the first black golfer to appear in the Ryder Cup.

Having kept the British lead down to one, Elder sank a twelve-foot birdie putt on the 455-yard sixth to level the match.

After a delay for another deluge, Oosterhuis had a thirty-foot putt, which slowed up so much on the saturated eighth green that it barely ran halfway to the hole. With a similar-length putt confronting him, Bean went to school on Oosterhuis's waterlogged putt and lagged up to within a couple of feet of the hole. The American made the birdie after Oosterhuis again came up short. Having taken advantage of the conditions and captured the lead, the Americans were not to be denied. The British pair had shot its bolt.

On his teaming with Bean: *"I had a good horse, and I rode him to death. He made a lot of birdies for us, and I sneaked in with a few every now and then. It was certainly a new experience for me, and we teamed well together."* —Lee Elder

Although Faldo and Oosterhuis finished six under, they went down 2 and 1, largely because of the eight birdies carded by the Americans, Bean claiming five and Elder three. This apparent disparity between the U.S. partners was due to the fact that Elder teed off first on every hole, allowing Bean to launch a monster drive—if his partner was safely on the fairway. The tactic paid huge dividends: Elder's selfless play gave his partner the required freedom to go bird hunting.

"Lee would make a birdie, and that would get me pumped up to make the next one. In match play there are always a few key holes, and we took turns playing real well."
—*Andy Bean*

Hale Irwin and John Mahaffey (USA) v. Bernard Gallacher and Brian Barnes (EUR)

Having seen the Europeans get off to a fast start in two of the first three matches, Irwin and Mahaffey made the first moves against Barnes and Gallacher.

Posting three wins in the first six holes, the Americans appeared to have the game in their grasp, but a rain delay came at the wrong time for them and washed away their momentum. On the 210-yard seventh, Barnes, who had complained of fibrositis in his left shoulder, shrugged off the pain and chipped in from just off the green to halt the Americans' early charge.

This would not be Barnes's only birdie two at the par 3s; he repeated the dose on the 175-yard eleventh. With his partner providing the spark to get them back into the match, Gallacher adjusted well to the wet conditions and fired birdies of his own at the 516-yard twelfth and 415-yard thirteenth to take the lead for the first time.

On the encouraging early-morning play of his team: "My fellows are 'up' and are working hard to accomplish their goal."
—*Billy Casper*

The two Brits, playing with greater assurance in the more familiar rain-soaked surroundings, not only caught but passed Irwin and Mahaffey, who failed to recapture their fair-weather form.

Barnes's third birdie two, at seventeen, was the coup de grâce that closed out the Americans, 2 and 1. This was the first-ever point gained for Europe and its only one of a miserable morning.

Morning fourball result: USA 3, EUR 1

Day One: Afternoon Foursomes

Hale Irwin and Tom Kite (USA) v. Ken Brown and Des Smyth (EUR)

"Tom and I played, with the exception of the sixth hole, reasonably solid golf. The fact of the matter is that they seemed to give us the match early on. The heart did not seem to be in the body. We were grateful recipients of their bad play. Ken hit some just terrible shots. Des hit some good ones, but when he did Ken promptly put him over in jail somewhere. The foursome is an unusual sort of game that we hardly ever play. You have to be able to communicate with your partner. I felt it was obvious there was no rapport between them. There was not even the slightest bit of idle conversation. Smyth didn't play very well, and Brown played like he didn't care."
—*Hale Irwin*

Hale Irwin had only a fifteen-minute break between matches, and he snatched a light lunch. Mark James had a cortisone injection in his shoulder for lunch and played three painful practice holes before pulling out of the afternoon session. He was replaced by the quiet and unassuming Des Smyth, who walked right into a hornet's nest.

Unhappy at not being paired with James, Scotland's Ken Brown refused to speak to his new Irish partner. This lack of team spirit led to a predictable result—an overwhelming American win.

Irwin and Kite were mere bystanders as the European pair lost six holes with bogeys. Brown strafed the nether regions of West Virginia with an array of shots that had the gallery both bewildered and in fear for their safety.

Had the Americans not double-bogeyed the 455-yard sixth hole, which the British pair took with another hideous bogey, the damage would have been far greater than it was. Out in 44 strokes, Smyth was powerless as Brown set about ruining the Irishman's big day.

On course for an 88, the British pair was smacked by the biggest loss in Ryder Cup foursomes history, as Irwin and Kite somewhat embarrassingly and far too easily won, 7 and 6.

"Smyth and Brown very likely established some kind of record with scoring which was nothing less than a disgrace. They had seven bogeys and two pars over the first nine holes. It was a relief when this travesty of a match ended on the twelfth hole."

—PETER DOBEREINER, *London Guardian*

In support of his rebellious player: "Ken Brown did nothing wrong, but he did fail to communicate."
—*John Jacobs*

Fuzzy Zoeller and Hubert Green (USA) v. Seve Ballesteros and Antonio Garrido (EUR)

Having failed to make a winning start to their European campaign, the two Spaniards found it tough going against Zoeller and Green as well. All square after the first nine holes, the tight match loosened up considerably on the next three.

Hubert Green badly misplayed his approach into the crowd around the 347-yard tenth hole, and a resultant American bogey gave the Spaniards the lead. Green hit an equally bad tee shot at the

175-yard eleventh, and Europe enjoyed a two-hole lead off back-to-back pars.

Given a boost by Green's generosity, the Spaniards made a hole-winning birdie at the par-5 twelfth to go three up. Although Green pulled his game back together, neither he nor Zoeller could crack the continentals, who coasted to a 3 and 2 win.

Against the American express, this proved to be not only the first point ever won by a non-British golfer, but also the only point won by a non-British player during the three days.

Lee Trevino and Gil Morgan (USA) v. Sandy Lyle and Tony Jacklin (EUR)

Strangely, John Jacobs delayed sending out his two most recent tournament winners, Lyle and Jacklin, until the afternoon.

The European captain was also criticized by the British press when he dropped his number one combo of Oosterhuis and Faldo and brought in rookie Des Smyth to partner the irascible Brown. It was argued that a senior player such as Oosterhuis or Jacklin would have been better placed to see Brown through his troubles.

Jacobs's reluctance to play Lyle and Jacklin in the morning appeared vindicated when they struggled against the well-oiled pair of Trevino and Morgan, who held a two-hole lead after eleven.

Like Green and Zoeller ahead of them, the Americans shot themselves in all four feet, taking four strokes to hole out from thirty feet on the 516-yard twelfth. The British pair leveled on the par-4 fourteenth but dropped behind again as the U.S. pair took the 440-yard fifteenth. With the lead back in their grasp, Trevino and Morgan let it slip away again when they had more putting problems, taking three more swipes on the par-4 sixteenth.

All square with two to play set up a dramatic finale—a rare sighting in the contest so far. Jacklin appeared to have given his team the upper hand at the 158-yard seventeenth with a tee shot to six feet of the flag. Morgan's tee shot left his partner a more difficult putt, but Trevino further dampened the British hopes when he slotted home his birdie. Lyle, faced with a sneaky six-footer for the half instead of the hoped-for win, could not answer Trevino's timely trump card, and the Americans were one up with one to play.

For the third time on the back nine, the Americans surrendered the lead with a costly bogey, and the Europeans escaped with a half when they took eighteen with a nervy par five.

Lanny Wadkins and Larry Nelson (USA) v. Bernard Gallacher and Brian Barnes (EUR)

"The quiet, unassuming Larry Nelson, a thirty-two-year-old Georgian who never has an unkind word for anyone and seldom displays emotion whether good or bad. He's been a golfer for all of eleven of those thirty-two years and prior to that didn't know a Ryder Cup from a Steuben glass."
—*Ron Coffman,* Golf World

The potent pair of Wadkins and Nelson struck again. Having seen off the combined efforts of two Spaniards in the morning, the two Americans made even shorter work of two Brits.

Gallacher and Barnes had also won their morning match, but they were no match for the U.S. players, who repeated their match-winning form (4 and 3). The Europeans seemed to lose their form against the all-out American attack of aggression and accuracy.

Wadkins and Nelson were the only pair to post two victories in the day, a feat they would uniquely repeat on the second day.

Afternoon foursomes result: USA 2½, EUR 1½
Day one result: USA 5½, EUR 2½

"Team golf, in which a player has to think for his partner as well as for himself, is a long way from the individualism of tournament golf, and an American team of professionals did the better job of mastering the art today than their European counterparts."

—JOHN S. RADOSTA, *New York Times*

Day Two: Morning Foursomes

Play was held up soon after the first pairs finished the opening hole, as fog rolled in and covered the course for almost an hour.

Having seen his opposing number take the heat from the press on day one, Billy Casper faced the music when his plan to rest three of his most experienced players backfired. Three-quarters of his Ryder Cup experience—Trevino, Irwin, and Green—were left on the sidelines in the morning as Casper gave rookies Hayes and Mahaffey a taste of the action.

Lee Elder and John Mahaffey (USA) v. Tony Jacklin and Sandy Lyle (EUR)

Lyle and Jacklin were in a positive frame of mind after their come-from-behind half against Trevino and Morgan the preceding afternoon, a performance that had proved their captain half wrong for ignoring them on the first morning. The pair took this momentum into the morning match with Elder and Mahaffey, and the Americans were swiftly swamped.

Jacklin and Lyle won the first three holes, and the Scot prevented an American revival by saving his side's half on the 167-yard fourth with a solid seven-foot putt. The European pair increased its lead to four by taking the par-3 seventh, combining wonderfully with play that was close to perfection. Having reached the turn in 34 strokes, Europe held a five-hole advantage, and the Americans were powerless to stop the flow of fabulous golf.

"I think there's a little more pressure in this type of match. You play a little bit different than you would if you were playing individual medal play. In match play, you have a tendency to be a little more aggressive. You hit a driver from some tees where you would hit an iron in medal play."
—*Lee Elder*

Despite gifting a hole back on the 347-yard tenth, where Jacklin made the Europeans' first mistake of the round by dumping a wedge shot into the water, the visitors held firm for a pulsating 5 and 4 win.

Andy Bean and Tom Kite (USA) v. Nick Faldo and Peter Oosterhuis (EUR)

Casper was also criticized for breaking up the pairing of Elder and Bean, who had melded so well on the first morning. With Elder going down in the previous match, Bean fared even worse with Tom Kite.

Oosterhuis's opening drive was way off line to the right and onto a pathway, but Faldo recovered magnificently with a four-iron to a couple of feet of the hole. This set up a win that had looked far from likely from the tee.

Giving up the early lead badly affected the Americans. Kite missed a crucial short putt on the second, while the fourth to the eighth holes saw the U.S. capitulate, losing all four holes to European pars.

A hole-winning birdie on the par-3 ninth gave Faldo and Oosterhuis a six-hole cushion that they rode on home for a crushing 6 and 5 win four holes later.

Lanny Wadkins and Larry Nelson (USA) v. Seve Ballesteros and Antonio Garrido (EUR)

With one win already over their Spanish opponents, the Americans went after them again like a bull after a red cape. Unfortunately, the Americans began more like a bull in a china shop, opening with a couple of bogeys. After this abominable start, Wadkins and Nelson set about restoring their unblemished record together.

Slowly and gradually, the Americans made up for their sluggish start. In particular, they gave the Spaniards a putting lesson on and around the lightning-fast greens, which had dried out surprisingly quickly after the previous day's drenching.

"Lanny coached me through those team matches. I didn't even know how to mark my ball in match play. He made most of the birdies; I just kept driving it in the fairway." —LARRY NELSON

"Blending as naturally as the scenic green Allegheny countryside and the bright blue sky overhead, Wadkins and Nelson beat Garrido and Ballesteros 3 and 2."
—*Barry Lorge,* Washington Post

Ballesteros and Garrido tried vainly to stay competitive but could not capitalize on the few chances the U.S. pair gave them on the greens. Finishing four under par in spite of their false start, the Americans ran out fairly impressive winners, 3 and 2, over the Spaniards.

This would not be the last time these players would meet, in pairs or even as singles.

Fuzzy Zoeller and Mark Hayes (USA) v. Bernard Gallacher and Brian Barnes (EUR)

In a scenario that became too familiar to Billy Casper, he saw one of his pairs throw away a midterm lead through negligence.

Zoeller and first-timer Hayes played superbly together for eleven holes, stretching out to a well-deserved two-hole lead against Barnes and Gallacher.

It was Zoeller who blew up first, firing his drive at the 516-yard twelfth out-of-bounds to lose the hole. Hayes magnified this error by making one of his own, as his drive found a bunker on the thirteenth.

Gallacher drove a hefty nail into the U.S. pair's self-sacrificial coffin with a sixteen-foot birdie putt on the par-4 fourteenth. Once they had a lead, the frugal Europeans refused to give it up, and they actually extended the advantage for a 2 and 1 win that the Americans found as hard to stomach as week-old haggis.

Morning foursomes result: USA 1, EUR 3

After Europe won three of the four morning matches: *"I think the captain made it clear that we had to make a major move today and try to get back in it. He got us thinking right, that we had to come out firing this morning."* —Peter Oosterhuis

Day Two: Afternoon Fourball

Lee Trevino and Fuzzy Zoeller (USA) v. Bernard Gallacher and Brian Barnes (EUR)

Having been put to the sword in the opening fourball match by the unstoppable pair of Wadkins and Nelson, Gallacher and Barnes gave this American duo a dose of their own medicine. They fired eight birdies at Trevino and Zoeller in sixteen holes. Barnes was in particularly outstanding form with five birdies on his own ball.

"The essence of team play was epitomized by the Americans in two slang phrases: 'ham and egging it' and 'brother-in-lawing it around.'" —*John S. Radosta,* New York Times

This 3 and 2 victory was the Brits' third in four matches together, their second against Zoeller in one day. Only Nelson and Wadkins had proved capable of beating them.

Lee Elder and Mark Hayes (USA) v. Nick Faldo and Peter Oosterhuis (EUR)

In a very tight match, the Americans trailed most of the time but refused to let their opponents establish a big lead.

"When Nick is playing well, I just try to stay out of his way and save a hole here and there." —Peter Oosterhuis

Coming to the last hole, the European pair still held a narrow one-hole advantage, and held on to that only courtesy of Faldo's tremendous recovery from sand at the last hole.

Hale Irwin and Tom Kite (USA) v. Tony Jacklin and Sandy Lyle (EUR)

Having set a Ryder Cup record for the biggest win in a foursomes match, Irwin and Kite were reunited to see what they could do with Jacklin and Lyle, who had been almost as impressive in their morning match together. As befits a battle of 7 and 6 winners dueling 5 and 4 winners, something had to give, and it was the British.

Irwin and Kite started out with three wins in the first four holes, but the Europeans fought back magnificently to not only rein in the trailblazing Americans but overtake them with a blazing trail of their own.

"Hale had to slow me down, even hold me back, because I was walking and playing too fast."
—*Tom Kite*

One up with four holes to play, Lyle and Jacklin were looking good for another sensational come-from-behind win, but they caught the American disease and threw away the advantage.

Lyle had a golden opportunity to put his side two up on the 440-yard fifteenth but squandered the chance from the back of the green. On sixteen, Jacklin hit his approach pitch into the water; Lyle still had two putts for a half, but he took three.

All square and back in the hunt at the 158-yard seventeenth, Irwin had a longer par putt than his partner's birdie putt but asked Kite to putt first. The tactic worked, as Kite holed a critical ten-foot birdie two to retake the lead.

On why he let Kite attempt his crucial birdie putt before he putted for a par: *"I let him putt first because his eyes were this big!"*
—HALE IRWIN

"Tom won the match for us because my coaching was of the highest quality."
—*Hale Irwin*

On the last green, Lyle's putting let him down again: he missed a birdie putt from nine feet that would have won the hole and halved the match. Irwin and Kite gladly settled for the 1-up win, their second win in two games together.

Lanny Wadkins and Larry Nelson (USA) v. Seve Ballesteros and Antonio Garrido (EUR)

These two pairs met for the third time in four sessions, and for the third time the U.S. pair came out on top, whereas Ballesteros and Garrido were undefeated against anyone else!

Wadkins and Nelson were pumped up to improve on their 2 and 1 and 3 and 2 victories against the Spaniards, and they made one of the greatest starts in Ryder Cup history.

The Americans opened up 3-3-4-2-3-3-3-3 for a nine-under start for eight holes. They actually bogeyed the 203-yard ninth, where a par would have given them an outward 27!

If Wadkins had been any more pumped up, he would have had Michelin tattooed across his chest. He started with a humble three-foot putt on the 428-yard first, stretched this to a ten-foot putt on the 409-yard second, and topped these opening offerings with a fifteen-foot putt on the 483-yard third. Three putts, three birdies, three wins.

When Wadkins finally faltered with a bunkered tee shot at the short fourth, Nelson birdied from three feet. Lanny kept the drive alive with an eagle putt from beyond forty feet at the 546-yard fifth and made it six birdies (or better) in a row with a twenty-footer at the par-4 sixth.

"We are both playing so confidently, it's unbelievable. We both drove excellently, and had the ball in play all afternoon."
—*Lanny Wadkins*

Against this blitzkrieg of birdies, the Spaniards were two under par and four down. The clinching blow came at the 501-yard eighth, where Nelson eagled from eight feet, with Ballesteros on the green for certain birdie.

"There were only a couple of holes in the round that we weren't both playing for birdies." —Larry Nelson

The Americans made the turn in 28, eight under par, just as they had in the pairs' first encounter. Not content with a mauling, they set about a total beheading of their opponents by making another birdie at the 347-yard tenth. They closed the lopsided match out at the fourteenth, where Wadkins approached to one foot for the Americans' eighth birdie or better of the afternoon.

The 5 and 4 result does not reflect how well the Spaniards played. They must have been sick of the sight of Wadkins and Nelson, and Ballesteros would have to live through the nightmare once more before the contest was done.

Coming into this contest, Wadkins was the PGA Tour money-list leader, with Nelson second. Having gone 4-0 over the first two days, the pair was a combined 11-0 lifetime (Wadkins 7-0 and Nelson 4-0) in Ryder Cup play to date.

Afternoon fourball result: USA 2, EUR 2
Day two result: USA 3, EUR 5

Unfortunately for Casper, his decision to play rookies Hayes and Mahaffey cost him three losses in their three appearances. This allowed the opposition to close the gap to one point after a day of European euphoria.

Overall match score: USA 8½, EUR 7½

On the importance of not getting too excited over the closeness of the overnight position: *"We have already made it a good performance. I must impress on my men that that is not enough, that we now are in a good position of winning."* —John Jacobs

Day Three: Singles

Gil Morgan (USA) v. Mark James (EUR)

James's injured ribs had not healed sufficiently to allow him to be competitive, and he was forced to withdraw. Morgan also complained of a sore shoulder after a bad fall on Friday, and asked to be dropped.

Following losses in all four of his previous Ryder Cup matches, this was the first point that James managed to gain for his team albeit a half-point for not playing!

This was the year the dreaded "envelope" was introduced. Each captain had to nominate one player who would sit out the singles if an opposing player could not go—and that name was sealed in an envelope. A completely confused Billy Casper had nominated his best player, Trevino, as his envelope player, but a fair-minded John Jacobs allowed Trevino to play and Morgan to sit the match out.

Des Smyth was widely regarded as the first name in the European envelope. In the original singles list, James was drawn last against Lee Trevino.

"I was told to put down the name of a player I wanted to protect. I thought putting in Lee's name meant he was guaranteed to play. It was just the opposite." —BILLY CASPER

Lanny Wadkins (USA) v. Bernard Gallacher (EUR)

Boasting two of the best records over the first two days, Wadkins and Gallacher were rightly chosen to lead their teams off on this crucial day.

Wadkins was unable to shake off Gallacher over the first five holes, as the Scot made two highly missable putts to deny the American wins.

On the 455-yard sixth, Wadkins could not match Gallacher's tenacity and lost the hole. Gallacher left his stamp on this match with a three-hole burst after the turn—two birdies and a par to take ten, eleven, and twelve.

With Wadkins's driving letting him down, he carded four bogeys the day after making five birdies, then settled his own fate by driving into the lake on sixteen.

The doughty Scot retained his unblemished singles record with a morale-boosting 3 and 2 win to level the overall match score.

This result gave Gallacher four wins out of five games, and it was Wadkins's first loss in eight Ryder Cup matches.

Larry Nelson (USA) v. Seve Ballesteros (EUR)

Having played Nelson three times in the first two days and lost all three, Ballesteros was keen to jump out fast on his older opponent. It was not to be, as Nelson snared three birdies on the first three holes.

After a disappointing start to his Ryder Cup career (1-3), Ballesteros was eager to prove that the expanded European tour was worthy of this biennial contest. From just off the par-4 sixth green, the Spanish superstar holed a forty-five-foot downhill putt for a birdie three to cut Nelson's lead to two.

The American was not finished with his own fireworks display: he chipped in from almost eighty feet away for a birdie two at the ninth to go back three up. Even better was to follow at the 516-yard twelfth. Nelson drove into the face of a steep bunker and had to play a ball lodged head high in the sand. The American did well to hack his ball out, let alone move it fifteen yards down the fairway. In danger of dropping the hole, Nelson pulled a four-wood out of his bag and smote an unforgettable strike to six inches of the hole.

"Seve's a rare kind of guy. He's an excitable golfer who can concentrate."
—*Larry Nelson*

Ballesteros needed and got a thirty-foot putt for a birdie on sixteen, but Nelson, not to be outshone, holed an eight-footer for the half and the match, 3 and 2.

Citing his opponent's wonder shots at nine and twelve, Ballesteros complained about Nelson's being "extremely lucky" and how the course was set up to suit the home side. Even in his rookie outing, Seve was honing his gamesmanship for more fruitful contests later.

"Today I probably hit the ball as well as I have all year. I learned a lot, too. I think this day will help me for years to come. I think I'm finally to the point where I can control my nerves, my emotions, and preserve a lead." —Larry Nelson

Finishing four under for his sixteen holes, Nelson was able to counter any move made by the Spaniard, just as he had all week, and ended with four wins out of four over him.

Thanks almost entirely to Nelson, Ballesteros finished his first Ryder Cup match with a sickly 1-4 record.

Tom Kite (USA) v. Tony Jacklin (EUR)

Tony Jacklin took a three-hole lead over the American after five holes, then missed a three-foot putt on the eighth that would have given him a commanding four-hole advantage.

Given the slimmest of chances, Kite then made five birdies in six holes—including three in a row from eleven—and took only ten putts over the next eight holes.

Jacklin tried to match Kite's barrage with a birdie of his own on the 306-yard fourteenth, but Kite had too many weapons and shelled Jacklin with a bomb on the fifteenth green to level the match again.

Kite's eight-iron pitch into the sixteenth landed close enough for him to side-foot the ball into the hole if he wanted to. This birdie gave Kite back the lead, which he kept to the last, halving the last two holes for a one-hole win.

Mark Hayes (USA) v. Antonio Garrido (EUR)

Both rookies experienced an unhappy introduction to the Ryder Cup, with five defeats and only one win between them in their six matches. With only that sort of negative record to build on, neither player proved capable of breaking the other, and so the match arrived at the last tee all square.

Hayes appeared to have blown his chance as he pushed his second shot to the par-5 eighteenth into the rough. Garrido was unable to capitalize on the American's error, and Hayes played a magnificent pitch to twelve feet and sank the birdie putt for a last-gasp 1-up win.

Andy Bean (USA) v. Michael King (EUR)

Playing in your first Ryder Cup singles is difficult enough, but when you have not played all week, it gets about as tough as a Scottish caddie's shoe leather. This was the dilemma faced by Michael King, who had sat out the first two days, while his opponent, Andy Bean, had a win and a loss already tucked under his rookie belt.

With little or no playing experience on American courses, King was hardly in his countinghouse, and the only commodity he counted during the first eight holes was the five American birdies. Bean roasted his opponent 4 and 3 with a scintillating start that more or less settled the match before the turn.

John Mahaffey (USA) v. Brian Barnes (EUR)

Having contributed nothing up to this point of the match, Mahaffey took on the hulking 6′5″ Brian Barnes. Barnes went out in 40 and allowed Mahaffey to take a three-hole lead with five holes to play.

The American then missed the fifteenth green and also lost the sixteenth, where Barnes stopped his approach two feet from the pin. The Brit almost threw away his comeback charge by not only missing the green at seventeen from the tee, but then chipping back six feet beyond the hole. With Mahaffey poised for a par, Barnes gamely rolled his putt in for a half to keep the game afoot.

This narrow escape signaled the end of Barnes's charge, because Mahaffey was able to par the final hole for another half to eke out a one-hole victory.

Lee Elder (USA) v. Nick Faldo (EUR)

Forty-five-year-old Lee Elder stormed out and surprised an opponent half his age by winning three of the first four holes. Slowly and gradually, in what would later become the unmistakable Faldo flow, the Englishman completely turned the tables on the American over the next twelve holes.

Having crept back into the match, Faldo holed a twelve-foot putt on the sixteenth to win his match, 3 and 2, after a six-hole swing in twelve holes.

This was Faldo's sixth win in seven Ryder Cup matches.

Nick Faldo holed his match-winning putt just seconds after learning that the United States had retained the Cup. Said Faldo: "It was disappointing to win my match and find out we had already lost. . . . We got knocked down like tin soldiers today."

Hale Irwin (USA) v. Des Smyth (EUR)

These two players had already crossed swords in the embarrassing foursomes blowout on Friday afternoon, and met again in the more conducive atmosphere of the solo format.

By winning three of the first eight holes, Hale Irwin pretty much wrapped up this singles match early on. Des Smyth was unable to mount any comeback challenge on the back nine and was dealt his second heavy defeat—both at the hands of Irwin—of the contest at 5 and 3.

Hubert Green (USA) v. Peter Oosterhuis (EUR)

Hubert Green, left out of the fourball matches on the second afternoon because of his poor form, faced the British player with the best singles record. Peter Oosterhuis was unbeaten in four previous singles matches and must have liked his chances of improving his record.

The match was close all along, with Green holding a one-hole lead after thirteen hard-fought holes. The 306-yard fourteenth was not a pretty sight, as Oosterhuis's bogey won the hole over Green's double.

All square, the next two holes were halved to set up a thrilling finish that saw the American reassert his game. Green made a decisive hole-winning ten-footer on seventeen and another birdie on the last hole to run out a 2-up winner.

This was Oosterhuis's first-ever singles loss, dating back to his debut in 1971.

When he went dormie at seventeen, Green earned at least a half-point, which was enough to retain the Cup for the United States.

Fuzzy Zoeller (USA) v. Ken Brown (EUR)

If ever a golfing matchup perfectly mirrored the Hare and the Tortoise story, this was it.

Reigning Masters champion Fuzzy Zoeller started out fast, while Ken Brown started cold, as though he still resented having to play in a regimented team format.

The American won the first two holes but was unable to protect his lead, as Ken Brown in his inimitably ambling, shambling, rambling manner clawed his way back into the match and won it going away—ever so slowly—1-up on the final green.

Lee Trevino (USA) v. Sandy Lyle (EUR)

After allowing Billy Casper to remove Trevino's name from the envelope: *"We are going to win this match fairly."* —JOHN JACOBS

Given a reprieve by the European captain after his own skipper had mistakenly put his name in the envelope, Lee Trevino was only too glad to be out on the course, and thrived in his role as anchor. He managed to hold off the very much in-form Sandy Lyle, who had been scheduled to go out early but also found himself last out in the revised order. The final score—2 and 1 to Trevino—showed how close this final match had been.

Day three result: USA 8½, EUR 3½

The only halved match in the twelve singles matches was the no result between the injured James and Morgan.

Overall match score: USA 17, EUR 11

Recap

The 17–11 result was a fair barometer of this first intercontinental Ryder Cup, as the European team showed some improvement on the road form of previous British sides. The six-point margin of victory was perhaps a little kind to the American team, which had profited from one particular cash-cow couple.

Disregarding the unbeatable pairing of Wadkins and Nelson, who went 4–0 in the first two days, the final match score was only 13–11. In fact, discounting the Spanish pair's going 0–3 against the two Americans, Europe actually won the first two days, 7½–5½.

Although things once again fell apart for the Europeans in the final-day singles, at last the U.S. side had been given a relatively tough match for the first two days. The Americans again proved much tougher when it came to the one-on-one battle, taking the singles by five clear points.

Downplaying his victorious captain's faux pas with the envelope: "Billy Casper only fouled up once. He never got the bar set up in the players' lounge."
—*Lee Trevino*

Europe may have expected its own men to do their duty, but it was a different Nelson (Larry, not Horatio) who stepped into the breach. The rookie went 5–0 and was named the unanimous MVP of the U.S. win. Said Nelson: "I don't think I'm the hero. If there was a hero, it was Lanny. He spent the first two days teaching me match play, and his aggressive nature got me going."

Only time would tell whether the inclusion of two Europeans had saved the Ryder Cup. One thing had been achieved, though: the first blow in chipping away at the foundation of archaic amateurism prevalent in British golfing society. Ten years after the historic moon landing, the events at The Greenbrier proved to be one small step for golf, one giant leap for golfkind.

Match Results (Winning side marked in *italics*.)

Friday, September 14—Morning Fourball

	USA	EUR	Score
1.	*Lanny Wadkins* *Larry Nelson*	Antonio Garrido Seve Ballesteros	2 and 1
2.	*Lee Trevino* *Fuzzy Zoeller*	Ken Brown Mark James	3 and 2
3.	*Andy Bean* *Lee Elder*	Peter Oosterhuis Nick Faldo	2 and 1
4.	Hale Irwin John Mahaffey	*Bernard Gallacher* *Brian Barnes*	2 and 1

Friday, September 14—Afternoon Foursomes

	USA	EUR	Score
5.	*Hale Irwin* *Tom Kite*	Ken Brown Des Smyth	7 and 6
6.	Fuzzy Zoeller Hubert Green	*Seve Ballesteros* *Antonio Garrido*	3 and 2
7.	Lee Trevino Gil Morgan	Sandy Lyle Tony Jacklin	halved
8.	*Lanny Wadkins* *Larry Nelson*	Bernard Gallacher Brian Barnes	4 and 3

Day one result: USA 5½, EUR 2½

Saturday, September 15—Morning Foursomes

	USA	EUR	Score
9.	Lee Elder John Mahaffey	*Tony Jacklin* *Sandy Lyle*	5 and 4
10.	Andy Bean Tom Kite	*Nick Faldo* *Peter Oosterhuis*	6 and 5
11.	*Lanny Wadkins* *Larry Nelson*	Seve Ballesteros Antonio Garrido	3 and 2
12.	Fuzzy Zoeller Mark Hayes	*Bernard Gallacher* *Brian Barnes*	2 and 1

Saturday, September 15—Afternoon Fourball

	USA	EUR	Score
13.	Lee Trevino Fuzzy Zoeller	*Bernard Gallacher* *Brian Barnes*	3 and 2
14.	Lee Elder Mark Hayes	*Nick Faldo* *Peter Oosterhuis*	1-up
15.	*Hale Irwin* *Tom Kite*	Tony Jacklin Sandy Lyle	1-up
16.	*Lanny Wadkins* *Larry Nelson*	Seve Ballesteros Antonio Garrido	5 and 4

Day two result: *USA 3, EUR 5*

Overall match score: *USA 8½, EUR 7½*

Sunday, September 16—Singles

	USA	EUR	Score
17.	Gil Morgan	Mark James	halved*
18.	Lanny Wadkins	*Bernard Gallacher*	3 and 2
19.	*Larry Nelson*	Seve Ballesteros	3 and 2
20.	*Tom Kite*	Tony Jacklin	1-up
21.	*Mark Hayes*	Antonio Garrido	1-up
22.	*Andy Bean*	Michael King	4 and 3
23.	*John Mahaffey*	Brian Barnes	1-up
24.	Lee Elder	*Nick Faldo*	3 and 2
25.	*Hale Irwin*	Des Smyth	5 and 3
26.	*Hubert Green*	Peter Oosterhuis	2-up
27.	Fuzzy Zoeller	*Ken Brown*	1-up
28.	*Lee Trevino*	Sandy Lyle	2 and 1

Day three result: USA *8½*, EUR *3½*

Overall match score: USA *17*, EUR *11*

---

* Match not played by agreement because both players were injured.

1981

Walton Heath Surrey England September 18–20	**United States 18½**	**Europe 9½**
	Ben Crenshaw	Jose-Maria Canizares (Spain)
	Raymond Floyd	Howard Clark (England)
	Hale Irwin	Eamonn Darcy (Ireland)
	Tom Kite	Nick Faldo (England)
	Bruce Lietzke	Bernard Gallacher (Scotland)
	Johnny Miller	Mark James (England)
	Larry Nelson	Bernhard Langer (Germany)
	Jack Nicklaus	Sandy Lyle (Scotland)
	Jerry Pate	Peter Oosterhuis (England)
	Bill Rogers	Manuel Pinero (Spain)
	Lee Trevino	Des Smyth (Ireland)
	Tom Watson	Sam Torrance (Scotland)
	Captain	**Captain**
	Dave Marr	John Jacobs (England)

United Strength of America

The powers that be thought opening up the Ryder Cup to European players would create a more level playing field for competition. But 1981 proved as level as a mogul slalom course.

As it turned out, the problem was not that the British (and now European) teams had been too weak, but that the U.S. teams were far too strong. Certainly the team Dave Marr captained at Walton Heath in the fall of 1981 was quite simply the best group of Americans to arrive in Britain since the GIs descended on war-torn England in 1941. Only this time the GIs who invaded the small island were Golf's Invincibles, and in Dave Marr they had a field marshal who maneuvered his troops with military precision.

"The forty-eight-year-old Marr, whose crumpled good looks and twanging accent make you think of a trail boss in some remake of *Rawhide*."
—*Christopher Plumridge,* London Guardian

"It's our Olympics. If you don't want to play your heart out for the good old red, white, and blue, you've got no business on the team."

—Dave Marr

Among Marr's recruits were three current majors winners: Watson (Masters), Rogers (British Open), and Nelson (PGA Championship). Amazingly, Bruce Lietzke was the only player of the thirteen, including Marr, not to win a major in his career. The U.S. side was stacked with talent that had won thirty-six majors (and two hundred tour victories), compared with a European squad that had yet to have a single major-winner on the entire team.

Dave Marr had a relatively good reason for not wanting to lose this Ryder Cup: his cousin Jack Burke, Jr., had been the last U.S. captain to do so, in 1957. He also echoed his cousin's famous words of warning: "The Ryder Cup is different than teeing it up for money. You can always talk to your landlord about the rent, but if we lose, we may not get back in the country . . . it could mean a posting to El Salvador."

The opposition, once again captained by John Jacobs, was if anything weaker than the first European team. The simple reason for that was the notable absence of their number one player, 1980 Masters champion Seve Ballesteros, and former number one Tony Jacklin—the only two Europeans to have won a major in recent memory. Jacobs and his selection team found valid reasons not to select either player.

Mark James had his own take on how he had mellowed since the 1979 incidents that cost him $3,000: "I got married since those days. My wife is in control now."

The average age of the European team was twenty-eight; of the American team, thirty-three.

"John Jacobs, the first captain of the European side, was having a lot of trouble in 1979 with some players. Then he left me out in 1981 in favor of one of the players who were being most disruptive [Mark James]."

—TONY JACKLIN

Unfortunately, the dozen European players who were selected just were not up to the task of taking on the full might of the United States. Two of the Euro-rookies would go on in later years to carve their own niche in Ryder Cup history: German Bernhard Langer (the leading European money-winner) and Scot Sam Torrance. Two Spaniards, Pinero and Canizares, also joined them, in a team that looked outgunned from the start.

Course Details

Walton Heath was so named because it stands on some rough and rugged heathland, fifteen miles south of London. One commodity the course had in abundance was heather, in which a great many golf balls found a permanent resting home.

"The rough looks like harmless heather . . . until you try to get out of it." —Golf Digest

Hole	Distance	Par	Hole	Distance	Par
1	410	4	10	340	4
2	513	5	11	488	5
3	391	4	12	462	4
4	422	4	13	470	4
5	174	3	14	517	5
6	489	5	15	404	4
7	390	4	16	475	4
8	404	4	17	165	3
9	180	3	18	373	4
		36			**37 = Par 73 (7,067 yards)**

Course designer: Herbert Fowler

Day One: Morning Foursomes

Both sets of players appeared on the first tee sporting dark blue golf sweaters. Fortunately for TV commentators and the gallery, the persistent rain meant the matching team colors were quickly hidden under a colorful array of waterproofs.

Despite the match's being sponsored by life insurance company Sun Alliance, the sun was not spotted too often on the first day.

"Today's opening matches drew a gallery of 10,700 who were unfazed by rain that ranged from drizzle to storm. There also was a cold wind blowing all day." —JOHN RADOSTA, *New York Times*

Lee Trevino and Larry Nelson (USA) v. Bernhard Langer and Manuel Pinero (EUR)

Having gone 5-0 in his first match in 1979, PGA champion Larry Nelson was sent out first as a psychological ploy—a reminder of the last contest.

Despite a lifetime 7–1 Ryder Cup record, Lanny Wadkins, who had combined with Nelson to go 4–0 in the 1979 pairs format, failed to qualify this time around.

The continental Euro-pairing of Langer and Pinero fought a losing battle against the confident coupling of Trevino and Nelson, who were two up after seven holes. Langer and Pinero did manage to make their way back level with two wins in the next three holes, but the Americans played as though they were well in control.

The 470-yard par-4 thirteenth proved a major headache for the home pair, who conceded the hole to give back the lead. Pinero's drive on fifteen again put his side in some difficulty, but Langer recovered well enough to win the hole. The Europeans were up against it again on sixteen, with Pinero holing a sneaky little putt for a half.

All square with two to play, Pinero followed another poor tee shot on the par-3 seventeenth by missing the par putt, after Langer had made another fine recovery. Fortunately for the Spaniard, the Americans could not birdie the hole, so the game was there for the taking on the eighteenth.

The eighteenth green had been vandalized three days before the matches started, but the grounds crew were able to patch up the dozen or so lumps dug out of the turf. The temporary repairs did not allow a favorable pin position all week.

After Larry Nelson won his sixth match out of six: "My baby-faced chicken killer."
—*Dave Marr*

However well they might have played the last hole, Langer and Pinero had no answer to Nelson's embarrassingly long birdie putt. Launched from forty-five feet away on the lower level of the green, Nelson's zip-code buster zeroed in on the cup and mailed itself for the win to snatch the match 1-up.

Bill Rogers and Bruce Lietzke (USA) v. Sandy Lyle and Mark James (EUR)

Almost as sweet a partnership as Tate and Lyle, former Walker Cup partners James and Lyle swiftly proved a bitter pill to swallow for Lietzke and Rogers. Off the first tee, Lietzke drove into the heather-clad rough. Following Rogers's hacking recovery, he failed to execute a relatively simple pitch shot and lost the first hole.

The Europeans soon found themselves three up after a birdie on the 391-yard third hole and another American bogey on the par-4 fourth. Lietzke and Rogers claimed one hole back by the turn, then lost the tenth to drop back to three down.

Sandy Lyle's strength allowed him to easily reach the 488-yard eleventh in two, while the Americans needed three shots to get inside of Lyle's second. James slammed home the twenty-footer for an eagle three to pad out a very comfortable cushion of four up.

Comfort counts for nothing in the Ryder Cup, and the British pair was immediately brought back to earth with a bump. Lyle's drive found the heather on twelve, and his approach on thirteen failed to find the green. These errors gave up both holes to American pars, and the lead was slashed to one off the back of an American birdie on the 517-yard fourteenth after James bunkered his approach.

Their tails up on the scent of a comeback, the United States carded a rally-busting double-bogey six on sixteen, Lietzke hooking dramatically into the heather and Rogers finding sand, as the more than grateful Europeans took the hole with a par four.

The Americans' double calamity on sixteen allowed James and Lyle to regroup, make a gentle half in par at the 165-yard seventeenth, and hold on for the win, 2 and 1.

Raymond Floyd and Hale Irwin (USA) v. Bernard Gallacher and Des Smyth (EUR)

Floyd hooked his tee shot on the first, and he and Irwin could do no better than a bogey five to immediately drop one down to Gallacher and Smyth. An American birdie on the third leveled the match until the par-4 tenth hole, where Smyth persuaded a difficult long birdie putt to drop for the go-ahead win. Smyth's putt broke a string of six halved holes.

"The main honors must be awarded to Bernard Gallacher who figuratively threw off his drab blazer to emerge in tights and T-shirt emblazoned with giant letters. Bam! Zap! Pow!"
—*Peter Dobereiner,* London Guardian

Gallacher broke the match open by sinking an eagle putt on eleven for a two-hole lead. The Americans briefly showed some hope as they birdied the twelfth, but they dropped the next hole with a bogey five.

The British held their two-hole lead until they dramatically brought the curtain down on the 475-yard sixteenth. Gallacher played a mighty recovery after Smyth's tee shot found the rough, allowing the Irishman to make amends by sinking another long birdie putt from the edge of the green for a 3 and 2 win.

Although the Americans had not played badly, three under par for their sixteen holes, the Europeans carded five birdies and an eagle in their bogey-free seven-under-par total.

Tom Watson and Jack Nicklaus (USA) v. Peter Oosterhuis and Nick Faldo (EUR)

Peter Oosterhuis had arrived from his home in California with a painfully swollen right hand, having been bitten by an insect, and had difficulty gripping a club properly, although he played this down, saying, "I am perfectly OK now. I got bitten by some sort of spider . . . but I have had penicillin treatment, and although I was sick on Sunday, there are no problems now."

The Americans' star pairing of Watson and Nicklaus got hit early by two birdies in four holes, giving Oosterhuis and Faldo a two-hole lead. Faldo essayed a splendid recovery from the heather up to the second pin for an Oosterhuis birdie putt. On the 422-yard fourth, Faldo assumed the putting duties, holing a birdie putt across a considerable portion of the wet green.

Oosterhuis gave a hole back on the par-3 fifth when he took a club or two too many for the 174-yard journey. After the sixth was halved, the Americans dug in and dragged themselves back into contention. Nicklaus made a seven-foot birdie putt on seven to get the American bandwagon rolling. Having found his first fairway off the tee in four drives, Watson holed his partner's excellent approach for a birdie and the lead after eight holes. Nicklaus left another awesome approach sitting a yard from the hole on nine, for a certain Watson birdie, but Faldo holed his long putt from the edge of the green to halve.

On the first homeward hole, Oosterhuis skinned a bunker shot across the green and off into the thick rough to double the U.S. advantage. Not wishing to stand on ceremony, the Americans harmonized for another win on the par-5 eleventh to go three up.

Watson's persistent problems off the tee continued: he visited the welcoming but inhospitable heather with another wayward drive. Nicklaus played a safe but sure recovery, but it was not enough to save the twelfth hole. Two up with six to play, the Americans not only defended their lead but also doubled it, closing out the ultimately disappointing European number one pairing, 4 and 3.

None of these four star names appeared in the second session: Marr demanded that his legends put their feet up for the afternoon, while Jacobs dropped his "log-ends." Oosterhuis was clearly troubled by his swollen hand. Faldo had no excuses except that he played poorly after the first few holes.

Morning foursomes result: USA 2, EUR 2

Day One: Afternoon Fourball

A thunderstorm midway through the afternoon halted play, the sky turning as black as night, mirroring the rain delay at The Greenbrier in 1979.

Tom Kite and Johnny Miller (USA) v. Sam Torrance and Howard Clark (EUR)

Kite and Miller were picked to sweep away Clark and the rookie Torrance but found themselves only one up after nine holes, as the European pair played tougher than expected.

The Americans quickly doubled their lead after the turn, but things got even tougher for them when they both made mistakes off and on the thirteenth green.

"The first Ryder Cup is wicked on your nerves."
—*Sam Torrance*

Torrance played as if he were to the manor born when it came to the perils and pressures of the Ryder Cup, and his eagle putt on fourteen squared the match. The European pair had chances to win each of the following three holes but spurned them all.

Had Torrance's ten-foot birdie putt on the last hole not lipped out, he would have stolen a much-needed and improbable victory off Kite and Miller. As it happened, both sides shot excellent 65s for a commendable share of the spoils.

Ben Crenshaw and Jerry Pate (USA) v. Sandy Lyle and Mark James (EUR)

Against Crenshaw and Pate, Scotsman Sandy Lyle had a round of golf that every twenty-handicapper knows only too well. Unable to buy a decent tee shot all day, he holed almost every putt he left himself. His first two drives were hooked into the rough, and his third drive was hooked clear over the rough. In the midst of this carnage, he kept his touch on the putting surface by holing a twenty-five-footer on the second for the win. At the par-3 fifth, he sank another birdie putt as the Europeans' tactics paid off.

"We meshed well today. The greens are probably slower than the Americans are used to. They're tricky, and I am used to them." —Sandy Lyle

Jerry Pate had a long-standing score to settle with Mark James, who had beaten him twice in the 1975 Walker Cup.

With Mark James playing the safe anchor role, Lyle was let loose to plunder as many birdies as he could capture. With two birdies in the first five holes, the Europeans hit pay dirt, making five more birdies in the next seven holes. Pate and Crenshaw vainly tried to keep up with the pace but found themselves three down at the turn, as their opponents carded an outward 31.

On the 340-yard tenth, with James safely in the middle of the fairway, Lyle unleashed a three-wood that cleared some trees and found a green that the Scot could not see. Holing one of his four putts from beyond twenty-two feet, Lyle increased his side's lead to four.

The lone American highlight of the round came on the 517-yard fourteenth, where Jerry Pate caught Lyle's putting fever and sank a twenty-five-footer for eagle. With halves until the end on sixteen, Lyle (five birdies) and James (three birdies) combined for an eight-under-par tally and a rousing 3 and 2 win.

On his partnership's second win of the day: *"We now know we can win individual matches. That has given us great confidence. Now we have to find out whether we can all win at the same time."* —MARK JAMES

Bill Rogers and Bruce Lietzke (USA) v. Des Smyth and Jose Maria Canizares (EUR)

John Jacobs gambled with this improbable pairing of a Spaniard and an Irishman, but he wanted to get all his men into the action on the first day.

In spite of a very nervous start by Canizares, the thirty-four-year-old Spanish rookie and his Irish partner were rarely in trouble, though they had set out as what many had thought to be the weakest home pairing. The Europeans did not have to play earth-shatteringly well, as Rogers and Lietzke were way off form, although the latter birdied the 513-yard second to take an early lead.

The Europeans took this promising American foundation and demolished it brick by brick. From the par-4 fourth, Rogers and Lietzke were undone in a seven-hole stretch where they lost six holes, two of them to European pars. The Spaniard, who had been uptight and downhearted over his debut, burst out with a dazzling array of strokes that brought him two birdies and an eight-foot eagle, while Smyth added a couple of birdies to complete the unexpected rout.

Six up after the Spaniard's eagle settled the eleventh, Smyth and Canizares quickly put the Americans out of their misery on the thirteenth with a 6 and 5 thrashing.

This was a day that Bill Rogers would like to forget. The British Open champion was humbled on his competitive return to the British Isles, as he and Bruce Lietzke easily lost both their matches together.

Canizares earned only the second "continental" point for Europe, after seven previous attempts had generated just one win (Ballesteros and Garrido on the opening afternoon in 1979).

Hale Irwin and Raymond Floyd (USA) v. Bernard Gallacher and Eamonn Darcy (EUR)

Late in the afternoon, there was a second delay of twenty minutes because of another severe storm, but this last match played through an official rain-and-thunder suspension at the end of the day.

Gallacher opened the encounter in grand style, dropping a forty-foot birdie putt on the first hole, but Floyd leveled on the second with his much shorter birdie putt.

Although this roller-coaster match saw both pairs twice pull back the other to level the score, the defining moments came from Floyd and Gallacher, Irwin and Darcy filling the minor supporting roles.

Locked at evens after nine holes, the Americans edged ahead at the par-4 tenth before Floyd's eagle at the 488-yard eleventh sprang open a two-hole lead with seven to play. This good work was partially undone with a double bogey on twelve. Having quickly seen the United States cut their own lead to one, Gallacher stepped up to sink his fifty-foot eagle putt on the par-5 fourteenth to level the match again.

"Gallacher was a bandit with his putter."
—John Radosta, *New York Times*

Back all square, the fifteenth was halved, but Floyd sensationally put the game away with birdies on sixteen and seventeen for a 2 and 1 win. Hole-winning putts from twenty and eleven feet gave the big man his fifth and sixth birdies of the round, as he overcame the added pressure of being watched by all his nonplaying teammates.

On playing through the storm warning: "Floyd managed to keep his putter warm enough to save a valuable point."
—*Peter Dobereiner,* London Guardian

Afternoon fourball result: USA 1½, EUR 2½

"We nearly got blitzed. But this has pulled the team together. They know now they are in a dogfight." —Dave Marr

"I'm disappointed. A couple of matches in the balance fell the wrong way for us." —John Jacobs

Day one result: USA 3½, EUR 4½

"It's nice to be in the game, as no one thought we would, but to be ahead as well. We have a chance to knock down the Americans."

—SANDY LYLE

"When the host Europeans took a surprising lead in the Ryder Cup matches, it seemed to give the Americans the incentive they needed to prove to all they were indeed 'the best ever assembled.'"

—MICHAEL MCDONNELL

With an overnight European lead, some ill-informed local wag suggested that the United States might need to call on Canadians and Mexicans to strengthen their team. How the U.S. team would make him eat his words . . .

Day Two: Morning Fourball

Following even more overnight rain, a beautiful sunny morning turned to miserable gray.

"Rain fell and the skies darkened to pewter above Walton Heath. . . . Play had begun under soft blue skies. Later in the morning, rain fell intermittently." —JOHN HOPKINS, *Sunday Times* (London)

Lee Trevino and Jerry Pate (USA) v. Nick Faldo and Sam Torrance (EUR)

Overnight, Dave Marr sought the advice of his senior players as to what had gone wrong on the first day. Trevino pointed out that Marr had teamed too many rookies together and they had suffered under the unique pressures of international match play. With this in mind, Marr sent out Trevino, at the head of his Strategic Response Team, with Jerry Pate.

The U.S. captain did not have to wait long to see how his new pairing would work out against Faldo and Torrance. Pate opened with a birdie three that was to set the tempo for a short, explosive day for the Americans.

Said Marr about his opening "teacher-student" pairing, "Sure enough, they won the first hole, and Jerry just kills a drive. Trevino hits his approach and then runs over to Pate's ball and asks him what he's planning to do. Pate said he was going to cut a little four-iron into the pin. Trevino put his hand over the four-iron, handed him the five-iron, and told him to just bust it. Sure enough, Jerry put the shot six feet from the hole. Trevino did this all the way round."

From here, the news only got better and better for Marr. The unlikely partnership of Trevino and Pate combined flawlessly: six up after nine, a remarkable score even in a fourball match. Faldo and Torrance were left drowning in the Americans' wake, as Pate played like an honor student under Trevino's tutelage, making six birdies in the first eleven holes.

On being paired with Pate: *"Jerry had everything . . . from the neck down. With my brains and his swing, we were unbeatable. I told him what clubs to play and even gave him the line of the putts."*

—Lee Trevino

Trevino had an easy, laid-back time as he and his partner took this first match 7 and 5, paving the way for one of the greatest days the Americans would enjoy in the Ryder Cup.

"I did the thinking for Jerry. Maybe I should have kept my mouth shut, because now I may never beat him back home."
—*Lee Trevino*

Pate was finally beginning to pay back his teammates, who had joked with him all week about the points he owed them from his four losses in the Walker Cup.

Larry Nelson and Tom Kite (USA) v. Sandy Lyle and Mark James (EUR)

This was a battle of the four in-form players: Lyle and James were 2–0 in matches together, Nelson was 6–0 lifetime, and Kite was the U.S. money-list leader. Something had to give . . . but not for eighteen glorious holes played in torrential rain.

An American win on the 391-yard third was matched by a European success on the one-yard-shorter seventh. All square after nine holes of engrossing match play, the U.S. pair took another lead with a win on the 340-yard tenth.

Lyle pegged the Americans back again with a wonder strike from way out on the 475-yard sixteenth. After the Scotsman's second shot almost rolled into the hole for an eagle two, the gimme birdie leveled the match with two to play.

Within sight of a well-earned half, Lyle and James had a half-point snatched from under their noses by some magical putting by Larry Nelson. After almost holing his approach on sixteen, Lyle almost holed his six-iron tee shot to the par-3 seventeenth. Having conceded the European birdie, Nelson promptly halved the hole with a looping twenty-foot birdie putt.

"I enjoy head-to-head playing. I can do things I couldn't do the rest of the week."
—*Larry Nelson*

The American repeated the magic act on the final green, just as he had done on Friday morning, with another long birdie putt. This time, he made his ball disappear from a mere fifteen feet, capturing the decisive win by one hole.

On Nelson's double-birdie finish: *"That was the turning point, the key match."* —DAVE MARR

In this outstanding match of quality and sportsmanship, neither pair was ever more than one hole ahead, the Americans finishing with a nine-under 64.

Raymond Floyd and Hale Irwin (USA) v. Bernhard Langer and Manuel Pinero (EUR)

In an early stretch of this match, Irwin and Floyd made four birdies in a row but did not win a hole. Langer and Pinero matched them stride for stride, stroke for stroke. The tenacity of the European pair was exemplified on the 404-yard eighth. With Irwin's ball sitting on top of the flag, Pinero chipped in from forty yards out to halve the hole.

Pinero put his side three up when he sank another birdie putt on the ninth, then repeated the act on the tenth for his side's sixth birdie of the match.

Without a hole to their name, the desperate and frustrated Americans arrived on the sixteenth tee three down with three to play. They opened their account to pull back to dormie two, but the writing (albeit in German and Spanish calligraphy) was already on the wall. On the 165-yard seventeenth, Pinero again proved to be the Americans' worst nightmare. The Spaniard's tee shot found the center of the green, and with neither American able to hole his birdie putt, Pinero two-putted for the half to wrap up the win 2 and 1.

This would prove to be the only European win and point of the second day.

Jack Nicklaus and Tom Watson (USA) v. Jose Maria Canizares and Des Smyth (EUR)

Canizares and Smyth were coming off one of the biggest wins against the Americans in Ryder Cup history, but this match would be totally different. For starters, they faced Nicklaus and Watson, who were well rested (after their own big win on Friday morning) and raring to go. Second, the whole American team had been stung into positive action following their disappointing first day.

This match as a contest was over by the halfway stage, but with two American legends in harness, there was still plenty for the gallery to marvel at. Watson and Nicklaus started out hot and gently turned up the heat: they were three up after nine, with five birdies between them, Watson claiming the honor at the third and ninth, Nicklaus making successive sub-par strikes at four, five, and six.

"I never thought Jack's short game was very good. Of course, he hit so many greens today, it didn't make any difference." —Tom Watson

More birdies on the way home gave the Americans seven in a dominating nine-hole stretch, but they allowed Canizares and Smyth an opportunity for damage control. The Europeans posted their first wins on fifteen and sixteen to delay a much larger defeat than the 3 and 2 loss they were handed.

Morning fourball result: USA 3, EUR 1

Day Two: Afternoon Foursomes

"After lunch torrential rain fell incessantly and a wind got up to blow at between 30 and 35 mph."—John Hopkins, *Sunday Times* (London)

Dripping Towards Defeat Across a Blasted Heath
—Sunday Times *(London) headline*

Three out-of-form Americans—Miller, Crenshaw, and Lietzke—volunteered to sit out the day for the benefit of the team.

Lee Trevino and Jerry Pate (USA) v. Peter Oosterhuis and Sam Torrance (EUR)

Playing with Oosterhuis, the rookie Torrance was with his third partner in three matches. Having suggested to Marr that the American rookies needed a guardian angel, Trevino all but sprouted wings and a halo, and was easily coaxed into playing his second match of the day with Pate, after the pair's romp in the morning.

Trevino-Pate Inc. got a ringside seat to a most remarkable opening burst by their opponents. Oosterhuis and Torrance exploded on the first hole, failed to detonate on the second, and imploded on the third and fourth holes. With birdie on the opening hole, Europe had its only lead in this match—and its only lead in any of the four afternoon matches. At the 513-yard second, the Anglo-Scottish alliance barely missed making another birdie to go two up.

After this confident start, the rot set in. The Europeans bogeyed the third and fourth holes to hand their opponents the lead, which the Americans built upon with a birdie two on the 174-yard fifth. On the par-5 sixth, it was the U.S. pair's turn to slip up, a bogey reducing the lead to one.

The match rolled through ten holes, Trevino and Pate holding on to their unstable lead until they lost the eleventh to a British birdie. The Americans hit back with two wins on thirteen and fourteen to reclaim a two-hole lead, on which Oosterhuis and Torrance could not make any impression.

The closest match of the afternoon was brought to its conclusion on the seventeenth. Trevino and Pate had their second win of the day, this time by the reduced terms of 2 and 1.

Jack Nicklaus and Tom Watson (USA) v. Bernhard Langer and Manuel Pinero (EUR)

The top American pairing had already won their first two matches with some ease—4 and 3, and 3 and 2.

The continental coupling of a German and a Spaniard could not produce the level of golf required to test Nicklaus and Watson, who, as expected, cruised to another comfortable win, 3 and 2.

Even when the Americans did falter, the Europeans were unable to make their birdie. On the thirteenth, Watson played a very poor tee shot, but the Europeans allowed the U.S. pair to halve the hole in a scrambling par.

Spurning the few chances they were given, Langer and Pinero were made to pay for their lack of a killer touch by two golfers who were at the very top of their game.

Bill Rogers and Raymond Floyd (USA) v. Sandy Lyle and Mark James (EUR)

At the turn, the U.S. players were in absolute ascendancy in all four matches, with three pairs out in 34 despite the worsening conditions. For Europe, only Lyle and James went out under par, but they still found themselves down to Rogers and Floyd.

During the match, a British player's ball disappeared into the crowd packed around a green, before reappearing and rolling back toward the hole: *"It was quite a few seconds before the ball came back. That kind of thing shocks you."* —Raymond Floyd

The Americans doubled the lead with Rogers's long, raking putt on the 462-yard twelfth. Having looked to be the best European pair of the first day, Lyle and James could not click quite as well as they had before and found the Americans too tough to crack. One win and four holes later, the Americans wrapped up the match, 3 and 2.

This match gave world traveler Rogers, who held the British and Japanese Open titles, his first point and his only-ever win in four Ryder Cup matches. This year was his sole appearance in the competition.

Tom Kite and Larry Nelson (USA) v. Des Smyth and Bernard Gallacher (EUR)

Having been paired together in the morning and produced a fighting finish for their fourball win, the Americans continued their good work together in the afternoon foursomes.

Larry Nelson kept up his incredible Ryder Cup run as he and Tom Kite quickly took control of this match, with a three-hole advantage after ten holes.

Smyth and Gallacher, having dropped behind on the front nine, could not mount any more of a challenge on the back nine, although they did manage to stave off the inevitable defeat until the sixteenth hole, going down 3 and 2.

On Larry Nelson's going 8–0 in Ryder Cup play: "There goes the most notorious man in Britain since Jack the Ripper."
—*Dave Marr*

Afternoon foursomes result: USA 4, EUR 0

Europe lost all four foursomes matches to an American side that was a collective eleven under par.

Day two result: USA 7, EUR 1

This was the biggest margin of victory in a single day since the Americans' 7½–½ second-day rout in 1967. "It's a miracle," said Dave Marr. "You don't win seven out of eight matches in Ryder Cup play. The Europeans played well. They just hit a slick spot in the road and spun out."

After avoiding a clean sweep on the day: *"The Americans played as well as we all knew they could, and they did it all on the same afternoon. It wasn't that our boys played badly. The Americans just excelled."*
—JOHN JACOBS

Overall match score: USA 10½, EUR 5½

Day Three: Singles

On his players' becoming complacent with a five-point lead: *"There's no such thing as a cinch in golf, but if they are the strongest team, then they've got to prove it."* —DAVE MARR

After more heavy rain overnight, Jacobs prayed for his own dramatic conclusion to the day ahead. Needing a miracle at the top of his order, Jacobs decided to send out three Scots in a hope that their brand of enthusiasm would bring an unexpected return.

Lee Trevino (USA) v. Sam Torrance (EUR)

Torrance lost the first and second holes with awful approach shots, leaving himself lengthy putts for par that he missed by some distance. Trevino built on this gifted lead, but the Scot holed a thirty-foot putt for the win at the 174-yard fifth.

A second Trevino birdie at the sixth increased his lead to four, and he reached the turn two under, six shots better than Torrance.

Despite driving way off course at the tenth, Torrance played a marvelous recovery to eight feet and made the birdie putt for the win. Having turned back the tide of Trevino's successes, the Scottish rookie cracked under the pressure of playing on his own in the Ryder Cup.

After tangling with the heather, Torrance sheepishly conceded the fourteenth to Trevino's eagle, before twice burying his ball in sand to concede the fifteenth. This final blunder gave the match to Trevino, 5 and 3, who finished five under, with three birdies, an eagle, and no bogeys.

With an alarmingly early 8:30 start, Trevino wanted to get out of the heavy rain so quickly that he finished off Torrance in just over two hours. So fast that he was drying himself off in the clubhouse well before Jack Nicklaus had teed off in the last match at 1:00 P.M. Trevino joked that he would go out again if Jack wanted to stay dry.

This proved to be Lee Trevino's last appearance as a player in the Ryder Cup. He had distinguished himself in six campaigns with a record of 17-7-6. At the time, his 20 points ranked him third on the U.S. all-time list behind Casper and Palmer.

Tom Kite (USA) v. Sandy Lyle (EUR)

"Then came a match of scarcely credible quality, perhaps the greatest Ryder Cup encounter in the history of the event."

—Peter Dobereiner, *London Guardian*

This proved to be the match of the day, if not the decade. Kite held a two-hole lead after five holes, having made birdies at the first three holes. Lyle hit back with a triple-birdie burst of his own, from the par-5 sixth, to take a one-hole lead.

Tom Kite was quite familiar with the vagaries of this course, having won the 1980 European Open at Walton Heath.

Overhauled by the three Scottish birdies in a row, Kite went one better. He carded four birdies in succession to regain a one-hole lead after twelve holes of breathtaking golf that had Kite seven under par. Lyle's noble challenge faltered under the onslaught of Kite's majestic play when he conceded his opponent's seven-footer on the twelfth. The Scot made his second consecutive bogey of the day at thirteen, before the par-5 fourteenth was shared with another birdie each.

Kite got a vital break, halving the 404-yard fifteenth with a putt that was so long that the genial American apologized to Lyle for his outlandish luck. This put Kite three up with three to play, and with another birdie, he halved the sixteenth for an amazing win, 3 and 2.

Although the Scot lost his match, the heroic manner of his downfall was seen in some quarters as a moral victory: Lyle Virtuosity Rescues Europe's Honor. —*London Guardian* headline

"If Sandy and I had played as a foursome, we would have beaten the lights out of anyone."
—*Tom Kite*

Going down to a glorious defeat, Lyle had amassed eight birdies. Kite had ten birdies and no bogeys, putting him ten under par for the sixteen holes played.

Bill Rogers (USA) v. Bernard Gallacher (EUR)

Bill Rogers and Bernard Gallacher were in disappointing form, each having mustered only a mediocre 1-2-0 record coming into the singles. Rogers dropped the first hole to Gallacher but quickly hit back with go-ahead wins on three and four. Showing the experience and poise of a seven-time Ryder Cupper, the Scot leveled with an unanswered birdie on the 390-yard seventh before taking his second lead of the match with a win on the tenth.

The British Open champion, who had struggled with his game, the course, and the conditions all week, evened up the match on the par-5 fourteenth, and the next three holes were halved to set up a showdown on the eighteenth.

All square on the final green, Rogers putted up close to the hole, walked over, and picked his ball up. Gallacher had not conceded the hole and could have rightly claimed the hole (and thus the match) by default. He did not, and proceeded to halve the hole and the match in gentlemanly fashion.

Gallacher's sportsmanship in not claiming the last hole was doubly admirable: since the two matches behind them were already decided, the half-point Rogers gained by halving the hole guaranteed that the United States would win the Cup outright.

Larry Nelson (USA) v. Mark James (EUR)

Playing with the confidence that eight wins out of eight gives you, Larry Nelson never trailed Mark James, who had exceeded most people's expectations by not only sticking close to the American but leveling the match after twelve holes.

Nelson's ninth consecutive win equaled Gardner Dickinson's record from 1967 and '71: "I wanted to win it. I wanted to do it just one more time."
—*Larry Nelson*

On fourteen, Nelson reached the front of the 517-yard hole with a two-iron for the go-ahead win that he rode to the seventeenth. Here the PGA champion was able to get up and down from a bunker to scrabble a half.

Nelson's par on eighteen was enough to take the hole. James was unable to get up and down from a bunker, giving Nelson a 2-up win.

Ben Crenshaw (USA) v. Des Smyth (EUR)

"An overnight storm left the Ryder Cup tented village sagging and swamped . . . and by the end of the final day's play, European golf was in the same state of disarray." —PETER DOBEREINER, *London Guardian*

Rookie Ben Crenshaw had not played since his Friday afternoon loss in the fourball format. Smyth, his Irish opponent, was one of only three players to play in all five matches. The rustiness in the Texan's game showed as he dropped the first hole, but he played his way back to a one-hole lead after seven.

His touch and confidence restored, Crenshaw lit up the gray skies with a match-winning burst of birdie-par-birdie-eagle-birdie that put him four up after twelve holes. Smyth hardly knew what had hit him; his bogey five allowed Crenshaw to win the 470-yard thirteenth and go five up.

In his blistering spell of five holes from the seventh onward, Crenshaw carded five consecutive threes to blow the game apart. Still only one up at the turn, Crenshaw won the next five holes to close out the match in grand style.

Crenshaw brought the curtain down in the most dramatic way possible. At the 517-yard fourteenth, his second eagle in four holes gave him a crushing 6 and 4 victory.

Despite his loss, Smyth ended up as joint top points scorer for his team, with two points from his five matches.

Bruce Lietzke (USA) v. Bernhard Langer (EUR)

Having struggled with Bill Rogers in their two losses on Friday, Bruce Lietzke did not suit up on Saturday, but he started out on Sunday as though he had something to prove. Against fellow first-timer Langer, the American carved out a three-hole lead after just eight holes and looked to be coasting to a well-earned victory.

Bernhard Langer was not the first German-born player to appear in the Ryder Cup. Peter Alliss, who was born in Berlin in 1931, claimed that privilege.

Lietzke would not play in the Ryder Cup again, while Langer would become a cornerstone of the future European successes. The German demonstrated some of the qualities that separated men from boys on the Ryder Cup battlefield as he methodically and almost mechanically dragged himself back into the match.

All square after seventeen holes, neither rookie could find that extra piece of magic needed to claim the final hole—the hole and the match were halved.

Finishing with an 0-2-1 record, Bruce Lietzke was one of only two Americans who failed to win a match all week. Johnny Miller was the other.

Jerry Pate (USA) v. Manuel Pinero (EUR)

Another all-rookie contest turned into a one-sided affair. Without the much-needed support of his mentor, Lee Trevino, Jerry Pate failed to show his sparkling Saturday form.

Both players proved to have good memories, as there was still some bad blood between them dating back to the World Cup in 1976.

Pinero was always in control of this game and held a three-hole advantage when news reached him that the Cup had been lost elsewhere on the course. Unperturbed, the Spaniard had other issues to settle, and with his win on sixteen he posted a creditable 4 and 2 win.

In the seventh match out, Pinero's win earned Europe's first full point of the day. With five birdies and an eagle, Pinero was seven under par for his sixteen holes.

Hale Irwin (USA) v. Jose Maria Canizares (EUR)

The experience of the 1979 U.S. Open champion proved too much for the Spanish veteran, and Hale Irwin appeared to be coasting to an easy victory once the Cup had been decided.

Whether or not Irwin let his concentration slip, at dormie three he allowed Canizares to get back into the match with wins on sixteen and seventeen. After this sudden loss of two holes, Irwin refocused his efforts and held on with a half at the last for a one-hole win.

Having played in three previous Ryder Cup contests, Hale Irwin would not appear again for ten years—in a fateful encounter at Kiawah Island.

Johnny Miller (USA) v. Nick Faldo (EUR)

With only one Ryder Cup singles match to his name—a loss to Peter Oosterhuis way back in 1975—Johnny Miller was unable to do any better against Oosterhuis's former pairs partner.

Having been one up when the Cup was lost, Nick Faldo eventually carded six birdies and no bogeys in the seventeen holes played, as he accounted for Miller 2 and 1.

Riding on the crest of a million-dollar wave in the United States, Johnny Miller failed to win either of his Ryder Cup matches, going 0-1-1: *"Money is not an issue. That sort of makes it extra pure. You're playing for your teammates and you're pulling for your country. All of a sudden, the game gets real special. It gets back to its roots."*

—JOHNNY MILLER

Tom Watson (USA) v. Howard Clark (EUR)

The fact that Tom Watson had topped the PGA Tour money list four straight years counted for naught against Howard Clark, who hailed from Yorkshire, where they know the value of every brass farthing.

Both players had similar Ryder Cup records, having made their debuts in 1977 and losing their respective singles matches. Neither golfer played in 1979.

Although Tom Watson was one down when the Cup was secured up ahead on the course, it is unlikely that he would use that as an excuse for his sudden collapse over the closing holes. The fact was that Clark, who had posted three birdies on the front nine to edge into a narrow lead over the Masters champion, burned up the wet course on the way home.

With five more birdies in the six holes played on the back nine, Howard Clark, regarded by some as the weak link of the European team, suddenly proved them all wrong by rolling over Tom Watson, 4 and 3. Clark finished as the only unbeaten European, with a 1-0-1 record. What made Clark's overall performance even more remarkable is the fact that every other home player lost at least two matches.

Raymond Floyd (USA) v. Peter Oosterhuis (EUR)

The onetime leading light of the British side, Oosterhuis was 14-8-3 coming into the contest, but he lost his only two pairs matches as he struggled with a painfully swollen hand. Iron man Ray Floyd was the only American to play in all five games, having won two and lost two matches before the singles.

Despite this apparent disparity, the match turned into a real dog-eat-dog fight, as neither player could get more than one hole ahead at any time. Floyd made the vital breakthrough by winning the 462-yard twelfth to go back up by one.

With the final six holes all halved, Oosterhuis could not pull back even again, and Floyd held on for a hard-earned win.

Sadly Peter Oosterhuis, who had played on some of the most one-sided British losses, bowed out of Ryder Cup play—with three losses—just as his side was on the verge of rewriting golfing history.

Jack Nicklaus (USA) v. Eamonn Darcy (EUR)

On sending out Eamonn Darcy against Jack Nicklaus for the final match: *"I knew how much courage he has."* —John Jacobs

Having not had the confidence to play Darcy more than once in the first two days, the European captain seemed to think his man had a chance of downing Jack Nicklaus "mano-a-Eamanno." The Irishman's record—0-1 in this encounter, 0-2 lifetime in singles—did little to suggest that Nicklaus had much to worry about.

And so it proved. Courage was not enough to knock down Nicklaus, who ran all over the Irishman, 5 and 3, as the great man was held back by Dave Marr for "insurance purposes" at the tail end of the day.

Nicklaus finished a perfect 4–0, along with Trevino and Nelson.

The Golden Bear brought a close to a glittering Ryder Cup career with another emphatic win. His record of 17-8-3 contained a few more losses than he would have liked, and his point total of 18½ fell short of some other Cup legends. But no one could approach what Jack Nicklaus had done for the Ryder Cup as a sportsman and as an ambassador. Without Jack Nicklaus's massive contribution, the Ryder Cup would be just another tin pot in golf's end-of-year silly season.

Day three result: USA *8,* EUR *4*

The 4½ points the United States needed to win the Cup came in the first five matches out. Conversely, 3 of Europe's 4 points came after the Cup had been lost, although all three players were up in their matches at the time.

Overall match score: USA *18½,* EUR *9½*

This was the largest margin of victory ever recorded by the Americans away from home.

Recap

U.S. CLASS TELLS IN BIGGEST VICTORY ON BRITISH SOIL

—*London Telegraph* headline

If the first day belonged unequivocally to the Europeans, the final two days were undeniably the Americans', as they won 15 of 20 points to keep a Vardonesque grip on the Cup.

"There is no danger to the future of the Ryder Cup. Our players are always anxious to get into the team. So long as men like Nicklaus and Trevino are keen to play, it will continue. In fact, I would like to see the match played annually, so that it would create more interest in the United

States. The trouble is that one country gets the match every four years . . . and people forget." —Dave Marr

This stunningly overwhelming victory for the United States saw them win almost twice as many points as the defeated and downhearted Europeans, a return to Ye Bad Olde Days of the Ryder Cup. It seemed that Europe's debut "success" at The Greenbrier had been another false dawn, since the combined scores over the last two matches—35½–20½—added up to a margin of defeat close to the long-standing 2:1 ratio of the previous encounters.

After being asked if he had any comment for his cousin, Jack Burke, Jr., who was still the last U.S. captain to lose the Ryder Cup: "Yeah. Tell him I've cleared up the mess he left twenty-four years ago!"
Dave Marr

So it appeared that the inclusion of continental players had had little effect on raising the competitive level against the all-conquering Americans. The three non-British players managed to win 3½ points out of a possible 8, while the British players contributed 6 out of a possible 24. In effect, the European players had been twice as productive, but the problem was that there just weren't enough of them to take on the Americans.

"I am very disappointed, but proud of my men. If we included the rest of the world in our team, there's no guarantee we would win against the Americans. I don't want to sound old-fashioned or detract from the splendid American performance, but the Ryder Cup isn't just about winning."
—John Jacobs

The different methods of selecting the European team continued to be a hot topic for discussion. Said Jacobs, "I don't think we've got things right. The players want a straight twelve to be determined by points. I feel that some of the young players might miss out either by playing in America or by not going there because of the system. I favor a system of designated tournaments, which would count for Ryder Cup places. This would give all players time to get back. Failing that, I would like to see the entire team selected, but finding the right selectors might be the problem."

The Americans had six players with three or more wins, while the Europeans had none, and even the most resilient European player, Peter Oosterhuis, crashed 0–3. However, this defeat at home was about as low as the Europeans would ever sink, as good times were just around the corner.

Throwing some cold water on his team's magnificent display, Dave Marr presciently warned that this might be the last time the forty-plus pair of Nicklaus and Trevino would be seen in Ryder

After his remarkable 5–0 in 1979, Larry Nelson kept up his perfect record with a 4–0 performance to stand 9–0 in his Ryder Cup career. In their last Ryder Cup appearances, Nicklaus and Trevino also went 4–0, while Tom Kite was unbeaten 2–0–1.

Cup action. Having had the great honor of leading his country, Marr nominated both legends as future captains.

Fittingly, both players finished their Ryder Cup playing careers with 5 and 3 wins in the singles matches. Nicklaus would return immediately as nonplaying captain in 1983, and both he and Trevino would later captain their countries in a losing cause.

Continuing his role as a golfing Nostradamus, Marr also predicted that Europe would one day win the Ryder Cup, but he was only half serious in his prophecy: "It will happen when you have been trailing for two days and then you will catch us giggling to ourselves and ambush us."

Match Results (Winning side marked in *italics*.)

Friday, September 18—Morning Foursomes

	USA	EUR	Score
1.	*Lee Trevino* *Larry Nelson*	Bernhard Langer Manuel Pinero	1-up
2.	Bill Rogers Bruce Lietzke	*Sandy Lyle* *Mark James*	2 and 1
3.	Raymond Floyd Hale Irwin	*Bernard Gallacher* *Des Smyth*	3 and 2
4.	*Tom Watson* *Jack Nicklaus*	Peter Oosterhuis Nick Faldo	4 and 3

Friday, September 18—Afternoon Fourball

	USA	EUR	Score
5.	Tom Kite Johnny Miller	Sam Torrance Howard Clark	halved
6.	Ben Crenshaw Jerry Pate	*Sandy Lyle* *Mark James*	3 and 2
7.	Bill Rogers Bruce Lietzke	*Des Smyth* *Jose Maria Canizares*	6 and 5
8.	*Hale Irwin* *Raymond Floyd*	Bernard Gallacher Eamonn Darcy	2 and 1

Day one result: USA 3 ½, EUR 4 ½

Saturday, September 19—Morning Fourball

	USA	EUR	Score
9.	*Lee Trevino* *Jerry Pate*	Nick Faldo Sam Torrance	7 and 5
10.	*Larry Nelson* *Tom Kite*	Sandy Lyle Mark James	1-up
11.	Raymond Floyd Hale Irwin	*Bernhard Langer* *Manuel Pinero*	2 and 1
12.	*Jack Nicklaus* *Tom Watson*	Jose Maria Canizares Des Smyth	3 and 2

Saturday, September 19—Afternoon Foursomes

	USA	EUR	Score
13.	*Lee Trevino* *Jerry Pate*	Peter Oosterhuis Sam Torrance	2 and 1
14.	*Jack Nicklaus* *Tom Watson*	Bernhard Langer Manuel Pinero	3 and 2
15.	*Bill Rogers* *Raymond Floyd*	Sandy Lyle Mark James	3 and 2
16.	*Tom Kite* *Larry Nelson*	Des Smyth Bernard Gallacher	3 and 2

Day two result: USA *7,* EUR *1*

Overall match score: USA *10 1/2,* EUR *5 1/2*

Sunday, September 20—Singles

	USA	EUR	Score
17.	*Lee Trevino*	Sam Torrance	5 and 3
18.	*Tom Kite*	Sandy Lyle	3 and 2
19.	Bill Rogers	Bernard Gallacher	halved
20.	*Larry Nelson*	Mark James	2-up
21.	*Ben Crenshaw*	Des Smyth	6 and 4
22.	Bruce Lietzke	Bernhard Langer	halved
23.	Jerry Pate	*Manuel Pinero*	4 and 2
24.	*Hale Irwin*	Jose Maria Canizares	1-up
25.	Johnny Miller	*Nick Faldo*	2 and 1
26.	Tom Watson	*Howard Clark*	4 and 3
27.	*Raymond Floyd*	Peter Oosterhuis	1-up
28.	*Jack Nicklaus*	Eamonn Darcy	5 and 3

Day three result: USA *8,* EUR *4*

Overall match score: USA *18 1/2,* EUR *9 1/2*

1983

PGA National Champion Course
Palm Beach Gardens, Florida
United States
October 14–16

United States 14½	**Europe 13½**
Ben Crenshaw	Seve Ballesteros (Spain)
Raymond Floyd	Gordon J. Brand (England)
Bob Gilder	Ken Brown (Scotland)
Jay Haas	Jose Maria Canizares (Spain)
Tom Kite	Nick Faldo (England)
Gil Morgan	Bernard Gallacher (Scotland)
Calvin Peete	Bernhard Langer (Germany)
Craig Stadler	Sandy Lyle (Scotland)
Curtis Strange	Sam Torrance (Scotland)
Lanny Wadkins	Brian Waites (England)
Tom Watson	Paul Way (England)
Fuzzy Zoeller	Ian Woosnam (Wales)
Captain	**Captain**
Jack Nicklaus	Tony Jacklin (England)

The Shape of Things to Come

This encounter at Palm Beach Gardens harked back to 1969, when Jack Nicklaus offered Tony Jacklin a most sporting half on the eighteenth in the final singles match of the contest to tie the overall scores. Both players were once again in opposition, this time as nonplaying captains. It was an honor that both would hold again, with quite different results.

"After we [captains] select our teams each day and hand in the piece of paper, all that's left is to go on course and act important."
—*Jack Nicklaus*

Following what was considered his last Ryder Cup match against Eamonn Darcy in the 1981 singles, it wasn't a shock when forty-three-year-old Nicklaus was named the American captain. Thirty-nine-year-old Jacklin, however, was a surprise, in view of his public disillusionment over the way the British and later European teams were chosen and treated.

When he was asked to mastermind the European challenge, he agreed to do so only on his terms. He demanded (and got) assurances that the players would be treated the same way the Americans had been for years. To this end, the European team and, for the first time, their caddies arrived in the States aboard Concorde.

"If Napoleon thought that an army marched on its stomach, and Montgomery (the general, not the golfer) insisted on a full English breakfast (even at two in the morning) before going into battle, then that was good enough for Jacklin."
—*Jock Howard,* Golf World *(1998)*

As Jacklin would later say, "Too many times in the past, the Ryder Cup had been run, it seemed, more for the officials than for the players. Priorities had been in the wrong places. If I was to be captain, it would be run and organized with the players in mind. . . . You can't expect golfers, who are perfectionists in their field, to be comfortable in the back of the bus. That was crystal clear to me."

Jacklin brought with him much the same-strength team that had been humiliated two years earlier, but importantly it included Masters champion Seve Ballesteros. The Europeans had four rookies: twenty-year-old Paul Way, forty-three-year-old Brian Waites, Gordon J. Brand, and Ian Woosnam.

"The first thing to be said about my captaincy is that I am not hell-bent on starting a third world war, unlike some previous British captains who have approached the match as though they were leading the Light Brigade into the valley of death." —TONY JACKLIN

"I remember the 1983 matches in Florida. There weren't a thousand people watching. It all changed after that."
—*Curtis Strange (1995)*

Playing on a course just twenty minutes from his Florida home, Nicklaus pointed to the fact that his side had one more rookie and that this lack of Ryder Cup experience would give an edge to the visitors. This was probably some attempt at gamesmanship by Nicklaus, since his new boys—Gilder, Haas, Peete, Stadler, and Strange—were obviously more than a match for the Euro-rookies.

The U.S. team must have been strong enough, since it could afford to overlook the services of Ryder Cup's "Mr. 100 percent," Larry Nelson, who—despite winning the U.S. Open—had not earned enough Ryder Cup points to book his place on the team.

"I may have a relatively inexperienced team, but I have to say that with the strength of competition on the U.S. tour, it does not make a whole lot of difference who plays on our side." —JACK NICKLAUS

The two captains had decidedly different game plans for this match. Nicklaus paired players he thought would get along with each other, and he tried to give all his players equal playing time. The only exception to the latter plan is that he played current British Open champion Tom Watson in all five matches, to maximize the psychological advantage of having the world's best player out on the course.

Jacklin, however, with less riches to divide up, decided early on to play his best pairings, irrespective of how the players got on with each other. He even took the unprecedented step of telling Brand (on-board Concorde) that he would play only in the singles. As it was, both captains' methods seemed to get the best out of their players.

Course Details

The long, tough, and aptly named Champion Course at the PGA National Resort and Spa—the headquarters of the Professional Golfers' Association of America—had opened only in 1981.

This was the only Ryder Cup not held in September in the last thirty years; all other fifteen matches from 1969 to 1997 were staged in September. Even so, experts felt that the visiting side would be seriously disadvantaged by the Florida fauna and sauna conditions.

On the local problems facing the visitors: *"The [ninety-five-degree] heat, the Europeans won't be accustomed to that. The Bermuda grass, they won't know too much about that. Then there's the fact that we win most of the time."* —Jack Nicklaus

Hole	Distance	Par	Hole	Distance	Par
1	369	4	10	412	4
2	417	4	11	577	5
3	539	5	12	428	4
4	187	3	13	393	4
5	423	4	14	452	4
6	492	5	15	167	3
7	227	3	16	443	4
8	432	4	17	191	3
9	410	4	18	578	5
		36			**36 = Par 72 (7,137 yards)**

Course designers: George and Tom Fazio

Day One: Morning Foursomes

Tom Watson and Ben Crenshaw (USA) v. Bernard Gallacher and Sandy Lyle (EUR)

Nicklaus didn't wait long to play his trump card: British Open champion Thomas Watson. Sent out first up, the pair of Watson and Crenshaw had little trouble accounting for Lyle and Gallacher, the latter suffering from a head cold. As it turned out, both Scots' games were woefully off; they coughed and spluttered to an outward 40 but somehow were only one down.

On the 412-yard tenth, it was Watson who was feeling poorly after a sickly looking drive. Crenshaw produced a cure-all recovery to leave his partner with a twenty-five-foot birdie putt that Watson gratefully accepted to atone for his tardiness off the tee. This put the U.S. pair two up; then Watson almost chipped in from a bunker alongside the eleventh, and settled for a half.

Lyle overhit his approach into twelve to drop three down, Gallacher came up short with his pitching wedge on the next to sink four down, and the Americans were still one over par when they wrapped up the match on the 452-yard fourteenth, 5 and 4.

Having started out as one of Jacklin's main pairings, after this imploding defeat the two British players were sidelined—at their own request—until the singles.

Lanny Wadkins and Craig Stadler (USA) v. Nick Faldo and Bernhard Langer (EUR)

Jacklin's number two pairing of Faldo and Langer certainly paid dividends with a comfortable 4 and 2 win over Nicklaus's highly favored pairing of Wadkins and Stadler. The European captain was so impressed with this performance that he played the pair in all five matches. The pair finished 3-1, and both players also won their singles matches.

"I figured we had come to win, and if it became obvious I had eight hot guys, then those eight were going to play. I never got a squawk from anyone about my plans. I told Nick and Bernhard they were going to really get to know each other because they were a permanent team. I wanted Bernhard's driver on the long holes and Nick's long iron in alternative stroke." —TONY JACKLIN

Separately Wadkins and Stadler were both short fuses in search of a lighted match. Together they became irritable and irascible, soon showing their anger—at their poor play and their opponents' success—by throwing clubs and making Faldo and Langer putt out from inconsiderately short distances.

At the treacherous 492-yard sixth, Faldo was asked to putt out from eighteen inches to go two up. After Wadkins badly hooked his tee shot on the par-4 ninth, a yip-free Langer was invited to putt from one foot away to put Europe three up.

Out in 38, the Americans were three down, and Faldo kept it that way with a fourteen-foot putt on the tenth to stifle any thoughts of a U.S. revival.

On playing with Stadler: "I thought we'd be an unbelievable team, but I'm out there trying to get him fired up and he just kind of looked over at me as if to say, 'Buzz off!'"
—*Lanny Wadkins*

The Europeans continued their relentless pursuit of birdies with another on the 577-yard eleventh to go four up on the strength of Langer's eighteen-footer. The Americans temporarily cut the lead at the par-4 twelfth but could not make any further inroads into the Anglo-German union.

On the 443-yard sixteenth, Faldo struck a mighty second shot over the lake to an elevated green, then Langer holed the birdie putt to silence their opponents, 4 and 2.

Tom Kite and Calvin Peete (USA) v. Seve Ballesteros and Paul Way (EUR)

One of the key talking points before the whole match was the identity of Ballesteros's partner. Few guessed that Paul Way would be the answer. Tony Jacklin's thinking was that if Way, who had shown prodigious form on the European tour, could be nurtured through his first few matches by a senior player, he would repay that faith with good results.

After a typical Ballesteros opening drive into a bunker, which Way could only hack out, the Spaniard finessed a tremendous recovery to five feet. Way shook off any rookie nerves by holing his first Ryder Cup putt for a half. After the Americans took a lead, Way's approach shot to the 410-yard ninth was close enough for Ballesteros to stroke home the birdie putt to square the match.

On the second-youngest rookie in Ryder Cup history: "Paul Way is one of the gutsiest young players we have."
—*Tony Jacklin*

Belying his years, Way hit a terrific three-wood over the water to the eleventh green, setting up another Ballesteros birdie putt for the lead.

On his poor approach into eleven: *"Goddamn! I missed the green with a wedge. I just don't believe it!"* —Tom Kite

Unable to match his younger partner's accurate approach shots, Ballesteros left his pitch well short of the 428-yard twelfth green, while Way found a bunker with his, allowing Kite to take the hole with a crucial putt.

"The ideal foursomes partner is someone who doesn't make mistakes—like Calvin Peete. . . . On tour, they say he misses greens about as often as Craig Stadler misses meals."
—*Jerry Tarde,* Golf Digest

Way hit the thirteenth green from a fairway bunker to help snatch a vital half, and Kite saved his half on fourteen with a clutch ten-footer. After Kite's tee shot missed the fifteenth green and found a horrible feathery lie, Peete made light of the error. He chipped down a slick slope and in, for a birdie two to win a hole that put the U.S. pair one up, as Way then missed his twelve-foot birdie putt.

Tom Kite staked his approach to the 191-yard seventeenth a yard from the flag, and Ballesteros followed him in to six feet. Way's nerve finally gave way, and he left the vital putt an inch short, as Peete continued his good work on and around the greens. He holed his putt for a birdie two to close the match out, 2 and 1.

For their growing pains together, the Europeans carded a one under par for their seventeen holes, while the Americans finished three under.

Raymond Floyd and Bob Gilder (USA) v. Jose Maria Canizares and Sam Torrance (EUR)

Canizares and Torrance jumped out early in this one with two hole-winning birdies on the first and third holes. Floyd and Gilder were back level within five holes, and the match was level after nine, both pairs out in par 36s.

Having evened out the match and held firm for a couple of holes, the Americans produced some of the ugliest golf of the week. Floyd missed the tenth green, and Gilder's recovery was not going to win any beauty contests. Ugly is as ugly does, and in trying to lay up in front of the water on the 577-yard eleventh, Gilder hit his ball into the water—two down.

After Torrance drove into a fairway bunker on twelve, Canizares hit a five-iron 175 yards out of sand, onto the green, and ran it up to the flag. In response, the U.S. pair bunkered its second by the green and failed to get down in five, conceding the hole without asking Torrance to putt.

Following Torrance's accurate tee shot on the par-3 fifteenth, Canizares holed the birdie putt from thirteen feet for the hole and a well-crafted 4 and 3 victory.

Morning foursomes result: USA 2, EUR 2

The 2-2 morning foursomes was the U.S. side's worst opening session at home since 1971, when they started 1-3 at Old Warson.

HOT-HANDS MAKE WARM START
—London Guardian *headline*

Day One: Afternoon Fourball

Gil Morgan and Fuzzy Zoeller (USA) v. Brian Waites and Ken Brown (EUR)

Morgan and Zoeller faced a makeshift pairing of Brown and Waites, thrown together at the last minute to replace the misfiring Lyle and Gallacher, who asked to be dropped from the afternoon session.

After being told at the last minute he was playing: *"This is the way to do it. I had no stage fright. I was actually twisting at a Chubby Checker concert in the hotel until after midnight because I thought I'd got the day off. As it was, I was completely relaxed."* —BRIAN WAITES

For Brown this was a major reprieve following his "silent protest" in 1979, and he grabbed his second chance with both hands. For Waites, it was his last chance, at the age of forty-three, to prove himself on the international stage.

Brown scrambled a half on the first hole after he put his tee shot among some palm trees, making a fine recovery to snatch a hole-sharing birdie. Knowing that certain people were watching his temperament as well as his play, Brown made a twenty-five-foot putt on the 410-yard ninth. This was for his fourth birdie of the front nine and gave his side a one-hole lead.

"It's marvelous to win your first Ryder Cup match, especially at the age of forty-three. After all, I may never play in another. I don't think they allow wheelchairs at The Belfry, where we play in 1985."
—*Brian Waites*

With the Americans in quiet mode for much of the match, Waites extended the European lead to two with a seventeen-footer on the par-5 eleventh. Zoeller and Morgan could not close the gap over the next five holes, as the reserve crew gave Europe an unexpected 2 and 1 win.

Tom Watson and Jay Haas (USA) v. Nick Faldo and Bernhard Langer (EUR)

Having crushed Lyle and Gallacher in the morning, Tom Watson—Jack Nicklaus's go-to guy—played even better off his own ball in the afternoon. In the first seven holes, Watson knocked down four birdies, and he and Jay Haas were able to spot themselves an early lead.

Faldo and Langer made only two birdies between them on the outward nine but upped the stakes coming home by making five birdies.

Up by two after ten holes, Watson could make only a couple of birdies on the inward journey, but it was enough to hold the Europeans at bay until the 2 and 1 finale on the seventeenth.

Raymond Floyd and Curtis Strange (USA) v. Seve Ballesteros and Paul Way (EUR)

"I'll never forget the first one I was involved in. I had tears and goose bumps . . . the whole bit. You felt you wanted to come out fighting and swinging like Rocky." —CURTIS STRANGE

Floyd and Strange matched Ballesteros and Way all the way to the last hole, as neither pair was able to hold on to a lead of any substance.

All square at the 578-yard eighteenth, the Spaniard ignored the water along the right-hand side of the green and reached the front of the putting surface with a massive drive followed by an equally good fairway wood. Neither Floyd nor Strange could match the Spanish birdie four that gave Europe a 1-up win.

Having played seven matches (three foursomes, three fourball, and one singles), Seve Ballesteros picked up only the second point of his career.

Ben Crenshaw and Calvin Peete (USA) v. Sam Torrance and Ian Woosnam (EUR)

The Americans were eight under par for the first thirteen holes played.

In his Ryder Cup debut, Ian Woosnam played a watching role as his partner Sam Torrance single-handedly matched the American challenge.

Early on, the British pair was one up after six, but Crenshaw and Peete played equally effectively on the front nine to stand all square. Both pairs playing some exceptional golf, the British covered seven holes in five under but saw their lead disappear as Crenshaw and Peete took two fewer strokes.

At one stage, the Americans carded seven birdies in a row, but Torrance more or less matched them off his own ball, making six birdies in the last twelve holes, including a cliff-hanger of a birdie putt on the eighteenth to halve the match.

Afternoon fourball result: USA 1½, EUR 2½
Day one result: USA 3½, EUR 4½

This was only the second time the Americans had been behind after the first day as hosts. For the visitors, it was the best start on U.S. soil since 1971, when the British opened up with the same score line.

In response to suggestions of a European victory: *"Golf has a way of coming back at you. We've a long way to go yet."* —Tony Jacklin

Day Two: Morning Fourball

Heavy overnight rain had drenched the course, but the players were greeted with another hot, sunny, and very humid day.

"As sure as God made little green apples, the American backlash had to come in the Ryder Cup, after the European team had taken a one-point lead from the first day's play." —John Hopkins, *Times* (London)

Craig Stadler and Lanny Wadkins (USA) v. Ken Brown and Brian Waites (EUR)

The British odd couple of Waites and Brown once again started well and hit Wadkins and Stadler with an early burst of four birdies in six holes. Three down, the Americans pulled two of these holes back when their opponents failed to make pars between them over the course of the next few holes.

The U.S. pair added a couple of birdies of its own to take a one-hole lead, but Brown quickly leveled the match again with another well-struck birdie.

The pairs were all square over the closing five holes, and the match reached a dramatic climax on the last green. Waites made his par five, and Brown just failed to hole his long birdie putt across the width of the green, but Stadler had already holed his nine-iron chip from twenty-five feet away from the back of the green. This last-ditch birdie four gave the Americans another last-ditch victory, 1-up.

Calvin Peete and Ben Crenshaw (USA) v. Nick Faldo and Bernhard Langer (EUR)

Bernhard Langer, who had been unhappy with his first day play, asked to be dropped, but Jacklin, who was quickly running out of topflight players—either those playing well or ones who simply wanted to play at all—persuaded the German to carry on. Langer was paired with Nick Faldo, and they took on the unbeaten pairing of Peete and Crenshaw.

Thanks mainly to two long putts by Nick Faldo on the eighth and ninth, the European pair was three up after nine holes. Faldo finished off Peete and Crenshaw with another long putt on the sixteenth for a comfortable 4 and 2 win.

Gil Morgan and Jay Haas (USA) v. Seve Ballesteros and Paul Way (EUR)

A new U.S. pairing of Morgan and Haas took on the established European blend of Ballesteros and Way, in a match that was as tight as a new grip on a fat shaft. With never a hole separating the teams at any time, Jay Haas made long putts on the third, fifth, tenth, and thirteenth but could not turn these masterstrokes into a lead.

All square after fourteen, Ballesteros, who was on antibiotics for a lingering illness, fired his six-iron tee shot to the fifteenth, the ball landing just nine feet from the flag. His birdie putt gave Europe a one-hole advantage with just three to play.

With his putter as hot as Ballesteros's fever, Haas holed another long one across the sixteenth green to level. On the par-3 seventeenth, Morgan took his turn to hole a long, snaking birdie putt to go one up with one to play.

Having failed to reach the final green in two on the first day, Seve covered the 578 yards (and more) in two mammoth shots. A drive over 300 yards set up a superhuman three-wood that ran fifteen yards through the green. In retaliation, the Americans could reach the green only in three to leave themselves two putts for par. With his tail well and truly up, Seve chipped back the forty-odd feet to within a yard of the pin. He holed the final stroke of the match for a staggering birdie that snatched the full point away from the hosts for a half.

Tom Watson and Bob Gilder (USA) v. Sam Torrance and Ian Woosnam (EUR)

Watson and his third partner in as many matches, Gilder, birdied the opening three holes to take a three-hole lead and never looked back.

The American number one increased the European troubles by chipping in from behind the 410-yard ninth green. Torrance and Woosnam were rarely a threat, save for Woosnam's eagle at eleven.

The Americans closed the match out on the fourteenth, 5 and 4.

In a move that was becoming both annoying and worrying for the two captains, Watson asked to sit out the afternoon session, because he felt his play might suffer from the nonstop workload. With three wins out of three, Nicklaus was not about to drop his star. "No way, I need the intimidation factor of Tom Watson in the lineup."

Morning fourball result: USA 2½, EUR 1½

Day Two: Afternoon Foursomes

Raymond Floyd and Tom Kite (USA) v. Nick Faldo and Bernhard Langer (EUR)

Having been persuaded to play in the morning, Bernhard Langer was still apprehensive about playing in the afternoon, but he and Faldo made a rampant start, taking a three-hole lead after just four holes.

Floyd and Kite hit back with three consecutive birdies of their own to level the match after seven holes. Floyd then missed a shortish par putt on the 432-yard eighth that would have given his side another win, but his bogey five was enough for a half.

"Ray Floyd is as hard as Stadler, but in the same Western saloon he would be the guy with the green eye-shade, dealing 'em in the poker school."
—*David Davies,* London Guardian

With the Americans blowing a chance to take the lead, Faldo and Langer made them pay by winning the ninth and tenth to go two up. Probably a little too overconfident, Langer overhit a chip for par on the 428-yard twelfth, when a bogey would have gained a half. In the end, an American five won the hole.

The Europeans once again struck back to increase their lead to two with three to play.

On the par-4 sixteenth, and with the game on the line, Kite almost pulled off a wonder shot, just failing to hole a sixty-foot chip for a birdie three. Langer's ball was also just off the green, but was a few feet closer than Kite's, and that made all the difference, as the German not only holed his birdie chip but won the match, 3 and 2.

Jay Haas and Curtis Strange (USA) v. Ken Brown and Brian Waites (EUR)

A two-time collegiate All-American and the 1975 NCAA champion, Jay Haas was also the nephew of former Ryder Cupper Bob Goalby.

Having played only once in the first three matches and lost, Curtis Strange was raring to get back out on the course to open his Ryder Cup rookie account. The twenty-eight-year-old partnered fellow first-timer and fellow Wake Forest golfing alumnus Jay Haas, who already had one win and a half to his name.

The former college teammates had a fairly easy match against the stopgap pairing of Brown and forty-three-year-old rookie Waites. The British pair had been brought down to earth, after its surprise win on Friday afternoon, with a narrow loss in the morning fourball. Brown and Waites completed an off day as they went down to their second defeat together, Strange and Haas giving their older opponents an education in team play by beating them 3 and 1.

Lanny Wadkins and Gil Morgan (USA) v. Sam Torrance and Jose Maria Canizares (EUR)

Nicklaus played a hunch and paired two players who had lost their first matches on Friday but had rebounded in the morning fourball. Jacklin was more or less forced to send out a far-from-cohesive Scottish-Spanish pairing that struggled all afternoon.

Wadkins and Morgan did not need to be at their best to register by far the biggest win of the weekend. Their opponents failed to card a birdie in thirteen holes and finished a disappointing four over par, as the Americans stuck a 7 and 5 tag on them.

Bob Gilder and Tom Watson (USA) v. Seve Ballesteros and Paul Way (EUR)

Jack Nicklaus should have paid heed to Tom Watson's request to sit out the afternoon session. The U.S. number one failed to sparkle at the start of his match, and he and Gilder were torn apart over the opening six holes. Ballesteros and Way reeled off five wins in a row, including a six on one hole to an American seven.

Down by five with six to play, the Americans staged something of a minor comeback with their own barrage of birdies, winning three holes out of four. This revival came too late to prevent an inevitable loss, which came on the seventeenth, 2 and 1.

Jacklin's plan of pairing Ballesteros with the rookie Way had paid off—two wins and a half from their four matches together.

Afternoon foursomes result: USA 2, EUR 2
Day two result: USA 4½, EUR 3½
Overall match score: USA 8, EUR 8

This was the first time the scores had been level going into the singles in the United States, and was the closest the Americans had been to a competitive match on home soil.

Day Three: Singles

With the match delicately poised at 8 points a side before the final-day singles, the U.S. captain spelled out what he expected from his players, "I do not want to be remembered as the first captain of an American team to lose on American soil! Now, you guys show me some brass."

Nicklaus's speech had the desired effect on his players: *"We came out of there as if Vince Lombardi had just hyped us for Baltimore."*

—Ben Crenshaw

As a safety measure, just in case his call to arms fell on deaf ears, Nicklaus put his top three players out last: Wadkins (tenth), Floyd (eleventh), and Watson (twelfth). As it happened, this defensive ploy may have kept the U.S. captain from living his nightmare.

Fuzzy Zoeller (USA) v. Seve Ballesteros (EUR)

Sensing victory, Jacklin sent out his three best players at the top of the order and asked his ace, Ballesteros, to lead the charge. Nicklaus opened with a sacrificial lamb in the shape of an injured Fuzzy Zoeller who was carrying a back injury inside a restrictive corset.

Said Zoeller, "I told Jack to put me out first because I figured Jacklin would put one of his cripples there too. Imagine my surprise! I started popping painkillers as soon as I learned. Thank goodness they don't give urinalysis to golfers. My eyes were spinning."

Whatever the captains' planning, it turned into one of the great Ryder Cup matches. Zoeller took the lead on the second, only to witness Ballesteros string together four wins in a row from the fourth hole, to go three up. Zoeller's bad back no doubt contributed to the outcome—he failed to make par on two of those lost holes.

Ballesteros continued to dominate a match he was expected to win easily, and he set about building a large lead in the hope of inspiring his colleagues behind him. Zoeller not only fought tough, holding the Spaniard to a three-hole lead with seven to play, but fought back.

"Being a professional, I just kept thinking that there is ebb and flow in match play and my time would come," Zoeller said. "He gave me some gifts, and for that I thank him."

"Seve had a little storm over the front nine, and I caught mine on the back nine."
—*Fuzzy Zoeller*

A birdie at the 428-yard twelfth triggered a tit-for-tat string of four wins from Zoeller, who played himself into the lead with three holes remaining. It was now a question of whether his back would hold out.

Ballesteros stopped the rout and leveled again on sixteen with a crucial twenty-foot putt, then missed a twelve-foot birdie at the 191-yard seventeenth and had to settle for the half.

On his missed birdie putt at seventeen: *"It was one of the worst I have ever hit."* —Seve Ballesteros

All square on the eighteenth tee, Ballesteros knew his fitness and superior driving gave an advantage he needed to cash in on. But the Spaniard hooked an awful drive into the heavy rough, and his hacking recovery shot traveled only twenty yards into a fairway bunker, more than 250 yards short of the green.

Zoeller, having also found the rough off the tee, managed to play a better recovery to the fairway. This forced Ballesteros's hand, and he took a three-wood into the sand trap with him. He came out of the bunker having dispatched one of the best Ryder Cup shots of all time. Playing a cut shot with huge slice, he smote the ball to the edge of the green, eighteen feet from the flag.

On Ballesteros's 250-yard bunker shot at eighteen: *"The finest shot I've ever seen."* —Jack Nicklaus

Not to be outdone, Zoeller hit a long raking two-iron onto the green and watched as it rolled up to within ten feet of the hole. Seve left his birdie putt four feet short, but Zoeller missed his shorter putt—close enough for a concession. Ballesteros was left with a putt to halve a match he was not only dominating but had been expected to put away some holes earlier. The Spaniard's nerve held, and he escaped with a half for the hole in quite extraordinary pars.

This half was a major blow for the Europeans, who had expected their best player to easily defeat the injured Zoeller, who had played one match in the previous two days.

Still, when the match finished, Europe was in a strong position in the other eleven singles: up in four, level in five, and down in only two. The golfing gods seemingly were smiling on the visitors.

Jay Haas (USA) v. Nick Faldo (EUR)

Known on the PGA Tour as a hot-and-cold player, Jay Haas could not get his hot hand going and rarely troubled Nick Faldo. Although the Englishman was only two under par for the match, a birdie putt on seventeen closed the match out 2 and 1.

This win put Europe up 9½–8½, and was Faldo's fourth win in five matches, his eleventh in fifteen Ryder Cup matches overall.

On Langer's well-publicized problems with the yips: "Langer holes fewer three-footers than any other top-class golfer in the world. . . . Just pray that if anyone in the European team is left with a three-footer for the match, it is not Langer. He may hole it; but not on purpose."
—*David Davies,* London Guardian

Gil Morgan (USA) v. Bernhard Langer (EUR)

Out in 32 strokes, Bernhard Langer was in control of this match against Gil Morgan, but the German, who had putted superbly on the front nine, began to let things slip coming home.

Down by as many as three at one stage, Morgan not only stayed in the match but pulled back to one down with one to play. On the last green, Langer rediscovered his touch and his confidence, from twenty feet, holing his fifth birdie putt of the day.

Back in 38, Langer had held just enough in reserve to pull out a two-hole win at the death.

This win put Europe two up in the match, as Langer mirrored his pairs partner Faldo with his fourth win out of five.

Bob Gilder (USA) v. Gordon J. Brand (EUR)

Not only was Brand unknown in his own country, but many of those who knew of him continually got him mixed up with fellow British golfer Gordon Brand, Jr. (no relation), who appeared in later Ryder Cups.

Perhaps this singles match should have been billed as the Battle of the Unknown Golfers, since neither player was well known in his own country. Whereas Gilder had played three times with two losses, Brand had sat out the first two days . . . and played like it.

Neither player really got into stride, although neither played badly enough to let the other establish a telling lead. As it happened, Gilder held all the aces as they came to the last hole, which he won to eke out a two-hole victory.

Ben Crenshaw (USA) v. Sandy Lyle (EUR)

Although Crenshaw made seven birdies in his round, he could not finish off a sadly out-of-touch Lyle until the seventeenth hole.

The Scot had sat himself down after his dismal display on the opening morning, and no amount of practice and tinkering with his swing made any difference.

Despite the failings of his opponent, Crenshaw was unable to close the match out early. One up with three to play, the Texan finished the match off with back-to-back birdies on sixteen and seventeen for a 3 and 1 win.

Calvin Peete (USA) v. Brian Waites (EUR)

This was the duel of the old-timers, as forty-year-old Peete took on a man three years his senior. Peete finally held sway in a tight tussle, with birdies on fourteen and fifteen.

Waites, who, it seemed, could never get over the fact that he was actually playing in the Ryder Cup, failed to cut the mustard, and Peete held on for a narrow 1-up win on the last green.

Peete's win gave the United States the lead for the first time in the overall match.

Curtis Strange (USA) v. Paul Way (EUR)

"Paul Way grew up ten years in three days."
—*Tony Jacklin*

Paul Way faced a tough task, taking on the moody Curtis Strange in a solo matchup. Just as he had done in the pairs, the young Englishman rose admirably to the challenge and gave Strange as good as he got.

With Strange mainly playing par golf, Way was able to sneak into the lead and hold on long enough for the holes to run out, leaving him with an important and impressive debut success in the singles, 2 and 1.

Tom Kite (USA) v. Sam Torrance (EUR)

Although behind for most of the match, Torrance nevertheless managed to keep himself within striking distance of Kite. Two up after fifteen, the American felt the pressure and lost the sixteenth with a bogey. Under the increasing tension of the occasion, the players halved seventeen and made their way to the last hole.

Short of the final green in two, Kite hit his approach over the green to the second cut of rough between two bunkers. Torrance found himself with an awful lie in the rough sixty yards shy of the green in two, and the wily Scot tried in vain to get a free drop out of casual water. His personal duel with Kite and the Ryder Cup on the line, Torrance went for broke, pitching his ball out and watching as it bounced on the front fringe. The ball slowed as it rolled down toward the hole, pulling up eighteen inches past the cup.

All the pressure was suddenly transferred onto Kite, who was unable to threaten the hole with his chip, his ball tamely running four feet past. Kite made his par, leaving Torrance to hole his birdie putt, which halved the match and leveled the overall standings, 13-13.

The match all square with two games left on the course, Nicklaus and Jacklin bumped into each other and discussed the ups and downs of the day. Both captains agreed that another tie would be the best result, as the U.S. captain intimated after the match: "It's a shame the match wasn't tied. My team might not have been happy, but I would have been happy with a tie. Nobody should have lost this one."

Craig Stadler (USA) v. Ian Woosnam (EUR)

Having been unable to recapture the highs of his career year, 1982, when he won the Masters and topped the money list with almost half a million dollars, Craig Stadler at least finished off his first Ryder Cup with a win against another rookie, Ian Woosnam.

Already with a victory under his belt from Saturday's fourball, the American held an important psychological edge over the winless Welshman. By the end of their match, this advantage had translated into a 3 and 2 win.

Lanny Wadkins (USA) v. Jose Maria Canizares (EUR)

At three down with seven to play and the Ryder Cup at stake, most golfers would crumble at the challenge. Not so Lanny Wadkins.

A born battler, Wadkins was known to blow hot and cold. And as for Canizares, the wind of change was about to muss with his hair and mess with his head.

"I put Lanny at the bottom of the order, because I knew if we needed something to happen he could make it happen."
—*Jack Nicklaus*

Wadkins called on his deepest reserves. He was playing as much for himself and his country as for his inspirational captain, who he knew was counting on him to pull through. Having pulled back two holes by the time he reached the eighteenth tee, Wadkins knew that he could finish the job and earn a half-point that might make all the difference in the final reckoning.

Wadkins laid up with his second shot sixty yards short of the green, but his spirits must have lifted when he saw Canizares's approach. From the fairway, the Spaniard knocked his pitch up and over a bunker but watched in horror as his ball came up short of the green, burying itself in the rough between two bunkers.

"Wadkins was the perfect guy for an occasion like this: cocky, a gambler, a thriver on pressure. He almost holed the shot, and his teammates swarmed over him as if he'd kicked a winning field goal with no time remaining."
—*Dan Jenkins,* Sports Illustrated

Sensing and seizing his chance, Wadkins nailed a perfect pitch to eighteen inches. Within seconds, teammates and his captain swamped him, and the ad hoc celebration that broke out on the fairway suggested that he had holed the shot to win the Cup.

To his happy captain: *"It was only the most important shot of my life, Jack. There's nobody I'd rather have hit it for."* —LANNY WADKINS

"It was the most pressure that I have ever felt in making one shot," Wadkins said later. "I've got a lot of satisfaction since, by knowing that I can handle that kind of pressure, knowing your gut holds up and your swing holds up."

Needing to hole his recovery, Canizares chipped his ball out of the rough, past the pin, and off the back of the green. With his cause all but lost, he failed to hole his par putt and immediately conceded Wadkins's birdie putt for an overall half.

Yet another valuable half-point had leaked away from the Europeans.

Raymond Floyd (USA) v. Ken Brown (EUR)

Having let himself, his country, and his sport down in 1979, Ken Brown repaid those who had stood by him and captured a valuable point.

The lanky Scotsman's finishing burst of three birdies in the last six holes not only sewed up the singles match but left Raymond Floyd with an ignominious 0-for-the-week label.

Floyd had experienced a desperately disappointing three days, losing all four of his games, probably the worst all-around result by any American in Ryder Cup play.

Rated as the second-best American player in the world after Tom Watson, Floyd was not able to stay with Brown over the closing stretch. The Scot carded five birdies in his 4 and 3 win.

Tom Watson (USA) v. Bernard Gallacher (EUR)

Nicklaus kept his key player, Watson, until last, guessing that Jacklin would do the same with Ballesteros. This ploy worked in favor of the U.S. side.

After seven holes, Watson was three up on the feisty Scot, who was still not on his best game (he had dropped himself after the first morning's foursomes). Gallacher got one of the holes back on his own before Watson bogeyed sixteen to cut his own lead to one.

With all matches in front of them in the record books, the destination of the Ryder Cup was still up for grabs. The outcome of this match would decide the Cup's home for the next two years.

Under the utmost pressure, both players missed the par-3 green at seventeen—Gallacher running through the back of the green, Watson missing to the right. Both also made a terrible hash of their resulting chip shots and failed to reach the putting surface.

Gallacher then lived a personal nightmare, taking three more shots, including a missed four-foot putt for the half in four.

"I had this four-footer for a half, and I still think to this day that I hit a good putt. There was a subtle break, but I missed and that was it, 2 and 1." —BERNARD GALLACHER

Watson did not play the hole any better, but he did putt up to the hole from off the green for a bogey four, enough to halve the hole, win his match, and retain the Ryder Cup by a solitary point.

"If Gallacher had managed even a bogey on seventeen, they would have gone to the final green with as much golf drama in the air as anyone could ever hope to witness. But Gallacher butchered the seventeenth worse than Watson had." —DAN JENKINS, *Sports Illustrated*

Day three result: USA 6½, EUR 5½

"It's a shame it wasn't a tie. I never expected it to be like that. It was an experience I will remember for a lifetime." —JACK NICKLAUS

"Golf won in the end today. All matches ebb and flow, and at the end we were on the ebb." —TONY JACKLIN

Overall match score: USA 14½, EUR 13½

"Europe's team of twelve professional golfers, far behind in power and depth of talent, came close to tying or beating the United States. In losing 14½–13½, the Europeans made their best effort in this country since the matches began in 1927." —JOHN RADOSTA, *New York Times*

Recap

"I didn't sleep well, not a wink one night, and this is the biggest thrill and more fun than anything I've done in golf. At the start of the day, we wondered seriously how we could halve this match, let alone win it. But then things started to go slightly our way."
—*Jack Nicklaus*

Not only was this the closest-ever Ryder Cup finish in the United States, but the home side had just held on by the narrowest of margins as the Europeans eclipsed any previous performance by a visiting team.

"Now it is a contest. The European Ryder Cup team frightened the money-laden breeches off their American counterparts."
—DAVID DAVIES, *London Guardian*

Just as pleasing for the Europeans was the fact that their three continental players had a hand in 9 of the 13½ points their side won. That was the obvious difference between this narrow defeat and the long line of lopsided losses suffered by the British teams before.

Not only had the newly assembled European team come of age by almost winning the Ryder Cup, but they had scared the mighty Americans in their own backyard. All the Europeans had to do was find five or six more continental players to fully complement the five or six top-class British players.

"We had done everything right and now we had nothing to show for it. I'm disappointed, but it could not have been any closer. Our boys put up a fantastic performance. I think the game of golf will benefit."
—Tony Jacklin

In Tony Jacklin, Europe had at last found a captain who was not scared of taking on the Americans and was more than capable of masterminding a victory. All he needed were the tools to finish the job.

With an expert eye to the future, both captains predicted better things for the revitalized Ryder Cup:

"One thing is certain, these matches are going to be as close as this from now on. There will be no more American walkovers." —Tony Jacklin

"We will not be the favorites when we go to The Belfry in two years. This score was no fluke. Let me tell you, most of the European players outdrove mine, and they made shots and putted well. I said before, it was the strongest team in years. It was no fluke." —Jack Nicklaus

On being asked if Ronald Reagan had made the traditional presidential phone call of congratulations: "No . . . and I voted for him."
—*Jack Nicklaus*

ABC TV had more or less given up covering the Ryder Cup and provided only minimal coverage of the matches to fulfill its contract with the PGA of America. Despite the close result, the network lost more than a million dollars on the broadcast.

Match Results (Winning side marked in *italics*.)

Friday, October 14—Morning Foursomes

	USA	EUR	Score
1.	*Tom Watson* *Ben Crenshaw*	Bernard Gallacher Sandy Lyle	5 and 4
2.	Lanny Wadkins Craig Stadler	*Nick Faldo* *Bernhard Langer*	4 and 2
3.	*Tom Kite* *Calvin Peete*	Seve Ballesteros Paul Way	2 and 1
4.	Raymond Floyd Bob Gilder	*Jose Maria Canizares* *Sam Torrance*	4 and 3

Friday, October 14—Afternoon Fourball

	USA	EUR	Score
5.	Gil Morgan Fuzzy Zoeller	*Brian Waites* *Ken Brown*	2 and 1
6.	*Tom Watson* *Jay Haas*	Nick Faldo Bernhard Langer	2 and 1
7.	Raymond Floyd Curtis Strange	*Seve Ballesteros* *Paul Way*	1-up
8.	Ben Crenshaw Calvin Peete	Sam Torrance Ian Woosnam	halved

Day one result: USA 3 ½, EUR 4 ½

Saturday, October 15—Morning Fourball

	USA	EUR	Score
9.	*Craig Stadler* *Lanny Wadkins*	Ken Brown Brian Waites	1-up
10.	Calvin Peete Ben Crenshaw	*Nick Faldo* *Bernhard Langer*	4 and 2
11.	Gil Morgan Jay Haas	Seve Ballesteros Paul Way	halved
12.	*Tom Watson* *Bob Gilder*	Sam Torrance Ian Woosnam	5 and 4

Saturday, October 15—Afternoon Foursomes

	USA	EUR	Score
13.	Raymond Floyd Tom Kite	*Nick Faldo* *Bernhard Langer*	3 and 2
14.	*Jay Haas* *Curtis Strange*	Ken Brown Brian Waites	3 and 1
15.	*Lanny Wadkins* *Gil Morgan*	Sam Torrance Jose Maria Canizares	7 and 5
16.	Bob Gilder Tom Watson	*Seve Ballesteros* *Paul Way*	2 and 1

Day two result: USA 4 1/2, EUR 3 1/2

Overall match score: USA 8, EUR 8

Sunday, October 16—Singles

	USA	EUR	Score
17.	Fuzzy Zoeller	Seve Ballesteros	halved
18.	Jay Haas	*Nick Faldo*	2 and 1
19.	Gil Morgan	*Bernhard Langer*	2-up
20.	*Bob Gilder*	Gordon J. Brand	2-up
21.	*Ben Crenshaw*	Sandy Lyle	3 and 1
22.	*Calvin Peete*	Brian Waites	1-up
23.	Curtis Strange	*Paul Way*	2 and 1
24.	Tom Kite	Sam Torrance	halved
25.	*Craig Stadler*	Ian Woosnam	3 and 2
26.	Lanny Wadkins	Jose Maria Canizares	halved
27.	Raymond Floyd	*Ken Brown*	4 and 3
28.	*Tom Watson*	Bernard Gallacher	2 and 1

Day three result: USA 6 ½, EUR 5 ½

Overall match score: USA 14 ½, EUR 13 ½

1985

The Belfry
Sutton Coldfield
England
September 13–15

United States 11½	**Europe 16½**
Raymond Floyd	Seve Ballesteros (Spain)
Hubert Green	Ken Brown (Scotland)
Peter Jacobsen	Jose Maria Canizares (Spain)
Tom Kite	Howard Clark (England)
Andy North	Nick Faldo (England)
Mark O'Meara	Bernhard Langer (Germany)
Calvin Peete	Sandy Lyle (Scotland)
Craig Stadler	Manuel Pinero (Spain)
Curtis Strange	Jose Rivero (Spain)
Hal Sutton	Sam Torrance (Scotland)
Lanny Wadkins	Paul Way (England)
Fuzzy Zoeller	Ian Woosnam (Wales)
Captain	**Captain**
Lee Trevino	Tony Jacklin (England)

The Empire Strikes Back

—*Sports Illustrated* headline

Recent history has shown that Ryder Cups are won and lost not so much on playing strength as on match-play experience. The two teams that squared off in 1985 were proof positive of this truism. The United States had only two players (Floyd and Kite) in their ranks who had played on the last visit to Europe. The home side had seven players from 1981 and nine from the close contest two years later.

The U.S. team also had four rookies (North, O'Meara, Sutton, and Jacobsen), compared with Europe's one (Rivero). With the weight of experience on their side, the home team surely had their best chance to finally win back the Ryder Cup after twenty-eight years in the golfing wilderness.

The American captain still liked his own team's chances. "I believe my team is stronger than it was in '83," said Trevino. "I have all the current money winners, tournament winners, and the ones that are playing extremely well. So I am very confident of winning this championship. . . . I may not have the best players in the world—I have the highest regard for Seve Ballesteros and Bernhard Langer—but when you take the whole team as a team of twelve players, yes, I think my team is extremely strong."

Trevino had good reason to be cautiously optimistic. Ray Floyd and Lanny Wadkins had won 31 Ryder Cup points between them; the rest of the ten U.S. players totaled 32.

"The American team is going to have its hands full—if they come out of there winning, we'll be lucky."
—*Jack Nicklaus*

Neither Jack Nicklaus nor Tom Watson had qualified for Lee Trevino's team, but the captain showed little concern over his side's lack of experience. He was more worried about his squad's lack of winning play on the PGA Tour, only three players having had Tour wins since May: Andy North (U.S. Open), Hubert Green (PGA), and Curtis Strange (who had three Tour wins in 1985: Honda Classic, Las Vegas Invitational, and Canadian Open).

"For the better part of the twentieth century, starting just about the time Harry Vardon brought his overlapping grip over to Massachusetts and had it undone by a bespectacled amateur named Francis Ouimet, the United States has enjoyed some semblance of supremacy in world golf."
—RON COFFMAN, *Golf World*

After the near miss at the PGA National in 1983, Tony Jacklin was retained as Europe's captain, granting him a golden opportunity to avenge his 1972 British Open loss to his opposing number—Lee Trevino.

"Tony and I have been very good friends for many, many years. I guess one of the greatest matches that Tony and I participated in was the old Piccadilly Matchplay at Wentworth, when we had twenty-six birdies and three eagles in thirty-six holes and I beat him 1-up on the thirty-sixth. As we walked down the first fairway, Tony turned to me and said, 'I just want to play golf today. I don't want to talk.' I said to him, 'I don't want you to talk . . . just listen!'" —LEE TREVINO

"It is not going to be easy to win, but if I have some control over the weaker end of the team—the top eight or nine should not be a problem—it might just tip the balance."
—*Tony Jacklin*

Jacklin was still intent on running things his way, and he managed to persuade the European PGA to change its rigid selection procedure, allowing him to make three wild-card choices: Faldo, Brown, and Rivero.

Against the Americans' two majors winners, Europe boasted two as well: Lyle (British Open) and Langer (Masters). So everything was finally balanced. Jacklin's side contained five continental players, the most in the four matches since Europe had joined forces with Britain.

"If my head says America, then my heart shouts Europe. There is feeling abroad that it is our turn, that it's our time to send the Yanks home mouthing platitudes about such results being good for the game. It may be irrational but I take us to win." —David Davies, *London Guardian*

Course Details

The PGA of Europe chose this site for the next three Ryder Cup matches in the east. It was also the site of the association's headquarters, a hotel complex ten miles northeast of Birmingham (England's second-largest city) in the Midlands.

In setting up the course, Tony Jacklin requested that the greenkeeper not cut the greens too close, which drew a general thumbs-down from the visitors.

"Nothing wrong with this course that some mowers wouldn't help."
—Hubert Green

"The Belfry's Brabazon course, with its manicured smooth fairways and manmade lakes, could have been lifted from a San Diego suburb, so American did it seem."
—*Barry McDermott,* Sports Illustrated

Hole	Distance	Par	Hole	Distance	Par
1	418	4	10	275	4
2	349	4	11	420	4
3	465	4	12	235	3
4	579	5	13	394	4
5	399	4	14	194	3
6	396	4	15	550	5
7	183	3	16	410	4
8	460	4	17	575	5
9	400	4	18	474	4
		36			**36 = Par 72 (7,176 yards)**

Course designers: Peter Alliss and Dave Thomas

Day One: Morning Foursomes

Tony Jacklin was hoping that Friday the thirteenth would prove unlucky for the Americans, since he knew the importance of building a lead on the first day.

Curtis Strange and Mark O'Meara (USA) v. Seve Ballesteros and Manuel Pinero (EUR)

The 1985 Ryder Cup got off to a less-than-auspicious start. O'Meara sliced his opening drive into the rough, just shy of some exhibition tents. Pinero also missed the fairway, and Ballesteros's first shot of the day found a bunker. A couple of fine recoveries from Strange and Pinero allowed both pairs to bounce back from their bad starts to make par fours.

On the second hole, twenty-eight-year-old O'Meara leaked his second shot into a bunker by the green, then failed to convert Strange's fine recovery to nine feet, and the Americans lost their first hole of the day. On the next hole, it was Strange's turn—he missed a four-foot par putt.

With the par-5 fourth halved in birdies, the Americans continued to struggle. O'Meara's poor drive on five and his bunkered approach on six gave the Spaniards both holes to par. The Americans did themselves little credit as a leadoff pair, covering the opening six holes in 28 strokes to find themselves four down.

On a last-minute switch to his original pairing: *"Jose Rivero was struggling with his driving. With four holes of the last practice round remaining, I took Manuel away from Jose Maria and linked him with Seve. I had a feeling. I went right to it, and they played the last four holes well. They know each other from past World Cups, and I owed it to the team to make a decision beneficial for us."* —TONY JACKLIN

Pinero contrived to lose the 183-yard seventh, hitting his tee shot wide of the green and missing a six-foot putt for par. The Americans got their act together and birdied the eighth—on Strange's well-judged twelve-foot putt—to cut the lead to two. On the tenth—a shortened 275-yard par 4 with a carry over a pond to the green—Strange, under captain's orders, laid up short of the water.

"The freaky little tenth measures only 275 yards and is either a blah of a par 4, played with something like a six-iron followed by a pitch across a

pond, or a white-knuckle three-shooter calling for a full wood to be directed through the narrowest air corridor in British golf. Deviate by a degree or so either side of that curving approach path and you find water, or trees, or sand or a flower bed. It is what our chaps call a 'bottle hole,' the Americans 'a right mother.' " —Peter Dobereiner

With a green light from his captain, Ballesteros drove over the water and found the green. His ball landed just a few feet from the stream on the left-hand side of the putting surface, then rolled some ninety feet past the pin to the back of the green. Pinero rolled his long putt up to within seven feet, and his partner holed the birdie putt to restore a three-hole cushion for the Europeans.

Ballesteros was the first player ever to drive the tenth green in one, and a plaque commemorates the feat.

With eleven halved in par, the Spaniards went four up at twelve with a par three, after both Americans failed to reach the green with their first two shots. Thirteen was halved in par, after which the U.S. pair won the par-3 fourteenth thanks to a Spanish bogey.

Three down, O'Meara found his form on sixteen, leaving his pitch shot a yard from the hole for Strange to make birdie, reducing Europe's lead to two. On the severe dogleg, 575-yard seventeenth, Seve was forced to lay up well short after Pinero's drive left him too much to do to make the green in two. Strange was also left with more than 300 yards to the green, but he sliced his wood into a fairway bunker. Pinero, with 170 yards to the flag, hit a six-iron perfectly on line but five yards short of the flag. O'Meara's recovery ran through and off the back of the green, leaving Strange to hole the comeback chip to keep the match alive. Strange left his attempt four feet short, giving the Europeans two putts for the match. Ballesteros rolled the first putt up to the hole for a half in par, enough to secure the first (and only) point of the morning for the home team, 2 and 1.

Calvin Peete and Tom Kite (USA) v. Bernhard Langer and Nick Faldo (EUR)

Before the contest had started, Trevino confidently named Peete and Kite as his best pairing, and they did not disappoint their captain.

Trevino put up a $1,000 prize for the best U.S. pair in the prematch foursomes practice round. Kite and Peete won the dash for cash with a joint 69.

Producing the best golf of the morning, the U.S. pair reached the turn in 33 strokes, four shots better than Faldo and Langer. The Europeans' dismal play was typified by their double bogey on the third hole. Faldo bunkered his tee shot, Langer scuffed his attempted recovery, and Faldo came up short of the green with a six-iron.

A forty-two-foot putt from the Americans on the 183-yard seventh increased their lead, but Langer's ten-foot birdie putt on eight meant his side was only one down. This slight lead was doubled at the ninth when Faldo hit another poor tee shot. The Europeans' game came completely apart on the tenth when Langer tried in vain to drive over the water in front of the green.

Three up soon became four for the U.S. pair when Langer again slipped up, blowing a four-foot putt for a half on the par-4 eleventh. Europe managed to pull one hole back after Peete found the bunker on the 235-yard twelfth, but the end was near. Trevino's money matchup cashed in on the sixteenth, 3 and 2.

Kite and Peete amply repaid Trevino's faith in them, carding the best round of the morning. They were on course for a three-under 69. Faldo and Langer, 3-1 coming into the contest since 1983, had played the last five pairs matches in a row together, but they were split up after this defeat (four over par).

Lanny Wadkins and Raymond Floyd (USA) v. Sandy Lyle and Ken Brown (EUR)

Floyd and Wadkins did not have to work hard for a three-hole lead by the turn, reached with a slovenly 38 on their card. Lyle and Brown fared worse (with a 41) and played worse, lucky to escape with a half on the second hole. Having twice failed to get out of the rough on the 465-yard third, Lyle could have halved the hole with a twenty-eight-foot putt for par. Somehow the Europeans contrived to play the sixth even worse, taking four shots to reach the par-4 green.

"For me the Ryder Cup is the ultimate, because you are representing your country. A lot of people come out and say that this is just a nice week off from the Tour. That's not true. It's an exciting, challenging week, which breeds camaraderie, as for once the players are actually pulling for each other."
—*Raymond Floyd*

The U.S. pair struggled to find pars on seven and eight but still emerged with halves. Brown missed an easy two-footer on seven, and neither pair played eight with any authority. Out in two over par, the Americans increased their lead to three at the turn after Lyle put his ball in the water on nine. The Europeans reached the turn five over, without a birdie or a three on their card.

Like Langer before them, the Europeans also found the water on ten, to gift-wrap a four-hole lead for their adversaries. The sorry Scottish pair won just one hole in this match, the 394-yard thirteenth, and that was courtesy of an American bogey.

A birdie two on the short fourteenth was more than enough to beat another European bogey, putting Wadkins and Floyd one step closer to a convincing 4 and 3 win.

The margin of victory, the biggest of the day, scarcely revealed how poorly the home pair played (six over for the round), a fact not overlooked by the Europeans' hard taskmaster of a captain, who immediately scratched their names from the afternoon fourball.

Craig Stadler and Hal Sutton (USA) v. Howard Clark and Sam Torrance (EUR)

Sutton and Stadler started out with an early lead on the strength of the latter's twelve-foot birdie putt on the second. Torrance and Clark managed to halve the next hole, with the U.S. pair three-putting and Clark having to make a five-footer for a matching bogey five. This narrow escape emboldened the Europeans to snatch the par-5 fourth hole, with Clark knocking his approach stiff for a tap-in eagle.

With Stadler finding water on the 396-yard sixth, Europe won the hole with a bogey five to lead for the first and only time in the contest. Torrance found sand with his tee shot on the par-3 seventh, and another European bogey on the par-4 eighth put the Americans one up at the turn.

The match was back level after Torrance's impressive tee shot at the "rip it or chip it" tenth secured a birdie three. The home pair bogeyed the 420-yard eleventh to fall behind again. Stadler and Sutton lost the par-3 twelfth to Clark's monstrous putt but were back ahead on thirteen after another British bogey. In trying to recover Clark's wayward drive, Torrance succeeded only in knocking the ball out-of-bounds.

The Europeans' game totally fell apart as the tension began to build, making a mess of fourteen, which they lost to par. Stadler and Sutton combined well on the 550-yard fifteenth with another hole-winning birdie, then took the match 3 and 2 on the next hole. This was another point presented to the Americans, who hardly had to break a sweat all morning, returning one over par for their troubles.

Morning foursomes result: USA 3, EUR 1

By losing three of the four morning foursomes, the Europeans had dealt any hopes of a home-team victory a massive blow. Jacklin responded by dropping all three of his wild-card choices (Faldo, Brown, and Rivero), as well as an off-his-game and none-too-pleased British Open champion. Sandy Lyle was furious, claiming fourball was his preferred format, and threatened that if he was omitted the following afternoon, "you will really hear some screaming."

Day One: Afternoon Fourball

Instead of going for Europe's exposed jugular, Trevino, armed with a healthy lead, decided to give every player a match on the first day. This traditional American act of amicable appeasement proved to be the side's undoing . . .

Fuzzy Zoeller and Hubert Green (USA) v. Paul Way and Ian Woosnam (EUR)

Leading off the afternoon session, Green and Zoeller teed it up against Woosnam and Way, all four players getting their first taste of action.

Having sat out the morning session, Ian Woosnam started like a Welsh cottage on fire, with birdies at the first three even holes to put Europe two up. Zoeller's birdie on the 579-yard fourth canceled Woosnam's, and the American made a ten-foot putt on the par-4 eighth for another birdie to pull another hole back.

Fuzzy Zoeller's ball had counted on seven of the first eight holes, as he single-handedly kept his pair in the match.

On the 400-yard ninth, Way hit an admirably accurate approach to the top tier to finish eighteen feet away. Green's approach ran off the back of the green, leaving him with a nasty downhill chip for a birdie. The American left his delicate chip a few inches short for a conceded par four, but Way's birdie putt was true and the ball rolled home to double his side's lead.

"If I could putt like Paul, we'd beat anybody in the world together."
—*Ian Woosnam*

Woosnam took on the tenth and lost. He drove into the water, but Way played a safe tee shot before pitching up to eight feet. Having also laid up and pitched on, Green putted first and just failed to curl in a tricky ten-footer for a three. Way repeated his straight-as-an-arrow birdie putt to put the Europeans up by three.

Zoeller and Green had no real answer for the European one-two bantamweight punch, as Woosnam and Way combined to play near-perfect fourball golf. But from looking desperately outmatched, the Americans suddenly found the solutions to their problems. Green birdied the short twelfth with a four-foot putt, and Zoeller returned the compliment on thirteen, his eight-foot downhill putt racing into the hole.

The 194-yard fourteenth was halved in par, and Woosnam and Zoeller again swapped birdies on fifteen for another half. Sixteen saw Zoeller's swinging twelve-foot putt barely take the bottom lip and drop into the cup to square the match. Woosnam (two putts from sixty feet away) and Green (one putt from fifteen feet) sank birdies on the 575-yard seventeenth for another half.

All four players safely found the last green with their second shots, Woosnam playing the most spectacular approach. His partner only ten feet from the flag with a fine two-iron approach of his own, the Welshman ripped a three-iron from a fairway bunker. His ball just cleared the water, then rolled around the contours of the green to within twenty feet. From some distance, both Zoeller and Green made impossible-looking long putts seem simple and came within inches of holing out for birdies. Woosnam almost holed his birdie putt, but it was left to Way to hole his ten-footer to wrap up the match, 1-up.

On the European pair, nicknamed the "Tiny Tots" by their colleagues: "Way and Woosnam, who both have to jump up and down in order to peep over their golf bags, cut Green and Zoeller down to size."
—*Peter Dobereiner*

The Americans finished fast, five under for the back nine, as they just failed to catch the Europeans, who carded the best round of the afternoon, 64 on their best-ball.

Andy North and Peter Jacobsen (USA) v. Seve Ballesteros and Manuel Pinero (EUR)

Trevino's second fresh pairing, Jacobsen and North, won the first hole, the latter holing an eight-footer for birdie. Ballesteros made a miraculous recovery from the sand on the 579-yard fourth to a few inches of the hole, saving a half in birdie fours. A nine-iron approach to three feet on the fifth gave Ballesteros another birdie, and he made it three in a row on the 396-yard sixth to take the lead.

The Americans leveled the match with a par on eight, as Ballesteros found the water and Pinero a bunker. Nine was halved in par, then Ballesteros again went for the "hit or miss" tenth green, nonchalantly knocking his three-wood to within twenty feet of the hole. Following his partner's lead, Pinero also found the green in one. Jacobsen, who had laid up, hit a pitch to within five feet, but the ball spun back twenty-two feet from the hole. The smaller Spaniard rolled his eagle putt right up to the hole, as did Ballesteros. Jacobsen had a chance to match the Spaniards' threes, but his putt sailed blithely past the hole, putting Europe one up.

Pinero kept the Spanish surge rolling with a four-foot birdie at eleven for a two-hole lead. The 235-yard twelfth saw the U.S. pair in prime position on the green, but Seve got up and down from a bunker for a half. Answering Ballesteros's pin-high tee shot on fourteen, Jacobsen pulled his tee shot wide left of the green. Faced with a thirty-five-foot chip, the American simply holed his second shot for a birdie that the stunned Spaniards could not match.

With two more halves in par, Europe retained a slight advantage until the seventeenth, where Ballesteros fired two shots at the 575-yard hole to almost reach the green. A fifty-yard bump-and-run wedge to the green left him with an eight-foot birdie putt. Jacobsen had also reached the green in three, but his thirty-foot birdie putt slowed up inches short of the hole. Seve's putt, which dripped into the left-hand side of the hole, was enough to secure the 2 and 1 win for Europe.

After carding five birdies in the 2 and 1 win: *"I like match play. It suits my game. But golf is difficult enough when you are playing for yourself. When you are also playing for Europe, it is so much more difficult."*

—SEVE BALLESTEROS

Craig Stadler and Hal Sutton (USA) v. Bernhard Langer and Jose Maria Canizares (EUR)

In a close match, Stadler captured the only hole won on the outward nine, with a birdie four at the fourth. Stadler and Sutton took 35 strokes to reach the turn, one better than Langer and Canizares.

Craig Stadler had warmed up for the Ryder Cup with two wins in Europe: the Swiss Open and the European Masters.

All four tee shots at the tenth were both disgusting and different in a manner all their own. Stadler's ball hit a tree before dropping into the water, so Sutton laid up way, way short of the water and the green. Both Europeans went for the green: Canizares put his ball out of view behind the crowd on the right of the green, and Langer finished closer to the adjacent sixteenth green, some distance from the green he had aimed at.

Sutton, the only player not in any real trouble, hit a rasping pitch shot to within a foot of the hole, but it spun back eight feet. With trees, a bank, a bunker, a slope, and the sun in his eyes to contend with, Langer lofted his chip high over the bank, landing the ball between the bunker and the fringe. His ball skipped onto the green and rolled down the slope to four feet of the hole. Sutton's birdie putt caught the right-hand lip and stayed out. Langer stepped up and, with his cross-handed grip, topped off a miracle recovery shot for a hole-winning birdie to square the match.

The German won the next hole with another excellent chip shot to five feet. Langer's third three in a row was only enough to halve the twelfth with Stadler, who rolled home a seventeen-footer for birdie at the next to pull back level. Sutton and Langer exchanged birdies on fifteen, and their partners did the same on seventeen.

Canizares came within an inch of holing his pitch shot at seventeen for a late lead. In reply, Stadler, from off the front of the green, played his third—a pitch-and-run—up the slope of the green to within two feet to cancel out Canizares's birdie.

On eighteen, Canizares's second shot landed on the slope ten feet in front of the pin but ran back another fifteen away from the hole. Stadler punched in a long iron that found the green pin-high, twenty-five feet to the left. Sutton suffered the same fate as Canizares, his ball rolling back away from the hole. Langer hit the best approach, landing his ball high and right of the flag, only fifteen feet away.

Convinced he had holed his long putt, Stadler raised his putter in salute, then quickly pulled it down as the ball ran out of speed and pulled up a foot short. Langer had a putt to win the match. Like Stadler's, it was right on line but, agonizingly for the Europeans, spluttered to a halt one revolution away from dropping in for a match-winning birdie. The hole and match were halved, as both pairs had combined for better-ball rounds of 68.

Raymond Floyd and Lanny Wadkins (USA) v. Sam Torrance and Howard Clark (EUR)

Following their morning win, Floyd and Wadkins were sent out against Clark and Torrance, who had played poorly in losing their first match. Clark's eleven-foot birdie putt put the Europeans one up at the first, but this was to be their only lead of the match. Wadkins wiped off this lead with a six-foot birdie putt on the second. A European bogey on the third and an American birdie on the fourth gave the U.S. pair a two-hole advantage.

Clark made his second birdie at six to cut the lead to one, and Wadkins countered with a birdie two at the seventh. Torrance claimed the ninth with a wonderful twenty-foot downhill putt that took its boots off and wiped its feet before dropping into the hole. More than adequately inspired, Torrance found the back of the tenth green with his rasping drive. As had been the Americans' plan, their pair laid up. Wadkins's approach pitched close and, like so many before his, spun back some distance. Torrance's eagle putt dropped off rather tamely underneath the hole, leaving Wadkins to hole his twelve-footer for a crucial half in threes.

"On the Tour you are an individual. You play only for yourself, and if you lose, it doesn't bother anybody else. Now, all of a sudden, you are representing the United States of America. When I stand out there and they raise the flag and play the national anthem, I get goose bumps."
—*Raymond Floyd*

The next five holes were halved in regulation, and the match remained level until the 410-yard sixteenth, where Torrance hit a superb approach from the rough to five feet of the hole. With his partner short of the hole in two, Wadkins's second finished well outside of both of his rivals. The American read the tricky line to the hole beautifully, and his twenty-five-foot putt slammed into the center of the cup for a birdie. With much shorter putts than Wadkins had, both Europeans missed, giving the Americans back their lead.

This proved the defining moment in the match, because seventeen was halved, assuring the U.S. side of at least a split. On the last hole, Clark hit the best second shot to the middle tier, within twenty feet of the flag. The Englishman's birdie putt to halve the match never challenged the hole, and the United States came away with a hard-fought point, 1-up.

Afternoon fourball result: USA 1½, EUR 2½

"I don't have any fingernails left, because I've been chewing them all afternoon. At one point it looked like we could be wiped out 4–zip."
—LEE TREVINO

Day one result: USA 4½, EUR 3½

"On a flawless day for world-class golf, a competition that in this country ranks second only to the British Open drew 24,896 fans, a record for the first day of a Ryder Cup match." —JOHN RADOSTA, *New York Times*

Day Two: Morning Fourball

Tom Kite and Andy North (USA) v. Sam Torrance and Howard Clark (EUR)

Having been beaten in both their games on day one, Torrance and Clark were a little surprised to be sent out first on the second morning.

The Europeans realized they had their hands full against North and Kite when the former chipped in from ten yards away, leaving Clark to halve the second hole with a six-footer.

Clark again stepped up on the third, where par was enough to beat Kite, who failed to make a ten-foot putt for his par, having found sand with his approach. The fourth was halved in par, as Clark quickly made his third decisive putt of the round, followed by a twenty-two-footer for birdie at the par-4 fifth—good for a two-hole cushion. With Torrance playing out of the water and Clark from a bunker, Kite's par four on the 460-yard eighth was enough to cut the lead to one.

The Europeans continued to plunder the shortened tenth, where Clark made a sixteen-foot birdie putt to restore the two-hole lead. Kite played an exquisite long-iron tee shot into the par-3 twelfth, and his first successful birdie putt, from eight feet, just about dribbled into the right-hand side of the cup. With his trademark putting grip—halfway down the shaft—North holed a four-footer on thirteen, and the match was back all square.

Having played the senior role for his side, Clark stamped his authority on the match. His approach into the three-tiered green at the 550-yard fifteenth landed on the first upslope, and the ball ran back away from the hole. This left the Englishman with a sixty-foot putt, made even longer by two rises to the flag. Clark set the ball off on its long journey way to the right of the hole, but the ball curled in off the two slopes and plunged straight into the cup for a much-needed birdie. So critical was this stroke of luck that the Europeans performed an impromptu jig in the middle of the green, once again holding the lead.

On sixteen, the mercurial Clark hooked his pitch shot left of the green, then holed the twenty-foot chip shot coming back for another birdie. Kite had a shorter chip shot from the same area, but his ball brushed past the hole to give Europe another win. This second stroke of good fortune for Clark put Europe two up with two to play.

After Torrance's approach shot almost hit the flag at seventeen, Clark nearly holed another chip shot from off the back of the green, but he'd used up his quota of luck for the day—his ball ran around the lip of the hole. Torrance's first birdie of the round was good enough to halve the hole with Kite and secure a 2 and 1 win for Europe.

Hubert Green and Fuzzy Zoeller (USA) v. Paul Way and Ian Woosnam (EUR)

Green and Zoeller were looking for instant revenge against Way and Woosnam, after the Europeans had beaten them the previous afternoon on the last green. The all-British pair was still on fire and gave the opponents little chance of turning the tables.

Woosnam sank a thirty-five-foot putt on the first for a birdie and a lead they never lost. Way's par at three and two more Woosnam birdies at four and five had the Americans struggling to get anywhere near the last green this time around. Their failure to make par on the eighth saw them go five down; the game had already slipped out of their grasp.

Ian Woosnam was in prime form, having shot a last-round 62 at the B&H International in August. He equaled a world record with eight consecutive birdies.

Just when Green and Zoeller thought they were down and out, their rivals gave them a glimmer of hope when they blotted their scorecard with a bogey five at the ninth, cutting the lead to four at the turn. Green birdied eleven thanks to a twenty-five-foot putt, and an American comeback seemed under way.

On the 235-yard twelfth, Zoeller added more fuel to the recovery by sticking his tee shot five feet from the flag. With Green and Way out of the hole, Woosnam produced his trump card, knocking his tee shot halfway between Zoeller's ball and the pin. Zoeller's makable putt now became eminently missable—which is exactly what Zoeller did, pushing the putt to the right of the hole. Woosnam's killer birdie restored a four-hole lead, which was made to count after three consecutive halves in par for a commanding 4 and 3 win.

Mark O'Meara and Lanny Wadkins (USA) v. Seve Ballesteros and Manuel Pinero (EUR)

Against the Spanish pairing of Ballesteros and Pinero, who had won both their matches on the first day, O'Meara and Wadkins needed to get hot from the start. On the first, Wadkins's thirty-three-foot putt furnished a birdie and a lead that was not to be relinquished. After halving the next four holes, the U.S. pair made three birdies in the next four to reach the turn in 32 strokes, good for a four-hole lead.

O'Meara holed from seven feet on the sixth, and Wadkins made hole-winning putts from twelve and twenty feet on seven and nine.

The irrepressible Wadkins defused any European comeback by matching Ballesteros's gimme three at the tenth, although the American did so with a drive, pitch, and seven-foot putt for his birdie. Wadkins proved to be holding the hot hand in this match, as he went on to birdie thirteen with a ten-foot putt.

Five down with five to play, the Spaniards threw caution to the wind and reaped a couple of birdies on fourteen (Pinero holing a massive putt from fifty feet) and fifteen (a second birdie from Ballesteros). The Spaniards ran out of steam and holes, going down 3 and 2 on the sixteenth, the Americans on course for a 66.

Craig Stadler and Curtis Strange (USA) v. Bernhard Langer and Sandy Lyle (EUR)

Playing with his third partner in three games, Langer delivered an inch-perfect pitch to the first that gave the Europeans their only lead of the clash against Strange and Stadler. On the next hole, Lyle missed a six-foot birdie putt, and he could only suffer in silence as he watched Strange make his two-footer to level the match.

The Americans proceeded to take a lead on Stadler's nine-foot birdie putt on the par-5 fourth, but the dogged Europeans kept hounding the U.S. pair, with Lyle making a birdie on the fifth. The par-3 seventh gave up a fifteen-foot birdie putt by Stadler that regained the lead, only for Europe to pull it back on the ninth. Lyle hit a great second over the water to the green and sank the ten-foot downhill putt for a birdie to square the match at the turn.

After Stadler and Langer birdied the tenth, Strange hit back at the par-3 twelfth, arrowing his tee shot to within ten feet. His dead-straight birdie putt put the United States one up again. On the 394-yard thirteenth, both Europeans missed good birdie opportunities, but Stadler made no mistake from ten feet to increase the U.S. advantage.

Making an eight-foot right-to-left putt, Lyle cut the lead to one with the only par on the par-3 fourteenth. Here Stadler had a seven-footer for a half with Lyle, but he pulled his second putt to the right of the hole. When fifteen was halved in par, the United States was one up with three to play.

In 1985, Bernhard Langer had five tournament wins coming into the Ryder Cup: Australian Masters, U.S. Masters, Heritage Classic, German Open, and European Open.

Langer safely found the heart of the sixteenth green, but Strange's superlative six-iron landed twenty-five feet from the flag, and the slope encouraged the ball to run right down to the hole. Having conceded Strange's gimme, Langer was unable to make his twelve-foot birdie putt, which appeared to run right over the hole. Strange's fortuitous "rub of the green" put the U.S. pair two up with two to play.

With Stadler's ball sitting just off the back of the seventeenth green in two, Lyle kept the match alive with a twenty-five-foot eagle putt. Stadler, who seconds earlier must have felt he had two shots to win the match, was now faced with having to hole his chip shot to win. His fifteen-foot attempt came up a few inches short.

With the United States one up on the last tee, three drives were safely dispatched, but Strange's found a bunker. The Europeans hit fine second shots to reach the green, with Langer the closest, twenty feet from the flag. All American eyes were on Stadler, who needed only to match the Europeans' highly probable par fours. He found the green forty feet from the hole. With the odds still stacked heavily in his favor, Stadler rolled his putt to within two feet of the hole and as certain a par as you could hope for in these conditions.

When Lyle and Langer narrowly missed their longish birdie putts, Stadler had a tap-in par four and the match at his mercy.

On Stadler's two-footer: "I had a look at it, and had we been out on the course, five down with five to play, I'd have conceded. But it was for victory on the final green, so we had to make him play it."
—*Sandy Lyle*

He got neither, mind-blowingly missing the short putt—wide left. In despair, he turned away from the hole and grabbed the back of his neck with his left hand, as if to garrote himself.

On Stadler, prior to the contest: *"Former U.S. Masters champion. Not the kind to crack under pressure. Powerful driver, inspirational putter."* —*Times* (London) player biography

Not only had Europe halved this match, but they had also pulled level in the overall match score—6 points each.

Morning fourball result: USA 1½, EUR 2½

Day Two: Afternoon Foursomes

Tom Kite and Calvin Peete (USA) v. Jose Maria Canizares and Jose Rivero (EUR)

Calling on a makeshift pairing to allow him to rest the weary Clark and Torrance, Jacklin sent out the two least-regarded Spaniards—Canizares and Rivero—against the number one American pairing, Kite and Peete. Not even in his dreams could Jacklin have imagined the response his understudies gave him. Not that the "backups" were without a chance—they had won the World Cup together in 1984, and Rivero had won the 1984 Lawrence Batley International at The Belfry by one stroke, holing a ten-footer on the last green for victory.

After trading holes to par with the Americans at the second and third, the Spaniards tore the course up. Over the next five holes, they made four birdies and took a four-hole lead against the suddenly down-and-out Peete and Kite, who played these five holes in seven more strokes than their unsung opponents. The highlight of this Spanish offensive came at the 183-yard seventh. Standing on the inclined fringe of the green, Canizares made a remarkable twenty-five-foot birdie putt that roller-coastered this way and that way into the hole.

Even after such a roaring start, the Europeans did not rest on their laurels. Once Peete found the water at ten, Rivero pitched his second to ten feet—par being good enough to win the hole after Peete's par putt ran by it. Europe went six up after Peete put another ball in the water on twelve.

At the 394-yard thirteenth, Canizares's approach finished pin high just off the right of the green. Peete played a steady recovery from a fairway bunker through the L-shaped green, leaving a most difficult chip shot across the fringe. Kite made the resultant chip look ridiculously easy, lagging the ball to four feet of the flag. From just off the green Rivero putted up to twelve inches. Refusing to concede the Spaniards' gimme for the outright win, Peete missed his own—to lose the hole and the match by an improbable 7 and 5.

This loss was doubly galling for Tom Kite, who now had a dual record, having inflicted the worst defeat in eighteen-hole competition (7 and 6 with Hale Irwin in 1979), and suffered the second-biggest defeat, 7 and 5.

The Americans contributed to their own downfall by taking ten more strokes than their conquerors (58–48) in only thirteen holes.

Craig Stadler and Hal Sutton (USA) v. Seve Ballesteros and Manuel Pinero (EUR)

In quick succession, Jacklin launched his remaining Spaniards on an afternoon that produced more Spanish treasures than the Armada ever managed to pillage. Sutton and Stadler were given the golfing equivalent of a keelhauling as they were blown out of the water by the Spanish broadside.

A home birdie on two, followed by Sutton's inexplicable miss from two feet on the third, gave Europe a two-hole lead. Ballesteros left his chip to the fourth green some eight feet away for Pinero to hole a birdie putt. Three down, after the fifth hole was halved in par, the shell-shocked Americans totally lost their way and the next three holes—two of them with bogeys—to fall six behind after just eight holes.

On the sixth, Sutton hit a long putt so far off target that BBC TV commentator Peter Alliss exclaimed, "That really is testing his partner . . . and his friendship!" Left with a testing five-footer for the half, Stadler left his putt on the lip of the cup again. "The Walrus" must have wondered whom he had upset to deserve such a morning *and* afternoon of undiluted tribulation and grief. To make matters worse, the Spaniards went from strength to strength, Pinero unleashing an irreproachable four-iron to eighteen inches of the seventh flag.

With par good enough to take the 460-yard eighth off the Americans, the European charge temporarily slowed with a bogey on nine and Sutton's emphatic eagle on the tenth. Stadler's day of woe continued on the "unlucky-for-some" thirteenth, where his tee shot drifted out of bounds.

Five up with five to play, Ballesteros almost aced the fourteenth: his ball bounced four inches from the hole, hopped up in the air, and stopped dead where it had landed. Sutton needed his own hole in one just to keep his side's interest alive, coming up twenty-five feet short. This was enough for Stadler to concede the hole and the match, 5 and 4, finally bringing an end to his dreadful day of misery and heartache.

In spite of the plundering, the Spanish players together were only two under par for their fourteen holes, their opponents failing to click as a pair.

Curtis Strange and Peter Jacobsen (USA) v. Paul Way and Ian Woosnam (EUR)

Two-for-two in their matches together, Woosnam and Way were full of confidence against Strange and Jacobsen, who were without a win in three separate appearances.

The first birdie of the match came at the fifth hole thanks to Way's five-foot putt. On the next hole, Jacobsen added his own birdie with a fifteen-foot putt. After an evenly matched power struggle over the first eight holes, the United States blew the game open with three wins in a row.

Jacobsen played the second shot over the water to within four feet of the ninth hole. Way followed suit to six feet, but Woosnam missed the putt, and Strange made his birdie for the win to put the Americans one up. Woosnam compounded his miss by dunking his ball in the water on ten. Once Way planted Europe's third shot on the back of the green, the U.S. pair had two comfortable putts for the hole in par. Jacobsen and Strange rolled on to take the eleventh and go three up.

From the seventh to the twelfth, Woosnam and Way managed to card six consecutive bogeys (4-5-5-5-5-4) but lost only three holes in the process.

On the 194-yard fourteenth, Jacobsen's tee shot was right on the flag but fell fifteen feet short. Woosnam knocked his reply to the right of the flag, drifting in on the wind to finish seven feet beyond the hole. Putting first, Strange read the cross-slope of the green to perfection, and his birdie putt was always on line for the hole. Way's tricky downhill putt never looked as if it would miss either—the hole was halved in birdie twos.

From the left-hand rough at sixteen, Strange hit a lofted iron to two feet of the hole, just failing to duplicate his perfect pitch from the previous afternoon's fourballs. Needing to hole his own pitch to save the match, Way clumsily overhit the shot. As his ball disappeared off the back of the green, Europe's last chance disappeared with it.

Woosnam failed to get his chip close, and Jacobsen quickly tapped in for a 4 and 2 victory, gaining his side's only point of the afternoon.

The previously unbeaten British pair, which had knitted so well, unraveled. They carded a nasty four over to the Americans' competent but hardly earth-shattering one under for sixteen holes.

Raymond Floyd and Lanny Wadkins (USA) v. Bernhard Langer and Ken Brown (EUR)

Floyd and Wadkins soon found themselves two holes down after three to Brown and Langer. The lanky Scot nailed a short chip to the second flag, and Wadkins missed a fourteen-foot putt for par on the third. Slowly but surely, the Americans got themselves back into the match.

They got a hole back on the 399-yard fifth with a par, then leveled the match on the sixth after Wadkins's long chip shot drifted in to three feet of the hole. With a chance to win the hole, Langer saw his long birdie putt trundle four feet past, but Brown missed the simple par putt coming back. Floyd's shorter putt horseshoed round the hole and dropped in for the win to level the match.

From a downslope off the back of the sixth green, Langer nudged his ball four feet past the hole. After Floyd just failed to make a putt from twenty-two feet away, Brown this time holed the four-footer for the win to put Europe one up again.

"Ken Brown looks like a walking one-iron."
—*Lee Trevino*

The visitors began to get the hang of the challenging tenth hole. Wadkins bailed out a long way to the left, finding dry land and the crowd. Langer badly sliced his tee shot, and all Brown could do was put his recovery into the water. Floyd made a magical pitch to ten feet, setting up the birdie and the win.

Two holes later, the Europeans were back in front after Wadkins missed his four-foot par putt on the 235-yard twelfth. Following a couple of halved holes, Wadkins missed much the same-length putt on fifteen that Strange (in the match ahead) had holed a few minutes earlier. In any case, Langer won this hole with a twenty-foot curling putt from just off the back of the green for a birdie four.

On sixteen, Langer pushed his tee shot to the right and hit a spectator. Wadkins uncorked a colossal drive that almost hit some more unwary spectators who were scurrying across the fairway, figuring they were safely out of range. From the rough, Brown almost holed an incredible pitch shot that landed in the heart of the green and rolled twenty feet up to within four inches of the hole. Floyd was unable to match this pinpoint accuracy, and when Wadkins failed to make the fifteen-foot birdie putt, Europe had won another match, 3 and 2.

Neither pair broke par; the Europeans carded an even score for the round, and their opponents were two over.

Afternoon foursomes result: USA 1, EUR 3
Day two result: USA 2½, EUR 5½
Overall match score: USA 7, EUR 9

A truly memorable day finished with the Europeans holding a priceless two-point lead going into the singles. This was the first time since 1949 that the Americans did not lead going into the final day's singles.

Many of the Americans found it hard to stomach the bad day behind them and the daunting prospect of the day ahead. But their captain noted, "I'm doing everything I can to lift them. They all seem fine. I like the singles draw."

The silence of dusk was broken by the noise of all the Americans on the practice tees trying to find answers that had eluded them over the first two days.

Day Three: Singles

Finding the U.S. team in an unaccustomed position, down by two going into the singles, Lee Trevino did what was expected of him. He packed the top of his order with his tough-guy trio—Wadkins, Stadler, and Floyd—in the hope they could muscle up some early points and generate some morale-boosting momentum for those lower in the order.

On a bright and breezy third day, Trevino's tough approach did not have the desired effect. Eight of his players managed to card a bogey before they made birdie.

Lanny Wadkins (USA) v. Manuel Pinero (EUR)

With a two-point lead, Jacklin gambled with his order of play and packed his strongest players in the middle of his lineup. Trevino did the opposite, splitting his best players top and bottom. First out for Europe was Pinero, whom Jacklin had written off as a loss, but the plucky Spaniard had his own ideas against the American bulldog Wadkins.

Jacklin: "You're playing top, and you've got Wadkins." *Pinero:* "He is exactly the one I wanted."

Both players were 3-1 in their earlier matches, but Wadkins held the head-to-head edge with a 3 and 2 win in the Saturday fourball over his opponent.

Twice Pinero fell behind to final-day specialist Wadkins on the outward nine, and twice he pulled back level. On the third hole, Pinero took three to get down from just off the putting surface, but he won the next hole when Wadkins took five shots to get down from a fairway bunker.

The American was back up again on the fifth, following a strongly struck putt from thirty-three feet for a birdie, but he took three putts on the eighth to fall back to all square.

"Lanny Wadkins . . . in just three appearances on the European tour last year won more money than Pinero did playing full-time."
—*Barry McDermott,* Sports Illustrated

The tenth again proved to be a pivotal hole. With Wadkins on the green looking at a straightforward birdie putt, Pinero was off the green in two. From forty feet away, Pinero holed his chip shot, while Wadkins missed his birdie putt to lose a hole he had looked sure to win. Instead of being one up, Wadkins found himself one down. On twelve, two wild shots cost the American another hole, as Pinero strapped a two-iron fifteen feet from the hole. Wadkins could sense the game slowly drifting away from him.

Pinero won the fifteenth with a seven-foot birdie four to take a three-hole lead with three to play. Under pressure, Wadkins produced a fighting birdie at sixteen to keep the match alive but was unable to follow up on seventeen. Thanks to a gutsy recovery from some heavy rough, Pinero's par five—after Wadkins missed a four-foot putt for par—won the penultimate hole to bring him a surprise win, 3 and 1.

Wadkins's fourth defeat in seventeen matches (13-4) proved costly, as his captain later confirmed: "That loss put us behind the eight ball."

Craig Stadler (USA) v. Ian Woosnam (EUR)

In a match of plain ugly golf, Woosnam took twenty shots to cover the first four holes but found himself down by only one against the almost equally inept Stadler. The quality of the golf was best illustrated when both players took it in turn to three-putt the first two holes.

Stadler eagled the 579-yard fourth, where a par would have accounted for Woosnam's waterlogged bogey five. On the 396-yard sixth, it was the American's turn to get wet, as his mistake leveled the match. The seventh saw Stadler miss a seventeen-foot putt for par to hand the Welshman the lead, but the American holed a thirty-five-foot birdie putt on eight to level.

On a roll, Stadler took the tenth with a par and was in pole position on thirteen after Woosnam put his one-iron drive out-of-bounds. Somehow, the Welshman matched Stadler's bogey despite the burden of a penalty stroke. Another Welsh birdie putt from off the green at the par-3 fourteenth leveled a match neither player apparently seemed to want to win—or, more correctly, deserved to.

As if to atone for the horror of the second day, Stadler stepped in with two decisive birdies at fifteen and sixteen, where a beautiful approach finished four feet from the flag. Woosnam had one last chance at the par-5 seventeenth, but he narrowly missed his eight-foot birdie putt, and the match was mercifully laid to rest, 2 and 1 in the U.S. side's favor.

This match was the last Stadler played in the Ryder Cup. He bowed out with a perfect singles record (2–0), both wins coming against Woosnam, having beaten him 3 and 2 in 1983.

Raymond Floyd (USA) v. Paul Way (EUR)

Ray Floyd, one of Trevino's leading hopes, found nine nightmares on the outward stretch and carded the worst front nine of the day. Forty-one strokes—including five fives—to the turn left Floyd four holes behind Paul Way, and he was extremely fortunate not to be further behind.

With everything seemingly going right for him, Way learned what Ryder Cup golf and Raymond Floyd were all about. The American had wins on eleven and twelve to halve the lead but couldn't improve his position over the next three holes.

On the 410-yard sixteenth, Way had a chance to close the big man out, but the tension got the better of him. With Floyd deep in the rough off the tee, Way's tee shot also found the rough, but he had a much clearer lie. All Floyd could do was chip out of the rough a long way short of the green. With the hole and match at his mercy, Way's technique and nerve let him down again: he squirted his second shot right through the green and the crowd, and almost into the lake beyond. To compound the error, the Englishman duffed his chip shot back after Floyd almost holed a carefully crafted chip-and-run. Europe's lead was back to one, and Floyd was on a Falstaffian charge.

Both tee shots landed in bunkers on seventeen, and the hole was halved in par fives. This was the first singles match to reach the last hole, which was to prove so crucial and so cruel.

Needing to win the hole for a half, Floyd went for broke and paid the price. He overhit his tee shot and landed in one of the two fairway bunkers to the right. Way played a textbook drive with enough draw to cut the corner off the doglegged fairway. His ball finished in a perfect position in front of the lake that guarded the last green. In an act of desperation, Floyd hauled a three-wood out of his bag for one final roll of the dice, but his topped shot crawled as far as the lake.

In a short career that spanned only two Ryder Cups, Paul Way won both his singles matches and finished with a very creditable 6–2–1 overall record.

With the hole and match at his mercy again, Way made no mistake this time, dispatching a full-blooded three-iron to the back of the green, grazing the flag on its way. After taking a drop, Floyd's pitch to the green spun back a long way—far enough to persuade the American to concede the hole without asking Way to putt. Floyd sportingly walked onto the massive green, picked his ball up, and walked over to shake hands with his vanquisher, conceding the 2-up victory.

Way was allowed to gain this vital point with a four-over-par 76, as Floyd came in two shots behind.

Tom Kite (USA) v. Seve Ballesteros (EUR)

Against Europe's number one, Tom Kite took an early two-hole lead with an unanswered birdie at the second, and Ballesteros bogeyed the fourth. The Spaniard made his first telling birdie at seven to cut the lead, but Kite got it back at nine with a birdie of his own.

The pair halved the next three holes, the eleventh spectacularly shared with birdie threes. Kite found himself three up with five to play after Ballesteros bunkered his wedge shot to thirteen and could not recover. As Kite surveyed his four-foot par putt on the 194-yard fourteenth, Ballesteros holed a runaway birdie putt from forty feet, which swung late to find the cup, snatching a hole back from the quiet American.

The par-5 fifteenth also went Europe's way—even after Ballesteros sent a wayward second shot forty yards right of the hole. Playing from the rough, Ballesteros chipped up to sixteen feet of the hole. Feeling the strain, Kite came up short on his longer putt, while Ballesteros holed his putt for another birdie and another win. Sixteen was halved, and the American still held a crucial one-hole advantage with two to play.

Kite was outdriven by 50 yards on the 575-yard seventeenth, which allowed Ballesteros to go for the green in two. With a trailing wind, he thundered a three-wood through the back of the green. Kite played his third shot twenty feet short of the hole, giving Ballesteros a short chip and a putt for the hole. The Spaniard remarkably muffed his chip shot, just about reaching the green, ten feet shy of the hole. As the advantage seemed to be slipping from his grasp, Ballesteros rammed his putt home for a win to level the match.

Having played the last four holes in regulation, Kite was taken aback to have lost three holes in that time. Ballesteros hit his final tee shot too straight, and it ran off the fairway into the light rough. Kite played a glorious fade across the corner and watched his ball dance up the fairway toward the hole. Standing in the rough, Seve spanked a three-wood that soared majestically onto the green twenty feet from the flag.

On his opponent's play: *"He hit shots I never even dream about."*
—TOM KITE

With both players on in two, Ballesteros carefully inspected his slightly longer putt and prudently rolled it up to the hole. This left Kite with a putt from eighteen feet to win the hole and the match. Knowing a half probably would not be good enough to rescue his ailing team, Kite attacked the cup, and the ball rolled five feet past. He confidently holed the return putt before stepping back to allow Ballesteros to hole out for the half.

From three down with five to play, Ballesteros—the European big gun—had dodged a live bullet, as both players finished with matching 71s. Another semiprecious half-point had been earned the hard way by the buoyant European side.

Peter Jacobsen (USA) v. Sandy Lyle (EUR)

Having played poorly on the first two days, Sandy Lyle regained the touch that won him the British Open. Peter Jacobsen also started with a hot hand, and both players holed missable birdie putts on the first green. The American played the third as though the fairway were out-of-bounds, taking a double-bogey six to Lyle's par four. Jacobsen rectified matters with a birdie at the fifth, but he put his ball in the water on the 460-yard eighth to reach the turn one down.

Lyle went two up at eleven, where Jacobsen failed to make par. After his putter saved his dropping the par-3 twelfth, the Scot lost his way with the driver, depositing his tee shot on thirteen out-of-bounds. Having dropped his only stroke of the day to par and lost the hole, Lyle won the fifteenth from a bunker, stroking his third shot to eight feet of the hole for birdie. Jacobsen had his chance, but he took three shots to get down from the edge of the green.

Two up, the Scot sealed another European victory on the 410-yard sixteenth, holing an outrageously long but perfectly weighted downhill birdie putt from all of forty feet. Lyle's ball appeared to have stopped on the lip before it dropped in for a 3 and 2 win.

On the European march to victory: *"I looked at my wife and said, 'Honey, our guys are getting a spanking out there.'"* —LEE TREVINO

Hal Sutton (USA) v. Bernhard Langer (EUR)

A misfiring Hal Sutton found himself two down after four holes, although Bernhard Langer had done nothing more spectacular than open in even par. The German made his first birdie on the 396-yard sixth to go three up, prompting Sutton into making a fight of it.

The American took seven and eight with two pars of his own, to trail by one hole. This comeback was short-lived: Sutton promptly lost the next four holes to the slow-paced, sure-putting German. Sutton took a triple-bogey six on the 235-yard twelfth to cap the disastrous run of four holes. Five down with six to play, an American par was enough to win the par-4 thirteenth.

On the jeering crowds that greeted every American mistake with a rousing cheer: "If this is an example of British sportsmanship, then it's a sad day for golf. Their behavior is disgraceful."
—*Hal Sutton*

Four up, Langer unleashed a magnificent five-iron tee shot to the fourteenth that did everything but go in the hole—rolling around the lip and dribbling fifteen inches away. Sutton made a brave attempt to hole his thirty-five-foot putt from off the green, but he came up two inches short of the hole. Langer's second birdie of the round was good enough to take the hole and the match by the widest margin of the day, 5 and 4.

The fifth hole was the only one of the fourteen holes not halved. Langer made only two birdies (on six and fourteen), as the American was six over when the German closed him out on the fourteenth.

Andy North (USA) v. Sam Torrance (EUR)

The way this match started, it hardly looked as if it would ultimately decide the outcome of the Ryder Cup.

Torrance, in particular, was well off his game early on, carding four bogeys on the outward nine. On the ninth, the Scot topped his drive into the water and made the turn in an appalling 40 strokes; only Ray Floyd had been worse all day. North covered the nine holes in only a couple of shots fewer, but more important, he held a two-hole lead.

Torrance butchered the tenth with a six, as he struggled to find any sort of rhythm at all.

"When I went three down, I just told myself to keep concentrating, keep trying, and hopefully my luck would change. It did on the next green, as North failed to find the green with his approach, chipped to eight feet, and missed the putt." —Sam Torrance

The pair halved the next three holes in almost respectable pars, before North missed a three-foot putt on fifteen to see his lead shrink to just one.

Torrance just failed to win the 410-yard sixteenth, his seven-foot birdie putt curling round in front of the cup. Unable to string two good holes together, both players found the rough on seventeen. Torrance, who had tried to cut the corner off the fairway, recovered much the better. From eighty yards out, he struck his third shot to five feet of the flag. North's third shot ran through the green, ending up sixteen feet away. The tall American was unable to match Torrance's birdie, which squared the match with one to play.

"The first thing I thought of when I stood on the eighteenth tee was my drive at the ninth, which I'd topped 130 yards into the lake."

—Sam Torrance

Up first and looking to take a psychological advantage, Torrance dispatched a mighty draw that disappeared more than 300 yards from the tee. The Scot's drive went so far that it almost ran into the lake in front of the green. The tension of the occasion and the pressure of Torrance's power drive got to North. Possibly caught in two minds, he neither played safe nor tried to follow Torrance's excellent lead. His fatal tee shot skied up and up and came down to a watery grave. The overly partisan home crowd immediately cheered another American misfortune, as they had done for much of the contest.

With the cheers and jeers of the crowd ringing in his ears as he walked down the fairway, Torrance's eyes filled with tears. He had the Ryder Cup firmly in his grasp.

On the victory march up the final fairway: *"I have dreamed about it all my life. It's just the greatest moment I have ever had. I've been crying all the way since the last tee."* —SAM TORRANCE

North took his drop and, without a shot in his bag long enough to clear the large lake, played his ball up the fairway behind Torrance's massive drive. The American put his fourth shot to the far left of the green, and with it went the United States' last hope of retaining the Ryder Cup.

Torrance hit what in normal circumstances would be a simple, nine-iron pitch shot to the huge green. With the crowd milling around him, he did not let his excited teammates down, floating his ball up to twenty feet of the hole. To the resounding cheers of the frenzied crowd, Torrance strode onto the final green brandishing his putter as though the lady of the lake had thrust it into his hand. Once the clamor had died down, North failed to make his five and slumped off with a disastrous double-bogey six. Torrance had four putts to halve the match and win the Ryder Cup. He needed only one.

Arms raised aloft, putter pointing skyward, Sam Torrance had done what no other European golfer had done for more than a quarter of a century: he had won the Ryder Cup.

"If I had known I was going to shoot that birdie on the eighteenth, I would have given Andy a par as we stood on the tee. At least he would have gone down with plenty of pride." —SAM TORRANCE

Torrance's struggling 76 had been enough to take the match and win the vital point that finally loosened the Americans' twenty-eight-year lock-tight grip on the Ryder Cup.

Mark O'Meara (USA) v. Howard Clark (EUR)

Mark O'Meara started dreadfully—four over par for the first five holes—and not surprisingly was three down to Howard Clark. The American recorded his first birdie on the 400-yard ninth, and it was enough for Clark to concede the hole. O'Meara cut the lead to one when he took the par-3 twelfth thanks to Clark's bogey.

The next four holes were halved in par, this sequence capped by O'Meara missing a birdie putt on sixteen that would have leveled the match. On seventeen, Clark had a chance to write his name in the record books. Having made a fine recovery from a fairway bunker, the Englishman had a four-foot putt to win the match and earn the point that would win the Ryder Cup.

"Before, when I'd played in the Ryder Cup, it had been in the company of Watson and Nicklaus. You felt two down as soon as they walked into the same room. This time it was different. The Americans had nobody with that charisma."
—*Howard Clark*

As luck would have it, a tentative putt ran around the cup and lipped out. Seconds later, a roar from the eighteenth told Clark that the Cup had been won . . . by Torrance.

With the Cup decided, the pair halved eighteen to give Clark some recompense for his fine fighting effort, a one-hole victory.

Hubert Green (USA) v. Nick Faldo (EUR)

A player who had rebuilt his game around shooting regulation golf, Nick Faldo surprisingly took seven holes to record his first par. The first six holes saw Faldo card three birdies and three bogeys that added up to a one-hole lead over the even more erratic Hubert Green, who had three bogeys and a solitary birdie.

If Faldo had started slightly the better, Green finished the stronger, one up after nine, thanks to Faldo's making double bogey and bogey at eight and nine. From here the American was never behind on the inward nine.

Yet another Faldo bogey at the par-3 twelfth put the U.S. side two up, but the Englishman birdied the 194-yard fourteen to lie one back. With many of his lesser-regarded teammates producing stunning wins all around him, Faldo's dismal day was complete when he bogeyed both sixteen and seventeen.

Faldo bogeyed nine of the seventeen holes, while Green needed only one birdie for a 3 and 1 win.

Calvin Peete (USA) v. Jose Rivero (EUR)

Having been hammered by Jose Rivero in his foursomes match, Calvin Peete was more than eager for some revenge.

Despite this extra incentive, the first seven holes were all halved in some uninspiring golf, neither player making a birdie. The lack of quality on the opening nine holes was emphasized by

Rivero's winning the eighth with a bogey, then claiming the ninth with the first birdie of the round.

Two up at the turn, Rivero looked to have Peete's number again, but full credit goes to the American, who came back home much the stronger.

With the Spaniard still holding a comfortable two-hole lead with four to play, Peete birdied the next three holes to clinch a somewhat unexpected last-gasp win on the final hole.

In the six singles matches that reached the final green, Peete was the only American to walk away with a win.

Rivero parred eight of the nine holes coming home, but it wasn't enough for him to hold on. Peete had gone out in 40 strokes but came back much the stronger to card a more convincing 34 for the one-hole win.

Fuzzy Zoeller (USA) v. Jose Maria Canizares (EUR)

Having matched birdies on the first hole, Jose Maria Canizares took the lead against Fuzzy Zoeller with a birdie at the par-5 fourth. The American soon hit back with his own birdie at the 396-yard sixth and took over the lead when Canizares conceded the eighth hole.

Zoeller could not hold on to his lead, bogeying the par-4 ninth to reach the turn all square. Neither player was able to assume control of the match as the pair halved the next seven holes in par. With the match building to a climax, Zoeller's game fell apart: he carded a bogey on the par-5 seventeenth and failed to hole out on the last to give the Spaniard a welcome two-hole win.

Surprisingly, Canizares—the oldest player in the whole contest—took 2½ points from his three matches, and was the only undefeated player on either team (2-0-1).

Curtis Strange (USA) v. Ken Brown (EUR)

Curtis Strange won this match with an outward nine of bogey-free golf, which he covered in 34 strokes, five shots better than Ken Brown. The American's only real concern was getting up and down for par from a bunker on the first hole.

Four up after six holes, Strange retained this lead to the turn, then went further ahead when Brown continued his bogey bonanza on the tenth. Although the Scot mounted something of a comeback with birdies at thirteen and fifteen, this was not enough. Strange was always far too strong for Brown, matching the birdie at thirteen and easing past the tenacious Scot with another birdie on sixteen, for a 4 and 2 win.

Strange was only the sixth player out of twenty-four to finish under par for his round—his gross 69 was matched only by Sandy Lyle. Tom Kite was the only other American to break par all day; his one-under-par tally was matched by three continental players: Ballesteros, Langer, and Pinero.

Day three result: USA 4½, EUR 7½
Overall match score: USA 11½, EUR 16½

"It's history, isn't it? I'm so proud of this team. And the way Torrance played the eighteenth hole. You just dream of winning the Ryder Cup that way. I've been fortunate to have won the U.S. and British Open championships, and this goes right alongside those as my greatest moments in golf. I didn't play this week, but I certainly felt I was a part of it."

—Tony Jacklin

Recap

And so the new order of golf had been ushered in. The European side, in only its fourth match against the United States, had finally produced the win that had painfully eluded the British side for twenty-eight years.

Coincidentally, the solid foundation of the European success was built around five players who were born around the time Britain last won the Ryder Cup, in 1957.

"Europeans have not been treated like U.S. golfers. This is a sign of progress in the European side. We need things like this to open people's eyes."
—*Tony Jacklin*

"The foreign group challenged and won and turned indifference into international intrigue because of that freak batch of child births in a calendar's time. You know the one, in 1957–58, when into the world came those named Seve Ballesteros, Nick Faldo, Bernhard Langer, Ian Woosnam, and Sandy Lyle. It is a rare overnight harvest second only to the unthinkable 1912 offering of Hogan–Snead–Nelson."

—Jeff Rude, *Golfweek* (1997)

What gladdened the hearts of all home supporters and put the fear of God into the visitors was the margin of victory—five points. The biggest U.S. defeat in Ryder Cup history was made even worse by the fact that the Americans actually held the lead after the first day.

"This doesn't signify any decline in American golf. It's a tremendous rise in European golf. . . . We took a smoking out there today. This is not a disgrace; we lost to a great team. I don't think my guys played as well as they can. Actually, I knew we were in trouble when we lost the fourball matches the first day." —LEE TREVINO

After Sutton complained about local British crowds: "I bet Hal Sutton can't wait to get back to America and head straight for McDonald's."
—*Tony Jacklin*

One unsavory aspect of the match was the effect the overly partisan and vociferous crowd had on the players. The jeering that greeted American mistakes was not new on either side of the Atlantic—but it did reach fever pitch on the highly emotional last day. This unfortunate by-product of the newly competitive Ryder Cup would be a necessary evil the players and officials from both sides would have to live with as long as they charged admission to get in.

"I knew how pumped up all the Europeans were, and all the players from Great Britain. I said to my guys, 'You are going to have a tough match. Also remember one thing: when you make a bogey, the crowd will scream like you've made eagle. These are things you have to deal with. The only way you can quiet a crowd down is with birdies.' And what happened was that my team just didn't make enough birdies. They were outplayed this week. It's evident from what has happened today." —LEE TREVINO

Jacklin was unable to have a final word with Trevino before the Americans left for the Concorde. But he noted, "I just wanted to tell him not to be too downhearted, because he won't be the last losing American captain."

The American postmortem began immediately after the Cup was lost. This team had been their weakest in many years, probably since the war. The superstar millionaires had grown fat off the uncompetitive PGA Tour that handsomely rewarded nonwinners. It was felt that Trevino, as captain, had not been strict enough or vocal enough in his instructions, although he skippered the side in the same time-honored democratic way most of his predecessors did.

What the Americans had found out was that the European tour had finally matured and was a viable opponent for the once-unconquerable Americans. From this momentous day forth, the Ryder Cup would no longer be a tap-in for the Americans; it had become a five-foot downhill putt with a nasty break at the end.

"European golf came of age when Sam Torrance sank his winning putt on the eighteenth against Andy North. . . . Nobody knew Seve when he came out. When Bernhard Langer came out, they asked, 'Who's this German guy?' Wait till the 1987 Ryder Cup match. You'll be seeing players from Sweden." —TONY JACKLIN

Match Results (Winning side marked in *italics*.)

Friday, September 13—Morning Foursomes

	USA	EUR	Score
1.	Curtis Strange Mark O'Meara	*Seve Ballesteros* *Manuel Pinero*	2 and 1
2.	*Calvin Peete* *Tom Kite*	Bernhard Langer Nick Faldo	3 and 2
3.	*Lanny Wadkins* *Raymond Floyd*	Sandy Lyle Ken Brown	4 and 3
4.	*Craig Stadler* *Hal Sutton*	Howard Clark Sam Torrance	3 and 2

Friday, September 13—Afternoon Fourball

	USA	EUR	Score
5.	Fuzzy Zoeller Hubert Green	*Paul Way* *Ian Woosnam*	1-up
6.	Andy North Peter Jacobsen	*Seve Ballesteros* *Manuel Pinero*	2 and 1
7.	Craig Stadler Hal Sutton	Bernhard Langer Jose Maria Canizares	halved
8.	*Raymond Floyd* *Lanny Wadkins*	Sam Torrance Howard Clark	1-up

Day one result: USA 4½, EUR 3½

Saturday, September 14—Morning Fourball

	USA	EUR	Score
9.	Tom Kite Andy North	*Sam Torrance* *Howard Clark*	2 and 1
10.	Hubert Green Fuzzy Zoeller	*Paul Way* *Ian Woosnam*	4 and 3
11.	*Mark O'Meara* *Lanny Wadkins*	Seve Ballesteros Manuel Pinero	3 and 2
12.	Craig Stadler Curtis Strange	Bernhard Langer Sandy Lyle	halved

Saturday, September 14—Afternoon Foursomes

	USA	EUR	Score
13.	Tom Kite Calvin Peete	*Jose Maria Canizares* *Jose Rivero*	7 and 5
14.	Craig Stadler Hal Sutton	*Seve Ballesteros* *Manuel Pinero*	5 and 4
15.	*Curtis Strange* *Peter Jacobsen*	Paul Way Ian Woosnam	4 and 2
16.	Raymond Floyd Lanny Wadkins	*Bernhard Langer* *Ken Brown*	3 and 2

Day two result: USA 2½, EUR 5½

Overall match score: USA 7, EUR 9

Sunday, September 15—Singles

	USA	EUR	Score
17.	Lanny Wadkins	*Manuel Pinero*	3 and 1
18.	*Craig Stadler*	Ian Woosnam	2 and 1
19.	Raymond Floyd	*Paul Way*	2-up
20.	Tom Kite	Seve Ballesteros	halved
21.	Peter Jacobsen	*Sandy Lyle*	3 and 2
22.	Hal Sutton	*Bernhard Langer*	5 and 4
23.	Andy North	*Sam Torrance*	1-up
24.	Mark O'Meara	*Howard Clark*	1-up
25.	*Hubert Green*	Nick Faldo	3 and 1
26.	*Calvin Peete*	Jose Rivero	1-up
27.	Fuzzy Zoeller	*Jose Maria Canizares*	2-up
28.	*Curtis Strange*	Ken Brown	4 and 2

Day three result: USA 4½, EUR 7½

Overall match score: USA 11½, EUR 16½

1987

Muirfield Village
Dublin, Ohio
United States
September 25–27

United States 13	**Europe 15**
Andy Bean	Seve Ballesteros (Spain)
Mark Calcavecchia	Gordon Brand, Jr. (Scotland)
Ben Crenshaw	Ken Brown (Scotland)
Tom Kite	Howard Clark (England)
Larry Mize	Eamonn Darcy (Ireland)
Larry Nelson	Nick Faldo (England)
Dan Pohl	Bernhard Langer (Germany)
Scott Simpson	Sandy Lyle (Scotland)
Payne Stewart	Jose Maria Olazabal (Spain)
Curtis Strange	Jose Rivero (Spain)
Hal Sutton	Sam Torrance (Scotland)
Lanny Wadkins	Ian Woosnam (Wales)
Captain	**Captain**
Jack Nicklaus	Tony Jacklin (England)

The Course That Jack Built, The Cause That Tony Built

"For sixty years the American sporting public has regarded the Ryder Cup, insofar as it was aware of its existence, as a quaint ritual of no competitive relevance. The one-sided results distressingly confirmed this judgment that the matches were on a rough par with the Tennessee Frog Jumping Festival. But times are a-changin' and the Europeans come to Dublin, Ohio, as holders of the beautiful golden chalice."

—Peter Dobereiner, *Golf World*

Quite simply, Muirfield Village was one of the best courses that had been privileged to host the Ryder Cup. Meticulously designed and built by Jack Nicklaus, it was named in deference to Muirfield, in Scotland, where the Golden Bear had many notable career moments (debut in Walker Cup, win in the 1966 British Open).

The Muirfield course in Scotland also hosted the Ryder Cup in 1973.

And so, in 1987, the name Muirfield would once again loom large in the personal annals of Jack Nicklaus—for all the wrong reasons. In the sixty-year history of the competition, the visitors to American soil had never won the Ryder Cup. In fact, the visitors had rarely and barely troubled their hosts. This year would change all that, as the United States lost the Ryder Cup for the first time on home soil and for the second time in a row (another unwelcome first).

"As nonplaying captain of the American team and host at his own golf club, Nicklaus has done everything humanly possible to insure that the matches will be a sporting occasion somewhere between the World Series and the Third World War, the way we in Europe have always esteemed the biennial confrontation between European and American professionals." —PETER DOBEREINER, *Golf World*

If Nicklaus was the architect of the golf course, his opposing captain, Tony Jacklin, was the architect of this historic European win. Once again, Jacklin was armed with the more experienced side, with only two rookies: Olazabal and Brand. Almost half of Nicklaus's team was fresh to the Ryder Cup: Calcavecchia, Mize, Pohl, Simpson, and Stewart.

"We all believe we can win on American soil for the first time. . . . I have been coming to America for twenty years, and this is the first time I am really confident of winning." —*Tony Jacklin*

Jacklin again did things in his own forthright, no-nonsense way. He warned three of his minor players they might not play until the obligatory singles; in the event, Rivero, Brand, and Darcy all played in the first two days. Jacklin told The Players Championship champion Sandy Lyle he would not be playing in the foursomes, since his game was not suited to it, although Lyle did play in the foursomes on day two.

Jacklin was not afraid to upset his players. Nicklaus, like many U.S. captains who had preceded him, took a more cautious, kid-glove approach. He paired Kite and Strange simply because they wanted to play together and he wanted both of them to play. Nicklaus worked it so that all twelve of his team played in the first six matches, which might have been a crucial slip. In these six matches, Europe opened up a vital two-point gap.

"Our guys are aware that they can be beaten. But the European side winning last time is more of an advantage to us." —*Jack Nicklaus*

The major impact Europe's 1985 win had on the Ryder Cup was to increase public and media interest—on both sides of the Atlantic.

For the first time in the United States, a major TV network (ABC) took full coverage of the three days of action. Plans were drawn up to add an extra day of singles especially for the TV audience, but Jacklin soon quashed this idea, if for no other reason than the fact the U.S. side had always dominated the singles. An extra day of singles would be a major handicap against Europe. So the format stayed the same and the Ryder Cup stayed in the same hands.

In an extraordinary show of player power, orchestrated by the team captain, the European players had a forthright meeting with their PGA executives the night before the tournament started. The players aired their many grievances about the way the tour was run and the way the players were treated. This was a masterstroke by Jacklin, since it focused his team's collective mind.

Course Details

Hole	Distance	Par	Hole	Distance	Par
1	446	4	10	441	4
2	452	4	11	538	5
3	392	4	12	156	3
4	204	3	13	442	4
5	531	5	14	363	4
6	430	4	15	490	5
7	549	5	16	204	3
8	189	3	17	430	4
9	410	4	18	437	4
		36			**36 = Par 72 (7,104 yards)**

Course designer: Jack Nicklaus

Day One: Morning Foursomes

A beautiful, fresh sunny morning brought temperatures in the mid-eighties by noon.

Curtis Strange and Tom Kite (USA) v. Sam Torrance and Howard Clark (EUR)

Europe's opening drive set the scene for its early-morning suffering: Clark found sand off the first tee to go one down to an American par. Strange won the second with a birdie putt from more than thirty feet, following Kite's fine five-iron to the green. Torrance and Clark steadied themselves by halving the next two holes in par but lost the plot on the fifth as they carded a double-bogey seven, only just beaten by an American bogey six.

Three up after five holes, the U.S. pair secured nine halves in par over the next ten holes—the exception being the 549-yard seventh, where Strange and Torrance exchanged twelve-foot birdie putts.

> "Sam and Howard didn't play to their capabilities, while we just had a nice solid round. When we were two up, it was just a case of making steady pars."
> —*Tom Kite*

Three up with three to play, the Americans' thirteenth par in sixteen holes sewed up the victory, after Torrance had bunkered his tee shot to the par-3 green. The first match went to the home side by a very comfortable 4 and 2.

Hal Sutton and Dan Pohl (USA) v. Ken Brown and Bernhard Langer (EUR)

With Dan Pohl not only making his Ryder Cup debut but also playing foursomes for the first time in his life, it was not surprising that he and Sutton dropped the first hole with a bogey to Brown and Langer. Having both made mistakes with their first shots, Pohl and Sutton knuckled down to the task at hand and profited as the Europeans' game fell apart at the seams.

Brown could not get out of a wicked lie in a bunker on the second, while Pohl made a confidence-boosting par putt from all of eighteen feet to square the match. Brown's tee shot at the 204-yard fourth failed to find the putting surface, allowing the U.S. pair two putts to win the hole in par and go one up.

European bogeys at eight and eleven (after three putts) were highly contagious, as the Americans bogeyed twelve to hold a two-hole cushion. When the visitors again failed to make par on the 442-yard thirteenth, the lead was back to three, but they made amends at fourteen with Brown's twenty-foot putt—the only European birdie of the day.

Pohl and Sutton managed to halve the next three holes in par for a second U.S. win of the morning, 2 and 1.

Lanny Wadkins and Larry Mize (USA) v. Nick Faldo and Ian Woosnam (EUR)

Nick Faldo and Ian Woosnam were paired in what turned out to be the start of a beautiful friendship—they formed one of Europe's main pairings of the next few Ryder Cups. In their first match together, they were faced with Lanny Wadkins and Larry Mize in a remarkable morning of up-and-down golf. Only one hole on the front nine was not won or lost—the 189-yard eighth, halved in par threes.

The Americans birdied the first hole, which, coupled with pars at the next two holes, was enough for a three-hole lead, as the Europeans played as if they were the worst partners since Samson and Delilah. In an amazing sequence of scoring, Wadkins and Mize went bogey, par, bogey, birdie to win, lose, win, win—four, five, six, and seven—somehow retaining their three-hole lead.

The eighth was halved in par, and another American par at nine was sufficient for a four-hole buffer at the turn, which the European juggernaut reached in a misfiring 40 strokes. The British players must have had a five-star tune-up at the halfway stage, because what followed bore no comparison to their early-morning woes.

Faldo nailed his three-iron to the shadow of the pin on the par-4 tenth, and Woosnam holed the five-foot birdie putt with a flourish to cut the lead to three. The tiny par-3 twelfth saw Wadkins find sand off the tee, and the lead was down to two. Having lost two holes in three after the turn, the Americans succumbed to the pressure, whereas their opponents were just starting to enjoy themselves.

"We don't need any motivation. We are playing for history. It's like playing for your life."
—*Nick Faldo*

Fourteen saw another disastrous drive from Wadkins, who had started to play like someone who had suddenly discovered that slicing was an art form. His tee shot found the creek and another bogey, leaving the U.S. pair one up.

With the dazed Americans on the ropes and fighting to save the match, Woosnam delivered the knockout punch. A superhuman one-iron from over 250 yards found the central core of the fifteenth green. Although Faldo could not hole the long eagle putt, birdie was good enough to square the match.

Woosnam continued his one-man comeback tour by holing a difficult putt on seventeen. Even at the death, the Americans shot themselves in the feet, as Wadkins had an eleven-foot birdie putt on seventeen to halve the hole. His downhill putt hit the hole and squirted out far enough for Mize to miss the return putt; the Americans were behind for the first time.

On the final hole, Woosnam played such a superb recovery from a bunker that Faldo was not asked to putt out from two feet.

A tale of two sickies: Europe limped out in 40 and the United States crawled back in the same score.

A disappointing and equally disappointed U.S. pair finished bogey-bogey, putting an error-ridden exclamation point on a remarkable six-hole swing on the back nine to give Europe their first point, 2-up.

Larry Nelson and Payne Stewart (USA) v. Seve Ballesteros and Jose Maria Olazabal (EUR)

Larry Nelson started this match with a perfect 9-0 Ryder Cup record and was entrusted with schooling the rookie Payne Stewart in the perplexities of match play. Ballesteros took on the task of tutoring a rookie of his own—Jose Maria Olazabal, who had struggled in the practice rounds.

It was the American rookie who made his mark first: Stewart holed a nine-foot birdie putt on the opening hole for the lead. Ballesteros and Olazabal answered with a birdie of their own on the second, easily accounting for an American bogey. When Nelson fired his tee shot to within a yard of the fourth flag, the lead was restored, and the veteran American holed from off the green at five for a birdie that doubled the lead.

After winning the 430-yard sixth and halving seven, the Spaniards also won the par-3 eighth, Ballesteros holing a putt just shy of thirty feet for a birdie. With the score all square, the U.S. pair needed three stabs on the putting surface at the ninth, reaching the turn behind for the first time in the match. The Americans would not hold the lead again.

Twenty-one-year-old Olazabal occasionally showed his rookie nerves with some wayward shot-making, but his irrepressible partner backed his own genius and more often than not got his side out of trouble. On ten, Ballesteros hit a three-iron 190 yards from a bunker up onto the green to save a half.

The Americans pulled level on the par-5 eleventh, Stewart leaving his third shot nine feet from the flag for Nelson to RSVP the birdie invitation. Nelson had trouble in a bunker on twelve, the resulting bogey costing his side the hole, the same fate that greeted Seve on the next hole.

All square after thirteen, the match was still there for the taking. Not surprisingly, Ballesteros was the player who did the taking, with a defining chip inside a yard of the fifteenth flag to set up Olazabal for a simple birdie putt.

The Europeans held this lead until the last hole, where Olazabal found another fairway bunker off the tee, Ballesteros once again making a matchless long-iron recovery to set up a thirty-foot putt. Meanwhile, Stewart's ball missed the green, back right, scattering a few spectators in its wake. From a precarious downhill and perilously downtrodden lie, Nelson played a superbly judged chip-and-run to four feet, recovering a seemingly hopeless situation.

Olazabal was also up to the task that his senior partner had left him, as he rolled his long putt around ninety degrees of slope, allowing the ball to run down to five feet of the hole. Ballesteros made the putt to halve the hole and take the one-hole win.

The Spaniards were the only pairing to break par all morning, with a two-under 70.

Morning foursomes result: USA 2, EUR 2

Having lost the first two foursomes matches, Europe had looked as if it might swallow a whitewash, but the side struck back strongly to share the morning spoils. In his final two selections, Jacklin had found two perfect pairings that would pay handsome dividends in the future.

Day One: Afternoon Fourball

The warming rays of the late-September sun quickly dried out the greens, and the Americans took longer to adapt to the changing conditions.

"The afternoon was a rout . . ."
—*John Radosta,* New York Times

Ben Crenshaw and Scott Simpson (USA) v. Gordon Brand and Jose Rivero (EUR)

With little or no preparation time, having replaced Clark and Torrance at the last minute, Brand and Rivero both bogeyed the first to go one down. From there on in, the favored pairing of Crenshaw and Simpson were put to the sword over the next three holes. On the second, Rivero got into his rhythm with a beautifully weighted birdie putt from eight feet, while on the third, both Europeans left their second shots close to the flag for certain birdies and a lead.

The unheralded Scot increased the lead to two, making his second birdie at the 531-yard fifth, and produced a thirty-foot birdie putt on the par-5 seventh to prevent Simpson from capitalizing on his almost perfect chip to eight inches. Brand was on fire on the greens, and he choked the hole with another long putt on the ninth—a twenty-five-footer that bought him his fourth birdie on the outward stretch.

Three down at the turn was soon four, as the U.S. players both failed to make par on the tenth. The Americans finally managed to record their first win since the opening hole when Crenshaw made his seven-foot birdie putt count at the par-3 twelfth.

With six holes left, the Americans knew they needed to play error-free golf to gain a chance of halving, let alone winning, the match. But the Americans made errors that proved to be very costly, both players failing to deliver critical putts.

First, Crenshaw clunked a six-footer on fourteen, and two holes later his partner was even more culpable. After Simpson had almost nailed his tee shot to the flag on the 204-yard sixteenth, Rivero had a four-foot putt that could have sealed the match, but it lipped out as so many had before. With the hole at his mercy, Simpson's three-foot stone-cold cert also brushed the lip of the cup and stayed aloft.

Finishing with four straight pars was enough for the Europeans to hang on to their lead and register a highly deserved—but highly unexpected—3 and 2 victory.

Andy Bean and Mark Calcavecchia (USA) v. Sandy Lyle and Bernhard Langer (EUR)

The basic idea of fourball play is for one of the partners to cover the other's error—it is not to have both partners three-putt the first green. This is how Bean and Calcavecchia started off, and they soon found themselves two down after the third hole, where Lyle made the first birdie of the match.

After the next three holes had been halved in par, the Americans tore off three straight wins with fine birdies. The 430-yard sixth fell to the twenty-seven-year-old rookie Calcavecchia, who needed only two solid putts from fifty feet. The seventh belonged to an Andy Bean eight-foot birdie putt, while the 189-yard eighth was tamed by Calcavecchia's impressive thirty-footer for a one-hole lead at the turn.

Lyle and Langer could muster only one birdie between them, and reached the turn in 35 strokes, one more than their rivals. The European birdie drought ended with a three on the 441-yard tenth to level the match, but Bean drained an eleven-footer on eleven to reinflate the one-hole cushion. With the twelfth halved in par threes, Calcavecchia continued his hot hand on the greens with a twelve-foot birdie putt on thirteen. This success meant Calcavecchia and Bean had turned a two-hole deficit into a two-hole credit within seven holes.

Just as the home team looked to be coasting to an easy victory, the more experienced European pair bravely fought back. Langer birdied the par-4 fourteenth with a treacherous-looking eight-foot downhill putt to cut the lead to one. Lyle saved the half on the sixteenth green with a crucial thirty-footer for par, and the Scot's par won the 430-yard seventeenth when the Americans both failed to make theirs.

All square at the last, the Americans hit their second shots through the green. Lyle safely found the target, but a long way from the flag. Neither American was able to get up and down in two, which allowed Lyle to run his putt to within a few feet, which he holed for the outright win by one hole.

"That's like stealing a point there. When you start losing these holes to pars, that's not good when you are playing best-ball."
—*Dave Marr,* ABC TV

Hal Sutton and Dan Pohl (USA) v. Nick Faldo and Ian Woosnam (EUR)

Jacklin retained the services of his two successful pairings from the morning, sending Faldo and Woosnam out against another winning combination in Sutton and Pohl.

Having halved the first ten holes (eight pars and two birdies), the Americans looked as if they would go one up—until Woosnam benefited from a stupendous slice of good luck on the par-5 eleventh. His extremely wild and wayward second shot crashed into an overhanging branch, bounced down onto the green, and rolled toward the hole. Instead of reaching for a machete and his wedge, Woosnam was able to reach for his putter to cut down an eleven-foot putt for an outrageous eagle to take the lead.

On the par-3 twelfth, Faldo hit a seven-iron tee shot over the large lake in front of the green and saw his ball just creep onto the putting surface. Sutton hit a similar shot right at the flag, ending up four feet away in pole position. With the Americans holding the advantage, Faldo sent his twenty-four-foot putt racing hopefully toward the hole; his ball rattled into the back of the cup and disappeared for a birdie two. Needless to say, Sutton missed his downhill birdie putt, lipping out on the left. Europe was two up, when they could so easily have been two down.

Woosnam's eagle on eleven was the first of the whole contest.

Sutton reversed the trend on thirteen when he made a sixteen-foot putt count for a birdie that the Europeans could have matched. After Faldo had knocked his own ball from a greenside bunker to inside a foot for a gimme par, Woosnam missed his own short birdie putt.

The Welshman atoned for his putting error, knocking his tee shot to within a couple of feet at fourteen for another birdie to restore the lead to two. Sutton and Pohl were unable to crack their opponents as the last three holes were halved.

The British better-ball blasted round in a net 65 (seven under), the best of the day . . . until the Spaniards behind them finished a few minutes later.

Woosnam sealed the win with a marvelous approach to seventeen that finished seventeen feet to the left of the flag, in the light fringe. Pohl played an even better shot, his ball rolling eight feet past the pin. Not to be denied any glory, Woosnam stroked his putt a few inches past the hole. Pohl could do no better, and the match went to Europe, 2 and 1.

Curtis Strange and Tom Kite (USA) v. Seve Ballesteros and Jose Maria Olazabal (EUR)

Ballesteros and Olazabal continued their mercurial form from the morning, taking the first hole off the tough American pair of Kite and Strange in typically cavalier fashion.

Ballesteros asked his partner to putt out for par on the first green to allow him to ponder his chip shot. Strange immediately refused this request, claiming Olazabal would have to step on his line to make the putt. Undaunted, Seve shrugged his shoulders and simply holed his chip shot from over forty feet away. The stuff that legends are made of.

Ballesteros continued to blow hot and cold, missing a four-foot birdie putt on the par-3 fourth for a win, then making a twenty-footer on the sixth to go two up. This typified the early European onslaught, as Kite had to hole a slippery eleven-foot birdie putt on seven to secure a half.

"This has nothing to do with money. It's bigger than that. This is playing for Uncle Sam, and Sam expects a lot."
—*Tom Kite*

Olazabal's twelve-foot birdie putt on eight saw the Spanish combo out in 32 strokes with a three-hole lead. Not to be outshone by his protégé, Ballesteros again brought the stupefied crowd to their feet with a fabulous fifty-footer that homed in on the tenth hole.

At four down, and sensing the match was ebbing away, Strange made a telling birdie four at eleven. With the Europeans contributing to their own downfall on twelve—a Ballesteros lip-out on a seven-foot putt that would have halved the hole—the lead was cut to two. The 363-yard fourteenth saw excellent approaches from both sides result in a pair of seven-foot putts for birdies.

On fifteen, it was Ballesteros's turn to make an eleven-foot birdie putt just for the half. With sixteen halved in par, Kite played an eight-iron pin high on seventeen, eleven feet from the flag, while Strange stapled his approach just inside his partner's ball. Ballesteros's second shot, from much closer to the green, finished almost twice as far from the hole as the Americans'. It made no difference to the Spaniard, who impassively holed his longer putt, for his seventh birdie of the round, sealing the 2 and 1 win.

On his having carded a net 64, the best round of the day: *"Today was the best I have played in three months. There are so many people here from Europe [two thousand fans], I didn't want to let them down. When you play for so many it makes you strong."* —SEVE BALLESTEROS

Afternoon fourball result: USA 0, EUR 4

Winning only ten of the sixty-eight holes played in the afternoon, this was the first time the Americans had been swept in a Ryder Cup session. The previous closest had been Great Britain's 3½ points out of 4 in the first day's foursomes in 1969.

Day one result: USA 2, EUR 6

Day Two: Morning Foursomes

Sending a warning out to his players: *"Everyone on my team has played now. From now I'll pick only the best players. I've told them, 'If you don't win, you don't play.'"* —JACK NICKLAUS

Curtis Strange and Tom Kite (USA) v. Jose Rivero and Gordon Brand (EUR)

Nicklaus's top-rated pairing of Strange and Kite lost the first hole to Brand's forty-foot birdie putt, but Strange holed his own longish birdie putt to level the match after two. The next three holes were halved, with Brand and Rivero conceding a lead to par when they could not recover from a bunker upside the sixth.

The visitors immediately pulled level with another birdie on seven, on the strength of Rivero's eight-foot putt. The Europeans' up-and-down play continued as Strange and Kite took eight and

Strange and Kite was the only pairing Nicklaus retained from the cataclysmic clean sweep the previous afternoon.

nine with pars for a two-hole lead at the turn. The lead would have been three if the Spaniard had not holed a monster fifty-footer on the ninth just to make a half.

With Rivero only six feet shy of the hole in three, Strange and Kite made bogey six at the 420-yard eleventh. Having played superbly, Rivero saw his game fall apart on the par-3 twelfth when his ball took a dip in the small lake, resulting in a double-bogey five to the Americans' almost wasteful birdie two.

Despite dropping fourteen to par, the U.S. pair won two of the last three holes played. Strange made a fifteen-foot birdie putt on the 490-yard fifteenth to go two up, and he closed out Rivero and Brand, 3 and 1, with a highly polished seven-iron approach to five feet of the seventeenth flag.

Hal Sutton and Larry Mize (USA) v. Nick Faldo and Ian Woosnam (EUR)

In a sloppy contest, all four players missed too many chances and made too many mistakes. Apart from the first hole, which Sutton and Mize won birdie to Faldo and Woosnam's bogey, the U.S. pair was down for most of the match. The Americans were unable to cut into the slim European lead, mainly due to Sutton's lack of finishing touch on the greens. Although the first six holes were won or lost, the U.S. players could not regain the lead they had on the first hole.

Faldo had wanted to sit out this match due to his inconsistent play on the first day. He was not much more fluent on the opening four holes, as Europe opened bogey-birdie-birdie-bogey.

With Sutton finding the sand on nine, the Americans limped to the turn having carded a double-bogey six to the Europeans' birdie three. Both pairs played the front nine over par, but it was the British who held a one-hole lead. Woosnam doubled the lead with a fourteen-foot putt on ten, but his English partner—still struggling with his swing and all-around play—cost his side the eleventh with their second six of the round.

On the next green, Mize jumped in jubilation, having holed a sixteen-foot birdie putt, but the American was brought crashing down to turf by Faldo's serenely stroked eight-footer for a matching birdie two. The far-from-happy Englishman needed to make another scrambling par putt at the 442-yard thirteenth hole to repel an American win.

With Europe still one up after sixteen, Woosnam hit a nine-iron pitch to four feet of the seventeenth hole to seemingly seal the victory, but Mize was able to hole his own twelve-foot putt for an invaluable half.

The British players were unable to protect their narrow lead on the final hole, taking four shots to reach the green, with the U.S. pair on in two. Sutton played his putt up to the hole from twelve feet away, allowing Mize to calmly hole out. Europe had to be content with walking off the eighteenth with a half, but the win had been theirs for the taking.

Lanny Wadkins and Larry Nelson (USA) v. Sandy Lyle and Bernhard Langer (EUR)

This was the first time Wadkins and Nelson had partnered each other since 1979, having been 4-0 in the matches they played together. Wadkins did not play in 1981, while Nelson missed out in the next two meetings.

A sense of comedy and tragedy pervaded the first green as Wadkins and Nelson started drive, pitch, putt, putt, chip, putt—for a double-bogey six. The trouble started after Wadkins had putted up to inside ten feet of the hole. Nelson charged his putt past the cup, and the ball continued rolling on and on and on and off the green. Suitably nonplussed, Wadkins chipped back for Nelson to make sure with his second putt of the round on the first hole.

The embarrassed Americans were soon back on level terms with Lyle and Langer when Wadkins holed a ten-footer on the 204-yard fourth hole. Sandy Lyle, who had previously been "banned" from the foursomes by Jacklin, proved he was a valuable team player with winning putts of six and twelve feet at the fifth and sixth holes.

The Americans' par reduced the lead on the seventh, and they made birdies on nine and ten, Wadkins holing from sixteen feet and Nelson from six feet. Having battled hard to remain all square after ten, the U.S. pair was ripped apart by a piece of pure magic from Lyle. On the 538-yard eleventh, the Scot crushed a two-iron inches from the hole. The Americans had no answer, conceding the gimme for an eagle and the hole to go one down.

Langer stretched the lead, accounting for the 442-yard thirteenth with a birdie putt from twenty-eight feet. After the Americans had double-botched the hole, Lyle applied the killer blow on fifteen, rolling his twenty-two-foot par putt up to the hole for the win.

Three down with three to play, Nelson hit a scorching tee shot to the par-3 sixteenth, his ball almost running right over the hole.

Wadkins knocked the eight-foot birdie putt into the middle of the cup and the lead was down to two.

On seventeen, Lyle's pitch came up twenty-five feet short of the hole, while Wadkins chipped out of a deep greenside bunker to within six feet. Langer putted up a few feet short, but Lyle closed out the match in par and a 2 and 1 victory.

Ben Crenshaw and Payne Stewart (USA) v. Seve Ballesteros and Jose Maria Olazabal (EUR.)

If Ballesteros had been Olazabal's guardian angel on the first day, the younger Spaniard returned the favor on day two. Three up after twelve against Crenshaw and Stewart, the Europeans looked to be coasting thanks to some excellent work by Olazabal. He made telling putts on the second and sixth, from thirty-three and sixteen feet, to give the Spaniards a two-hole lead.

When the Spanish players lost their ball in the water on nine, Crenshaw and Stewart not only failed to make them pay, but contrived to lose the hole with a disastrous double-bogey six of their own.

"Seve is a genius, one of the few geniuses in the game. The thing is, Seve is never in trouble. He's in the trees a lot, but that's not trouble for him. That's normal."
—*Ben Crenshaw*

The Americans dragged themselves back into the match with a win at fourteen, despite Olazabal's brilliant recovery after Ballesteros put his shot into another water hazard. Seve was unable to convert Olazabal's chip, which pitched past the hole and ran back down the slope to within eight feet. Crenshaw read the sloping green to perfection, his thirty-foot birdie putt looping a few feet past the hole, and Stewart holed the come-backer for the win.

On seventeen, Crenshaw's pitch almost ran straight into the hole, coming to rest eight inches short of the cup. Conceding the gimme, Ballesteros was faced with an eighteen-foot putt that could settle the match, but he raced the ball by the hole.

Having got back into the match by reaching the eighteenth one down, the Americans blew their chance. Crenshaw put his drive into a bunker, and Stewart left a poor recovery short of the green. Too delicate with his short chip shot, Crenshaw found sand for the second time in as many shots, this time at the front of the green. The only saving grace for the self-destructing Americans was that Ballesteros had not played the hole any better. After Olazabal's fine tee shot, Ballesteros put his approach into a different greenside bunker. With the touch of a low-handicap angel, Olazabal played a beautiful recovery to the green, the ball curling and settling six feet behind the hole. After Stewart had knocked his own excellent recovery shot to seven feet, Crenshaw made the must-make bogey putt.

With a dastardly downhill par putt of similar distance, Ballesteros delicately rolled his seven-footer down the green and watched incredulously as the ball gathered speed, slipping six feet beyond the hole.

Having played the hole perfectly, Olazabal was left to pick up the pieces again, needing to hole a six-foot teaser to halve the hole and secure the overall win. A shamefaced Ballesteros held his head in his hands as the youngster went back to work. Olazabal was more than up to the task, his nerveless putt securing Europe another point. A thankful Ballesteros rushed over and bear-hugged his partner off the ground.

Morning foursomes result: USA 1½, EUR 2½

"This is the hardest job I've ever had in my entire career. Every other time I've been on a golf course, I've been in control, and I don't like this one little bit." —Jack Nicklaus

Day Two: Afternoon Fourball

Having struggled in the first three sessions to read the pace of the drying greens (14 on the stimpmeter), the Americans fared much better off their own ball in the afternoon.

Curtis Strange and Tom Kite (USA) v. Nick Faldo and Ian Woosnam (EUR)

With three birdies from Faldo and two from Woosnam, the British pair produced one of the greatest starts in Ryder Cup history (3-3-3-2-4). The shell-shocked Kite and Strange parred the first five holes and were five down.

Woosnam started the rout by bolting his second shot to two feet at the first hole. Faldo carried on the carnage with two short birdie putts on the second and third. Woosnam made a birdie two on the fourth from fourteen feet, and Faldo birdied the 531-yard fifth with the shortest putt the British had needed to make.

"I don't think the Americans knew what hit them, because Woosie and I birdied the first five holes. I remember we both played like dreams. . . .

Sometimes when you're playing with Woosie, you feel like putting a pair of reins on him and holding him back. Not on this day: we both played some unbelievable golf." —NICK FALDO

The overwhelmed Americans actually birdied the sixth to get their pride back on track and the lead back to four, but Faldo struck again, with a birdie two at the eighth. The British players reached the turn in a scintillating 29 better-ball score, and they were not yet through with sticking a sizable suffering on the Americans.

Woosnam pitched up to a yard on the tenth for the Europeans' seventh birdie in ten holes, good for a commanding six-hole lead. The U.S. pair finally salvaged something from this savaging with its own unanswered birdies on eleven (Kite from nine feet) and twelve (Strange from eight feet).

Four up with six to play, Faldo and Woosnam slammed the door on the number one American combination when Faldo's fifteen-footer at thirteen left his side dormie five.

Woosnam, who had been dazzling all the way, hit a telling second to within four feet at fourteen. Kite and Strange followed with equally impressive pitches, the former holing his fourteen-footer for a birdie three. Almost disdainfully, Woosnam drove his own birdie putt home for the crushing 5 and 4 win.

The British pair not only collared Nicklaus's top dogs but also tamed his course, carding an unbelievable ten under par for the fourteen holes.

Andy Bean and Payne Stewart (USA) v. Eamonn Darcy and Gordon Brand (EUR)

With their backs against the wall, Bean and Stewart came out firing and reached the turn in 29 strokes, matching the bombs Faldo and Woosnam were detonating ahead of them. Like the British pair in front, the Americans birdied the first five holes, but they had only a four-hole lead. Darcy and Brand managed their first birdie at the 392-yard third to puncture the Americans' perfect start.

Without a five on their card, Bean and Stewart failed to make birdies at only two of the first ten holes. Six up with eight to play, the Americans would have set a new record for the biggest margin of victory with back-to-back wins, but the European pair was not yet ready for the record books.

To Brand and Darcy's credit, with the Irishman playing his first match of the weekend, it was they who won three out of the next four holes to cut the lead in half. This spirited British rally was too little too late, and they bowed out 3 and 2 on the sixteenth.

Hal Sutton and Larry Mize (USA) v. Seve Ballesteros and Jose Maria Olazabal (EUR)

As the two pairs ahead of him set the fairways and greens on fire, Hal Sutton turned into a one-man trailblazer, with four birdies of his own in the first seven holes. Larry Mize was happy to play a watching role, as two birdies from Olazabal—on three and six—prevented Sutton from blowing Europe's lights out before the turn. Olazabal and Ballesteros failed to make par on the ninth and sank to three behind at halfway.

The first two holes home were halved in par, before the Spanish made their expected move. Olazabal started with a birdie two at the twelfth, while Ballesteros finally contributed to the match with his own birdie at thirteen. The United States was now only one up with five to play—and facing a surging Spanish offensive.

Olazabal's second to fourteen landed twelve feet from the target, and Sutton followed him in, stopping his ball in the shadow of the flag. Mize outdid his partner's fine effort as his ball circled a few inches round the back of the hole. Having conceded Mize's gimme, Olazabal holed his birdie putt for the half.

On the par-3 sixteenth, Sutton's tee shot was straight at the flag, six feet shy of the hole. After missing the green with his first two shots, Ballesteros chipped his ball in from ten feet for a par. Not letting Ballesteros's showmanship affect him, Sutton calmly rolled his birdie putt straight into the hole to go two up with two to play.

On seventeen, Seve faced a ten-foot putt from the back of the green to keep Europe's hopes alive, but he pushed the ball to the right of the hole and the match went with it, 2 and 1.

Lanny Wadkins and Larry Nelson (USA) v. Sandy Lyle and Bernhard Langer (EUR)

Having been beaten for the first time in five matches, by Lyle and Langer in the morning foursomes, Wadkins and Nelson were glad to be given an immediate chance to get back on the winning trail.

For the fourth match in a row, the first hole gave up a decisive win to set up another contest of quality golf under pressure. Sandy Lyle struck first, holing his eight-foot putt to gain an opening advantage. Langer matched his partner's birdie with one from fifteen feet on the second hole, but Wadkins neutralized the German's strike with a twelve-footer of his own.

With birdies on the fourth and sixth, the Americans turned a one-hole deficit into a lead, which they lost on the seventh to a European birdie. All square through nine holes, both pairs were out in a modest 33 strokes.

Upside the tenth green, Langer encountered some ugly rough but dug his ball out and sent it scurrying into the hole for another birdie. No one was more stunned at the result than the German, who collapsed in joy. With his side back up by one, the Scot got his name on the scorecard with a hole-winning birdie at twelve, for two up.

With Langer and Nelson planting their approach shots within eight feet of the hole on the par-4 fourteenth, Lyle calmly rolled in his eighteen-foot par putt. Langer missed his birdie putt, leaving Nelson with a downhill eight-footer for a win, but his attempt rolled tamely past the left of the cup.

From 230 yards back on the fifteenth fairway, Lyle hit a three-iron to the left of the green, where it bounced out of the light rough, curled round the back of the putting surface, and came to rest ten feet from the hole. Wadkins's third shot pitched near Lyle's ball but spun back toward the flag to leave a five-foot putt. On in two, Lyle stroked his second eagle putt of the day into the right-hand side of the cup to put his side three up with three to play.

On sixteen, Lyle overhit his tee shot to run off the back of the green. His twelve-foot birdie attempt—to win the match—didn't quite swing enough at the business end of the putt to find the cup. Having hit a terrific tee shot, pin high six feet away, Wadkins made his birdie two to keep the match alive.

As on the previous hole, Lyle overhit his nine-iron to the back of the seventeenth green, scattering his watching teammates and opponents alike. Wadkins's reply was swift and deadly: he cleared the massive drop bunker in front of the green, his ball rolling up to seven feet of the hole. The American's putt was on line all the way, good for his second consecutive birdie.

Having pulled back to one down, and with a slim chance for a half, the American pair took on the last hole with renewed gusto. In the gathering evening gloom, Lyle responded with a glorious second shot that ended up nine feet from the hole. Nelson's approach landed thirty feet past the hole, but Wadkins hit a draw shot that sent the ball over the flag, coming to rest fifteen feet beyond. With their slim chance of halving the match having gained a few pounds, the Americans were smacked hard when Langer almost holed his pitch shot. With the German's ball just eighteen inches away, the Americans gracefully accepted their fate, conceding the putt and the match.

On their second defeat of Nelson and Wadkins in the day: "The last nine holes were unbelievable—five birdies and an eagle, and still they kept coming back."
—*Sandy Lyle*

Afternoon fourball result: USA 2, EUR 2

In an exhilarating afternoon of low scores, the worst card of the day was a net five under par. The fourball matches gave up eighty-seven birdies and two eagles in sixty-five holes played.

Day two result: USA 3½, EUR 4½
Overall match score: USA 5½, EUR 10½

Day Three: Singles

On his team's needing to win nine of the twelve singles against a rampaging Euro-team: *"Emotion in golf is fantastic when you're playing well, and so far the Europeans have drowned us with it. But it can work against you, too."* —Jack Nicklaus

Nicklaus was onto something. Under the pressure of defending a large lead, five of the first seven Europeans bogeyed the opening hole.

Andy Bean (USA) v. Ian Woosnam (EUR)

Andy Bean (all 6′4″ of him) was in no mood to play Goliath to Ian Woosnam's David (all 5′4″of him), and he jumped out to a two-hole lead after four holes. Par was good enough on the first hole, and he went one better on the par-3 fourth. Recovering from a bunker, Woosnam pulled back a hole on the fifth with his own birdie, after Bean had three-putted the par-5 hole.

Bean extended his lead to two on the short eighth and reached the turn two up in a tidy 34 strokes.

After both players bogeyed the tenth, Woosnam birdied the eleventh but once again failed to answer Bean's birdie two at the short twelfth. Woosnam had more success on the long par 5s, making three of four birdies. Bean three-putted the thirteenth, and he could birdie only one par 5, as he was unsettlingly overpowered on the longer holes.

"It hurts when a little itty-bitty fellow outdrives you." —*Andy Bean*

One down on fourteen, Woosnam had a chance to level the match but missed a six-foot birdie putt, having seen Bean hole from farther away for par. Woosnam threw another chance away on fifteen, missing an eagle putt and having to settle for a half in birdie.

On sixteen, it was Bean's turn to miss a short putt that would have gone a long way toward settling the match. With Bean's drive deep in the trees on seventeen, Woosnam again failed to take advantage, hitting his approach into a bunker. He almost knocked his sand wedge into the hole, but the ball ran five feet past. Having played another poor shot out of the trees, Bean hit his third through the back of the green, thirteen feet beyond the flag. His chip back came up three feet short, but he holed that for a five. With yet another golden opportunity to win the hole and level the match, Woosnam knocked his par putt three and a half feet past and suffered the ignominy of a half in a wretched bogey five.

With time running out, on eighteen Woosnam hit his approach to fifteen feet and waited for Bean's reply. The tall American, conscious of the pressure on him, stepped aside and consulted his captain as to which shot to hit. He eventually matched Woosnam's solid approach to the green and was rewarded with a half in par, taking the match by one hole.

Dan Pohl (USA) v. Howard Clark (EUR)

Dan Pohl's par on the second gave him a lead he held until he bogeyed the next hole to Howard Clark's birdie. Pohl's flirtation with the lead was fleeting: he never got back up again during the rest of this close encounter of the third class. In a game where more holes were lost with bogeys than won with birdies, Pohl's second bogey, at five, gave Clark a lead. But this was immediately canceled out by the Englishman, who played the par-4 sixth in twice as many shots as his rival's birdie three.

Halving the next four holes in par, Pohl dropped another shot and another hole at the eleventh to give Clark his second lead of the match. Once again Clark's advantage was short-lived: the American made his second birdie of the day at twelve. But Pohl again followed with bogey at unlucky thirteen.

Clark shot himself in the foot with a four at the par-3 sixteenth to bring the match back all square for the fifth time. Clark blew a hole-winning chance at seventeen, wasting a superb pitch shot to within four feet, by missing his birdie putt that would have put him dormie one up.

Coming off two disappointing putts on sixteen and seventeen, Clark knew that following Woosnam's surprise demise, he needed a full point to settle the European nerves.

All square up eighteen, Clark was pumped up, and he fired a 310-yard drive with a slight draw on it. Pohl found a bunker with his tee shot, and his recovery came up thirty yards shy of the green. Granted relief from behind a TV tower, Clark hit a sensible seven-iron onto the green, but the ball spun back into the front fringe. With his opponent up on the green, Pohl skinned his chip from the ankle-high rough, sending the ball flying into a bunker guarding the back of the green. After knocking his bunker shot back past the pin and almost into another bunker, Pohl eventually made a six to Clark's par four, as the game and the match swung toward the Europeans by one hole.

On matching Pohl's three-over 75: "It was like drawing teeth out there. I'm just sorry that such a close game had to end in this fashion."
—*Howard Clark*

Larry Mize (USA) v. Sam Torrance (EUR)

Having retaken the lead on the par-3 fourth with his second hole-winning par, Larry Mize lost two holes in a row (bogey-par) to hand the lead to Sam Torrance, who took the sixth with a birdie three. The Scot was no more secure with his lead than the American, and he returned the lead to Mize with the same bogey-par scenario on seven and eight, Mize capitalizing on a superb tee shot to the par-3 eighth for a one-putt birdie. The 452-yard second was the only hole halved on the front nine, as Torrance birdied the ninth with a seventeen-foot putt to reach the turn level, both players over par.

Another American bogey on the 538-yard eleventh gave Torrance a one-hole lead he held until he bogeyed fourteen. Mize won seventeen with a wonderfully judged chip-and-run across the length of the big green to within four feet. Torrance could not get his bunker shot close enough to the cup for par. Mize accepted the hole to assure him of a half, but the American rookie knew that he needed a full point for his side to have any chance of recapturing the trophy.

On eighteen, with the mounting pressures of his team's hopes on his shoulders, Mize hit a terrible tee shot that left his ball teetering on the bank of a small stream. After some minutes of discussion over line-of-sight drops and the like, Mize took a penalty drop. He had been allowed a free line-of-sight drop, but the only place he could have legally dropped his ball was in the stream.

From beside the water, Mize swung a hopeful three-wood at the ball, succeeding only in depositing his third shot in a greenside bunker. With the pressure off him, Torrance was able to hit an arrow straight at the flag, finishing ten feet short of the hole.

Although Mize got up and down with a gutsy fifteen-foot putt for bogey, the Scot took his two putts to win the hole and halve the match.

Torrance's valuable half-point retrieved Europe's five-point lead, but the news from the course was not so good. The United States was up in six of the nine matches and well in touch in the other three.

Mark Calcavecchia (USA) v. Nick Faldo (EUR)

Faldo's concerns over his play were still apparent as he bogeyed the first hole along with his opponent. Calcavecchia made another bogey on three but birdied the par-5 fifth to draw level, his only win on the front nine. The Englishman recorded his first birdie at the par-5 seventh and held the one-hole lead through ten tainted holes of match play.

The American pulled level for the second time on eleven, when Faldo failed to make his par five. After the next two holes were halved in par, Calcavecchia took his first lead of the match thanks to another English bogey at the 363-yard fourteenth. The American tried to increase his lead, making a seven-foot birdie putt at fifteen, but Faldo refused to give in and rolled home his own shorter putt for birdie.

After sixteen was halved, both players found greenside bunkers on seventeen. Calcavecchia played out first to three feet of the flag, before Faldo, with a much harder shot, managed to stop his ball five feet past the hole and made the putt coming back. Calcavecchia also sank his par putt, and he was in the happy position of being one up with one to play.

On eighteen, the American's second shot found a bunker to the left of the green. With a five-iron from 180 yards out of the rough, Faldo's second also found a bunker on the front right of the green. The Englishman recovered his composure to set up the chance of another superb sand recovery. Calcavecchia knocked his ball out of the bunker to the back of the green, sixteen feet beyond the flag. The American's putt rolled past the hole by three feet, leaving Faldo with an eight-foot putt to halve the match. As so many shortish putts had done throughout the three days, Faldo's caught the right-hand lip, boomeranged around, and stayed out. The short putt was conceded, and Calcavecchia calmly stepped up and holed his putt for a full point.

Payne Stewart (USA) v. Jose Maria Olazabal (EUR)

For the third time in three days, Payne Stewart and Jose Maria Olazabal crossed swords on the golf course. The Spaniard had prevailed on both previous meetings, twice walking off the eighteenth green with a one-hole win over the American. In this rematch, which was every bit as close as their pairs matches, Olazabal never had the luxury of being in front.

After matching pars for the first three holes, the stalemate was broken by Stewart's excellent tee shot to two feet for a go-ahead birdie two on the fourth. Olazabal could not reduce this lead until the ninth, where his first birdie of the day, an impeccable putt from over twenty feet, brought him level.

Stewart quickly regained his lead off a six-foot birdie putt at ten and did enough to halve the next four holes in regulation. With holes running out, Olazabal birdied fifteen to square the match with three to play. For the second time in the match, Stewart retrieved his lost lead on the very next hole, canning a birdie on the 204-yard sixteenth.

At seventeen, Olazabal had to make a tricky five-foot putt for a half, leaving Stewart one up with one to play.

Stewart's 70 was the best round of the first five matches out; Andy Bean, with a 71, was the only other player to break par. Olazabal's 72 equaled Sandy Lyle's level par as the best European score in the first five matches.

On the last hole, Stewart pushed his drive into the right-hand rough, from where he did extremely well to find the green with his second shot. His ball ran up the green and nestled twenty-five feet away in the fringe at the back of the green. The American hardly touched his long putt, but it ran quickly down the slope to twelve inches of the hole, and Olazabal, who could not match the par four, immediately conceded for a two-hole loss.

Scott Simpson (USA) v. Jose Rivero (EUR)

Some putt-ugly golf sent this match out on the wrong foot, as the first two holes were halved in bogeys. Simpson brought some much-needed quality back into the match with a birdie at the third to go one up. He quickly relapsed, making his third bogey in four holes to relinquish a lead that he got back with his second birdie of the day at the par-5 fifth.

Rivero's normally solid game never materialized as he posted five fives and no birdies on the outward nine, while Simpson made his third birdie at nine for a two-hole cushion.

Not content with a lead, Simpson bogeyed the tenth and saw his lead completely disappear on twelve, where Rivero finally produced his first birdie of the day.

After the next two holes were halved in gratefully accepted pars, Simpson reeled off back-to-back wins on fifteen and sixteen to break the back of the Spaniard's resistance.

Two down with two to play, Rivero had a six-foot putt to stay in the match, but he underborrowed right to left and his ball stayed out. Simpson took the match, 2 and 1, and had pulled back a vital point for the Americans.

Tom Kite (USA) v. Sandy Lyle (EUR)

Both Tom Kite and Sandy Lyle were in top form and eager for this match. It was Lyle who would get out to the faster start, but Kite who would prevail over the stretch.

Kite's bogey on the first was enough for Lyle to stand one up after four holes. The thirty-five-year-old Texan produced his side's first and only eagle at the fifth hole to level, then took a lead on Lyle's bogey at six.

Kite pushed his lead to four with unanswered birdies on eleven (from seven feet), thirteen (from thirteen feet), and fourteen to take a firm grip of his match.

On fifteen, Kite, with the ball below his feet, hit a short pitch to ten feet of the hole. On in two, Lyle made his thirteen-foot putt to try to save the match. Kite overborrowed on his birdie putt and Lyle got a hole back, to put him three down with three to play.

On the 204-yard sixteenth, Lyle had a monster putt of sixty feet or more, which he slowly played up two inches short of the hole. To win the match, Kite had two putts from forty feet, and he left his first try two feet short, then sank his second after Lyle refused to concede, comically measuring Kite's putt as longer than his shoe length.

Tom Kite returned in the best round of the day—four under for the sixteen holes played and the 3 and 2 victory.

Ben Crenshaw (USA) v. Eamonn Darcy (EUR)

With two defeats in his two previous matches, Ben Crenshaw may have had his mind elsewhere, since his wife was at home in Texas waiting to give birth.

Little did Ben Crenshaw know, after holing from forty-five feet on the first for a go-ahead birdie, that he would have one of his most testing days on the putting surface.

Little did anyone realize that the mild-mannered Eamonn Darcy would be capable of reeling off four consecutive wins to take a surprise but well-deserved three-hole lead after seven.

"Darcy swings like an octopus falling from a tree."
—*Anonymous TV commentator*

The Irishman's run of success started with unanswered birdies at four and five to level, then lead the match. If this double strike upset Crenshaw, the sixth hole literally proved to be crunch time for the normally unflappable Texan.

Despite his outlandish success from another zip code on the first green, Crenshaw—widely regarded as the best clutch putter ever—became increasingly unhappy with his putter and his putting. Three strokes on the sixth green made Crenshaw see red, and he took his frustrations out on his trusty Wilson 8802 putter, nicknamed "Little Ben," which he had owned since he was fifteen. Crenshaw smashed the club into the ground, snapping the old shaft.

"I remember breaking my putter on the sixth green. I just tapped it down on a walnut, and it snapped. It was like somebody shot me. I had to resort to using my sand wedge for a couple of holes. After that, I used my one-iron for the rest of the round. I actually holed a couple of long putts to stay in the match." —Ben Crenshaw

At three down after the next hole, Crenshaw's uncharacteristic show of petulance had the desired effect on his game—even when he was putting with wedge or iron. Galvanized into fighting a rearguard action, he gradually pulled back the lead. He got one hole back on the eighth thanks to a Darcy bogey but gave the advantage straight back with a bogey of his own on the next, after driving into the trees.

With ten and eleven halved in bogey and par, respectively, Crenshaw reeled off three wins. On the par-3 twelfth, it was Darcy, wielding his putter as though caught in a strobe light, who three-putted from the back of the green. Having hit a superb tee shot to twelve, with the ball on line for the hole but pulling up four feet shy, Crenshaw missed his birdie putt with a one-iron. This left Darcy with his second putt from just four feet, but his hesitant putting stroke dragged the ball wide for a bogey.

On thirteen, Crenshaw used a wedge to scoot the ball to within six feet of the hole and proceeded to hole his birdie putt with his one-iron. Darcy's lead was down to one, which quickly vanished on fourteen after he played an ugly shot way over the green, over a cart path, and into the crowd some forty yards from the flag. As luck had it, his ball dribbled down the gallery bank and back across the path to within twenty yards of the green. From the middle of the fairway, Crenshaw found the middle of the green in two. Darcy was unable to cash in on his good luck; he did all he could to stop his delicate chip on the green, but the frightening slope took the ball off the other side. Crenshaw's four to Darcy's five gave the American his third win in a row to level the match.

The Irishman did not realize until after the match that Crenshaw had broken his putter: "I figured he was using the irons because he wanted to slow the ball down on the fast greens."
—*Eamonn Darcy*

The Irishman stopped the hemorrhaging on fifteen, but it took a fine birdie putt from over fifteen feet just to match Crenshaw for a half. The American's dead-eye tee shot at the 204-yard sixteenth almost landed in the hole, ran on six feet past the flag, stopped . . . then dribbled back a couple of feet. Darcy took three to get down from just off the green, and he was behind for the first time in the match.

Many expected the Irishman, the owner of one of the worst playing records in the Ryder Cup, to collapse over the final two holes.

Ignoring his abysmal Cup record (winless in ten matches), Darcy played like a champion, and it was the more experienced American who wilted under the pressure, in another remarkable twist of fortune.

Crenshaw's blind approach to seventeen was off target to the back of the green, landing in a grassy tongue above a bunker. The American's cramped recovery barely cleared the bunker, and the ball rolled back down into it. Unable to hole his fourth shot from the sand, Crenshaw conceded the hole to Darcy, who had hit his second to four feet.

Level at the last hole, Darcy's reasonable drive was followed by a calamity for Crenshaw, whose drive found the stream down the left of the fairway. Worse was to follow for the Texan: having dropped his ball, he knocked it into a bunker beside the green.

With the green, the hole, and match at his mercy, Darcy hit his 200-yard approach into the same bunker as Crenshaw, but in one shot fewer. The drama continued when Crenshaw softly lifted his ball up and out to six feet of the hole in four. Darcy dug out his ball to finish inside Crenshaw, but he had left himself a nasty downhill putt of about four feet. Still using a long iron, Crenshaw made his bogey putt, and all the pressure shifted to the genial Irishman. He made the telling putt to win his first-ever Ryder Cup match. As well as picking up a point, Darcy received a sporting pat on the back from Jack Nicklaus.

"While for three days the Americans fought snap hooks, snapped nerves, and finally, Ben Crenshaw's snapped putter shaft, the European side displayed international homogeneity."
—*Jaime Diaz,*
Sports Illustrated

Darcy's completely unexpected point could not have come at a better time for his side. Behind him, his teammates had been dropping like flies at an insecticide salesmen's convention.

Larry Nelson (USA) v. Bernhard Langer (EUR)

Larry Nelson played par golf for eight of the first nine holes (with a birdie at eight) and twice enjoyed a two-hole lead. Bernhard Langer, with bogey fives at the first and third, birdied the fifth and eighth to struggle to the turn one down.

Having started the competition with a perfect record from nine games, Larry Nelson then went 0–3 in the first two days, with two losses at the hands of his singles opponent.

Nelson extended his advantage on the first two homeward holes; Langer failed to make par on the tenth, and a par five at eleven was canceled by the American's second birdie of the day, which earned him a three-hole lead. This buffer was catastrophically eradicated as Nelson bogeyed twelve through fourteen (4-5-5 to 3-3-4).

The players got their acts together and parred the next three holes to reach the final tee all square. The match, as well as the fate of the Ryder Cup, would be decided here.

With his third shot at eighteen, Nelson chipped up from off the front of the green to three feet. Langer—in his own exacting way and time—surveyed a twenty-five-footer for the match. The German prudently rolled his ball up inside Nelson's and cheekily offered the American a half. Nelson, after a few seconds' thought, cordially accepted, despite the need for maximum points. Langer's thinking had been that this half-point gave Europe 14 points in the match, enough to retain the Ryder Cup.

Although Nelson should have putted out on the last green in the hope of stealing a full point, his captain fully understood the thinking behind his player's actions, having been there himself in 1969: *"Larry thought that was the right thing to do, and I accept that. It was a proper gesture on Larry's part."* —JACK NICKLAUS

Curtis Strange (USA) v. Seve Ballesteros (EUR)

In this eagerly awaited clash of two players, each described by his respective captain as the "best golfer in the world," the Spaniard chipped in from a bunker on the first and never surrendered his lead. Back-to-back bogeys on three and four by Strange endowed his rival with a three-hole lead.

In his fourth singles match, Ballesteros was still looking to record his first win, having lost one and halved two previously.

Both players lived up to their captains' billing with superbly matched birdie fours at the fifth and seventh. Strange managed to pull one hole back on nine with his third birdie of the day. Seve reached the turn in a creditable 33 strokes and added to his lead by making his fifth birdie on the tenth. The Spaniard made his first mistake on eleven, his bogey six giving Strange some slim hope of saving the match and the Cup.

The American's position looked even better—until Ballesteros was forced to hole a nasty putt on twelve just to retain his two-hole cushion. When Seve bogeyed thirteen after Strange had made par from four feet, he was left clutching a fragile one-hole lead. The Spaniard noticeably redoubled his efforts and doubled his lead on fourteen after Strange failed to make par.

With the American trying everything he could to cut the lead, Seve holed a five-foot birdie putt on fifteen to deny Strange, who then holed a shorter birdie putt of his own. On the short sixteenth, the Spaniard's tee shot finished six feet from the flag, while Strange had a birdie putt of twice that distance. The American misjudged the amount of borrow on his putt, and the ball swept below the hole. Ballesteros was left with a putt for the match. He also missed but was still well placed at two up with two to play.

On seventeen, the Spaniard made no more mistakes, firing his eight-iron second into the heart of the green. From the right-hand rough, Strange put his four-iron approach through the green in two. Seve putted up to within eighteen inches and holed the putt, which was enough to settle the match for Europe and brought a much greater reward: the vital point that won the Cup.

In his vital win, Ballesteros carded the best score by his side on the final day—a net 69—and finished as top points scorer, with four from five games.

Lanny Wadkins (USA) v. Ken Brown (EUR)

Having played in only one match (the morning foursomes on day one) prior to the singles, Ken Brown was in no real form to deal with Lanny Wadkins—one of the Ryder Cup's most belligerent battlers.

At times, the Scot flattered to deceive: when his birdie at the second gave him a one-hole lead, and when he almost aced the 189-yard eighth.

At other times, Brown was downright awful, sandwiching his birdie on the second between an opening bogey and a double bogey. Playing slightly more consistent golf, which is the polite way of saying Wadkins stank less than Brown did on the front nine, the American was two up at the turn.

Making one birdie, Wadkins managed to increase his lead at ten, eleven, and twelve to hold a five-hole grip on the game. Although Brown pulled back a couple of holes, with birdies at fourteen and fifteen, Wadkins eased to a 3 and 2 win for his thirteenth Ryder Cup victory.

A week after the Ryder Cup, Brown played some of the best golf of his career to win the Southern Open, in Columbus, Georgia, by seven shots. He became only the fourth British player to win an official U.S. tour event.

Hal Sutton (USA) v. Gordon Brand (EUR)

Gordon Brand, Jr., left his mark on the opening of this match, carding three consecutive wins from the third to the fifth, then adding another at the seventh just for good measure—and a four-hole lead. Hal Sutton had been to blame for half of this disparity, having bogeyed three and four, while Brand birdied the par 5s at five and seven—the latter accomplished with a remarkable pitch-in from almost a hundred yards.

The pair traded hole-losing bogeys on nine and ten, but Sutton's emphatic eagle on eleven gave him hope to build on. With momentum running his way, the American birdied twelve to reduce the lead to two with six to play. Down the stretch, the 1983 PGA champion applied the pressure, making decisive birdies at fifteen and seventeen to square a match that had looked all over six holes earlier.

Having played the previous seven holes in five under par, Sutton was unable to win the final hole to cap a sensational comeback.

"I never thought I'd live to see golf played at the level it was played on Friday and Saturday. Today? I've never been so worried."
—*Tony Jacklin*

After being in the driving seat—four up on the way home—Brand had to settle for a half, but fortunately for him, the Ryder Cup had already been captured some time earlier.

Day three result: USA 7½, EUR 4½
Overall match score: USA 13, EUR 15

Recap

As if to prove that the long-awaited victory in 1985 was not a blip on the golfing cosmos, Europe showed, for the very first time, that they could produce the goods on American soil. Jack Nicklaus had warned his team in 1983 that he did not want to be remembered as the first U.S. captain to lose on home soil. This time around he dared not even ask; he knew how tight the match was going to be. But Nicklaus had already demonstrated that the Ryder Cup was as much about winning friends and respect as about winning matches.

What troubled the great man more than the loss was the manner of the loss. He had seen his team outfought and out-thought, and that hurt him deeply.

"Well, it wasn't a total loss. After all, we *did* win the opening ceremonies. And the closing ceremonies weren't too bad either. But in between those two bits of pomp and circumstance, the twenty-seventh playing of the Ryder Cup Matches was quite a different story, and anyone who left Dublin, Ohio, thinking the United States still had a corner on the golf ability market has his head in a bunker."
—*Ron Coffman,* Golf World

"They almost pulled it out, but we did not win the eighteenth hole in any match, and we lost the eighteenth in three crucial matches. That was the difference right there. . . . We just weren't as tough in the stretch as the European guys." —JACK NICKLAUS

The one saving grace in the one-sided matches of the '50s, 60s, and 70s was that it was a clear indication of the strength of the U.S. PGA Tour and its members. The back-to-back defeats in 1985 and 1987 showed up a fatal weakness that had festered in the domestic game: the U.S. PGA Tour paid handsome rewards for top ten finishes, so the need to win was not as urgent as had once been the case. Nicklaus also felt that the European tour bred better top-class players, who were honed on winning week in, week out.

"The problem is really with the American golf system. Because it is so difficult to win, our guys rarely get in position to contend down the stretch. Instead of being aggressive, they develop a percentage type of style. On the European tour, there is less competition, which puts players in contention more often and makes them better, more aggressive finishers."
—JACK NICKLAUS

As confirmation of Nicklaus's fears over the relative strength of the two sets of players, Europe had six players contribute three or more points in 1987, while the United States had only two: the ever-reliable Kite and the unsung Sutton.

After Jose Maria Olazabal had finished his now famous Spanish jig on the eighteenth green, Tony Jacklin joined his victorious team in the almost as famous high-kicking line. Knowing that it took two teams to tango, and with the U.S. side having suffered back-to-back defeats for the first time, Jack Nicklaus suspected that things would not get any easier next time around. The 1989 Ryder Cup Matches would be played back at the European HQ—The Belfry, with its infamous eighteenth hole.

Match Results (Winning side marked in *italics.*)

Friday, September 25—Morning Foursomes

	USA	EUR	Score
1.	*Curtis Strange* *Tom Kite*	Sam Torrance Howard Clark	4 and 2
2.	*Hal Sutton* *Dan Pohl*	Ken Brown Bernhard Langer	2 and 1
3.	Lanny Wadkins Larry Mize	*Nick Faldo* *Ian Woosnam*	2-up
4.	Larry Nelson Payne Stewart	*Seve Ballesteros* *Jose Maria Olazabal*	1-up

Friday, September 25—Afternoon Fourball

	USA	EUR	Score
5.	Ben Crenshaw Scott Simpson	*Gordon Brand* *Jose Rivero*	3 and 2
6.	Andy Bean Mark Calcavecchia	*Sandy Lyle* *Bernhard Langer*	1-up
7.	Hal Sutton Dan Pohl	*Nick Faldo* *Ian Woosnam*	2 and 1
8.	Curtis Strange Tom Kite	*Seve Ballesteros* *Jose Maria Olazabal*	2 and 1

Day one result: USA 2, EUR 6

Saturday, September 26—Morning Foursomes

	USA	EUR	Score
9.	*Curtis Strange* *Tom Kite*	Jose Rivero Gordon Brand	3 and 1
10.	Hal Sutton Larry Mize	Nick Faldo Ian Woosnam	halved
11.	Lanny Wadkins Larry Nelson	*Sandy Lyle* *Bernhard Langer*	2 and 1
12.	Ben Crenshaw Payne Stewart	*Seve Ballesteros* *Jose Maria Olazabal*	1-up

Saturday, September 26—Afternoon Fourball

	USA	EUR	Score
13.	Curtis Strange Tom Kite	*Nick Faldo* *Ian Woosnam*	5 and 4
14.	*Andy Bean* *Payne Stewart*	Eamonn Darcy Gordon Brand	3 and 2
15.	*Hal Sutton* *Larry Mize*	Seve Ballesteros Jose Maria Olazabal	2 and 1
16.	Lanny Wadkins Larry Nelson	*Sandy Lyle* *Bernhard Langer*	1-up

Day two result: USA 3½, EUR 4½
Overall match score: USA 5½, EUR 10½

Sunday, September 27—Singles

	USA	EUR	Score
17.	*Andy Bean*	Ian Woosnam	1-up
18.	Dan Pohl	*Howard Clark*	1-up
19.	Larry Mize	Sam Torrance	halved
20.	*Mark Calcavecchia*	Nick Faldo	1-up
21.	*Payne Stewart*	Jose Maria Olazabal	2-up
22.	*Scott Simpson*	Jose Rivero	2 and 1
23.	*Tom Kite*	Sandy Lyle	3 and 2
24.	Ben Crenshaw	*Eamonn Darcy*	1-up
25.	Larry Nelson	Bernhard Langer	halved
26.	Curtis Strange	*Seve Ballesteros*	2 and 1
27.	*Lanny Wadkins*	Ken Brown	3 and 2
28.	Hal Sutton	Gordon Brand	halved

Day three result: USA 7½, EUR 4½
Overall match score: USA 13, EUR 15

1989

The Belfry
Sutton Coldfield
England
September 22–24

United States 14	**Europe 14**
Paul Azinger	Seve Ballesteros (Spain)
Chip Beck	Gordon Brand, Jr. (Scotland)
Mark Calcavecchia	Jose Maria Canizares (Spain)
Fred Couples	Howard Clark (England)
Ken Green	Nick Faldo (England)
Tom Kite	Mark James (England)
Mark McCumber	Bernhard Langer (Germany)
Mark O'Meara	Christy O'Connor, Jr. (Ireland)
Payne Stewart	Jose Maria Olazabal (Spain)
Curtis Strange	Ronan Rafferty (N. Ireland)
Lanny Wadkins	Sam Torrance (Scotland)
Tom Watson	Ian Woosnam (Wales)
Captain	**Captain**
Raymond Floyd	Tony Jacklin (England)

Honors Even

For the first time in Ryder Cup history, the U.S. team had suffered back-to-back defeats. Before this, they had lost only three matches in the previous fifty-six years. The U.S. PGA swiftly appointed a no-nonsense captain, Raymond Floyd, to spearhead the challenge to get the Cup back. To reinforce Floyd's position as overlord, he was given two wild-card choices—something his opposite number, Tony Jacklin, had demanded when he assumed his position in 1983.

Floyd used his two choices on Tom Watson and Lanny Wadkins, going for experience over recent success in the latter's case, since Wadkins had missed six of his last eight cuts.

On choosing Wadkins: "If you haven't played in a Ryder Cup, you can hardly get through it the first time."
—*Raymond Floyd*

Jacklin was saved from making a difficult choice over one of his picks when Sandy Lyle phoned him and requested that he not be considered. At the time, Lyle's run of bad play made Wadkins look like a world-beater. Although Sandy Lyle declined to play for Europe because of his bad play on the U.S. tour, he had actually accumulated enough U.S. PGA points to qualify for eighth spot on the U.S. Ryder Cup team.

With three wild-card choices, Jacklin chose Langer, Clark, and O'Connor, knowing that he had the more experienced lineup, with only one newcomer to his team: Ronan Rafferty. Jacklin, who in the past had often viewed some of his automatic players with less than a welcoming glance, did not see the Northern Ireland player as a weak link. Rafferty not only qualified by right but also was the leading money winner on the European circuit; no one on the Continent was playing better golf.

"The first time I played in the Ryder Cup, I couldn't breathe."
—*Fred Couples*

Floyd had a worry in that five (Azinger, Beck, Couples, Green, and McCumber) of his ten automatic players were new to the Ryder Cup. He knew that the value of experience in the heat of battle was what won Ryder Cups, not money in the bank or padded-out column inches in flattering press reports.

On learning that George Bush had hosted a presidential dinner for the U.S. Ryder Cup team: "We have had no such threats of that kind from Mrs. Thatcher."
—*Tony Jacklin*

Europe was back home at The Belfry, scene of their tumultuous triumph in 1985, giving them a huge psychological advantage over the visitors, who had struggled the last time. In 1985, the last hole had proved pivotal in the outcome of the overall match, and 1989 would be no different, with more than half (fifteen of twenty-eight) of the matches finishing on the eighteenth green.

The contest proved to be one of the most closely matched and closely fought Ryder Cup encounters ever.

Course Details

The Ryder Cup returned to The Belfry, which had hosted the European win in 1985.

Hole	Distance	Par	Hole	Distance	Par
1	418	4	10	275	4
2	349	4	11	420	4
3	465	4	12	235	3
4	579	5	13	394	4
5	399	4	14	194	3
6	396	4	15	550	5
7	183	3	16	410	4
8	460	4	17	575	5
9	400	4	18	474	4
		36			**36 = Par 72 (7,176 yards)**

Course designers: Peter Alliss and Dave Thomas

Day One: Morning Foursomes

The first match teed off at 8 A.M. under very gloomy gray skies littered with ominous rain clouds.

Tom Kite and Curtis Strange (USA) v. Nick Faldo and Ian Woosnam (EUR)

Not standing on ceremony, Ian Woosnam hit the first drive of the contest to the right of the fairway. Nick Faldo recovered nicely to set up a par for the opening half with Tom Kite and Curtis Strange.

The opening match proved embarrassing for the starting official, who called upon Ian Woosnam to play the first drive of the day. Tradition has it that the visitors always take the first cut.

The British pair, who had worked well together in the past, quickly got into gear, taking the second and third holes, highlighted by a five-foot birdie putt on two for Faldo, followed by his approach to two feet for a second straight birdie.

Two down, the Americans stabilized themselves by halving the next three holes before unleashing their own salvo of success, winning four holes in a row. Strange birdied the par-3 seventh with a ten-footer after Kite's excellent tee shot, and they took the eighth and ninth with par fours for a one-hole lead at the turn.

Out in par, one shot more than their rivals, Faldo and Woosnam played the tenth about as badly as two top professionals could play it. Faldo's tee shot missed the green and went over the bank up on the right. Woosnam overhit a chip back down that did not stop on the kidney-shaped green until it went splash! After a penalty drop, Faldo put the new ball straight back into the water to go two balls down, two holes down, with five to play.

The home pair steadied its listing ship by making a couple of birdies in a row. At the 194-yard fourteenth, Faldo hit his seven-iron to seven feet, and at the par-5 fifteenth, Woosnam's short jab of a pitch set up Faldo's birdie putt from two feet.

All level on eighteen, Kite's second shot had difficulty carrying the lake in a strong head wind. With his feet almost on the edge of the lake, Strange played a fine chip onto the green to seven feet of the hole. Woosnam deposited Faldo's drive in a bunker guarding the front of the green, though the Englishman played a superb chip-out, stopping the ball on its second bounce five feet from the hole.

Kite rewarded his partner's excellent chip by holing their seven-footer for par. This left Woosnam under some considerable pressure to repay Faldo's fine recovery, which he did, but not

Coming back in 33, the British pair carded a 69, a couple of shots better than the competition, although the match was halved.

before the ball executed a full 360 round the rim of the cup. The last hole was halved in par to split the match and set the tone for the twenty-seven matches to come.

Lanny Wadkins and Payne Stewart (USA) v. Howard Clark and Mark James (EUR)

The early skirmishes in this close match saw Wadkins and Stewart birdie the fifth for a lead, but consecutive birdies by Clark and James on six and seven swung a one-hole advantage their way.

The match continued to swing. The Americans leveled on eight with a par four, then took the ninth with a birdie three after the Englishmen had bogeyed both holes to the turn.

With ten halved in par fours, Clark and James carded four threes in a row, but the net result of this fine scoring was merely to level the match. Stewart and Wadkins matched the par three at twelve, then lost thirteen to a birdie to go one down, before an American deuce on the 194-yard fourteenth squared the match.

With the next two holes halved with pars, Wadkins uncorked the shot of the morning on the 575-yard seventeenth. After Stewart pushed his second shot to the back right off the green, Wadkins sent his twenty-yard chip curling across the green as though it were being sucked into a black hole, for an eagle three. This gave the Americans a one-hole lead they kept on the last, where Wadkins almost holed another chip from off the right-hand side of the green. This time, though, as his thirty-yard effort rolled up to the hole, it drifted past the left-hand side, stopping twelve inches past for a bogey five that should have lost the hole and the lead.

Wadkins and Stewart carded two 34s for the best round of the day, a four-under 68.

Clark had a nine-foot putt up the green for a chance to halve the match, but the Englishman's feeble attempt never looked threatening, tailing off limply a few feet short. This clutch miss secured the Americans a one-hole win.

Mark Calcavecchia and Ken Green (USA) v. Bernhard Langer and Ronan Rafferty (EUR)

The poorest of the opening matches saw Rafferty and Langer limp to the turn in 41 strokes. Calcavecchia and Green were one-under, for a three-hole lead.

Rookie Rafferty, the top-earning European, and Langer started off disastrously, dropping the opening holes to two birdies by good friends and partners Calcavecchia and Green. A far-from-amicable American bogey on the par-5 fourth gave the Europeans a glimmer of hope, but the Americans made another birdie on six—that was quickly canceled by their bogey on the 183-yard seventh.

Having weathered an early storm, Langer and Rafferty undid their good work by bogeying the ninth. The overall quality of play did not improve much on the inward nine: the Americans lost the eleventh and thirteenth with bogeys, and the Europeans sandwiched their own bogey in on twelve.

On the change in emphasis to team spirit over individual egotism: "We are even cheering for Ken Green."
—*Curtis Strange*

The standard of shoddy workmanship was typified by the way both pairs played the 550-yard par-5 fifteenth. Up by two, the Americans put their second shot into the ditch that runs across the fairway. With a great chance to get the lead back to one, Europe played follow-the-leader and dunked its ball into the same ditch. Both pairs took four more shots to get down—for a woeful half in seven!

The Americans took their two-shot lead and mercifully put the five-over-par Europeans away on the seventeenth, with Calcavecchia leaving his twenty-foot eagle putt a few inches from the hole for a conceded birdie and a 2 and 1 victory.

Finishing on the seventeenth hole, this was the only match of the opening morning that did not reach the last green.

Tom Watson and Chip Beck (USA) v. Seve Ballesteros and Jose Maria Olazabal (EUR)

Watson and Beck took a lead off Ballesteros and Olazabal with a birdie on the 465-yard third hole, but they were reeled in on the next hole by the Spanish pair's first birdie. Three holes later, the Americans were staring at a two-hole deficit after they slipped in a bogey at six and the Spaniards got their two at the 183-yard seventh. The U.S. pair could not capitalize on the Spaniards' first bogey in eight holes, as they themselves followed suit.

The Spaniards continued in a typically swashbuckling manner, going after the drivable tenth hole. An eagle two brought a concession from the struggling Americans, who slumped to three down.

Watson and Beck were not downhearted at this seemingly terminal shortfall, as they grimly fought back to take three holes out of the next four to level the match. This concerted comeback was mainly due to a brace of birdies from Watson, and to Ballesteros's knocking his tee shot into a bunker on the 394-yard thirteenth.

Beck's putting touch deserted him on the fifteenth green, and he ran his par putt for a half by the hole. The Spaniards failed to make their own crucial par putt on the next hole, and the match was back level. On seventeen, Olazabal was forced to sink a twelve-foot pressure putt just to keep the match even.

From the eighteenth fairway, Olazabal played the Spaniards' third shot from right in front of the lake to the top tier of the green, some eighteen feet short of the flag. Beck played his side's third beyond the flag a little farther away than Olazabal's ball. Watson, with a downhill par putt, judged the subtle left-right break to perfection but was an ounce short of speed, as the ball pulled up on the lip.

Conceding the U.S. ball for a bogey five, Ballesteros had an uphill putt for the match. His ball set off for the middle of the cup, then suddenly juked right at the death and agonizingly ran by a couple of inches—to halve the match.

Morning foursomes result: USA 3, EUR 1

Day One: Afternoon Fourball

In true U.S. tradition, Floyd brought in the four players who had not played in the morning and paired each of them with a player who had: three rookies with three veterans. Jacklin made one change, swapping his third pairing from the morning for the Scots Torrance and Brand.

Curtis Strange and Paul Azinger (USA) v. Sam Torrance and Gordon Brand (EUR)

Playing against Curtis Strange and Paul Azinger (in his first match), Gordon Brand, Jr., played an approach shot from the left-hand rough that bounced three feet in front of the opening flag and rolled over the hole to stop a few inches past. This conceded birdie put Brand and Sam Torrance one up, and they went further ahead after six holes with another birdie, but the Americans pulled a hole back immediately on the next with a birdie two.

After this quick exchange of holes, both pairs canceled each other out as the next nine holes were all halved, with birdies balancing the books on nine and ten. Strange and Azinger had not played badly, but their first real strike on the way home arrived late, at the seventeenth hole. Here Strange had a putt from just off the green to level the match. His twenty-five-footer locked in on the hole and dived in for an eagle three, leveling the match for the first time since the first green. Having trailed from the get-go, the American pair had a chance to win the match but had to conquer the specter of the eighteenth hole.

"The atmosphere was great. The spectators were clapping us all the way. You feel two up before you start."
—*Gordon Brand, Jr. (it actually took him six holes to go two up)*

From in front of the lake, Azinger hit a pitch directly at the flag that landed and stopped nine feet short. Having bunkered his second shot, in the front-right trap, Brand knocked a supreme third shot some sixty-five yards up onto the green, reaching the top tier, his ball stopping pin-high six feet from the hole. With his ball on the middle tier, Strange saw his uphill putt run on line for twenty feet, then veer off left as the ball approached the hole. Conceded for a five to match Torrance's bogey, this left the two remaining players a putt each that could win (or lose) the hole.

Azinger's nervous nudge of a putt was never on line or up to the hole, and the Americans now sweated on the last European putt. From much closer, Brand had a golden opportunity to become a hero, which he duly took—rattling the ball home to the cheers of the crowd for a one-hole win at the death.

Fred Couples and Lanny Wadkins (USA) v. Howard Clark and Mark James (EUR)

"There is nothing that prepares you for the Ryder Cup. In England, you get there and even in practice you're nervous. You have fun around your teammates, but when you tee off on Friday, you're going against two other guys, and the fans are screaming. It's a totally different feeling."

—Fred Couples

Fred Couples made his Ryder Cup debut in tandem with Lanny Wadkins, taking on the All-England ensemble of Clark and James.

From the fringe on the second green, James was faced with a very awkward chip over a ridge that ran across the putting surface. He not only figured out how to get the ball close enough for a concession, but he holed it for a birdie. Wadkins leveled immediately with a birdie on the third, but he and teammate Fred Couples, who found the early pace and pressure too much, could do very little over the next ten holes to prevent their opponents from staking a three-hole lead.

Scoring wins on five with a second birdie, eight with a par, eleven off Clark's birdie, and twelve with James's par, the Englishmen found themselves three up with six to play. The only U.S. success in that decisive European stretch came at the tenth, where Wadkins made his second birdie of the day.

Thirteen through fifteen were halved in par, and Europe found itself dormie three.

On sixteen, Wadkins had a chance to cut the lead with a thirteen-foot birdie putt. Looking for hole or nothing, he pushed his ball a couple of feet past on the left, leaving James with two putts from about the same distance to close the match out. He rolled his first putt right up to the lip of the cup and wasn't asked to make a second, for the 3 and 2 decision.

Mark Calcavecchia and Mark McCumber (USA) v. Nick Faldo and Ian Woosnam (EUR)

With birdies on two and four, the first six holes were halved in what promised to be an entertainingly equal encounter between the two American Marks and the proven and battle-hardened British pair of Faldo and Woosnam.

Europe drew first blood with a splendid birdie two on the 183-yard seventh, but the Americans hit back on the next to level the affair with a par to take the hole.

Following the pattern of the opening third of the match, the next five holes were also halved; it was turning out to be an extremely close contest, as four pars were mixed with a birdie apiece on eleven. Having found the long bunker alongside the thirteenth green with his approach, Woosnam got his chip not only up but in—for a birdie to restore the one-hole lead.

This advantage was doubled by Faldo's par on the 550-yard fifteenth, but Calcavecchia made a putt from fifteen feet to win the sixteenth.

On seventeen, Woosnam pushed his tee shot into the right-hand rough and proceeded to hit a prodigious long iron up onto the green, which came to rest thirty feet short of the hole. Having seen Woosnam leave his eagle putt four feet short of the hole, McCumber, from much the same distance and also on the lower tier of the green, had an eagle putt to level the match. Totally misjudging the pace and the upslope, he was six feet short, leaving a tester for birdie to stay in the match. The American was not short with his second putt. Woosnam calmly sunk his four-footer and was quickly on his way to the last tee, still leading by one.

With the wind playing havoc with drives off the eighteenth tee, McCumber, needing to win the hole, was forced into taking a driver out for his second shot. The ironic cheers of the home crowd soon told him that he had failed to clear the lake. Some way in front of the American, Woosnam also broke out the lumber. His all-or-nothing swing barely saw his ball creep over the lake, coming to rest at the front of the green by a bunker.

Realizing that Woosnam had only just cleared the water with a wood, Calcavecchia also took out his driver. Like McCumber, he also found the water. The ball never got up and instead skipped across the surface, just managing to make it to dry land on the far side. Faldo, having played up to a few feet in front of the lake, hit a very poor third, coming up way short of the flag in the light rough to the left of the green.

McCumber took his drop and played his pitch to the very back of the green in four. With half a shot at his ball on the stony "beach," and standing with his heels in the water, Calcavecchia got all ball and watched as it flew off the back of the green into the photographers.

From a difficult lie, Woosnam struck an almost unbelievable chip-and-run that arrowed in on the flag, hit the hole, looped up into the air, and stopped three feet beyond the cup. With his partner out of the hole, Calcavecchia, needing to hole his fourth shot from off the back of the green, could only knock his short chip tamely past the hole. Woosnam's putt was conceded, and Europe had another win on the last hole, to end up with a two-hole victory.

"We were determined to get the full point because the others had, and we knew we might get taunted at dinner."
—*Ian Woosnam*

Tom Watson and Mark O'Meara (USA) v. Seve Ballesteros and Jose Maria Olazabal (EUR)

Ballesteros and Olazabal tore the heart out of Watson and O'Meara, winning the first five holes. Olazabal set the scene immediately by chipping in from off the back of the first green for a twenty-five-foot birdie. He followed this with a birdie putt that found nothing but hole on the second.

The Americans got in on the scoring act—negatively—by handing the third over with a bogey. Ballesteros's first birdie at the 579-yard fourth was followed by another costly American bogey.

Five down, Watson and O'Meara staged a mini-comeback—with two wins of their own, courtesy of birdie threes at the sixth and ninth holes.

"I let Jose Maria win the first five . . . then I took over because he was a little tired."
—*Seve Ballesteros*

Purveying a purple patch of his own, Ballesteros stopped the U.S. fight-back dead in its tracks. At his favorite hole, the tenth, he cut his drive back in with the wind to finish twelve feet past the hole. With his partner in a superb position for an eagle, Olazabal hit one of the greatest shots ever seen at this challenging hole. His drive landed five foot shy of the flag and dug its heels in to pull up four feet past the hole. With both Americans unable to challenge, Seve rolled his eagle putt left to right into the hole to push the lead back to four.

With the success Ballesteros and Olazabal enjoyed at this hole over the years, it should have been renamed "The Spaniard's Inn," because one or the other was always in.

On eleven, Ballesteros made a four-foot birdie putt to halve the hole and keep the lead at four. At the par-3 twelfth, Ballesteros hit a magnificent tee shot that stopped two feet from the flag for another certain birdie putt, which he almost dragged left and short. Five up with six to play, Seve was on a king-size roll.

"When Seve gets his Porsche going, not even San Pedro [St. Peter] in heaven can stop him."
—*Jose Maria Olazabal*

With his motor running, and helped by a tailwind, Ballesteros drove the 394-yard thirteenth, pushing his "tee shot approach" to the left-hand side of the green. This act of Spanish bravado shocked Mark Calcavecchia, who was trying to putt out on the green in the match ahead. From thirty feet away in the fringe, Seve knocked his putt four feet past. O'Meara was also in the fringe, on the right of the green, in two, but much closer than Ballesteros. He lagged his putt up to the side of the hole, which allowed Seve to hole his short putt for birdie and to win the match in double-quick time.

This spellbinding series of scores (2-3-2-3) from the Spaniard closed the match out 6 and 5.

Despite the very windy conditions, the Spaniards were an astonishing seven under par for their thirteen holes. Although last out, this was the first match to finish in the afternoon, and it set the European team on their way to sweeping their opponents for only the second time in a Ryder Cup session.

Since 1985, the United States had gone 4-13-1 in fourball play, which dumbfounded Curtis Strange: "Who can make reason out of that? There's just no logic to it."

Nick Faldo had an answer: "We were motivated by a few criticisms. We know there's a hell of a long way to go. But we've done this before."

Afternoon fourball result: USA 0, EUR 4
Day one result: USA 3, EUR 5

Day Two: Morning Foursomes

Another 8 A.M. start was greeted with a better weather outlook: hazy sunshine and little wind.

Lanny Wadkins and Payne Stewart (USA) v. Nick Faldo and Ian Woosnam (EUR)

Faldo and Woosnam were sent out first to repel an early American charge, as Wadkins and Stewart were entrusted with launching the U.S. offensive.

With the first three holes halved in par fours, this looked as if it would be a close match. After finding trouble at the 579-yard fourth, the Americans could make only bogey six to lose the hole to par. The United States got this hole back with their first birdie at the fifth, while the sixth was halved in birdie threes.

Faldo and Woosnam made their third birdie in eight holes to retake the lead but lost it immediately on the next. Faldo failed to extricate Woosnam's poor drive from the rough, and the match was all square at the turn.

On his players helping each other too much: "These men win hundreds of thousands of dollars, and they are used to consulting only their caddie when they're standing over a shot. If you bring in a third party, it's a new consideration and it doesn't seem to help."
—*Raymond Floyd*

With everything to play for on the back nine, Stewart found more trouble off the tenth tee, but this time trouble was of the liquid variety, and the European lead was back to one. The home pair birdied eleven with a fifteen-foot putt from Woosnam, and two holes later he holed another birdie putt from twelve feet to go three up.

After halving the next two holes, Woosnam fired his second shot at sixteen over the flag to the fringe at the back of the green. Stewart's approach was even better, pulling up ten feet short of the hole. Faldo's putt started on line but slipped to the right as it got close to the hole. The Americans conceded the putt, the hole for a half, and the match, 3 and 2.

Paul Azinger and Chip Beck (USA) v. Gordon Brand and Sam Torrance (EUR)

Floyd was forced to pit two rookies together, and Azinger and Beck took on the two Scots Brand and Torrance. After the first hole was halved in par, the next four holes gave up five birdies: one by Europe at the second and a pair of American sub-par strikes at three and four, topped by a share of the par-4 fifth. This gave the U.S. side a one-hole lead that they held on to, halving the next couple of holes.

The Scots bogeyed eight and birdied nine on the back of Torrance's ten-footer, reaching the turn just one down against what would later prove to be the Americans' best pairing.

Azinger and Beck blew the match open with birdies on eleven and twelve before halving the next two holes in par. Three up with four to play, Azinger and Beck looked to close the game out on the 550-yard fifteenth, where Azinger coaxed a short pitch to four feet. Torrance needed to hole his approach, but it drifted nine feet past the flag. After Brand missed his putt, Beck holed his for a birdie four to take the match by 4 and 3.

The impressive Americans jelled well together, covering their fifteen holes in six under par (two shots better than any other pair in the morning).

Mark Calcavecchia and Ken Green (USA) v. Christy O'Connor and Ronan Rafferty (EUR)

Having paired Scots in the preceding match, Jacklin linked up his two Irishmen and got much the same result against Ken Green and Mark Calcavecchia.

In this turbulent match, only three holes were halved in regulation, only one on the front nine—the par-4 eighth. The first hole was halved in birdie, the United States bogeyed the second, Europe followed suit on the third, the United States made their second birdie on the par-5 fourth, Europe birdied five and bogeyed six, and the United States birdied the par-3 seventh.

At the end of this fluctuating opening, Calcavecchia and Green were only two up, which soon became three after Rafferty blew a five-footer for par on the 400-yard ninth.

The tenth was a walkover, as the Americans' eagle two laughed loudly in the face of Europe's bogey five. Eleven was the second hole halved in par—after Rafferty continued his nightmare on the greens by missing a birdie putt from four feet. The par 3 twelfth played host to a reprise of Rafferty's putting atrocities, as he missed another four-footer to go five down.

A ray of Irish hope appeared on the thirteenth, where their only birdie on the back nine accounted for the hole. Fourteen was the third and last hole to be halved in par. With the United States four up with four to play, O'Connor's third shot to fifteen pitched twelve feet past the pin and spun back directly toward the hole, coming to rest four feet away. Calcavecchia's third shot also spun back but finished up farther away. Green could not make his ten-foot putt, and Rafferty cast aside his demons to hole his frightening four-footer to cut the lead to three.

"Ken and I played well. We made a couple of mistakes, but by then we were five up, and if you're going to do something wrong, then that is a good time to do it."
—*Mark Calcavecchia*

On sixteen, O'Connor guided his second shot inside ten feet of the flag, and Calcavecchia seriously underclubbed and failed to hit the putting surface with his second. The Americans' ball finished up in the front fringe, twenty yards short of the flag, from where Green putted up on line but watched as his ball stopped eight inches short. The putt was conceded, and Rafferty had to hole his putt to keep the match alive. Drained of all confidence on the putting surface, Rafferty pulled his putt to the left of the hole to hand the Americans a solid 3 and 2 win.

Tom Kite and Curtis Strange (USA) v. Seve Ballesteros and Jose Maria Olazabal (EUR)

After Kite and Strange won the opening hole off the latter's pitch to five feet, Ballesteros and Olazabal birdied the 399-yard fifth and 396-yard sixth to go one up. Out in two threes and seven fours, Ballesteros and Olazabal had a two-hole lead when the Americans bogeyed the eighth.

The Spanish players walked off ten with their customary birdie, but this was well matched by their opponents. Olazabal settled his seven-iron approach to eleven no farther than seven feet from the flag, and Ballesteros made the birdie putt to go three up. The Spaniards let the Americans back into the game with back-to-back bogeys. On the 235-yard twelfth, Olazabal pushed his tee shot and left Ballesteros in the right-hand bunker alongside the green. Seve played out nine feet beyond the flag, but Strange made a three-foot par putt to win the hole.

After Ballesteros drove into a bunker on thirteen and Olazabal had played out, Seve knocked his approach six feet from the hole. Olazabal had his par putt catch the left-hand lip and stay out. Strange made his two-foot putt for par, cutting the lead to one. Fifteen was halved in birdies, and sixteen was shared with pars.

With two holes to play, the Americans were on the front of the seventeenth green in three, with Olazabal's second shot way right of the green among some thick bushes. With a small fir tree interfering with his backswing, it was all Ballesteros could do to chop his ball into the bunker in front of him. Strange knocked his long putt four feet past the hole to look all over winning the hole. With very little green to work with, Olazabal jabbed his ball out of the trap, somehow stopping it five feet from the target. Seve made the putt for a par five. Kite tentatively made his slippery downhill par putt to go to eighteen still one down.

"We knew we had to win because . . . of the boost it gives the whole team psychologically. I just had to sink that last putt."
—*Seve Ballesteros*

Ballesteros's long iron from the eighteenth fairway found a bunker to the right of the green, while Kite's second shot also beached itself in the same strip of sand. Olazabal's recovery lobbed onto the fringe and rolled up to six feet of the hole. Strange flew his sand shot farther, bouncing it pin-high but rolling it on three feet past. Needing to hole his putt to secure the match, Ballesteros safely slotted his par putt into the middle of the cup.

Morning foursomes result: USA 2, EUR 2

Day Two: Afternoon Fourball

Having promised to play all twelve of his players on each day, Floyd reneged, leaving out Couples, O'Meara, and Watson (one of his wild-card picks) for the second time on this second day.

Paul Azinger and Chip Beck (USA) v. Nick Faldo and Ian Woosnam (EUR)

In an incredible match, the likes of which may never have been seen in any class of golf, let alone the Ryder Cup, Azinger, Beck, Faldo, and Woosnam managed to birdie the first eleven holes.

The Americans reached the turn in an astonishing 30 strokes but could open up only a one-hole lead, as the British pair carded a 31. The die was cast on the very first hole. Woosnam, having pulled his approach to the left of the green behind a bunker, made a miracle chip shot. After landing inches beyond the bunker on the fringe, his ball ran on at some pace toward the hole and dived in like a scared rabbit outrunning a fox. Nailing his second right in front of the flag had left Azinger with a seven-foot birdie putt for the half, which he rolled home to cancel out Woosnam's wonder chip.

The European's magic faded after this opening, and they could only par the next three holes between them. The Americans continued in sparkling form as Azinger made two more birdies at two and three, while Beck birdied the fourth hole to open up a three-hole lead.

On the fifth green, Woosnam made a ten-foot putt for a birdie to cut the lead to two, and on the 396-yard sixth Woosnam again showed everyone else the way home. From out of the right-hand rough, he fired a long iron over a bunker at the front of the green, his ball galloping up the green to four feet of the hole. Beck's second also found the green, coming up twelve feet short of the pin, and he sank the birdie putt to prevent Woosnam from pulling another hole back. Not to be denied, Woosnam stroked his ball home for his half in birdie threes—disappointment writ large over his face.

Having allowed his partner to work hard for a win and two halves, Faldo looked to be off form as he guided his tee shot into a bunker at the par-3 seventh. Faced by a steep wall of sand, Faldo did well to loft his ball out, but he was repaid as his ball took two kind bounces and ducked into the hole for another birdie. Azinger got back in on show time, on the eighth, with an accurate approach pin-high four feet from the hole, for a birdie putt.

On the 400-yard ninth, Woosnam stole the show with an immaculate pitch over the corner of the lake to six feet of the hole at the back of the green. Nine holes out of nine had all given up birdies, and the United States held only a slender one-hole lead.

On ten, Woosnam badly hooked his tee shot into the woods, so Faldo played up short of the green with an iron. Azinger took out a wood and hit a tree on the right, while Beck knocked his tee shot onto the front of the green. Faldo pitched to the back left of the green, while Woosnam had left himself a shot between two trees over the fat part of the water, with a third of the green to aim at. All he could do was thread his shot onto the green and through the back. Azinger, with a much more straightforward chip, lobbed his ball up to fifteen feet of the flag.

Beck's eighty-foot eagle putt finished three feet from the hole, forcing one of the Europeans to hole his next shot for a half. Faldo tried vainly but finished a foot to the right of the hole, but, from fifteen feet away, Woosnam chipped in again to snatch a half off the shocked Americans. After Azinger made a woeful attempt at his putt, Beck needed to hole his three-footer for a half, which he did quite easily.

Some good-humored fans politely booed all four players for failing to make a birdie on twelve.

With his tail up, Beck also birdied the eleventh, but so did Faldo for another half. Finally, the magical spell of birdies was broken: twelve and thirteen stood firm, yielding to no man. Both holes were halved in par, leaving the United States up by one.

On the par-3 fourteenth, Woosnam made his par, allowing Faldo to concentrate on another birdie putt. Faced with a very tricky twenty-five-foot putt across the slope in the green, he read the line perfectly—sinking the putt for a two. Beck missed his birdie putt, but Azinger, from twenty feet behind the flag, slipped his ball in the left-hand side door of the hole. Another hole had been halved in birdie.

Still one down, Woosnam slammed his second shot along the right-hand side of the green at the 550-yard fifteenth, but Azinger had already left his second shot on the right-hand edge of the green. Faldo's third found the heart of the green, eleven feet from the flag, while Beck managed to put his third shot inside of Faldo's, below the cup. Woosnam's chip shot rolled six feet past the hole, and Azinger's thirty-foot putt came to a halt fifteen inches past the hole. Conceding Azinger's ball, Faldo attempted a birdie putt for a half, but the ball rolled at the hole, just caught the left-hand lip, and spun out. With Woosnam also missing his birdie putt, the Americans doubled their lead with three to play.

After sixteen was halved in par, Beck powered his second through the back of the green at seventeen, and Woosnam and Faldo followed suit with their approaches. The American's chip back rolled to within two feet of the hole. Faldo needed to hole his chip but came up a few inches short, and all Woosnam could do was knock his chip beyond the hole. Beck applied the knockout par putt to take a most incredible match, 2 and 1, with his side carding a joint eleven under par for their round.

On Azinger's carding seven birdies on his own in this match: *"Boy! Did they ever make a hell of a lot of birdies!"* —NICK FALDO

On the first-ever loss by the European pairing after being unbeaten (5-0-2) in the previous seven matches together: *"We beat two thoroughbreds today, and we're real excited. I don't know that I've ever been this happy, not even winning a golf tournament."* —PAUL AZINGER

Tom Kite and Mark McCumber (USA) v. Jose Maria Canizares and Bernhard Langer (EUR)

Widely regarded as the slowest player on the European PGA Tour, (if not in the world), Bernhard Langer was paired with the oldest man in this contest, forty-two-year-old Jose Maria Canizares. Neither deliberation nor age was of any help to the Europeans, who never really got into the match against Tom Kite and Mark McCumber, although the sides traded winning birdie putts on the first two holes.

With the next five holes halved—the par-5 fourth with birdies—the Americans took a lead into the turn by making another birdie at the 460-yard eighth. Of the four players, only McCumber really showed any sign of consistent form. The highlight of this encounter was his tee shot at the tenth to ten feet of the hole, setting up a superb eagle.

On the strength of this, the United States made birdies at the next two holes to open up a three-hole lead. Following a tremendous tee shot at the par-3 fourteenth, Langer failed to convert his six-foot birdie putt, and any hopes of Europe's recovering vanished.

Standing two up with two to play, McCumber punched his second shot into seventeen, planting his ball pin-high—eight feet from the flag. With two putts for the match, he rolled his first up to within a foot for a conceded half and the match, 2 and 1.

Payne Stewart and Curtis Strange (USA) v. Howard Clark and Mark James (EUR)

Clark and James stormed out with a pair of birdie threes to open with a two-hole lead over Stewart and Strange. On the fourth, Stewart's second shot nearly rolled into the hole for an eagle, and the hole was finally halved in birdie fours. After this close shave, the Americans trimmed the lead back with birdie threes of their own on five and six.

All square, the match reached the turn without any further change of lead, until the Americans got their heads in front for the first time with a birdie at the tenth. Stewart's drive not only found the green but stopped fifteen feet from the pin, and two putts were sufficient to win the hole.

Clark made a nine-footer for his birdie on thirteen to level, but Strange stuck his tee shot at the par-3 fourteenth within a stride of the hole. In a match that saw no pair up by more than two holes, and the score pulled back to all square three times, the U.S. pair found itself with a precarious one-hole lead with four to play.

The last four holes produced some heart-stopping golf of the highest (and on occasions lowest) quality.

From a greenside bunker on the long fifteenth, James almost holed his recovery, but the ball spun ninety degrees around the pin, denying the Englishman an eagle three. From the back of the green, Strange holed his ten-foot birdie putt to deny James the hole. Strange had a fifteen-foot putt for birdie at sixteen, which edged left of the hole and stayed out. Following an exquisite eight-iron, Clark stepped up and sank an eight-footer for birdie to level the match.

With adrenaline pumping, Clark sliced his drive into the trees at seventeen, then fashioned a recovery shot down the fairway and some way short of the hole. From the left-hand rough, James hit a rasping three-wood that crept up the right-hand fringe of the green. Whether the tension got to the two Americans or not, they both appeared to play the hole in the worst possible way—as though it were a kind of sinister side bet. With his second shot, Stewart hit a salacious slice way short and way right of the hole, threatening the spectators' safety rather than the green. From the middle of the fairway, and some yards in front of Stewart, Strange managed to conjure up an even worse five-wood toward the same besieged fans.

With the U.S. side in trouble short and right of the green, Clark played a dream third shot that ran right over the hole, stopping a few feet beyond. From among some small trees, Strange had only a narrow "window" to hit through and could only chip his ball into the bunker in front of him.

Stewart fared even worse as his muffed chip didn't even reach Strange's bunker. Although Strange got up and down to make his par five, James chipped up close to the hole with his third, then made his six-foot birdie putt to win the hole, taking an invaluable one-hole lead up the eighteenth. Having won the last two holes to move from one down to one up, the Europeans knew they could not lose this vital dogfight.

On eighteen, James was faced with a dreadful lie for his second shot; his drive had run off the fairway, leaving his ball on the edge of the bunker—half in and half out. With the lake looming large in front of him, James had no margin for error as he went for the green with a three-iron. He picked the ball perfectly and sent it flying at the flag, finishing pin-high, twenty feet to the right. Stewart bailed out too far to the right with his second and landed nearer the blue-and-white-tented village than the green, twenty yards from the flag. Strange was unlucky with his second, which pitched onto the brow of the first upslope, fifteen feet short of the hole; his ball stopped for a moment before rolling back fifteen yards. Watching in anticipation as the Americans self-destructed, Clark had the luxury of having hit a most wondrous draw off the tee, bouncing his ball six inches over the stream, where it launched itself toward the fairway, curling round in front of the lake.

Waiting for the players to tee off on eighteen, Raymond Floyd parked his buggy "out of range" and behind the trees. Clark's monster cut drive almost caused the U.S. captain to fall out of his cart in amazement.

From pole position in the fairway, Clark flew his second shot onto the middle tier of the green, pin-high from the flag and only seventeen feet away. Stewart's short chip briefly threatened the hole but ran on by a few feet. With his partner out of the equation, Strange completely misread the line and weight of his putt, sending it way past the hole. The British pair had two putts each for the match, and James all but holed his sixteen-foot birdie putt, close enough for the Americans to concede defeat.

Four holes earlier, the U.S. pair had stood one up, but the side walked off the last green with heads bowed, having to take a distressing one-hole loss on the chin. The Americans' excellent round of 66 was also one worse than their rivals'.

Mark Calcavecchia and Ken Green (USA) v. Seve Ballesteros and Jose Maria Olazabal (EUR)

Ballesteros and Olazabal proved to be the pairing of the tournament, and they played almost as well as they had in their previous day's annihilation of Watson and O'Meara. They were soon three up against Calcavecchia and Green, thanks to a birdie from Olazabal on the second and a brace of birdies from Ballesteros on three and four.

This was the battle of the undefeated pairings; the Spaniards were 2–0–1 in their matches, while Calcavecchia and Green were 2–0

An American birdie at the eighth did little to repel the Spaniards' unstoppable quest for points, epitomized by Ballesteros's scorching long iron in to the ninth. Seve's second shot was almost too good to be true; it did everything but land in the hole, spinning back a couple of feet for an assured birdie.

Seve set off even more fireworks on the tenth, when his chip from the back of the green hit the pin to serve up another birdie and a four-hole lead. After their fine victory in the morning, Calcavecchia and Green had no real answer to this sort of attacking golf, although they birdied the 394-yard thirteenth to cut the lead to three. Having won only their second hole of the round, the Americans suffered at the hands of another Spanish birdie on fourteen.

Ballesteros had a simple chance to snuff out the match on fifteen, but he blew his three-foot par putt, his ball running around the cup and sliding out the side.

Having dodged one bullet, the U.S. pair was well and truly gunned down on the next hole. From the left-hand side of the sixteenth fairway, Olazabal found the green pin-high to eight feet, and his partner pitched up even closer. Calcavecchia almost holed his eighteen-foot putt from just off the green, but this miss brought an immediate concession to give Europe the win, 4 and 2.

Afternoon fourball result: USA 2, EUR 2
Day two result: USA 4, EUR 4
Overall match score: USA 7, EUR 9

The Americans had not enjoyed a lead going into the last-day singles since 1981. Going into the final day, the score stood exactly the same as it had in 1985, when Europe had also won at The Belfry.

Day Three: Singles

The final day was treated to perfect sunny weather, with little or no wind, and everything was all set fair for another historic day of golf.

Paul Azinger (USA) v. Seve Ballesteros (EUR)

Jacklin sent out his ace first up, in the hope that Ballesteros could spark off a tidal wave of European success in his wake. Fired up against Paul Azinger, the Spaniard blasted off with a two-hole lead after birdies on the second and fourth holes.

Azinger repaid Floyd's faith in him, leading off the American counterattack by taking four of the next five holes.

Two Azinger birdies coupled with two Ballesteros bogeys allowed the American to turn for home up by two. The Spaniard leveled with a birdie at ten (a surefire gimme from the tee all week for Seve), and a par at eleven also won a prize.

With a hang-tough birdie four at the 550-yard fifteenth, Azinger regained a one-hole lead that he defended to the eighteenth.

With the match his for the losing, the American tried his best to lose it and his ball, by driving into the water. With the door flung open wide, Ballesteros, chasing a half the way a hungry lion chases a limping gazelle, unleashed his drive across the water and across the fairway into the light rough beyond.

After his penalty drop, Azinger hit a prodigious third—with a wood—over two stretches of water. His ball just scraped over the lake and dribbled into the bunker at the very front of the green. With his ball wrapped up in the rough, Seve took a three-iron and pressed too hard, probably jolted by Azinger's amazing act of aggression. The Spaniard could only watch in dismay as his ball ducked into the lake, and a door slammed shut in his head.

After his drop, Ballesteros pitched his fourth up onto the top tier. Again, he could only stand and stare in expectation as his ball started to spin back, but it stopped just short of the slope that would have rolled it down to the flag. The American played a divinely delicate lob out of the sand to run his ball up to four feet of the hole. This forced Ballesteros into having to make his treacherous twenty-foot putt down across the ridge.

With one of the most incredible putts, under the most incredible pressure, Ballesteros barely touched his shot. The ball raced down the incline and was in danger of running off the green into the lake at the bottom had it not been struck with the precision of a master craftsman. The packed crowd could hardly believe their eyes. The cheer that rose as Ballesteros's ball dropped into the

Despite the friendly backslaps on the last green, this was the match that stoked the coals of a "feud" between the two players that was to burn even more fiercely at Kiawah Island in 1991. Apart from many niggling complaints, it had been quite obvious that Ballesteros had deliberately walked over, stood in Azinger's line of sight, and put his hands on his hips as the American prepared to play out of the bunker on eighteen. On other occasions, the Spaniard was reported as standing in Azinger's view and shuffling his white shoes as the American was about to hit. Azinger returned the gamesmanship by hovering over Seve's ball, intimating that if he were not there, the Spaniard would improve his lie.

center of the cup was crowned by a most sporting slap on the Spaniard's back by Azinger.

Azinger had to wait for the crowd to quiet down, only to hear cheers echoing around the course signaling other home successes. The American knew that his short putt meant much more than settling a personal duel. Having played two shots of the highest quality to put himself in a position to win the match, Azinger was not going to let it all come to naught. He slowly and deliberately stroked his putt into the middle of the hole. Ballesteros was the first to congratulate him, returning the genial slap on the back.

Chip Beck (USA) v. Bernhard Langer (EUR)

Having been off his game during his two losses in the pairs matches, Bernhard Langer did not put up much of a contest against Chip Beck, who had played some wonderfully consistent golf all week.

Beck did not start out this match too consistently, though. A birdie first up gave him a lead, but he bogeyed three and birdied four. The German, showing glimpses of his past Ryder Cup and majors form, birdied the fifth to level, but Beck was back on top with his third birdie at the 396-yard sixth. Langer bogeyed the ninth, but Beck's birdie would have won him the hole in any case.

Two up at the turn, Beck held this lead until another Langer bogey—on thirteen—stretched the lead to three. A German birdie two at fourteen was the last note of cheer for the home team, as Beck birdied the par-5 fifteenth to go back up by three. Langer conceded an inglorious defeat on seventeen when he failed to finish the hole in answer to Beck's birdie four.

With three wins and a half, rookie Chip Beck was the only undefeated American in three days. He also inflicted Langer's first-ever defeat in the singles, and the German's third loss in three games.

With six birdies and only one bogey in his round, Beck clinched a fine 3 and 1 win. Beck's point brought the United States level (9–9) for the first time since Friday afternoon.

Payne Stewart (USA) v. Jose Maria Olazabal (EUR)

From the start, this match quickly marked itself as a classic in the making. As with his pairs matches on the first two days, Olazabal stepped out to an early two-hole lead with birdie threes on the first two holes.

Stewart replied with birdies at four and five to level the match. And so the match progressed. The twenty-three-year old Spaniard claimed the 460-yard eighth with his third birdie on the outward nine, for a one-hole lead.

Having owned the tenth hole all week in his pairs matches with Ballesteros, Olazabal seemed to miss his partner's guiding hand and bogeyed the hole. With his opponent handing him the hole, Stewart rammed home the psychological advantage by making a birdie three at the 420-yard eleventh to go up in the match for the first time.

Showing why he had ousted Ballesteros as his team's best player, Olazabal struck back with another birdie at the thirteenth to level. With the next two holes halved in par, it was Stewart's turn to make a hole-winning birdie at fifteen, and he halved sixteen to leave himself in control of the match: one up with two to play.

Staring defeat in the face, Olazabal made an invaluable two-foot birdie putt to square the match at the long seventeenth. This gave the Spaniard the psychological upper hand, because he was now able to take on the last—the American graveyard—on level terms.

Olazabal's final drive ran through the fairway into the shallow rough beyond. Sensing a chance to take the match, Stewart tried to get cute with a draw off the tee, but his cute draw turned into an ugly hook, finding the stream that cut across the fairway. Donning waterproofs, Stewart took up a stance in the water and looked more like a fly fisherman than a professional golfer. A mighty swing and an even mightier splash confused the American, who looked all around for any sign that his ball had come out. Once the ripples subsided, he realized the ball was still lying in the water. With a sense of failed destiny and with a good sense of humor, Stewart opined, "We're gonna try this again."

Fair play to the amphibious American, his second swipe succeeded in moving his ball out of the water—six inches, to be exact—and onto the muddy shelf of the stream. Essaying the air of a man not born to quit, Stewart lifted his fourth shot out of the hazard and onto the fairway ahead. He acknowledged the good-natured cheers and sympathetic applause from the crowd and quickly disrobed back to his plus fours, taking full stock of his watery demise.

Olazabal had one aim in mind: to knock his ball over the lake for a certain win. He cleared the water with something to spare and was not worried to see his ball dribbling back down the green, having just failed to make it onto the second tier. Refusing to be beaten or give up, Stewart pondered how he was going to hole his fifth shot.

Around in 68, Olazabal was the only unbeaten European, with 4½ points out of a possible 5, making him the undisputed MVP of the contest.

Deep in thought, he was almost hit by Rafferty's monster tee shot from behind. If Stewart needed reminding how badly he had played the hole, having someone chase his first shot up his backside while he contemplated his fifth probably was a touch cruel. All he could achieve was to find the front bunker with an underhit pitch. Cutting a sad and lonely figure, he strode manfully around the lake to concede the match one down.

Mark Calcavecchia (USA) v. Ronan Rafferty (EUR)

With birdie threes at the second and third, Ronan Rafferty took a two-hole lead, but Mark Calcavecchia was back on even terms by the sixth. After the par-5 fourth was halved in offsetting birdies, Calcavecchia took the 399-yard fifth with a birdie and the sixth with a par.

This was another mishmash of a match on which neither player stamped his authority. Rafferty went one up with a birdie three on the ninth that easily beat the American's bogey, but Calcavecchia leveled immediately with his own birdie on the tenth. The American took his only lead of the match when the Irishman bogeyed the 235-yard twelfth, but the match was all square again on the next when Rafferty made his fifth birdie at thirteen.

With the next three holes halved, the match would be decided on the last two holes. All square on seventeen, Calcavecchia had a fourteen-foot putt to win the hole with one to play, but he failed to take the opportunity.

"I thought that we had the team to win it. We had problems again with the eighteenth hole. We had three boys in a row hit it in the water. You can't do that and beat world-class players."
—*Raymond Floyd*

Level on eighteen, Rafferty unleashed a mammoth drive that awoke Stewart from his reverie ahead. Whether it was this drive or the prolonged wait for Stewart to clear the fairway, Calcavecchia hit a wretched drive that found the middle of the stream.

With the match on the line, Calcavecchia knew there would be no point laying up in front of the lake in three, since Rafferty was already there in one. So he dropped his ball and drew out his three-wood for one last mighty gamble. An extra thirty yards on the shot would not have kept his ball dry, as he found the water for the second time in two shots. By the time the American reached Rafferty's ball, he already knew his fate, and conceded before they reached the green.

Tom Kite (USA) v. Howard Clark (EUR)

Quite simply, Tom Kite played some of the best and most devastating singles golf ever seen in the Ryder Cup. Those who witnessed his massacre of Howard Clark felt that two players playing fourball against Kite would not have held their own.

At one stage during the day, with eleven matches still out on course, the U.S. players were up in eight, all square in two, and down in this one. Had the match finished at around midday, Ray Floyd's men would have triumphed by a whopping 17–11 score line.

Reeling off three consecutive wins after the second hole (birdie-par-birdie), Kite added birdie-inspired wins on six, eight, and nine with four threes in a row. Five birdies and four pars to the turn saw the American up by six and out in an astounding 31 shots.

Clark hardly helped his cause by making the turn in three over par, but he had little to offer in the way of resistance. The Englishman failed to complete the tenth, and Kite's sixth birdie in eleven holes was amply rewarded with a record singles win, 8 and 7.

Kite's remarkable card read 4-3-4-4-4-3-3-3-3-3-3 for a net six-under total. Kite's record margin of victory in Ryder Cup singles was later equaled by Fred Couples's demolition of Ian Woosnam in 1997.

"Howard Clark was handed a dog license today by American Tom Kite."
—Peter Alliss

In the United Kingdom, dog licenses used to cost seven shillings and sixpence, or 7 and 6, and any heavy defeat by more than 7 and 6 was called a "dog license."

Mark O'Meara (USA) v. Mark James (EUR)

Mark O'Meara, who had suffered a poor Ryder Cup, took the lead on the second with a birdie three, which was eventually canceled out by Mark James's three on the fifth. From this point on, the Englishman never looked back: two more birdies claimed the sixth and eighth for James, who reached the turn two up.

With four birdies on the front nine, James was in complete control coming home. O'Meara bogeyed the par-3 twelfth, while the Englishman carded his fifth birdie on thirteen to go four up with five to play.

O'Meara briefly kept the match alive with his third birdie of the round at fifteen, but was unable to pull back any more ground. Three up with three to play, the Englishman had two putts from twelve feet to settle the outcome on sixteen. His first putt came up three feet short, but he holed out for a 3 and 2 win.

James covered the front nine in just 32 strokes, one more than Kite ahead of him, but the American held a six-hole lead, whereas James was only two up.

Fred Couples (USA) v. Christy O'Connor (EUR)

Neither Couples nor O'Connor could establish a lead after the first nine holes, which both reached in 34 strokes. O'Connor had taken a lead on the second, and Couples leveled on the third, each with birdie threes. The Irishman bogeyed the 399-yard fifth to go one down but leveled the match at the turn with his second birdie three. These two players were so well matched that they even shared the par-3 seventh with a brace of deuces.

"The last day of the Masters, you're nervous if you're near the lead. In the Ryder Cup, if it's the first hole or the fourth or the eighteenth, your stomach never stops churning. It lasts all day long. Anyone who tells you they're not nervous is lying." —FRED COUPLES

The "hit-or-bust" tenth saw Couples's brave birdie give him a lead he held through fifteen holes. On sixteen, O'Connor Junior unleashed a shot that Senior (his uncle) would have been proud of. His pitch from a hundred yards almost landed in the hole and came to rest four feet past. In reply, Couples also struck a fine shot but was nine feet short of the pin. Unable to hole his putt, Couples could only stand back and watch his opponent tentatively roll his ball at the right-hand side of the cup. Looking for all the world as if he had pushed his vital putt, the ball wavered on the lip before toppling in with the luck of the whole Irish nation willing it on. O'Connor sighed deeply, looked to the heavens, and offered a silent prayer of thanks.

All square with two to play, seventeen was halved in par, although Couples missed a vital three-foot birdie putt for the lead. Maybe he felt the ominous call of eighteenth, which loomed large once again for the hydrophobic Americans.

O'Connor hit one of the better drives of the day, curling his ball into the middle of the L-shaped fairway. Unlike many of his colleagues before him, Couples did not flirt with the stream. Instead, he scorched a thunderous drive way over 300 yards and was closer to finding the distant lake than the adjacent stream. With the win in his sights, Couples left himself a nine-iron to the green, while Christy O'Connor was about to hit the most famous two-iron shot in Irish golfing history—and one that not only his uncle but the whole of Ireland would be proud of.

"Coming down the fairway, Tony Jacklin said to me, 'If you put him under pressure, I promise you will win the hole and the match. Just have a good swing.' And that's all I thought about. I had a big two-iron, I made a good turn, and just hit it." —Christy O'Connor

From 240 yards, he singularly nailed his approach to three and a half feet of the hole. The tumultuous reception from the massed gallery was possibly heard as far away as the Emerald Isle. In response to the Irishman's supreme second, Couples played one of the worst shots of his life. He shanked his short pitch so far to the right of the green, the TV cameras almost failed to pick it up. It seemed even the unflappable Couples had yielded to the pressure, just as so many of his colleagues had done before on this fine, finishing hole.

With the gallery now at fever pitch, O'Connor was almost carried onto the green on a carpet of cacophonous cheering. Couples's chip from the side of the green came up short enough for him to putt first. From five feet, Couples already knew the Ryder Cup was, once again, slipping from the Americans' clutches. His putt raced over the top of the hole, and his only redress was to concede to the Irishman, who was immediately overcome by tears (and his wife, Ann) as he stood and offered another prayer to the sky.

A few weeks after he returned home to the West of Ireland and a hero's welcome, O'Connor sold his magical two-iron at an auction for fifty thousand pounds, which he donated to a hospital near his hometown of Galway.

Ken Green (USA) v. Jose Maria Canizares (EUR)

The first hole again gave up a birdie, and Jose Maria Canizares doubled his lead on the par-5 fourth with his second birdie. In reply, Ken Green holed a twenty-two-foot putt on the sixth, and the players traded birdies to pars on eight and nine to give the Spaniard a one-hole lead on the outward stretch.

Coming home, Green went on a remarkable run, covering the next five holes in fifteen shots—all threes (three birdies and two pars). Despite this impressive scoring bonanza, Green could pick up only two holes on the Spaniard and led him by one after fourteen.

Having failed to see off his older opponent, Green saw Canizares pitch up to inches of the flag on fifteen for a birdie four to level the match. Sixteen was halved in par, leaving two holes to play.

From the seventeenth fairway, the Spaniard unleashed an ugly-looking swing with his three-wood, but the result was quite beautiful. His ball ran up and onto the back of the massive green, leaving him an equally massive putt back down. Green had left an even longer eagle putt, plus he had a ridge in the green to play over. He did, however, manage to knock his ball up to three feet of the hole, while Canizares, closer but still forty feet away, could only run his ball up to five feet of the hole. In terms of the destiny of the Ryder Cup, Canizares was faced with the sort of putt that no man should be asked to take on single-handed. But that is the stuff that Ryder Cups are made of, and Canizares proved he was made of the right stuff, holing his knee-clanking five-footer for a half in birdie fours.

Canizares again kept his nerve off the tee at eighteen, playing a marvelously controlled drive to the middle of the fairway. Green also hit a fine tee shot, but much straighter, and finished on the edge of the fairway some way behind Canizares. The American hit a mighty wood at the green but suffered the agonizing fate of seeing his ball roll back down the slope to the front of the putting surface. Not wanting to flirt with the lake up front, Canizares deliberately played a strong second to the very back of the green.

From sixty feet beyond the flag, Canizares had a devilish putt back down the slope, but his perfectly weighted stroke seemed to take an age to reach its destination—three feet to the right of the hole. Green's putting touch deserted him as he sent his fifty-foot putt up to the slope, past the hole, and six feet yonder. This left him a nasty, sharp breaking putt back downhill to halve the hole. The American slightly underborrowed, and his ball slipped by the right of the hole.

Canizares was left with his three-footer for the 1-up win. He calmly rolled the ball in for the point that saw Europe retain the Ryder Cup. The older Spaniard could barely conceal his delight as he danced off the green to be engulfed by his fellow countrymen, Olazabal and Ballesteros.

As well as retaining the Ryder Cup, Canizares's hard-earned point meant that his side needed only half a point from the remaining four matches to win the Cup outright.

Mark McCumber (USA) v. Gordon Brand (EUR)

Amazingly, Mark McCumber birdied the first hole against Gordon Brand, Jr., and held on to this lead through the remainder of the front nine as the next eight holes were halved. The fourth and fifth holes were halved in birdies, whereas the other six holes were covered in regulation.

The American started home par-birdie-bogey to lose the lead, regain it, and lose it again. A birdie two at the 194-yard fourteenth gave McCumber the lead back again, but he eventually let it slip with a damaging bogey at seventeen. With the scoreboards informing them that their match would be crucial to the final outcome, both players knew they had a part to play in destiny.

Both safely negotiated the strips of water up eighteen and were safely on the green, faced with par putts. McCumber made his to guarantee at least a half-point, while Brand was faced with a putt for a half that would allow Europe to win the Ryder Cup outright. The Scot was unable to sink his ten-foot putt, and the United States still had a chance to escape with their pride intact.

This was the first American win on eighteen after thirteen previous visits there. They had managed to halve some holes, but recorded mostly losses. With a mighty round of 67, McCumber had broken the jinx on eighteen, though it was too late to help the United States regain the Cup.

Tom Watson (USA) v. Sam Torrance (EUR)

After his captain had left him on the bench for the whole of the second day, Tom Watson came into this singles match with something to prove. Sam Torrance had played twice, with one win and one loss, and he was looking for more glory on the same venue as his 1985 triumph.

This match went the way of Watson's pride rather than Torrance's pursuit of glories past, as the American birdied the first and never looked back. Torrance gave up the fourth with a bogey, birdied the par-3 seventh, and bogeyed the eighth as his round blew more cold than hot. With a birdie at the 396-yard sixth, Watson held a three-hole lead after nine.

Four up with a birdie two on the twelfth, Watson may have eased up slightly, as Torrance won the next two holes with a birdie and a par. With his lead suddenly slashed in half, the American was in no mood to let the match slip away. Nerve-settling halves on the fifteenth and sixteenth set Watson up for a glorious finish: his fifth birdie of the round, earning him a pride-restoring win, 3 and 1.

This was Tom Watson's last Ryder Cup appearance as a player, although he would return as a victorious captain in 1993. He left behind a 10-4-1 career record that may not stack up against the earlier legends' records, but it must not be forgotten that he played primarily in the modern, more competitive European era. The fact that he did not play in the '85 or '87 losses shows just how much his country missed him. A true golfing gentleman and a consummate team player, Watson lost only two of eleven pairs matches.

Lanny Wadkins (USA) v. Nick Faldo (EUR)

The Masters champion, Nick Faldo, struggled all day to stay with Lanny Wadkins, and he failed to make a single birdie on the front nine. The Englishman had taken a lead on the first hole thanks to a Wadkins bogey, but that would prove to be his only lead of the match. The American was level after his second-hole birdie, and further birdies on five and eight put him comfortably three up at the turn.

When the players halved the eleventh in pars, it was Faldo's tenth par in eleven holes. He had bogeyed the eighth (won by Wadkins's birdie three).

Wadkins's fourth birdie—on the tenth—pushed his lead to four. Faldo was still searching for his first birdie.

Both players bogeyed the par-3 twelfth, a nasty habit Wadkins carried to the next hole, where his lead was cut to two, on Faldo's first win since Wadkins's first-hole bogey. Wadkins's bogey habit turned into an addiction on sixteen, where he gave the birdie-less Faldo his third win of the match. The American's third bogey in five holes cut his own lead to one, and awoke a sleeping giant.

Faldo finally struck off his own ball, on the seventeenth, to level the match. His eighteen-foot putt from just off the green was his first and only birdie of the round.

On eighteen, it was finally an Englishman's turn to drown his drive in the drink. Pressing for the win, when a half would have won the Cup outright, Faldo cut off too much of the corner. His drive had too much draw and gave his ball too much to do to clear the stream, coming up a couple of feet short of clearing the water hazard.

With his opponent in trouble, Wadkins hit a sweet drive into the heart of the fairway. After Faldo laid up in front of the lake in three, Calcavecchia's second shot safely found the front of the green. The Englishman needed to hole his pitch and very nearly did so, planting his ball three feet from the cup. Unable to convert this excellent chip shot, Faldo saw his putt lip out and conceded the match to a very grateful Wadkins, who had been three up with six to play.

Curtis Strange (USA) v. Ian Woosnam (EUR)

Both captains saved their toughest battler for last, and the first four holes could not separate Curtis Strange and Ian Woosnam. The Welshman was the first to crack, bogeying the 399-yard fifth hole. Strange rammed home the psychological advantage by taking the sixth with the first birdie of the match.

Two down, Woosnam brought his battling qualities to the fore. He won the next two holes with his first birdie on the seventh and Strange's first bogey on eight.

All square at the turn, both battlers had battled out in 35 strokes, and the battle continued unabated as the next six holes were halved. This time it was Woosnam's turn to break the sequence in a positive fashion. His birdie at fifteen seemed to have given him the vital edge, but the American responded to his team's battle cry.

Strange pulled back level with a three-foot putt on sixteen, then left his third to seventeen stone dead for a birdie four. Woosnam was unable to match the American's accuracy, failing to hole a forty-foot birdie putt on seventeen to drop one down with one to play.

Strange more or less settled matters on eighteen with a supreme two-iron to within eight feet of the hole, a shot bettered only by O'Connor's career two-iron earlier.

When he successfully found the green on eighteen, U.S. Open champion Curtis Strange was the only one of the four reigning majors champions to have done so without finding the water.

Having been much longer off the tee, Woosnam, armed with an eight-iron, still could not match the American's accuracy. Finding the left-hand fringe, the Welshman could not hole his twenty-foot chip and conceded Couples's putt for the final 2-up win, ensuring only the second tie in Ryder Cup history.

Having picked up only a disappointing half-point from his first four matches, Strange took great delight in earning the final point, which secured a share of the trophy. "For a while it looked like we could win all but one match," he noted. "It's not like a win and it's not like a loss."

Day three result: USA *7,* EUR *5*

Eight of the twelve singles reached the final green, with each side claiming four wins. If the sixty minutes between 3:35 and 4:35 P.M. belonged to Europe with five straight wins, the final thirty-five minutes were all America, as they fought back to take the last four matches to earn a share of the Cup.

Overall match score: USA 14, EUR 14

"Every man will lay his head on the pillow tonight and have his own story. Thinking he lost it. Or whatever." —TONY JACKLIN

Recap

OLD HANDS MAINTAIN GRIP ON CUP
—*Times (London) headline*

The second tie in Ryder Cup history did little for either side: the Europeans were upset at not winning outright at home after two wins, while the U.S. players were upset at just plain failing to win for the third time running. Tied matches may be like kissing your sister, but this result smacked of kissing your grandmother with her teeth out. Maybe after the next tied match, the captains should embark on a sudden-death play-off to decide the outcome.

BIG MOUTH YANKS GET THEIR OWN BUTTS KICKED
—London Daily Star *headline*

Of the two captains, Tony Jacklin was by far the happier, because the result meant he kept the trophy. It also meant that he was the first captain (from either side of the Atlantic) to lift the trophy three times in succession. However, soon after this momentous third "win," Jacklin announced he would no longer captain the European side, since he had nothing else to achieve in the role. He had captained four times, and his overall points record was most impressive: 59–53—a winning record to be proud of for the man who put European golf on the world map.

On retiring as captain: *"What else is there for me to do? The dream has been realized: first to win it and then victory in America for the first time."* —TONY JACKLIN

"As I said at the beginning of the week, 'I hope the game of golf will be the winner when it is all over,' and it has truly been the winner here. The Ryder Cup was won by the game of golf, and that is what we are all about."
—*Raymond Floyd*

With honors even, it was difficult for anyone to feel good or bad about the outcome. Each team had chances to win and each team had moments when it looked as if they would lose. In the end, "golf won."

One thing was sure: the American team would be looking for a new spiritual leader in its playing ranks. With Tom Watson having played his last game, the U.S. side lacked that inspirational figure to turn to. In the past they had Hagen, Hogan, Snead, Palmer, Nicklaus, Trevino, and Watson, all of whom stepped up and answered their country's call to arms. Who would the next American Ryder Cup hero be?

Match Results (Winning side marked in *italics*.)

Friday, September 22—Morning Foursomes

	USA	EUR	Score
1.	Tom Kite Curtis Strange	Nick Faldo Ian Woosnam	halved
2.	*Lanny Wadkins* *Payne Stewart*	Howard Clark Mark James	1-up
3.	*Mark Calcavecchia* *Ken Green*	Bernhard Langer Ronan Rafferty	2 and 1
4.	Tom Watson Chip Beck	Seve Ballesteros Jose Maria Olazabal	halved

Friday, September 22—Afternoon Fourball

	USA	EUR	Score
5.	Curtis Strange Paul Azinger	*Sam Torrance* *Gordon Brand*	1-up
6.	Fred Couples Lanny Wadkins	*Howard Clark* *Mark James*	3 and 2
7.	Mark Calcavecchia Mark McCumber	*Nick Faldo* *Ian Woosnam*	2-up
8.	Tom Watson Mark O'Meara	*Seve Ballesteros* *Jose Maria Olazabal*	6 and 5

Day one result: USA 3, EUR 5

Saturday, September 23—Morning Foursomes

	USA	EUR	Score
9.	Lanny Wadkins Payne Stewart	*Nick Faldo* *Ian Woosnam*	3 and 2
10.	*Paul Azinger* *Chip Beck*	Gordon Brand Sam Torrance	4 and 3
11.	*Mark Calcavecchia* *Ken Green*	Christy O'Connor Ronan Rafferty	3 and 2
12.	Tom Kite Curtis Strange	*Seve Ballesteros* *Jose Maria Olazabal*	1-up

Saturday, September 23—Afternoon Fourball

	USA	EUR	Score
13.	*Paul Azinger* *Chip Beck*	Nick Faldo Ian Woosnam	2 and 1
14.	*Tom Kite* *Mark McCumber*	Jose Maria Canizares Bernhard Langer	2 and 1
15.	Payne Stewart Curtis Strange	*Howard Clark* *Mark James*	1-up
16.	Mark Calcavecchia Ken Green	*Seve Ballesteros* *Jose Maria Olazabal*	4 and 2

Day two result: USA *4,* EUR *4*

Overall match score: USA *7,* EUR *9*

Sunday, September 24—Singles

	USA	EUR	Score
17.	*Paul Azinger*	Seve Ballesteros	1-up
18.	*Chip Beck*	Bernhard Langer	3 and 1
19.	Payne Stewart	*Jose Maria Olazabal*	1-up
20.	Mark Calcavecchia	*Ronan Rafferty*	1-up
21.	*Tom Kite*	Howard Clark	8 and 7
22.	Mark O'Meara	*Mark James*	3 and 2
23.	Fred Couples	*Christy O'Connor*	1-up
24.	Ken Green	*Jose Maria Canizares*	1-up
25.	*Mark McCumber*	Gordon Brand	1-up
26.	*Tom Watson*	Sam Torrance	3 and 1
27.	*Lanny Wadkins*	Nick Faldo	1-up
28.	*Curtis Strange*	Ian Woosnam	2-up

Day three result: USA 7, EUR 5

Overall match score: USA 14, EUR 14

1991

The Ocean Course Kiawah Island South Carolina United States September 13–15	**United States 14½**	**Europe 13½**
	Paul Azinger	Seve Ballesteros (Spain)
	Chip Beck	Paul Broadhurst (England)
	Mark Calcavecchia	Nick Faldo (England)
	Fred Couples	David Feherty (N. Ireland)
	Raymond Floyd	David Gilford (England)
	Hale Irwin	Mark James (England)
	Wayne Levi	Bernhard Langer (Germany)
	Mark O'Meara	Colin Montgomerie (Scotland)
	Steve Pate	Jose Maria Olazabal (Spain)
	Corey Pavin	Steven Richardson (England)
	Payne Stewart	Sam Torrance (Scotland)
	Lanny Wadkins	Ian Woosnam (Wales)
	Captain	**Captain**
	Dave Stockton	Bernard Gallacher (Scotland)

Golf War Syndrome

"The teams are playing for their countries, their families, their teammates, Uncle Sam, the Queen, Mom and Dad, the Fatherland, and the legends of the Leprechaun, all rolled into three days of golf."

—*Charleston News*

Not only was the course new, but Dick Stockton and Bernard Gallacher were fresh to the captaincy. Stockton's career playing record was 3-1-1 (from 1971 and 1977), while Gallacher's was a modest yet even 13-13-5 (eight appearances from 1969 to 1983). Only Tony Jacklin and Nick Faldo had scored more points than Gallacher's 15½. So the Scot had a major edge in Ryder Cup experience, including his having been Tony Jacklin's right-hand man on previous winning teams.

Stockton welcomed back nine players with Ryder Cup experience, and he had only three rookies to nurture: 1990 PGA Tour Player of the Year Wayne Levi (thirty-eight years old), leading money winner Corey Pavin (thirty-one), and the man-in-form Steve Pate (thirty). Unfortunately for Stockton and the team, Pate was involved in a car crash after the Grand Opening Ball, damaging his ribs and left hip, and was doubtful for the opening matches. This was a major blow to Stockton, as the rookie's form and excellent touch on the treacherous greens had made him a shoo-in for all five matches.

The United States could have called up a replacement for Pate (Tim Simpson—tenth on the points list), but as Stockton pointed out, "By the time Tim gets here, he won't have time to practice."

Stockton had also elected not to select surprise PGA champion John Daly as a wild-card player (taking Beck and Floyd instead), which Daly duly understood, and he sent a heartfelt fax to the U.S. captain: "Good luck. Now go kick butt!"

Gallacher had two more rookies than his opposite number, four of whom were in their twenties: Paul Broadhurst (twenty-six years old), David Gilford (twenty-five), Colin Montgomerie (twenty-eight), and Steven Richardson (twenty-five), with the oldest Euro-rookie David Feherty (thirty-three).

One advantage Gallacher had over Stockton was that he could pick three wild-card players rather than two, a consequence of a strange irregularity in the selection procedure. The Scot wisely chose Faldo, Olazabal, and James.

"The disappointing thing is that even though we've won on the last three occasions, the Americans won't recognize we're number one."
—*Nick Faldo*

"Are we talking about the same match here? One team [Europe] is picked on '91 performance, the other goes back twenty-one months. One gets three wild-card picks [Europe], the other two . . . Why go through this agony to pick twelve guys, then for days only eight get to play? Eight fine players get to twiddle their thumbs Friday and Saturday."

—STEVE HERSHEY, *USA Today*

The Sony World Rankings at the time of the match revealed that the Europeans had the greater strength, with four of the top five players in the world. The home side, however, had seven players ranked in the top sixteen, whereas Europe had only one other player ranked that high.

Ryder Cup players in the Sony World Rankings (Top 20):
1. Woosnam 2. Olazabal
3. Faldo 5. Ballesteros
6. Stewart 7. Couples
8. Azinger 9. Langer
12. Irwin 13. Floyd
15. O'Meara 16. Pavin

The Americans managed to upset their visitors with a couple of shows of bad taste. In his opening welcome speech, Dave Stockton appeared to gloat over the riches his players had amassed in their careers: "This team has collectively won $50 million, or better than $4 million apiece."

In the nights running up to the match, Charleston DJ Michael D started a "Wake Up the Enemy" campaign, encouraging his listeners to ring up the Europeans' hotel rooms in the early hours of the morning. The disruption got so bad that Gallacher threatened serious action: "Gill Faldo had an obscene phone call, and if any of them get any more, I'm going to phone the FBI about it."

Course Details

The 1991 Ryder Cup was originally scheduled for PGA West in La Quinta, California, but the European broadcasters objected to the nine-hour delay on their side of the pond. This had not been a problem when the site was chosen, since U.S. and British TV had shown little interest in the competition. After the run of European success in the '80s, continental broadcasters suddenly became interested, but not if it meant showing live action at 3 A.M. GMT.

Not wanting to upset the European broadcasters (or turn down their substantial broadcast fees), the PGA of America switched the match to the East Coast. Kiawah Island was chosen as the new site, because The Ocean Course was owned by the Landmark Land Company, which also happened to own PGA West. The late switch was complicated by the delicate matter that the new course was still being built.

"The powers that be were seduced into taking this grand old event to a brand-new golf course, the Pete Dye–designed Ocean Course at Kiawah Island (so new, in fact, that the carpet had barely been laid in the clubhouse in time for the opening ceremony)."
—*Jock Howard,* Victory! *(1995)*

Hole	Distance	Par	Hole	Distance	Par
1	381	4	10	405	4
2	531	5	11	575	5
3	370	4	12	466	4
4	453	4	13	404	4
5	185	3	14	219	3
6	455	4	15	468	4
7	537	5	16	579	5
8	175	3	17	197	3
9	463	4	18	438	4
		36			**36 = Par 72 (7,301 yards)**

Course designer: Pete Dye

Not only was the course brand new, but it was almost impossible to play. Pete Dye had constructed a tortuous route that partly ran in line with the ocean, and the crosswinds were perilous. The outstanding feature of the course, especially to European eyes, was the vast waste areas of sand and reeds, which were not true bunkers, in that a player was allowed to ground his club. This local rule did little to make the course any easier to circumnavigate.

The NBC TV blimp gave a magnificent aerial view of irregularly shaped greens and massive waste bunkers that looked like microscopic amoebae.

Day One: Morning Foursomes

"Pete Dye's tormenting Ocean Course on Kiawah Island, S.C., now known as the Transition Area Golf Club, thanks to TV announcers."
—*Dan Jenkins,* Golf Digest

Dense fog rolled over the seaside course, and not even the seemingly gale-force winds could persuade it to move until two hours after the official start time.

With an enviable first-morning record of never being behind after the opening session in eighteen years, the U.S. team set out to recapture the Ryder Cup.

Paul Azinger and Chip Beck (USA) v. Seve Ballesteros and Jose Maria Olazabal (EUR)

One of the few sour notes to come out of the amicable 1989 tie was the festering feud between Paul Azinger and Seve Ballesteros. Both players publicly accused the other of "cheating," and matters did not cool down in the white-hot crucible of Kiawah Island.

Realizing that a winning start was psychologically imperative, both sides sent out their best pairing first. Stockton dealt the pair of Azinger and Beck, who won two matches together in 1989, while Gallacher looked no further than the almost unbeatable and inseparable Spaniards.

This stellar matchup provided one of the greatest and hardest-fought encounters ever seen in pairs play, and laid the table for a banquet-cum-battle, a feast-cum-joust, as superlative golf was needed to win matches and to tame the course.

"Before the end of the second hole we were embroiled in another conflict over what I considered to be a controversial drop of their ball. We had another question over their lost ball on number four. It went like that all day long, just one bit of controversy after another."
—*Paul Azinger,* Zinger *(1995)*

The opening hole was halved in par fours, but Ballesteros and Olazabal, noted for their explosive starts, imploded at the second. Despite receiving a beneficial (and questionable) free drop, the Europeans were unable to recover a bad situation and conceded the hole to go one down.

A rare sequence at the fourth saw both star pairings card double-bogey sixes for a half, neither pair able to cope with the gusting winds. The lingering bitterness and open hostility between the pairs came to a head after the Americans won the ninth in par to go three up.

"By the ninth hole I was livid. When Jose hit his drive off to the right, I was right there to help spot the drop. The referee was intimidated by Seve and Jose, so he simply stood aside and waited to see how we would settle things. Seve and Jose wanted to drop the ball much farther up the fairway from where I thought the ball had gone into the water. 'You need to drop it right back here,' I said as I pointed to the original position I had indicated. Reluctantly Seve dropped the ball at that spot."

—Paul Azinger, *Zinger* (1995)

Azinger: "I can tell you we're not trying to cheat." *Ballesteros:* "Oh no. Breaking the rules and cheating are two different things."

Three down at the halfway point, and sensing the match was slipping away from them, the Spaniards officially complained to the match referee that their opponents had illegally changed balls on the seventh hole. Neither Beck nor Azinger denied hitting the wrong ball, but the much-consulted official correctly ruled that since the Spaniards had not raised the issue at the time, no penalty could be assessed. Although Ballesteros and Olazabal lost the battle with the rule book, this incident only served to spark the impulsive Spaniards into greater efforts to win the war.

On the tenth tee, Seve was in no mood to hang about, and he unleashed an almighty drive that split the fairway, while Olazabal's approach work was equally dynamic—pin-high, eight feet from the hole. With Beck's second shot safely on the back of the green, Azinger putted up to four feet. Seve rolled his birdie putt twelve inches past the cup for a concession, but Beck missed his par putt to lose the hole.

This was the first hole the Americans had lost in ten holes, and the momentum had shifted dramatically.

"Although Seve and Jose had not received a favorable ruling [on the tee], they had succeeded in breaking our momentum. That's no excuse, of course, but Chip and I were so shaken by all this commotion that we three-putted the next green. Our game went downhill from there."

—Paul Azinger, *Zinger* (1995)

After Olazabal almost holed his approach to the twelfth, Ballesteros sank the three-foot putt for the Spaniards' first birdie of the day to cut the lead to one. Azinger made a solid seven-footer for par on the thirteenth but lost the hole to Olazabal's similar-length birdie.

Both Spaniards wasted shots into the sand rather than use the fifteenth fairway, but Olazabal's recovery from forty yards out ended up a yard from the pin. Beck putted from off the front of the green to five feet, but Azinger missed another crucial putt for a half.

Not only had the Spanish pair won four holes out of six since the "complaint," but they also held their first lead of the day.

Then it was on to the notorious par-3 seventeenth, a risky "heart-in-your-mouth" 200-yard tee shot over brackish water, with the right-hand side of the massive green cut into a lake that stretched back to the tee.

With his side in the ascendancy, Olazabal landed his ball on the narrow strip of green between the flag and the water, running on twenty-five feet past the hole. Beck found the front half of the green, leaving a wickedly long putt up to the middle level. Azinger's sweeping uphill putt swung by the hole and carried on six feet past. Seve's downhill putt kept on curling right to left, turning at the hole in the last few revolutions to drop in for a birdie two.

The unbeatable Spaniards had beaten the previously unbeaten American pair, 2 and 1, in a bitter match that lasted four and a half hours, setting the scene for the rest of the weekend.

Azinger was also widely reported as saying: "Seve always develops a cough at the Ryder Cup."

"The American team has eleven nice guys . . . and Paul Azinger."
—*Seve Ballesteros*

"Throughout our matches—throughout the entire '91 Ryder Cup, actually—Seve continued to pull little stunts that helped me better understand why, prior to the '89 Ryder Cup, Curtis Strange had warned me not to let Ballesteros pull anything on me. During these '91 matches, Seve seemed to come down with a severe case of sporadic throat clearing. It usually struck just as a player was approaching his ball. Seve later blamed the problem on allergies to sand and dust." —PAUL AZINGER, *Zinger* (1995)

Raymond Floyd and Fred Couples (USA) v. Bernhard Langer and Mark James (EUR)

With only two wins against six losses from his last two Ryder Cup appearances, wild card Floyd became the first (and only) player to reappear after being a nonplaying captain. Said Floyd, "Nobody on the outside understands the value of experience, the intense pressure the players are under."

Despite reaching the turn one over par, Floyd and Couples found they had a comfortable three-hole lead over Langer and James. The basis of the Americans' success came at the two par-3 holes, where they made hole-winning birdies. Out in 40, the

European pair had been seriously affected by the strong wind, carding two bogeys, with a double on the sixth.

Another European bogey at ten pumped up the American lead, and all looked set fair for an early finish. Once eleven was halved in birdie fours, the Americans may have eased off the throttle a little, carding nothing but fives (bogey-bogey-double) to gift-wrap the next three holes.

Langer's yard-perfect pitch to thirteen was outdone by James's ticklish downhiller from off the green to two feet of the cup on fourteen, giving the Europeans hole-winning pars when they were most needed. Hauled back to only one up, much by their own wrongdoing, Couples and Floyd needed to refocus their efforts on the fifteenth. Floyd answered the call, holing the longer and much trickier of two par putts for a welcome half.

On sixteen, Couples—with an iron—tried to lay up between the encroaching lateral bunkers but found the one on the right, some way shy of the green. With his opponents' ball in the sand, James—with a wood—decided to go for the green but almost landed on top of Couples's beached ball. Floyd and Langer failed to hit the green with their recoveries, but then Couples chipped up to seven feet, and James got one foot closer. Floyd holed his par putt; Langer did not.

"Less than a year before joining the Seniors Tour, forty-nine-year-old Ray Floyd was bouncing around the sand dunes like a kid on a trampoline."
—Philadelphia Enquirer

Two up with two to play, Couples thumped his tee shot over the lake and eight feet over the flag, rolling on a few feet more. Once Floyd carefully rolled his putt up to the hole for a par, the Europeans conceded the match for a 2 and 1 American win. Both pairs were round in four over par, accentuating the dual difficulties of the course and conditions.

Having gone 0–2 in his rookie appearance in 1989: "I finally won a Ryder Cup game."
—*Fred Couples*

Lanny Wadkins and Hale Irwin (USA) v. David Gilford and Colin Montgomerie (EUR)

Against Wadkins and Irwin, a pair of forty-plus veterans with twenty-six Ryder Cup wins and thirty-nine Tour wins between them, Europe sent out a couple of twenty-plus rookies—Montgomerie and Gilford—with no Cup wins and only three Tour wins to their credit.

The American veterans began with a birdie to a rookie bogey, and added a second birdie at the next hole to cancel out Montgomerie's sixteen-footer. Irwin, who had replaced the ill-fated Pate in the starting lineup, struck a brilliant approach to a couple of feet on the third, and the United States was two up, having opened with three birdies in a row.

The Europeans finally managed their first par of the match at the 185-yard fifth hole, but it was a labor in vain. Wadkins planted a tee shot four yards from the flag, and Irwin sank the Americans' fourth birdie to go three up.

The slightly built Gilford had particular trouble with the increasingly windy conditions, as his chip shot from sand to the sixth green went way too far left. All the Europeans could do was salvage another bogey to their opponents' precise par.

On the seventh, the Americans were unable to match Gilford's approach, which he somehow managed to coax onto the putting surface. Montgomerie's putt up to the hole was quickly conceded for the visitors' first success of the day. Irwin immediately hit back, sticking his tee shot a few feet from the flag on the par-3 eighth.

"Some of Hale Irwin's shots today were godlike. We played steady enough golf, but under that kind of fire there isn't much you can do."

—COLIN MONTGOMERIE

With the 463-yard ninth halved in regulation, the Americans held a commanding four-hole lead, having gone out in 31 strokes—five better than any of their morning compatriots.

Another bogey cost Europe the eleventh to put the United States five up with just seven to play. After Gilford lagged a swinging forty-foot putt up to two feet of the twelfth hole, Wadkins kindly conceded the missable putt for par and the half. Almost blown over by the fierce wind on the next green, Gilford was unable to hole a five-foot par putt for the win.

The 219-yard par-3 fourteenth proved difficult for both pairs: Irwin's tee shot missed the green, and Wadkins's chip shot came back to where he was standing. In the end, the Americans' second double-bogey five of the round was untidily seen off by a European bogey four to cut the lead to dormie four.

With the match still firmly in their grasp, the Americans encountered even more trouble on fifteen. Wadkins drove wildly into some reeds and rushes, leaving Irwin to carve the ball out into sand. Two shots later, Wadkins had a fifteen-footer that he gave up on and started to walk after it. The nearer he got to his ball, the closer it came to dropping into the hole. With Wadkins willing his ball on, it ran out of steam and drifted past the left side of the cup, cutting the U.S. lead to three with three to play.

Having been five down a few holes earlier, the Europeans must have been surprised to reach the par-5 sixteenth, where they sensed a slight chance for a complete comeback. Irwin silenced any European hopes by knocking his three-iron approach into the center of the green. From just off the back right of the green, and needing to win the hole, Montgomerie had a twelve-foot putt that stayed left and stayed out. This final miss brought an immediate concession from the gangly Scot, handing the United States a 4 and 2 win.

Wadkins and Irwin were the only pair to break par in the morning round, but by only one stroke. The Europeans, who had struggled most of the way round, were six over—the worst score of the session.

Payne Stewart and Mark Calcavecchia (USA) v. Nick Faldo and Ian Woosnam (EUR)

As their teammates did before them, Stewart and Calcavecchia started faster than their opponents, making a birdie at the second, then going two up after Faldo and Woosnam conceded the 453-yard fourth hole.

The Europeans finally got their game going on the sixth, where Faldo chipped to within eight feet for Woosnam to make par. The U.S. pair missed a shorter par putt and saw its lead cut to one.

Earlier in the season, Ian Woosnam was not only crowned Masters champion, but he also won the USF&G Classic.

On the par-5 seventh, Stewart—with an awkward stance and a restricted backswing—played a breathtaking chip from a dense clump of grass to four feet of the hole. Calcavecchia's birdie putt cruelly lipped out for a half—not the win that Stewart's remarkable recovery deserved.

After a couple more halves in par, Stewart's third shot from in front of the eleventh green came up fifteen feet short of the hole. Much closer to the green, Woosnam chipped up two foot shy. Calcavecchia was unable to make his birdie putt, whereas Faldo smoothly guided his home to level the match. The Europeans' equilibrium was short-lived—they proceeded to drop another stroke at the 466-yard twelfth, and Stewart made no mistake with his partner's impressive approach to five feet of the thirteenth hole.

Woosnam needed a deft chip to two feet to save par on the short fourteenth, just to stay two down. The next two holes were also halved in par, with Calcavecchia surprising even himself as he chipped in on sixteen to maintain the two-hole cushion.

Dormie two, Stewart's tee shot missed the seventeenth green to the right and found water—the first of many. Woosnam, with an open green and a shot in hand, fired his four-iron low and straight at the flag. The ball landed on the upslope at the front of the green and held its ground, fourteen feet left of the flag. Calcavecchia's careless third shot from the drop zone also found the water. A sorry and soggy concession gave the Europeans fresh hope of sneaking a half-point.

Woosnam's seven-iron pitched safely on the extreme left-hand side of the final green, fifteen feet from the hole. Stewart's approach, with an eight-iron, drifted in on the cross-breeze, settling eleven feet front-right of the flag. Needing to hole his putt, and with a nasty borrow from left to right, Faldo could only watch in despair as his ball faded by the hole. With two putts to win, Calcavecchia almost holed the first one as the ball slipped across the cup and stopped inches away, for the win by one hole.

Having lost only one of their previous eight games together (5-1-2), Faldo and Woosnam were never ahead in their second loss. Strangely, the British pair was round in 74, only to be beaten by a U.S. pair who carded a 76.

Morning foursomes result: USA 3, EUR 1

Only one pairing came close to breaking par for its round. The four American pairs combined to be eleven over, while Europe suffered even more with a combined total of fifteen over.

Day One: Afternoon Fourball

In deciding not to give every player an outing on the first day, Stockton left the injured Pate (who reportedly had not broken any bones in his car crash) and the luckless Levi (who reportedly had not broken 80 in practice) on the sidelines.

Lanny Wadkins and Mark O'Meara (USA) v. Sam Torrance and David Feherty (EUR)

"Kiawah was so difficult in 1991 that it was possible to drop a shot between the locker room and the first tee. The greens were harder to hit than Oscar De La Hoya's nose." —DAVID FEHERTY, *Golf* magazine (1997)

In his Ryder Cup debut against Wadkins and O'Meara, Irishman Feherty (paired with Sam Torrance) was obviously more nervous than most other rookies, despite the comfort of a half in four at the first hole.

To his jittery partner on the second tee: *"If you don't pull yourself together, I'm going to join them, and you can play all three of us, you useless bastard!"* —SAM TORRANCE

This quiet word of "advice" from his partner did little to ease Feherty's worries, as the British pair promptly bogeyed the second to go one down. From this point on, the match settled in to some fine golf, both pairs halving the next five holes in better than regulation.

The Europeans halted the run of halves by bogeying the par-3 eighth, then went three down at the turn when Wadkins and O'Meara birdied the ninth.

Just as it seemed the United States was coasting to a cozy win, up stepped a more insouciant Irishman on the eleventh to give renewed heart to his whole team. From the downslope on a bank off the back of the green, the chirpy chappy chipped up onto the crest of the slope and watched in joy as his ball rolled home some thirty feet away. Europe's second birdie four of the round cut the American lead to two.

The players found that the gusting conditions had slightly eased in the afternoon, making shot making easier and more rewarding.

This spark of success served to give Feherty nerves of steel, and he continued his good work on the 219-yard fourteenth. His tee shot not only stayed on the green, but it rolled up to six feet of the hole. Having struggled thus far with a highly strung putter, Feherty sneaked his ball in the left-hand side of the hole. With two birdies in four holes, the Irishman had single-handedly pulled his side back into the match, one down.

Pumped with his success, Feherty overplayed a putt on the sixteenth that would have squared the match. With his partner reining in the Americans, Torrance took his best shot at the devilish seventeenth. The Scot almost holed a remarkable tee shot that sailed over the water, bounced on the corner of a bunker, and skipped on down two feet from the pin—set right at the front left of the green. Not to be outdone, O'Meara landed his ball five feet farther on than the Scot, but it rolled eight feet beyond the hole. O'Meara holed his putt to guarantee his side an overall half.

On the eighteenth tee, Feherty got twitchy again and drove into a morass of sandy stuff. Surrounded by dunes and bush, the Irishman found a good flat lie and struck a long iron out into more sand short of the green. From here he lofted out short of the hole, and the ball trickled up a few yards, coming to a halt eleven feet short of the pin.

O'Meara's long putt was on line all the way but straightened too much and caught the right-hand lip. The American fell to his knees as the ball stayed out. Wadkins still had a putt for the match from twelve feet, but he pulled his putt short and left, and no amount of waving his putter after the ball helped it get any closer.

In his Ryder Cup career, Lanny Wadkins played in twenty-six pairs matches, and this was the only one that he halved.

Locked into a cocoon of nervous tissue and self-doubt, Feherty barely seemed able to swing his putter back, but the forward stroke was hard enough to propel the ball straight into the cup to win the hole and halve the match.

"I ended up with a twelve-footer to win the hole and halve the match. I had read the greens like a Russian newspaper all day, so I asked Sam to aim me. To his eternal credit, he said, 'Hit it firm on the left edge,' in a manner that made me feel he was completely positive. Somehow I made a controlled spasm and the ball rolled into the center of the cup. The crowd roared; I almost fainted. Sam and I had made my first Ryder Cup half-point!" —DAVID FEHERTY, *Golf* magazine (1997)

Chip Beck and Paul Azinger (USA) v. Seve Ballesteros and Jose Maria Olazabal (EUR)

Gallacher out-thought his opposing number by moving his star pairing to second in the order. Stockton had wanted to protect his top pairing of Azinger and Beck from meeting their morning antagonists again, and he assumed the Spaniards would lead out the Europeans in the afternoon. Wrong!

In this Spanish-American rematch of bad blood from the morning, Azinger and Beck took another early lead thanks to a birdie three at the third hole. Olazabal again proved the more dependable of the Spaniards; his tee shot to the 185-yard fifth left him within a yard of the hole for a birdie to level the match. A second U.S. birdie landed the home team the sixth to go back up by one, but they could not get more than a single hole ahead.

If it wasn't Olazabal sticking one on them, it was Ballesteros. On seven, from sand off the back right of the green, Seve caressed his chip up onto the green and let it curve slowly down eighteen inches past the cup. Neither American could match the birdie, and they unhappily conceded another hole.

After the European win at seven, Ballesteros knew the Americans would be mentally down. Now was the time to hammer them physically—and hammer them he did. Up first, he fired his tee shot to the middle of the steeply shelving green, fifteen feet from the flag, and let the ball roll down to within four feet. Needless to say, he made the birdie putt to put his side up for the first time. Azinger and Beck twice had the lead and lost it; Seve felt that if they didn't want it, he did, and he took it.

With the Spaniards one up at the turn, neither pair—in true fourball style—had carded a bogey. Even when the Americans threatened a win on ten with a birdie, Seve and Olazabal combined to thwart their hopes. With the pin only ten feet on, Seve played a delicate short chip out of sand at the back of the green, stopping his ball three feet from a par. With his partner's par safe, Olazabal was able to concentrate on holing his eight-foot birdie putt to match the U.S. birdie.

On the next two holes, Olazabal again proved the European savior, holing from ten feet for birdie at eleven, and three feet for another half on the 466-yard twelfth.

With his side narrowly ahead, Seve's game momentarily faltered.

On thirteen, Ballesteros continued to have trouble. He found the water, but this time his youthful guardian angel could not match the American birdie, and the match was back level.

"In fact, if Ballesteros regularly inspires romantic associations with Don Quixote, for most of Friday's play Olazabal was cast in the role of Rozinante. Not that he played like a feeble horse, but he did carry Seve for much of the day."
—*Robert Green,* Sunday Times *(London)*

Now was the time for the Americans to step up their game. With Ballesteros struggling, they needed to stamp their authority on the match, but they came up short, as Seve recovered his form on fourteen. His tee shot bounced right on the front of the reverse-sloping green, having just cleared an expanse of sand, and his ball rolled up pin-high. With neither American able to threaten the hole in two, Ballesteros holed his straight-shooting seven-footer to reclaim the lead.

The crowd erupted as Azinger sank a twenty-five-footer for a much-needed birdie on sixteen, forcing Olazabal not only to battle a nasty ten-footer for his own birdie, but also combat the noise of the raucous assemblage. Nothing the Americans or the crowd threw at the young Spaniard seemed to faze him, as he calmly popped his putt in to silence the cheering hordes and maintain a one-hole lead with two to play.

Whether or not this counterblow affected the Americans, they did not seem to recover their composure on the next tee.

Seve's tee shot caught the extreme right-hand side of the seventeenth green and held its ground, pin-high twenty-five feet adrift. Beck's head was bowed in disgust and disgrace as he quickly realized his tee shot had missed the green. Twenty feet right of the putting surface meant one thing—SPLASH!

With the match on the line, Azinger also got into the head-hanging act, his tee shot finding the water between Beck's splash and the green. With two putts to win the match, Seve barely got his putt within five feet of the hole. Having dropped and pitched on, Azinger had a twelve-footer that could have put some pressure on Seve. As the American's ball sailed harmlessly past the hole, he conceded the hole and the match to go down 2 and 1.

"Chip and I played Seve and Jose again. I played the match of my life, making eight birdies, and they still beat us! We lost 2 and 1 again. That loss was really heartbreaking for Chip and me."

—PAUL AZINGER, *Zinger* (1995)

Corey Pavin and Mark Calcavecchia (USA) v. Mark James and Steven Richardson (EUR)

Two more rookies saw their first tour of duty: Pavin partnered Calcavecchia, and the Europeans sent out new boy Richardson with old hand James. For a pleasant change for Bernard Gallacher, one of his pairings actually got off to a winning start.

With the first hole halved in par, Mark James's putter caught fire on the following two greens, yielding a couple of birdies to go two up. This unusual early European advantage was maintained with a pair of halves in par, before Richardson, overcoming his rookie nerves, drilled home a twenty-foot birdie putt to go three up. This birdie strike galvanized the blond Englishman into holing his sand recovery at the 537-yard seventh for an eagle to stretch the lead to four.

Having been overshadowed in the rookie nursery stakes, Corey Pavin announced his intentions on the par-3 eighth. His tee shot almost repeated Ballesteros's shot before him, his ball landing in the middle of the green and crawling down to within four feet of the hole. Carding a fourth three in a row, the English pair still lost the hole to Pavin's birdie two.

The Americans continued their minirevival, cutting the British lead to two, when their opponents bogeyed the 463-yard ninth —their only five of the round.

James's match-play experience was well matched with Richardson's youthful blitzkrieg medal play. Having birdied the eleventh, the rookie had two putts—from eighteen feet on twelve—for the win to move back to four up with six to play.

With James and Richardson out in 32 to their opponents' 34, Gallacher rejoiced in a new pairing that worked well together.

The Europeans needed only two holes to close the match out. A half in par on the 404-yard thirteenth set up the last rites on fourteen.

From twenty feet off the back of the green, and thirty feet from the hole, James chipped into the steepish downslope of the elevated green to leave his ball three feet behind the pin. Calcavecchia, with a seven-foot putt for a three, pulled it to his left and missed the hole by some way.

This left James to knock in his shorter putt for a very impressive 5 and 4 win.

This was a vital morale-boosting victory for the European team, since it was the only non-Spanish win they had on the first day. The margin of victory also pleased Gallacher: his pair was five under compared with the Americans' level par tally.

Fred Couples and Raymond Floyd (USA) v. Nick Faldo and Ian Woosnam (EUR)

Raymond Floyd lost his ball off the first tee, but Fred Couples was not distracted and holed a birdie putt from off the green to take the lead against Faldo and Woosnam. The U.S. lead soon doubled when neither European could make par at the second. Woosnam, who putted poorly in the first session, holed a good birdie putt to win the third and had a five-foot birdie to level the match on the fourth.

Floyd left himself with a seven-footer to win the 455-yard sixth, and he slowly rolled his putt down the green into the hole to regain the lead. A British birdie two at the eighth leveled the score, and the turn was reached in an equitable 33 strokes.

Whereas the front nine had been a close encounter, the inward session became a blowout of biblical proportions.

With a fifteen-footer for a win on the 405-yard tenth, Floyd walked after his birdie putt, pumping his fist as he almost caught the ball before it dived into the hole. After Faldo fluffed his chip to eleven, Floyd squeezed home another birdie putt from eleven feet. Woosnam had a three-footer to halve but squibbed his putt.

All four players had birdie putts on the par-4 twelfth, but Couples was the only one to convert—from five feet.

> "Faldo and Woosnam, who lost more points than they won, . . . seemed more concerned with which of them deserved to be ranked No. 1 in the world than with team play. In particular, it looked as if a map of the course would have helped Faldo immensely. By the end of the week, they were better known as 'Waldo and Foozie.'"
> —*Dan Jenkins,* Golf Digest

At the next green, Couples manufactured himself another birdie putt, making no mistake from eight feet. Four American birdies in a row bought four wins and a four-hole lead with five to play. A fifth consecutive birdie was rewarded with only a half on the difficult par-3 fourteenth, but it left the Americans dormie four.

With Woosnam again out of the hole, Faldo pushed a fifteen-foot putt to the right of the fifteenth hole and conceded the match, 5 and 3.

For the second time in the day, Gallacher had given Faldo and Woosnam the anchor role, but again they had sunk without a trace. Woosnam's form was so poor, he was dropped from the next day's morning session. In complete contrast to their opponents, Floyd and Couples enjoyed two fine wins on the first day. This American win—with the best round of the day, a net eight under—was crucial, because a loss would have left the home side winless in the afternoon session and facing an overnight deficit.

Faldo and Woosnam had not been beaten in their first seven matches together (5-0-2). This loss was their third in a row, dating back to 1989, and they were split up on day two, never to partner each other again.

Afternoon fourball result: USA 1½, EUR 2½
Day one result: USA 4½, EUR 3½

Day Two: Morning Foursomes

The second day saw little respite from the gale force winds that starched the flags solid and dried the lightning-fast greens out even more.

With temperatures reaching a very humid eighty-five, Europe responded by donning flamingo pink shirts; Team USA countered with bright red.

Lanny Wadkins and Hale Irwin (USA) v. David Feherty and Sam Torrance (EUR)

With the greens slicker than on the first day, the opening three holes were all lost to par—two of European origin. Wadkins put his opening tee shot into some trees, from where Irwin chipped out but could not advance the ball. Wadkins's poor start continued, as he missed the green with his approach to lose the hole with a double bogey.

"It was apparent from the first putt of the day that the greens were more perilously faster than ever." —Nick Pitt, *Sunday Times* (London)

The Americans returned to normality as they took the par-5 second, but Irwin's missed putt from under three feet on the third gave the lead back to the Europeans, which they held until the sixth.

Further American pars accounted for six and eight, but their third outward bogey leveled the match at the turn. A second birdie of the round restored the U.S. lead on the tenth, but ugly golf returned as the 575-yard eleventh was shared in bogey sixes. Wadkins's three-foot par putt won the twelfth and stretched the lead to two.

Amazingly, only two holes in sixteen were halved in par: the fourth and the fifth.

Feherty's pitch from the thirteenth fairway flirted with the water on the right of the green, but the ball stayed dry and rolled around the contours of the putting surface fifty feet from the flag. Torrance used his long-handled putter to handle the long putt with almost perfect precision. He aimed his putt up the bank, some yards to the right of the hole, but the ball drifted back down, just missing the hole and coming to rest a few feet past. Wadkins holed a three-footer for bogey, allowing Feherty to hole out from less than a yard to bring the deficit back to one.

As Torrance and Feherty struggled on the next two greens, par and bogey were sufficient to extend the American lead to three up with three to play.

On sixteen, Feherty played his side's second shot from the comfort of the wide fairway but found another wide expanse of sand. Irwin played the Americans' third from closer to the green, and left it pin-high twenty-five feet to the right. Torrance found Feherty's bunkered shot sitting at the foot of a massive incline, with more than a dozen steps to get back up to the green. Unable to see the flag, Sam blasted his ball through the green, stopping it twenty feet beyond in the fringe. With the Americans closer in four, Feherty's fifth shot came up four feet short and brought an instant concession of the match, 4 and 2.

Mark Calcavecchia and Payne Stewart (USA) v. Mark James and Steven Richardson (EUR)

Although Richardson's treacherous downhill putt lipped out by a yard away, James had the comfort of holing the come-backer to win the opening hole; the Americans could manage only bogey between them. As in the first match out, par took the prize at the initial three holes, this time with the Americans emerging with an early lead, which they lost with another bogey on the par-3 fifth.

Both sides had to wait until the seventh hole before a birdie putt dropped. From the greenside sand, Richardson blasted his third shot to three feet of the hole, leaving James to make the all-elusive putt for a birdie four and a one-hole lead.

Spurred into action by the Europeans' breaking par, Calcavecchia and Stewart went on a scoring spree, firing not one but two birdies in a row. Covering the next three holes in an almost unprecedented nine strokes, the U.S. pair turned a one-hole deficit into a one-hole lead.

Just as the Americans appeared to have mastered the tricky conditions, they went and bogeyed the eleventh, with James playing a killer sand shot to four feet of the hole for a winning par.

On the next hole, Stewart's pin-high pitch gave Calcavecchia the luxury of two putts from seven feet for par. He needed only one putt to regain the two-hole lead. After thirteen and fourteen were halved in par, Richardson played a class approach to thirty inches that could not be matched by Stewart. Having been left an eighteen-foot downhill putt, Calcavecchia's ball found nothing but an empty hole waiting for it. James tidied up his end of the deal, walking away with a half, when he must have thought he would have a putt for the win.

After four holes of error-free golf, the gremlins returned to the Americans' game on sixteen. Calcavecchia hated his third shot the instant he sliced a three-wood behind the backs of the gallery on the right. With the pressure off him, James flew his approach from 120 yards to the back edge of the green. From a lie on the "beach," Stewart sent a flyer whistling past the pin and off the back of the green, scattering the photographers beyond. Making up for his slice of bad fortune, Calcavecchia coolly laid a chip back to three feet of the cup, but the Americans had taken one more shot than their opponents to reach the green.

Although Richardson's ball was tucked up on the edge of the green, he was faced with a downhill-breaking putt. The good news was that he had two putts for the hole. He underborrowed from the left and overhit the ball by four feet. With a shortish putt to win the hole, James never gave the ball a chance: he started it out to the right, and it never came back. The United States escaped with a half in sixes and was now dormie two.

Needing only to find dry land at seventeen, Stewart started his tee shot way out to the left, but the unpredictable gusts of wind took the ball back across the green and over the water. Richardson's low tee shot safely cleared the water, coming up short of the green. Playing his side's third, Calcavecchia also put that in the water. Not for the first or last time, the Americans ignominiously conceded the crucial hole from the drop zone.

Europe was now just one down, highlighting how damaging James's missed putt on sixteen had been.

Calcavecchia smacked his final drive to the perfect place on the right of the fairway, from where Stewart struck a long iron into the sand on the front right of the green. Unsure as to whether he could make the green from his own sandy lie, Richardson decided to lay up with a five-iron, then found that he reached the front edge of the green in two. Calcavecchia chipped out to nine feet, while James was faced with a thirty-foot putt across a sweeping gully. His putt broke both ways as it traversed the slopes and ended up four feet to the right of the hole.

Stewart's par putt brushed the left of the hole, giving Richardson a chance to level the match from four feet, but he pushed his putt wide. Calcavecchia was forced to hole out the short putt Stewart had left him for the half and the overall win, 1-up.

Once again, the scoring was not a sight to behold. The Americans carded a 77 to a European 78, in a session where only one pair broke par.

The Europeans were left to ponder how they had both blown short winning putts on two of the last three holes.

Paul Azinger and Mark O'Meara (USA) v. Nick Faldo and David Gilford (EUR)

With Paul Azinger twice beaten by Ballesteros and Olazabal on Friday, Dave Stockton hoped his key player would avoid them on day two: *"I was having a heart attack when Bernard had not named them [the Spanish] in his first two teams. I knew Azinger was in the third match. I thought, 'This is not good.'"* —DAVE STOCKTON

"Faldo's surliness and Gilford's painful shyness ensured a pairing with less conversation than Trappist monks." —*Lauren St. John,* Sunday Times *(London)*

The ordinarily par-perfect Faldo and the timorously tidy Gilford carded seven fives or worse on the front nine to more or less gift-wrap the match for their grateful opponents.

Opening with four fives, Europe dropped two down to Azinger and O'Meara, who birdied the par-3 fifth to go three up. American pars at six and seven left them sitting pretty with a five-hole lead. Faldo's short game self-destructed: the taller Englishman twice failed to hold the green with seemingly simple short chips.

The Americans were the only pair to break par in the morning session. Their net one-under total was five shots better than that of any of the other U.S. pairings.

Although the British pair had failed to mount much of a challenge on the front nine, the American pair was out in level par, no mean feat in the difficult and trying conditions.

On the tenth, O'Meara left his partner a testing thirty-foot putt up and over a ridge in the green. Azinger appeared to have underhit the ball, as it never looked like it would reach the hole, but it kept on coming and coming until it dropped in to put the U.S. side six up.

In his eighth Ryder Cup, Nick Faldo suffered his biggest defeat. His worst setback had been the 7 and 5 drubbing by Lee Trevino and Jerry Pate in 1981 at Walton Heath.

With the eleventh halved in par fives, O'Meara again left his partner with a thirty-footer on the 466-yard twelfth. As before, Azinger's putt took its time to get to the hole, but this time it fell away two feet to the right. Having seen enough on this morning of misery, and unable to win the hole, Faldo picked up his marker and conceded the match by the resounding score of 7 and 6.

Raymond Floyd and Fred Couples (USA) v. Seve Ballesteros and Jose Maria Olazabal (EUR)

This final foursomes match was an eagerly awaited clash of the only 2-0 pairings from the first day.

The youngest of the four veterans, Olazabal immediately had a problem judging the speed on the first green, and his side three-putted for an opening bogey and a loss.

If observers thought this might be the day the Spaniards' bubble would burst, they were wrong. On the second hole, the Spanish pair clearly demonstrated why it was such a tough nut to crack. Olazabal bravely rescued Seve's sliced drive, saving par and the loss of a second successive hole. Olazabal had plenty of practice in playing his rescue shot. This was the third time in three rounds that Seve sliced his drive at the second hole.

With a shaky start behind them, the Spaniards soon crashed back, winning three of the next four holes to take a two-hole advantage. The Americans gave away the third hole with a bogey five, the fourth was halved in par, while Olazabal's tee shot at the fifth landed pin-high, inside the shadow of the flag. Left with a dead-straight nine-foot birdie putt for the win, Seve did what he does best and finished off Jose Maria's heroic handiwork.

Ballesteros repaid the compliment at six, firing his third shot to four feet, allowing Olazabal to sink a par putt for a two-hole advantage.

With the seventh halved in fours, Olazabal again rescued his partner's wayward tee shot into sand alongside the par-3 eighth. Ballesteros accepted the four-footer left for him, but Floyd matched putts from much the same distance for another half in par.

The elder statesman was not so fortunate on the ninth green: he raced a ten-foot downhill par putt at the hole, but it caught the left-hand lip and rolled on by a couple of feet. Ballesteros made his eight-footer for another winning par to steal the hole.

On the effect the Spaniards—who were out in 35, three shots better than their opponents—would have on the outcome of the overall match: *"One European pair cannot beat four American teams."*

—Anonymous American TV commentator

Three up on eleven, Ballesteros had a chance to extend the lead, but faced with a twelve-foot putt for the win, he pushed his stroke past the hole, and the Spaniards settled for a half in par fives.

The next green saw Olazabal squander a chance to take the hole, failing from five feet.

The 404-yard thirteenth required Ballesteros to hole a knee-trembling seven-footer to escape with a half, as the U.S. pair tried its utmost to climb back into the match. Any fleeting chance of an American revival vanished on the frightening fourteenth, where Olazabal again conjured up an immaculate short chip to four feet. Floyd missed his tricky putt for a half, before Ballesteros calmly extended his side's lead to four with four to play.

Thanks to a rare Spanish bogey on fifteen, Couples and Floyd finally won their second hole of the match, their first seemingly having come in a different match on the first hole.

On sixteen, Ballesteros had a seven-footer for the match that dribbled across the face of the hole and stayed alive, as did the Americans' slim chances. Floyd addressed his three-foot putt by facing sideways to the hole and, not surprisingly, sending his ball past the left-hand edge to halve the hole and lose the match, 3 and 2.

On his Spanish pair's third win in three matches: *"They are keeping us in the Ryder Cup."* —BERNARD GALLACHER

Morning foursomes result: USA 3, EUR 1

Day Two: Afternoon Fourball

"Pars were often like birdies in the brisk wind which swept the links on an afternoon of glistening sunshine. It was terribly difficult to either hole putts or lay them close, the ball time and again seeming 'dead' but rolling on another three feet." —MICHAEL WILLIAMS, *London Telegraph*

Paul Azinger and Hale Irwin (USA) v. Ian Woosnam and Paul Broadhurst (EUR)

Having been dropped from the morning foursomes, Woosnam was reprieved, to very good effect, for the afternoon own-ball format, although he played second fiddle to his rookie partner's virtuoso lead.

Dave Stockton also made changes from the morning; he surprisingly split up his two biggest winning pairs, but combined the two leading lights in Azinger and Irwin. As it turned out, Stockton's expected victory from his top two players did not transpire; they combined to win just two holes in the seventeen they played.

The Americans' opening win at the second hole came as the result of both British players' failing to make par on the 531-yard hole. The match stayed tight as the next five holes were halved, with both sides claiming their first birdie on the second par 5 of the round.

A stroke of luck helped the Europeans level the match on the par-3 eighth: Broadhurst chipped out of sand alongside the green, hit the base of the pin, and finished inches from the hole. Neither American could match Broadhurst's good fortune or his par three.

On the ninth green, a British bogey gave the two Americans their second and final success of the day, although they carded a birdie three between them just to make sure.

On the tenth, the match started to swing the British players' way. Broadhurst's thirty-foot birdie putt up the green swung in from the left and had just enough action to crawl into the hole before it expired. From the opposite end of the green, Azinger had a slightly shorter putt for the half; he started it to the left of the hole, and it kept straight as it ran by the cup.

"The [three thousand] European fans, bless their smelly little underarms, actually issued a verbal challenge on Saturday when they began singing rowdy English football songs as they celebrated their team's amazing comeback. Our fans, bless their lemon-scented Evian breath, are still cheering and applauding as they do at a concert when they want Barry Manilow to sing 'I Write the Songs' just one more time. We simply aren't accustomed to such raucous behavior on the hallowed grounds of a golf course, but it's time for a change."

—*Ken Burger,* Sunday Post-Courier

All square through eleven, Woosnam had a chance to put Europe up for the first time, but his birdie putt from twenty feet skinned the left of the twelfth hole for a half in fours.

Broadhurst's approach from the thirteenth fairway finished inside both American balls—four feet from the target. Having been left out of the first three sessions, the English rookie demonstrated that he should have been blooded earlier, holing his putt for another birdie three and the win.

With their noses in front, the British were not to be denied, and the next three holes were halved in par-bogey-par. It was Broadhurst who had the best chances over this stretch, but he failed to make hole-winning putts from eight feet on fourteen and twelve feet on sixteen.

Avoiding the water at all costs, Woosnam hooked his tee shot into the crowd on the left of the seventeenth. Going after the win and the flag, Irwin sent a tracer bullet at the green, but it drifted right, hit one of Pete Dye's infamous wooden supports, and bounded back into the water.

Forewarned is forearmed, so Azinger and Broadhurst hit safe shots, but both missed the green. From a nasty lie with the ball beneath his feet and in the rough sand, Woosnam came up two feet shy of holing his recovery. Having pulled his tee shot to the left, Azinger needed to hole his twenty-eight-foot putt from off the green to move onto the eighteenth. His attempt never seriously threatened the hole, although it finished only a few inches to the left. Woosnam made his par to sew up the 2 and 1 win.

The all-British four-under-par round was not bettered over the course of the afternoon, while the Americans' hard-fought 69 was not too shabby either.

Steve Pate and Corey Pavin (USA) v. Bernhard Langer and Colin Montgomerie (EUR)

For the final afternoon of pairs play, Dave Stockton made two decisions he may well regret. One was to give some match practice to his two unemployed players: Pate and Levi. Second, he allowed Desert Storm camouflage hats to be worn as a means of engendering some patriotic spirit in his players and in the crowd. Pavin and Pate not only looked silly and out of place in their hats, but they were never ahead in the match.

On their Desert Storm caps: "Frankly, Pavin and Pate looked like house-painters who had put down their ladders and brushes and buckets and wandered onto a golf course. Like house-painters, they lost."
—*Dan Jenkins,* Golf Digest

For the only time in twenty-eight matches, the first three holes were halved in par, 4-5-4. Langer and Montgomerie broke the opening stalemate with a birdie on the fourth, after Steve Pate received attention from the team doctor. The brave American was clearly not fit enough for such a grueling and demanding round of golf, whereas his partner was caught on one of his rare off days.

A second European birdie on the par-5 seventh extended the lead to two. The Scottish-German combo bogeyed the next two holes to reach the turn all square again. Both pairs played nine holes in even par, not overly impressive for better-ball competition; amazingly, the U.S. pair actually parred all nine holes.

The Americans' opening run of pars was halted by a bogey at the tenth, where Langer's par recaptured the lead. The German doubled the lead on the 466-yard twelfth, where another par proved damaging to the Americans, who started back with three fives.

The standard of play improved as the next few holes were all halved in threes. Pavin planted his approach to thirteen a mere three inches from the cup, while Montgomerie's ball arrived a few seconds later three feet away. The 219-yard fourteenth was halved in par, while Pate—in a rare glimpse of his true form—sank a fifty-footer from off the fifteenth green. This roc-size birdie was soon canceled out when Montgomerie holed a twenty-foot downhiller to retain the European lead.

With sixteen also halved, the Europeans stood confidently on the seventeenth tee, dormie two up and looking for immediate closure.

Montgomerie's tee shot parked itself on the back tier of the green only twenty feet from the pin. Pavin's one-iron was right at the flag but landed on the front tier and just about crawled up to the top level, thirty feet short. Pavin had little chance of holing out across the steeply sloping shelf of the green, doing well to terminate his travels three feet to the right.

Pinpointing the main "culprit" for the five-hour-and-ten-minute round: "The chess world must hope that Langer never takes up chess. His games might take years to finish."
—Charleston News

With two strokes for the match, the Scot rolled a nicely judged putt up to a foot of the hole for a concession and a 2 and 1 win.

Lanny Wadkins and Wayne Levi (USA) v. Mark James and Steven Richardson (EUR)

Wayne Levi, who came off a career year in 1990, had a careworn year in 1991. His form was so bad and his confidence so low that even in the friendly confines of the practice rounds, he barely strung two par holes together.

Facing Levi and Wadkins was one of the few successes of Europe's misfiring campaign. James and Richardson were coming off a narrow one-hole defeat in the morning, having thumped the highly rated pair of Calcavecchia and Pavin, 5 and 3, on Friday afternoon.

With both Americans starting with bogeys to lose the first hole, the Europeans promptly combined for back-to-back birdies to go three up after three. Wadkins's pars at the second and third were to no avail—his partner was as much help as an incontinent caddie with the hiccups.

Wadkins's third par in a row finally paid off when the British pair failed to match his mark on the 453-yard fourth. Having cut the European lead to one, Wadkins held the opposition close as the next eight holes were halved.

In 1990, Wayne Levi had four wins on the PGA Tour: the Atlanta Classic, the Western Open, the Greater Hartford Open, and the Canadian Open.

The 537-yard seventh was halved in birdies. James almost holed a forty-footer for an eagle on the twelfth but settled for a half in birdie fours.

The run of halved holes was broken on thirteen, where Richardson continued in feast-or-famine fashion by gorging himself on a ten-footer to go three up.

James needed to steer home a nasty three-footer on fifteen for a half, and the Americans found themselves still three down but with only three to play. Having kept his side in the match, Wadkins set about trying to win the contest on his own. His birdie putt at sixteen was conceded after both British players made a mess of the par-5 hole.

"Poor Lanny Wadkins had to carry Wayne Levi around like baggage all afternoon; the reigning player of the year (cue laughter track) started bogey-double bogey-bogey, then later picked up on four straight holes."
—*Thomas Boswell,* Washington Post

James hit one of the better approaches of the afternoon at seventeen, planting his ball fifteen feet from the hole on the top tier. From the left-hand rough betwixt green and gallery, Wadkins played a gentle chip off the trailing slope of a bunker and let his ball roll down three feet past the hole. Almost matching his partner's outstanding tee shot, Richardson rolled his seventeen-foot putt up to a few inches of the target, and the match was over, with Europe winning, 3 and 1.

Payne Stewart and Fred Couples (USA) v. Seve Ballesteros and Jose Maria Olazabal (EUR)

The American pair could manage only pars for the first five holes, but against the normally razor-sharp Spaniards, they were only one hole down. Having made their par at the 185-yard fifth, the Americans reeled off three more threes in a row to take a one-hole lead. A U.S. birdie at the sixth leveled the score, but better was to follow on the 537-yard seventh. After Ballesteros executed a sand recovery to two feet for a birdie, Couples's putt from off the green changed directions twice and snaked into the hole for an eagle and a one-hole lead.

Stewart continued the run of threes when his tee shot just stopped off the front left of the eighth green. Olazabal's eight-iron reply pitched alongside the flag but carried on and slowly rolled off into the bunker, from where he chipped up to four feet short. Stewart putted up and left his ball on the front lip of the hole for a "birdie and a half" par. Olazabal safely holed his full par putt for a slightly fortuitous half.

With nine and ten halved in par, the scene was set for a battle royal over the closing eight holes. The Americans held a fragile one-hole lead over the previously unbeaten Spaniards.

Off the side of the green at the par-5 eleventh, Couples had another lengthy putt for an eagle. Uncharacteristically, he completely misread the break and started his twenty-five-foot putt way out to the right of the hole, where it stayed. He made no such mistake with his seven-foot birdie putt to take the hole and go two up.

"As the sun set, the only American with his dignity entirely intact may have been Couples. But he was walking tall indeed. For all intents, he played Europe's best team alone after U.S. Open champion Payne Stewart packed his knickers and headed for home as soon as the match turned in to the wind." —Thomas Boswell, *Washington Post*

Safely finding the thirteenth fairway off the tee, Ballesteros saw his second shot come to rest eight feet shy of the cup, and he made the birdie putt look simple to pull to within one. On fourteen, Stewart and Olazabal swapped nine-foot par putts for a half, as the match began to heat up even as the sun went down.

Having seen both Americans fail to hit the fifteenth green in two, Ballesteros fired his approach at the flag and drilled it four feet past. Spurred on by Seve's masterstroke, Couples produced one of his own, chipping in—blind—from the deep recess of a sand pit for a four that suddenly wiped the broad grin off the Spaniard's face. Seve got the smile back when his birdie putt, which looked to have run past the hole, caved in at the back door. Once again the Spanish pair had mounted a sudden comeback—two wins in three holes—when all had seemed set against them.

On sixteen, with Stewart out of the hole again, the other players had medium-range birdie chances, but each missed, and Couples emerged with another half to his credit. On the seventeenth, Olazabal's tee shot was even better than James's a few minutes earlier, pitching on the top of the upslope and rolling six feet past the hole for a truly remarkable result. Unfortunately for Olly, he couldn't sink his birdie attempt, his ball drifting past the left of the cup.

Of the eighteen players who drove off the seventeenth tee in the afternoon fourballs, only seven found the putting surface, of which only two were American: Pavin and Couples.

Again it was left to Couples to rescue the American cause. He still had a five-foot putt for the half in three, which he made under the soul-searching spotlight of competitive stress, taking the match to the eighteenth all square.

"Fred's putt was huge . . . gigantic. If anybody ever questions his courage again . . ."
—*Paul Azinger*

After five and a half hours of play, dusk settled in as the last match reached the last hole.

Couples drove into the sand and played a mighty recovery to the green, rolling up to fourteen feet of the pin. Olazabal also found the green in two, twenty-five feet short right, and made a mess of his putt, misreading the line and speed across the slope. Couples's birdie putt swung by the left of the hole, and Olazabal holed his second putt from four feet for par. To tie up all the loose ends, Stewart sank a three-foot putt for an honorable and well-deserved half.

Afternoon fourball result: USA ½, EUR 3½
Day two result: USA 3½, EUR 4½
Overall match score: USA 8, EUR 8

Day Three: Singles

Realizing that this match would probably come down to the last stroke, Stockton kept three of his big names—Couples, Wadkins, and Irwin—back until last, and sent the inspirational old-timer Ray Floyd out first. Gallacher did likewise with the bottom of his order—Torrance, James, and Langer—using his best one-on-one player, Nick Faldo, as his leadoff man.

Steve Pate (USA) v. David Gilford (EUR)

After barely getting through his fourball match on Saturday evening, Steve Pate finally bowed to the fact that the injuries he had suffered in the car crash would not allow him to complete another round of golf.

Unfortunately for David Gilford, his name was in the European envelope and he had to sit out the final day, the only reward being that the half-point he earned for his team was his first in the Ryder Cup.

Gilford became the second European player to earn his first half-point courtesy of the injury/envelope system. Mark James suffered the same fate when he pulled out of the singles in 1979.

Raymond Floyd (USA) v. Nick Faldo (EUR)

A fascinating opening singles match saw a rematch of the 1990 Masters play-off where Faldo beat Floyd on the second hole. This time around, Faldo was clutching an unwanted 0-3 record, while Floyd was 2-1 with a fourball win over his opponent.

Floyd singularly failed to find his form of the first two days, starting bogey-par-double bogey to Faldo's par-birdie-par, and was three down before he could almost draw breath.

Over the next three holes, it was Faldo's turn to blow a fuse: he carded two bogeys to cut his lead by one. From the ridiculous to the sub-par, Faldo slammed home an eagle putt from twelve feet at the seventh, followed by a birdie at the par-3 eighth to recapture the three-hole lead by the turn.

On the 405-yard tenth, both men finally achieved the level of quality normally associated with their names. Floyd's second bounced on the right-hand bank of the green and rolled down toward the flag, stopping two feet in front to be conceded for a birdie. Faldo's pitch came up a lot shorter, but from over thirty feet away his putt started way out to the right and took advantage of the bank that Floyd's ball drifted in on. Faldo's ball curled right at the hole and dropped for a matching birdie that maintained his three-hole buffer.

Faldo, out in 35 to Floyd's 39, was three up as the two players underwent a reversal of form from the first days.

With Floyd floundering like a beached whale in the sand on eleven, Faldo carded another birdie to go four up. He was close to putting this match away, but he bogeyed twelve and scrabbled a half on thirteen.

The 219-yard fourteenth had promised to be a pivotal hole all week, but most of the players had coped admirably with a green that unusually sloped away from the tee. Although he held a three-hole margin, the overly fastidious Faldo took an age to select a club to hit from the tee. Worried about keeping his ball on the green, Faldo finally hit his tee shot into a waste area and found a lie so bad that he could not hit the ball toward the flag. He eventually conceded the hole, having still not figured out which club to use to get on in three.

"You wouldn't get me here for stroke play. You stand on fourteen and wonder what the hell you've got to do. I had a bad lie in the waste area. If you're there you're dead. The golf course is so hard, it's unbelievable. In these conditions, I don't know how you could finish with a scorecard."

—Nick Faldo

Two down, Floyd had a chance on fifteen to close even further, but he missed a winning par putt from less than four feet. Feeling his lead starting to erode, Faldo—from a waste bunker 160 yards short of the sixteenth—landed his second shot eighteen feet from the hole. After Floyd answered with his third to three feet for par, Faldo's birdie attempt slipped off to the right.

"On this blustery day on the South Carolina shore, replete with a howling wind that made the last four holes a swirl of false hopes and broken dreams."
—*Leonard Shapiro,* Washington Post

Floyd's safety-first two-iron at seventeen found a grassy lobe between the sandy areas on the left of the green, leaving a precarious chip over more sand. Faldo went at the flag and came up twenty feet short in the heart of the green. After Floyd chipped up to five feet, Faldo rolled his birdie attempt at the hole, but the ball drifted right and kept rolling on by five feet. Still his turn, Faldo missed his second putt, which would have won him the match. With another chance to dance, Floyd took aim, and his ball rolled into the left-hand lip of the cup. The first singles match out moved on to the last hole.

After bogeys at twelve, fifteen, and seventeen, and a double at fourteen: *"I was petrified. No way do I want to do that again. I've never known such pressure. I hated every minute of that round. It's been such a tough week. . . . I've had a bad week. But in the real world, having a bad week is waking up and finding you're a steelworker in Scunthorpe."*
—NICK FALDO

"The golf course is so hard, it's unbelievable. Nick Faldo and I have just said we don't know if we could have finished if we'd had a card in our hands.
—*Raymond Floyd*

With his idiosyncratic backswing that appears to freeze at its zenith, Floyd fired his third shot up toward the final green but found sand to the left. Faldo was already on in two, albeit forty feet short of the hole. He almost holed his meandering putt, but it drifted a few feet past. Sensing this might be his last Ryder Cup, Floyd did not concede his opponent's putt but strode over to his ball in the sand for one last hurrah. He left the bunker with more a harrumph than a hurrah, his chip coming nearer to hitting Faldo than the hole. The concession was given with a hearty handshake and customary slaps on the back. Faldo had earned Europe a valuable victory by two holes.

Payne Stewart (USA) v. David Feherty (EUR)

A strangely nervous and below-form U.S. Open champion bogeyed the first two holes and doubled the fourth to drop three down.

Feherty, for his part, started with four straight fours and seemed to be enjoying himself in that impish, Irish way of his. Stewart got serious on the sixth, carding his first birdie to cut the lead to two. Both players made birdie at the seventh and proceeded to halve the next three holes in par.

Feherty was out in 35, two shots and two holes better than Stewart.

On eleven, Feherty showed why he was the European tour putting leader, holing a tough twelve-footer for par to go back three up as Stewart logged another bogey. Another American bogey was recorded on thirteen, where Stewart dropped four down with five to play.

With holes running out, and dormie four to the bad, Stewart finally pulled what was left of his game together. He scrabbled a winning par on the fifteenth with a clutch three-foot putt. Sixteen saw Feherty disappear into a waste bunker, but a fine recovery left him with an eight-footer for the match. The par putt just failed to drop, and he remained dormie as Stewart collected another hole-winning par.

Stewart safely found the seventeenth green forty feet short of the hole, while Feherty's tee shot finished fifteen feet in front of the American. Stewart miserably misread his long putt, missing the hole by eighteen inches as his ball scurried eight feet by. Having got a partial read off his opponent's total misread, the Irishman had a putt for the match, safe in the knowledge he probably had two bites at the cherry. His second bite was not going to be as big as his first: he almost holed the twenty-five-foot putt, leaving the ball a matter of inches past.

Stewart conceded, and, finishing before Faldo ahead, Feherty took the 2 and 1 win for Europe's first point of the day—the first and only full point of his all-too-brief Ryder Cup career.

"I got behind the eight ball early and hit some bad shots. I kept beating myself. He played better than I did, so he deserves to win."
—*Payne Stewart*

Mark Calcavecchia (USA) v. Colin Montgomerie (EUR)

After Calcavecchia birdied the first hole, the two players exchanged alternate sixes that more than set the tone for a match fated from the outset to conclude in the type of human tragedy found only on a golf course. With the rancid run of sixes out of their systems, both players bogeyed the par-3 fifth just for good measure.

The American pulled himself together with a couple of birdies at seven and nine, and Montgomerie clunked five bogeys on the outward journey. When the math had been done at the turn, the angry Scot, who had been delightfully described as "a bear hug waiting to happen," was more like a bear trap waiting to snap on. Out in 42, Montgomerie was five down on Calcavecchia's nice round par figures.

Without a three to his name in the first nine holes, Montgomerie bunkered his second shot to the tenth but emerged with a three on his card after he bounced his recovery five feet short of the hole and saw it disappear for his first birdie. His second birdie quickly followed at the par-5 eleventh, and Calcavecchia, who had started home par-par, was only three up.

The following two holes were halved, but the Scot appeared to have finally blown his chance when he conceded on the unforgiving fourteenth.

Back four up with four to play, Calcavecchia was in the catbird seat, but the doghouse was barking his name. To crash from hero to zero in four holes takes a lot of undoing, and the American crashed as hard as the Atlantic breakers on the Carolina shoreline.

On fifteen, he pulled his second to the left of the green and somehow contrived to take five more to get down. Montgomerie was just happy to card a five for a bogey and the win.

Sixteen saw Calcavecchia on and through the green in three. After chipping back to fifteen feet, he pushed his par putt to the left of the hole and another four feet past. Montgomerie was on in three and only eleven feet away. The bad news for the Scot was that he had a slippery downhill putt; the good news was that he had two putts for the hole. Judging the pace and line almost to perfection, the Scot missed the hole by fractions of an inch, but close enough to cut the American's lead to two with two to play.

Standing on the exposed seventeenth tee, Montgomerie realized that his opponent had been struck by the Ryder Cup equivalent of stage fright. Needing one good honest shot to keep the pressure up, Montgomerie also fell afoul of the Ryder Cup tension. His tee shot drifted off line and found the reeds and weeds on the very edge of the water. Reprieved and back in control of his own destiny again, all Calcavecchia had to do was find dry land. What he did was to produce the worst shot of the week from this tee: a wave-hugging slice-cum-shank-cum-scuff that failed by thirty yards to carry the water. The crowd was stunned, the players were stunned, the captains were stunned.

"The worst thing you can do to me is put me into a 30-mph crosswind with my snap slice. I peeled one off into the ocean; I hit another one in the lake." —MARK CALCAVECCHIA

On the American's finding water in his second successive singles match: "If Mark Calcavecchia were a ship's captain, nobody would want to sail with him, such is his propensity for ending up in the water at crucial moments."
—*Malcolm Hamer,* The Ryder Cup Players *(1992)*

This misfiring match restarted from the ignominy of the drop zone. Montgomerie put his third shot twenty feet to the left of the pin, while the American's third shot also found the green—thirty feet below the pin. Calcavecchia's putt rolled past by three feet, and the Scot put his flat-iron approach stone dead. The American had a three-footer for the match and blasted it across the top of the hole.

Having lost the last three holes, Calcavecchia smacked his ball into the water and must have seriously thought about jumping in after it to swim off somewhere quiet—or perhaps meet a watery fate with the alligators—rather than face the sharp teeth of the hostile media sharks. With renewed hope and vigor, Monty strode off purposefully—as only Scotsmen with a purpose can stride—to the eighteenth tee, still one down.

With his game and nerves in tatters, Calcavecchia did well to put his second shot through the green, and his chip back came up nine feet short of the flag. On the front of the green in two, Montgomerie had a thirty-foot putt to win the hole. The ball rolled up and over the ridge and made a beeline for the hole, rolling on and on, closer and closer, coming to a halt one revolution short—draping itself all over the front lip. Calcavecchia knew he could erase all the troubles of the previous three holes with one stroke—but it was not close.

"Sometimes it's good to look at the other guy and realize he's feeling awful too. It's easy to forget that if you are scared yourself."
—*Colin Montgomerie*

The apoplectic American walked after his disappointing putt as soon as he hit it. Having traded a four-hole lead for a half-point, Calcavecchia was so upset that he could not look his opponent in the eye when they shook hands.

In losing the last four holes, Calcavecchia finished triple bogey, bogey, triple bogey, bogey, while Montgomerie came home bogey, par, double bogey, par—to win the four holes. Between them they finished eleven over par for these last four unforgettable holes. For the whole round, the American took one more stroke than his opponent, carding the worst round of the week—an 81. Between the two of them, they were a staggering nineteen over par.

If Calcavecchia had not faltered down the finishing stretch, the score would have read Europe 10½-9½. Instead it was 11-9 in the visitors' favor.

Paul Azinger (USA) v. Jose Maria Olazabal (EUR)

Having taken the first hole with a birdie, Azinger took a bogey six on the second to Olazabal's birdie, falling further behind when the Spaniard holed a seven-footer for birdie on the third. The American got his hole back with a bogey on the fourth, where it was Olazabal's turn to card a double bogey. In this wild four-hole start, the two aces managed to remain all square. They returned to normality and halved the fifth in par threes.

On the 455-yard sixth, Olazabal played a magnificent four-iron approach, but Azinger's second finished closer, four feet from the flag, and the American made his birdie putt after Olazabal missed his. Azinger was unable to hold on to a lead as he promptly bogeyed the par-5 seventh to level.

"The Spaniards are tough. But we'll see on Sunday. Jose won't have 'Dad' telling him what to do every shot, and Seve will have to play his own ball."
—*Mark Calcavecchia*

Even without his "mentor," Seve, Olazabal still knew how to try to bend the rules to his advantage. There was a fifteen-minute delay at the eighth green as Jose Maria sought relief from a sprinkler head. A free drop was not given, so he took his lumps and chipped up to two feet for a half in threes. Olazabal's putting let him down on the ninth, where he missed making par from three feet, and the Spaniard then asked Azinger to make his par from six inches closer to win the hole.

On the 405-yard tenth, Azinger missed his birdie putt from eighteen feet, but Olazabal leveled the score with his birdie from nine. After conceding Azinger's par putt on the next hole, Olazabal again missed a crucial putt from eleven feet to go back down. Roles reversed on the twelfth as Azinger conceded a short par putt, then failed to hole his own seven-footer.

In a match that was up and down more than a jack-in-the-box overdosing on Energizers, Azinger's twelve-foot birdie on thirteen gave him back his lead. Needless to say, Olazabal parred the tricky fourteenth, Azinger did not, and the American's bogey cost him the hole and the lead—again.

For a change, the fifteenth was halved, not in birdies or in pars, but in bogeys, after both players missed par putts of about six feet. With three holes to play and the match all square, neither player could afford to make a fatal slip.

Both found sand on sixteen. Olazabal launched his second shot to twenty-five feet, while Azinger's spectacular third finished half that distance from the hole. The Spaniard putted to the edge of the hole for a conceded par, and Azinger made a clutch putt for his par.

"I had to save par on sixteen with a huge sand-wedge blast, followed by a twelve-foot putt that slammed into the hole to keep me even with Jose."
—PAUL AZINGER, *Zinger* (1995)

On his tee shot at seventeen: "I absolutely killed it! If I missed it the slightest bit, I would have been in the water on the line I took."
—*Paul Azinger*

Having sprung a leak on Friday and landed in the crowd on Saturday, Azinger hit a blistering two-iron onto the penultimate green, but fifty feet off line. Olazabal's tee shot found a heel print in the sand; then he cleverly chipped onto the green but could not make his par putt. With two telling putts, the American made sure of going one up with one to play by draining his second putt from all of eight feet.

This was the sixth time Azinger had taken a one-hole lead on Olazabal, and on the previous five occasions he had promptly lost the next hole.

From 220 yards out and into the teeth of a gale, Olazabal's one-iron second shot from the right of the fairway plunked into a sandy waste area to the right of the green. Azinger's two-iron second was more fortunate, finding a sand-free hollow to the left of the green. Jose Maria played a controlled chip out of the sand, landing his ball on the fringe to keep it from bounding past the hole, but it pulled up fourteen feet shy.

Azinger played his seventy-footer up from the hollow, the acute downslope guiding his ball underneath the hole to finish within two feet. The Spaniard had to hole his putt, but his ball swerved off line and ran wide left. Olly quickly conceded Azinger's quite missable short putt to give America the 2-up win.

Corey Pavin (USA) v. Steven Richardson (EUR)

With the 185-yard fifth the only hole halved out of the first seven, this dogfight lived up to its billing as an explosive encounter. Richardson had already whacked Pavin, 5 and 4, in the Friday fourball, so the American was more than up for the rematch.

Richardson started out as though Pavin were in for another drubbing, a birdie at the first setting him on his way. Revered as a born battler, Pavin leveled on the second with a birdie of his own, then took the lead when Richardson conceded the third.

Richardson's game let him down again on the fourth, where a bogey cost him another hole to go two down. After his winning start, the Englishman had lost the next three holes.

Richardson, who towered over his rival, pulled a hole back on six with a par but bogeyed the seventh to go back two down. With the next two holes halved in pars—and the ninth in bogey fives—Pavin grimly clung to his two-hole advantage.

"I had waited a long time to play in the Ryder Cup and was more nervous than I had ever been in any golf tournament. Not only was I playing for my country and my teammates, but for my tour, and that meant so much to me."
—*Corey Pavin*

Half of the American's lead disappeared at the eleventh when he could do no better than a bogey six. The lead completely vanished on thirteen, where Pavin made his fourth bogey in eight holes.

Having fought back level, Richardson lost the momentum he had built for a driving finish, and on fourteen it was his turn to card a bogey.

Back one up, Pavin scrabbled a half on fifteen before rolling a twenty-five-foot putt up to the hole on sixteen to make a par five. Richardson failed to make his par from the edge of the green.

Two up with two to play, Pavin knew the time was right to finish his man off.

Hitting into a strong breeze, Pavin took no chances and teed off seventeen with a testosterone-packed three-wood. The extra power of the club and the increased adrenaline rush caused the little American to pull his drive, badly plugging his ball in the back of a rugged bunker. Needing to win the hole, Richardson hit a spectacular shot that bounced pin-high fifteen feet left of the flag, then bounded on another ten feet to the back left of the green.

With a cockeyed stance, halfway up the sandbank, the ball well below his feet, and facing a downhill slope with the consistency of an overpolished bowling alley, Pavin produced the second-most-defining moment of this Ryder Cup.

On Pavin's bunker recovery on seventeen: *"I think he's just trying to whack it out. . . . Oooh! He's played it very well indeed. . . . Fantastic shot!"* —PETER ALLISS, BBC TV

From the bunker, Pavin deftly scooped up his ball as though he had lobbed it underhanded, landing it on the downslope just beyond the fringe. Leaping out of the sand trap almost as fast as his ball, Pavin raced after the ball as it gathered pace down the slope. First it threatened to curve away from the hole, then—with Pavin urging it on from right behind—the ball curled back toward the hole. By the time the American had caught up with his ball, it had run out of breath two and a half feet short of the hole—but dead on line.

From favorite to win the hole, Richardson had to hole his putt just to stay in the match. After he had waited for the crowd to calm down, his nervous-looking putt rolled harmlessly past the left of the hole and five feet beyond. Pavin gallantly holed his putt for the match, then almost swung himself off his feet in celebratory delight.

The chants of "USA! USA!" from parts of the crowd were in response to the first point of the day for the home team, thanks to Pavin's 2 and 1 win, since this match concluded before Azinger's.

Wayne Levi (USA) v. Seve Ballesteros (EUR)

Wayne Levi faced a tough task in taking on Seve Ballesteros, who had dropped only half a point in his first four matches. Brought into the starting lineup on Saturday afternoon for some match practice, Levi contributed very little in a losing cause.

The American started off his singles match well enough, with a par four at the first hole for a half with the great Spaniard. After this promising start, things went bad for Levi.

Despite the criticism leveled at Levi's inclusion on the team, he was the fourth-winningest player on the U.S. side, with twelve titles, after Floyd, Irwin, and Wadkins.

Having laid up short of the par-5 second, the American hit his next two shots into the water and ended up with an eight. The worst thing about this triple bogey was that Seve also hit the water twice, but got down for a hole-winning seven.

Two down, Levi parred the third but lost that as well to Seve's twenty-five-foot birdie putt.

The American held firm for a few holes and even cut the Spaniard's lead by making his first birdie on the 537-yard seventh. This success was short-lived: Levi bogeyed the par-3 eighth, which Seve birdied from thirty-five feet for good measure to go back up by two.

When Ballesteros sank a ten-footer on the ninth for another birdie, he was three up at the turn. Seve was out in 35 for his three-hole lead, while Levi was credited with a slightly forgiving 39.

Levi conceded eleven to drop further behind, with no obvious way back into the match.

The American was not going to give in easily. He made his second birdie at thirteen and halved the treacherous par-3 fourteenth, one of the few players to find the back-to-front green from the tee. The American caught a glimmer of hope when Seve bogeyed fifteen to stand two up with three to play.

With time running out on sixteen, Levi's putt from seventeen feet weaved like a drunken snake and slithered past the left of the hole by the thickness of a reptile's scale. Ballesteros made his three-footer for par to win the match, 3 and 2, giving Europe its third win of the day. Once again, Severiano Ballesteros proved the mainstay of the European team, taking 4½ points out of a possible 5.

"Wayne Levi—losing to Seve Ballesteros—looked like a Sunday hacker."
—Washington Post

Chip Beck (USA) v. Ian Woosnam (EUR)

With the first hole halved in par, Beck won the next two holes with fours. He was pegged back when Woosnam took the fourth and fifth on a concession and a par.

Back level at the par-5 seventh, Woosnam blew through the green in two, leaving a treacherously bad lie, and he was able only to get down in par. Beck had a birdie putt to retake the lead but blew a great chance to take the hole. The American did take the lead again with a long birdie putt at the par-3 eighth, but the Welshman immediately squared the match on nine, winning his second hole with a par after Beck three-putted.

In the sand on eleven, Beck flipped his ball up onto the raised putting surface but did not call upon his putter—the ball rolled gently into the hole on its own. The American did not see his ball go in, because he was too far below the surface of the green. Only when he climbed up onto the green did he realize that his ball had gone underground for an eagle and another lead.

Remarkably, the next four holes were all halved in straight fours, and the fourteenth hole claimed two more bogeys.

Woosnam found more strife than he needed on sixteen, driving into the water. Taking a drop, he reached the green in five, but Beck was already there in three, so the Welshman conceded the hole without bothering to putt, going two down.

At seventeen, Beck was armed with a two-iron on the tee, but Dave Stockton persuaded him otherwise: "I told him to hit a three-wood. I said he wanted to get the ball past the hole. I told him Corey Pavin hit a three-wood and couldn't get it past the trap, so hit three-wood, go ahead and get it back up there."

Beck—a captain's choice—took his captain's advice and struck a three-wood from the tee that ran through the back right of the green only fifteen feet from the hole. In reply, Woosnam pulled his tee shot into the sand on the left of the green. With Woosnam's ball eighteen inches below his feet, his recovery looked plastered all over the pin, but it failed to bite as it pitched, bounding past the hole by ten feet or more, threatening to run off into the water beyond. With two putts for the win, Beck almost holed out with his first, but the ball decided to stay up top, six inches to the right, for a tap-in win and a 3 and 1 result.

On another singles defeat for Woosnam: "How could the world's number one have played in five Ryder Cup singles and lost the lot?"
—*Peter Alliss, BBC TV*

Mark O'Meara (USA) v. Paul Broadhurst (EUR)

Having pulled out of the afternoon fourball on Saturday with a recurring back strain, O'Meara pronounced himself fit to play in the singles after overnight treatment had eased his injury.

Broadhurst's bogey six at the second presented O'Meara with an early lead that lasted as long as it took the American to bogey the next hole. Whether or not O'Meara's bad back affected his early play, he dropped further strokes at the third and fourth, falling three down to a very grateful Broadhurst, who took the three holes with nothing more malicious than par.

The Englishman's first birdie came at the par-3 eighth, where he chipped up from just short of the green, then could see just enough of the raised green to watch his ball dribble into the hole. With a chance to cancel the chip, O'Meara missed a birdie putt from fifteen feet.

Out in 36, Broadhurst took three fewer shots than O'Meara in building his three-hole lead.

Broadhurst gave a hole back on the tenth, which he bogeyed, but the American just as quickly repaid the compliment on eleven. O'Meara claimed his first birdie of the round on the 404-yard thirteenth to pull back to two down.

With halves at fourteen and fifteen, O'Meara was unable to cut any further into Broadhurst's lead, then had to make a priceless putt at sixteen just to stay alive.

O'Meara's one-iron missed the seventeenth green to the right and found the water ten feet in. Needing only to keep his ammunition dry, Broadhurst badly plugged his ball in the same bunker visited by Pavin and Woosnam before him. O'Meara's third shot from the drop zone got eight feet closer than his first but still drowned, and he hastily conceded the match, 3 and 1.

"I've been on a winning, losing, and tying team, and to tell the truth, I didn't have much fun in any of them."
—*Mark O'Meara*

Twenty-six-year-old rookie Paul Broadhurst (who once shot a 63 at St. Andrews) had only one birdie—on the eighth—but his maximum of two points from two games gave him as many points as the powerhouse duo of Faldo and Woosnam managed from their eight starts.

This was the second American loss of the week to have been proffered at the seventeenth-hole drop zone, and it left Europe one point away from retaining the Cup, at 13-12.

Fred Couples (USA) v. Sam Torrance (EUR)

This "battle of the buddies" failed to produce much in the way of memorable magic on the course, the two carding one three each in sixteen holes of pretty poor play. Couples was handed the lead on the first hole when Torrance missed a par putt, and the long-time friends halved the next five holes, notably bogeying the par-3 fifth in close harmony.

Couples was in control of the match after nine holes, three holes up and three shots fewer than Torrance's 39. All in all, the Scot carded eight fives or worse in sixteen holes.

Couples went two up on the sixth, again thanks to a bogey by Torrance, and the American carded the first birdie of the day at the 537-yard seventh to go three up. The par-3 eighth hole was notable for the fact that both players carded the only threes of the round there.

Torrance continued to struggle on the way home, making costly bogeys at eleven and twelve to go five down. Couples generously returned the gesture by bogeying thirteen and double-bogeying fourteen, where Torrance escaped with a bogey himself.

Couples twice found himself in the sand on fifteen, but he was able to keep his three-hole lead intact with a half in bogey fives, after Torrance missed a par putt from eight feet.

Dormie three down, Torrance, faced with a sixteen-footer from the right-hand fringe across the sloping sixteenth green, made a mockery of his earlier play by draining a miracle par putt. His success was fleeting—Couples holed out from three feet for par to take the match, 3 and 2.

"If the Americans win, they ought to let Couples keep the Cup. If the Europeans win, they can just fill the Cup with cough syrup and give it to Seve."
—*Thomas Boswell,* Washington Post

Couples proved to be one of the strong men of the American side, with 3½ points from five matches, the half-point against the Spaniards on Saturday afternoon a crucial result in the overall context of the match.

"It's the highlight of my career. I just felt like two years ago I lost my match and we lost the Cup. There's more pressure here than you can ever imagine. It's a weird experience." —FRED COUPLES

This point leveled the match score, 13–13, with just two matches left.

Lanny Wadkins (USA) v. Mark James (EUR)

After dropping the opening hole with a careless bogey, Wadkins took the next two holes with a birdie and a par to go one up. Both players bogeyed the par-4 fourth, and Wadkins putted up from the fringe on the fifth green, over a ridge and in, for a birdie two to double his lead.

The American went further ahead at the next par 3 hole, the eighth, where James made another bogey. The Englishman, who was not enjoying his round, carded a double bogey to lose the ninth to Wadkins's bogey. Four down at the turn, James had only himself to blame, having made five bogeys on the way out.

Whatever affliction James suffered on the front nine, Wadkins caught it coming home, inexplicably bogeying four of the next six holes but remarkably still retaining a two-hole lead.

The only good news from this trail of Wadkins's woe came with a par at twelve, and an unbelievable birdie at the unbirdieable fourteenth.

Back to two down with three to play, James looked as if he might have a shot at a half-point from this poor encounter. On sixteen, the Englishman was allowed to replace his ball in a waste bunker after a spectator moved it. From there, he just failed to reach the green. Wadkins rolled his putt, from off the right-hand side of the green, up to six inches for a concession by James, who needed to hole his next shot to stay alive. James, from five feet off the green, played his putt up to the hole and looked to be a lock for holing it—until it took a vindictive veer to the left and finished off the putter's hopes, 3 and 2.

Previously, only two players had birdied the unfairly ferocious fourteenth. Feherty and Ballesteros achieved the feat in the comfort and safety of fourball play on Friday afternoon.

On being close to tears after his eighteenth Ryder Cup victory: *"That's only happened to me once before, and that was at the 1983 Ryder Cup. . . . That just shows you how much this means to everybody on the team."* —Lanny Wadkins

This result from the penultimate singles match left the score tantalizingly poised at 14–13 in the Americans' favor, with the last pair still to finish. The Americans needed to win or halve the last match to regain the Cup.

Hale Irwin (USA) v. Bernhard Langer (EUR)

In this battle of the titanic anchormen, Langer faltered at the first hurdle, losing the hole with a bogey to Irwin's par.

Irwin went two up with another par effort as Langer conceded the second hole, only to see Irwin do the same on the third. The fourth was halved in par, and the par-3 fifth was shared in bogey fours. In an ugly round of golf, Langer struck his first successful

"On that course, in that wind, under that pressure, the shots played were ugly and we were made to look ugly."
—*Hale Irwin*

birdie putt on the sixth, but Irwin failed to follow his example, and the match was back all square.

After the seventh was halved in par fives, the American finished off the front nine with two threes and two wins, as Langer bogeyed eight and parred nine. En route to a two-hole lead at the turn, Irwin was out in 37 to Langer's 39.

Ten was halved in par, and Langer got a hole back on eleven thanks to Irwin's bogey six. Twelve and thirteen were halved in par, but Langer got into terrible trouble on fourteen. Still off the par-3 green in two, he hit a putt he fully expected to turn at least a foot. Left with a teasing four-footer, the German saw his putting woes continued as his ball lipped out for double bogey and sent him back two down. Irwin, who holed out with a winning bogey, was about to face his own demons.

"When I was out there on ten, eleven, twelve and I kept hearing that 'USA!' I'm telling you what, I couldn't breathe, I couldn't swallow, I couldn't do anything. And making that turn back in on fourteen, I could barely hit the ball." —HALE IRWIN

Having driven into sand on fifteen, Irwin took three to reach a green his opponent was through in two. Langer chipped up to four feet to leave himself a par putt for the win. With the echoes of his miss on fourteen still ringing in his ears, Langer looked pensive as he wiped something off the heel of his putter. They say time waits for no man, but it certainly does if Langer is on the course in front of you, which is one reason Gallacher let him out last.

The German's hands took an eternity to clamp themselves into a split-lock grip. Fully prepared, he dragged the blade back six inches and tapped forward—the ball rolling slowly into the hole. One doubts if Langer has ever bolted the ball into the back of the hole in his life or in his dreams. Whatever his preparation or method of execution, he was back to one down with three to play—and the Ryder Cup was about to witness one of its most unforgettable finishes.

On the 579-yard sixteenth, Irwin hit his third shot into the gallery way out to the right. Langer, with 140 yards to the green, took a seven-iron when he needed a six, coming up five yards short in the bunker in front of the pin. Irwin's fourth, a masterful chip-and-run trundling up to three and a half feet, seemed to have settled the match and the Ryder Cup. Langer's recovery ran right at the flag but carried on five feet. Both were on in four. Langer putted first: his cross-handed style did not look pretty, but the result was most attractive. Irwin made his par putt to remain one up with two to play.

The formula was simple for Langer—he needed to win the last two holes for Europe to retain the Ryder Cup with a tied score. What was not so simple was the terrifying tee shot on seventeen that immediately faced him.

With the weight of a continent on his slight shoulders, Langer swung lustily into the breeze and sent his ball into the crowd on the left of the seventeenth green, only to see it run down toward but not reach the green.

With the wind in his face and tension wrapped around his thoughts, Irwin placed his trust in a small wood and was repaid. On first sight, his ball appeared to bounce back onto the green from the same area Langer's ball had alighted. On second sight (and not spotted by NBC TV), it transpired that some joker in the gallery had thrown another ball onto the green.

On the mystery of Irwin's ball at seventeen: *"We had no way of knowing. It was purely a freak thing. The replay we showed was exactly what happened. When I saw Irwin putting the ball, my spotter said to me, 'Why is he putting the ball from there?' To tell you the truth, in all the excitement, I let it go."* —Larry Cirillo, NBC TV producer

Irwin's ball had remained where it had landed just off the green, forty feet left of the pin, but closer than his opponent. In light of his much-publicized putting woes, Langer's decision to stick with his putter from way off the green was surprising. He knocked his ball over the ridge and it rolled down toward the hole, miraculously coming to rest within four feet. Under even more pressure, Irwin putted up from off the green and saw his ball gather speed where Langer's had died, rolling five feet past the hole. Irwin's shaky comeback putt waddled like a pregnant duck and went past the hole, presenting Langer with a golden opportunity to wrestle the Cup away from the U.S. side's tightening grasp. Taking his usual amount of time, Langer calmly stroked his putt home—and the match was well and truly joined.

"People ask me how Bernhard Langer stood up to all that pressure over the last three holes of the Ryder Cup. How about me? I not only had to stand up, I had to carry the bag as well."
—*Peter Coleman*

Langer safely found the left of the final fairway. Irwin found the gallery on the left, but his ball luckily bounced back onto the fairway.

With a three-wood from 230 yards out, Irwin tried to bring the crowd on the right of the green into play, but his ball dug into the lush grass around the green and rolled back toward the putting surface. Sixty yards closer in, Langer put his ball between Irwin's and the hole, just short of a sandy hollow. Irwin's critical seventy-five-foot chip slowed up the instant it landed on the green, abjectly sloping away twenty feet short of the hole. The chorus of groans from the gallery was almost enough to persuade Irwin to bury his head in the nearest pot bunker.

"There is no way I would ever, ever wish what happened on the last hole to anyone. My disappointment after my pitch shot . . . no one on this team will ever know what it's like. I hope they never know."

—HALE IRWIN

Thrown a lifeline, Langer drew his putter out again and almost knocked the ball into the hole, but it ran five, maybe six feet past. Irwin had a twenty-foot putt to win the Ryder Cup, but his chances were slim to none, and he finished two feet short and to the left.

Langer courteously conceded the putt and went to work on his own, holding the destiny of so many hopes and dreams in his shaking hands.

"The greatest pressure putt in the history of golf."
—*Michael Bonallack*

The bravest and cruelest putt of the week slipped agonizingly by the right of the hole, halving the match.

"I saw two spike marks on my line. It looked like a left-left putt. I talked to my caddie [Peter Coleman]. He said, 'Hit it left-center and firm to avoid the spike marks.' That's what I tried to do. It did not go in."

—BERNHARD LANGER

"The right kind of pressure finds diamonds. But it's hard to putt when you see three golf balls and don't know which one to putt at."
—*Johnny Miller,* NBC TV

Having performed a minor miracle in sinking crucial putts on fifteen, sixteen, and seventeen, just to keep the match and Cup alive, Langer could not fourpeat on eighteen. The miss brought the Ryder Cup back to America; the miss brought two golfing nations closer together; the miss brought Bernhard Langer months of nightmares.

"Imagine the shock and now the exultation of what happened. It was a 180-degree turnaround over the simple matter of a six-foot putt."

—HALE IRWIN

"I've been in golf all my life, and my father before me, but I think this will stay in my memory: The sadness of Langer's putt, on the final hole, having played so well. The mistakes of Calcavecchia, the braveness of the players. . . . It really has been an incredible event."
—PETER ALLISS, BBC TV

"No one in the world can make that putt. It is too much pressure for anyone. Not even Jack Nicklaus in his prime will make that putt. . . . Not even me!"
—*Seve Ballesteros*

Day three result: USA 6½, EUR 5½
Overall match score: USA 14½, EUR 13½

The 14½–13½ final score was exactly the same as the score the last time the United States won the Cup, in 1983.

Recap

To celebrate the first U.S. win since 1983, the victorious captain and some of his players (Pavin, O'Meara, and Irwin) took a celebratory dip in the ocean.

"Our celebration was like no party I had ever attended. Golf doesn't have the tradition, like NFL football, of dousing the coach at the end of a super performance. Instead, we simply tossed our captain into the Atlantic Ocean, as part of our celebration." —PAUL AZINGER, *Zinger* (1995)

Stockton's decision to "pull" Pate from facing Ballesteros in the singles may have been the deciding factor in winning back the Cup for the United States, since this envelope half-point (with David Gilford) was crucial in the final outcome. Had Pate played and lost, the extra half-point would have been the difference between winning and losing the Cup.

Not only had this match been close, but the total points from the last three Ryder Cups gave Europe a single-point advantage after eighty-four matches.

Against the backdrop of a nation still celebrating the Gulf War victory some months after the event, many partisan Americans seemed to forget that Europe had been its main ally in sharing the bloodshed. Still, war was war and golf was golf, though the edges were blurred on numerous occasions on an oceanside battleground like no other. "The War on the Shore" would prove to be the defining match in the entire litany of the Ryder Cup. It was not what Samuel Ryder had intended, but he sold penny seeds, not million-dollar dreams, or billion-dollar defense contracts

"I have never felt excitement like this in my whole life. The country's pride is back! We went over and thumped the Iraqis, and now we have won this."
—*Paul Azinger*

Another part of the match that would have been entirely alien to a post-Victorian benefactor like Samuel Ryder was the concentrated pressure that seemed to hang on every stroke under the watching eyes of the TV millions. Never again would the Ryder

Cup be seen as just another gentlemanly game of golf, no matter how both sides would try to play down such stressful situations in future years.

"In today's world, all of the festive flag-waving, song-singing, and champagne-spewing rest on the ability or inability of a single golfer, American or European, chosen by fate, dog-tired and emotionally drained from previous battles, to make or miss a putt that looks on a TV screen or in person to be almost inside the leather for any member of your Sunday foursome at Fragrant Swamp Country Club."

—DAN JENKINS, *Golf Digest* (1991)

In a positive happy-ever-after to the match, repeating a fate that befell Densmore Shute after he missed the putt that lost the Cup in 1933, Bernhard Langer was able to bounce right back with a big tournament win. A week later, Langer holed a twelve-foot putt on the final green of the German Masters to force a play-off, which he went on to win. Still, whatever Langer achieved after that fateful Sunday in September in South Carolina, nothing would ever wipe away the misery of the moment.

On how long it would take for him to get over his final missed putt: *"It's going to stick with me for a lifetime, that putt. . . . I will never forget it, that's for sure."* —BERNHARD LANGER

"To some there was a quality so raw and cruel in the circumstances of the U.S. victory as to leave a residue of hollow sadness. When a match—ballyhooed for two years and viewed all over the world—comes down to the last putt in the last match on the last hole of the last day—you'd think the result would be sublime stuff. Yet so many fine citizens of golf were reduced to caricatures of themselves for the sake of that tableau that you wonder if the prize was worth the pain."

—THOMAS BOSWELL, *Washington Post*

Match Results (Winning side marked in *italics*.)

Friday, September 13—Morning Foursomes

	USA	EUR	Score
1.	Paul Azinger Chip Beck	*Seve Ballesteros* *Jose Maria Olazabal*	2 and 1
2.	*Raymond Floyd* *Fred Couples*	Bernhard Langer Mark James	2 and 1
3.	*Lanny Wadkins* *Hale Irwin*	David Gilford Colin Montgomerie	4 and 2
4.	*Payne Stewart* *Mark Calcavecchia*	Nick Faldo Ian Woosnam	1-up

Friday, September 13—Afternoon Fourball

	USA	EUR	Score
5.	Lanny Wadkins Mark O'Meara	Sam Torrance David Feherty	halved
6.	Chip Beck Paul Azinger	*Seve Ballesteros* *Jose Maria Olazabal*	2 and 1
7.	Corey Pavin Mark Calcavecchia	*Mark James* *Steven Richardson*	5 and 4
8.	*Fred Couples* *Raymond Floyd*	Nick Faldo Ian Woosnam	5 and 3

Day one result: USA 4½, EUR 3½

Saturday, September 14—Morning Foursomes

	USA	EUR	Score
9.	*Lanny Wadkins* *Hale Irwin*	David Feherty Sam Torrance	4 and 2
10.	*Mark Calcavecchia* *Payne Stewart*	Mark James Steven Richardson	1-up
11.	*Paul Azinger* *Mark O'Meara*	Nick Faldo David Gilford	7 and 6
12.	Raymond Floyd Fred Couples	*Seve Ballesteros* *Jose Maria Olazabal*	3 and 2

Saturday, September 14—Afternoon Fourball

	USA	EUR	Score
13.	Paul Azinger Hale Irwin	*Ian Woosnam* *Paul Broadhurst*	2 and 1
14.	Steve Pate Corey Pavin	*Bernhard Langer* *Colin Montgomerie*	2 and 1
15.	Lanny Wadkins Wayne Levi	*Mark James* *Steven Richardson*	3 and 1
16.	Payne Stewart Fred Couples	Seve Ballesteros Jose Maria Olazabal	halved

Day two result: USA 3½, EUR 4½

Overall match score: USA 8, EUR 8

Sunday, September 15—Singles

	USA	EUR	Score
17.	Steve Pate	David Gilford	halved*
18.	Raymond Floyd	*Nick Faldo*	2-up
19.	Payne Stewart	*David Feherty*	2 and 1
20.	Mark Calcavecchia	Colin Montgomerie	halved
21.	*Paul Azinger*	Jose Maria Olazabal	2-up
22.	*Corey Pavin*	Steven Richardson	2 and 1
23.	Wayne Levi	*Seve Ballesteros*	3 and 2
24.	*Chip Beck*	Ian Woosnam	3 and 1
25.	Mark O'Meara	*Paul Broadhurst*	3 and 1
26.	*Fred Couples*	Sam Torrance	3 and 2
27.	*Lanny Wadkins*	Mark James	3 and 2
28.	Hale Irwin	Bernhard Langer	halved

Day three result: USA 6½, EUR 5½

Overall match score: USA 14½, EUR 13½

---

* Match not played by agreement because Steve Pate was injured.

1993

The Belfry
Sutton Coldfield
England
September 24–26

United States 15	**Europe 13**
Paul Azinger	Peter Baker (England)
Chip Beck	Severiano Ballesteros (Spain)
John Cook	Nick Faldo (England)
Fred Couples	Joakim Haeggman (Sweden)
Raymond Floyd	Mark James (England)
Jim Gallagher, Jr.	Barry Lane (England)
Lee Janzen	Bernhard Langer (Germany)
Tom Kite	Colin Montgomerie (Scotland)
Davis Love III	Jose Maria Olazabal (Spain)
Corey Pavin	Costantino Rocca (Italy)
Payne Stewart	Sam Torrance (Scotland)
Lanny Wadkins	Ian Woosnam (Wales)
Captain	**Captain**
Tom Watson	Bernard Gallacher (Scotland)

Elementary, My Dear Watson

"I have to reduce this war-by-the-shore mentality we created in the last couple of Ryder Cups. . . . This isn't war. This is golf. We're going to go over there and try like hell to kick their butts. And they're going to try like hell to kick ours. That's as it should be. But when it's over, we should be able to all go off together, lift a glass, and toast one another. That's what the Ryder Cup is about." —Tom Watson

"If Watson wants to play the gentleman sportsman, that's fine for making a nice little speech at the opening ceremony. But let's not take all the bellicosity out of the Ryder Cup. When the competition begins, it's time to take off the blue blazer and put on the flak jacket. Military history is filled with men who can do the job. If Watson can't do it, let's find someone who will." —Peter Andrews

After the martial memories that still lingered like the smell of napalm in the morning, the Ryder Cup needed and, in Tom Watson, found the right impetus to redress the open hostilities from Kiawah Island. Not only was Watson the least bellicose of all

American captains, but he also was revered in the British Isles (having won six of its Opens) as much as he revered the country and its golf courses and its people. Tom Watson was not just the United States captain; for the week, he supplanted the U.S. ambassador with his diplomacy and brought a new level of decency and—that endangered species of golfing virtue—etiquette back to the Ryder Cup.

"I definitely wanted to be captain over there. Winning at home just wasn't quite the same challenge. I love golf in Britain. I love the fans, and I love their knowledge of the game."
—*Tom Watson*

Watson was not a kid-glove captain, making tough decisions when required. With two wild card picks, the U.S. captain went for the unmatchable experience and unquenchable team spirit of Floyd and Wadkins over the flamboyant and flammable talent of John Daly. Despite his wildly erratic performances, Daly had forced himself into the Ryder Cup reckoning, but his hit-or-miss approach to the game did not fit with Watson's carefully thought-out plans.

"I'll only play in the Ryder Cup if my teammates approve."
—*John Daly, just before checking into a rehab clinic*

Watson knew he needed to rely on his veterans, because he had four players new to the Ryder Cup in Cook, Janzen, Gallagher, and Love. All four had proved themselves on the U.S. tour, but Watson realized that the step up onto the international stage is one that is even greater than playing in your first major.

"There is no question that the pressure created by the Ryder Cup is greater than playing in the British Open. You are testing the human bottle, the human spirit, the human capacity to the utmost."

—TOM WATSON

Following the near miss in 1991, Bernard Gallacher was kept on as the European captain, and was also faced with some tough decisions over selection. He gave wild-card berths to Ballesteros and Olazabal, even though neither Spaniard won an event during the year, and he gave the final spot to a player who was almost unknown in his own country. Swedish rookie Joakim Haeggman had finished tenth in the European PGA Order of Merit and was the next in line after the nine automatic qualifiers.

Haeggman was joined by three other Euro-rookies—Baker, Lane, and Rocca—as the home side took on the feel of a worn-out pair of carpet slippers, with half the side making at least their sixth appearance.

Though Tom Watson wanted to remove the nasty taste left in the mouth after Kiawah Island, he inadvertently sank his teeth into a tabloid-size incident during the $300 gala banquet. It had been customary for the players to sign each other's menus, which normally led to the paying guests' also wanting their pound of flesh from the assembled superstars.

Wanting to avoid having his players sidetracked before their big match, Watson refused Sam Torrance's request to sign his menu. Torrance, who was "too angry to talk about it," took this as a personal rebuff, and the British tabloids championed his cause the next day. Watson quickly apologized, pointing out that he merely wanted to sign menus at a more convenient time and place, which Torrance eventually accepted.

"I don't want to talk about it. It's simply more fuel for us, and tomorrow I'll show them exactly how I feel." —Sam Torrance

Asked about the previous night's difficulties: *"As far as the European team is concerned, it was a small incident that shouldn't have been blown up. Sam was a bit embarrassed, but I know Tom Watson's signature, so he is happy."* —Bernard Gallacher

The menu signing was not the only official occasion that required Watson's diplomatic touch to smooth over a few cracks. As had become traditional, before the Ryder Cup the U.S. team was invited to the White House to meet the president. This time Watson faced out-and-out dissension from among his own ranks, as politics superseded golf and national pride. Watson was quick to point out that his team of superstars should treat an invite to the Oval Office the same way a twenty-eight-handicapper from Boise, Idaho, would treat an invite to play at Augusta National.

On the prematch audience with Bill Clinton at the White House: "Where I grew up you were better off telling people you were a garbageman than a Democrat."
—*Lee Janzen*

"It doesn't matter who the president is; if you're invited to the White House, you go. The president is the country's First Golfer. We'll be there. . . . Mr. Clinton told me my job was to bring the Cup back. They were the last words he said to me." —Tom Watson

"I don't want to shake hands with no draft dodger."
—*Paul Azinger*

Course Details

This was the third time in a row that the Brabazon Course at The Belfry had hosted the European leg of the Ryder Cup, and with good reason. The home side had an unbeaten record in the previous two encounters with a win and a tie, totaling 30½–25½ points in doing so.

Hole	Distance	Par	Hole	Distance	Par
1	418	4	10	275	4
2	349	4	11	420	4
3	465	4	12	235	3
4	579	5	13	394	4
5	399	4	14	194	3
6	396	4	15	550	5
7	183	3	16	410	4
8	460	4	17	575	5
9	400	4	18	474	4
		36			**36 = Par 72 (7,176 yards)**

Course designers: Peter Alliss and Dave Thomas

On the lack of rough: "[It's] Seve rough. They've got it set up so he can play."
—*Paul Azinger, as the feud continued*

On the par-4, 275-yard tenth hole: *"Beautiful as it may be, its driveability is the key to the hole's distinction as the greatest, most exciting match-play hole in golf."* —GEOFF RUSSELL, *Golf World*

"Lay up and you're looking at a safe five." —MARK JAMES

On his first look at the hole: *"I think it would be a tough call to lay up."* —DAVIS LOVE III

Day One: Morning Foursomes

The start was delayed, as seems normal in Britain, by early-morning fog. After a two-and-a-half-hour delay, the sun broke through the clouds to leave a warm, mostly calm day.

"The foursome format adds psychological burdens because you know your partner has to pay for your mistakes. You have to play to your partner's strengths and away from his weaknesses, rather than just play to your own strengths and weaknesses." —TOM WATSON, *Strategic Golf* (1993)

Corey Pavin and Lanny Wadkins (USA) v. Sam Torrance and Mark James (EUR)

On being the first to tee off after the fog delay: *"I couldn't get the tee in the ground; my hand was shaking a little. The whole week rides up to that shot, and we had a lot of extra time to think about it. I made a real nice slow swing and hit a solid one down the fairway."*

—COREY PAVIN

Following Pavin's "solid one" down the middle, Torrance deposited his opening drive in a fairway bunker on the left, and the U.S. pair was one up. An American bogey on the third leveled the score, and Torrance holed a four-footer on the 399-yard fifth for the lead.

Wadkins rammed in an eighteen-foot birdie putt on six, and almost holed out from a bunker on the next green. The Europeans recovered to halve the par-3 eighth after Torrance lost control of his tee shot, but the American pair took control of the match.

"The only thing that scares me about the Americans now is their dress sense."
—*Mark James*

"Sam and Mark didn't play very well, so they gave us a break. They made it a little easier on us. I made some birdies early and kinda turned Corey loose on 'em, and he struck hard and often." —LANNY WADKINS

James missed a birdie putt to match the Americans on the 400-yard ninth, and Wadkins's ten-foot downhill birdie putt from the right-hand fringe of the tenth green put the U.S. pair three up. Two American pars followed and produced two more wins, as the British pair dropped five behind.

An American bogey that cost the par-3 fourteenth was soon forgotten when Pavin holed a two-footer, on fifteen, for the half and the match, 4 and 3.

Torrance ended the four-over round in some discomfort with a recurrence of a painful toe infection, which would force him to sit out the rest of the contest.

Paul Azinger and Payne Stewart (USA) v. Ian Woosnam and Bernhard Langer (EUR)

The 183-yard seventh was remarkable for two reasons. First, it was halved in magnificent birdie twos with all four players playing their parts, and second, it was the first hole halved in the match.

Azinger and Stewart made as bad a start as any U.S. pair had ever made—bogeying the first three holes with straight fives. Woosnam and Langer started par-birdie-par to accept a three-hole lead without any real effort.

This was the first time Woosnam and Langer had played together in the Ryder Cup, although they had been on the team since 1983.

The Americans' luck changed so violently, they must have been tempted to leave the course in search of lottery tickets. From 111 yards short of the par-4 sixth, Stewart's pitch to the green bounced right by the side of the hole and skipped back in for an eagle three.

The American celebration was curtailed when Woosnam canned a fifteen-footer on the next hole to respot the three-hole cushion, which stretched to four when the U.S. pair relived the bogey-five nightmare on the 396-yard sixth.

The Europeans continued to feed off the Americans' mistakes. Four became five up with the fourth U.S. bogey in the first eight holes, as Stewart badly hooked his tee shot and found the lake alongside the fairway. Five down on the front nine, the U.S. couple tried to get things going on the "rip it or dip it" tenth, where Stewart, forced into taking on the green, again badly pulled his tee shot—off a bank and into the stream.

Three more steady European pars did in the struggling Americans, who conceded the hole and the match on thirteen to crash 7 and 5.

The 7 and 5 win equaled the best ever by a European foursomes pair: Canizares and Pinero in 1985.

On the Americans' carding seven bogeys in their fifteen-hole thrashing: *"I didn't play very well. After the match, I told Ian I felt like Santa Claus out there."* —PAYNE STEWART

Tom Kite and Davis Love III (USA) v. Seve Ballesteros and Jose Maria Olazabal (EUR)

On the Spaniards' nine wins and two halves against one loss in a dozen matches together: *"Seve and Jose Maria are the best team that has ever played in the Ryder Cup in foursomes match play. That is something we hope to change as far as their wonderful percentage is concerned. If we could win this match . . ."* —TOM WATSON

Handing Love a pack of cough drops on the first tee: "First time Seve coughs, take this out and give it to him."
—*Anonymous U.S. player's wife*

Noted for bending the rules of golf and developing a "Ryder Cup cough," Ballesteros did not wait long to unleash his tricks on the suspecting Americans.

On the very first green, after Kite had marked and lined up his two-foot par putt, Seve loudly conceded the putt, claiming he had already said the putt was good. Kite diplomatically claimed the crowd noise must have drowned it out.

On the very next hole, Love answered Ballesteros's mind games with a game of his own: leave your ball as near to the flag as possible. After Love's approach to five feet of the second hole, Kite's birdie putt put the United States one up, which became two after a second U.S. birdie on the par-5 fourth.

With Kite missing a shorter par putt than his opponent's on the 399-yard fifth, the U.S. lead was cut to one. An American birdie on six was canceled by a Spanish birdie on seven, where Kite missed a chance to halve with a relatively short par putt. On the 400-yard ninth, Kite made amends for his putting lapses with a clutch five-footer for par and the half, after Ballesteros spectacularly holed his own par putt from twenty-five feet away.

At the tenth—a hole where the Spaniards had owned the bragging rights (and probably the drilling rights) in the past—the U.S. players were keen to stamp their authority. This time was different, as the Europeans made a major tactical error.

"When I didn't make the team last time, I made up my mind to make it this time and come over here and play well."
—*Tom Kite*

With Ballesteros's play off the tee the past season being at best erratic, it seemed a mistake to have him take the drive on this pivotal hole. In the past, Olazabal had played this hole as well as, if not better than, his partner, but Seve took a nine-iron this time and laid up short of the water. The wily ol' Kite quickly saw and seized his chance. Pulling a three-wood out of his bag, he assuredly dispatched his ball straight at the flag. Five feet from the hole—advantage United States.

"In that instance, Seve issued one type of challenge, and we responded with another. The guy who hits first drives the wagon. It totally determines what your opponent does." —Tom Kite

"The swashbuckling Ballesteros laid up at the go-for-broke semi-par-4 tenth in Friday morning's foursome, only to watch Tom Kite, who rarely buckles his swash, knock a gutsy three-wood onto the green."

—Gary Van Sickle, *Golf World*

Not used to playing catch-up at their favorite watering hole, Olazabal showed why he is one of the best short-iron exponents in the world, leaving his pitch nine feet from the pin. Seve might have lost all his confidence off the tee, but his touch on the green was still as good as ever—he holed his birdie putt. Faced with a five-foot eagle putt for the hole, Love calmly sank it for a valuable two-hole lead and an invaluable psychological advantage.

On the 394-yard thirteenth, Olazabal missed a ten-foot birdie putt after Kite had stopped his 115-yard wedge approach a yard from the flag for Love's birdie putt. The Americans had played themselves into a winning position, three up with five to play—but could they finish off the unbeatable Spaniards?

Fourteen and fifteen came and went with pars, Kite and Love holding on to their lead. Ballesteros holed a breathtaking thirty-footer to pull back to two down with two to play, leaving more than ample time for the Houdinis of golf to escape with a half.

Fittingly, it was the rookie who ended the Spaniards' unbeaten run: Love sank the critical two-foot putt for a half on seventeen to win the match, 2 and 1.

Having been unbeaten in six previous foursomes matches, the Spaniards had their impressive winning percentage dented, although they did not card a bogey: *"We played well, but I must tell the truth . . . they played fantastic."* —SEVE BALLESTEROS

Not only was the Spanish pair beaten, but they also never held a lead in the whole match, although the Americans needed to finish five under for the win.

Raymond Floyd and Fred Couples (USA) v. Nick Faldo and Colin Montgomerie (EUR)

At fifty-one years and twenty-one days of age, Raymond Floyd, in his eighth and final Ryder Cup, became the oldest-ever player on either side.

As was usual, the Americans opened the scoring on the first hole. Unusually, it was with a bogey to give the lead to Europe, but the Americans soon leveled with a birdie on the third hole.

Montgomerie left his pitch to the fourth hole five feet right of the pin, leaving Faldo to sink their first birdie putt for the lead again.

Eighteen feet away, Monty chipped in from the third cut of rough of the eighth green, putting Europe two up. After his side had bogeyed the ninth to fall three down at the turn, Floyd had no choice but to attack the tenth green. The fifty-one-year-old struck a mighty three-wood to five feet, and Couples swept up the crumbs on the green for a morale-boosting eagle.

With the win theirs for the taking, the European players picked a fine time to card their first bogey of the round—after thirteen holes. Having let Couples and Floyd back into the match, the British pair proceeded to close them out in the next two holes.

On fourteen, Montgomerie's tee shot landed twelve feet front left of the pin. Faldo drained the birdie putt to go three up again, and another unanswered birdie on fifteen gave Europe a 4 and 3 win. The Americans could only combine for level par figures in the match, and the British pair came in three under for the win.

Morning foursomes result: USA 2, EUR 2

On this being the first time since 1987 that Europe had not been behind after the opening session: *"This is what the Ryder Cup is all about. The competition was so intense that you could have written a novel about it." —Tom Watson*

Day One: Afternoon Fourball

Lee Janzen and Jim Gallagher (USA) v. Peter Baker and Ian Woosnam (EUR)

Belying his nervous start, Peter Baker sank a thirty-footer on the second green, but it was matched by an American birdie. Not to be dissuaded so easily, Baker repeated the birdie dosage on the 465-yard third to take a lead.

The Americans hit back at once, making birdie on the par-5 fourth to level the score, which remained that way to the turn, as the next five holes were halved in par.

On his rookie start: "I was so nervous, I felt like changing my underpants."
—*Peter Baker*

In a concerted effort to keep the Europeans from dominating the pivotal tenth hole, Tom Watson ordered his men to take the green on from the tee. Obeying his captain, Gallagher courageously found the left of the putting surface with his all-or-nothing driver. Two easy putts accounted for the eighteen feet of green, and he walked off with a birdie and a one-hole lead.

Not to be outdone by a fellow Ryder Cup rookie, Baker fired another accurate approach into eleven, landing ten feet in front of the flag and rolling on to leave a four-foot birdie putt to square the match.

Baker's tee shot missed the green on the par-3 fourteenth, but he trundled home his birdie putt from sixteen feet for birdie and a lead his side would not relinquish. The fifteenth was halved in birdie fours, while sixteen and seventeen were shared in comparatively boring pars.

"It was a great, great day. Woosie tells me the clubs, and I just fire away."
—*Peter Baker*

This match, in which no pair was ever more than a solitary hole ahead, came down to the last hole with the Europeans narrowly ahead. One down with one to play, Gallagher ripped a rasping drive up the fairway and dispatched an equally impressive six-iron over the lake to within ten feet of the hole. Not wanting the U.S. rookie to steal his thunder, Baker rose to the challenge. His approach from the right-hand edge of the rough finished on the middle tier, twenty-two feet to the left of the pin. Faced with an oil slick of a downhill putt across a slippery slope, the English-

Baker made five birdies to Woosnam's one: "I just had a stroll this afternoon. Peter played all the golf."
—*Ian Woosnam*

man (later dubbed the "Fabulous Baker Boy" by the media) calmly rolled home his fifth birdie of the round to safeguard the one-hole victory.

Corey Pavin and Lanny Wadkins (USA) v. Bernhard Langer and Barry Lane (EUR)

As expected, the fiery fourball of Pavin and Wadkins started in a blaze of aggression. With birdies at the second, fourth, and fifth, the U.S. pair led by three. The Europeans got a hole back on six with their first birdie, and the seventh was shared in birdie twos. With their third birdie in as many holes, the two BLs—Langer and Lane—cut the lead to one after eight holes.

In a clinical finish to the match, the Americans carded five threes in the final six holes. Pavin was the main instigator of this triple-play climax, coaxing a six-foot birdie putt down a delicate incline on the eleventh. The par-3 twelfth was halved, and Pavin claimed another birdie three on thirteen to go three up.

"Pavin, anxious to remind Europeans of the excellence of his golf rather than the fact that at Kiawah Island two years ago he had worn that silly cap, did so with interest."
—*David Millar,* London Telegraph

Pavin continued his fine work. His ten-foot birdie putt on fifteen was aimed straight at the hole for a half, and was closely followed by his fourth birdie in six holes, bringing an end to the match, 4 and 2.

With this win, Lanny Wadkins tied Billy Casper with twenty Ryder Cup victories. Only Arnold Palmer had more.

Paul Azinger and Fred Couples (USA) v. Nick Faldo and Colin Montgomerie (EUR)

The best match of the first two days took two days to finish, as the action spilled over into Saturday morning. The first two holes were halved in fighting birdies as neither team gave an inch to the other, which is how the match would progress. Only the 465-yard third hole failed to give up a birdie in the first eight played.

The Americans gained their third birdie in four holes at the par-5 fourth, for a lead that was offset by a British birdie at five. But the U.S. pair was back up after another birdie on six. Faldo produced the shot of the front nine, chipping in from nine feet for birdie to win the seventh, before a couple of birdies canceled each other out on the 460-yard eighth.

All square at the turn, both pairs were out in 31, but it had become obvious that the real match was between Azinger and Faldo.

With Azinger laying up in front of the lake at ten, the other three took on the lake. Couples found the water, while Faldo found some trees to the right and Montgomerie landed in the multicolored flower bed in front of the green. Standing among the floras with a diabolical lie, the Scot made a recovery that was hardly worthy of the name, his ball flying over the gallery beyond the green and out of sight. Monty could only stand and laugh at his predicament, having uprooted a small nursery of plants. Azinger pitched nine feet past the flag for yet another birdie to take the lead for the third time.

"Nick Faldo carried Colin Montgomerie and the whole European team on his back (hard to say which one's heavier)."
—*Gary Van Sickle,* Golf World

For the only time in the match, two holes in a row were halved in par, before Azinger and Faldo continued their personal duel. The ever-efficient Englishman leveled the score on thirteen, pitching up to leave himself a left-to-right birdie putt from ten feet.

Receiving as much help from his partner as Faldo was getting from his, Azinger took matters into his own hands, reeling off three birdies over the next three holes. The American nailed his tee shot at fourteen just five feet from the flag. Faldo failed to find the green in one but drained his second with a chip of almost twenty feet. The Englishman's second pitch-in of the skirmish halved the hole in birdie twos.

The 550-yard fifteenth was halved in birdie fours, as Azinger's best shots could not beat two men. On sixteen, Azinger finally broke down the British resistance, but it required him to almost hole his eight-iron from the right-hand rough. His chip stopped twelve inches from the cup for a conceded birdie and the hole, regaining the lead for the Americans.

With darkness dropping like a black blanket all around, Bernard Gallacher wanted his troops to call it a day to regroup and consider their battle plan. Faldo thought otherwise, but he might have wanted to reconsider after everyone had played his tee shots. Couples suddenly awoke and exploded off the seventeenth tee. Faldo watched his opponent rip his ball down the fairway, only to pop his own drive up into the air. Faldo's shot barely traveled 200 of the 575 yards to the par-5 green.

Couples crashed a long iron to the green, unluckily finding a bunker, while Faldo and Azinger took two more shots to get on.

From 160 yards out, Faldo's seven-iron zeroed in on the hole, finishing four feet away to put the pressure on Couples.

On his "night-sight" approach to seventeen: *"It was getting dark, but I knew where the pin was, I knew the yardage, and I hit the shot as quickly as I could."* —NICK FALDO

From the bunker, the American could not get down in two and had to settle for a par, missing the birdie from twelve feet, while Azinger also just missed making his fourth birdie in a row. Faldo's four-footer flattened the match score, and he promptly called it a night. Darkness had fallen with Europe in overall ascendancy, 4–3, with this close encounter of the bird kind to conclude in the morning.

The match resumed at eight o'clock on a freezing cold and windy morning, with the score level. The Americans had never been behind, nor had they been more than one hole up.

Montgomerie opened with a long, straight drive through the fairway, leaving a long shot to clear the water from the rough. Faldo just cut the corner and made the fairway in front of the lake. Trying to repeat his monster drive off seventeen, Couples hauled his tee shot into the water and took no further constructive part in the contest. Azinger hit the best tee shot, his ball bounding twenty yards beyond Faldo's.

"It was probably the best drive I've ever hit, under the circumstances."
—PAUL AZINGER

Struck with a five-iron from a ridiculous lie, Montgomerie's second clipped off the top of a mound to join Couples in the water and on the sidelines. With his six-iron approach, Faldo came up fifty feet short of the flag on the front tier, while Azinger, from 160 yards out, hit his second glorious eight-iron approach in a span of three holes—eighteen feet right of the hole on the middle tier. Faldo left his long putt ten feet short on the slow, wet green—as it just crested the rise. For the match, Azinger's putt was dead on line until the last few feet, when it drifted to the right. With his near miss conceded for a par, Azinger left the stage for Faldo.

The Englishman, with his systematic "seeing-eye" help from caddie Fanny Sunesson, had no problem sinking his vital putt in the right-hand lip of the hole to halve one of the great duels in fourball history.

"We are not surprised. We were expecting them to chip in; we expected them to hole putts on top of us. Nothing surprises us. We stood out there and said, 'You realize he's going to make this to tie.' " —*Paul Azinger*

Finishing nine under par, both pairs notched nine birdies each: Faldo seven, Azinger six, Couples three, and Montgomerie two.

Tom Kite and Davis Love III (USA) *v. Seve Ballesteros and Jose Maria Olazabal* (EUR)

Not only were the Spaniards looking for revenge on the pair that had inflicted a rare foursomes defeat, but they were looking to do so in the most explicit way possible. Nine birdies and an eagle in fifteen holes for a net eleven under par proved most explicit.

Realizing the Spanish pair would try to dominate the match from the opening drive, Kite and Love were able to prevent them from taking the first hole. But the Americans' only lead of the match disappeared with the Spaniards' first birdie at the 349-yard second.

The third and fourth holes were halved, the latter in birdie fours, while a Spanish birdie on five gave the Europeans their first lead of the match. Despite their fourth birdie in five holes, Ballesteros and Olazabal could not extend the lead, as Kite and Love matched them. The U.S. pair went one better on the par-3 seventh with a birdie two to level the match, but they could manage only par between them on eight, losing that and the lead to another opposing birdie.

The Americans went out in a four-under-par 32 but were a hole down as the Spanish Armada set full sail for home after a 31 on the front nine.

After faltering when he laid up at the tenth in the morning, Seve bounced his three-wood tee shot off a bank on the right of the green, where it rolled down twenty feet from the flag. Olazabal followed his partner in with an equally impressive drive to twenty-five feet, while both Americans cracked under the pressure. Kite's ball just cleared the narrow bridge, while Love's one-iron went a few feet farther—but both balls got wet. With two putts each for the hole, the Spanish pair needed just one to make eagle and double the lead.

With both cannons blazing on the Spanish galleons, the eleventh was halved in birdie threes and the Americans were in danger of being swamped. Twelve was also halved—in pars—but when Olazabal chipped in on thirteen for another birdie, the lead was up to three and the Americans were close to hanging out the white flag. On the par-3 fourteenth, Ballesteros sent his tee shot rolling up the green to five feet of the flag, and walked off with another birdie and a four-hole advantage.

The Americans birdied the 550-yard fifteenth but could not better Olazabal's approach to three feet for the Spaniards' eleventh birdie of the round and a revenge win, 4 and 3.

Afternoon fourball result: USA 1½, EUR 2½
Day one result: USA 3½, EUR 4½

On the role of nonplaying captain: *"There's a feeling of helplessness. It's a bit like kicking the kids off to school. It's been one of the longest days of my life. Pressure does that; it makes things go so slowly."*

—TOM WATSON

Day Two: Morning Foursomes

Lanny Wadkins and Corey Pavin (USA) v. Nick Faldo and Colin Montgomerie (EUR)

Neither pair got off to the start it had wanted, halving the first six holes—in par with the exception of the par-4 third, which generated two bogeys after both balls encountered sand. The Americans recovered to get up and down for their bogey, and Montgomerie was unable to convert Faldo's fine sand recovery into a par to win the hole. On the fifth green, it was Faldo's turn to miss a birdie putt from ten feet.

Without a birdie recorded in six halved holes, this match came alive on and around the 183-yard seventh green. Faldo's tee shot finished twenty yards from the target, and Pavin's reply was much closer but off the putting surface. Montgomerie struck his lengthy putt with such calculated confidence that it was hardly a surprise when the ball found the bottom of the cup. Not to be outdone, Wadkins took out his wedge, addressed the ball in the light rough, and struck a short, stabby shot that leapt obediently onto the green and just as dutifully found the hole. A stunning half was exchanged with the first two birdies of the round.

"When Lanny is on his game, it's like having a cobra in the basket with the lid off."
—*Tom Watson*

On the next hole, Pavin looked long and hard at his four-footer, but he was unable to get his ball to drop, losing the hole to go down by one for the first lead of the match.

Declining to take on the water at ten, Montgomerie and Wadkins played safe tee shots up the fairway. Faldo's approach to the right of the hole spun back to the edge of the flowers, and Pavin tore the heart out of the green with a pitch to a few inches. Montgomerie could not repeat his monster putt heroics, and the Americans' birdie three leveled the match, but they bogeyed eleven after Wadkins found sand, handing the lead right back.

Worse was to follow for the U.S. pair, as Wadkins contrived to put his tee shot in the stream running along the front of the twelfth green. With a double-bogey five to lose the hole to a par, the Americans fared little better on the next par-3 hole. Montgomerie's tee shot came within twenty feet of the cup at fourteen, but it was just off the green. Faldo chipped in for birdie at such an alarming rattle that had his ball missed the hole, it would have disappeared off the other side of the green. This crafty combination of potluck and dogged accuracy put Europe three up with four to play.

The Americans fell short on fifteen, where Wadkins's thirty-five-foot birdie putt up the slope rattled into the back of the cup and stayed out, for a half in par fives. Dormie three up, Monty had another mega-putt from over forty feet across the sweeping undulations of the sixteenth green for birdie. This was much more complicated than the bomb he dropped on the seventh, and the Scot did brilliantly to lag the ball up close. Wadkins was left with a twenty-five-footer to win the hole. He missed his birdie attempt and the match was lost, 3 and 2.

Fred Couples and Paul Azinger (USA) v. Bernhard Langer and Ian Woosnam (EUR)

Although their birdie four on the fourth hole gave the Europeans a halfway lead, Woosnam and Langer missed four good chances to add to it on the way out.

Couples and Azinger finally got something going on the tenth after the latter laid up rather than go for the green. Couples produced a stunning lob pitch to within a couple of yards, while Woosnam could not match the American's pinpoint accuracy, finishing twenty feet from the hole. Langer came up well short with his putt before Azinger stroked his birdie putt home to square the match.

Tom Watson described the Europeans as a couple of "panthers," while he dubbed his own players a pair of "tigers."

The Europeans squandered another chance to regain their lead on the twelfth, where their opponents found water, took a drop, and could only hole out for a bogey. Langer, with a makable par putt, blew his chance, and Woosnam blew on another cigarette. On the next hole, the U.S. pair fell behind again. Langer stroked his approach from the right-hand rough to within five feet of the thirteenth hole for a Woosnam birdie putt and the lead, as Azinger's four-foot par putt lipped out to the left.

Somehow Couples and Azinger halved the fifteenth without ever touching the fairway; the former hooked his drive way into the rough, and the latter's recovery flew across the fairway into the rough on the right. Couples plowed his ball out of the bad stuff and was somewhat fortunate to find the green. Two American putts were enough to share the hole with the Europeans, who had played the 548 yards in strict regulation via the fairway.

At sixteen, the Americans' luck ran out, although Couples's approach landed two feet closer than Woosnam's. Langer nonchalantly holed the longer putt, and Azinger had another attempt cruelly lip out to give the home pair a two-hole advantage with two to play.

With defeat staring them in the face, Azinger tried to cut off the dogleg, but it bit him back. On the green, Azinger was left with a twenty-eight-footer to save the match, but his too-strong putt lipped out again. The Europeans' day was done, and they had a 2 and 1 victory that could easily have been worse for the Americans.

Raymond Floyd and Payne Stewart (USA) v. Peter Baker and Barry Lane (EUR)

This was a battle of the six-time major winners from America against the two-time Ryder Cup rookies from Britain. In deference to Stewart's fashion-conscious sensibilities, Tom Watson allowed Stewart to wear his trademark knickerbockers.

The omens did not look good for Europe when Peter Baker blew a four-footer on the third to hand an early lead to the U.S. pair, who opened with six straight fours. Lane's ground-hugging wood to the heart of the fourth green gave Baker a chance to redeem himself, but his eagle putt ended up only close enough for a conceded birdie. From almost twenty feet away, Stewart matched the concession for a half.

With his third miss in as many holes, Baker was so frustrated with his six-foot blunder that he asked Floyd to win the hole with a short putt that would have normally been conceded. Stewart was asked to do the same on the next hole to make a half.

From the left-hand rough, Floyd closed out a fine front nine for his side, firing his second onto the slope running through the green, where the ball rolled down to three feet for a three-hole lead.

Sensing that his rookies were being put to the sword by their more experienced opponents and by their own ineptitude on the green, Gallacher had a quiet calming word with them. This chat had a positive impact: Baker sank a twelve-foot putt on the tenth for a birdie three and the British pair's first (and only) win of the round.

The captain obviously forgot to mention the courtesy of conceding putts, because Floyd was again asked to hole out a very short gimme for the half on eleven. Baker found thirteen particularly unlucky as his putting problems reared their ugly head again, paper-clipping a four-footer to push the U.S. lead to three.

With halves in par at fourteen and fifteen, Floyd had a ten-footer for birdie on sixteen, but he ran it by the left of the hole, close enough for a concession and a very comfortable 3 and 2 win.

On the U.S. side's two-under round: "We were fairway and green, nothing spectacular, but we kept the pressure on. . . . Actually, it was easy for us."
—*Raymond Floyd*

Tom Kite and Davis Love III (USA) v. Seve Ballesteros and Jose Maria Olazabal (EUR)

These pairs played their third consecutive match against each other, having split the first two on Friday.

Third time around it was the Spaniards who drew first blood. Olazabal struck a mighty iron from a fairway bunker to a dozen feet of the first flag for the go-ahead birdie. On the second, Ballesteros converted Olazabal's perfect drive into a perfect approach, three feet from the pin, but Olazabal was unable to provide the perfect putt, the ball drifting off line for a half in fours.

Having found a bunker with his opening drive, Ballesteros hit an even worse second tee shot over the gallery on the left. Olazabal's recovery struck a branch and left Ballesteros in even more trouble. The older Spaniard, used to such impossible positions, produced an eight-iron shot of miraculous proportions to three feet of the hole. Meanwhile, the Americans must have realized this was not going to be their day when they left their birdie putt short and settled for a dispiriting half in par.

Kite's approach to the fourth came up well short of the pin, and the Spaniards gratefully added to their lead. The fifth hole was halved, but on the sixth Love found water with his seven-iron approach and Europe found itself three up. As if to repay Love's error on six, Olazabal selected a three-wood on eight, against his partner's vehemently expressed wishes, and promptly hit his ball into the lake.

The Ryder Cup is never complete unless Ballesteros can find some official ruling to argue about or some official to argue with, and this day was no different. After another typical Ballesteros altercation over playing rules (this time regarding the exact drop area), Kite settled the hole with an approach to twelve feet, cutting the deficit to two.

The U.S. pair also took the ninth when Ballesteros found more wood than grass off the tee and Olazabal could only lay up short of the lake. From just off the right-hand side of the fairway, Kite hit another tremendous approach to four feet of the hole, and the turn was reached with the Spaniards only one up.

"What the tenth hole is, more than anything else, is golf's version of that old carnival game where you swing the sledgehammer and try to ring the bell. Drive the green, you win a stuffed animal for your girl. Miss the green and find the water, hey—at least you impressed her."

—GEOFF RUSSELL, *Golf World*

The Americans' minirevival was quickly halted on the tenth. Trying to emulate his game-busting drive of the first morning, Kite again took a three-wood off the tee and failed to find the green or the water—finding sand to the right of the green. With his opponents in trouble, Olazabal responded with a tee shot through the trees that bounced off the bank onto the green, fifteen feet beyond the hole. With an unforgiving downhill green in front of him, Love could only transfer his ball from a sandy lie to a watery grave, and the hole was lost. And how the local crowd cheered as Love's ball ran across the green and dove off the edge into the stream.

The Americans struck back again on eleven to be one down, but Ballesteros decisively holed from all of thirty feet across the slope on the twelfth. The thirteenth went the Americans' way—

as they were determined not to let the Spaniards dominate the back nine—with Love faultlessly judging a curling eight-footer from just off the green.

The next two holes were halved despite some erratic play from the leading pair, but Olazabal settled matters on the sixteenth green with a four-foot birdie putt in reply to an American bogey. Seve's five-footer for par halved seventeen, giving the Spaniards their second win over Kite and Love in two days, although by a much-reduced score of 2 and 1.

With Olazabal missing the next Ryder Cup because of a foot injury and Seve the nonplaying captain in 1997, this was the swan song of the greatest partnership in Ryder Cup history. Notching eleven wins as a pair, the Spaniards easily eclipsed the next-best pairs—four pairs tied—who had five wins apiece.

Morning foursomes result: USA *1,* EUR *3*

Day Two: Afternoon Fourball

Bernard Gallacher was forced to go without two major stars. Ballesteros tried to hide his unhappiness with his snap hook by claiming he needed the rest, while Langer ruled himself out with a sore neck (possibly sustained while looking back at the matches stacking up behind him).

After requesting to be left out of the afternoon session: *"I'm feeling tired, and the cold did not help my back this morning. I was hitting some very bad tee shots. I will practice in readiness for the singles."*

—Seve Ballesteros

European players appeared for the afternoon wearing bright flamingo-pink sweaters, while the Americans donned rather somber but foreboding black and blue, possibly a signal of the bruising they were about to inflict.

John Cook and Chip Beck (USA) v. Nick Faldo and Colin Montgomerie (EUR)

Rather than split them up, Watson threw two fresh players at one of the top European pairs, who had dropped only half a point in three matches.

"Faldo and Montgomerie probably thought they drew an easy match. This afternoon was very important for us. Tom told Chip and me he needed our point. The way he said it, he *needed* it. That's all that was said."
—*John Cook*

Faldo made an eighteen-foot birdie at the first, but Cook, from just off the back of the green, answered in kind from four feet closer. The second and third were halved in par fours, as, not for the first time, Faldo and Cook locked horns: Cook had finished runner-up to Faldo in the 1992 British Open.

Faldo and Cook again swapped birdie putts for a half on the par-5 fourth, the American seemingly shadowing the Englishman's every move. From off the back of the fifth green, Faldo chipped in from ten feet for a birdie four, but he could not shrug off Cook's close attention, as the American sank an eight-footer for another half.

Finally, Faldo was able to make a telling putt on the sixth green. Following a rapierlike five-iron to fifteen inches, his hole-winning birdie brought the first lead of the match. Not content to be cast in Faldo's shadow, Cook emerged with a tormenting three-iron tee shot to four feet of the seventh, squaring the match.

Cook went one better on the 460-yard eighth. Faldo found a bad lie in a fairway bunker and was out of the hole, while Montgomerie's approach came up short of the green. The Scot knocked his chip to four feet, with the American pair sitting pretty for par. Cook holed out, but Monty missed his par putt, and the U.S. pair were up for the first time in the match.

With Beck deep in the woods on nine, Cook halved the hole on his own in par, despite finding a greenside bunker and Faldo having a shot at a fifteen-foot putt for birdie. Cook was the only player to go for the tenth green, but he found the water as the others laid up. Beck knocked his approach through the green and just missed his twenty-foot putt back for birdie, while the British pair missed birdie putts from fifteen and twelve feet to halve in fours.

After two poor British drives on the 420-yard eleventh, Faldo looked to have rescued the situation with another fine approach, but he blew his birdie putt for another half in four. The Englishman continued to have trouble getting crucial putts to drop—he had two more birdie putts shave the hole—while Beck kept the American lead intact, getting up and down, from around the green, on three straight holes.

Beck produced a stunning sand save on fifteen, leaving a four-foot birdie putt to match Faldo's eight-footer. Monty then pitched seven feet beyond the sixteenth flag, but he caught Faldo's fever and his birdie putt lipped out off the left of the hole. Cook stepped in to halve the hole with a steady par putt.

Answering a reporter's post-match question, "Is this the greatest pressure you have ever faced?": "Undoubtedly. And without the partner I had, I couldn't have handled it."
—*Colin Montgomerie*

One down with two to play, the British pair needed to make a move or kiss their unbeaten run goodbye. From the right-hand rough behind a bush, Faldo left his approach twelve feet past the pin. Like his partner before him, Faldo lipped his birdie putt off the left of the hole, as Cook proved equal to the task with a half in par.

With his confidence bubbling over, Cook hit a glorious drive up the eighteenth fairway. He followed this with an equally good four-iron approach to twelve feet, just perching on the brow of the upslope, threatening to roll back to the lower tier. Repeating his morning performance, Montgomerie more or less played himself out of the hole, but Faldo improved on his early-morning work by firing a five-iron between Cook's ball and the hole, running twelve feet past the pin. Unlike his play in the morning rounds, Faldo missed his putt, which rolled by the left of the hole. After a few seconds' thought, Faldo conceded Cook's putt, as Cook had two for the hole and a win by two holes.

Looking back after the contest to define the pivotal moment: *"I believe the heart of our victory was Cook and Beck winning their fourball yesterday afternoon. Last night was a night we will remember. It was one of revelry, fun, and laughter which stemmed from Chip and John's win."*
—Tom Watson

Corey Pavin and Jim Gallagher (USA) v. Mark James and Costantino Rocca (EUR)

Missing the valuable services of Ballesteros and Langer, the European captain was forced to use two "second-string" players, James and Rocca.

In a fourball match in the Ryder Cup, playing the first six holes in a joint one under par is not going to get the job done. If you were playing Corey Pavin at the peak of his form, you would count yourself lucky to be only four holes down after six. This is exactly how the American maestro greeted James and Rocca.

Fortunately for the Europeans, they managed to halve the first and third holes; otherwise they would have been six down.

Pavin birdied the second after his wedged approach came to rest two feet from the flag, then sank a twenty-five-footer on the par-5 fourth to go two up. On a roll, he pitched in from 140 yards away on the fifth for an eagle two, when both his opponents had birdie chances from inside six feet.

On his long pitch-in for eagle: *"There were some cheers . . . and some stunned-like noises."* —Corey Pavin

Pavin applied the coup de grâce on the 396-yard sixth with another birdie putt for a four-hole lead and a personal five-under start for six holes, including three birdies and an eagle. Although he did not need one, Pavin did have a partner—Jim Gallagher, who fully enjoyed the free ride.

"Corey Pavin's swing has more planes than British Airways."
—*Mel Webb*, London Telegraph

The seventh hole was halved in par threes, and the Europeans tasted their first success of the day on the eighth with a birdie. But the U.S. pair went back up by four at the turn when Gallagher holed his five-foot birdie putt.

Two holes later they were six up, with Pavin's eight-foot downhill birdie at the tenth and a complete hash by James at eleven doing the damage.

Twelve was halved as the Europeans tried to staunch the bleeding, and Rocca stole thirteen when his magnificent eight-iron from a fairway bunker to four feet of the hole was rewarded with a birdie three. Up by five with five to play, the Americans parred the short fourteenth and brought a 5 and 4 closure to the Europeans' sorrows, both Rocca and James narrowly missing birdie putts.

Fred Couples and Paul Azinger (USA) v. Peter Baker and Ian Woosnam (EUR)

Although they twice held an early lead, Couples and Azinger never really jelled as a pair. Once Baker had found his putting touch on the 399-yard fifth hole to level the match, the visitors were never in it.

From one down after four, Baker and Woosnam totally dominated the next nine holes, with Baker reeling off six birdies of his own. He started the onslaught at the fifth by burying a fifty-footer to level the score, then sank one of half that length on six to put Europe up for the first time in the match.

The Fabulous Baker Boy continued to set the greens on fire, as he sank a twelve-footer for birdie on eight, then canned a ten-footer on the ninth for a three-hole lead.

At the turn the highly touted Americans were struggling three down, and they tried to get them all back at the tenth. Both British players laid up in front of the lake, so the Americans went for the green. Azinger bounced off the left bank into the stream, while Couples overshot the bank and found the second bend of the stream. Despite both men having ten-foot putts to halve the hole, the U.S. pair was soon four down.

With the twelfth falling to another British birdie, Baker put the exclamation point to a fine individual round as he drained a five-foot birdie putt on thirteen to clinch an "in-yer-face" victory, 6 and 5.

Couples continued his poor play—his ball counted in only four of the thirteen holes played. On the other side, Baker had six birdies to top his five from the previous afternoon—in five fewer holes.

Raymond Floyd and Payne Stewart (USA) v. Jose Maria Olazabal and Joakim Haeggman (EUR)

Watson was happy to send out his solid pairing of Floyd and Stewart, who were coming off a workmanlike win in the morning foursomes. Gallacher pieced together another makeshift partnership, giving the Swedish rookie his first appearance, alongside the Seve-less Olazabal.

The Continental couple did not couple well in the opening holes. They were three down after just four holes, as American birdies on the second and fourth holes sandwiched a European bogey.

Floyd's sixteen-foot birdie on the 396-yard sixth stretched the early advantage to four, while the par-4 eighth was halved in birdie—the Europeans' first of the round. Stewart missed a putt for par on the ninth, so the second European birdie pulled them back to three down at the turn.

Floyd and Stewart took 33 to cover nine holes and found themselves three up against a far from fully functioning rival outfit, who were just beginning to jell.

Missing his normal partner's guiding hand, Olazabal found water on ten, while Haeggman found the gallery on the right. Both Americans laid up, but Stewart's birdie putt was matched by a fine recovery and putt from the Swede, who was beginning to feel more at home. Two holes were halved in par before Olazabal and Stewart made birdies to balance out the 394-yard thirteenth.

Olazabal was unable to repeat his birdie touch on fourteen, where his ten-footer would have won the hole and cut the lead to two.

The par-5 fifteenth was the site of one of those remarkable moments that are found only in the Ryder Cup. On in two, Stewart completely misread his first putt and came up forty feet shy of the still-distant flag. Rather than embarrass his partner any further, Floyd decided to hole out from six inches, but even more embarrassingly, he missed. Haeggman holed his birdie for what seemed like the win, but Stewart was able to recover his (and his partner's) blushes by holing his second putt for an unbelievable half. The U.S. pair was more than fortunate to remain three up with three to play.

"I fed off Raymond like a leech. He would be pumping me up and all of a sudden I would just do it."
—*Payne Stewart*

Having pulled his drive left at sixteen, Olazabal plugged his second into the face of a greenside bunker, but he holed out from there for birdie, while the other three players all missed makable putts.

All four played two fine opening shots up the seventeenth fairway. Haeggman drilled his third just past the pin and had it spin back almost into the hole, stopping three feet in front. After asking the Swede to run up and mark his ball, Olazabal showed why. He not only hit his approach at the flag, but he hit the pin, and his ball dropped dead by the hole. Two great approach shots left two certain European birdie fours, but they were matched by Stewart from twelve feet for his own birdie and the win, 2 and 1.

Afternoon fourball result: USA 3, EUR 1

Laying the afternoon setback firmly at the door of Gallacher's selections, the British tabloids typically headlined with BERNIE'S CLANGERS, in response to the omission of Ballesteros and Langer, although both asked to sit the session out.

Day two result: USA 4, EUR 4
Overall match score: USA 7½, EUR 8½

Day Three: Singles

A bitingly cold and blustery morning greeted the players on the crucial last day.

The U.S. team were in beige sweaters with a large imprint of the Ryder Cup on the front; the Europeans were in bright red.

Europe made a bad start, seven times losing the opening hole, six times to par. Things quickly changed, as by one o'clock in the afternoon Europe was leading in the first five singles matches. One hour later, the United States was back on top.

Lanny Wadkins (USA) v. Sam Torrance (EUR)

Overnight the U.S. team heard that Sam Torrance had had a nail removed from a badly infected toe and, being unable to walk, would almost certainly be scratched from the singles.

This left Tom Watson with the decision no Ryder Cup captain wants to make. As it happened, this Ryder Cup captain did not have to make the decision. Having heard the news of Torrance's toe, wild-card pick Lanny Wadkins, who was due to face Ballasteros, volunteered.

"I offered to Tom to put my name in the envelope. It would not have been fair to the guys who qualified. A lot of the guys came up to me and said I was crazy to do it. But those guys earned points to get on the team."
—Lanny Wadkins

Watson initially tried to talk the eight-time Ryder Cupper out of it, but he realized it was the logical step—since the other ten players had qualified on merit.

"I think the other guys understood the sacrifice he was making, because no one wanted to play more than Lanny. It was one of the great gestures I've ever seen anyone make." —Tom Watson

To each of his players on the first tee: *"Play this one for Lanny. And if you get down, just think what a fighter Lanny is, and that will help you get through a tough spot."* —Tom Watson

Fred Couples (USA) v. Ian Woosnam (EUR)

Having driven poorly in his pairs matches, Fred Couples was also unhappy with his play on the greens, noting, "I didn't make a big putt anytime in the first two days." While Couples had only a half-point from his first four matches, Woosnam was 4-0.

Woosnam's opening drive found the trees, and he found himself one down after Couples made an opening birdie. Couples lost the second by missing the green with his approach, chipping fifteen feet beyond the flag and taking two putts.

The seven holes that followed were all halved in par, except for bogeys at eight, as neither player appeared capable of breaking par. These two star names carded a total of one birdie on the front nine—Couples's opening strike.

The Welshman ended his birdie drought by knocking his approach into the tenth green for a four-foot birdie attempt, which he made to go one up. Having got the birdie touch, he went two up with a thirty-foot birdie putt from the far left of the eleventh green.

Not to be out-birdied, Couples put away a seven-footer on thirteen to even the birdie count at two apiece. The 550-yard fifteenth saw Couples's two-iron second perch itself precariously on the brow of the upslope twenty-two feet from the hole, which Couples covered in two easy putts to square the match.

Woosnam pushed his approach onto the grassy crown of a greenside bunker alongside the seventeenth green. His delicate chip landed softly on the green, rolled at the hole, ran into the pin, and bounced out a few inches. Couples matched the par, and they took on the eighteenth as they had started.

Fred Couples reprised his failure in 1989 against Christy O'Connor, but instead of missing the green, he hit a majestic eight-iron to eight feet. Woosnam's eight-iron bounced inside Couples's excellent approach and settled seven feet from the final pin. Couples's putt appeared to be heading for the center of the cup, but it ran out of steam and rolled under the hole by six inches.

With a chance to win, the Welshman sent his downhill putt by the hole, then watched in disbelief as his ball dribbled on and on—four feet past. He had to hole the return for an overall half. Somewhat nervously under the circumstances, Woosie's return putt faded to the left of the hole and just dropped in. Couples, who may have thought he had won at the death, put both hands to his head in exasperation—or perhaps relief that the match was finally over.

Apart from after the first hole, Couples was never ahead. This was Woosnam's first-ever half-point in the singles. The Welshman finished undefeated with 4½ points out of 5, while Couples came away winless (0-3-2) for the second time in three Ryder Cups.

Chip Beck (USA) v. Barry Lane (EUR)

Playing like a player who had lost both his previous matches, Barry Lane opened with a bogey at the first hole, but Chip Beck's bogey at the third leveled the match. Lane went for the fourth green in two, just clearing the stream in front, then, from over thirty feet, he two-putted for a birdie to take a lead. Beck's first birdie followed at the fifth, and they were back all square.

The American gave up the lead with another bogey at seven, and the Englishman made his second birdie at nine to reach the turn two up.

Beck continued to have trouble finding his range and gave up another bogey on eleven. Lane failed to hit his marks on the par-3 twelfth, and his bogey cut back the lead. He got it right back at thirteen when an approach, aiming for the flag, bounced just to the right for a five-foot birdie putt. This left him three up with five to play, well in control of a match Beck had barely gotten into.

"My game just wasn't firing on all cylinders. I was just waiting for my game to come around. Trying to persevere. Giving myself a chance to come back is so rewarding." CHIP BECK

The American was quickly back in it when the Englishman three-putted fourteen, and his own slow-rolling, thirty-foot putt went straight into the hole for eagle at fifteen. With his third win in three holes, courtesy of Lane's bogey at sixteen, Beck had evened out the match with two to play. A half at seventeen meant the second singles match out reached the eighteenth tee all square. Unlike the previous match, this one would end with a clear decision.

Beck safely found the middle of the fairway, but Lane's drive ate sand and his three-iron recovery drank water—eight feet short of dry land. Beck's approach safely cleared the water and settled in the light rough to the right of the hole. Lane only just missed making par with a chip that ran seven feet past the hole.

"Pressure and choking are things the pros don't like to talk about. The last two Ryder Cups have produced more multiple collapses than the annual trade show for deck chair manufacturers."
—Golf Digest

Beck's chip back downhill was judged perfectly, and his ball slowly trundled down to a few inches from the hole. Having been three up with five to play, Lane conceded the putt to hand Beck a win by one hole. Beck had won by taking four of the last five holes!

Beck's inspirational turnaround win leveled the score at 9½ with nine games on the course: three all square, the United States up in three, Europe up in three. Beck played in only two matches —and won them both, ending his brief Ryder Cup career with three singles wins out of three and an overall record of 6-2-1. Not playing Beck more than twice may have been Tom Watson's only blunder of the week (apart from the menu incident).

Lee Janzen (USA) v. Colin Montgomerie (EUR)

Lee Janzen started cold with two bogeys but retrieved half of the damage with a fine eight-foot birdie putt at the par-5 fourth hole. Montgomerie made his first birdie on six, bogeyed the par-3 seventh, and held on to his one-hole lead until the fourteenth hole.

The Scot had trouble with the short holes, and he bogeyed his second par 3 of the round to give Janzen a share of the lead.

Suitably inspired, Janzen overpowered his bigger opponent, hitting his second to the 550-yard fifteenth four feet closer than Monty's three-wood to twelve feet. The Scot drilled his eagle putt home to a crescendo of cheers from the local supporters, which unnerved the American, who drifted his eagle putt to the right and drew an even louder response from the crowd.

On missing his eagle putt on fifteen: *"All I could think as I was standing over it was if you miss, you're going to hear an unbelievable roar."* —LEE JANZEN

With the American one down at the last hole, Janzen's "death-or-glory" approach from the right-hand rough in front of a bunker sailed high over the lake and almost landed in the hole, unluckily bounding on by sixteen feet. Montgomerie was also on in two, leaving his first putt two feet short, but it was most surprisingly yet most sportingly conceded by Janzen, who missed his downhiller from sixteen feet to hand victory to the Scot, 1-up.

On the lengthy concession on the last: "He was a gentleman."
—*Colin Montgomerie*

Janzen was one of three Americans not to register a win in the three days. He went 0-2 for his efforts.

Corey Pavin (USA) v. Peter Baker (EUR)

Peter Baker's eleven-month-old daughter, Georgina, was rushed to the hospital on Saturday night with suspected meningitis. Fortunately, it proved to be only a viral infection. Baker stayed up most of the night and arrived back on the course a few hours before play was due to begin.

Baker, still to warm up after his night of anxiety, allowed Pavin to win the first hole with an easy par. Baker quickly warmed to his task on the second as Pavin dropped the hole with a bogey. By the third green, Baker was hot: he holed a seventeen-footer for a half, a feat he repeated on the sixth to save another half.

Baker's putter stayed hot as he rolled in an eight-foot birdie from the fringes of the eighth green to take the lead. Pavin took a turn to conjure some magic out of his putter, draining a nine-foot birdie on the ninth to level.

Just to prove the old golfing adage "He who hath the hottest putter shall maketh the byrdie," Baker produced a twenty-five-foot birdie putt up the slope of the tenth green to regain a lead he would not give up.

Baker increased his advantage by almost holing his approach to eleven, the ball running across the hole and ten feet past. The come-back putt found the bottom of the hole for a two-hole lead.

Recognizing a charge when he saw one, Corey Pavin realized he needed to make his own move and grabbed a birdie two at the twelfth to halve the Englishman's lead. It was to little avail, as Baker rattled home another putt—from eleven feet—for a birdie two on fourteen, and a two-hole lead with four to play.

Local boy Peter Baker, who lived less than forty-five minutes from the course, needed only fifteen putts to cover the first eleven holes: "I have putted the lights out this week."

Pavin had a chance to get a hole back on fifteen, but he blew a short birdie putt and settled for a half in par. The American made no such mistake on the next hole, taking sixteen with a nine-foot birdie putt that had him punching the sky with his trademark uppercut.

The tension and the rookie got to Pavin on the seventeenth green, where he toppled over after narrowly missing a twenty-five-foot putt that refused to turn enough to find the hole. Spread-eagled on the putting surface, Pavin put his hand behind his head and crossed his legs as if to fall asleep. Baker was not to be distracted from his ten-footer from the edge of the green. With a putt to win the match, his ball just stayed atop the hole, finishing alongside the cup.

With two putts for the match from just off the eighteenth green, Baker holed a tricky twenty-foot downhiller to birdie and win by two holes.

With three wins out of four matches in his only-ever appearance, Baker turned in one of the greatest rookie performances, from either side, in recent Ryder Cup history.

John Cook (USA) v. Joakim Haeggman (EUR)

With a defeat in his only match of the week, Haeggman faced John Cook, who had single-handedly dismantled Nick Faldo's game in the Saturday fourball. The Americans had this down as point already earned, but the Swede was a man who did not like to count his birdies before they were hatched.

In a remarkably tight start, the first seven holes were halved in par, before Haeggman stepped in with an eight-foot birdie putt on the eighth to break the ice.

Three more holes were then halved in par before all hell cut loose on the par-3 twelfth. Cook carded his first bogey, and Haeggman retaliated with his first double bogey—having three-putted, with his second putt lipping out from four feet.

Back to all square, the next five holes were halved—but not all to par, as the fifteenth fell to matching birdies. Haeggman had to hole a nervy six-footer for a par on seventeen to keep the match balanced, while Cook had to follow the Swede in with a slightly shorter par putt.

Haeggman just cleared the water off the final tee, his ball bounding onto and up the fairway, almost running on into the second stretch of the stream. With his drive, Cook disastrously found the back of a fairway bunker. The American tried to get clever and clear the lake, but his bunker shot ballooned, took a bite out of a bank on the far side of the lake, leapt up, and dribbled back into the water.

From an uncomfortable lie, Haeggman gave his second shot all he could give it, even waving his ball on and over the lake onto the front of the massive final green. Only after managing to make a six did Cook eventually concede Haeggman's par putt for a surprise one-hole win for the home side.

In a match he was expected to wrap up early, John Cook never even took a lead, finishing two over par and making only one birdie—at the par-5 fifteenth, which had given up birdies all week like a magician's top hat.

Payne Stewart (USA) v. Mark James (EUR)

This one-sided match was done and dusted by the turn, though Payne Stewart, who birdied four holes on the front nine, almost let the match slip.

The dour-faced Englishman started badly, with a bogey on the first hole, and he never really recovered. Stewart doubled the opening agony for James, pitching up to ten feet and holing the birdie putt to go two up after two holes. The 579-yard fourth was shared in birdie fours, but Stewart kept up a birdie pace that James could not live with.

Having extended his lead to three on the 399-yard fifth, Stewart dropped his tee shot on the par-3 eighth within five feet of the hole, landing inside James's fine tee shot to ten feet. James missed his longer putt, while the American made his shorter putt. Stewart went five up at the turn when James bogeyed the ninth, and the American was coasting to a big win.

Stewart was unable to extend his lead over the next three holes, causing some concern in his camp when he bogeyed the thirteenth and failed to match James's second birdie of the round at fourteen. His advantage down to three, Stewart had to birdie fifteen just to keep his fast-diminishing lead intact.

Three up with three to play, Stewart breathed a huge sigh of relief when his four-footer for par dropped on sixteen for the match, 3 and 2.

This win by Stewart brought the overall match score to 10½–12½, with Europe still needing only two more points to regain the Cup and five games left on course.

Davis Love III (USA) v. Costantino Rocca (EUR)

In a tension-filled match that saw neither player more than one hole ahead, the action on the front nine did little to suggest the drama that would unfold over the final five holes. Rocca bogeyed the third; Love bogeyed the fifth and seventh but birdied the eighth on Rocca's concession.

With the score all square after nine, this lackluster display continued home, Rocca having to make a long putt on eleven to save his par and the hole. Having saved his bacon, Rocca made a hamfisted bogey at the par-3 twelfth that left him one down. The Italian then made an impressive up and down on thirteen to save par.

Known as a streak player, Rocca rode this streak through the next two holes, holing a storming thirty-footer for birdie at fourteen to level, then a five-footer for birdie and the lead on fifteen. With the 410-yard sixteenth halved in par, Rocca and Europe were well placed to put the champagne on ice. The Ryder Cup looked as though it would not be making the journey back to the States.

"I'm a rookie; I couldn't figure out that scoreboard. But when I saw all those people [around the sixteenth], I knew my match would be critical."
—DAVIS LOVE III

Pumped up with expectation, Rocca overhit his third, a three-iron, to the seventeenth, running his ball twenty feet past the pin. Love was left with a wedge onto the green and just got inside Rocca's three-iron. With a putt to win perhaps the biggest match of his life, the Italian rolled his ball a yard past the hole. Love could not make his birdie putt either, but refused to concede his opponent's three-footer, as he had done on earlier holes.

"I knew he was thinking about it. He had so much pressure. I had given him a couple from a foot or two, and he had made some long ones. His luck was due to run out." —DAVIS LOVE III

"My agent was yelling, 'Don't move your head!' at me all day. When I move my head before I putt, I get in trouble. On that putt, I looked at the hole too soon."
—*Costantino Rocca*

With an air of nonchalance, Rocca took very little time over his second putt, which he almost casually swatted at the hole. The ball lolled round the lip and stayed out. The Italian stormed off the green, swiping the grass with his putter, his precious lead gone in three putts.

Love stayed behind on the seventeenth green to practice his putting stroke, hoping this delay would allow Rocca to think about his miss. Love's mind games worked, as the Italian confirmed afterward: "Between seventeen and eighteen, I realized that it was all down to me. But everyone has told me that it is a team game and you win or lose as a team."

A keen student of the mental approach to the game, Love knew that a good drive would heap even more pressure on Rocca's already sagging shoulders. The American was greeted with a unanimous "Beautiful" as his big drive split the narrow, angled fairway.

"I knew if I was out there in the middle with a big drive, it would be a tough drive for him. He's got to be thinking, 'Shoot, he's got a nine-iron in there.' And he didn't hit a very good one." —DAVIS LOVE III

With the pressure even greater than that of a few seconds earlier, Rocca was a rotisserie of mixed emotions, pumped up and let down. He sent his drive soaring between the two bunkers beyond the fairway, way right of Love's drive.

From the gallery's feet off the right side of the fairway, Rocca hit a flat two-iron with just enough power to clear the lake but not much more. It bounced on the bank and leaped forward, but short of the green. With 150 yards to go after his perfect drive, Love took a nine-iron but also came up short, his ball rolling off the slope across the green and back toward Rocca's. Having got within twenty feet of the hole, Love's ball just stayed on the putting surface forty feet away.

"I'm walking across the bridge to the eighteenth green, thinking, 'What in the world are you doing that far below the hole?' I can't imagine any more pressure than that last putt. I knew I had to make it."

—Davis Love III

Rocca's chip looked bound for the hole, but it skimmed by the cup and carried on fourteen feet past the pin. Love underhit his long putt up the big slope, and it stopped four feet short. Rocca's tricky downhiller for par refused to curl into the hole and drifted eighteen inches too far, but surprisingly was conceded by his opponent.

Love stood astride a four-footer for the match and steadied himself over the ball. Nervously he backed off. He took a deep breath, composed himself again, took fresh aim, and stroked the ball through a graceful arc into the center of the cup.

"You dream about having a putt for something like this. . . . I didn't really make any putts all day except that one on eighteen. . . . I'll always remember that putt going in and looking over at the guys and being frozen to the ground. I still don't know where that ball is." —Davis Love III

With the win secured, Love immediately adopted the same triumphant two-arms-raised victory salute used by Sam Torrance in 1985, on the same green, although the Cup was not won yet.

Love's crucial point brought the U.S. side to within half a point of the fourteen they needed. The point also marked the first time since the first day that the Americans had been in front.

As Love's final putt rolled in: "The Cup is on the Concorde! The Cup is coming home!"
—*Lanny Wadkins*

On Rocca's blowing a lead with two holes to play: *"Italy cost us two world wars. Now they have cost us the Ryder Cup."*

—Anonymous German spectator

On missing the putt: *"I go anywhere, they know me. I go to Japan, they know me. I never see a player miss a putt and become so famous. I just miss a putt. I don't kill anybody."* —COSTANTINO ROCCA

Jim Gallagher (USA) v. Seve Ballesteros (EUR)

Lanny Wadkins had been due to face Ballesteros, but the Spaniard teed off against Gallagher, who had been slated to play the injured Sam Torrance.

"Sadly for Ballesteros, and Europe, the route he followed seldom embraced the fairway as he visited parts of the course few others have been. . . . He was into the crowd, the water, or the bunkers seven times in the first seven holes."
—*David Millar,* London Daily Telegraph

The Spaniard had asked to be dropped from the previous afternoon's fourballs so he could work on his ailing swing. The rest and practice did not help him, and the first eight holes of this match read like a rap sheet for a golfing delinquent. First hole: bunkered—bogey; second hole: chip short of the green—bogey; third hole: missed eight-foot putt for win—bogey; fourth hole: water—bogey; fifth hole: bunkered again; sixth hole: hooked drive into bushes—bogey; seventh hole: bunkered again; eighth hole: approach through the green—bogey.

After the dust had settled on Seve's opening, Gallagher was left holding a three-hole lead, the Spaniard having taken 42 strokes to reach the turn. The American had played a part in his own ascendancy, with birdies at the second and fourth holes, but he also had bogeys at three and six; otherwise he may well have sewn the match up by the turn.

Gallagher made his third and final birdie at the par-4 tenth, when Ballesteros, who failed to drive his favorite green, found sand for the fourth time and could only make par. The Spaniard won his second hole of the match at the twelfth, having taken the sixth with a bogey to Gallagher's double bogey.

"I never thought a Gallagher would beat a Ballesteros."
—*Bernard Gallacher*

The last four holes were shared, as Gallagher made no mistakes coming home and Seve had no more fire left in his fatigued body, despite the urgings of the crowd. The end came for Seve on sixteen, where he missed a nine-foot birdie putt that curled in front of the hole for a 3 and 2 defeat.

King of the pairs format, Ballesteros had a very average singles record. In seven singles, he had won only two, lost three, and halved two. *"I played very badly. You can blame me. I tried my best, but it was not to be. I am sorry."* —SEVE BALLESTEROS

Raymond Floyd (USA) v. Jose Maria Olazabal (EUR)

Jose Maria Olazabal was a completely different and less effective player without the support of his mentor, Seve Ballesteros. Dropping two bogeys in the first three holes, he spotted Ray Floyd a two-hole lead that he got back with birdies on five and six.

Floyd, who was still on the practice range well after darkness fell the previous night, played with the zeal of a fresh-faced rookie rather than a flush-faced veteran, the oldest player in Ryder Cup history.

Floyd thoroughly enjoyed his "farewell round." He nailed his approach to the ninth four feet from the flag for birdie to go one up. Then he sank a thirty-footer on twelve for birdie, and holed a fifteen-foot birdie putt on thirteen to go two up. His five-iron tee shot arrowed in on the fourteenth flag, hit the pin, and bounced out twelve inches to the left for a concession and three up.

"Floyd was knocking down flagsticks like a slalom skier."
—*Gary Van Sickle,* Golf World

Olazabal was playing some pretty handy golf himself but could not keep pace with the senior American, who was relishing his last Ryder Cup match.

The Spaniard gave himself and his team some hope with a birdie on fifteen, two down with three to play. It came too late, as Floyd's three-foot par putt on sixteen guaranteed the United States a half-point, enough to retain the Ryder Cup.

"It was so exciting for me to be here at fifty-one and be part of this spectacle. Kiawah Island was the biggest sporting event in America for a decade, and this must rank alongside it."
—*Ray Floyd*

Playing for pride, Olazabal birdied the seventeenth to cut Floyd's lead to one, but he hooked his final drive into the stream and conceded Floyd's ball, on the green in two, before the two players crossed the bridge. This full point lifted the Americans to 14½ points, and the Cup was theirs outright.

Olazabal was never ahead, while Floyd was the only American not to card a bogey. Floyd said good-bye to the Ryder Cup with a 12-16-3 record that belied the tremendous service he had given his country, having been the only golfer to play in four decades—1969-93. "That's about as good as I can play. It was fabulous. It's just been a thrill to be part of it. It's a memory I'll never forget," Floyd reminisced after his final match.

Tom Kite (USA) v. Bernhard Langer (EUR)

Having defeated Howard Clark 8 and 7 in a record singles win on his last Ryder Cup visit, Tom Kite did not quite inflict the same beating on Bernhard Langer, but he did record the biggest win of the day.

Suffering from an injured neck, Langer dropped the first stroke on the third, where his bogey five gave Kite a lead he would give back for only one hole. With his first bogey—on the par-3 seventh—Kite momentarily lost his lead, but his second birdie of the round—at eight—not only put him back on top but also started a run of four consecutive birdies.

On the ninth Kite knocked his approach nine feet from the flag for birdie and a two-hole lead over the reigning Masters champion. As he had done on the very first morning, Kite drove the tenth with a three-wood and found the front of the green, forcing Langer to follow suit. The German, still bothered by his stiff neck, found water, and Kite sank his fifteen-foot putt for an eagle and the hole.

Full of confidence, Kite made his fourth consecutive birdie or better at eleven and was four up, as Langer's resistance crumbled.

On his opponent's neck injury: "Anyone coming up against him would count himself lucky if he wasn't 100 percent, because we all know what a great player he is when he is firing on all cylinders."
—*Tom Kite*

Not only was Langer bothered by a stiff neck and a high-flying Kite, but he also ran out of luck and time on fifteen. The German's forty-foot birdie putt negotiated the slope across the green and rattled into the back lip of the cup, staying out. This left Kite, on in two, with a twenty-foot eagle putt, which he stuffed home for the most emphatic win of the day, 5 and 3.

Kite was eight under par for his last seven holes. He finished 3-3-2-3-3-4-3-3, winning five holes in the last eight played.

As with Ray Floyd ahead of him, this would prove to be Tom Kite's last Ryder Cup after six previous outings, and he finished with a splendid winning record of 15-9-4 and 17 points. In seven singles matches, he won five and halved two (against Torrance and Ballesteros), and he did not lose a single singles match—the only player in Ryder Cup history to have been unbeaten in seven solo starts.

Paul Azinger (USA) v. Nick Faldo (EUR)

Having dropped the first hole to par, Faldo made amends on the next with an emphatic approach from the right-hand rough to four feet. The third was halved in bogey fives, while Azinger took the par-5 fourth with his first birdie to go back up by one. Faldo immediately leveled with a birdie at five, and an American bogey at eight gave the Englishman the lead for the first time.

Faldo enjoyed a brief two-hole lead after pitching up to the hole on ten for an unanswered birdie.

In the twenty-seven matches that passed through the tenth hole, there were four eagles, fifteen birdies, and six par fours, as well as two bogeys—reducing the hole's stroke average to 3.63.

It had seemed all day that once a player got in front, he self-destructed, handing holes back to his opponent. Faldo was no different, blowing his two-hole lead with bogeys on eleven and thirteen, where a twelve-footer for par was way wide right of the hole on a major misread.

Azinger's tee shot at the 194-yard fourteenth found the green, forty feet from the flagstick, though Faldo's six-iron was considerably closer. His tee shot was on line all the way, and Faldo sensed—before he even hit his shot—he had something special. His ball landed directly in front of the pin, ran at the flag, rolled round the lip, and dropped for an ace.

Faldo's hole-in-one was only the second in Ryder Cup history after Peter Butler in 1973, and was Faldo's fifth career ace—all made with a six-iron.

"I told Monty earlier in the week that I was going to hole in one this week. I said birdies aren't good enough. That's how you must play matches like this. You are trying to get the ball close, but close is not good enough. You have to think about holing shots. . . . After losing two of the last three holes, I brushed a few leaves out of the way and said it was a good time to hole one now, and boom—I knocked it in."

—Nick Faldo

Once the United States had retained the Cup, the pair shook hands after halving the sixteenth and agreed to play on.

After he had finished his singles match: "I was so into our game, I didn't even know we'd won until three holes ago. Nick had to tell me. I played the last two holes with tears in my eyes. I told our guys the previous night at dinner, 'Don't make my match matter.' They didn't."
—*Paul Azinger*

On seventeen, Faldo almost holed his approach shot for an eagle but settled for a conceded birdie and the lead with one to play. After waiting for the American celebrations on the green ahead of them, Faldo knocked his pitch beyond the flag and watched as it started to roll back toward the hole. The Englishman raised his club and pretended to reel his ball back toward the hole—ten feet away.

After a perfect drive that carved up the fairway, coming to rest in front of the lake, Azinger, unleashed an equally good approach. His ball bounced on the upslope, which ran across the green, taking the pace off the ball and letting it stop six feet away from the hole. Faldo's putt down the slope curled too much and ran by the hole. Azinger, with the putt for a half, sank it without any problem and topped off a great day for the Americans.

Although this had been a good week for the U.S. team as a whole, Paul Azinger had struggled and was winless in five games: 0-3-2—the same record that Fred Couples had.

Day three result: USA 7½, EUR 4½

At the start of the week, it was thought that Europe's experienced Ryder Cuppers held the key to a home victory. On the final day, five of these veteran players—Faldo, Woosnam, Langer, Ballesteros, and Olazabal—combined to bring home just two half points among them in the singles, as they all finished winless. Faldo's half-point came after the Cup had been lost. If these five could have scraped together three more half-points among them on the last day, Europe would have regained the trophy.

Overall match score: USA 15, EUR 13

"Under no circumstances did we lose the Ryder Cup. The Americans won the Ryder Cup. We tried our best. It's best not to think about the score line too much. I did not think anyone was to blame."

—BERNARD GALLACHER

Recap

This was the first time the United States had won the Ryder Cup on foreign soil since 1981, when Dave Marr led the blowout at Walton Heath.

"My team performed with the guts that typified our American teams. I told them at the opening ceremony and I'll tell them to their faces right now how proud I am of all of them. . . . This is the finest experience I have had in the game of golf, being captain of the Ryder Cup, even though I didn't hit a shot all week. This is better than all of my major championships."
—*Tom Watson*

His Royal Highness Prince Andrew presented the Ryder Cup to a delighted Tom Watson, who had seen all the hard work and homework he had put into this contest pay off. In his closing address, Watson read some favorite lines from Teddy Roosevelt's "Man in the Arena" oration.

Perhaps pride of place in Watson's victorious team goes to the old American warhorse Raymond Floyd, who showed all the younger players how to play match play. Floyd won two matches on Saturday, and in his singles on Sunday, his putt on sixteen won the Cup for the United States. Most of all, it had been a triumph for Tom Watson and the culmination of a lifelong dream—to not only captain a winning U.S. team but to do so in Great Britain.

Not only had Watson retained the Cup, but he had also gone a long way in regaining the event's prestige, which may have been tarnished in 1991. After the unfortunate "egg-on-his-face" incident over the menu signings before the matches got under way, there was hardly a ripple on the millpond of controversy during the three days of competitive action. For this both captains, all twenty-four players, and the more appreciative galleries should be congratulated.

In three days of exceptional camaraderie and sportsmanship, one example of a player's sacrifice for the good of his team shone above all others. Lanny Wadkins's selfless act in sitting out the singles would not go unrewarded: he was destined to follow Tom Watson into the captain's hot seat in 1995 at Oak Hill.

"Some guys had a tough time at the end, but if you give your best, it's OK. . . . It's only a game! Well done to the American team. Best of all, it was great Ryder Cup."
—*Nick Faldo*

Contemplating his skipper's role in 1995: *"The toughest thing is to just stand by and watch. It's one thing to play and then go watch, but to sit out and not be able to help the team is something I wouldn't wish on anybody. If the captaincy is anything like that, I'll have enough stomach acid to wear the chrome off a set of irons."* —Lanny Wadkins

Match Results (Winning side marked in *italics*.)

Friday, September 24—Morning Foursomes

	USA	EUR	Score
1.	*Corey Pavin* *Lanny Wadkins*	Sam Torrance Mark James	4 and 3
2.	Paul Azinger Payne Stewart	*Ian Woosnam* *Bernhard Langer*	7 and 5
3.	*Tom Kite* *Davis Love III*	Seve Ballesteros Jose Maria Olazabal	2 and 1
4.	Raymond Floyd Fred Couples	*Nick Faldo* *Colin Montgomerie*	4 and 3

Friday, September 24—Afternoon Fourball

	USA	EUR	Score
5.	Lee Janzen Jim Gallagher	*Peter Baker* *Ian Woosnam*	1-up
6.	*Corey Pavin* *Lanny Wadkins*	Bernhard Langer Barry Lane	4 and 2
7.	Paul Azinger Fred Couples	Nick Faldo Colin Montgomerie	halved
8.	Tom Kite Davis Love III	*Seve Ballesteros* *Jose Maria Olazabal*	4 and 3

Day one result: USA 3½, EUR 4½

Saturday, September 25—Morning Foursomes

	USA	EUR	Score
9.	Lanny Wadkins Corey Pavin	*Nick Faldo* *Colin Montgomerie*	3 and 2
10.	Fred Couples Paul Azinger	*Bernhard Langer* *Ian Woosnam*	2 and 1
11.	*Raymond Floyd* *Payne Stewart*	Peter Baker Barry Lane	3 and 2
12.	Tom Kite Davis Love III	*Seve Ballesteros* *Jose Maria Olazabal*	2 and 1

Saturday, September 25—Afternoon Fourball

	USA	EUR	Score
13.	*John Cook* *Chip Beck*	Nick Faldo Colin Montgomerie	2-up
14.	*Corey Pavin* *Jim Gallagher*	Mark James Costantino Rocca	5 and 4
15.	Fred Couples Paul Azinger	*Peter Baker* *Ian Woosnam*	6 and 5
16.	*Raymond Floyd* *Payne Stewart*	Jose Maria Olazabal Joakim Haeggman	2 and 1

Day two result: USA 4, EUR 4

Overall match score: USA 7½, EUR 8½

Sunday, September 26—Singles

	USA	EUR	Score
17.	Lanny Wadkins	Sam Torrance	halved*
18.	Fred Couples	Ian Woosnam	halved
19.	*Chip Beck*	Barry Lane	1-up
20.	Lee Janzen	*Colin Montgomerie*	1-up
21.	Corey Pavin	*Peter Baker*	2-up
22.	John Cook	*Joakim Haeggman*	1-up
23.	*Payne Stewart*	Mark James	3 and 2
24.	*Davis Love III*	Costantino Rocca	1-up
25.	*Jim Gallagher*	Seve Ballesteros	3 and 2
26.	*Raymond Floyd*	Jose Maria Olazabal	2-up
27.	*Tom Kite*	Bernhard Langer	5 and 3
28.	Paul Azinger	Nick Faldo	halved

Day three result: USA 7½, EUR 4½

Overall match score: USA 15, EUR 13

*Match not played by agreement because Torrance was injured.

1995

Oak Hill Country Club
Rochester, New York
United States
September 22–24

United States 13½	**Europe 14½**
Fred Couples	Seve Ballesteros (Spain)
Ben Crenshaw	Howard Clark (England)
Brad Faxon	Nick Faldo (England)
Jay Haas	David Gilford (England)
Peter Jacobsen	Mark James (England)
Tom Lehman	Per-Ulrik Johansson (Sweden)
Davis Love III	Bernhard Langer (Germany)
Jeff Maggert	Colin Montgomerie (Scotland)
Phil Mickelson	Costantino Rocca (Italy)
Corey Pavin	Sam Torrance (Scotland)
Loren Roberts	Philip Walton (Ireland)
Curtis Strange	Ian Woosnam (Wales)
Captain	**Captain**
Lanny Wadkins	Bernard Gallacher (Scotland)

Soak Hill

With the United States returning to winning ways with two victories in a row—1991 and 1993—albeit down-to-the-wire triumphs that could have gone either way, the U.S. media started early with their forecasts of doom and gloom for the future of the Ryder Cup.

According to the naysayers, the thirty-first reenactment of what had turned into golf's most eagerly awaited contest would signal the watershed in European competitiveness, as the Ryder Cup looked destined to become U.S. permanent property again.

THE LAST DANCE, IF EUROPE CAN'T WIN, THE RYDER CUP WILL TAKE A GIANT STEP BACKWARD
—Sports Illustrated *headline*

Fortunately for golf lovers everywhere, the media were to be proved wrong again. The 1995 Ryder Cup once more reached heights of drama and depths of despair unmatched by any other gathering of golfers.

European captain Bernard Gallacher squared off against his third opposing captain in Lanny Wadkins, having beaten the American 3 and 2 in the opening singles match in 1979. This had been Wadkins's only loss in five singles matches to that point, and he went on to record a 4-2-2 record in the solo format against Gallacher's similar 4-3-4.

There was one fact the American media had got right: the European team was not getting any younger. With the side's average age of thirty-six, Gallacher was in charge of seven players over thirty-seven and only one under thirty. The Americans, however, were not any younger than their opponents: their team was the same average age and had five forty-year-olds, with only Phil Mickelson under thirty.

Faldo (in his record-equaling tenth appearance), Ballesteros, Clark, James, Langer, Torrance, and Woosnam totaled fifty matches among them—an average of seven matches per veteran.

Since age would not be a factor, the difference between the teams could lie in their experience. The European players had won thirteen majors and had fifty-one Ryder Cup appearances, and numbered just two rookies among them: Johansson and Walton. The United States, however, had fewer majors (six) and fewer appearances (fifteen) but more rookies (five): Faxon, Lehman, Maggert, Mickelson, and Roberts.

More important, perhaps, Europe had five players with a winning Ryder Cup record, whereas the United States barely had one: Jay Haas, who had played four matches way back in 1983, posting a 2-1-1 record.

"One of the toughest jobs that we face is getting guys to get the hell out of the team room at night and quit joking around, playing games. Last night they were playing 'Pass the Pigs' until all hours."
—*Lanny Wadkins*

Wadkins had gone out on a limb and a prayer when selecting his wild-card players, Couples (3-6-3 in Ryder Cup play) and Strange (without a PGA tournament win in six years). Gallacher had less leeway with his two choices: Nick Faldo had played mostly on the U.S. PGA Tour, and Ian Woosnam finished twelfth in the Ryder Cup rankings after a midseason slump. The European team was severely weakened by the loss of the 1994 Masters champion, Jose Maria Olazabal, to a long-standing toe injury.

Course Details

In an attempt to return the Ryder Cup to a more traditional setting, the U.S. PGA chose one of its perennially favorite courses. With ten par-4 holes more than 400 yards long, but only two par-5s, Oak Hill is one of America's premier championship courses. By 1995, it had hosted three U.S. Opens (1956, '68, and '89), as well as the 1980 PGA Championship.

"The key is keeping the ball out of the rough. . . . Since I get to decide how much rough there'll be, I can tell you right now there will be plenty. You're going to see rough up to your knees. You can bet on that."

—LANNY WADKINS

Hole	Distance	Par	Hole	Distance	Par
1	440	4	10	429	4
2	401	4	11	192	3
3	202	3	12	372	4
4	570	5	13	598	5
5	406	4	14	323	4
6	167	3	15	184	3
7	431	4	16	439	4
8	426	4	17	458	4
9	419	4	18	445	4
		35			**35 = Par 70 (6,902 yards)**

Course designer: Donald Ross

"America had rigged the whole thing. It had picked one of its hardest courses, grown the rough higher than June corn, cut a little footpath for fairways, and dried out the greens. The teams would play a U.S. Open and a Ryder Cup at the same time. Let's see the Euros handle that."
—*Rick Reilly,* Sports Illustrated

Day One: Morning Foursomes

With a customary eight o'clock start, the players were soon greeted by steady rainfall, which arrived around nine-thirty and, like the capacity crowd, stayed for the rest of the day. The rain even turned into hailstones by late morning.

"Under dreary skies and wrapped in a biting chill, weather fit for a Scottish moor, things will heat up." —LARRY DORMAN, *New York Times*

Corey Pavin and Tom Lehman (USA) v. Nick Faldo and Colin Montgomerie (EUR)

Teeing off first for the United States, Lehman unleashed an unforgettable 290-yard drive from his three-wood—right down the middle of the fairway.

Pavin matched Lehman's drive with a delightful approach to seven feet of the flag for his partner to top off the perfect start by holing the birdie putt for one up. On the second, Faldo sent a chip shot scurrying across and off the putting surface, into the deep rough beyond.

Thirty-six-year-old rookie Tom Lehman was in no doubt over his selection: "On the first tee this morning, I felt, 'I should be here. I should hit this [opening] shot.' I was so calm, it was unbelievable."

The Englishman was still annoyed with himself when he chastised Lehman for holing out a fifteen-inch par putt that the Americans had not heard Faldo concede, barking, "When I say it's good, it's good!"

On his opening pair of blue-collar battlers: "I felt like I was going to stick two bulldogs out there. Nobody's going to intimidate either one of those gentlemen."
—*Lanny Wadkins*

"I told him to speak clearly. Then he claims he said a couple of times that my putt was good. I wasn't going to put up with any crap, especially after he stretches his arms out as if to say, 'Put the ball in your pocket, you idiot!' I was hot." —TOM LEHMAN

After a few calming words from Pavin, Lehman got his game face back on before firing his tee shot to seven feet of the flag on the 202-yard third. Having played the peacemaker, Pavin, in his inimitable Chaplinesque splayfooted putting style, emphatically rolled home another birdie, extending the U.S. lead to three. The British pair staunched the bleeding by halving the fourth, but Faldo missed a simple putt from outside a yard that cruelly lipped out in front of him to give the Americans a four-hole lead after five.

Rewarded with a thump on the back from his partner, Montgomerie got things going for the visitors by finishing off Faldo's six-iron to twelve feet of the sixth flag, after Lehman had just failed to do the same with Pavin's similar-length tee shot.

"This was a day that began with almost equal parts bad golf and good drama. The pounding rain, quickening pulses, and raw nerves led to some high numbers."
—*Larry Dorman,* New York Times

On seven, Lehman compounded his missed putt by drowning his ball in Allen's Creek, while Pavin hit the dropped ball with his driver into a willow tree. Pegged back to two up, Pavin visited the deep rough along the eighth fairway, as Europe took two putts from forty feet—for the second hole in a row—to nail a hole-winning par.

From the ninth on, four holes were halved. Lehman's long game was faltering—he pulled a drive on nine and missed a green on eleven. Pavin worked wonders with the Lehman miscues, first holing a clutch four-footer on nine, then chipping up to a couple of inches to save the half and the one-hole lead on eleven.

"You know you're never out of the hole when Corey's your partner. No matter how bad a shot you hit, you know you're going to have a chance to make a par." —TOM LEHMAN

On the 598-yard thirteenth, in the driving rain and hail, and from the light rough, Montgomerie banged a beautiful three-wood to the green. Faldo capitalized superbly on his partner's offering by holing the huge swinging putt from way over forty feet. Europe was back level in the match. Pleased with finding some form on the greens, a semi-stunned Faldo tripped over his putter in jubilation.

On the next hole, Pavin swiftly retaliated with a twenty-five-foot birdie putt to regain the slender lead. Aiming at the par-3 fifteenth, Lehman pulled his five-iron into the gallery and it bounced back off a spectator into the deep rough, beside a bunker. Standing in the sand, Pavin was unable to leave his recovery shot close; the ball ran right across the green, and the match was back all square.

After another rough-seeking drive from Pavin, it was Lehman's turn to lay up short, before Pavin saved par at sixteen with a spirited pitch from forty yards away, leaving his ball two feet from the flag. Faldo was unable to get his twenty-five-foot birdie putt to roll the extra few inches into the cup, which would have given Europe their first lead of the match.

Seventeen was also halved with bogeys, after both pairs visited the woods as the pressure began to build in the first match out. After two bad shots from his partner (a drive into trees and a poor bunker recovery), Faldo was unlucky not to hole his long uphill birdie putt. Having spurned two great chances to take a lead in the match, the Europeans were made to pay on the final hole, where the pairs lined up on the tee all square.

With a chance of completing a fantastic comeback, Faldo drove into the rough on the right. Pavin, with his opponents' ball in some trouble, also failed to find the fairway, leaving his tee shot in the lighter rough on the right. All Montgomerie could do with his recovery was play the ball out into the middle of the fairway, halfway to the green. From almost 200 yards out, in the driving rain, Lehman had the problem of a downhill lie in the slippery rough.

"Before I hit the shot, I said, 'Corey, I need a pep talk. I'm not hitting it too well.' He said, 'Pick your best club, get committed, and swing really hard.' After I hit it, I'm thinking, 'Don't make me putt.' But I think maybe I needed to make a three- or four-foot putt to win the match."

—Tom Lehman

Pavin's advice to his partner was simple: "Rip it!" From 186 yards, Lehman hit a consummate five-iron safely onto the very front of the waterlogged green. Faldo erred for the second time in as many shots, misfiring a wedge into a bunker off the back right of the green. From there, Montgomerie was unable to threaten the hole for par, and Pavin left his forty-foot putt short on the saturated green. After waiting for the greens staff to squeegee away the water between ball and hole, Lehman calmly slotted his four-foot putt home for the narrow win.

"They got back even, and we just hung in there. We worked hard and stayed patient. When we got to eighteen, we were able to win the last hole and win the match. It was a nice script."
—*Corey Pavin*

In every Ryder Cup there has always been one match that has set the tone for the overall contest; in 1995, this opening encounter was it. As Lehman later said, it was "a statement that Europe's best team can be beaten."

Jay Haas and Fred Couples (USA) v. Sam Torrance and Costantino Rocca (EUR)

"This pairing is a roll of the dice for the Europeans. Rocca has never played alternate shot and Torrance has a 1–7 record in it."

—LARRY DORMAN, *New York Times*

After Torrance had outdriven Couples off the first tee, Rocca holed a putt of eerily similar distance to the one he missed in 1993 to hand the Ryder Cup back to the United States. This time his putt earned him a half.

With the ghosts of 1993 exorcised, Rocca calmly chipped out of a bunker on the second to within a couple of feet for another half.

Couples hit his tee shot to the short third over the back of the green, from where Haas could only chip back to twenty feet. Couples missed the long par putt, and Europe found itself one up after Torrance holed from six feet.

Couples's ten-footer leveled the score after Torrance made a mess of a chip from the edge of the fourth green, while Jay Haas more than matched his partner's previous putt with a fifteen-foot curving strike for another half.

All level after the first five holes, the wheels—all five of them—fell off the American wagon. Five holes later, Europe found itself five up on their opponents, whose game disintegrated like an egg caught in a ball washer.

After Haas's errant tee shot, Couples overhit a flop shot thirty feet beyond the sixth flag. Torrance's chip lipped out, and Rocca made the resulting three-footer for a par three to regain the lead, as the Americans two-putted.

A second U.S. bogey in a row, thanks to Haas's error after Torrance putted up dead from fifty feet away for par, dropped the Americans two down. The Americans both hit poor shots before they reached the eighth green: Haas's tee shot found the rough, and Couples's attempted recovery found the sand. Another bogey, another lost hole, as Rocca putted up stiff from twenty-five feet.

"Costantino was a rock out there, right from the very first hole. He's so strong and has so much talent." —Sam Torrance

On nine, Torrance's recovery to two feet, from under the lip of a greenside bunker, saved par and won the hole from yet another U.S. bogey. The Europeans held a four-hole lead at the turn, having won the previous four holes with pars.

The Americans' plight did not improve any on the tenth. From off the back of the green, Rocca laid up a delightfully delicate chip to twelve inches of the flag—another par, another win. Things looked to be getting even worse when Haas hooked into more rough off the twelfth tee, but Couples laced a recovery between some trees, to within thirty feet of the target, but off the putting surface. Haas finally found his touch and chipped in on one bounce to stop the decay.

"Sometimes when you get five down, you relax a little bit and good things start to happen."
—*Fred Couples*

Back to four down, Couples's next drive landed safely on the fairway . . . the wrong one—the tenth, not the thirteenth. Haas took the easiest route home, firing his second up the wrong fairway, from where Couples was able to lift the ball over the crowd between him and the green. When the Americans finally reached the green, they found their ball closer to the hole than their opponents' ball was, and the Europeans had played down the correct fairway. The U.S. pair transformed this piece of luck into another win: three down with five to play.

Couples, the youngster of the foursome at age thirty-five, pulled another hole back with a superb approach to fourteen, which must have had the Europeans quaking in their soaking golf shoes.

Pushing too hard after their comeback to two down, Couples badly missed the right of the par-3 fifteenth green, whereas Torrance's six-iron left his ball twenty feet away from the pin for a reassuring win to go back up by three with the same to play.

"It got a bit smelly when they got us back to two after we had been five up."
—*Sam Torrance*

Having blown three holes in a row before, the European pairing were not to be pegged back again. They played the sixteenth in fine fashion for a match-winning par, with Rocca rolling a twenty-four-foot birdie putt up to the edge of the hole for a 3 and 2 win, their team's first point of the day. Europe did not make a birdie in sixteen holes of play, nor did they have to.

Davis Love III and Jeff Maggert (USA) v. Howard Clark and Mark James (EUR)

Mark James was the only player not to find the opening fairway, while Love's spot-on approach to three feet left Maggert a simple birdie putt for the win. The U.S. pair combined well again on the third, with Love stroking home Maggert's tee shot to thirteen feet for a second winning birdie in the first three holes.

"We hit what you can't hit in foursomes—three destructive shots. I was guilty of two, Howard of one."
—*Mark James*

Howard Clark got his side back on track, holing an eight-footer to win the fourth, but the pair totally derailed in the next three holes. James drove into water on five, Clark hooked into water on the par-3 sixth, and James topped his three-wood on seven, handing the three holes to the Americans, who had started with four birdies in seven holes for a four-up lead.

After such a bad start, Europe never got back into the match. Love and Maggert combined well enough to retain a healthy lead, with just one hiccup on their card: a bogey six at the monster 598-yard thirteenth.

"Love and Maggert played the puddles better than Clark and James."
—Los Angeles Times

The match was closed out on the 184-yard fifteenth, as the U.S. pair swept to a convincing 4 and 3 win over a far-from-fluent English pair.

Ben Crenshaw and Curtis Strange (USA) v. Bernhard Langer and Per-Ulrik Johansson (EUR)

Rookie Johansson had to earn his colors right away with a putt that saved the half after he had made a poor approach to the first green.

On how he chose his first and fourth pairings: "Corey and Tom like to get up early, and Ben and Curtis like to sleep in."
—*Lanny Wadkins*

The match stayed close for the first eight holes, and then the German dropped a bomb on the ninth green. Langer's forty-foot semicircular birdie putt trundled across the rain-soaked green and amazingly curled right into the hole. Somewhat taken aback by Bernhard's birdie, Strange missed from a mere fifteen feet.

Langer's monster putt upset the Americans' poise, and they proceeded to bogey the next two holes to hand the Europeans a three-hole lead in as many holes.

With this pair dominant in the morning play, Gallacher named them as one of his pairs for the afternoon fourball. Little did the European captain realize that the match was far from over and that his pair would face a strength-sapping slog to the final hole.

From such a dominating position, it was expected that Europe would close out the match, but the persistent heavy rain made club selection and shot-making a lottery, and the match was slowed up with continual stoppages for mopping up the greens.

Despite hailing from the rainier regions of their continent, the two Europeans fared worse in the inclement conditions. They double-bogeyed thirteen, bogeyed fourteen, and doubled again at seventeen—where Langer failed to get out of a bunker—and saw their three-hole lead washed away with one to play. Along with the three holes the Americans won, Strange also made a couple of clutch putts for halves on the increasingly sodden greens: from thirteen feet on twelve and from eight at fifteen.

Both sides failed to hit the final fairway, Crenshaw hitting the deep rough on the right, the Swede hitting an elm tree. Langer, from a trampled lie on the left, was able to hit a longer layup, and Johansson chipped over some casual water to within five feet of the hole. After Strange pitched out, Crenshaw hit a poor approach and left his partner with a thirty-footer for a half that never came. Langer holed the five-footer to win the hole and the match, which had taken more than five hours, 1-up.

Morning foursomes result: USA 2, EUR 2

All three Ryder Cup rookies who played in the morning won their matches: Lehman, Maggert, and Johansson.

Day One: Afternoon Fourball

Gallacher dropped Woosnam—his wild-card selection and the all-time Ryder Cup leader with eight wins in fourball matches. The hitch was that in his last three stroke-play tournaments, Woosnam had missed the cut and finished thirty-third and thirty-fourth.

The afternoon turned out to be even wetter than the very wet morning: *"I didn't find it difficult playing. The wind was blowing, and it was chilly. But I'm an Oregonian with Norwegian blood, so I can handle that."* —Peter Jacobsen

Peter Jacobsen and Brad Faxon (USA) v. Seve Ballesteros and David Gilford (EUR)

On not playing the Spaniard in the opening foursomes: *"Seve's game is bogies and birdies. Foursomes is not about that."*

—Bernard Gallacher

A superb tee shot to the par-3 sixth set up Gilford's birdie putt to level the match after the Americans had crept into a one-hole lead, Jacobsen having notched a couple of birdies at two and four.

After his partner had holed out from eight feet on the seventh green, Jacobsen, from just off the green, attacked the hole with his chip for a birdie three, but it ran four feet past. Jacobsen picked up his ball and turned to celebrate his partner's par—but Faxon was in no mood to celebrate. Having driven behind a willow tree beside Allen's Creek, he had taken a penalty drop. Despite a scorching third shot to the front edge of the green, a chip and a putt gave Faxon a bogey five.

"The only rookie mistake made by an American player all day was made by a veteran, Peter Jacobsen."
—*Larry Dorman,* New York Times

"I picked up and gave him a little high-five. I said, 'Great four,' and he said, 'That was a five.' It hit me like I had taken a Muhammad Ali punch to the solar plexus. I feel like an idiot. I want to cry."
—PETER JACOBSEN

With Gilford comfortably making his par from ten feet, the quiet Englishman had won back-to-back holes, although it could be argued that the miscommunicating Americans had conceded the hole. Whoever took the blame or credit, Europe was up for the first time in the match.

Unnerved by his blunder, Jacobsen hit a poor tee shot and a poor chip shot, and picked up his ball on the eighth hole.

"Ballesteros brought with him to Rochester a sore back, an erratic game, and the confidence of a right-handed novice borrowing Bob Charles's clubs."
—*Alex Spink,* Victory! (1995)

On ten, Ballesteros slowly rolled in a downhill putt from twelve feet for a birdie and the win. This was a brief show of good play from the Spaniard, who could not get much of anything going all day, except pumping up his partner, repeatedly telling him he was "the best player out here today."

Although his own game was suffering, Ballesteros weighed in mightily with a crucial half on nine, recovering from the trees, and his birdie two on ten doubled the lead. Overall, Seve's main contribution proved to be as the guiding light for his silent partner.

"Seve wanted to win so much that it was infectious. To have him as a partner was very special for me. I listened to him, but I still played my own game." —DAVID GILFORD

Gilford's approach to the long thirteenth finished on the very edge of the deep fringe, leaving a perilous putt back twenty feet down an undulating green. Despite being out of the hole, the Spaniard still had an important role to play. Using his putter, he pointed to a spot ten feet left of the perpendicular between ball and hole. Gilford did not argue. Taking careful aim at Seve's imaginary *X*, he gently persuaded his ball onto the green, where it hit the Spaniard's spot and rolled round and round and round and into the hole for an incredible birdie four. A shocked and bemused Faxon missed his ten-foot putt for the half, and Europe was three up.

This killer blow on thirteen just about did in Jacobsen and Faxon, who had struggled ever since their fateful error on seven. They kept the match close but could not make the shots or drop the putts necessary to sustain a challenge.

Gilford's twenty-foot birdie on the 184-yard fifteenth wrapped up the match by the comfortable margin of 4 and 3.

Although he did not contribute much to this win, Seve was the first player to post twenty wins against the Americans, as he took his career mark to 20-15-5. Also coming into the match with nineteen wins, Nick Faldo had a chance to be the first European to reach twenty wins, but he lost both his matches on the first day.

Jeff Maggert and Loren Roberts (USA) v. Sam Torrance and Costantino Rocca (EUR)

On how he chose his pairings: *"Maggert and Roberts was my big guess of the afternoon. . . . I knew those guys would hit fairway after fairway, and green after green, and just wear somebody out."*

—Lanny Wadkins

The American captain's gamble paid off as his pair fused flawlessly into the fourball format. Playing the perfect foil, Maggert made thirteen straight pars, allowing Roberts to go for his shots and go for the birdies.

"The weather and the U.S. outlook improved considerably after Wadkins had played a hunch, putting rookies Maggert and Roberts together."
—Los Angeles Times

Roberts produced the goods with a fine array of attacking shots that brought him a clutch of birdies on the front nine and a three-hole lead after just eight holes. Even when his approach work let him down, Roberts was able to recover in devastating style.

On the 419-yard ninth, Roberts missed the green by six feet and left his ball on the lip of a bunker in thick grass. The only shot he had at the ball was to stand with his right foot in the bunker and his left foot fifteen inches higher on the lip. With a shortened grip, he made short work of the chip shot by knocking his ball onto the green and into the hole.

"Neither [Torrance nor Rocca] fits anybody's description of an athlete. They shamble around the place like an improbable alliance between an unsuccessful Dodge City undertaker and a particularly gloomy Neapolitan waiter. And that was how they played."
—*Richard Williams,* London Guardian

This reduced the European pairing, which had seen off Couples and Haas in the foursomes, to impotent bystanders, as they had dropped the last three holes to go four down at the turn.

The European outlook went from bleak to black on the par-3 eleventh, when Roberts's two-iron tee shot rolled to a couple of feet for his fourth birdie of the round. Five up soon became 6 and 5, as the Europeans could not reproduce their morning sparkle, with only one birdie between them in thirteen holes. They finished a desperate five over par—in a fourball match!

Fred Couples and Davis Love III (USA) v. Nick Faldo and Colin Montgomerie (EUR)

Couples and Love were seen as a natural pairing, having won the World Cup three times (1992, '93, and '94), and they soon hit Faldo and Montgomerie with some world-class "déjà vu" golf.

The top-ranked European pair found themselves four down after six holes for the second time in a day. One up after three, Love birdied the fourth from six feet, and two European bogeys on five and six did the rest of the early damage.

Having lost their touch, their match in the morning, and their collective tempers, the European number ones were nicknamed "Snooty and the Blowfish" by some U.S. sportswriters.

With the visiting pair feeling the effects of the typically British cold and wet conditions more than their hosts, Montgomerie finally made his side's first birdie of the round—a twenty-footer on twelve. Faldo vainly tried to build upon his partner's good work, but after a fine six-iron into thirteen, he could not sink a six-footer for the win.

"The Americans took to a rainy Friday and jumped to a 5–3 lead, mostly by beating Europe's King and Kong, Faldo and Montgomerie."
—*Rick Reilly,* Sports Illustrated

To add insult to his partner's wounds, Montgomerie stepped up again, at the 323-yard fourteenth, to nail his second birdie in three holes, cutting the American lead to two.

Had Faldo holed his putt on the previous green, the match would have been there for the taking. The Americans had not won three World Cups by being generous, and they gave their opponents no more chances, closing out the match on sixteen, for a 3 and 2, condemning the top Euro-pair to its second narrow defeat of the day.

Corey Pavin and Phil Mickelson (USA) v. Bernhard Langer and Per-Ulrik Johansson (EUR)

On why he did not send out his dry pairing of Woosnam and Walton instead of Langer and Johansson: *"I made an error, and it was an error because when I put the pairings in, Per-Ulrik and Bernhard were three up. I didn't foresee that they would have a stressful finishing five holes, and I didn't also foresee that they'd have such heavy rain and they would have only half an hour to be dried out and get back on the golf course."* —BERNARD GALLACHER

The Europeans had only a half-hour break between the finish of their morning match—which had gone the full eighteen in the rain—and the time they were due back on the first tee.

The weary and weather-beaten Europeans were hoping that their opponents would cold start in the wet conditions, but Corey Pavin had other ideas. Firing two great shots up onto the first green, the U.S. Open champion drained an eye-popping forty-foot birdie putt to hot-wire his side's start.

This blazing birdie opening not only helped settle Mickelson's rookie nerves but also paved the way for an opening blitz by the Americans, who were on fire in the wet conditions. Before the European players could get their game faces back on, they were four down after four.

With three birdies of his own during the round, Mickelson threw a jaw-dropping stroke into the Americans' opening offense. From the wet rough and an uphill lie, he hooked a miraculous shot around a tree trunk, ten feet in front of his ball, onto the front fringe of the green.

From such an explosive opening, the Europeans were in no condition to fight back. Johansson fared much worse than Mickelson, his former Arizona State roommate, as he covered the front nine in four over par. The experienced Langer was not any more effective, picking up on three holes in a row.

With this sort of self-destructive help from their opponents, Pavin and Mickelson had a relatively easy ride for their 6 and 4 win. Although they carded a four under par in the fourteen holes played, Langer and Johansson were buried before they had shaken off their morning hangover.

Afternoon fourball result: USA 3, EUR 1

"Not since Cornwallis has the United Kingdom's finest arsenal looked so helpless in transatlantic warfare. In Friday's drizzle turned downpour, in conditions blissfully endorsed by the men dressed in life preserver orange, the Good Ship Europe capsized like Ryders on the storm."

—JOHN HAWKINS, *Golf World*

Day one result: USA 5, EUR 3

"Riding a rookie wave that rolled inexorably across a soggy Oak Hill Country Club course, the United States Ryder Cup team opened a commanding 5–3 lead over Europe."
—*Larry Dorman,* New York Times

As well as holding the largest margin after a first day's play since 1979, Lanny Wadkins had also been able to give all his players some action and had seen his five rookies combine to give him five wins. The only rookie setback had been Faxon—and he had fallen victim to the more-experienced Jacobsen's error, while Jeff Maggert proved the cream of the new crop with two wins out of two.

Since 1979, the team ahead after day one had won only four of the eight overall matches. So the team trailing is just as likely to win the Cup as the side in the lead. But figures also show that no team since 1973 had lost after scoring five or more points on the first day. Go figure!

Day Two: Morning Foursomes

The opening-day rain was replaced by some most welcome hazy fall sunshine, but it was still unseasonably chilly.

Needing some instant inspiration to turn the match around, the European players appeared on the second morning wearing their lucky "champagne bottle green" sweaters. Decked out in their so-called celebration outfits, the visitors would prove to have more "bottle" than their rivals and were definitely very bubbly by the end of the day.

Curtis Strange and Jay Haas (USA) v. Nick Faldo and Colin Montgomerie (EUR)

Strange and Haas, like captain Wadkins, played their college golf at Wake Forest. The American partners had played three times before, twice in the 1975 Walker Cup and once in the 1983 Ryder Cup—and were 3-0 in harness.

After Montgomerie hit a peach of an opening drive, Strange found the rough underneath an overhanging tree with his. Haas could only hack into more rough, before Strange fluffed his chip into a bunker, gift-wrapping the hole to the British, who had made a flawless par.

Biting off more of the dogleg than he could chew on the 570-yard fourth, Montgomerie hit a poor shot into the trees but was fortunate to have his ball rebound out the other side onto the fairway. Faldo accepted this good fortune by knocking his 200-yard approach onto the green to set up Monty for a birdie putt that doubled their lead.

"Roars erupted like bombs all over the Oak Hill Country Club course, reverberating off the thousands of trees that frame the spectacular old Donald Ross layout."
—*Larry Dorman,*
New York Times

Jay Haas made a three-footer on five after Faldo's eight-foot par putt lipped out, and the U.S. pair had its first win of the round. Both pairs contrived to bogey the par-3 sixth, but the Europeans played seven much the better. After Haas had put his second into woods, Monty nailed his short chip to two feet for par and a two-up lead.

At the ninth, Faldo, who had left his partner with garbage duty much of the time, finally found a shot worthy of a six-time major winner. His perfectly weighted five-iron left the Scotsman with a fifteen-foot birdie putt that he did not squander. This second British birdie on the front nine put them three up, as they were out in 35 to their rivals' 38.

Neither pairing set the world on fire on the front nine. The Americans were especially ineffective on the greens, as they failed to capitalize on a number of European mistakes.

Two more bogeys halved the 429-yard tenth hole, and the par-3 eleventh was shared in pars. On twelve, Monty caught his approach fat and missed the green, then missed a six-footer for the half, as Strange holed a three-footer for par and the win.

Montgomerie made amends on the par-5 thirteenth, stroking a nine-iron to eight feet of the flag, which Faldo drilled home for birdie to reclaim their three-hole lead.

"The key hole for me was on thirteen, a ridiculously treacherous green. I asked Monty to give me a straight uphill birdie putt with his approach shot, and that's exactly what I got. It was perfect." —Nick Faldo

The Americans had their chances to cut the lead but blew shortish hole-winning putts.

Haas failed to reward Strange's tee shot into fifteen, by missing a six-footer for birdie. Strange missed a thirty-foot par putt on sixteen that signaled the end for the Americans, who finally conceded the match, going down to a very sloppy 4 and 2 defeat.

Having played fifty holes in their first three matches, the "Euro Dream Team" of Faldo and Montgomerie were a disappointing four over par for their two losses and a win.

Davis Love III and Jeff Maggert (USA) v. Sam Torrance and Costantino Rocca (EUR)

American hopes were high for a pair that had won one match together on Friday morning and won in the afternoon with different partners. With Maggert having handed the same European pair a 6 and 5 beating in the first fourball, the visitors' chances seemed bleak, but they caught the United States cold.

In the week before the Ryder Cup, Sam Torrance had won the British Masters title and displaced Colin Montgomerie from atop the Order of Merit (the European equivalent of the money list).

Having driven into the rough, Maggert and his partner were unable to get on the first green in four, and their double-bogey six was swamped as the Europeans, on in two, made a comfortable winning par.

Rocca extended the lead at the second with a left-to-right eight-foot birdie putt that caught enough of the right-hand lip to fall back into the cup, just as it looked to have rolled by. Torrance's par putt on the third was too much for another U.S. bogey.

Three down after three holes, Love holed from three feet for par and a win as Rocca missed his par putt, but the Italian had a bogey putt on five that won the hole, as the Americans found more trouble than you could shake an oversize driver at. With the U.S. pair liberally sprinkling double bogeys all over the front nine, Rocca went to the other extreme.

The undisputed highlight of Europe's fast break came at the par-3 sixth, which Rocca won from the tee. His five-iron arrowed in on the flag and jumped into the hole, and Rocca rolled his eyes and jumped into Torrance's arms.

"I asked Sam about the wind. I wanted to hit a six-iron but ended up hitting a half five-iron. It started two or three meters to the right, and it went in the cup. It was a great moment for me and my partner. It's hard to lose the hole with a one." —COSTANTINO ROCCA

"I don't know what their side did before they got out here, but they're holing shots from the tee and making a lot of putts."
—*Davis Love III*

Love tried to answer the Italian's ace, and he came mighty close by hitting his self-proclaimed "best shot of the round" to within three foot in a vain attempt at a half, as Torrance and Maggert found themselves redundant on this hole.

No one, it seemed, was overly inspired by Rocca's ace, as the Italian was forced to hole a putt on the seventh for a half in bogey fives, and the 426-yard eighth was shared in par.

The scorecards made for rather interesting reading. From the fourth through seventh holes (par 5-4-3-4), Europe went 6-5-1-5, while the United States went 5-6-2-5, as both pairs played some sublime and rather ridiculous golf.

Love's missed par putt on nine cost the Americans the hole, as Rocca again stood firm in holing his three-foot putt for the win, to go five up at the turn. The Europeans continued to play the more inspired golf, Torrance digging his ball out of a bunker alongside the tenth to leave a two-footer for the half.

After Rocca made his twelve-foot putt for birdie on twelve, Love made no mistake from half the distance for a splendid half. The taller American continued to have an up-and-down day on the greens; he missed another birdie putt on thirteen that brought an abrupt end to the match, 6 and 5.

On the Europeans' reversing their 6 and 5 loss to Maggert on the previous afternoon: "I can tell you one thing—it's a much better feeling *winning* 6 and 5."
—*Sam Torrance*

Loren Roberts and Peter Jacobsen (USA) v. Ian Woosnam and Philip Walton (EUR)

Such was the European dominance in their "lucky green sweaters" that the U.S. side was in contention in only one match at the turn—this one. Jacobsen and Roberts were the only pair standing between the Europeans and a demoralizing clean sweep of the second morning.

Roberts started off poorly, missing a par putt from five feet to drop the first hole. A British birdie followed two halves in par, as Woosnam and Walton took a two-hole jump on the Americans after the first four holes.

After the first U.S. birdie of the round cut the lead, Walton replied on the 167-yard sixth green, running in a twenty-five-foot putt for a two-hole lead, as Jacobsen missed his birdie opportunity.

Two down after six, the U.S. pair took the seventh despite visiting the rough, as Roberts, with memories of his five-foot miss on the first still fresh, slotted one home for par to win the hole. Confidence restored, Roberts lagged up from forty feet away on the eighth to level the match, with Europe not in sight of their par.

The match all square after eight, the next two holes were halved in par, as the Americans looked to build on their comeback. Jacobsen short-circuited those ideas of grandeur, firing his tee shot at eleven into a bunker, but Roberts rescued the situation, chipping out to a yard of the flag. Walton had just found the putting surface with his tee shot, but this did not worry Woosnam, who rammed home a forty-five-foot putt, across eight feet of break, for a blistering birdie and the lead.

"Woosie could use a regular putter and it would look like a broom-handled putter."
—*Lanny Wadkins*

Ian Woosnam had seemingly recovered from his midseason putting worries, when he carried two putters in his bag during the Volvo Masters—a broom handle for short putts and a standard length for longer putts. Unlike Torrance, James, and his partner Walton, the Welshman left his broom handle behind for this contest.

Having made only one birdie in the first eleven holes, the Americans soon changed all that on the next two holes. Back-to-back birdies gave the U.S. side their first lead of the day in any of the foursomes. Jacobsen nailed his nine-iron approach to five feet for Roberts's birdie at twelve, and from 140 yards out on thirteen, Jacobsen emptied an eight-iron ten feet from the flag for a one-hole lead.

Jacobsen and Walton put their second shots into bunkers on fourteen, but Roberts pulled off a great escape as he recovered to a yard for a U.S. par, while Europe took four to get up and down with three putts from eighteen feet.

Two down, Woosnam halved the U.S. lead with a brave twenty-footer after Roberts just missed his twenty-two-footer on the 184-yard fifteenth.

Both British players found rough or trees on sixteen, and Walton missed a six-footer to level the match, after Jacobsen overhit his approach through the green into heavy rough, and the Americans took three more to get down. The hole was halved in bogey fives as the pressure began to bite all four players.

Woosnam had to make a ten-footer on seventeen just for a half in par fours to set up a showdown on the final hole, with the Americans still one to the good. Jacobsen clipped a nine-iron out of the grabbing rough to ninety yards of the hole, from where Roberts—who had missed his only fairway from the tee in two days—rediscovered his accuracy by nailing a ninety-five-yard approach to within a yard of the pin.

On his crucial wedge shot into eighteen: *"The softness of the green really helped. It allowed me to play more aggressive. I was really happy to hit such a good wedge shot and nail down the match. I knew it was a crucial match, and we were fighting to get it in."* —Loren Roberts

From the snagging rough guarding the front of the green, Woosnam needed to hole his chip to save the match. He failed by only a matter of millimeters. A quivering bundle of nervous tissue and shaking muscles, Jacobsen kept his concentration and poise as he found nothing but the center of the cup for par and the win.

The American team all breathed a collective sigh of relief as this point was secured. The U.S. captain quickly realized the value of this result: "That win kept us boosted up. We used that as a very positive influence heading into the afternoon."

Trying to describe—to the media—the pressure of his final putt: "I wish I could do a Vulcan mind meld here so you can feel it. You're thinking you're going to miss the hole, you're going to drop the putter, you're going to whiff the ball, anything."
—*Peter Jacobsen*

Corey Pavin and Tom Lehman (USA) v. Bernhard Langer and David Gilford (EUR)

The quiet and unassuming Gilford let his approach shots do the talking in the first three holes. The Englishman hit an eight-iron to within a foot of the second hole for a half, then followed up with an even more impressive three-iron to a yard on the third green for the win.

With Pavin and Lehman often struggling to find the fairways from the tees, they bogeyed eight and nine. Against such a display of shoddy workmanship, the European pairing had little to do to retain a two-hole lead through eleven holes.

A few feet short of the twelfth green, Langer pushed the match beyond the Americans' grasp, as he swished a chip out of shin-deep rough and into the hole for a birdie. Pavin was left with a forty-footer for the half and could not respond in kind.

The Europeans' three-hole lead was safely protected and even built upon, as Langer and Gilford combined for a crushing 4 and 3 win over the heavily favored pair of Pavin and Lehman.

"If you hit a bad shot, you always feel Bernhard is going to be there. He's such a great chipper-and-putter."
—*David Gilford*

Morning foursomes result: USA 1, EUR 3

"If Friday's dinner went down easy for the American side, Saturday's lunch might have been served with Maalox consommé."

—Chris Millard

In the sixty-two holes played during the four morning matches, the U.S. team made only four birdies: three by Jacobsen and Roberts, and one by Love—his gimme concession after Rocca's ace.

Day Two: Afternoon Fourball

"The morning defeat gave my guys a jolt. I'd probably told them a dozen times last night to stay focused and get after them, but the Europeans were better. So I just said, 'We've had a bad morning, but we're still tied, so let's go out and put some wins on the board.' And we did it."

—LANNY WADKINS

Brad Faxon and Fred Couples (USA) v. Sam Torrance and Colin Montgomerie (EUR)

All square after five holes, Couples broke this tightly contested match open with a birdie two at six, when par would have been enough to see off the Scots' bogey.

To make the U.S. team, Brad Faxon holed a fifteen-foot putt on the last green of the PGA Championship at Riviera for a 63, assuring himself of a top five spot and enough points to finish tenth in the Ryder Cup points standings.

After the turn, Faxon showed why he had long been regarded as one of the leading lights in the U.S. PGA's "flat-iron society," when he sank a seven-foot putt to halve the tenth hole with Montgomerie's birdie, and followed that with a winning birdie putt from sixteen feet for the lead again.

After Faxon's one-two punch had left the Scottish pair reeling like an overweight drunk at a Glaswegian wake, Couples flattened the Scots with his first killer blow of the afternoon. He stapled his wedged approach to eighteen inches of the flag for a two-hole lead, but Couples still had some more hurt to lay on the Scots.

On the par-5 thirteenth, Torrance fired his pitch to seven feet front right of the hole. The ball bounced on past the hole, dug in, and spun back around the hole, coming to rest a few inches to the left. With a certain birdie, and with Couples on the front left fringe of the green in three, the Scots looked to have won the hole and staunched the flow of U.S. success. They had not reckoned on "Boom-Boom" blasting their slender hopes.

Couples chipped up the twenty-five feet across the green, past where Torrance's ball had finished, and his ball kissed the pin to drop into the hole for a half, countering the Scots' conceded birdie that they thought would win the hole. The crowd had erupted in anticipation with the ball still some way short of the hole, and the crescendo of cheers was the loudest Johnny Miller (in the NBC TV commentary box) had "ever heard in championship golf."

"When I chipped it in on thirteen, I tried to jump up and down and get everybody going [Faxon rushed over to deliver a high five]. Chipping in

to tie was a thrill I'll never forget, and I figured I might as well let the people realize it. I don't do this very often." —Fred Couples

Unable to find his true form, which had seen him ranked among the top three golfers in the world, Montgomerie narrowly missed a twenty-foot birdie putt on the sixteenth, where Faxon dropped his fourth birdie of the round. This was the final nail in the Scottish pair's coffin, as they were buried 4 and 2.

"Brad got a good win today. We'll have to scrape him off the ceiling tonight to bring him down."
—*Lanny Wadkins*

Davis Love III and Ben Crenshaw (USA) v. Ian Woosnam and Costantino Rocca (EUR)

Wadkins sent out his pair of Love and Crenshaw in an intriguing matchup. Crenshaw and Woosnam were former Masters winners, while Rocca had heavily beaten Love in the morning foursomes. Love had asked to play with Crenshaw to allow Faxon to team up with Couples.

His game well suited to the tight, long course, Rocca continued his single-handed assault on a course that had multiple majors winners begging for mercy. The thirty-eight-year-old Italian, who was enjoying his newfound starring role in the world of golf, birdied the 401-yard second to grab an early lead.

Not to be outshone, Woosnam repeated the birdie dose on the par-3 third. His tee shot landed on the extreme right of the green and ran back to the heart of the green to finish three feet in front of the flag.

"I feel a little at home around here in Rochester. There are so many Italians here shouting 'Paisan, Paisan!'"
—*Costantino Rocca*

Quite remarkably in the birdie-fest fourball format, all four players halved the next six holes, and the Europeans retained their two-hole advantage through the turn. Then—shock, horror! The Americans actually birdied a hole. Recording his side's only birdie of the round at the 429-yard tenth, Davis Love reduced the lead to one.

Spurred on by this sudden American offensive, and as if to show his opponents how easy it was to make a birdie, Rocca rolled off two in a row, at eleven and twelve.

Three down with six to play just about did in the almost impotent Americans, and Rocca's articulate approach to six feet at sixteen spelled T-H-E-E-N-D for the United States, 3 and 2.

The U.S. pair could manage only one birdie in the equivalent of thirty-two holes, as Ben Crenshaw ended his Ryder Cup career with only one win in five fourball matches (1-3-1).

On failing to make a single birdie in sixteen holes: "Making all those pars was just like a dial tone. I kept it in play, had opportunities, and nothing, just nothing."
—*Ben Crenshaw*

Jay Haas and Phil Mickelson (USA) v. Seve Ballesteros and David Gilford (EUR)

With the first and third holes halved in par, Jay Haas proved the difference between the sides as he birdied the second and fourth for a two-hole lead.

The 406-yard fifth hole, where the creek comes into play twice, is nicknamed "Double Trouble" and is acknowledged as the hardest hole on the course by the Oak Hill regulars. Here the Europeans found themselves in plenty of trouble. Gilford's second shot plugged in the creek, and Seve's chip came up short of hole, but Seve somehow scrabbled his par for a half. The Spaniard again made a fighting par on the par-3 sixth, from six feet, which Mickelson covered from four feet for another half.

Fighting for their lives, Europe needed Ballesteros to make another ten-footer for his half in par on seven. Having unexpectedly jelled so well the previous afternoon, Ballesteros and Gilford came up empty for Gallacher the second time. Despite his hole-saving exploits, the Spaniard found only three fairways on nine outward holes.

Putting like a demon, Mickelson parred the first ten holes, then drained a sweet-looking thirty-foot birdie putt at the 192-yard eleventh. This put the U.S. players three up—a lead they enjoyed all the way to the fifteenth.

On his partner's thirty-foot birdie putt on eleven: *"It was quick and there was not as much break as there looked, and Phil poured it in like Vermont maple syrup."* —JAY HAAS

"Seve's game is simply just awful. I am amazed that he's even playing."
—*David Leadbetter*

Seve's tee shot was unerringly attracted to the pond on the right of the green, as though it had been specially placed there for him. Gilford's tee shot landed twenty-five feet from the flag, but he was unable to make the birdie. With a chance to seal the match, Haas also missed a birdie putt from twelve feet that brutally lipped out, for a half in par.

The only player on sixteen in two, Gilford missed a twenty-two-foot birdie putt to win the hole, but Haas chipped up to a yard and holed the match-winning putt for a 3 and 2 triumph.

Unable to make a birdie between them in sixteen holes, the European pair could not find the same magic from the previous day. Ballesteros obviously missed the company of his regular partner, Jose Maria Olazabal.

Corey Pavin and Loren Roberts (USA) v. Nick Faldo and Bernhard Langer (EUR)

This last fourball out came down to a knock-'em-down-and-drag-'em-out dogfight that ranks among the finest ever played in Ryder Cup history.

Setting the scene for the match, Pavin led off with a first-hole birdie—from fifty feet—having drained a forty-footer earlier at the first hole.

When both Europeans caved in with bogeys on the seventh, the Americans held a two-hole lead. Langer finally got the visitors' game into gear, making a ten-footer at nine after both Americans missed the green and made bogey. One up at the turn, it was the Americans' turn to card hole-losing bogeys on the 429-yard tenth. The match had leveled up with the players heading for home.

Pavin had already beaten Faldo in the opening foursomes match, and had also defeated the Englishman in the final of the 1993 World Matchplay at Wentworth.

Knowing that his captain was looking for an American to stand up and be counted, 5′9″ Pavin knew he would not win any high-jump contests, but he answered his captain's clarion call and rose above those around him. His seven-foot birdie at twelve reinstated the U.S. lead and set the match up for an ending of epic proportions.

On the longest hole of the course, the 598-yard thirteenth, Pavin played a marvelous third shot from the right-hand fringe of the fairway to pin-high, fifteen feet right of the flag. Into the sun, Faldo answered with a third shot that almost pitched into the hole but spun back five feet to leave a welcoming uphill putt for his birdie. Pavin was unlucky with his birdie putt, the ball running right around the lip and heading off back the way it had come. To add salt to Pavin's wounds, Faldo solidly stroked home his five-footer for birdie to level the match again.

On Corey Pavin's trademark technique: "A swing that looks like a woodchopper's and length that wouldn't pass the longest hitters on the LPGA. . . . That warm-up move he does, where it looks like he's starting a lawn mower with his right hand, is designed to keep him from coming over the top."
—*Tim Rosaforte,* Heartbreak Hill

With six holes to play, this match had truly come alive, but the next four holes were halved, neither team feeling it could afford to make a slip. Pavin missed the best chance to snatch a lead when he let a six-foot birdie putt get away on the short fifteenth. Faldo made the half with a three-footer, despite a joker in the gallery yelling "Miss it!" on his downstroke.

The par-4 sixteenth saw Faldo miss a chance to make a hole-winning birdie from seven feet, and it was left to the pumped-up Pavin to play a miracle recovery from the trees to make a half from five feet.

With Faldo in a bunker on seventeen, Langer's putt for the win veered away from the hole at the death. Another lofted recovery from the rough alongside the green gave Pavin a putt to halve the hole, again from five feet away.

"Nick hit a good drive on seventeen. I got on eighteen and said, 'OK, Loren, hit it in the fairway.' But I forgot to do it myself."
—*Corey Pavin*

All square on eighteen, Faldo, from the middle of the fairway, hit an impressive approach to within five generous paces of the flag. Langer had found rough with his second shot, but he chipped his third up to six feet of the final hole, standing in a deep swath of rough some 190 yards away. Pavin was faced with an almost impossible approach of his own from a terrible-looking lie, but the ball was sitting up nicely, albeit some inches below his feet.

Without a three in his bag, Pavin drew a four-iron out and threw all 150 pounds into his ball, sending it flying at the flag. It landed ten feet from the hole but had no way of slowing up until it nestled in the fringe at the right-hand back side of the green—eighteen feet away.

"The chip? I paced it off, because I didn't know if Nick was farther away or me, so I was eighteen feet. It was six paces exactly." —COREY PAVIN

After Pavin's wonder shot, Roberts's approach from the fairway swung left of the hole fifty feet away. Playing first, Roberts rolled his birdie putt up to the hole for a par, allowing Pavin to attack the hole with his treacherous downhill chip.

"I had the luxury of being able to have a free run of the chip, because Loren hit a magnificent putt and I knew he was going to make par, so I had a free run at the chip. I didn't care if it went ten feet past. It looked like it might pop out of the hole for a second, but it sank right down to the bottom." —COREY PAVIN

"When Pavin's chip danced around the rim of the cup and finally fell in like the salt on a margarita glass, it put the United States into an intoxicating position."
—*Larry Dorman,* New York Times

The crowd's roar that started as the ball hit the back of the hole, leapt up, and suddenly dropped into the hole more than matched the one that Couples had elicited earlier with his crucial chip-in on thirteen.

The U.S. side could now do no worse than halve the match, as Langer had already taken three and Faldo still had his fifteen-footer for birdie. Once he had waited for the cheers to quiet down, Faldo surveyed his line from all angles, but for all his preparation he misread the line by inches, and the ball sailed past the hole by some distance.

The United States had not only won this final match of the second day but also extended their overall lead to two points.

In his three paired wins, Corey Pavin had partnered three different teammates: Mickelson, Lehman, and Roberts. "If his fellow Americans don't win Sunday, they can blame only themselves and leave Corey Pavin out of the team picture," wrote Bob Verdi of the *Chicago Tribune*.

Afternoon fourball result: USA *3,* EUR *1*
Day two result: USA *4,* EUR *4*
Overall match score: USA *9,* EUR *7*

On the U.S. team's first lead going into the singles since 1981: *"Yeah, I'm real confident. I have twelve guys playing well, but this is golf. And a two-point lead is not big enough. The last two days, there were matches I thought we were dead cinches to win and we ended up losing, and that's golf."* —Lanny Wadkins

Wadkins's rookies had played a part in all but one U.S. win in the first two days, combining for a debut record of 9-3.

Two of the top European players had very different views of how the final day would pan out. Said Nick Faldo, "Nobody was down. In a way, it's a good position to come from. Nobody can muck about." Ian Woosnam wasn't as optimistic: "Phone it in, mates. It's time to catch the Concorde home."

Day Three: Singles

The U.S. team came into the singles with not only a two-point lead but also a clear superiority over their rivals on the final day. In the previous six meetings, the United States had won 39½ points on the final day to 32½ for the Europeans. The only problem for the Americans was that only two of their number had won more than two singles matches—Crenshaw and Strange (both would lose on this fateful Sunday). The combined record of the whole U.S. team in the singles was 7-7-1.

Observers felt that the captains were a little tight coming into the final day: *"Lanny's so wound up, he's about 130 compression. I don't even think they make 130-compression balls, but if he were a Titleist, he'd be 130 compression."* —PETER JACOBSEN

"Gallacher had nothing to lose, so he gambled when he made the final pairings. The man who is wound tighter than a 100-compression golf ball chose inspiration over fairways, emotion over birdie putts. He put a struggling Ballesteros in the leadoff spot in singles where he would meet Lehman." —MARK MCCORMACK, *World of Professional Golf* (1996)

Tom Lehman (USA) v. Seve Ballesteros (EUR)

Knowing Wadkins would lead off with one of his trump cards, Gallacher took a calculated gamble in sending Seve out first. Although Tom Lehman was a Ryder Cup rookie facing a seven-time legend, this contest, from an American point of view, was a fairly futile matchup. Wadkins would have preferred to have had Lehman taking on one of Europe's in-form players.

Knowing that Ballesteros had been firing off the tees like a loose cannon on a sinking Spanish galleon, the European captain hardly gave him the most positive pep talk: *"I am sending you out first in the singles because you cannot lose us the Ryder Cup in that position."*
—BERNARD GALLACHER

Gallacher's worst fears were immediately confirmed when Ballesteros dispatched his opening drive deep in the woods on the left, found an unplayable lie, and took a drop to bogey the first hole against Lehman's winning par. On the second hole, the swashbuckling Spaniard went from pauper to prince. A second sorry tee shot was followed by an equally bad approach short of the green and behind a bunker, from where Seve deftly guided his chip into the hole, to improbably level the match.

Lehman was forced to hole out from two feet for a half on the 202-yard third hole, as the Spaniard tried all his tricks to keep competitive.

Almost losing his ball with another misdirected drive at the fourth, Ballesteros twice visited the rough, hit a tree, and still emerged with a half after Lehman failed to take advantage.

The Spaniard made an even more improbable par on the fifth, after driving the wrong side of the creek, and he had to hole from eight feet for a half on seven, having missed the fairway again. Up to now, Lehman had barely been off the straight and narrow.

On the fifth: *"Seve's hooked drive had put him perhaps fifty yards off the fairway, which on yesterday's form was pretty good going. . . . He hit a nine-iron out of the swamp, over the towering willows and on to the green 150 yards away, almost bringing down the television airship on the way to making his par [with two putts from seventy feet]."*

—Richard Williams, *London Guardian*

Seve's luck ran out on eight, where he drove into a bunker and his bogey was beaten by another workmanlike par from Lehman for a one-hole lead. On nine, Seve's drive found a footpath and his second flew across the fairway, but he still halved the hole.

On the outward nine, Seve did not hit a single fairway, while Lehman hardly hit a bad shot. Despite this disparity in shot-making, the American remarkably reached the turn only one hole up. Seve finally hit his first fairway off the tee on the tenth, and the gallery broke out into spontaneous applause.

"I only played in three matches, and I hit three fairways the whole week, but I cleared out a lot of rough and all the branches on the golf course. I'm sure the members of Oak Hill aren't going to lose any balls anymore. . . . My biggest contribution was to get the team colors for Sunday changed from green to my lucky blue."

—*Seve Ballesteros*

After missing a seven-foot birdie putt on ten, Lehman went two up when Ballesteros missed his par putt on eleven. On the 372-yard twelfth, Lehman lagged up from seventeen feet away and tapped in, but he was totally bemused when Seve asked him to replace his ball and mark his six-inch gimme. The match official (who must have cursed when he drew Ballesteros in this match) defused a potentially high-explosive situation by loudly explaining that Seve had every right under match-play rules to ask his opponent to mark his ball, since Lehman had putted out of turn. Seve purportedly wanted to aim at Lehman's marker. Whatever the reason, he missed his fifteen-foot birdie putt, and both players amicably agreed on another half in par.

On the Spaniard's increasingly desperate gamesmanship: *"I felt that if I could play steady golf, it would eventually get him."* —Tom Lehman

The Spaniard again traversed the fairway with a couple of wild shots, visited a greenside bunker, and lost the thirteenth hole to Lehman's straight-up par. Another fairway-free drive from Seve, on fourteen, meant Lehman's birdie three put him dormie four.

Despite the plethora of wayward shots, Seve carded only four bogeys, while Lehman had a bogey-free round: *"Seve kept the club face shut at the top of the backswing; as a result, the ball was liable to go anywhere. And it generally did. I find it hard to believe that he took me to the fifteenth. If any other player in the world had been playing Seve's second shots, I would have beaten him 8 and 7. "* —TOM LEHMAN

Lehman found the heart of the fifteenth green, while Ballesteros drove way over it but chipped back on and made his par putt. Lehman lagged up to a yard before sinking his par putt for the overall win, 4 and 3. This first point from the singles put the United States three points up.

In eight singles matches, Ballesteros managed to win only twice (against Wayne Levi in 1991 and Curtis Strange in 1987). This would probably prove to be the Spaniard's last Ryder Cup outing as a player, and he ended with a record of 20-12-5, and a total of 22½ points (bettered only by Faldo, Casper, and Palmer).

Peter Jacobsen (USA) v. Howard Clark (EUR)

On Howard Clark's first match since his opening-morning foursomes loss: *"With five previous appearances and a 6–8–1 record, Clark was no stranger to the Ryder Cup competition; he was just a stranger to this Ryder Cup competition."*

—BILL BRINK, *New York Times*

On the second hole, Jacobsen had left himself a four-footer for par, with his opponent still off the green in three. The American could only watch as Clark (emulating Ballesteros ahead of him) holed his fifteen-foot chip shot from the rough for par. Jacobsen was forced to hole his short putt for a half, and thus the match progressed. Whatever Jacobsen threw at Clark, the Englishman not only coped with but, more often than not, topped.

After Clark pulled back level four times: "Every time I knocked, he answered."
—*Peter Jacobsen*

Although Clark holed another short chip, Jacobsen fought back to be level at the turn, and he took a lead on a twelve-foot birdie putt at the tenth. Just as it looked as if Clark's early bubble had burst, he struck back on eleven in the best way possible.

The forty-one-year-old Clark hit what he thought was a poor six-iron—his body English revealing obvious disgust—but dismay quickly turned to joy as he glanced up to see the ball bounce twice and skip straight into the cup. In the true spirit of this event, Jacobsen was the first person to congratulate Clark, wrapping his arms around him. This stroke of English luck leveled the match and gave Clark the kick-start-in-the-pants that he needed.

Despite his apparent annoyance with his tee shot on eleven: "The ace set the day for me. I really hadn't hit a good six-iron all week, and that was just about the sweetest shot I hit in my life. It was a straight shot. I knew I had 184 yards in the air and five yards of roll and there was no wind." —Howard Clark

This was the fourth hole-in-one in the Ryder Cup: Butler ('73), Faldo ('93), Rocca ('95), and Clark—none by Americans.

The score stayed level for the next four holes, as neither player dared make a mistake—the added pressure of going out early playing on their minds.

On sixteen, Clark made the decisive move, leaving his recovery from a greenside bunker within twelve inches of the hole for par. Jacobsen safely found the green in two, sixty feet from the flag, but he took three putts to get down, losing the hole and—at a vital time—the lead for the first time.

Jacobsen's third shot to seventeen was a twelve-foot chip, from two inches off the green, to eight inches off the hole for a conceded par. After the longest drive of the week at this long par-4 hole, Clark had pulled his second shot to the left of the green before chipping up to three feet, from where he holed for par to retain his one-hole lead.

From the extreme right-hand side of the final fairway, Clark flew his second shot onto the putting surface some way from the flag but safely over the rough in front of the green. From the middle of the fairway, Jacobsen hit a pitch at the flag, but it came up thirty feet short on the front of the green. Clark putted up from all of fifty feet away and saw his ball roll tantalizingly four feet above the hole.

With the chance of a half, Jacobsen started his thirty-footer out to the left of the hole, and it looked as if it would stay out there until it started to cave in as the hole got closer. Just as the ball looked certain to drop in, it brushed past the left-hand lip and ran on by fifteen inches.

Conceding Jacobsen's unlucky leave, Clark was faced with a ticklish putt back downhill to win the match. Taking as little time as he could afford—to prevent his nerves from rising up in a neural chorus line to dance to the silent beat of tension—Clark carefully stroked the ball home for an excellent win and an invaluable point for his team. A one-hole European victory . . . courtesy of the ace on eleven.

"It was like 1987 for me. I only played in the foursomes on the opening day at Muirfield Village, then came out and won my singles."
—*Howard Clark*

Jeff Maggert (USA) v. Mark James (EUR)

The Englishman opened with some inconsistent golf: he holed a twenty-foot putt on the second for a birdie, but at the 570-yard fourth, his third shot found the sweeping bunker on the right of the green. With Maggert waiting to shoot a nine-foot birdie putt, James scampered his ball out of the sand, over the bank, through two cuts of rough, and down the short stretch of green into the hole for his second birdie. When Maggert finally pulled the trigger on his putt, all he had in the barrel was a blank, his ball missing the target.

Under duress and two down, Maggert found it hard going and badly hooked his approach into the stream alongside the fifth green to drop three down.

"In match play, it helps when you get a gift, and after the hole-out from the bunker, Mark just never messed up. I was three down early, and I never had a chance to close the gap." —JEFF MAGGERT

James had further birdies at six and eight. The American offset these and more with life-preserving birdies of his own at seven and eleven—but these strikes proved his only successes of the round.

With his lead dwindling to one, James drew on his vast reserves of experience and cunning, putting the game away with three more birdies. Maggert drowned any hopes of a comeback by leaking his tee shot into the pond at the par-3 fifteenth. Although he recovered for a fighting bogey, he was dried out by James's four-foot par putt for the match, 4 and 3.

Fred Couples (USA) v. Ian Woosnam (EUR)

The halved encounter between these two players in 1993 was the only time Ian Woosnam had not lost a singles match in six previous outings.

The same pair had halved their singles match two years earlier at The Belfry, and this wouldn't be the last time they met on the final day.

Couples started well-OK-badly-badly-badly. An opening par won him the first hole, the 401-yard second was halved, then Boom-Boom went Plop-Plop-Plop—three-putting the next three greens. Woosnam had hardly warmed up before he was two up.

The misfiring American quickly got back in sync with his game and won the next two holes to stand level after seven. Woosnam finally warmed up and let fly with a double strike: a birdie on eight, before curling in a sixteen-footer on the next hole for another birdie to go back two up.

The Welshman gave a hole back with a bogey on eleven, but Couples spurned a seven-footer on the 372-yard twelfth to level. Halving the next four holes brought some semblance of order to a game that neither player could control.

Every course has a pivotal hole. Oak Hill's was the par-4, dogleg-right seventeenth, and all 458 yards lived up to its reputation of being a killer stretch of real estate. With Woosnam safely down the fairway, Couples lived up to his reputation and boom-boomed his drive fifty yards past his opponent. He followed his 300-plus-yard drive in equally aggressive style with a 150-yard eight-iron to eighteen feet of the flag. Woosnam had no reply to this titanic show of strength, and Couples, as cool as an iceberg, calmly collected the first birdie of the week at seventeen to level the score.

On the final hole, Woosnam put his tee shot into the deep rough off the right of the fairway, a few inches short of a bunker. His second shot flew to the back of the green, coming to rest eighteen feet from the flag, giving him an excellent chance of a birdie. Meanwhile, the adrenaline-rushed American had run his drive through the dogleg and into the rough beyond, guided his second shot through some fir trees into a bunker waiting at the front of the green, and blasted out four feet past the hole.

With an opportunity to win the match, Woosnam saw his tricky six-yard downhill birdie putt meet the same fate as Jacobsen's two matches earlier, his ball drifting unerringly toward the center of the cup, only to squirt by the lip. The emotional Welshman fell to his knees, burying his head in his hands as he saw the winning putt get away from him. He could only console himself with the thought that Couples also had a difficult downhill putt for his par and the half.

"I couldn't have hit a better putt. I thought I got it. I was just concentrating on the pace, because I knew Freddie had a tricky putt."

—Ian Woosnam

The American's nerve held firm, he made no mistake, and both players had to settle for a half on the hole and in their match—for the second time in two years.

As Woosnam slumped to his seventh singles match without a win, Couples more than repaid his captain's faith with a 2-1-1 record as a wild-card pick.

This was the only match of the twenty-eight that was halved in the three days.

Although this had been the fourth match out, it was the seventh match to finish, and it ensured that the United States held a lead, 11½-9½, proving just how important half-points were to both sides.

Davis Love III (USA) v. Costantino Rocca (EUR)

As with the match ahead of them, this was another repeat from the 1993 singles, which Love had won to regain the Ryder Cup for the United States. The two players had also met twice on Saturday in the pairs formats, with Rocca gaining double revenge.

"I was more nervous today than last time. I felt that Lanny was leaning on me and counting on me."
—*Davis Love III*

The American started this one rather messily, squirting his opening drive far enough into the rough to need a pitch-out, just recovering for a half in par, but then bogeying the second to go one down. Love was trying too hard too soon to fulfill his captain's wishes.

Winning the 406-yard fifth, Love leveled the match and steadied his nerves. With the match still even after six holes, the thirty-one-year-old American knocked in four unanswered birdies in the next five holes, with only the 419-yard ninth holding out on its own for an American par.

Four down, Rocca played as if he had burned himself out with his sterling efforts on the first two days. He managed to pull one hole back after fifteen, but holes were running out fast.

On sixteen, Rocca nailed his approach to three feet to further lift his hopes of a late charge, only to see Love plant his second shot a couple of feet farther away. With the confidence of a man ranked number two on the PGA Tour in putting, Love holed his longer putt for his sixth birdie to close out the lackluster Italian, 3 and 2.

The United States looked set to retain the Ryder Cup with ease after Love's win. They held an 11-8 advantage—but Europe proved they were not going to be counted out.

Brad Faxon (USA) v. David Gilford (EUR)

Two of the quieter men from either side squared off in a match that began quietly, proceeded quietly, but ended with a mighty crescendo.

The match was all square after the first thirteen holes, and neither player was ever ahead by more than one hole. Gilford scraped a par at fourteen and edged into a crucial lead. On fifteen, the Englishman faced a very tricky seven-foot putt for his par, which he made with a solid strike, retaining his one-hole lead. Sixteen was halved, and Gilford was forced to make another clutch par putt on seventeen, his five-footer keeping him one up with the last to play.

With the overall match score as close as their game score, both players showed the obvious signs of stress and strain as they played the final nerve-racking hole. Having found the middle of the fairway with his drive, Gilford overhit a career-bad four-wood at the green, which took off, hooked left, and crash-landed under a spectators' stand. With a chance to win the hole for an invaluable half, Faxon's second hung in the wind and dropped short of the green in the sand. Gilford took a free drop, then scuttled his chip out of the dense rough, failing to reach the putting surface and leaving him an even harder shot.

Brad Faxon managed only one birdie in eighteen holes. His two at the 167-yard sixth was offset by Gilford. This birdieless golf would return to haunt Faxon in the 1997 Ryder Cup.

Faxon had a great chance to win the hole, and he almost won it outright: his sandblast skimmed past the pin but ran on six feet past the finishing post, leaving a putt to level the match. Gilford looked at his slippery downhill chip and landed the ball exactly where he wanted—on the short fringe of the green—but the ball took an unexpected and unkind leap forward, running nine feet past the hole. The only saving grace for Gilford was that he had left himself an uphill putt. The Englishman not only holed his nine-footer for bogey but made it look so easy that he almost seemed embarrassed as he picked his ball out of the cup. This stunning recovery under pressure put more than enough doubt into Faxon's mind to worry him over his shorter putt.

"If you lose a tournament, as time goes by you feel better. With this, you feel worse. It's hard to take. . . . After he hit his second shot, I really thought I was going to win the hole." —Brad Faxon

With the chance to win the hole and sneak a priceless half in the match, what Faxon did next was to become enshrined in a "Kodak moment" in the most negative sense of the phrase.

The master putter pushed his putt to the right of hole, and the image of a golfer, eyes closed in total anguish, graced the cover of the book *Heartbreak Hill*—forever reminding Faxon of his fate. Gilford's win tied the score at 11½. Europe needed just three points to win the Cup, the United States a half-point less to retain.

The biggest surprise of the week on either side was the performance of shy and retiring David Gilford. In four starts he won three times, and the only American with more points than Gilford was Corey Pavin, with four points from five matches.

Ben Crenshaw (USA) v. Colin Montgomerie (EUR)

Although he was easily Europe's top-ranked player, Montgomerie still felt he had a lot to prove to the American golfing public, since he had not garnered the respect he felt he deserved after his play-off loss in the PGA Championship. An equally determined Ben Crenshaw was staring at an 0–2 record after the first two days and, in all honesty, never looked like opening his account.

In a game that was too close to call on the front nine, Montgomerie held a slim advantage after ten holes. Crenshaw managed to level but missed his ten-foot birdie putt after the Scot birdied fourteen with a precipitous sixty-footer. Like a B-movie gargantua sucking on glowing radioactive waste, Montgomerie grew in stature and confidence after his monster putt and lumbered on to card four threes in a row.

After halving the 184-yard fifteenth in par, Montgomerie planted his second shot four feet beyond the sixteenth flag, the ball obediently stopping on the same spot it landed on. Once the Scot made birdie to stand dormie two, Crenshaw knew he was in deep trouble with the nightmarish seventeenth to follow.

This was Crenshaw's eighth loss in a dozen Ryder Cup starts, and he failed to make a birdie all day. "I have never been wrung out like that before."
—*Ben Crenshaw*

With the win firmly within his grasp, Montgomerie played the hole as well as anyone all week, his approach pulling up six feet from the flag for only the second birdie at seventeen of the contest. Crenshaw hung his head as Montgomerie hung a 3 and 1 loss around the Texan's neck.

Curtis Strange (USA) v. Nick Faldo (EUR)

The players all square after four opening pars each, Faldo was forced to hole an unfriendly five-footer to halve the fifth in another par.

Faldo set a record by playing in his forty-first Ryder Cup match, while Strange's overall playing record was a poor 6–11–2.

Slightly miscuing his tee shot, Strange left himself a twenty-foot chip from just off the sixth green, with a nasty bank and slope between him and the flag. Judging the weight and line perfectly, he barely lifted the ball into the air, landed it on the brow of the bank, and let it curl down the slope into the center of the cup—to go one up.

Faldo immediately hit back to take the seventh hole in par, and the match stayed level until Strange's ten-foot birdie putt dropped at the par-3 eleventh. The American had the narrow lead back and set about repaying Wadkins's faith in picking him as a wild carder, keeping Faldo at bay for the next four holes.

One up and in touching distance of closing out a player he long admired, Strange proceeded to play the worst three-hole stretch of his career. He mishit his approach to sixteen and missed a four-foot par putt, Faldo also missing a ten-foot par putt—for an unhappy half in bogey fives.

The next hole was almost a reenactment, as Strange hit another woeful approach shot into the crowd that was greeted with an echoing "Fore right!" From 180 yards out, Faldo also played a poor second into a front left bunker. With his ball fifteen inches above his feet in the heavy rough, Strange played an almighty recovery, over a bunker, to eight feet. Faldo scooped his ball out of the sand, deliberately leaving his ball below the hole seven feet shy of the pin—on exactly the same line as Strange's putt.

The American generously allowed for a right-hand break that never came, and he took another bogey five square on the chin. Having seen that Strange's putt did not drift off the straight, Faldo hit his putt directly at and into the cup to level the match. For the first time on the final day, the Europeans were in, with a definite chance of snatching their second win on American soil.

If Strange was struggling with his inner doubts, this was also a time for the Englishman to exorcise his personal demons. In the previous two days, Faldo had twice reached the eighteenth hole level, only to lose both matches.

This reunion of the 1988 U.S. Open play-off at Brookline, which Strange won, was accurately described by NBC TV's Johnny Miller as "like watching two glaciers at work."

Off the final tee, Strange held a clear advantage. Faldo hooked his tee shot into the right-hand ankle-deep rough and decided to lay up ninety-five yards short of the flag, his ball running off the fairway into the light rough. With a much longer drive up the fairway, Strange hit a terrible three-iron, snagging the nasty rough short of the green—even worse, it was on the steep slope up to the raised green.

Faldo produced the sort of golf shot that is worthy of winning major titles, wedging up to within four feet of the flag. Inspired by the supreme effort of his distinguished rival, Strange lifted his chip shot out of the entangling rough and laid the ball six feet from the flag. With his putt first, Strange knew his reputation as a wild-card choice was firmly on the line—make it and he would have fully justified his controversial inclusion.

Alas, if golf games were fairy tales, putters would be magic wands and caddies would be fairy godmothers.

Strange's putt was something out of a Grimms' fairy tale—pushed hard at the hole, it caught the right-hand lip but never dropped. Faldo was so overcome with nerves that he closed his eyes during Strange's putt. The crowd's collective disappointment told him that there was a chance of a "happy ever after" for him.

Having played one of the shots of the week to arrive on the green, Faldo was not about to waste such a stroke and managed to calm his nerves enough to stroke the ball home for a sensational come-from-behind win.

"That was the greatest scrambling par of my life. It was as good as Muirfield in '87. Actually, it was tougher, because if I miss, it goes four feet past and I have to start negotiating with Curtis." —NICK FALDO

Not only did this win give Europe another vital point (13½ points and the lead for the first time in three days), but it elevated Faldo to the winningest European player in Ryder Cup history—with 21 victories and 23 points. For Strange, there was nothing to look forward to except private anguish and very public recrimination.

"What do you want to know? Bogey, bogey, bogey. The press can't beat me up more than I'll beat myself up. That's what happens under a great deal of pressure. Your swing doesn't hold up. I was escaping with Band-Aids on my swing. . . . These are the same swing problems I've fought for years, and I'm not sure how much longer I'm going to fight it. . . . I can't believe we lost, to be perfectly honest. All I've got to do is make four and we win. It's a frightening thought how I'm going to feel when I wake up and realize we didn't win and eleven guys played their heart out and I didn't." —CURTIS STRANGE

"When Strange got to the hardest miles—the three last holes against Europe's finest, Faldo, with the Cup on the line—he staged his own Heimlich festival, making three straight bogeys when one measly par would've been enough. It was Bill Buckner letting three straight balls through his legs. It was Jackie Smith dropping three straight in the end zone." —RICK REILLY, *Sports Illustrated*

Loren Roberts (USA) v. Sam Torrance (EUR)

Sam Torrance entered this match with an abysmal Ryder Cup record of 6-15-6, and his singles form was even worse. His only solo success had been his triumphant Cup-winning defeat of Andy North in 1985. Roberts came into this match with three wins out of three in his rookie start and must have liked his chances of going 4-0 first time up.

The Scot started the better and held an early lead after four holes, but on the next hole, Roberts's game went from the ridiculous to the sublime. He put his second into a water hazard, dropped out, then sent his fourth shot to a few feet in front of the flag, where it bounded a few feet past, only to spin back, stop on the lip, and finally drop in. Not only was this good enough for a par four, but it leveled the match.

Having worked his way into a two-hole advantage, Torrance fired his tee shot to four feet of the eleventh hole for a two, but Roberts matched this with an equally excellent birdie. After Roberts had cut the lead to one, he left his approach short at sixteen, coming to rest on the lip of a bunker at the front right of the green. Torrance's reply landed two feet behind the flag and rolled around, stopping six feet away. The Scot holed his sneaky swinging six-footer for birdie to go dormie two up on the American.

On in two at the "untamable" seventeenth, Torrance had two putts from thirty feet to win the match, and he lagged his putt just past the hole. That was close enough for Roberts to concede the match, 2 and 1.

In Roberts's only Cup appearance, this was his first loss (3–1–0) in four matches.

Corey Pavin (USA) v. Bernhard Langer (EUR)

After Pavin's heroics of the previous two days, it was going to take a bravura performance from Langer to thwart the American. Coming into the match on a roll, Pavin continued by rolling in a couple of birdies in the first four holes, but Langer dug in and halved the lead after six.

The American was not to be denied, and he slotted home an eighteen-footer on the 426-yard eighth to go two up. Once again, Langer fought back to cut the lead, but Pavin was two up again after twelve. The German was playing tough, but he could not haul his opponent back to level.

Pavin dropped the killer blow on thirteen, a remarkable ninety-degree putt that traversed an eight-foot quadrant into the cup for birdie. The American dropped his putter in disbelief and joy at his shot and his three-hole lead: he had finally broken Langer.

The German did not go down without a fight. His twenty-foot birdie putt came up just two feet short of the sixteenth hole, bringing an end to the match, 3 and 2.

Jay Haas (USA) v. Philip Walton (EUR)

Gallacher took a massive gamble and placed his two rookies out last: "I saw the players from three to eight as the main part of the team, but I had a job trying to convince myself that Philip and Per-Ulrik wouldn't have too much pressure on them."

Walton won back-to-back holes to start with and took an immediate two-hole lead.

On thirty-three-year-old Philip Walton's rekindling a sputtering playing career when he switched to the broom-handle putter: "Walton. . . . an Irishman who spoke softly but carried a big stick."
—*Gary Van Sickle*

Haas quickly realized that he would have to weave his own magic, and he produced a winning spell to pull back level after six holes. The American soon ran out of momentum, however, and the Irishman reeled off three wins as they approached the par-3 fifteenth hole.

"I figured I was in a key match around the eleventh or twelfth hole. I had a feeling. There were a lot of people around the green."

—PHILIP WALTON

Walton left his six-iron tee shot pin-high within four feet for a birdie two and a seemingly impregnable three-hole lead with three to play. But a seemingly impregnable lead cannot be guarded against acts of God or freaks of nature, and Haas resorted to a freak shot from a bunker adjacent to the fifteenth green. With Walton three feet from the flag with a par putt to win the match, Haas chopped his sandblast out and watched as the ball flew up, bounced a foot in front of the flag, hit the pin hard, and dropped into the hole. The ball would have disappeared off the other side of the green save for the pin's intervention.

On his anonymity in the United States: "Maybe the Americans know me now. Tell 'em I'm related to all those Waltons on that TV show."
—*Philip Walton*

This gave the American an audacious birdie to win the hole and deprive Walton of a par putt for the match—one that would have also won the Ryder Cup.

On seventeen, both players missed the fairway and left their drives behind trees. Haas played his second successive magical recovery; his ball fought its way through the rough at the front of the putting surface and kept rolling up the green to within ten feet of the flag. Walton, laid up forty yards short of the green, produced a stunning bump-and run through the rough at the front of the green to get within four feet of the hole.

Haas had his ten-footer to win the hole, but his ball just drifted by the left of the cup. After being cruelly denied on the previous hole, Walton got another chance for a par putt to win the match and the Cup, but his putt caught the left-hand lip and spun out.

Having won the last two holes, Haas and the United States were still alive.

Beneficiary of a miracle on sixteen and some magic on seventeen, Haas now needed the most perfect drive of his life. What he got was a dreadful, short hook into a hellish position. But it was a good lie, behind a tree in the left-hand rough among the gallery.

On Haas's wayward drive on eighteen: *"It was 3:02 P.M., and Haas had hit it in a spot only Seve Ballesteros and the club's 15-handicappers had seen. It was deep in the trees."*

—Tim Rosaforte, *Heartbreak Hill*

A very nervous-looking Walton barely managed to hit a better reply, badly leaking his ball into the ankle-high rough on the right. Haas made as good a recovery as he could in the circumstances, other than the fact that he needed to win the hole. Walton, faced with 200 yards to the flag, took a five-wood from a sunken lie, managing to fire his ball to the front of the green and find the rough that fronted it like an unkempt beard.

"I really didn't think he could get up and down. It would've been hard enough during a Tuesday practice round. I just wanted to get mine within ten feet and have a try at it." —Jay Haas

Haas launched his approach to the green and watched in despair as it spun back viciously to the very front fringe of the green. From eight feet down the bank, Walton stabbed his wedge at his ball, which had barely enough impetus to reach the top of the bank and roll toward the hole, fortuitously finishing ten feet short. Haas was unable to hole his forty-foot chip, knocking it wide and eight feet past the hole.

With two putts from ten feet to win his match and the Ryder Cup, Walton nervously trickled his putt twelve inches by the hole. Haas conceded, and the match was over. Europe, with 14½ points, had regained the Ryder Cup from a most unlikely source.

On his knee-clanking putt on the final green: "I thought it was somebody else's legs."
—*Philip Walton*

"Irish eyes are crying. . . . Philip Walton has won it for Europe."
—DICK ENBERG, NBC TV

Bernard Gallacher jumped for joy as he hopped and skipped onto the green to congratulate Walton, while Lanny Wadkins could only shake his head in total disbelief.

Phil Mickelson (USA) v. Per-Ulrik Johansson (EUR)

This was a clash of former Arizona State University roommates from the 1990 NCAA championship team, and the only twenty-somethings on either side. Twenty-five-year-old Mickelson and twenty-eight-year-old Per-Ulrik Johansson made up one of the youngest-ever singles matches in the Ryder Cup. Mickelson was 2-0 in his fourballs, while the Swede had a win and a loss to his name.

The American's plea to his captain to go out last as the anchorman seemed to have backfired after the first few holes, as the Swede made four birdies in five holes on the front nine. With wins on five and eight, Johansson took a two-hole lead over the left-hander.

Over his walkie-talkie linkup: "Tell Mickelson he better win that damn match or I'm gonna kick his butt . . . and tell him I said that!"
—*Lanny Wadkins*

With the news that his side was faltering and his captain was threatening, Mickelson fired three birdies in a row from the tenth to put himself one up.

"At the turn, I looked at the board and saw the Europeans were beating us in almost every match. We needed to do something to turn around, which I thought I could do by making some birdies. I thought it would be a lift for the entire team if they heard the roars." —PHIL MICKELSON

The American fired his second shot on the tenth hole, landing the ball just four feet from the flag for a slow-rolling birdie putt that cut the Swede's lead to one. Mickelson followed this with a six-footer on eleven and a thirty-five-footer downhill across the twelfth green for his third birdie in a row, to move from two down to one up.

Phil Mickelson was the first American left-hander to play in the Ryder Cup and the second overall, after Peter Dawson played reverse hand in 1977 for Britain.

Having taken the lead, Mickelson almost extended it on thirteen. From the rough on the left, he landed his ball ten feet behind the flag to roll back half the distance for his fourth birdie putt in a row, but he lipped out.

Mickelson faced another birdie putt on sixteen for two up, but again his twenty-five-footer rolled by the hole for a half with Johansson's two-and-a-half-foot par putt. Having failed to take advantage of his accurate approach play, the left-hander won the seventeenth, where he closed out the Swede, 2 and 1.

The Ryder Cup having long since been returned to Europe, all Mickelson could claim for this win was bragging rights and the honor of being the only 100 percent player, with three wins in three starts.

"Mickelson, who would emerge as the only unbeaten American, was still out on the course [when Europe won the Cup], forging a victory in the last pairing. He might as well have been in Buffalo. The U.S. let Europe play through on this memorable Sunday." —Bob Verdi, *Chicago Tribune*

"Obviously you're looking at thirteen very disappointed people. We all thought we were going to retain the Cup, and we did not. We're all sharing in this defeat except for Phil Mickelson. Everybody here lost a point this week except for him." —Lanny Wadkins

Day three result: USA 4½, EUR 7½

Europe Victory Offers a Lesson in Teamwork
—*New York Times* headline

Hankie Doodle Dandy! Tears As We Spank Yanks in Ryder Cup —*London Sun* headline

"The champagne flowed Sunday at 3:09 P.M. So did the tears. European champagne. American tears."
—Michael Mayo, *Ft. Lauderdale Sun-Sentinel*

"Call it the most stunning comeback in Ryder Cup history since the long-forgotten Yorkshire Terror of 1957, when Great Britain went 6½–1½ the final day to win." —Gary Van Sickle

Overall match score: USA 13½, EUR 14½

Recap

From Oak Hill to Soak Hill to Choke Hill

For only the sixth time in sixty-eight years, the United States had lost the Ryder Cup, and for only the second time in their country.

In the fifty years of the Ryder Cup, only five teams had come back to win after going into the singles down in the match:

"There's nothing like watching a USA team supposedly head and shoulders above Europe in the talent pool sink like a range ball in a lake."
—*Thomas Bonk,* Los Angeles Times

1929 (GBI)—1 down to win by 2
1949 (USA)—2 down to win by 2
1957 (GBI)—2 down to win by 3
1993 (USA)—1 down to win by 2
1995 (EUR)—2 down to win by 1

So how did Europe come from behind to land the big one? Of the twelve singles matches, five got as far as the final green—where the American players lost four and halved one (which Couples almost lost to Woosnam), making three bogeys among them in the crunch, when just one extra half-point would have kept the trophy in the United States.

"To be honest, I thought it was going to be one of those 17–11 routs, that there was no way they'd come close. I think that was the way most of the guys felt."
—*Tom Lehman*

"What happened today was that we had a strong desire to win this trophy back. I don't think there was any choking. In fact, eighteen is one of the toughest finishing holes in golf. Our desire over that last hole was very, very strong, and the players were very determined to win it back."

—BERNARD GALLACHER

While the American players were overcome by the curse of the last hole, three of Gallacher's unsung makeweights—Clark, James, and Gilford—played out of their skins to record wins that not even their captain could have dreamed about.

"The Europeans played inspiring golf. . . . They just played awfully well. Sometimes you just have to hand it to the guys who win."
—*Lanny Wadkins*

Many experts blamed the American loss on the selection process. No U.S. player had won a tournament since June, while four (Faxon, Haas, Maggert, and Strange) hadn't won in two years. The question that had been raised vociferously before the match reared its ugly head again: Should Wadkins have selected young guns Lee Janzen (who actually won the International after Wadkins made his selections) and Jim Gallagher, Jr.? Both had two wins on the Tour in 1995 but did not have enough points to qualify automatically, because performance from the previous year counted in the final eligibility process.

"America lost the Cup in a week Nick Faldo made two birdies, Seve Ballesteros hit three fairways, and the European captain forgot that Ian Woosnam existed. America lost the Cup with the No. 1 U.S. player on the PGA Tour money list, Lee Janzen, sitting on his couch at home. . . . America lost the Ryder Cup . . . in the greatest come-from-ahead pratfall since DEWEY DEFEATS TRUMAN."

—RICK REILLY, *Sports Illustrated*

During his final speech, Lanny Wadkins was struck by a serious case of wet-eye, and he was consoled by Bernard Gallacher, who had twice experienced the emotions of losing a close one:

Gallacher: "Let me help you through this, Lanny."

Wadkins: "You been there and done that."

After the two men embraced, Wadkins fought back the tears and replied with some typically fighting words, "Enjoy your two years with this pretty little thing, because we're going to be back fighting like hell in 1997 in Spain."

Gallacher had his own reasons to be emotional as he resigned as captain, after never having been on the winning side in nine previous Ryder Cups as a player and captain: "I expected it, I did, I did. It took ten times, but I finally won. I'm going out with the trophy."

"The Ryder Cup brings out the best—and worst—in people. The one played at Oak Hill was no different, but what made this one so special was the way it all turned around within a matter of an hour on Sunday afternoon. An anticlimax developed into another classic Ryder Cup cliffhanger, where heroes would become labeled as chokers, losers would emerge as winners, and tears would flow with champagne. Tears of joy. Tears of sorrow. Enough tears to fill the cup they played for."

—Tim Rosaforte, *Heartbreak Hill*

"Everybody says the 1987 team was the strongest team we have ever had. But we are all eight years older now, and everybody has climbed their own mountain this week."
—*Nick Faldo*

Match Results

Friday, September 22—Morning Foursomes

	USA	EUR	Score
1.	*Corey Pavin* *Tom Lehman*	Nick Faldo Colin Montgomerie	1-up
2.	Jay Haas Fred Couples	*Sam Torrance* *Costantino Rocca*	3 and 2
3.	*Davis Love III* *Jeff Maggert*	Howard Clark Mark James	4 and 3
4.	Ben Crenshaw Curtis Strange	*Bernhard Langer* *Per-Ulrik Johansson*	1-up

Friday, September 22—Afternoon Fourball

	USA	EUR	Score
5.	Peter Jacobsen Brad Faxon	*Seve Ballesteros* *David Gilford*	4 and 3
6.	*Jeff Maggert* *Loren Roberts*	Sam Torrance Costantino Rocca	6 and 5
7.	*Fred Couples* *Davis Love III*	Nick Faldo Colin Montgomerie	3 and 2
8.	*Corey Pavin* *Phil Mickelson*	Bernhard Langer Per-Ulrik Johansson	6 and 4

Day one result: USA 5, EUR 3

Saturday, September 23—Morning Foursomes

	USA	EUR	Score
9.	Curtis Strange Jay Haas	*Nick Faldo* *Colin Montgomerie*	4 and 2
10.	Davis Love III Jeff Maggert	*Sam Torrance* *Costantino Rocca*	6 and 5
11.	*Loren Roberts* *Peter Jacobsen*	Ian Woosnam Philip Walton	1-up
12.	Corey Pavin Tom Lehman	*Bernhard Langer* *David Gilford*	4 and 3

Saturday, September 23—Afternoon Fourball

	USA	EUR	Score
13.	*Brad Faxon* *Fred Couples*	Sam Torrance Colin Montgomerie	4 and 2
14.	Davis Love III Ben Crenshaw	*Ian Woosnam* *Costantino Rocca*	3 and 2
15.	*Jay Haas* *Phil Mickelson*	Seve Ballesteros David Gilford	3 and 2
16.	*Corey Pavin* *Loren Roberts*	Nick Faldo Bernhard Langer	1-up

Day two result: USA 4, EUR 4
Overall match score: USA 9, EUR 7

Sunday, September 24—Singles

	USA	EUR	Score
17.	*Tom Lehman*	Seve Ballesteros	4 and 3
18.	Peter Jacobsen	*Howard Clark*	1-up
19.	Jeff Maggert	*Mark James*	4 and 3
20.	Fred Couples	Ian Woosnam	halved
21.	*Davis Love III*	Costantino Rocca	3 and 2
22.	Brad Faxon	*David Gilford*	1-up
23.	Ben Crenshaw	*Colin Montgomerie*	3 and 1
24.	Curtis Strange	*Nick Faldo*	1-up
25.	Loren Roberts	*Sam Torrance*	2 and 1
26.	*Corey Pavin*	Bernhard Langer	3 and 2
27.	Jay Haas	*Philip Walton*	1-up
28.	*Phil Mickelson*	Per-Ulrik Johansson	2 and 1

Day three result: USA 4½, EUR 7½
Overall match score: USA 13½, EUR 14½

1997

Valderrama Golf Club Sotogrande Spain September 26–28	United States 13½	Europe 14½
	Fred Couples	Thomas Bjorn (Denmark)
	Brad Faxon	Darren Clarke (N. Ireland)
	Jim Furyk	Nick Faldo (England)
	Scott Hoch	Ignacio Garrido (Spain)
	Lee Janzen	Per-Ulrik Johansson (Sweden)
	Tom Lehman	Bernhard Langer (Germany)
	Justin Leonard	Colin Montgomerie (Scotland)
	Davis Love III	Jose Maria Olazabal (Spain)
	Jeff Maggert	Jesper Parnevik (Sweden)
	Phil Mickelson	Costantino Rocca (Italy)
	Mark O'Meara	Lee Westwood (England)
	Tiger Woods	Ian Woosnam (Wales)
	Captain	**Captain**
	Tom Kite	Seve Ballesteros (Spain)

Seve Reigns in Spain

"Let's face it, if the Europeans didn't keep winning or retaining the Ryder Cup, it wouldn't be nearly so much fun for those of us who derive perverse pleasure out of seeing some of our spoiled, pampered American millionaires get dusted every two years by a bunch of guys whose names are hard to spell, harder to pronounce, and no doubt grew up learning the best use for something as curious as a golf club was to herd goats."

—Dan Jenkins, *Golf Digest* (1997)

The Ryder Cup was normally about twenty-four golfers.

The Ryder Cup was normally played in the United States or the United Kingdom.

The Ryder Cup captains were normally seen, not heard.

The Ryder Cup in 1997 was not normal. It was played in Spain, it was about one man . . . and he wasn't even playing.

Despite his obvious reluctance to accept a nonplaying captain's role, Seve magnificently overplayed so many other roles that he could quite easily have sustained a lengthy run on Broadway with his one-man magic show. He juggled his players, he seemingly cast magical spells, he appeared out of thin air, he conjured up a famous victory . . . he even made one player disappear!

The United States was seen as an overwhelming favorite to regain the coveted Cup, but not by Seve—he only had eyes for EU. If Kiawah Island, in 1991, had been the "mother of all golf battles," then Seve made sure that 1997 would be the golfing equivalent of the Spanish Inquisition, with himself cast as a latter-day Torquemada, asking all the questions and sparing no one in his quest for the ultimate prize.

The unlucky player who fell foul of Seve's scheming mind was fellow countryman Miguel Angel Martin, who had qualified as an automatic choice. Just before the competition, Martin needed surgery on an injured wrist, giving Seve the glimmer of a chance to solve a major selection headache. With only two wild-card choices, Seve wanted and needed to have nonqualifiers Faldo, Parnevik, *and* Olazabal on his team. He achieved this by forcing Martin to pass a fitness test. Martin declined and was deselected, disappearing almost without a trace. And—hey, presto!—Olazabal, next in the order of merit, was given the vacant automatic spot, leaving wild cards for Faldo and Parnevik.

Many "experts" forecast that an American blowout was as likely as conceding your boss a two-foot gimme for an eight on the last hole, with the imminent threat of rain. The United States was a lock . . . but Europe was a stock and two smoking barrels.

"The beginning of the end is here . . . for Europe has too many old Faldos and Langers and no youthful duplicates. . . . So we go back to lopsided, maybe for decades again, or until Europe permits two-legged cloning. To think Europe will win this Ryder Cup is to think Clinton gets a third term." —JEFF RUDE, *Golfweek*

With three majors champions (Woods, Love, and Leonard) in their ranks, the U.S. side looked dominant in every department. As many of the American players started to believe the hype, Seve and his underdogs began to bite back. Colin Montgomerie mentioned that Brad Faxon's marital difficulties might prevent him from performing well. Seve deliberately targeted and taunted the young, and supposedly unbeatable, Masters champion: "This is the first time Tiger Woods plays in the Ryder Cup. I think any of my golfers can play against Tiger Woods and beat Tiger Woods."

This European verbal sniping barely rankled a visiting team that was in great shape, hell-bent on avenging their emotional loss at Oak Hill. So the stage was set for the 1997 Ryder Cup in the sunny south of Spain . . . but this was to be no normal Ryder Cup.

Even the normally reticent Nick Faldo added his voice to the mental and verbal prematch barrage: "Since 1985, the European team has a better record in the Ryder Cup than the American team."

"A lot of people would say it's the number one golf event in the world right now. It makes for a very intense, pressure-packed week for all the players." —Tom Kite

Tom Kite, the American captain, had played very well himself during 1997 and must have seriously considered selecting himself as a wild card. Kite also possessed an unblemished singles record in the Ryder Cup, unbeaten in his seven matches, halving a titanic struggle against Ballesteros in 1985. Among other notable performances during the year, Kite finished second at the Masters and fifth in the PGA.

The U.S. captain had far fewer problems than his opposite number over his wild-card choices, taking Lee Janzen (fifteenth on the Ryder Cup points list) and Fred Couples (seventeenth on the list).

"The team is more relaxed than the others I have played on in the Ryder Cup. We are more at ease. Tom Kite as captain has made us come together. He's not being extra strict, standing over us, demanding we hit every shot perfect. He is stressing that we can work hard and have fun at the same time." —Davis Love III

The U.S. team also had the edge in world rankings: Kite's men occupied nine of the top sixteen spots, while Seve's team contained just two. Man for man the U.S. team stacked up better, as well: the team's average world ranking was fourteen to Europe's thirty-five. Many experts translated this quality and extra firepower as making the Americans twice as good as the host side.

For the first time, the European team was less than half British—with two Spaniards, two Swedes, an Italian, a Dane, and a German.

Course Details

Valderrama, set in the deep south of Spain on the Mediterranean coast, was definitely a jewel on the European PGA Tour. Not only was it regarded as one of the most testing continental courses, but it also was certainly one of the most beautiful and well maintained—from the impeccable carpet greens and manicured fairways right down to the natural flora: cork and olive trees, brightly burgeoning flower beds, and even a waterfall by the fourth green.

"This, I have to say, is probably the best, most immaculate course anywhere at the moment. I was actually talking to some of the teams and caddies, and they were all saying they were worried about taking a divot out of the course!" —PRINCE ANDREW, the Duke of York

Hole	Distance	Par	Hole	Distance	Par
1	389	4	10	364	4
2	399	4	11	547	5
3	173	3	12	197	3
4	535	5	13	402	4
5	381	4	14	370	4
6	163	3	15	200	3
7	461	4	16	422	4
8	345	4	17	511	5
9	441	4	18	434	4
		35			**36 = Par 71 (6,734 yards)**

Course designer: Robert Trent Jones

"How do you say 'Augusta National' in Spanish? Valderrama!"
—*Ron Whitten,* Golf Digest *(1997)*

In the precompetition press conferences, Seve avoided the sensitive question of how, despite Ireland's much earlier connections with the Ryder Cup, Spain was chosen as the site for the first non-British venue. At a press conference unveiling Valderrama, the European captain failed to impress his critics.

"Seve poured so much oil on troubled waters . . . that he was in danger of creating an environmental disaster to rival the 'Exxon Valdez.' "
—DERMOT GILLEECE, *Irish Times*

If Seve's wheelings and dealings over selection were cold and calculated, then his golf course was crafty and clinical. Seve had redesigned Valderrama with the intention of blunting the Americans' superior firepower off the tee. Narrow, tree-lined fairways with small, tricky greens were deliberately set up to favor the home team.

One hole in particular upset many of the players (and, much less important, the media), Valderrama's signature hole, the 511-yard seventeenth. Ballesteros had rebuilt and reshaped the whole

hole, from growing the rough across the fairway to shaving the banks of the lake in front of the narrow, sloping green.

"With its water in the front and to the left of the green and the intruding rough across the middle of the fairway, it has undergone so many face-lifts that it has become known as the 'Michael Jackson of golf holes.' "

—Dan Jenkins, *Golf Digest* (1997)

Looking forward to playing the course, Fred Couples noted, "It's a great course. You're going to see some very close matches." And how very right the American was. Only four of the sixteen "doubles" matches failed to reach the seventeenth, with Couples himself suffering two losses on the final hole.

"I never much cared for a par 5 where you hit driver, sand wedqe, sand wedge."
—*Iom Lehman (1997)*

Day One: Morning Fourball

Despite all the prematch hype and controversy, there was only one talking point on the first morning: the rain in Spain fell mainly on the playing—as thunder and lightning storms delayed the start. With the course in danger of flooding under the watery onslaught, it was feared play might not be possible at all on the opening day.

Against all odds, the ground staff's Herculean efforts enabled play to start only one hour and forty minutes late . . . and it was not long before the golfing action lived up to the great expectations.

Under the watchful gaze of two nervous captains, who stood alongside each other for the opening salvos off the first tee, the 1997 Ryder Cup finally got into full swing.

In the past, the opening morning had always been the domain of the best-ball foursomes matches. Knowing the Americans traditionally played foursomes better and, therefore, usually got off to the better start, Ballesteros managed to switch the formats around, with the fourballs first. Kite claimed he was not bothered which format they played first. One up to Europe before the match had even begun.

Davis Love III and Phil Mickelson (USA) v. Jose Maria Olazabal and Costantino Rocca (EUR)

Wearing a dark blue thermal vest, PGA champion Love had the honor of the first shot: a crisply hit one-iron found the middle of the rain-drenched fairway. Mickelson cracked a three-wood past him, while the Europeans were led into battle by Rocca's full-blooded driver, which split the two Americans. Ironically, Olazabal, who eight months earlier had almost been forced to give up the game due to a recurrent foot injury, toe-ended his drive into the right edge of the fairway. Four creditable second shots to the soft, receptive green were capped by Love's twenty-foot curling birdie putt to draw first blood for the Americans.

Just as the early morning had been a washout, so this early strike for the United States proved to be a false dawn. The Europeans quickly pulled back level with a birdie at the par-3 third, and this tight encounter remained all square through the turn, as the next six holes were all halved.

The Americans birdied ten and eleven to go two up with seven to play, and looked to have the upper hand. On the 547-yard eleventh, Mickelson lobbed his pitch over the flag, spinning his ball back as if on a piece of string, to three feet for birdie. Having sprung into another lead, the U.S. found itself back level within three holes.

Rocca made a seven-foot birdie at thirteen to touch off a European comeback, and the first day was spectacularly ignited at the 370-yard fourteenth. The Spaniard's 130-yard pitch from the middle of the fairway bounced beside the pin before skipping sideways into the hole for an eagle two.

The home team finally got their noses in front thanks to a magical birdie three at sixteen on Rocca's nine-iron pin-high pitch.

"The players who don't like the seventeenth are those players who really don't know how to play the hole. I'm very proud of what I have done there. It's very spectacular, very dramatic, and many things can happen there. You can make a three or a seven. I think it's a great hole."

—SEVE BALLESTEROS

On the infamous 511-yard seventeenth hole: "I'm not a fan of the rough in the middle of the fairway. It doesn't make sense to me."

—*Phil Mickelson*

With the ball lying above his feet, Olazabal's second shot to seventeen flew over the narrow neck of water in front, found the heart of the narrow green, and rolled down to twenty-five feet of the pin. In reply, Love's approach landed pin-high but rolled on and through the back of the green, leaving a nasty twenty-foot downhill eagle putt. Olazabal allowed for a break that was not there, pushing his putt high to leave Love with a chance to halve the match. Putting downhill and out of the second cut around the green, the American left his ball a few tantalizing inches short and settled for a half in birdie fours.

At the 434-yard eighteenth, the U.S. pair needed to win the hole just to halve the match. Europe was in trouble, with Olazabal in the greenside bunker in two, and Rocca already out of the final equation. Love, standing in the right-hand rough with the flag obscured by a giant cork tree, stroked a magnificent iron shot to fifteen feet of the hole, allowing Mickelson to go for the flag.

The left-hander did not disappoint his partner, his lazily lobbed ball landing between Love's and the pin. With the prospect of letting a half-point slip away, Olazabal lived up to his short-game reputation and almost holed his recovery blast from the sand. He was rewarded with a conceded putt for par, but his look told everyone that he felt it was not going to be enough.

The Americans each had a putt to win the hole and halve the match. Love left his putt stone dead, again laying the table for Mickelson to win the hole with his much shorter putt. The left-hander cracked under the mounting pressure and pushed his crucial putt wide left of the hole.

This meant Mickelson lost his perfect record in the Ryder Cup, after three wins out of three in his debut at Oak Hill in 1995.

On his missed putt at eighteen: "I'm happy I got myself in that position, but sorry I missed it."
—*Phil Mickelson*

After almost five hours of play, the Europeans had hung on bravely for a nail-bitingly dramatic win on the last green, 1-up.

Fred Couples and Brad Faxon (USA) v. Nick Faldo and Lee Westwood (EUR)

The second match saw Faldo and the first rookie on show, Westwood, against an experienced U.S. pairing of Couples and Faxon. The rookie soon earned his stripes with a birdie at the second, sufficient only for a half with Couples. Undaunted, Westwood birdied the 173-yard third from twelve feet—this time for a lead.

Europe held the slender lead for four holes, but Couples's sand-wedge approach to the 345-yard eighth flew past the pin, dug in, and almost spun back into the hole. This gave the Americans a birdie putt to pull back level. Faldo sank an elliptical eighteen-footer on the next hole to put Europe back one up. At eleven, the British could only scrape a bogey six between them after Faldo found the sand.

Nick Faldo was appearing in a record eleventh Ryder Cup, having started out as the youngest-ever player in 1977.

The match was all square until the par-3 fifteenth. Here the visitors again won the hole to par, courtesy of Westwood, who let his rookie nerves show for the first time, missing a five-foot par putt. Significantly, this mistake put the United States ahead for the first time in the match.

"After three practice rounds, we knew where to hit it. More important is that the course didn't fit the length of Tiger, Davis, Freddie, and Phil. It took the driver out of their hands." —BRAD FAXON

After the pairs halved the 422-yard sixteenth in par, they took on the frightening sight of seventeen. Couples elected to take the sting out of the hole by laying up with his second, firing an exquisite eighty-five-yard chip to a stride of the pin for a certain birdie. This calculated pitch followed Faldo's equally outstanding second shot to ten feet to set up a relatively easy eagle putt. Couples's pinpoint pitch may have unnerved Faldo, as his eagle putt burned the hole on the top side. The highly partisan crowd's cheers quickly turned to groans as they, along with Faldo, realized he had let slip a golden opportunity to level the match with one to play.

Having reached the final green with a pin-high wedge shot, Faldo again lost his touch and his concentration when an American press photographer "accidentally" fired off some shots as the Englishman addressed his crucial birdie putt. Despite backing away, Faldo failed to regain his composure, failed to make the eight-footer, and failed to win the hole. His miss allowed one of the leading putters on the U.S. tour, Brad Faxon, a chance to erase the memory of his costly missed six-footer against David Gilford in 1995.

"The thing about the Ryder Cup that separates it from a major is its intensity. Not even a glare from Faldo could cut through the tension."
—*Dave Allen,* Golfonline

Taking a read from Faldo's miss, Faxon stroked his five-foot putt into the center of the cup to halve the hole and win the match, 1-up.

"Sinking this one helped all of us to believe things will be different this time." —BRAD FAXON

The difference between these pairings was on the greens, as Faxon, who did not make a birdie all round, acknowledged, "We were really decisive. Good putters are decisive. Fortunately, my last putt went in."

Having missed three crucial putts of ten feet or less in the last four holes, Faldo and Westwood spurned a great chance for Europe to gain a psychological advantage by sweeping the first two matches.

Tom Lehman and Jim Furyk (USA) v. Jesper Parnevik and Per-Ulrik Johansson (EUR)

In the third match, the Swedish pairing of Johansson and another rookie, Parnevik, were pitted against Lehman and the first of Kite's rookies, Furyk. The Americans were quickly two up after three holes, with Lehman making a three on the first and holing a twenty-footer for his second birdie on the third.

"Lehman holed putts the length of Route 66."

—Alister Nicol, *Golf.com*

Dealt the hot hand, Lehman had a massive slice of good luck on the 535-yard fourth. His five-iron approach drifted toward the lake to the right of the hole but just held its line, bouncing high off the rocks and landing in the rough behind the green. The American got up and down for his third birdie to halve the hole.

The ice-cool Swedes were not to be overpowered and quickly pulled one back at the par-3 sixth, thanks to Johansson's twenty-foot birdie putt. Another Johansson birdie at the 345-yard eighth saw Europe back on level terms, and Parnevik's par gave Europe a lead on the 441-yard ninth, capping a three-hole swing in four holes.

With the European logo proudly sewn into the trademark-upturned brim of his cap, Parnevik happily explained, "I couldn't wear a regular [team] hat because I haven't done it in so long. I might not have been able to hit the ball."

The ever-vigilant European captain obviously spotted a weakness nobody else saw in Johansson's play, and he decided early on in the proceedings to replace him with Garrido in the afternoon foursomes. Unusually, Ballesteros gave Parnevik the news in the middle of his round—between the twelfth and thirteenth holes—to the Swede's obvious displeasure. But the prospect of a fresh partner did little to spoil Parnevik's play and may even have spurred him on to greater efforts.

Another Parnevik birdie doubled the lead on the fourteenth, but the Americans leveled matters over the next two holes. Lehman superbly birdied the 200-yard fifteenth, chipping in from way off the green after a wayward tee shot, while the rock-steady Furyk slowly rolled home a twenty-two-footer for birdie on the sixteenth.

Furyk's birdie on sixteen was his first of the match, whereas his partner Lehman had already made five.

With the match all square and two to play, this roller-coaster contest continued a-rolling and a-coasting. Parnevik committed the cardinal Valderrama sin in missing the seventeenth fairway with his drive. Forced to lay up short of the water, he made amends for his earlier aberration by planting his eighty-five-yard pitch fifteen feet from the flag. The brave uphill putt that followed—curling in against the grain of the green—restored Europe's narrow lead. By failing to answer Parnevik's superbly timed birdie, the Americans had ensured Europe at least a half-point.

Parnevik finished birdie-birdie to single-handedly snatch victory from the stunned Americans. To say that Parnevik carried his partner is a little harsh on Johansson, whose three birdies were crucial in the overall outcome, but Parnevik's scores counted on thirteen of the eighteen holes. "It's very good for Jesper's confidence. He has come close to winning the British Open twice, so it's nice for him to show he can hole those kinds of putts under pressure."

—*Per-Ulrik Johansson*

Further drama was squeezed out of the final hole. Parnevik somehow followed a perfect drive with an even better approach, nailing a nine-iron inside twelve feet. Not to be outdone or go down without a fight, Furyk and Lehman (handicapped by a poor lie in the rough) more than matched the younger Swede, with approaches to ten feet.

With his partner Johansson out of the hole, and this being the last match out on the course, Parnevik felt the mounting pressure on his frail shoulders. He shrugged off the burden of a team's hopes by calmly stroking home his twelve-foot putt for another birdie, not only snatching the hole from the grasp of the disbelieving Americans but also taking the full point, 1-up.

Tiger Woods and Mark O'Meara (USA) v. Colin Montgomerie and Bernhard Langer (EUR)

The last, but not the least, of the morning fourballs saw the sides' two big guns—Woods and Montgomerie—enter the fray. Neither big gun was supposedly looking forward to shooting up the course, which had been set up under Seve's strict instructions.

"If you are going to pick a course in the whole world that would be a bad course for Tiger Woods, this is it. It is the narrowest course and has the smallest greens I've ever seen. It's got trees overhanging the fairways. This is a precision course. This is a Ben Hogan course . . . it is not a Tiger Woods course."

—JOHNNY MILLER, NBC analyst and three-time Ryder Cupper

His course or not, Woods made his mark on it. He played the 535-yard fourth hole as though the course were set up for him: a two-iron instead of a driver, a nine-iron layup, a sand wedge to twenty-four feet of the hole, and a typically languid putt for birdie. This put the United States one up—a lead they would not abandon.

Having experimented with different ball positions in his stance, Montgomerie was erratic off the tee, hooking his first drive into the gallery, and was never much of a threat all morning, except to innocent bystanders. Not only was his long game proving bothersome but he'd missed a golden opportunity to take the lead on the first green. After Woods had missed his birdie putt from five feet, the Scot failed to make his four-foot birdie putt.

The lead soon doubled when both Europeans failed to par the 163-yard sixth, and the American pair carried a two-hole lead to the turn. Woods made his second birdie on the par-4 tenth with a seven-foot putt to go three up against a dispirited European duo.

Compared with the fireworks in front of them, the Americans were rarely troubled in a contest that barely sparked into life, as their opponents won only one hole—at the relatively easy thirteenth, surprisingly handed to them in par.

Any hopes that a win at thirteen might prompt a late European revival were quickly quashed by the reliable O'Meara. Playing the steadiest and best golf of the four, he hit an immaculate approach to within four feet of the fourteenth flag and walked away with another birdie. This put the U.S. pair back three up, signaling an embarrassingly early exit for Ballesteros's top pairing.

The two experienced Europeans, both former winners of the Volvo Masters at Valderrama, failed to make a single birdie.

Fittingly, it was O'Meara who wrapped up a sloppy 4 and 2 win, at the sixteenth, with a thirty-foot birdie putt from just off the green. O'Meara's putter had been as hot as the two Europeans' had been cold.

This loss meant the Scot had won only one point in his last six fourball matches. "Monty didn't play his best. The Americans made the putts and we didn't. That was the difference between us."
—*Bernhard Langer*

Despite his Masters victory and an outstanding Amateur match-play record, Woods never really looked at home on this course, just as Johnny Miller had suggested . . . and Ballesteros had planned.

Woods had enough on his mind to worry about apart from a course that did not suit him: prematch taunts from the Europeans over how beatable he really was, the pressures of being the youngest-ever Masters champion, the hopes of a nation sitting squarely on his shoulders. Nor was it likely that the young Tiger was in the best frame of mind after the row concerning his father, Earl, who had boycotted the event when he was not included in the official U.S. tour party.

Morning fourball result: USA 2, EUR 2

Day One: Afternoon Foursomes

Having broken the news to Parnevik that he would be playing with Garrido in the afternoon, Ballesteros once again proved that he was fully prepared to put his players' reputations on the line for the

"I'm sure Seve will want to give us each an experienced partner, but Seve's Seve, and who knows what he might do."
—*Darren Clarke*

good of his team. An irate Ian Woosnam and the two untried rookies, Bjorn and Clarke, learned that they had been left out of the opening day only when they saw their captain announce the afternoon pairings on television.

On the traditional European selection strategy: *"You don't need depth for this. They just put out their eight show horses."*

—PAUL AZINGER

Far from being focused, Ballesteros's side was seemingly in some disarray: Langer was blaming Monty, Faldo couldn't buy a putt, Parnevik was upset at losing Johansson as a partner, while Woosnam was madder than hell at his captain.

All in all, Tom Kite was the happier of the two captains after the opening skirmishes. Taking a split of the morning fourballs into the afternoon foursomes, where the Americans had always proved to be the tougher team, Kite must have believed he would finish the day with a slight lead.

"Isn't the Ryder Cup neat? It's so much fun, it's really exciting stuff. I wish I was playing, but just to be involved in the matches is fantastic. The so-called experts who said it would be a blowout for one side or the other are going to be badly wrong." —TOM KITE

Reflecting none of Ballesteros's steely isolation from his players, Kite acted more as a first-base coach than a major-league manager to his team of strutting superstars. He was happy to let them "do their own stuff" as long as they kept on winning. Ballesteros, on the other hand, was determined his team would play his way—and win.

Scott Hoch and Lee Janzen (USA) v. Constantino Rocca and Jose Maria Olazabal (EUR)

The Americans knew the importance of a fast start, so Hoch and Janzen, left out of the morning play, did not waste any time making an impact. Hoch's pinpoint wedge to the first left Janzen a five-foot putt for birdie, which he duly holed to put them one up.

A second birdie doubled the Americans' advantage at the next hole, but they faltered on the 535-yard fourth, allowing the Europeans to wrestle a hole back to par. The Europeans won the next two holes, with another par on the short sixth and Rocca's four-foot birdie putt on the seventh. The Mediterranean pairing failed to hold on to Europe's only lead of the match, as it was their turn to lose the next hole to par.

This seesaw skirmish continued, with wins being posted on four of the next five holes. The Americans managed to take three steps forward on nine, eleven, and thirteen, but one back on twelve. All four holes were won in par, as all four players had problems coping with the drying conditions and the building tension.

"Best drainage: Valderrama after downpours.
Worst drainage: All those U.S. putts that didn't seep in during doubles."
—*Jeff Rude,* Golfweek

After the 370-yard fourteenth had been halved in par, the United States were two up with four to play.

Sadly, neither pair had gotten this sickly golf out of its system, and the 200-yard fifteenth was halved in bogey fours. To make matters worse, the Americans produced their second bogey in a row to lose the sixteenth.

Taking his captain's advice, Olazabal took the water out of the equation on seventeen, deliberately playing his second shot—with a three-wood—toward the far right of the green. His ball came to rest in the light rough just off the green, only twenty feet from the pin. The Americans had chosen to lay up in front, and Janzen landed his wedge shot ten feet from the flag, but it bit too hard on the soft turf and almost spun back into the water. Hoch's long birdie putt snaked up the green and finished within a foot of the hole to put some pressure on their well-placed opponents.

Thanks to Olazabal's tactical approach, Rocca was able to float a chip shot onto the fringe of the green and slowly roll his ball down to within a foot of the cup. The birdie putt was conceded, as was the hole, and brought an immediate pat on the back for Rocca from his ecstatic captain, who must have felt he had played the hole himself.

All square, and with only five of the previous seventeen holes having been halved, it was no surprise when the deciding hole fell to one side or the other.

Europe's birdie on seventeen was the first in the match since Rocca's hole-winning putt on seven.

Rocca's remarkable recovery, from the rough underneath some cork trees, almost landed in the hole but rolled ten feet beyond. Janzen retaliated with equally spectacular accuracy, landing and crucially stopping his six-iron approach four feet in front of the hole to grab the advantage. Olazabal winced as his crucial downhill putt swung late and skirted the hole. In contrast, Hoch's face was pure joy as he made no such error with his putt—the U.S. pair had its birdie three and a hard-fought one-hole victory.

"We had a huge momentum-swing there this afternoon, with Scott and Lee making a birdie on that last hole to win the match. That was a big match. That match went up and down and all around, and they held on to it." —TOM KITE

Jeff Maggert and Justin Leonard (USA) v. Lee Westwood and Nick Faldo (EUR)

In a far cry from the early days of the Ryder Cup, Faldo and Westwood were the only two Englishmen of the twelve on the European team.

In this mesmerizing match, over sixteen holes of exciting match play but slightly inconsistent stroke play, only three holes were halved.

The European pair was first to strike. Westwood's approach landed three feet from the first hole but spun back, leaving his partner an awkward eight-footer, which Faldo calmly struck home. An all-English bogey at the next leveled the score, and the Americans birdied the 173-yard third to go up, after Maggert stuck his tee shot three feet left of the flag.

Playing the fourth shot on the fourth hole, Maggert pinned his approach three feet from the flag, but Westwood outdid him with his side's third, which bounced between the Americans' ball and the hole. This European birdie was quickly followed by another bogey at the 381-yard fifth, leaving the U.S. pair one up. Maggert and Leonard repaid the favor by bogeying the seventh, only to have the Europeans birdie the eighth to go one up. Another American bogey at nine meant Faldo and Westwood reached the turn two up.

Having made only one birdie between them on the outward nine, Maggert and Leonard started home with a birdie at the tenth to cut the lead to one. The 547-yard eleventh produced the shot of the match: Faldo almost holed his approach for an eagle, but the birdie regained the two-hole lead.

"If you don't enjoy pressure, you are in the wrong place. I'm not saying I'm a great pressure player, but that's when I learn the most about myself."
—*Justin Leonard*

Leonard's tee shot at the par-3 twelfth came close to equaling Faldo's previous approach shot, landing within a foot of the hole. The conceded birdie putt again halved the Europeans' lead. Just when it appeared that both pairs had finally come to grips with the course, another American bogey on the thirteenth dropped them two down again.

The next two holes were halved in par as the English pair looked to consolidate on its two-hole cushion.

Up on the sixteenth tee, the gathering gloom persuaded the four players to agree to play one more hole before calling it a night.

With the sun swiftly setting in the west, Maggert's approach came up twenty feet short of the pin. Sensing a chance to close the match out that night, Faldo smoothly launched a towering shot directly over the flag, coming to rest seven feet above the hole. When the players reached the green, the American pair requested that play be called because of the poor light.

"I've learned a great deal about being a team man in the last two matches."
—*Nick Faldo (one wonders what he was doing in his first eight Ryder Cups)*

Nick Faldo was less than happy with the Americans' change of heart, noting, "We agreed to play one more hole and that's it, but they changed their minds and said it was too dark."

Next morning after the rain delay, Leonard's tantalizing twenty-footer came up one inch short of the hole—Leonard may have misread the soaking wet green—but the U.S. pair made its par four. Not wanting to let his record-breaking partner down, Westwood had practiced all morning on the length of putt he faced to win the match.

Practice did indeed make perfect. Westwood confidently rolled the ball straight into the middle of the hole, and the rookie from Nottinghamshire punched the sky in celebration before the ball had even dropped for a 3 and 2 win.

With this early-morning win, Nick Faldo became the all-time leading points scorer in Ryder Cup history with his twenty-fourth, moving a half-point ahead of Billy Casper. As ever, the Englishman was happier with the win than the record, declaring, "We played long and hard yesterday. It's great to get a result like that."

Tom Lehman and Phil Mickelson (USA) v. Jesper Parnevik and Ignacio Garrido (EUR)

For the first six holes, the only difference between the two pairs was an American birdie four on the fourth, where the Europeans could only scrape a bogey six.

Lehman's seven-foot par putt on the seventh doubled the Americans' advantage, before Europe won their first hole with their first birdie on the par-4 eighth. Under the ever-watchful eye of their captain, unmistakable in his bright blue golf cart, Parnevik knocked his approach two feet past the hole, and Garrido's putt reduced the deficit to one.

Three consecutive halves allowed the U.S. pair to stay one up until the 197-yard twelfth. Faced with a testing ten-footer for his par, Lehman failed the test, and the match was all square once again. In the dark, the players agreed to suspend play for the night.

After the laboriously slow play resulted in incomplete matches by nightfall: "Yet again the pace of some of the play was positively funereal, encouraging the thought that perhaps the Ryder Cup should not have come to Spain but gone instead to Akureyri in the north of Iceland in June, when the sun never sets."
—*Alister Nicol*

Soon after the early-morning resumption, Lehman hit another superb eight-iron pitch from the rough to three feet of the pin on thirteen. In reply, the Europeans' approach barely made the green, and Mickelson made the short birdie putt to regain the lead. Mirroring Lehman on the previous hole, Parnevik stroked an eight-iron to three feet on fourteen—but this time from the fairway, setting up a birdie putt for Garrido.

Having swapped birdies on thirteen and fourteen, and halves in par on the subsequent three holes, the players arrived on the last hole all square. After both approach shots missed the green, the hole and the match were there for the taking.

From sixty feet away, Lehman produced an exquisite chip-and-run that grazed the lip of the cup and ran eighteen inches past for a conceded par. Garrido's chip shot was much shorter but complicated by a lump of mud on his ball. However, he matched Lehman's shot and the hole was halved, as was the match.

Mark O'Meara and Tiger Woods (USA) v. Bernhard Langer and Colin Montgomerie (EUR)

Ballesteros showed the utmost faith in his star pairing by pitting them against their morning conquerors. Both Europeans had headed straight for the practice area after their dismal opening showing, and the extra work quickly paid off.

Having been given a second chance together, Langer and Montgomerie were two up after three holes thanks to an American bogey at the second and their first birdie in nineteen holes of play, at the 173-yard third.

"Tiger: Not the Full Monty"
—*T-shirt slogan on a spectator*

This lead was immediately cut back when Woods's extra distance enabled the Americans to counter with their own birdie at the 535-yard fourth hole.

The Europeans remained one up until back-to-back birdies at eight and nine put them three up. Montgomerie had been striking the ball much more fluently following his lunchtime session with coach Bill Ferguson, and Langer's adroit putting touch had returned.

On his improvement from the morning loss: *"I changed putters and started putting well again. I went back to my spare putter, and it worked. I always carry two."* —Bernhard Langer

"Go on, Tiger! Chew 'em up!"
—*Anonymous U.S. fan*

On the par-4 ninth, the Europeans combined perfectly for their third birdie of the day. Montgomerie's long-iron approach landed eight feet from the flag, and Langer's long-handled putter did the rest. The pair reached the turn in 33 shots, three fewer than their rivals, and three fewer than they had carded in the morning.

Woods and O'Meara were unable to make any progress against the revitalized Europeans, who won the fourteenth after Woods's six-foot par putt paper-clipped the hole, sending Europe four up with four holes to play.

With the touch of a master showman, the German's tee shot put the seal on the match at the par-3 fifteenth, plugging itself two feet from the hole. Under pressure of needing to win the hole, Woods pulled his tee shot wide and right, thirty feet from the hole. O'Meara failed to hole the must-make long putt, but Montgomerie had no such difficulty, tapping in for an avenging 5 and 3 win for Europe.

"Mark and I made some key putts this morning, but in the afternoon we didn't. And Colin turned his game around completely. I've got to give him credit for that."
—*Tiger Woods*

Langer and Montgomerie had five birdies between them after drawing a blank in the morning round, and the Scotsman could barely hide his delight as he walked off the green, saying, "We were brilliant this afternoon. It was a wonderful afternoon, a wonderful, wonderful afternoon and a great way to leave the course after a long day. . . . I struggled today physically . . . usually I struggle mentally."

Afternoon foursomes result: USA 1½, EUR 2½
Day one result: USA 3½, EUR 4½

On his side's up-and-down day: *"We started well, then it looked bad, then it was all right, then good and, in the end, very good. But that's golf, and that's what makes the Ryder Cup so special."*

—Seve Ballesteros

Day Two: Morning Fourball

The overnight fireworks display aboard Johnny Walker's (the main sponsor) luxury yacht moored in the harbor presaged the natural pyrotechnics of the early morning. A severe thunder and lightning storm flooded an already saturated course, as bunkers burst their banks and needed to be drained.

On day two, the European team had His Royal Highness Prince Andrew among their traveling fan base, while Team USA had His Royal Airness Michael Jordan, who received a front-row seat in the captain's golf cart.

Davis Love III and Fred Couples (USA) v. Colin Montgomerie and Darren Clarke (EUR)

Tom Kite finally decided to send out what was widely regarded as his number one pairing, Love and Couples, against the tenacious Celtic pairing from Scotland and Northern Ireland.

Love and Couples had won the World Cup four times for the United States (1992–95) and had beaten Montgomerie (with Faldo) in a 1995 fourball.

The American pair showed brief glimpses of its past glories on the outward journey. Having come up short and to the left in the rough at the par-5 fourth, Love chipped his third shot up to five feet of the hole, and the ensuing birdie could not be matched. On the following hole, Montgomerie's reply was as immediate as the Americans' concession. The Scot launched his approach at the flag and failed to connect by only a few inches, to level the match.

From 76 yards out at the 345-yard eighth, Couples struck a stunning pitching wedge ten feet past the pin. As if by remote control, his ball dug in and spun back into the hole for an eagle two, putting the U.S. pair one up at the turn. The fact that six of the opening nine holes were halved in par and the four players could make only three birdies among them showed how difficult the course was playing.

On pitching his final two rookies—Clarke and later Bjorn—into the fray: "If they win, it was a good decision. If they lose, it will be my fault."
—*Seve Ballesteros*

The Americans increased their lead at the tenth thanks to Couples's birdie from eight feet, but they saw their two-hole advantage disappear over the next two holes.

At the 547-yard eleventh, Clarke holed an eleven-foot birdie putt to cut the lead to one, and at the 197-yard twelfth, Montgomerie left his five-iron tee shot five feet off the pin. Couples's huge swinging birdie putt came up just short, and the Scot rattled in his five-footer to level the match.

Despite being one of the leading money-winners on the European tour, Darren Clarke was given a lesson in bunker play by his captain during a practice round.

As was the pattern in this Ryder Cup, as soon as one pair birdied a hole, it invariably seemed to bogey the next. Europe did just that at the thirteenth. With Montgomerie cavorting among the cork trees, Clarke missed a six-foot putt for par to hand the lead back to the United States.

With five holes to play, the American superpairing looked to have paid dividends, but Europe had other ideas. Undaunted by the quality of his partner and opponents, Clarke smacked his approach to twelve inches on fourteen, and Love, best placed to neutralize it, failed with his twelve-foot birdie putt.

The match remained all square after Clarke and Love missed birdie putts on the 200-yard fifteenth. The par-4 sixteenth was halved in threes, Montgomerie's birdie, courtesy of a superb eight-iron to twenty feet, was canceled out by Couples's gutsy left-to-right twelve-footer.

And so the pressure was turned up a notch as they arrived at the pivotal seventeenth, where Ballesteros instructed his players in how to play the hole. From the unforgiving rough, Clarke put his second shot into the water, forcing his partner—also in the rough—to play safe and lay up in front.

On his overzealous captain, who needlessly interrupted his crucial third shot to the seventeenth: *"We're going along OK until he arrives, then the whole thing bustles and shuffles around. Seve gets a little bit too intense. You wish he would relax a bit, maybe stay in his buggy and watch, especially on the seventeenth. There are so many ways to play the hole, yes, but there is only one way to play it at the time."*

—Colin Montgomerie

Love produced the best second shot, but he still left himself a tricky downhill twelve-foot birdie putt. Montgomerie found the heart of the green with his third and watched as the ball slowly trickled back down the slope toward the flag, finishing within five feet. Love tried to caress his downhill putt, but it gathered speed and blew two feet by.

Up stepped gentle giant Montgomerie. He provided enough encouragement to set the ball on its way, and the slope did the rest, guiding the ball into the hole for a birdie, garnering a priceless one-hole lead. The home crowd, knowing the Scotsman had earned at least a half in this vital opening match, rose in salute.

To the eighteenth, where Clarke's second shot was aimed straight at the flag but came up twelve feet short. Montgomerie, with a blind shot from the rough, produced another magnificent shot to the center of the green. With both Europeans on the putting surface, Couples found a bunker, while Love pushed his approach beyond the hole into the light rough between green and bunker. With a putt for the match, Montgomerie watched as his shot stayed on target until it wobbled off line at the end, caught the lip of the cup, and rolled away. This gave Love one last shot at saving the match. He needed to sink his putt from off the green, but the ball never troubled the hole, forcing the U.S. pair to concede the hole and a one-hole loss.

Brad Faxon and Justin Leonard (USA) v. Thomas Bjorn and Ian Woosnam (EUR)

With something to prove to his captain, Woosnam came into this match having won a record nine fourball matches, one more than Ballesteros. In Woosnam's fourteenth fourball match, Bjorn was his seventh different partner, after Torrance, Way, Faldo, Broadhurst, Baker, and Rocca.

With the match all square after three holes, Leonard's 110-yard pitch to the par-5 fourth landed softly on the downslope of the lush green and rolled slowly back into the hole for eagle. From here the U.S. pair was on fire, especially Leonard on and around the greens, making two more birdies in a row. His eleven-foot birdie putt from the fringe at the 381-yard fifth was answered by Woosnam, while Leonard's ten-footer from the back of the par-3 sixth nullified Woosnam's almost perfect tee shot to two feet at the fifth. After the first seven holes, Justin Leonard was a jaw-dropping six under par on his own ball—five birdies and an eagle—but the American pair was only one up.

"Justin Leonard did everything except win." —THOMAS BJORN

Not to be outdone, the young Dane got serious on the eighth, adding a fifteen-footer of his own to level the scores. Leonard struck back with another birdie on nine, after his approach dug its heels in four feet short of the hole. The tenth was halved in birdie threes, with Leonard continuing his solo assault by holing from off the green.

Despite his apparent inexperience, Bjorn again stepped up on the 547-yard eleventh and knocked his third shot stiff to three feet. His calmly struck birdie putt leveled the score and signaled the turning point of the match.

At the 402-yard thirteenth, the Americans lost the hole to Woosnam's par. On this "No Bunker" hole, both Americans managed to hit shots behind trees, and they soon found themselves behind for the first time in the match. Without any conspicuous support from Faxon, the British Open champion had single-handedly kept his side in the battle.

Leonard's nerve finally cracked under the Europeans' two-handed assault, as the par-3 fifteenth found a chink in his putting stroke. He hit a superb four-iron over the flag, stopping it ten feet past the pin, but Woosnam's answer was as devastating as it was demoralizing. The Welshman's tee shot pulled up fifteen feet from the flag, and he slammed it home with gusto before punching out the sky with both hands. This must have felt like a two-fisted blow to Leonard's solar plexus, and he overcompensated on his own birdie putt and let another hole slip away.

Two up with three to play, Europe looked to end matters as soon as possible. The sixteenth was halved in par, setting up another memorable battle on the seventeenth. Faxon took too much greenery with his second shot out of the right-hand rough. His loud groan of displeasure told its own story as his ball scooted across the fairway and into the water hazard running up the left-hand side of the fairway. Before the tournament, no one had even bothered to pay much heed to this innocuous stretch of water, but Faxon found it.

"I can't tell you how many times I rode up to a green when our guys were inside them, and we come away with just a halve [or worse!]. They made a lot more six-footers than we did."
—*Tom Kite*

Knowing a half was good enough, Bjorn had no such troubles. His approach safely found the green forty feet to the left of the pin. Two putts produced the half Europe needed to clinch another vital point, 2 and 1.

Faxon completed thirty-five holes of fourball without making a single birdie. Without saying so, Leonard may well have been blaming his partner for the loss by remarking, "That's match play. You can play really well and lose or play mediocre and win. Unfortunately, I was in category A."

Mark O'Meara and Tiger Woods (USA) v. Nick Faldo and Lee Westwood (EUR)

Both highly touted pairings came into this third match with a win and a loss under their belts.

As with the two matches in front, the first three holes were halved in par. Tiger Woods was again the first to make a move, chipping in a twenty-five footer at the par-5 fourth to go one up. Spurred on by Woods's wonder shot, Europe's young titan, Lee Westwood, produced one of his own on the fifth, planting a pitch three feet in front of the hole. Answering the challenge, Woods went one better and knocked his second shot twelve inches beyond the pin. The youngsters, who were leaving their senior partners gawking in their wake, halved the hole in birdie threes.

O'Meara's fifteen-footer birdied the long fourth hole, and Woods chipped in on the 461-yard seventh, from twelve feet away, to go up by two.

With Faldo not playing up to his normally high standard, Westwood took control of the European counterattack, pulling a hole back on the 441-yard ninth with a twenty-five-foot birdie putt. On the tenth, Westwood's eight-iron to the green landed beyond the pin but quickly spun back pin-high six feet away. He made the birdie putt to level the match score.

"On the eleventh tee Woods munched an apple. It was green and it did not sweeten his expression."
—*Hugh McIlvanney,* Sunday Times *(London)*

From ten feet away on eleven, the English rookie needed his third birdie in a row just to save a half with Woods, who holed from closer in. The score remained tied until Westwood again made the move at the par-3 fifteenth with a thumping three-iron that crept up the left of the green, ten feet from the hole. His uphill putt started left, seemed to sense where the hole was, and found its way into the center of the cup. Europe was now ahead for the first time in the match, with three holes to play.

Having let his junior partner carry him thus far, Nick Faldo took over the European responsibilities on the 422-yard sixteenth. With his game back under control, Faldo and his eight-iron attacked the pin, placed at the very front of the green, to leave a fifteen-foot return birdie putt. Woods more than answered with a supreme shot of his own high over the cork trees, spotting his ball inside of Faldo's for a huge psychological advantage.

The three-time Masters champion fed off the mental part of his game and stroked his birdie putt in as though he were on the practice green. A montage of blue and gold EC flags proudly dotted the galleries, and the packed stands needed no invitation to rise and salute the return of their king. Now was the time for the young pretender to call upon all of his mental reserves, but Tiger was running on empty: he badly misread the line and tailed off two feet past the hole. This put Europe in the driver's seat at two up with two to play.

Once again the seventeenth played host to more drama and horror than Alfred Hitchcock could have imagined. Faldo, from a difficult downhill lie in the middle of the fairway, powered a wondrous three-wood second, up and over the water, to the heart of the narrow green. O'Meara, having found the left-hand rough, and faced by Faldo's accurate approach, was forced into taking the green on in two with a three-iron. His ball barely cleared the water and plugged on the top of the perilous downslope with only water below.

Having had difficulty reading the greens, Tiger Woods said of the heavy rain, "it screwed up my sense of the greens."

Balancing a small measure of safety with an overdose of attack, Woods badly overhit his three-iron approach. The ball bounced on the green near Faldo's ball but hurtled through and off the back, leaving a very long and almost impossible downhill putt toward the water. With his partner best set in the middle of the green, and with the longest drive under his belt, Westwood drilled one of the shots of the day: a two-iron to fifteen feet beyond the hole, where the ball stopped, had a thought, and slowly rolled back nearer the hole.

Under the studious eye of former president George Bush, who appeared to have taken up official residency at the seventeenth, Woods sank to the ultimate ignominy. His wildly erratic and brazenly overstruck downhill putt breezed wide of the hole, over the lip of the green, and plunged into the water beyond. Needless to say, a Tiger in the water elicited more than a few jeers from the delighted crowd. This only heaped more pressure on O'Meara, whose well-judged chip from the edge of the green almost dropped for eagle but stayed out for a conceded birdie. With Faldo and Westwood both having two shortish putts for the half and win, the Americans knew when they were beaten and graciously conceded the match, 2 and 1.

With this victory, Nick Faldo went past Arnold Palmer's all-time record of twenty-two Ryder Cup wins.

This gave Europe three wins out of three in the morning session; a rout was well and truly on.

Tom Lehman and Phil Mickelson (USA) v. Ignacio Garrido and Jose Maria Olazabal (EUR)

"The atmosphere is something I cannot explain. We could play 100 holes and we would not be tired because the spectators would carry us in their arms." —IGNACIO GARRIDO

Another of Tom Kite's powerhouse pairings soon found themselves a hole down after a European birdie on the par-3 third, but the Americans were back level with a birdie of their own at the 535-yard fourth. The match remained all square until the seventh,

Olazabal's twelve-foot birdie putt giving Europe a one-hole lead that they still held after nine.

On the 364-yard tenth, Mickelson was so sure of his twelve-foot birdie putt that he was off after the ball before it had gotten halfway to the hole.

On missing two nine-foot putts at thirteen and fourteen that could have stretched the U.S. lead to two or even three: "I could have separated us from them a little with those two, but I didn't."
—*Phil Mickelson*

Halving the par-5 eleventh in regulation, thanks to Lehman's great recovery from a greenside bunker, the Americans struck again on the 197-yard twelfth. A birdie two saw them take a lead for the first time in the match, which they held until the sixteenth, where a fourth European birdie brought the match back level.

"They definitely are doing all the things you need to do to win matches. When one guy is in the tank, the other guy makes a birdie. There hasn't been one guy that's played well from start to finish. It's been mostly ham and egging it." —TOM LEHMAN

Up to this time, the seventeenth had seen its fair share of drama and great shots, but nothing like what it was about to witness. First, Lehman tried to sneak his second shot up the right of the green, but he was a few yards short. His ball dived into the shaved swale and started to roll back toward the water, and only the mud on the ball stopped it from rolling back all the way.

On the complete lack of U.S. success on the second day: "I've been waiting here all day [mostly at the seventeenth green] for an American victory. I just wanted to hear what the sound of an American victory was like."
—*George Bush*

With his partner in a precarious, if not impossible, position ahead of him, Mickelson faced an almost hopeless task of his own just to reach the green from the edge of the right-hand rough. With 240 yards to carry the water, the left-hander took a two-iron, took aim, and almost swung himself off balance. He yelled "Go!" as soon as he hit the ball, knowing it would need everything to clear the water. The ball, which Mickelson probably did not see, landed on the very front of the green right in front of the pin and bounced on up the slope and started to roll back toward the hole. Mickelson's miracle shot finished just five feet away.

On Phil Mickelson's miraculous two-iron out of the rough: *"The single greatest shot I've ever seen."* —TOM LEHMAN

From the middle of the fairway, Garrido took a three-wood—much too much weapon—sending his ball flying over the green and into one of the treacherous bunkers guarding the back of the green. Trying to sneak in via the Lehman side-door route, Olazabal also came up short, but his ball was clean and slowly trickled its way down into the water.

Faced with getting out of the downslope of the bunker and needing to stop his ball before it joined his partner in the lake, Garrido bravely played a stabbing flick shot. His ball flew out, bounced, and amazingly rolled slowly down past the pin to finish some six feet away, only a couple of rolls from the fatal drop into the drink.

On Ignacio Garrido's recovery shot: *"Maybe the second-greatest shot I've ever seen."* —Tom Lehman

Lehman's eagle attempt from short of the green whistled past the pin by ten feet. He underborrowed on the return birdie putt, his ball slipping by the hole, while Garrido stepped back up to hole his troublesome putt without any trouble.

Staggered by the Spaniard's miracle up and down for birdie, Mickelson faced an eagle putt that must have seemed as if it had doubled in length. Hardly daring to touch the ball, the left-hander putted and lipped out the left of the hole, much to his and the U.S. side's dismay.

On his missed eagle putt at seventeen: "That was the match right there. I thought I had made it."
—*Phil Mickelson*

Forced to settle for a half on seventeen, the Americans had blown a great chance to win the match, although it was still all square with one to play. On the eighteenth green, with Lehman all over a four-footer for his par, Olazabal sank a twelve-footer for a valuable half to keep the United States winless in the morning session, sending the already hyped-up crowd into a fiesta-like frenzy.

Morning fourball result: USA ½, EUR 3½

For Seve's men, the final halved fourball was welcomed as a win. Restricting the U.S. team to just half a point proved to be the turning point of the whole three days for the Europeans.

In the fourball matches, U.S. pairs finished six under, seven under, seven under, and six under, but did not win a single match and picked up only a half-point. *"The team I started with on Friday in the morning was almost as good. The team I started out with today was my A-Team . . . and they got hammered!"* —Tom Kite

"The Americans got off to a great start on the first nine, and we just plowed back and plowed back. We've played the best golf over the last few days." —Ian Woosnam

Day Two: Afternoon Foursomes

Lee Janzen and Jim Furyk (USA) v. Colin Montgomerie and Bernhard Langer (EUR)

As usual, the Americans got off to a faster start with a birdie three at the first, but they let the advantage slip by losing two of the next three holes. The European pair birdied the second, and an American bogey on the par-5 fourth gave the home side a lead they would not relinquish over the remaining fifteen holes.

Bernhard Langer has had the most partners of any player in the history of the Ryder Cup Matches. His twelve accomplices have been: Manuel Pinero, Nick Faldo, Jose Maria Canizares, Sandy Lyle, Ken Brown, Ronan Rafferty, Mark James, Colin Montgomerie, Ian Woosnam, Barry Lane, Per-Ulrik Johansson, and David Gilford.

After this rambunctious opening, both pairs settled down and halved the next four holes, although the 461-yard seventh was covered in bogey fives. Europe doubled their lead at the ninth when Montgomerie's long iron to the very back of the green left Langer a ten-foot downhill birdie putt.

The Americans got their game going again when they birdied ten and eleven, but they could not close the gap on the Europeans, who matched them stroke for stroke. Furyk and Janzen finally pulled a hole back at the 402-yard thirteenth with a par, but Montgomerie and Langer went two up on the 422-yard sixteenth with their own par.

Seventeen produced its usual diet of drama and disaster—this time with the Europeans suffering. Montgomerie missed an eight-foot uphill birdie putt, leaving it short of the hole. Janzen seized his chance and knocked in a three-footer for birdie and the hole. Europe was now just one up with one to play, and the Americans had their tails up.

Lee Janzen was without his normal caddie—as Englishman Dave Musgrove had decided the Ryder Cup might cause an embarrassing conflict of interest.

Up the eighteenth in the gathering gloom, the players could have used the poor conditions as an excuse for some atrocious play. Furyk found himself under the cork trees, and his half-scampered shot just found the front of the green some distance from a flag positioned right at the back. Montgomerie's wayward tee shot meant Langer could play only a hacking recovery shot onto the fairway. To make amends for his error, Montgomerie played Europe's third—a wonderful nine-iron—to five feet of the hole.

Under the pressure of the moment and in the darkness, Janzen fired his fifty-foot putt ten feet past the hole, handing the advantage back to Europe. The responsibility passed to Furyk, whose own putt stormed five feet past the hole. Faced with the obvious conclusion, Janzen offered Europe the half for the hole, enough to give them victory 1-up, and an unprecedented 9-4 overall lead.

"Europe led 9–4, which in a Ryder Cup is like saying Dallas 52, Buffalo 7 halfway through the third quarter. There were fifteen matches left, in which the Americans would need to score 10½ points. In other words, they were slightly more dead than Franco."

—Rick Reilly, *Sports Illustrated*

Scott Hoch and Jeff Maggert (USA) v. Nick Faldo and Lee Westwood (EUR)

As early as the fifth hole, it looked as though the scratch pairing of Hoch and Maggert were dead and buried—a tired Faldo and an inspired Westwood had them three down. British birdies at two and five sandwiched an ugly American bogey at the par-5 fourth to leave the Americans in trouble.

Westwood continued his phenomenal form from the morning, and the Americans were forced to hole some lengthy putts just to make their halves. By the turn, the United States had fought back to one down, thanks to a birdie at six and a European bogey at nine, where Hoch made a par-winning putt from all of twenty-five feet.

"Nick Faldo is as much fun as Saddam Hussein."
—*Scott Hoch*

On the 364-yard tenth, Hoch continued his hot hand, making a sixteen-footer for birdie to level the match.

The U.S. pair took the lead when both Europeans made a hash of the par-3 twelfth. After the next two holes were halved in par, the match was called because of bad light, leaving Faldo and Westwood unfinished for the second night running, and trailing by one.

Directly after the resumption the next morning, the U.S. pair stretched its lead on the strength of Maggert's majestic tee shot to the par-3 fifteenth that landed fifteen inches from the flag. Sixteen was halved in pars as the British pair tried all it had to reduce the deficit.

Dormie two on the seventeenth, the U.S. pair took no chances with the water, and Maggert was rewarded with a sensible four-foot putt for a half in par and the match, 2 and 1. The Americans were never ahead on the front nine, but, much more important, never behind on the back nine.

Justin Leonard and Tiger Woods (USA) v. Jesper Parnevik and Ignacio Garrido (EUR)

A rare Battle of the Rookies—all four players were new to Ryder Cup play, although the Americans were both majors winners that year.

The Americans' birdie at the first was the epitome of foursomes play: Woods's long accurate drive, Leonard's approach to two feet, and Tiger's birdie putt for a quick unanswered strike.

After this explosive opening, the next five holes were disappointingly halved in par. Another rasping iron shot from Leonard set up Woods for a four-foot birdie putt on the 163-yard sixth, but Tiger, still having trouble reading the greens, failed to convert.

"I always said Tiger would not win the Ryder Cup on his own. He has not played badly, but he has not played well, either, under a great deal of pressure. But he is young and he's only human." —TOM KITE

After blowing a chance to go two up, the Americans were soon back level on the 461-yard seventh, where the Europeans grabbed their own birdie, with Parnevik chipping in from off the green. In a state of equilibrium, the match was suspended for the night.

"Everybody thought Tiger would do better, but I don't think he's doing that badly. It's just that the Ryder Cup is very tough."
—*Seve Ballesteros*

The next morning, both pairs quickly traded birdie threes on nine and ten to keep things level, and eleven through fourteen were all halved in regulation. As if woken from the early-morning slumber, Parnevik and Garrido birdied fifteen with the Spaniard's twenty-five-footer, then bogeyed sixteen in self-defeating succession to keep the match tied as tight as Parnevik's drainpipe pants.

Not without its moments, seventeen was also halved in par, where Woods had a chance for glory but blasted his forty-five-foot downhill eagle putt fifteen feet past the hole. With Parnevik sitting on a ten-footer for his par, Leonard was faced with a comeback putt for birdie that never looked good, allowing the Swede to fearlessly roll in his par putt for the half.

"Seve hasn't been so much a captain as a father to us. Every time I was thinking, 'What can I do here?' he'd appear out of nowhere and tell me what to do. We put our hands on the clubs, but he's the one who played the shots."
—*Ignacio Garrido*

Neither side proved capable of winning the last hole or the match, as par fours left the pairs as they had started—all square.

Having sat out the first session, Garrido played in three halved matches to earn 1½ valuable points for his team.

Fred Couples and Davis Love III (USA) v. Jose Maria Olazabal and Costantino Rocca (EUR)

Once again Kite sent out his World Cup–winning tandem, and his pair got off to the better start, aided by Couples's nine-foot birdie at the second.

The fourth hole was halved with birdies, when a Rocca seven-footer was offset by Love's three-footer to maintain the American advantage. The Italian made his second successive birdie putt, this time from eight feet on the 381-yard fifth, to level the match.

With the light worsening by the second, Couples found himself beside the gallery ropes deep in the left-hand rough on the seventh. From there he fired an immaculate iron to the heart of the green. Rocca also found himself in the rough, between a bunker and the green, with an awkward stance. One would hardly have known the trouble Olazabal had left for his partner: Rocca not only managed to extricate his ball from the rough but holed his chip.

"If you are a bad putter, you will not make a putt. If you have a tendency to chili-dip wedges, you'll be chili-dipping them all over the place for sure. Whatever your weakness, it will come up in spades during the Ryder Cup."
—*Johnny Miller, NBC TV commentator*

Stung by this surprise birdie, Love needed to hole Couples's fine approach for a half instead of the expected win. He left the ball draped all over the front lip of the cup, and Europe snatched an important advantage—just as the match was called for the night.

"The way the U.S. players putted, they couldn't hit the Mediterranean from the Rock of Gibraltar." —Thomas Bonk, *Los Angeles Times*

Couples and Love must have had a sleepless night, because they carded bogey fives on the opening three holes after the resumption of play in the morning. In reply, Olazabal and Rocca opened par-birdie-par on the eighth through tenth to go up by four, and the damage had been wrought.

This knocked the stuffing out of the four-time World Cup champions, who rarely looked as if they would challenge the Europeans after their dreadful triple-bogey restart. Further birdies at thirteen and fourteen gave Olazabal and Rocca a truly convincing 6 and 4 win, the Spaniard closing out the match in magnificent style by holing a twenty-footer on fourteen.

Despite their previous World Cup form, Couples and Love lost both their matches at Valderrama. This 6 and 4 loss against Olazabal and Rocca was the heaviest defeat of the first two days.

It must be noted that although the Americans had won four World Cups in a row (1992–95), that event is a stroke-play rather than match-play format, and does not have such a built-in pressure-cooker effect.

Afternoon foursomes result: USA 1½, EUR 2½

VAL-DRAMA BELONGS MAINLY TO EUROPE

—*Los Angeles Times* headline

Day two result: USA 2, EUR 6
Overall match score: USA 5½, EUR 10½

Tom Kite invited George Bush to give his beleaguered team a fighting pep talk on Saturday night, which the former president gladly accepted, saying: "I love being with them, and just being able to pass on a word of encouragement was easy for me, since I have been in tough situations in sports and in politics. There's no reason to get down on something; you just bounce back, and these guys are doing that now. Whether we can pull it out at the end, I don't know, but I am so proud of them—those who win and those who lose."

Day Three: Singles

History was not on the U.S. side. The British team in 1957 was the only side ever to achieve a five-point turnaround on the final day, which is what the U.S. team needed to achieve just to retain the Cup.

"I think those guys can be had. I like our chances in singles."
—*Tom Lehman*

With a big lead, Ballesteros decided to go with his experienced players at the end. Kite, needing to get some quick points back, opted to lead with his big guns, who were not short of misplaced confidence.

Fred Couples (USA) v. Ian Woosnam (EUR)

This was the third time in a row that Couples and Woosnam had squared off in the Ryder Cup singles. The previous encounters were both halved, with the two opponents also leading off the singles in 1993.

Thirty-seven-year-old Couples was ranked twelfth in the Sony World Rankings, while thirty-nine-year-old Woosnam had slowly slumped all the way to thirty-fifth, having been number one.

With the United States five points adrift at the start of the day, Ian Woosnam knew his main task was to stop "Boom-Boom" from making an explosive start to blast off the American challenge. The Welshman bogeyed the first hole as badly as anyone had bogeyed it all week . . . and that was pretty much that.

"The tone for the match was set off the first tee, from which Fred Couples hit a corker and Woosnam hit a cork tree. His recovery shot hit another one so violently that the two people perched in it did well not to fall out. One down and very nearly two spectators down."

—Martin Johnson, *London Telegraph*

The American warmed up on the second hole with a birdie, but this was matched by Woosnam, who had no idea what was about to hit him. One up after two, Couples proceeded to take the difficult course apart hole by hole.

Woosnam handed over the 173-yard third, failing to make par, and this was all the impetus Couples needed to launch his blistering attack on Woosnam, the course, and the record books. In the final eight holes played, Couples won seven of them in just twenty-six strokes (seven under par).

Couples started the carnage on a 535-yard par-5 fourth that he tried his best to reduce to a par 3. From the left-hand rough and hit blind over the massed ranks of a gallery all agog, Couples's second shot pitched three feet short of the pin, almost bouncing straight in for an albatross. His ball came to rest four feet past the hole, and he settled for a hole-winning eagle rather than a more-worthy seagull. Woosnam's second birdie in three holes was simply no match for a man who had just caught fire.

Couples's third three in a row put him three up after five, and he went one better with a hole-winning birdie two at the sixth. The 461-yard seventh was halved in par, but another birdie on the par-4 eighth put Couples five up.

"Nearly thirty-eight . . . Couples is an appealing Peter Pan whose singular charm has always been that he would rather be thought of as just another of the Lost Boys."

—*Tom Callahan,* Golf Digest

After his miraculous mid-iron recovery from a hanging lie in a fairway bunker found the middle of the ninth green, Couples made a twelve-foot birdie putt for a six-hole lead by the turn—out in 30 shots to Woosnam's one-over 36.

Save for shooting him in the back, the Welshman had absolutely no answer to Couples's charge as the American continued to plunder the course with his sixth three or better in ten holes. Couples dropped his birdie putt from ten feet for seven up.

" 'I think if Fred and me are drawn against one another for a third time,' Woosnam joshed earlier in the week, 'we'll probably shake hands on the

first tee, settle for a half-point each, and walk in.' It would not have been a bad idea." —MIKE SELVEY, *London Guardian*

In the rough, well short of the 547-yard eleventh, Couples casually chipped up to eight feet for a chance to close out Woosnam early. Nonchalantly, he buried another birdie putt and buried the bowled-over Woosnam, 8 and 7.

When his final putt dropped, after just 130 minutes of play, Couples looked slightly embarrassed by this early finish, and he glanced almost apologetically across at the demoralized Welshman.

Woosnam did not win a single hole in his loss, and this defeat meant he had not won a singles match in eight attempts. His solo record stands at 0–6–2, but he was philosophical about his failures: "Someday I'll win one."

With five birdies, one eagle, and five pars in eleven holes, Couples equaled Tom Kite's record for the biggest margin of victory in an eighteen-hole singles match (against Howard Clark in 1989).

This was exactly the start Tom Kite wanted and got from Couples—the U.S. side quickly pulled back to four points down, which boosted the other American players—those on the course and those still in the clubhouse.

After his early demise, the Welshman took his life in his own hands by riding shotgun in his captain's buggy. *"Ballesteros was so conspicuous, he was almost beside himself. When he gave Ian Woosnam a lift in the captain's golf cart, the Welshman complained about the speed of the Spaniard's driving. . . . Considering he's hardly hit a fairway all year, driving has not been one of Seve's strong points."*

—TIM GLOVER, *London Independent*

Davis Love III (USA) v. Per-Ulrik Johansson (EUR)

On the PGA champion, ranked number ten in the world: "He is Grade A large."
—*Tom Kite* (Unfortunately for Kite, the yolk was on him, as his superstar laid an XXL duck egg during the contest.)

Having opened with his inspirational leader, Fred Couples, the American captain put all his eggs in one basket and sent out his three majors-winning champions in the next three spots. Ballesteros, on the other hand, led off with four players who had yet to win a single singles match among them in eleven attempts.

Thirty-three-year-old Davis Love was ranked tenth in the world, while thirty-year-old Per-Ulrik Johansson was ranked thirty-third.

When he started this match, Davis Love knew he not only had the fortunes of his country riding on his shoulders but he also had a personal score to settle, having not contributed anything tangible to his team's cause after taking three losses on the chops. He started off like a true PGA champion, making a fine fifteen-foot birdie putt from the back fringe of the first green to go one up.

Johansson quickly hit back at the second, his chip shot bouncing a foot beyond the hole and almost screwing back in for an eagle two. The third and fourth holes were halved in nervous pars, neither player wanting to make any early mistakes. With the pin placed right at the back of the fifth green, Johansson's approach managed to find the narrow neck of green between the flag and the fringe, leaving a four-foot downhill putt. He made his birdie to go up for the first time in the match.

The Swede lost his lead when he bogeyed the seventh, but he birdied the 345-yard eighth to pull ahead again. Johansson retained his narrow lead when the ninth was halved, and he reached the turn in 33 strokes to Love's 34.

Knowing a strong finish was required of him, Love started home with back-to-back birdies. The first claimed the 364-yard tenth to level the match, but Johansson also birdied the par-5 eleventh to keep the score tied. The twelfth was also halved, in par, as the match reached its most crucial phase.

On thirteen, with three trees staring him in the face, Love blasted his long iron out of the rough and through the green, taking a ruinous double bogey to go one down. From the fourteenth fairway, the Swede went for the flag and finished a few feet away on the elevated green. He made the short birdie putt, which Love could not equal, and the lead had suddenly stretched to two.

The American made a mess of the 200-yard fifteenth, carding another bogey to go three down with three to play, and the writing was on the wall in large capital neon letters.

Coming into the Ryder Cup, Love had carded a final-round 65 in the Canadian Open, having recorded three 66s to win the PGA Championship the month before.

From the left-hand rough on sixteen, Love's second shot landed pin-high eight feet away to give him a chance. From almost twice as far away, the Swede holed his downhill putt for par, heaping the pressure back on Love's shorter birdie putt to keep the match alive. With Ballesteros stalking like a hungry predator in the background, the American pushed the putt past the hole to give Europe their first singles win of the day, 3 and 2.

Love lived up to his name (albeit in the tennis sense) and finished without a single point from four crushing losses.

This was the second match to finish, increasing Europe's lead to five points: 11½-6½.

Tiger Woods (USA) v. Costantino Rocca (EUR)

This seemed to be a point in the bag for the United States. At the age of forty, Costantino Rocca was given slim chance of beating a player half his age. Added to this was the fact that Woods was ranked number two in the world and the Italian only forty-third.

After a wayward tee shot left him in the left-hand rough and almost under the cork trees, Rocca's approach not only found the first green but rolled up to within four feet of the flag. Woods's answer was to fly the green, but he was fortunate enough to see his ball roll back down the bank and onto the green. It was the Italian who took better advantage of his luck, holing his birdie putt for a lead Woods would not haul back.

"I'm feeling a lot of pressure. I felt it on the first day, on the second day, and I'm feeling it now on the third day. I felt it all the way around. It's definitely out there, no doubt about it."
—*Tiger Woods*

In a far-from-inspiring opening nine holes, Woods was lamentably off his game on the subtle greens, which he had not been able to read all week. By the turn, Rocca found himself with a commanding four-hole lead, as Woods had bogeyed the third (having flown the par-3 green) and ninth (having blown a par putt) without winning a hole himself. Rocca made his second birdie on the 381-yard fifth and was out in a gentle two under par compared with his opponent's four over.

The Tiger was playing more like a neutered tom.

Woods's woes were highlighted on the par-4 ninth, where he missed the fairway to the right with his drive, then recovered to hit his third shot to within five feet of the hole. In true match-play spirit, Rocca filled the cup with a fourteen-footer for par, leaving Woods looking at a downhill five-footer for a half. He pushed it, and instead of making the turn just two down, he headed for home four down to the underrated Italian.

The youngest-ever Masters champion finally made his first birdie of the day, from four feet, to pull back to three down after eleven, although Rocca had left the door ajar, missing his birdie from ten feet. Try as he might, Woods could not close the gap any further as the next four holes were shared in regulation.

Three up with three to play, Rocca again found himself under some cork trees where he was protected from the driving rain. From there he threaded an incredible skimming one-iron shot through the trees and through the green to keep the hole alive.

On Rocca's one-iron to sixteen: *"It was a gutsy shot, and he pulled it off."* —Tiger Woods

Woods, having badly missed the sixteenth green from the middle of the fairway, chipped up to leave an eight-footer for his par. As with so many of his other putts on the tricky Valderrama greens, he failed to read the insidious slopes correctly, pulling the putt left to lose the match.

"I've hit the ball well this week, but I just couldn't get the putter to roll and build any momentum that way. Consequently, I will have a disappointing record."
—*Tiger Woods*

Woods made only one birdie in sixteen holes, while Rocca made only one more to win by 4 and 2. The American was 1-3-1 on the week, but he was philosophical about his fate: "It's called golf. You can't always win. I gave it all I had today. Unfortunately, it just wasn't enough. Sometimes, that's just what happens."

Justin Leonard (USA) v. Thomas Bjorn (EUR)

Having been beaten 2 and 1 by Bjorn (and Woosnam) in the Saturday fourballs, despite carding five birdies and an eagle in the first seven holes, Leonard did not play quite so well, but he still found himself four up after four holes.

The American started by sinking a twenty-footer on the 389-yard first hole to go one up on the Dane, whose raw nerves were exposed on the second green, where he missed a tricky four-footer for par to hand a second hole to Leonard.

With his Danish rookie visibly unnerved and two down after just two holes, the European captain quickly stepped in and tried to calm Bjorn, telling him to "play his own game." With the sort of form Leonard was in, it would have been hard even for a vintage Ballesteros to stay with him over the first four holes.

Suitably warmed up, the British Open champion showed his true class, knocking his tee shot close enough to the par-3 third to collect another birdie for three up. But the best was still to come. Leonard's third shot over the water came to rest just eighteen inches from the fourth flag, and he was four up in as many holes—one of the fastest solo starts in Ryder Cup history.

Somehow and somewhere, something suddenly went wrong with Leonard's lightning start. Bjorn hit his approach to two feet of the 381-yard fifth and cut the American's lead to three with his first birdie of the day. The sixth and seventh were halved in regulation, as Leonard almost holed a chip shot at seven but settled for a half. Having scrambled a par on the previous hole, Leonard was

The par-3 sixth and par-4 seventh were the only two holes to be halved in this remarkable match.

not so fortunate on the eighth, where he carded his first bogey of the day to drop another hole.

Bjorn, continuing his own recovery, birdied the 441-yard ninth with a carefully judged twelve-foot putt. The Dane had reached the turn in 34 strokes, one more than Leonard, but more important, he had trimmed the four-hole lead to one. Leonard leveled the match with his second bogey in three holes, which meant that Bjorn had won four of the last five, after having dropped the first four.

The American was stunned to have been sidetracked so quickly and instantly rectified matters on eleven, where his pitch finished within a few inches of the pin to put him one up again. Thanks to an accurate recovery chip from in front of a greenside bunker, par was good enough on twelve for Bjorn to peg Leonard back after the American bogeyed the par 3.

The American was back in front when he birdied the 402-yard thirteenth, but he shot himself in the foot again on the next hole. After coming up short of the fourteenth green on the front lip of a deep bunker, Leonard hit a chip shot that dribbled up the green, rolled around the hole, and stopped a foot away. He could only get down for another bogey five, as Bjorn played the hole superbly for birdie to level yet again.

Having made one of the greatest starts in a Ryder Cup singles match, Leonard had become totally hit-or-miss. On fifteen, he hit—making his sixth birdie of the day to go up again.

Unbelievably, the 370-yard fourteenth saw Leonard card only his second par in seven holes of amazing peaks and tormenting troughs. Having hung tough early on and continued to fight for his life, Bjorn leveled the match—for the third time in five melodramatic holes—with his third birdie of the day.

"Tiger wasn't alone in his frustration. Other . . . stars like Lehman, Couples, and Mickelson also took lumps from guys with v's and z's in their names, guys whose names end in vowels, guys who sound like waiters. A Dane, for God's sake! Bjorn. Guy with a j wandering around in his name."
—*Dan Jenkins,* Golf Digest

This far-from-mellow drama had not yet been fully played out by these two young stars. The sinister seventeenth loomed large on the horizon—the first singles match to reach this far.

Bjorn's third shot pitched pin-high three feet to the right of the pin, rolling four feet behind a flag placed at the back of the green. In reply, Leonard's third shot matched Bjorn, coming up four feet short of the hole. The American pushed his birdie putt to the right of the hole, expecting more break than he got. Bjorn, faced with a tricky downhill putt, made no such mistake with his cross-handed grip and finally took the lead with one to play. The

Dane had managed a fantastic five-hole swing to blunt Leonard's early firepower.

With the adrenaline still pumping, Bjorn badly hooked his final tee shot into the cork trees. From deep under cover and in the deep rough, he could only scuttle his ball up toward but just short of the green. Leonard found a pin-high bunker with his second shot, but he had a vital stroke in hand. His sand shot was disappointing, eight feet short of the hole.

"It was pretty crazy out there. We were either stiffing it or missing the green."
—*Justin Leonard*

Off the green and below the hole, Bjorn chipped up and just failed to hole the shot, the ball rolling a few feet past. This left Leonard to hole his eight-footer, which he did, to halve a match he should have blown away by the turn.

In an extraordinary finish to this match, the last eleven holes were won or lost. Bjorn claimed seven to Leonard's four, and the Dane overturned the American's four-hole opening burst.

Tom Kite must have viewed this as a vital half-point dropped. His plan of unleashing his three majors winners had totally backfired, Leonard's par on the last hole earning the only half-point the three champions managed among them in the singles.

"I feel like I aged about five years out there on Sunday's back nine."
—*Justin Leonard*

Phil Mickelson (USA) v. Darren Clarke (EUR)

This was the match that Darren Clarke needed to win to earn a Ferrari from his sponsors. Unfortunately, Phil Mickelson's racing start left skid marks all over the Irishman.

The first hole was halved in neutral pars before Mickelson slap-shifted into top gear: birdie-birdie-eagle. The American went three up after holing a chip-and-run for eagle from off the left-hand side of the par-5 fourth green.

Darren Clarke had a deal with his club sponsor (MacGregor) that would net him a $180,000 Ferrari Testerossa if he finished the Ryder Cup with a perfect record. Having won his only previous match, the Irishman was playing for more than his team.

Clarke probably did not know what hit him in this spell, but he settled down and halved the next three holes, with both players bogeying the par-4 seventh.

Having seemingly punctured Clarke's hopes of landing the Ferrari, Mickelson appeared to run out of gas as he approached the turn. Back-to-back bogey fives on eight and nine saw his solid lead crash to a ticklish one up, with both men out in 34.

The Irishman made his second birdie on nine courtesy of a ten-footer, showing that he had some mileage left on his clock.

The 364-yard tenth was halved in par, and then Mickelson got his defective steering back on track. Proving he was still a clutch player with a lob wedge in his hands, the left-hander gracefully arced a chip shot from the rough over a greenside bunker. Mickelson's ball landed on the green as nimble as a kitten wearing Goodyear slippers, then rolled gently into the cup for his second eagle of the day. Back two up, he held this lead until he bogeyed the par-4 fourteenth.

Clarke was playing tough and refusing to give up on his point or the red sports car, but Mickelson had too many maneuvers and pulled away from him again, as the Irishman's challenge finally stalled. The American's third birdie of the round—his first in thirteen holes, not counting the two eagles—put him back up by two.

"He had two incredible eagles on the par 5s, and he got up and down from impossible places quite a few times as well. It's tough to win holes when your opponent's short game is as sharp as his was."
—*Darren Clarke*

Having lived through a few earlier nightmares with Seve's severe test at seventeen, Mickelson was relieved to gently roll in a five-foot downhiller for his second birdie in a row, wrapping up the match with a half and a win, 2 and 1.

Suffice to say, Clarke missed out on his Ferrari, but he consoled himself with the fact that his teammates were playing with the class of a fleet of Rolls-Royces.

Mark O'Meara (USA) v. Jesper Parnevik (EUR)

Having warmed up with a gentlemanly half in par on the first hole, Mark O'Meara (3-0 in singles play) announced his intentions on the second green by holing a twenty-five-footer from off the green for birdie to win the hole.

Parnevik, who looked jaded before he even teed it up on the first, birdied the 173-yard third hole, but the American delivered a one-two punch.

"The whacko from Sweden in his silly cap and skinny dancer's pants always looks like the last guy to climb out of the clown car at the circus."
—*Dan Jenkins,* Golf Digest

Back-to-back birdies on four and five were met with little resistance from the Swede. After Parnevik could muster only a bogey on the par-4 fifth, O'Meara holed an eighteen-foot birdie putt, although the ball looked as though it would stop on the lip.

Unlike some of his teammates before him, O'Meara did not let this early advantage slip. Like a good heavyweight boxer with his man on the ropes, O'Meara hit Parnevik with another one-two combination.

In an incredible run of scoring from the second to the eighth, O'Meara carded six threes and one four to establish a four-hole lead.

"When someone makes six or seven birdies straightaway, and you get three or four down, it's tough to get something going. Every time I had a chance, he'd hole a ten- or fifteen-footer and I'd miss my birdie putt. He never even gave me a chance to get any momentum going."

—JESPER PARNEVIK

For the second time in five holes, the American carded two birdies in a row to go four up after eight. On the 461-yard seventh, he struck his second shot inside a yard of the hole, and he followed up with another stunning birdie putt from twelve feet on the par-4 eighth.

Out in 30 strokes against 36, and four up, O'Meara was in complete control of his tired-looking opponent, who could not reproduce his stunning form of the previous two days.

The American's seventh birdie in thirteen holes stretched his lead to dormie five, and he finished off the match in fine style at the 370-yard fourteenth. As the rain beat down, O'Meara's pitch from the fairway landed two feet from the hole, and, with his own ball off in the fringe, the Swede conceded the hole to go down, 5 and 4.

"This is nice. My record was 0–3 in singles coming into today. I've shot under par in every round but gotten beat by somebody who did what I did today. I'm pleased that I hung in there and played pretty well."
—*Mark O'Meara*

Lee Janzen (USA) v. Jose Maria Olazabal (EUR)

In the first four holes, the only difference between the two players was Olazabal's immaculate tee shot on the par-3 third that left him an easy three-footer for birdie and the lead. Janzen produced his first birdie of the day on the fifth but spoiled this by making his first bogey at the next hole to drop back one down.

Janzen's pile driver of a twenty-foot birdie putt on the eighth was sandwiched between two ugly bogeys: Olazabal's five on the 461-yard seventh and Janzen's own five on the 441-yard ninth. By the turn, both players had contrived to win or lose six of the last seven holes, but the score remained all square.

Olazabal continued the sequence of decisive holes by making another birdie on the tenth, but he held the lead only until the par-3 twelfth. The Spaniard pushed his tee shot, missing the green wide right, and found a shallow bunker. The "king of the short game" made the recovery for par, but Janzen was looking at an eighteen-footer from the opposite edge of the green for the hole. His putt was true all the way, a white blur that disappeared from sight.

Coming into this singles match, Olazabal had won only one of his previous four solo encounters—against Payne Stewart, who should by rights have halved the match in 1989. All four of the Spaniard's previous singles matches went to the last hole, as did this one.

From the middle of the thirteenth fairway, Olazabal started and finished dead on line with the flag, pulling up inches short of the pin for yet another go-ahead birdie. Fourteen was halved before Janzen continued to have trouble with the short holes. He bogeyed his second par 3 of the round to fall two back of the Spaniard, who sensed he was at last getting the upper hand with holes running out.

On seeing the day's events on the scoreboards: "I saw our guys who had won, and all our guys who were hanging in there. I needed to make something happen."
—*Lee Janzen*

From the middle of a shallow bunker alongside the sixteenth, Janzen flopped his ball out and saw it roll eighteen inches past the pin for a par putt that would win the hole and avoid the loss.

With the game still in the balance, and his rival in the right-hand rough on seventeen, Olazabal lobbed his third shot into the center of the green, trying to protect his precious one-stroke lead. Janzen, needing a win, went directly at the flag and came up twelve feet short to keep his slender hopes alive. Olazabal's birdie putt for the match drifted left, up the slope, and never looked as if it would trouble the hole. On the other hand, Janzen's must-make putt never looked as though it would finish anywhere but underground—squaring the match with one to play.

On his crucial birdie putt on seventeen: *"I could stand there all day and not make that putt again."* —LEE JANZEN

Now feeling the pressure, Olazabal pulled his final drive into the rough among the trees, and from a bad lie he pulled his second shot short of a greenside bunker into some more tangling rough.

After hitting a variety of recovery shots on the eighteenth, while under the ever-watchful eye of his team captain: *"Olly not only made a barkie, a chippie, a droppie, and a sandie, but he also survived a Seve, which ought to be worth an Emmy."*

—RICK REILLY, *Sports Illustrated*

Known as the best chipper on the European tour, Olazabal did not let his reputation slip and laid a delicate recovery to within a foot. But the look on his face told everyone that he had been looking to hole the shot. Having played a priceless seven-iron from the middle of the fairway, repeating his match-winning shot from Friday's foursomes, Janzen calmly slotted home his four-footer for another match-winning birdie three.

"We played great today, but we were too far behind. That's what it amounted to—we dug ourselves too deep a hole."
—*Lee Janzen*

With a magnificent finishing burst of three wins in the last three holes, Janzen snatched victory away from Olazabal by one hole.

This was the tenth result of the day, cutting Europe's lead to two (14-12). With just two matches left out on the course (Montgomerie v. Hoch and Faldo v. Furyk), this come-from-behind win by Janzen gave the U.S. team renewed hope that they might halve the contest with two final wins.

Brad Faxon (USA) v. Bernhard Langer (EUR)

Thirty-six-year-old Brad Faxon was ranked sixteenth in the world, while forty-year-old Bernhard Langer had slowly dropped down the rankings to twentieth, making this the closest match on paper.

With the first two holes halved in par, Faxon looked to have made the first positive move on the 173-yard third hole. His tee shot landed three feet from the flag, halfway inside Langer's. The German holed his longer putt, heaping the pressure on Faxon, who missed his birdie putt to go one down. It was that sort of day for the Americans.

"The greens are so good, you can start celebrating when the ball is six feet away." —*Bernhard Langer*

After that rush of excitement, the match returned to normal levels of service, with the next three holes halved in par. Although the par 4s at seven, eight, and nine were all claimed, it was not as the result of any overly impressive golf. Faxon bogeyed seven and eight to fall three back, but Langer semireturned the compliment by bogeying the ninth.

With the match turning for home, a miracle happened: Brad Faxon made not one but two birdies off his own ball. In his two previous fourball matches, the American had failed to make a single birdie in thirty-five holes of play. After nine birdieless holes against Langer, Faxon uncaged two birds in three holes to level the match on the twelfth, where his birdie two embarrassed Langer's double-bogey five.

Having played eighteen holes with Fred Couples on Friday, and seventeen holes with Justin Leonard on Saturday, Brad Faxon went another nine holes against Bernhard Langer before making his first solo birdie at the tenth.

If Langer had not sunk a difficult downhill par putt from nine feet on the par-5 eleventh, Faxon would have been sitting on a lead.

Rather than inspire the American on to greater efforts, this sudden burst of sub-par golf served only to highlight how poorly he had played all week. With a brace of birdies under his belt, Faxon missed the thirteenth green and missed a ten-foot par putt, then doubled his agony on fourteen when he bunkered his approach to swiftly drop back two down after two soul-destroying bogeys.

"I'd love to go back to the thirteenth tee and start over." —Brad Faxon

The 200-yard fifteenth was halved in par as Langer resolutely held on to his second two-hole lead of the match.

The German had a chance to win the match outright on the 422-yard sixteenth, where his blind second shot, right to left around the trees, finished on the front edge eighteen feet below the pin. For the win, his birdie putt stayed on the right line but then tailed off, finishing a tantalizing few inches short.

Down by two with two to play, Faxon deliberately overhit his third shot beyond the seventeenth flag, stopping the ball on the green eight feet away. Some eighty yards short of the green, Langer, in the same rough stuff Janzen had got up and down from a few minutes earlier, played a similar shot with an even better result—to six feet.

On his approach to seventeen: *"The ball was sitting down in the long grass, which was not a pretty sight. I was just a bit worried about catching a flyer and going over the green, so I had to catch it just right."*

—BERNHARD LANGER

With time, holes, and results running out for the United States, Faxon needed to make his putt to give his side any chance of winning the trophy. The master putter let his putt slip to the left of the hole, allowing Langer the chance to close out. The German also misread his downhill putt, but Faxon conceded the hole and the match, 2 and 1.

This win meant a lot to Bernhard Langer in terms of his overall playing record. Langer had been an ever-present player since 1981, and his largely unsung contributions to a winning European cause had earned 17½ valuable points over the years. This win over Faxon gave him an overall winning record, 15–14–5.

Although Faxon made two rare birdies in this match, Langer needed to make only one (at the par-3 third) for his 2 and 1 win.

Europe had retained the Ryder Cup, and Langer was mobbed by his teammates as his nightmare at Kiawah Island slowly melted away. This was the ninth singles result of the day, and it gave Europe a 14-11 lead that could not be surpassed. It was just a question of whether they could find the extra half-point to win the Cup outright.

Jeff Maggert (USA) v. Lee Westwood (EUR)

Two of the surprise players of the week combined to produce the best all-around start to a singles match. With Maggert off the back of the first green with mud on his ball, Westwood looked certain to take a lead. Having pitched his second shot to seven feet of the hole, the English rookie could only stand and watch as Maggert rolled his ball, mud and all, straight into the hole. Not expecting to have the added pressure of putting for a half, Westwood failed to sink his birdie putt to go one down.

On the 399-yard second, Westwood improved on his opening approach, his shot ricocheting off the flag and stopping dead for a gimme. For the second time in as many holes, Maggert rained on Westwood's parade. Having left his second shot fifteen feet from the hole, the American sank his putt for a half and dashed Westwood's hopes yet again. Westwood must have thought he should be two up, but the scoreboard clearly showed he was one down.

After this dramatic opening, the match settled down, with the next three holes shared in par-birdie-bogey. Both players hit exemplary approach shots into the par-5 fourth for their offsetting birdies: Maggert got to three feet, while Westwood retaliated with his own shot that pitched beyond the hole and spun back to five feet below the pin.

On Maggert's making the squad at the last minute thanks to his third-place finish in the final U.S. ranking event, the PGA Championship: "I wanted him on my team. He's real solid."
—*Tom Kite*

On the shortest hole on the course, Maggert's tee shot to the sixth challenged the pin from the start and almost found it, landing a couple of inches beyond and spinning back a couple of feet below the hole. Westwood dug deep into his bag of tricks but had no reply this time and fell two back.

The Englishman, who had impressed so many observers with his maturity and stroke play all week, could manage only three pars as he reached the turn in 34 strokes. Maggert matched him on the seventh and eighth, but then carded his fifth birdie of the front nine to go out in 31, well in control at three up.

Westwood finally broke his run of pars on the tenth with a seven-foot downhill putt for the win, but Maggert quickly got a hole back at eleven with another fine birdie.

From here on in, whatever Westwood threw at the American was answered in kind. Pars at twelve and fourteen were matched, while Westwood's brilliant birdie at the 402-yard thirteenth was also equalized by Maggert's own fine effort.

With the end in sight, the Englishman, all guns blazing, birdied the sixteenth, but Maggert holed an uphill twenty-footer in reply to capture a magnificent match in magnificent style, 3 and 2.

Maggert closed the match out with his eighth birdie in sixteen holes to card a net 64 for his round. This fourth American win brought them to within two points of the European lead at 13-11, although Langer was in the throes of closing out Faxon (and the Cup) on the hole ahead.

Scott Hoch (USA) v. Colin Montgomerie (EUR)

Forty-one-year-old Scott Hoch was the oldest player on either side, but his world ranking of thirteen belied his advancing years. Thirty-four-year-old Colin Montgomerie, number five in the world, was the first European out who was ranked higher than his American opponent. With a combined world ranking of eighteen, this was the best matchup on paper.

This was the only singles match to start off halving the first three holes, all achieved in par figures. Not to be inconsistent, Hoch and Montgomerie also halved the par-5 fourth in par. With this solid start behind them, and knowing any points from this match would be decisive, the two evenly matched players were determined not to give anything away.

The string of pars was shattered when Montgomerie bogeyed the fifth, while Hoch birdied the hole for good measure and a one-hole lead. The Scot bogeyed the next hole as well to drop two down, but he quickly got his act together on the 461-yard seventh, where his second shot landed and stuck four foot behind the flag for an unanswered birdie.

Some normalcy returned to this encounter as the next six holes were halved. The ninth was shared in bogey fives, and an anguished Montgomerie missed a downhill five-footer that would have claimed the eleventh.

"At the tenth, I was happy because it looked like we might get a walk in the park. But it didn't turn out that way. My caddie and I became aware around the twelfth or thirteenth hole that it might come down to us. It was quite a nerve-racking experience." —COLIN MONTGOMERIE

Still holding a priceless one-hole advantage, Hoch relinquished his lead with an untimely bogey on fourteen. This would be the last time he held a lead, which proved crucial when the final accounting was done.

The 200-yard fifteenth was shared in par, then Hoch's second bogey in three holes gave the Scot his first and only lead of the match with two holes to play.

On losing his focus on the sixteenth tee after an official wrongly informed him that Europe had gained 14½ points and had won the match outright: *"It was right after a big roar, but the official said he heard it over the earphones. I momentarily let my guard down and hit it in the right rough."* —Scott Hoch

With the heavy rain and wet conditions underfoot making it almost impossible to reach the seventeenth in two, both players laid up well short of the water. Hoch played a match-saving pitch to twelve inches of the hole for a birdie that Montgomerie could not match. Back all square, this match found itself the only one left out on an increasingly sodden golf course and the eyes of the golfing world staring down at it.

The eleven results before them had panned out in such a way that Montgomerie needed to finish with a half to win the Cup outright for his team, while Hoch needed a win to gain a share of the spoils for his country.

The driving rain and gloom did not make for the best of conditions in which to play world-class golf, but it did make for wonderfully dramatic viewing.

Hoch hauled his tee shot off the left-hand side of the fairway, and sensed his chance had gone. This feeling was enhanced when Montgomerie, with the pressure lifted, hit a perfect three-wood straight down the middle.

With nothing to lose and everything to gain, Hoch tried for a miracle second out of thick wet rough, but he could only play up short of the green. Montgomerie continued his triumphant march down the middle of the fairway, knocking his nine-iron 140 yards onto the green and stopping pin-high, eighteen feet left of the hole.

With the inevitable about to happen, the European cheers rang out loud and hard.

"I did all I could, but I just didn't have it this week."
—Scott Hoch

All Hoch could do was play his third shot up to the green and try to avoid the exultant crowd that spilled onto the fairway. Hoch's ball finished up slightly closer than Montgomerie's eighteen-footer, but the American could only watch as the Scot readied himself for at least two putts for the half and the overall win.

With the green getting wetter by the second, Monty's putt dragged itself through the surface water and pulled up just short. Hoch needed to hole his thirteen-foot putt for a half as Monty strolled over to pick up his conceded ball. From the edge of the green, Seve urged his player, "Give it to him!" On his captain's orders, Montgomerie offered a gentleman's half to Scott Hoch.

"Let's face it, if somebody told you Scott Hoch would go 2–0–1 and the Americans would still get waxed like a piece of fruit in a Cézanne still life, you would have told them to make an appointment with Bob Rotella, pronto."
—*Michael Mayo,* GolfWeb

This final command by the European captain put the icing on the cake not only for his team of twelve brave battlers but also for himself. Montgomerie had managed to hold on for the vital half without making a single birdie in the final eleven holes.

Despite losing his opening fourball and donating a charity half to Hoch in the singles, Montgomerie still emerged as the top points scorer of the week with 3½ points (3-1-1). Coincidentally, Hoch was the top American, with 2½ points.

Jim Furyk (USA) v. Nick Faldo (EUR)

Playing in his eleventh singles match, Faldo opened up in brilliant fashion, firing his second shot into the first green and coming away with a three-foot birdie putt for the lead over Furyk, who was playing in his first singles match.

After a most promising start, Faldo showed why he had slipped down the world rankings by slipping in a bogey five at the second. Furyk's short chip to within a couple of inches was enough to level the match. The enigmatic Englishman was just as quickly back in front, a soaring seven-iron tee shot to fifteen feet giving him his second birdie in three holes and his second one-hole lead.

Having made a spirited opening to his crucial match, Faldo allowed Furyk to not only get back into the match but also dominate the remaining holes. Faldo bogeyed the 163-yard sixth before Furyk made his first birdie of the day at the par-4 eighth to go one up. Both players then let their game falter, carding bogey fives on the ninth.

In his record eleven Ryder Cup appearances, Nick Faldo had broken or equaled eleven other records.

The tenth hole produced some much better golf. Faldo holed a ten-footer for a birdie to force Furyk to make an eight-footer for a half to retain his narrow advantage. The American was in the middle of a purple patch of play and made his third birdie in four holes, then took a two-hole lead after eleven with another eight-footer.

With twelve and thirteen halved in par, the 370-yard fourteenth saw both players at the peak of their form. Faldo played a "you-have-to-see-it-to-believe-it" blind second shot round the trees that only just skipped over the hole and stopped two inches away. In reply, Furyk left his approach just off the green, fourteen feet from the flag. He conceded Faldo's gimme and proceeded to chip his ball into the hole for a hammer blow of a half. The American was answering everything the Englishman could launch at him in order to keep his two-hole lead intact.

After Furyk faltered slightly off the tee at the par-3 fifteenth, Faldo again upped the stakes by nailing his tee shot twelve inches in front of the pin. Standing in a bunker, left of the green and forty feet away from Faldo's conceded birdie, Furyk took a deep breath and calmly chipped in again to halve the hole. The American was playing inspired golf—and he needed to just to keep Faldo at bay.

"If somebody said Jim Furyk would not only beat Nick Faldo but play like he was possessed by the ghost of Ben Hogan, dropping in chip-in upon chip-in, and it wouldn't matter a whit, you'd say lay off the sangria." —Michael Mayo, *GolfWeb*

Realizing he needed something superhuman to climb back into the match, Faldo overreached himself on the 422-yard sixteenth and allowed Furyk's par to win the hole and seal the 3 and 2 victory.

As a match official was deciding which player was to play first from the sixteenth fairway: "It doesn't matter; he'll probably hole it anyway." —*Nick Faldo*

Tom Lehman (USA) v. Ignacio Garrido (EUR)

Thirty-eight-year-old Tom Lehman was ranked sixth in the world. Only Tiger Woods was higher among the Americans, while twenty-five-year-old Ignacio Garrido, the lowest-ranked player in the contest, at seventy-six, was patently overmatched. Both players came into this match without a win to their names: Lehman was 0-1-2 and Garrido 0-0-3, although all six of their matches (including their halved fourball match on Saturday) had reached the final green.

With the responsibility of being last man out, Tom Lehman started as if there were a house on fire and he was the chief marshal.

With five birdies on the front nine at two, five, six, eight, and nine, Lehman reached the turn five up on Garrido, who could answer the American's birdie blitz only on the par-4 eighth. The Spaniard added to his problems with a bogey on the third and again on the seventh, which was matched by Lehman for an otherwise spotless front nine in 31 strokes.

With the tenth halved in par, Garrido did not look as if he would get back into the match, since he was doing all he could just to stay within reach. The Spaniard went further behind when Lehman collected another birdie on the 547-yard eleventh to go six up with seven to play.

"We almost pulled it off. It would have been the greatest sports comeback of any sport in history. You have to hand it to our team. We didn't quit."
—*Tom Lehman*

A four-foot par putt on twelve was all Lehman needed to win the hole and inflict Garrido's first loss in four matches, 7 and 6, with six birdies in twelve holes. This was the second-biggest win of the day, sandwiching the other ten singles between the 7 and 6 closing match and Couples's 8 and 7 opener.

Day three result: USA *8,* EUR *4*
Overall match score: USA *13½,* EUR *14½*

"I have done nothing. It is always the team. They play great, very consistent. Before the singles on Sunday, it was the first time in the history of the Ryder Cup that every player made one point. I think that speaks for itself." —SEVE BALLESTEROS

"It was great this week. The fans were spectacular, the players were great. I certainly wish that the outcome had been different, but other than that, I couldn't wish for anything more." —TOM KITE

"Most Americans don't think we lose the Ryder Cup even when Europe wins the Ryder Cup." —DAN JENKINS, *Golf Digest*

Recap

VICTORY FOR SEVE-HANDED STYLE
—London Guardian *headline*

Not only had he masterminded another European win, but Severiano Ballesteros also had joined a select band of four nonplaying captains to have beaten the Americans: J. H. Taylor, Dai Rees, Tony Jacklin, and Bernard Gallacher. Seve is the only one of this quintet who had also won the Ryder Cup as a player. George Duncan was the only playing captain to win it—in 1929.

"My heroes? I have twelve of them! Everyone on my side was a hero. This was the first time in history that every player contributed to our points total before the singles began." —SEVE BALLESTEROS

"My hat's off to the Europeans. They did what they had to do when they had to do it. We're disappointed, of course we are. But I'm proud of my team. They were magnificent." —TOM KITE

In his congratulatory phone call to Seve Ballesteros: "I got very nervous when things looked complicated."
—*King Juan Carlos of Spain, who left the official trophy presentation to his daughter, Infanta Elena*

Everyone had expected Seve to be Seve, but no one had quite expected the U.S. side to be so quite unlike normal U.S. sides. The visiting team was nowhere near as overpowering as many experts had predicted. But neither did the 1997 Ryder Cup send the competition back into the dark ages of the 1950s, '60, and '70s.

On the unexpected American defeat that saw the Cup go to Europe for the fifth time in seven contests: *"To us, golf is not a team game. You don't pass the ball around; you just pass the blame around."*

—Art Spander

Even though the U.S. team achieved some measure of respectability—nearly pulling off the biggest comeback since Payne Stewart first donned knickerbockers—the media inquest had started before the final putt dropped.

The most startling cause of the Americans' downfall was the form—or singular lack of it—of the three majors champions. Among them, Woods, Love, and Leonard combined for 2½ points out of a possible 13, and it does not take a Rhodes scholar to work out what that shortfall meant.

"Woods, Leonard, and Love were a combined 1–9–3—Woods was 1–3–1, Love 0–4, and Leonard 0–2–2—and none of them won after the first day. If each one of the three had won only one point, the Ryder Cup would be heading back to the United States instead of sitting up there on the mantel of Seve Ballesteros's fireplace."

—Thomas Bonk, *Los Angeles Times*

Some of the U.S. players felt they had the Europeans licked everywhere but on the greens, while the U.S. captain felt his team had been beaten by the course.

"I thought we had the best twelve players before the Ryder Cup started, and I still think so. We just got outputted." —Tom Lehman

"In the long run, they knew the golf course better than we did."

—Tom Kite

The plain fact was that the Americans had not bothered to familiarize themselves with the course, since only three team members—Love, Woods, and O'Meara—accepted Kite's invitation to play Valderrama the week before the British Open. Though, this enlightened trio hardly set the course on fire in competitive play: they combined to win only two matches among them.

"If we had played it at Augusta National, Tiger Woods would get more than 1½ points."
—*Bill Ferguson, Ian Woosnam's coach*

The more highly rated and much more highly ranked American rookies were also outplayed by their European counterparts. The U.S. team's new boys contributed 5½ points in fourteen appearances, while the Euro-rookies earned 7 points in one game more.

On the over-forty brigade: "I just hope they have facilities for wheelchairs at the next Ryder Cup."
—*Lee Westwood*

The big prematch concern with the home side was that the players were too long in the tooth for modern match play. Although this was proved a fallacy at Valderrama, the same misgiving will be raised again in 1999 when Faldo, Woosnam, Langer, and even Ballesteros—who vowed to come back as a player—will all be that much older.

Whatever the postmortems and postmatch analyses throw up, one fact does remain: the Ryder Cup has been such a closely fought contest that only one point has separated the two sides over the last six meetings combined. The United States has totaled 83½ points since 1987, while Europe has a one-point edge with 84½, but—more important—Europe has won three, the United States two, and the two sides have tied once.

Following are match scores from the past six Ryder Cups (winning side marked in *italics*):

1987: USA 13, *EUR 15*
1989: USA 14, EUR 14
1991: *USA 14½*, EUR 13½
1993: *USA 15*, EUR 13
1995: USA 13½, *EUR 14½*
1997: USA 13½, *EUR 14½*
Total: USA 83½, *EUR 84½*

One other stunning fact reveals where the American problem might lie. In the last seven contests, 114 matches reached the seventeenth tee, with the U.S. team winning only 40 of them. In winning or halving almost two-thirds of the close matches, Europe proved to be the better team in the clutch—a trait that had been strictly an American preserve in the early Ryder Cup matches.

"The ring of a dozen stars on the European flag was the perfect symbol for Europe's victorious twelve. Theirs was an unbreakable constellation that had Ballesteros as its Spanish sun."
—*Paul Hayward,* London Guardian

As happened at Valderrama, the Americans held the lead in many more matches than they ended up winning—they could not protect a lead over the closing holes. This lack of a finishing killer touch may be a negative reflection on the U.S. PGA Tour, where too many different players battle it out on the final day. With the millions of dollars in prize money and sponsorship at stake on the U.S. tour, there is no need to be competitive week in and week out.

On the European circuit, with far less money to be shared, the same dozen players always seem to be around when it is time to hand out the currency. It was these dozen players who won the 1997 Ryder Cup.

An anonymous BBC radio commentator closed out his Ryder Cup report by informing listeners that the 1999 Ryder Cup would be played in Brooklyn. Of course, he meant Brook*line*, Massachusetts.

"'Next time,' I advised Tom Kite, 'start off against an easier land mass . . . like Saudi Arabia or Antarctica.'"
—*"The Good Doctor,"* Inside Sports *(1998)*

Match Results (Winning side marked in *italics*.)

Friday, September 26—Morning Fourball

	USA	EUR	Score
1.	Davis Love III Phil Mickelson	*Jose Maria Olazabal* *Costantino Rocca*	1-up
2.	*Fred Couples* *Brad Faxon*	Nick Faldo Lee Westwood	1-up
3.	Tom Lehman Jim Furyk	*Jesper Parnevik* *Per-Ulrik Johansson*	1-up
4.	*Tiger Woods* *Mark O'Meara*	Colin Montgomerie Bernhard Langer	4 and 2

Friday, September 26—Afternoon Foursomes

	USA	EUR	Score
5.	*Scott Hoch* *Lee Janzen*	Costantino Rocca Jose Maria Olazabal	1-up
6.	Jeff Maggert Justin Leonard	*Lee Westwood* *Nick Faldo*	3 and 2
7.	Tom Lehman Phil Mickelson	Jesper Parnevik Ignacio Garrido	halved
8.	Mark O'Meara Tiger Woods	*Bernhard Langer* *Colin Montgomerie*	5 and 3

Day one result: USA 3½, EUR 4½

Saturday, September 27—Morning Fourball

	USA	EUR	Score
9.	Davis Love III Fred Couples	*Colin Montgomerie* *Darren Clarke*	1-up
10.	Brad Faxon Justin Leonard	*Thomas Bjorn* *Ian Woosnam*	2 and 1
11.	Mark O'Meara Tiger Woods	*Nick Faldo* *Lee Westwood*	2 and 1
12.	Tom Lehman Phil Mickelson	Ignacio Garrido Jose Maria Olazabal	halved

Saturday, September 27—Afternoon Foursomes

	USA	EUR	Score
13.	Lee Janzen Jim Furyk	*Colin Montgomerie* *Bernhard Langer*	1-up
14.	*Scott Hoch* *Jeff Maggert*	Nick Faldo Lee Westwood	2 and 1
15.	Justin Leonard Tiger Woods	Jesper Parnevik Ignacio Garrido	halved
16.	Fred Couples Davis Love III	*Jose Maria Olazabal* *Costantino Rocca*	6 and 4

Day two result: USA 2, EUR 6

Overall match score: USA 5½, EUR 10½

Sunday, September 28—Singles

	USA	EUR	Score
17.	*Fred Couples*	Ian Woosnam	8 and 7
18.	Davis Love III	*Per-Ulrik Johansson*	3 and 2
19.	Tiger Woods	*Costantino Rocca*	4 and 2
20.	Justin Leonard	Thomas Bjorn	halved
21.	*Phil Mickelson*	Darren Clarke	2 and 1
22.	*Mark O'Meara*	Jesper Parnevik	5 and 4
23.	*Lee Janzen*	Jose Maria Olazabal	1-up
24.	Brad Faxon	*Bernhard Langer*	2 and 1
25.	*Jeff Maggert*	Lee Westwood	3 and 2
26.	Scott Hoch	Colin Montgomerie	halved
27.	*Jim Furyk*	Nick Faldo	3 and 2
28.	*Tom Lehman*	Ignacio Garrido	7 and 6

Day three result: USA 8, EUR 4

Overall match score: USA 13½, EUR 14½

Ryder Cup Records

Biggest Margin of Victory

USA	in USA	$23^{1}/_{2}$–$8^{1}/_{2}$	1967, Champions (most points)
		11–1	1947, Portland (largest winning percentage)
	in Europe	$18^{1}/_{2}$–$9^{1}/_{2}$	1981, Walton Heath
EUR	in Europe	$16^{1}/_{2}$–$11^{1}/_{2}$	1985, The Belfry
	in USA	15–13	1987, Muirfield Village

Most Ryder Cup Appearances

USA	8	Billy Casper	(1961, '63, '65, '67, '69, '71, '73, '75)
		Raymond Floyd	(1969, '75, '77, '81, '83, '85, '91, '93)
		Lanny Wadkins	(1977, '79, '83, '85, '87, '89, '91, '93)
GBI/EUR	11	Nick Faldo	(1977, '79, '81, '83, '85, '87, '89, '91, '93, '95, '97)
	10	Christy O'Connor, Sr.	(1955, '57, '59, '61, '63, '65, '61, '63, '65, '67, '69, '71, '73)

Most Matches Played

USA	37	Billy Casper	**GBI/EUR**	46	Nick Faldo
	34	Lanny Wadkins		40	Neil Coles
	32	Arnold Palmer		38	Bernhard Langer
				37	Seve Ballesteros

Most Points Won

USA	$23^{1}/_{2}$	Billy Casper	**EUR**	25	Nick Faldo
	23	Arnold Palmer		$22^{1}/_{2}$	Seve Ballesteros
	$21^{1}/_{2}$	Lanny Wadkins		$20^{1}/_{2}$	Bernhard Langer

Most Matches Won

USA	22	Arnold Palmer	EUR	23	Nick Faldo
	20	Billy Casper		20	Seve Ballesteros
		Lanny Wadkins		18	Bernhard Langer

Highest Career Percentage (minimum 4 matches)

USA	1.000	Jimmy Demaret	(6–0–0)	GBI/EUR	0.722	Paul Way	(6–2–1)
		Billy Maxwell	(4–0–0)		0.666	Abe Mitchell	(4–2–0)
	0.900	Gardner Dickinson	(9–1–0)			Manuel Pinero	(6–3–0)
		Bobby Nicholls	(4–0–1)				
	0.875	Jack Burke, Jr.	(7–1–0)				
		Horton Smith	(3–0–1)				
		Clayton Heafner	(3–0–1)				
	0.833	Walter Hagen	(7–1–1)				
		Mike Souchak	(5–1–0)				
	0.818	Tony Lema	(8–1–2)				
		J. C. Snead	(9–2–0)				

Highest Career Percentage (minimum 25 matches)

USA	0.719	Arnold Palmer	(22–8–2)	GBI/EUR	0.620	Jose Maria Olazabal	(14–8–3)
	0.667	Lee Trevino	(17–7–6)		0.608	Seve Ballesteros	(20–12–5)
		Gene Litter	(14–5–8)		0.554	Peter Oosterhuis	(14–11–3)
	0.661	Jack Nicklaus	(17–8–3)		0.543	Nick Faldo	(23–19–4)
	0.635	Billy Casper	(20–10–7)		0.540	Bernhard Langer	(18–15–5)
	0.632	Lanny Wadkins	(20–11–3)		0.532	Ian Woosnam	(14–12–5)
	0.607	Tom Kite	(15–9–4)		0.500	Bernard Gallacher	(13–13–5)

Most Singles Matches Played

USA	11	Arnold Palmer	GBI	15	Neil Coles

Most Foursomes Matches Played

USA	15	Billy Casper	EUR	18	Nick Faldo
		Lanny Wadkins			

Most Fourball Matches Played (started 1963)

USA	12	Billy Casper	EUR	17	Nick Faldo
	11	Lanny Wadkins			Seve Ballesteros
	10	Lee Trevino		14	Ian Woosnam

Most Wins—Singles

USA	6	Arnold Palmer	GBI/EUR	6	Peter Oosterhuis
		Billy Casper			Nick Faldo
		Lee Trevino			
		Sam Snead			

Most Wins—Foursomes

USA	9	Arnold Palmer	EUR	10	Seve Ballesteros
		Lanny Wadkins			Nick Faldo

Most Wins—Fourball

USA	7	Arnold Palmer	EUR	10	Ian Woosnam
		Lanny Wadkins		8	Seve Ballesteros
				7	Nick Faldo

Most Losses (all matches)

USA	16	Raymond Floyd	GBI	21	Christy O'Connor, Sr.
					Neil Coles

Most Losses—Singles

USA	4	Raymond Floyd	GBI	10	Christy O'Connor, Sr.
		Jack Nicklaus			

Most Losses—Foursomes

USA	8	Raymond Floyd	GBI	9	Bernard Hunt

Most Losses—Fourball

USA	5	Curtis Strange	**EUR**	9	Nick Faldo

Most Halved Matches—Career

USA	8	Gene Littler	**GBI**	8	Tony Jacklin

Most Halved Matches—Singles

USA	3	Gene Littler	**GBI**	4	Bernard Gallacher
					Neil Coles

Most Halved Matches—Foursomes

USA	2	Billy Casper	**GBI**	4	Tony Jacklin
		Lee Trevino		3	Charles Whitcombe
		Gene Sarazen			
		Julius Boros			

Most Halved Matches—Fourball

USA	4	Gene Littler	**GBI/EUR**	3	Tony Jacklin
					Brian Huggett
					Sam Torrance

Most Matches Without a Halved Result

USA	13	Corey Pavin	8–5–0
		Davis Love III	5–8–0
EUR	13	Ken Brown	4–9–0

Most Successful Ryder Cup Partners (based on number of wins)

USA	5–0–0	Arnold Palmer and Gardner Dickinson
	4–0–0	Jack Nicklaus and Tom Watson
	4–2–0	Larry Nelson and Lanny Wadkins
EUR/GBI	11–2–2	Seve Ballesteros and Jose Maria Olazabal
	5–3–2	Nick Faldo and Ian Woosnam
	5–6–1	Peter Alliss and Christy O'Connor, Sr.

Biggest Winning Margin—36-Hole Pairs

USA	10 and 9	Walter Hagen and Densmore Shute def. Duncan and Havers (1931)
		Lew Worsham and Ed Oliver def. Cotton and Lees (1947)
GBI	7 and 5	Aubrey Boomer and Charles Whitcombe def. Diegel and Mehlhorn (1927)

Biggest Winning Margin—18-Hole Pairs

USA	7 and 6	Hale Irwin and Tom Kite def. Brown and Smyth (1979)
		Paul Azinger and Mark O'Meara def. Faldo and Gilford (1991)
	7 and 5	Lee Trevino and Jerry Pate def. Faldo and Torrance (1981)
EUR	7 and 5	Jose Maria Canizares and Manuel Pinero def. Kite and Peete (1985)

Biggest Winning Margin—36-Hole Singles

USA	9 and 8	Leo Diegel	def. Abe Mitchell (1929)
GBI	10 and 8	George Duncan	def. Walter Hagen (1929)

Biggest Winning Margin—18-Hole Singles

USA	8 and 7	Tom Kite	def. Howard Clark (1989)
		Fred Couples	def. Ian Woosnam (1997)
GBI/EUR	5 and 4	Bernard Hunt	def. Jerry Barber (1961)
		Christy O'Connor, Sr.	def. Frank Beard (1969)
		Peter Dawson	def. Don January (1977)
		Bernhard Langer	def. Hal Sutton (1985)

100% Winning Record (minimum 2 matches)

USA	6–0–0	Jimmy Demaret
	4–0–0	Billy Maxwell
	3–0–0	Ben Hogan, Billy Burke, and Johnny Golden
	2–0–0	Chick Harbert, Wilfred Cox, Lew Worsham, Ralph Guldahl, and Bob Rosburg
GBI/EUR	2–0–0	John Jacobs
		Paul Broadhurst

100% Winning Singles Record (minimum 3 matches)

USA	3–0–0	Chip Beck
		Phil Mickelson

100% Losing Record (minimum 3 matches)

USA	0–3–0	Andy North
GBI	0–6–0	Alf Padgham
		Tom Haliburton
	0–5–0	John Panton
	0–4–0	Malcolm Gregson
		John O'Leary

Youngest Ever Player

USA	Horton Smith	age 21 years, 4 days (in 1929)
GBI	Nick Faldo	age 20 years, 1 month, 28 days (in 1977)

Oldest Ever Player

USA	Raymond Floyd	age 51 years, 21 days (in 1993)
GBI	Ted Ray	age 50 years, 2 months, and 5 days (in 1927)

Players' Career Records

United States of America

Player	Record	Year/s
Tommy Aaron	1–4–1	1969, '73
Skip Alexander	1–1–0	1949, '51
Paul Azinger	5–7–2	1989, '91, '93
Jerry Barber	1–4–0	1955, '61
Miller Barber	1–4–2	1969, '71
Herman Barron	1–0–0	1947
Andy Bean	4–2–0	1979, '87
Frank Beard	2–3–3	1969, '71
Chip Beck	6–2–1	1989, '91, '93
Homero Blancas	2–1–1	1973
Tommy Bolt	3–1–0	1955, '57
Julius Boros	9–3–4	1959, '63, '65, '67
Gay Brewer	5–3–1	1967, '73
Billy Burke	3–0–0	1931, '33
Jack Burke, Jr.	7–1–0	1951, '53, '55, '57
Walter Burkemo	0–1–0	1953
Mark Calcavecchia	5–5–1	1987, '89, '91
Billy Casper	20–10–7	1961, '63, '65, '67, '69, '71, '73, '75
Bill Collins	1–2–0	1961
Charles Coody	0–2–1	1971
John Cook	1–1–0	1993
Fred Couples	7–9–4	1989, '91, '93, '95, '97
Wilfred Cox	2–0–0	1931
Ben Crenshaw	3–8–1	1981, '83, '87, '95
Jimmy Demaret	6–0–0	1947, '49, '51
Gardner Dickinson	9–1–0	1967, '71

Player	Record	Year/s
Leo Diegel	3–3–0	1927, '29, '31, '33
Dave Douglas	1–0–1	1953
Dale Douglass	0–2–0	1969
Ed Dudley	3–1–0	1929, '33, '37
Olin Dutra	1–3–0	1933, '35
Lee Elder	1–3–0	1979
Al Espinosa	2–1–1	1929, '31
Johnny Farrell	3–2–1	1927, '29, '31
Brad Faxon	2–4–0	1995, '97
Dow Finsterwald	9–3–1	1957, '59, '61, '63
Raymond Floyd	12–16–3	1969, '75, '77, '81, '83, '85, '91, '93
Doug Ford	4–4–1	1955, '57, '59, '61
Ed Furgol	0–1–0	1957
Marty Furgol	0–1–0	1955
Jim Furyk	1–2–0	1997
Jim Gallagher, Jr.	2–1–0	1993
Al Geiberger	5–1–3	1967, '75
Bob Gilder	2–2–0	1983
Bob Goalby	3–1–1	1963
Johnny Golden	3–0–0	1927, '29
Lou Graham	5–3–1	1973, '75, '77
Hubert Green	4–3–0	1977, '79, '85
Ken Green	2–2–0	1989
Ralph Guldahl	2–0–0	1937
Fred Haas, Jr.	0–1–0	1953
Jay Haas	3–4–1	1983, '95
Walter Hagen	7–1–1	1927, '29, '31, '33, '35
Bob Hamilton	0–2–0	1949
Chick Harbert	2–0–0	1949, '55
Chandler Harper	0–1–0	1955
Dutch Harrison	2–1–0	1947, '49
Fred Hawkins	1–1–0	1957
Mark Hayes	1–2–0	1979
Clayton Heafner	3–0–1	1949, '51
Jay Hebert	2–1–1	1959, '61
Lionel Hebert	0–1–0	1957
Dave Hill	6–3–0	1969, '73, '77
Scott Hoch	2–0–1	1997
Ben Hogan	3–0–0	1947, '51
Hale Irwin	13–5–2	1975, '77, '79, '81, '91
Tommy Jacobs	3–1–0	1965
Peter Jacobsen	2–4–0	1985, '95
Don January	2–3–2	1965, '77

Player	Record	Year/s
Lee Janzen	2–3–0	1993, '97
Herman Keiser	0–1–0	1947
Tom Kite	15–9–4	1979, '81, '83, '87, '89, '93
Ted Kroll	3–1–0	1953, '55, '57
Ky Laffoon	0–1–0	1935
Tom Lehman	3–2–2	1995, '97
Tony Lema	8–1–2	1963, '65
Justin Leonard	0–2–2	1997
Wayne Levi	0–2–0	1991
Bruce Lietzke	0–2–1	1981
Gene Littler	14–5–8	1961, '63, '65, '67, '69, '71, '75
Davis Love III	5–8–0	1993, '95, '97
Jeff Maggert	4–3–0	1995, '97
John Maheffey	1–2–0	1979
Tony Manero	1–1–0	1937
Lloyd Mangrum	6–2–0	1947, '49, '51, '53
Dave Marr	4–2–0	1965
Billy Maxwell	4–0–0	1963
Dick Mayer	1–0–1	1957
Mark McCumber	2–1–0	1989
Jerry McGee	1–1–0	1977
Bill Mehlhorn	1–1–0	1927
Phil Mickelson	4–1–2	1995, '97
Cary Middlecoff	2–3–1	1953, '55, '59
Johnny Miller	2–2–2	1975, '81
Larry Mize	1–1–2	1987
Gil Morgan	1–2–3	1979, '83
Bob Murphy	2–1–1	1975
Byron Nelson	3–1–0	1937, '47
Larry Nelson	9–3–1	1979, '81, '87
Bobby Nichols	4–0–1	1967
Jack Nicklaus	17–8–3	1969, '71, '73, '75, '77, '81
Andy North	0–3–0	1985
Mark O'Meara	4–7–1	1985, '89, '91, '97
Ed Oliver	3–2–0	1947, '51, '53
Arnold Palmer	22–8–2	1961, '63, '65, '67, '71, '73
Johnny Palmer	0–2–0	1949
Sam Parks, Jr.	0–0–1	1935
Jerry Pate	2–2–0	1981
Steve Pate	0–1–1	1991
Corey Pavin	8–5–0	1991, '93, '95
Calvin Peete	4–2–1	1983, '85
Henry Picard	3–1–0	1935, '37

Player	Record	Year/s
Dan Pohl	1–2–0	1987
Johnny Pott	5–2–0	1963, '67
Dave Ragan, Jr.	2–1–1	1963
Henry Ransom	0–1–0	1951
Johnny Revolta	2–1–0	1935, '37
Loren Roberts	3–1–0	1995
Chi Chi Rodriguez	0–1–1	1973
Bill Rogers	1–2–1	1981
Bob Rosberg	2–0–0	1959
Mason Rudolph	1–1–1	1971
Paul Runyan	2–2–0	1933, '35
Doug Sanders	2–3–0	1967
Gene Sarazen	7–2–3	1927, '29, '31, '33, '35, '37
Denny Shute	2–2–2	1931, '33, '37
Dan Sikes	2–1–0	1969
Scott Simpson	1–1–0	1987
Horton Smith	3–0–1	1929, '33, '35
J. C. Snead	9–2–0	1971, '73, '75
Sam Snead	10–2–1	1937, '47, '49, '51, '53, '55, '59
Ed Sneed	1–0–1	1977
Mike Souchak	5–1–0	1959, '61
Craig Stadler	4–2–2	1983, '85
Payne Stewart	8–7–1	1987, '89, '91, '93
Ken Still	1–2–0	1969
Dave Stockton	3–1–1	1971, '77
Curtis Strange	6–12–2	1983, '85, '87, '89, '95
Hal Sutton	3–3–3	1985, '87
Lee Trevino	17–7–6	1969, '71, '73, '75, '79, '81
Jim Turnesa	1–0–0	1953
Joe Turnesa	1–2–1	1927, '29
Ken Venturi	1–3–0	1965
Lanny Wadkins	20–11–3	1977, '79, '83, '85, '87, '89, '91, '93
Art Wall, Jr.	4–2–0	1957, '59, '61
Al Watrous	2–1–0	1927, '29
Tom Watson	10–4–1	1977, '81, '83, '89
Tom Weiskopf	7–2–1	1973, '75
Craig Wood	1–3–0	1931, '33, '35
Tiger Woods	1–3–1	1997
Lew Worsham	2–0–0	1947
Fuzzy Zoeller	1–8–1	1979, '83, '85

Great Britain 1927–'77/Europe 1979–'97

Player	Record	Year/s
Jimmy Adams	2–5–0	1947, '49, '51, '53
Percy Alliss	3–2–1	1933, '35, '37
Peter Alliss	10–15–5	1953, '57, '59, '61, '63, '65, '67, '69
Peter Baker	3–1–0	1993
Seve Ballesteros	20–12–5	1979, '83, '85, '87, '89, '91, '93, '95
Harry Bannerman	2–2–1	1971
Brian Barnes	10–14–1	1969, '71, '73, '75, '77, '79
Maurice Bembridge	5–8–3	1969, '71, '73, '75
Thomas Bjorn	1–0–1	1997
Aubrey Boomer	2–2–0	1927, '29
Ken Bousfield	5–5–0	1949, '51, '57, '59, '61
Hugh Boyle	0–3–0	1967
Harry Bradshaw	2–2–1	1953, '55, '57
Gordon Brand, Jr.	2–4–1	1987, '89
Gordon J. Brand	0–1–0	1983
Paul Broadhurst	2–0–0	1991
Eric Brown	4–4–0	1953, '55, '57, '59
Ken Brown	4–9–0	1977, '79, '83, '85, '87
Richard Burton	2–3–0	1935, '37, '49
Jack Busson	0–2–0	1935
Peter Butler	3–9–2	1965, '69, '71, '73
Jose Maria Canizares	5–4–2	1981, '83, '85, '89
Alex Caygill	0–0–1	1969
Clive Clark	0–1–0	1973
Howard Clark	7–7–1	1977, '81, '85, '87, '89, '95
Darren Clarke	1–1–0	1997
Neil Coles	12–21–7	1961, '63, '65, '67, '69, '71, '73, '77
Archie Compston	1–4–1	1927, '29, '31
Henry Cotton	2–4–0	1929, '37, '47
Bill Cox	0–2–1	1935, '37
Fred Daly	3–4–1	1947, '49, '51, '53
Eamonn Darcy	1–8–2	1975, '77, '81, '87
William Davies	2–2–0	1931, '33
Peter Dawson	1–2–0	1977
Norman Drew	0–0–1	1959
George Duncan	2–3–0	1927, '29, '31
Syd Easterbrook	2–1–0	1931, '33
Nick Faldo	23–19–4	1977, '79, '81, '83, '85, '87, '89, '91, '93, '95, '97
John Fallon	1–0–0	1955
Max Faulkner	1–7–0	1947, '49, '51, '53, '57
David Feherty	1–1–1	1991

Player	Record	Year/s
Bernard Gallacher	13–13–5	1969, '71, '73, '75, '77, '79, '81, '83
John Garner	0–1–0	1971
Antonio Garrido	1–4–0	1979
Ignacio Garrido	0–1–3	1997
David Gilford	3–3–1	1991, '95
Malcolm Gregson	0–4–0	1967
Joakim Haeggman	1–1–0	1993
Tom Haliburton	0–6–0	1961, '63
Arthur Havers	3–3–0	1927, '31, '33
Jimmy Hitchcock	0–3–0	1965
Bert Hodson	0–1–0	1931
Tommy Horton	1–6–1	1975, '77
Brian Huggett	9–10–6	1963, '67, '69, '71, '73, '75
Bernard Hunt	6–16–6	1953, '57, '59, '61, '63, '65, '67, '69
Geoffrey Hunt	0–3–0	1963
Guy Hunt	0–2–1	1975
Tony Jacklin	13–14–8	1967, '69, '71, '73, '75, '77, '79
John Jacobs	2–0–0	1955
Mark James	8–15–1	1977, '79, '81, '89, '91, '93, '95
Edward Jarman	0–1–0	1935
Per–Ulrik Johansson	3–2–0	1995, '97
Herbert Jolly	0–2–0	1927
Michael King	0–1–0	1979
Sam King	1–3–1	1937, '47, '49
Arthur Lacey	0–3–0	1933, '37
Barry Lane	0–3–0	1993
Bernhard Langer	15–14–5	1981, '83, '85, '87, '89, '91, '93, '95, '97
Arthur Lees	4–4–0	1947, '49, '51, '55
Sandy Lyle	7–9–2	1979, '81, '83, '85, '87
Jimmy Martin	0–1–0	1965
Peter Mills	1–0–0	1957, '59
Abe Mitchell	4–2–0	1929, '31, '33
Ralph Moffitt	0–1–0	1961
Colin Montgomerie	9–6–3	1991, '93, '95, '97
Christy O'Connor, Jr.	1–3–0	1975, '89
Christy O'Connor, Sr.	11–21–4	1955, '57, '59, '61, '63, '65, '67, '69, '71, '73
John O'Leary	0–4–0	1975
Jose Maria Olazabal	14–8–3	1987, '89, '91, '93, '97
Peter Oosterhuis	14–11–3	1971, '73, '75, '77, '79, '81
Alf Padgham	0–6–0	1933, '35, '37
John Panton	0–5–0	1951, '53, '61
Jesper Parnevik	1–1–2	1997

Player	Record	Year/s
Alf Perry	0–3–1	1933, '35, '37
Manuel Pinero	6–3–0	1981, '85
Lionel Platts	1–2–2	1965
Eddie Polland	0–2–0	1973
Ronan Rafferty	1–2–0	1989
Ted Ray	0–2–0	1927
Dai Rees	7–10–1	1937, '47, '49, '51, '53, '55, '57, '59, '61
Steven Richardson	2–2–0	1991
Jose Rivero	2–3–0	1985, '87
Fred Robson	2–4–0	1927, '29, '31
Costantino Rocca	6–5–0	1993, '95, '97
Syd Scott	0–2–0	1955
Des Smyth	2–5–0	1979, '81
Dave Thomas	3–10–5	1959, '63, '65, '67
Sam Torrance	7–15–6	1981, '83, '85, '87, '89, '91, '93, '95
Peter Townsend	3–8–0	1969, '71
Brian Waites	1–3–0	1983
Philip Walton	1–1–0	1995
Charles Ward	1–5–0	1947, '49, '51
Paul Way	6–2–1	1983, '85
Harry Weetman	2–11–2	1951, '53, '55, '57, '59, '61, '63
Lee Westwood	2–3–0	1997
Charles Whitcombe	3–2–4	1927, '29, '31, '33, '35, '37
Ernest Whitcombe	1–4–1	1929, '31, '35
Reg Whitcombe	0–1–0	1935
George Will	2–11–2	1963, '65, '67
Norman Wood	1–2–0	1975
Ian Woosnam	14–12–5	1983, '85, '87, '89, '91, '93, '95, '97